At War

War Culture

Edited by Daniel Leonard Bernardi

Books in this series address the myriad ways in which warfare informs diverse cultural practices, as well as the way cultural practices–from cinema to social media–inform the practice of warfare. They illuminate the insights and limitations of critical theories that describe, explain and politicize the phenomena of war culture. Traversing both national and intellectual borders, authors from a wide range of fields and disciplines collectively examine the articulation of war, its everyday practices, and its impact on individuals and societies throughout modern history.

Tanine Allison, *Destructive Sublime: World War II in American Film and Media*

Brenda M. Boyle and Jeehyun Lim, eds., *Looking Back on the Vietnam War: Twenty-first-Century Perspectives*

Jonna Eagle, *Imperial Affects: Sensational Melodrama and the Attractions of American Cinema*

Aaron Michael Kerner, *Torture Porn in the Wake of 9/11: Horror, Exploitation, and the Cinema of Sensation*

David Kieran and Edwin A. Martini, eds., *At War: The Military and American Culture in the Twentieth Century and Beyond*

Delia Malia Caparoso Konzett, *Hollywood's Hawaii: Race, Nation, and War*

Nan Levinson, *War Is Not a Game: The New Antiwar Soldiers and the Movement They Built*

Matt Sienkiewicz, *The Other Air Force: U.S. Efforts to Reshape Middle Eastern Media Since 9/11*

Jon Simons and John Louis Lucaites, eds., *In/visible War: The Culture of War in Twenty-First-Century America*

Roger Stahl, *Through the Crosshairs: The Weapon's Eye in Public War Culture*

Simon Wendt, ed., *Warring over Valor: How Race and Gender Shaped American Military Heroism in the Twentieth and Twenty-First Centuries*

At War

The Military and American Culture in the
Twentieth Century and Beyond

EDITED BY DAVID KIERAN AND EDWIN A. MARTINI

Rutgers University Press
New Brunswick, Camden, and Newark, New Jersey, and London

Library of Congress Cataloging-in-Publication Data

Names: Kieran, David, 1978– editor of compilation. | Martini, Edwin A., 1975–
    editor of compilation.
Title: The military and American culture in the twentieth century and beyond
    / edited by David Kieran and Edwin A. Martini.
Description: New Brunswick, New Jersey : Rutgers University Press, [2018] |
    Includes bibliographical references and index.
Identifiers: LCCN 2017012145| ISBN 9780813584300 (pbk. : alk. paper) | ISBN
    9780813584317 (hardcover : alk. paper) | ISBN 9780813584324 (epub) | ISBN
    9780813584331 (web pdf)
Subjects: LCSH: War and society—United States. | Militarism--United States.
    | United States--History, Military—21st century. | United
    States—History, Military—20th century.
Classification: LCC E181 .M523 2018 | DDC 355.00973—dc23 LC record available at https://
lccn.loc.gov/2017012145

A British Cataloging-in-Publication record for this book is available from the British Library.

♾ The paper used in this publication meets the requirements of the American National Standard for Information Sciences—Permanence of Paper for Printed Library Materials, ANSI
Z39.48–1992.

www.rutgersuniversitypress.org

Manufactured in the United States of America

In memory of the brave, smart, and generous mentors whom we've recently lost:

James O. Horton
James A. Miller
Marilyn B. Young

Contents

At War

Introduction

War, the Military, and American Culture

DAVID KIERAN AND

EDWIN A. MARTINI

If you have grown up in the twenty-first century, you have grown up at war. The United States war in Afghanistan began on October 7, 2001, and continues in 2017, making it America's longest war.[1] President Obama declared the Iraq War, which began on March 21, 2003, officially over on October 21, 2011, but the emergence of the self-proclaimed Islamic State has led U.S. political leaders to once again commit troops to conflicts in the Middle East.[2] And while these two countries have occupied much of the news coverage about U.S. military engagements abroad, they are hardly the only two countries where U.S. troops have been active. As the use of drones in Pakistan, Yemen, Somalia, and Syria or the September 2015 revelation that U.S. special forces troops had been active in well over 100 countries makes clear, the United States has not been shy about deploying military power abroad.[3]

And yet your connection to those wars may seem distant, at best. After all, most Americans don't serve in the military and don't know anyone who does or has. As of 2015, there are about 1.4 million Americans who serve in uniform, but that represents less than one-half of 1 percent of the population.[4] If you include military dependents—the spouses and children of U.S. service members—that figure increases to 2.1 million Americans—still less than 1 percent.[5]

However, nearly every aspect of American culture, and significant parts of your own everyday life, have been shaped by the histories of war and militarism in American society. Of course, the military fights in conflicts small and large. And while most Americans are familiar with the largest—the world wars, the Korean War, the War in Vietnam, the 1991 Persian Gulf War, and the twenty-first-century Wars in Afghanistan and Iraq, many of the smaller conflicts are less well-known.[6] At the behest of its civilian overseers, the United States has deployed troops more than 100 times since 1898, ranging from the well-known to the obscure.[7] According to historian Mary Dudziak, "the only non-war period after World War II, other than a period of seven months in 1990, was from October 15, 1976, to November 4, 1979."[8] Moreover, she explains, examining the "eligibility criteria for combat-service medals and membership in American veterans' organizations" leads to the inescapable recognition that "these criteria cause wartime to swallow much of American history."[9] Following her one example, during the Second World War the United States Army began awarding the Combat Infantry Badge to soldiers in infantry units who come into direct combat with an enemy force. Those criteria are relatively narrow— the soldier must be assigned to a *particular kind* of unit (infantry, as opposed to armor, artillery, aviation, and so on), and she or he must experience a *particular kind* of action (direct combat with the enemy). Since its inception, soldiers have been awarded the Combat Infantry Badge for service in major conflicts like World War II and the Iraq War, as well as in smaller missions like the 1983 invasion of Grenada and the 1993 United Nations mission in Somalia. Yet how widely the U.S. military has been deployed, and that those missions have frequently involved conditions that look a lot like war, comes into sharp relief if you consider that U.S. soldiers have earned the Combat Infantry Badge in lesser-known engagements in El Salvador and the Demilitarized Zone between North and South Korea.[10]

The military also plays an outsize role in American life outside of war. The Obama administration's budget request for the Department of Defense (DOD) in 2017 amounted to nearly $583 billion—much more than, for example, the requested $69.4 billion for the Department of Education or the $50.1 billion requested to fund the State Department.[11] The United States also vastly outspends other nations on defense. China, in second place, spends $145 billion annually; to equal U.S. spending, it would have to add the totals from the next seven highest-spending countries on defense.[12] And U.S. military spending shows no signs of abating. Following his 2017 inauguration, President Donald J. Trump proposed a $54-billion increase in the Defense Department's budget, with that spending offset by cuts to other government departments and agencies.[13]

All of that money goes a long way. The Department of Defense, which oversees the different branches of the military (the U.S. Army, Air Force, and Navy, of which the U.S. Marine Corps is a part) and the various agencies that support it, remains, as it proudly touts itself, "the nation's largest employer," with 742,000 civilian employees.[14] It also provides billions of dollars in contracts to U.S. corporations each year for services that range from designing and building military equipment to considering how the Arctic will be impacted by the changing climate to serving food on U.S. military installations. The military's internal and contracted research has produced a long list of products whose absence from civilian life is almost unimaginable. Military-funded research is responsible for the jet engine technology essential to air travel and the global positioning systems that allow pilots to easily find their destinations.[15] It has provided medical technology ranging from tampon and tourniquet design to the very idea of an emergency medical technician.[16] It has given us the microwave that we use to cook our food and the internet that we use to keep in touch with friends, conduct research, and procrastinate.[17] If you own aviator sunglasses or a navy blazer with brass buttons, your wardrobe owes a debt to U.S. military uniforms, and the next time you reach for duct tape or super glue to fix something, you can thank the researchers who developed them for the military.[18]

The DOD is also one of the largest landholders in the United States, with a real estate portfolio of more than 500,000 buildings and twenty-four million acres worldwide.[19] Troops are deployed on every continent and nearly every country. As of 2015, there were 37,704 troops stationed in Germany and 27,558 in South Korea, but troops are almost everywhere the U.S. government operates; for example, in 2011 there were five U.S. service members stationed on the island of Gibraltar.[20] By treaty, the United States is obligated to defend both Japan and the countries of NATO in the event of military aggression. The United States Air Force maintains a network of nuclear and antinuclear missiles that stretches from the plains of southwest Wyoming to northern Europe, the United States Navy provides antipiracy patrols that keep the sea lanes open in all of the world's oceans, the United States Marines guard every U.S. embassy, and U.S. Army soldiers regularly train and conduct missions alongside their counterparts from other countries. Like the British Empire of the nineteenth century, it is not an overstatement to say that in the twenty-first century the sun does not set on the Stars and Stripes.

And because the military has always been composed of Americans of all kinds, it has been an important space for thinking about important questions within U.S. culture. Over the course of the twentieth and twenty-first centuries, the military has been the site of pitched battles over social issues. While many African Americans in the first half of the twentieth century viewed military service as a way of demonstrating good citizenship and challenging the assumptions of a segregated country, by the middle of the century many black and Latinx Americans viewed military service as facilitating what they considered an imperialist, genocidal foreign policy.[21] Women have also used military service as an avenue to achieve greater equity in American culture, most recently surrounding the question of whether women should serve in combat. In the last quarter of the twentieth century and the first decades of the twenty-first, significant legal and rhetorical battles have been waged over the role of gay men and lesbians in the U.S. military.[22] Perhaps most significantly, the question of who should serve in the military—of whether military service is an obligation of all citizens or the province of specialized professionals—and whether military recruitment offers opportunity or exploits the most vulnerable among us has persisted from the Vietnam-era draft to today's All-Volunteer Force.[23] The military, meanwhile, has responded to the challenges that each of these issues pose, often fitfully, buffeted by both outside criticism and internal dissent.[24]

The military and its actions abroad also play a decisive role in American political culture. In many cases, American voters have perceived a candidate's military service as a strong indication of fitness for office, and a lack of military service has sometimes been perceived as suspect. Presidential candidates from Dwight D. Eisenhower to John F. Kennedy to George H. W. Bush, for example, all campaigned on biographies that included wartime heroics. In contrast, Bill Clinton's avoidance of service in Vietnam left him vulnerable to claims that he was a "draft dodger" and thus unfit for the presidency.[25] During campaigns, a candidate's attitude toward the military and vision for how the military should be used are crucial bellwethers. Ronald Reagan promised that he would rebuild the U.S. military and, with it, restore American leadership. Barack Obama's campaign for the presidency was founded on his opposition to the Iraq War and promise to extricate the nation from it. As well, concerns about whether a candidate could be an effective commander in chief often shape voters' anxieties. Former secretary of state Hillary Clinton, for example, had to contend with misogynistic fears that a woman might not be sufficiently dispassionate in a moment of crisis.[26] And once a candidate is in office, appropriately "supporting the troops" (whatever that happens to mean in a particular context) and, often, keeping lucrative defense contracts flowing to constituents are crucial criteria for re-election.

And of course the military touches civilian life in another important way—it entertains us. Movies about the military—many times made with its cooperation—are often box-office hits, and anyone with an expanded cable package now has access to several channels devoted to military history.[27] Americans read histories of wars, travel to battlefields, and play military-themed video games. In the twenty-first century, it's impossible to watch an NFL or Major League Baseball game without seeing some reference to the armed forces.[28] The National Guard sponsors a NASCAR team, while the Navy Seals seek out recruits among competitors at road races and triathlons.[29] No other institution can claim as pervasive a presence in our popular culture.

It is no exaggeration, then, that the military intersects with—is shaped by and shapes—nearly every aspect of American culture. To be a well-informed citizen—one capable of engaging in the most important political and cultural debates of our moment—thus requires a nuanced understanding of these complicated intersections. However, traditional military history has often paid insufficient attention to them. With its focus on tactics, strategy, and leadership, the field has often emphasized the decision making of politicians and generals or the movement of troops on battlefields and the equipment they carry. This approach is valuable, and it certainly has its place in academic study, in college classrooms, and in public debate. But it also has its downsides.[30] Because of this approach, many Americans understand "military history" as something that happens elsewhere and military battlefields as both geographically and temporally remote. In this approach, conflicts can seem to happen in a vacuum, and the histories of the people fighting these wars, on all sides, and of the regions themselves often receive short shrift. These conflicts' intersections with other aspects of American life are often obscured, and sometimes ignored, and "military history" can often be reduced to a timeline of conflicts, a series of leaders' biographies, and a set of debates about weapons and tactics. And yet, as the preceding paragraphs have made clear, the history of the U.S. military, its conflicts, and its place in American life are much more complicated. We need to acknowledge and grapple with that complexity.

To illustrate what we're getting at, imagine a traditional timeline of U.S. major military engagements since 1898. It would probably include the War of 1898, World War I, World War II, Korea, Vietnam, the Persian Gulf War, the War in Afghanistan, and the War in Iraq. One necessary first step to understanding the intersections of the military and U.S. culture would be adding additional, lesser-known interventions, from the occupation of Haiti in the early twentieth century to the use of drones in Pakistan and Yemen today.[31] But we can also imagine a series of other timelines that cover a similar period, each of which tells the story of some important aspect of American culture. One might chart the African American struggle for civil rights. Others might focus on the struggles for equity and representation by women, Latinx, and LGBTQ Americans. Still others might chart the development of technology, business, politics, or the environmental movement in American culture. Yet another might reveal changing patterns of consumption and the evolution of popular culture. On top of those, we might consider similar timelines based on the social, political, or economic developments within all the various regions and countries of the world. The list goes on, but the point is clear: the history of the U.S. military and its activities must be approached in the context of the other histories with which they intersect, that they have shaped, and that have shaped them.

The authors whose essays appear in this volume contend that those histories are not distinct from the history of American military conflicts. Rather, they have often intersected, and the moments at which they have collided have often changed the directions of one or the other or both. To cite one example, in the Second World War, African American newspapers claimed that black Americans should fight fascism abroad in order to secure rights at home, but African American soldiers returned to a country in which segregation rendered them second-class citizens and rampant racial violence placed their lives at risk.[32] In the 1960s, leaders in the Black Power Movement called on African Americans to resist fighting in Vietnam and argued that both black Americans and Vietnamese civilians were the victims of a racist, imperialist U.S. government, while inside the army racial tensions ran so high that some African American soldiers killed white officers whom they considered racist.[33] By the time the United States fought in the Persian Gulf War, the chairman of the Joint Chiefs of Staff, Colin Powell, was an African American four-star general who claimed that his success could only have occurred in the army.[34] Over recent years, African American women have joined the U.S. Army in higher numbers than white and Latina women.[35] This is a history of what happened inside the military—of African Americans and their military service during five wars, of who served, why they did, and what their experiences were—but it is a history that is shaped by and which intersects with the larger histories of structural racism, civil rights, imperialism, and competing ideas of social mobility and economic opportunity in the United States over the seventy-five-year span from 1940 to 2016. Similar examples can easily be imagined for any other aspect of American life's historical intersections with American militarism.

The essays included in *At War* invite you to consider these intersecting histories. Drawing on the emerging field that has variously been called "New Military History," "War and Culture Studies," or "War and Society Studies," the authors ask how the U.S. military and the conflicts in which it has participated have intersected with issues of race, class, and gender; how the military is an important social actor shaping both the lives of Americans in and out of the armed forces and the social movements that have remade American culture; and how war-fighting and militarism impact the environment and the lives of those who live where U.S. troops are stationed and where the United States projects military force. At the same time, the scholars whose work appears here have not abandoned the more traditional study of diplomacy, intervention, and strategy but use new approaches to ask more nuanced and complex questions.

The collection's seventeen chapters are arranged to introduce concepts sequentially. *At War* is organized thematically, but within most chapters, the authors proceed both thematically and chronologically. This volume is not meant to be comprehensive, but it provides an overview of the defining issues during each conflict, asking how those issues and questions have changed or remained the same over the period. The book begins with topics familiar to traditional military history courses—chapters on war and the law, U.S. imperialism, the domestic politics of war, and the military-industrial complex—and moves to a consideration of topics that are central to the study of "New Military History." Here you will find chapters that focus on race, class, gender, technology, and environmentalism, among others. These include chapters that address who serves in the military and what their experiences have been like, how war impacts those who fight and the civilian populations who endure war's violence, and how the environment is impacted when wars are fought, weapons are tested, and bases are built. Before ending with a timeline of key events in U.S. military history, the book examines how Americans have represented and remembered wars, with chapters on visual culture, film, and memorialization.

Each chapter places its topic in a broad historical context, beginning in the late nineteenth century and examining how the issue has evolved over the past 125 years. You will learn, for example, how the military-industrial complex that Eisenhower warned of has changed over the past sixty-five years, how the twentieth century was marked by competing memorial impulses that served different ideological purposes as Americans sought to commemorate war, and how Americans have confronted the reality that wars significantly damage human bodies. In doing so, these essays place contemporary debates about American militarism, remembrance, and veterans' affairs in a broader historical context. Beyond this historical and thematic overview, each chapter explicitly places contemporary debates in a theoretical and historical context that will allow students to critically engage with and meaningfully discuss them. Should the United States intervene to stop the spread of ISIS or use military force to prevent an unfriendly state from attaining a nuclear weapon? What are the implications for women serving in combat roles? How should the Iraq and Afghanistan Wars be memorialized?

At the end of each chapter, our authors have included tools for discussion and further research. Discussion questions invite you to consider important aspects of these histories and connections across chapters. Suggestions for further reading point you to the best recent, accessible scholarship on the topic. We thus invite you to consider *At War* as the starting point for your consideration of how the histories of the United States military and the conflicts that it has waged are central to, shaped by, and themselves shape the broader history of American life and U.S. global engagement in the twentieth century and beyond.

In that spirit, we encourage you to keep four questions in mind as you read these chapters. They are, of course, hardly the only important questions, but they highlight key issues for the study of war and society in U.S. culture:

1. What is the value of an approach that looks beyond the study of battles and bullets to examine issues of war and militarism from multiple perspectives, taking into consideration the experiences of diverse peoples and intersections with the broader sweep of twentieth- and twenty-first-century American culture?
2. What types of questions do these writers ask and what types of evidence do they use to answer them? Do you find some approaches and analyses more persuasive than others? Why?
3. What were the defining issues during each conflict? How did those issues and questions change or remain the same over the period?

4. What are the everyday ways in which war and militarism have seeped into domestic life, and what are the ways in which those same everyday experiences have supported or contributed to American militarism and American empire? Why is this important?

Considering these questions, and reading these essays, is more than an academic exercise. In the era of a vast, often-utilized, but all-volunteer military, understanding the myriad ways in which the military and its activities have intersected with and shaped American society more broadly is a way of becoming more fully engaged in one of the central problems of democracy in the contemporary United States.

Notes

1 Mark Lander, "Obama Says He Will Keep More Troops in Afghanistan Than Planned," *New York Times*, July 6, 2016.
2 Matt Compton, "President Obama Has Ended the War in Iraq," *The White House*, October 21, 2011, https://www.whitehouse.gov/blog/2011/10/21/president-obama -has-ended-war-iraq. As Mary Dudziak has pointed out, the United States has continued to award medals to troops in Iraq despite the war's ostensible conclusion. Dudziak, *War Time: An Idea, Its History, and Its Consequences* (Oxford: Oxford University Press, 2012), 130.
3 Tim Craig, Antonio Olivio, and Missy Ryan, "Obama Takes War Back to Pakistan with Drone Strike Aimed at Taliban Leader," *Washington Post*, May 23, 2016; "Report: U.S. Drone Strike Kills 3 in Yemen," *Democracy Now*, August 31, 2016, http://www .democracynow.org/2016/8/31/headlines/report_us_drone_strike_kills_3_in_ yemen; Scott Shane, "Drone Strike Statistics Answer Few Questions, and Raise Many," *New York Times*, July 3, 2016; Nick Turse, "U.S. Special Ops Forces Deployed to 135 Nations: 2015 Proves to Be Record-Breaking Year for the Military's Secret Military," *TomDispatch*, September 24, 2015, http://www.tomdispatch.com/post/176048 /tomgram%3A_nick_turse,_a_secret_war_in_135_countries/.
4 Mona Chalabi, "What Percentage of Americans Have Served in the Military?," *FiveThirtyEight*, March 19, 2015, http://fivethirtyeight.com/datalab/what-percentage -of-americans-have-served-in-the-military/.
5 Ash Carter, *2017 Defense Posture Statement: Taking the Long View, Investing for the Future* (Arlington, VA: Department of Defense, 2016), 9, http://www.defense.gov /Portals/1/Documents/pubs/2017DODPOSTURE_FINAL_MAR17UpdatePage4 _WEB.PDF.
6 Dudziak, *War Time*, 32.
7 Zoltan Grossman, *From Wounded Knee to Syria: A Century of U.S. Military Interventions*, n.d., http://academic.evergreen.edu/g/grossmaz/interventions.html.
8 Dudziak, *War Time*, 30.
9 Ibid., 28. What follows builds upon Ibid., 28–32.
10 *Section 578.69—Combat Infantryman Badge, Code of Regulations, Title 32—National Defense* (Washington, DC: Government Printing Office, 2008), https://www.gpo. gov/fdsys/pkg/CFR-2008-title32-vol3/xml/CFR-2008-title32-vol3-sec578-69.xml. Dudziak, *Wartime*, 31.

11 Carter, *2017 Defense Posture Statement*, 1; Department of Education, *Fiscal Year 2017 Budget Summary and Background Information*, 2, http://www2.ed.gov/about /overview/budget/budget17/summary/17summary.pdf; Department of State, Foreign Operations, and Related Programs, *Congressional Budget Justification*, February 9, 2016, http://www.state.gov/documents/organization/252179.pdf.

12 Edward Wong and Chris Buckley, "China's Military Budget Increasing 10% for 2015, Officials Say," *New York Times*, March 4, 2015.

13 Mara Liasson, "Trump Administration to Boost Defense Spending in Budget Proposal," *National Public Radio*, February 27, 2017, http://www.npr.org/2017/02/27 /517563151/trump-administration-to-boost-defense-spending-in-budget-proposal.

14 Department of Defense, *About the Department of Defense*, August 27, 2015, http:// www.defense.gov/About-DoD.

15 Les Shu, "DPS, Drones, Microwaves and Other Everyday Technologies Born on the Battlefield," *Digital Trends*, May 26, 2014, http://www.digitaltrends.com/cool-tech /modern-civilian-tech-made-possible-wartime-research-development/.

16 Tom Currie, "10 Everyday Items We Can Thank the Military for Inventing," *Mandatory*, October 23, 2012, http://www.mandatory.com/2012/10/23/10-everyday-items -we-can-thank-the-military-for-inventing/10; Rosean M. Mandziuk, "'Ending Women's Greatest Hygenic Mistake': Modernity and the Mortification of Menstruation in Kotex Advertising, 1921–1926," *Women's Studies Quarterly* 38, nos. 3&4 (2010): 46; John F. Kragh et al., "Extended (16-Hour) Tourniquet Application after Combat Wounds: A Case Report and Review of the Current Literature," *Journal of Orthopedic Trauma* 21, no. 4 (2007); David Van Stralen, "The Origins of EMS in Military Medicine: How Combat Medicine Influences the Advent of Today's EMS Model," *Journal of Emergency Medical Services*, September 30, 2008, http://www.jems.com/articles /2008/09/origins-ems-military-medicine.html.

17 Currie, "10 Everyday Items We Can Thank the Military for Inventing"; John A. Alic, *Beyond Spinoff: Military and Commercial Technologies in a Changing World* (Cambridge, MA: Harvard Business Press, 1992), 56; Stephanie Ricker Schulte, *Cached: Decoding the Internet in Global Popular Culture* (New York: New York University Press, 2013), 4.

18 Currie, "10 Everyday Items We Can Thank the Military for Inventing"; Wilson Wong, *Emerging Military Technologies: A Guide to the Issues* (Santa Barbara, CA: ABC-CLIO, 2013), 4; Ted Allen, et al., *Queer Eye For the Straight Guy: The Fab 5's Guide to Looking Better, Cooking Better, Dressing Better, Behaving Better, and Living Better* (New York: Clarkson Potter, 2004), 204; Chantelle Champagne, "Serendipity, Super Glue, and Surgery: Cyanoacrylates as Hemostatic Aids in the Vietnam War," paper presented at the 18th Annual History of Medicine Days, Calgary, Alberta, 2009, http://prism.ucalgary.ca/bitstream/1880/48962/1/2009_HMD_Champagne.pdf.

19 Office of the Assistant Secretary of Defense for Energy, Installations, and Environment, *Real Property Accountability*, n.d., http://www.acq.osd.mil/eie/BSI/BEI_RPA .html. We first encountered this concept in Aaron B. O'Connell's presentation at the roundtable "Left Alone in American Studies: The American Military and Military Culture in America," Annual Meeting of the American Studies Association, Washington, DC, November 24, 2013.

20 Julia Zorthian and Heather Jones, "Boots on the Ground," *Time*, October 16, 2015, http://time.com/4075458/afghanistan-drawdown-obama-troops/; "U.S. Military Personnel by Country," *CNN*, n.d., http://www.cnn.com/interactive/2012/04/us /table.military.troops/.

21   On this more generally, see Kimberly Phillips, *War! What Is It Good For? Black Freedom Struggles and the U.S. Military from World War II to Iraq* (Chapel Hill: University of North Carolina Press, 2012); Lorena Oropeza, *Raza Si! Guerra No! Chicano Protest and Patriotism during the Viet Nam War Era* (Berkeley: University of California Press, 2005).

22   Beth Bailey, "The Politics of Dancing: 'Don't Ask, Don't Tell,' and the Role of Moral Claims," *Journal of Policy History* 25, no. 1 (2013): 89–113.

23   See, e.g., Christian G. Appy, *Working Class War: American Combat Soldiers in Vietnam* (Chapel Hill: University of North Carolina Press, 1993); Andrew Bacevich, *Breach of Trust: How Americans Failed Their Soldiers and Their Country* (New York: Metropolitan Books, 2013).

24   On these issues, see among others Beth Bailey, *America's Army: Building the All-Volunteer Force* (Cambridge, MA: Harvard University Press, 2009); Jennifer Mittelstadt, *The Rise of the Military Welfare State* (Cambridge, MA: Harvard University Press, 2015).

25   Peter Louis Goldman, *Quest for the Presidency, 1992* (College Station: Texas A&M University Press, 1994), 356, 528.

26   Dan Merica, "Clinton Nods to Trepidation around First Female Commander in Chief," *CNN*, July 25, 2016, http://www.cnn.com/2016/07/25/politics/clinton -female-commander-in-chief/.

27   Mark Glassman, "Military Channels Are Competing on Cable TV," *New York Times*, January 24, 2005.

28   For a critique of this practice, see Bacevich, *Breach of Trust*, 1–5.

29   Tom Vanden Brook, "Army Found NASCAR's Price Too High," *USA Today*, May 9, 2014; Tim Sohn, "Swim. Bike. Run. Shoot. Kill," *Outside*, August 27, 2007, https:// www.outsideonline.com/1825256/swim-bike-run-shoot-kill; Deborah Carson, "Naval Special Warfare Sponsors SEAL at Ironman World Championship," *America's Navy*, October 24, 2005, http://www.navy.mil/submit/display.asp?story_id=20717.

30   For an overview of the debate between "traditional" and "new" military history, see John Southard, "Beyond 'A Company, B Company' History: A Military History State of the Field," *American Historian* (August 2014): 20–23.

31   Mary Renda, *Taking Haiti: Military Occupation and the Culture of U.S. Imperialism, 1915–1940* (Chapel Hill: University of North Carolina Press, 2001); Ian G. R. Shaw, "Predator Empire: The Geopolitics of U.S. Drone Warfare," *Geopolitics* 18, no. 3 (2014): 536–559.

32   On this history, see Phillips, *War! What Is It Good For?*, 20–111.

33   Ibid., 188–272.

34   Melani McAlister, *Epic Encounters: Culture, Media, and U.S. Interests in the Middle East, 1945–2000* (Berkeley: University of California Press, 2001), 254.

35   James Dao, "Black Women Enlisting at Higher Rates in U.S. Military," *New York Times*, December 22, 2011.

1

War and Justice

SAHR CONWAY-LANZ

Like other peoples around the globe, Americans have a long history of struggling to justify the destructiveness and the human cost of the wars they fight. The United States has not been a noticeably more peaceful nation than other major powers in the modern world. Since the late nineteenth century, the country has fought in dozens of wars and smaller military actions, including both world wars. Creating the most powerful armed forces the world has ever known, Americans have the unique distinction of being the only people to have ever used nuclear weapons against an enemy. The repeated exercise of U.S. force abroad has resulted in the deaths of hundreds of thousands of American soldiers and even more enemy combatants and noncombatants. Added to this death toll is the expenditure, waste, and ruin of immeasurable wealth and resources.

This enormous human cost has challenged Americans, like others, to justify the ends and means of war. Few questions have generated as much debate and conflict in American society as when to go to war and what methods are acceptable to wage it. While Americans have expressed a great diversity of views on these questions, what has come to be known as the "just war" tradition and the realist and pacifist critiques of it have been the most influential. On the question of when to fight a war, the just war tradition has centered its answers around the ideas of self-defense and the protection of victims. On the question of how to fight a just war, the tradition has advocated for discrimination—the avoidance of harm to noncombatants—and proportionality—the avoidance of needless destruction and suffering. The realist critique has claimed that any idealistic justifications for war are merely a facade obscuring the exercise of power and pursuit of national interests. The pacifist critique, on the other hand, has argued that no true justice could come from war with its terrible human cost.

Despite the undeniable influence of the realist and pacifist critiques through-out American culture, modern American leaders have never offered the further-ing of national interests as the primary reason for going to war and the United States has yet to abandon war completely. Instead, justice in war has remained a central concern and struggle for Americans.[1]

The Just War, Realist, and Pacifist Traditions

The question of how to reconcile justice and war, along with the common answers the question has generated, is often called the just war tradition, which, like realism and pacifism, has deep cultural roots. Despite the diversity of reli-gious belief, each major world religion has reinforced aspects of the just war tradition. Hinduism, Judaism, Buddhism, Christianity, and Islam have each, to a certain extent, sanctioned self-defense and the protection of victims as the legitimate motivations for war and condemned the harming of noncom-batants and disproportional destruction in the waging of war.[2] In early Chris-tianity, pacifism was the dominant attitude toward war, but this orientation shifted toward just war ideas as Christianity became the ruling religion of the Roman Empire, with its provinces and interests to defend. Early Christian just war thinkers focused on the question of when fighting a war might be justified and emphasized war as a means to right a wrong or rectify an injustice. Based on the fifth-century teachings of Augustine and systematized by Thomas Aqui-nas during the Middle Ages, thinking on the question of just cause coalesced into a just war doctrine promulgated by the Catholic Church. Late medieval Christian legal theorists also articulated an alternative to just war thinking—the idea that war was a right of sovereigns. Niccolo Machiavelli and other pragmatic political thinkers adopted this idea and helped to build this school of thought into a critique of just war thinking that would come to be called "realism" in the twentieth century.

Supplementing this thinking on the question of when to fight wars, early shared European ideas of just conduct within war developed along several paths. Christianity fostered the value of mercy and encouraged restraints on war's vio-lence such as the medieval Peace of God movement that sought to spare clerics, peasants, and other noncombatants. Medieval chivalric traditions viewed com-bat as a contest between equals and saw little honor in killing the defenseless. These nascent ideas of noncombatant immunity and other restraints on the bru-tality of war would later be elaborated by legal thinkers after the religious wars of the sixteenth and seventeenth centuries.[3]

The Nineteenth-Century Background

As the United States emerged as a world power in the second half of the nine-teenth century, a widely shared international understanding about justice and the initiation of wars was coming to an end. For two hundred years, European states had tacitly agreed that war was a right of sovereignty and that the justice of going to war over any particular dispute could not be easily judged. The terrible religious wars of the sixteenth and seventeenth centuries, with each side proclaiming the blessing of God for its cause, had convinced European rulers of the difficulties of making such judgments. In any war each side claimed to be in the right. Who could judge the justice of these competing claims? In a religiously divided Europe, even a figure like the pope could not convincingly claim to speak for all Europeans, and few other institutions had the international reach that Christianity possessed among Europeans at the time.

This acceptance of war as a right of sovereigns and the resulting inattention to justifications for engaging in war certainly did not mean that European rulers abandoned the practice of claiming to be in the right. States still offered justifications for the wars they started and often these justifications claimed that they were pursuing self-defense or the protection of some victimized population. However, until the early twentieth century, there were few efforts to establish international norms, institutions, or laws to regulate or scrutinize the motives of sovereign states for going to war. Reason of state, meaning the needs or requirements of a state as defined by its leaders, became a normal and accepted justification for engaging in warfare.[4]

In this way, the nineteenth century can be seen as the historical high point, at least in Europe and the United States, of a "realist" challenge to the just war tradition on the question of justifying belligerency, even though the term "realist" was not applied to this way of thinking until the twentieth century. By the end of the nineteenth century, European states through battle and conquest had spread their empires around the globe. Although many claimed to be spreading Christianity and civilization and saving colonized peoples from savagery and despotism, these imperial conquests also secured access to trade and economic resources as well as to military recruits and strategic locations to station armed forces, serving the particular national interests of material gain and military power for a state.

As empires expanded, imperial states had more to protect and self-defense claims could grow correspondingly. However, outside the case of fighting back against an armed invasion, distinguishing between self-defense and the furthering of national interests has usually been tricky. Can certain interests be so vital to a state that a threat to them is a threat to the state's survival? Countries have claimed that defending access to a vital resource like oil or control over a strategic waterway, like the Suez Canal, were acts of self-defense. If other countries had claims to those resources or strategic areas, such assertions of "self-defense" often failed to convince. The lines between self-interest and self-defense are easily blurred, which has given the realist critique of just war thinking much of its influence. It can be difficult to trust noble-sounding justifications when concrete interests are also at stake.

While the late nineteenth century was a low point for international attention to the question of when war was justified, it was a significant period for the formal articulation and institutionalization of norms for regulating how military struggles were to be fought justly. Although states had difficulty agreeing on what might constitute a just cause for war, they found many shared interests in limiting the violence that conflicts unleashed. The United States was instrumental in this move to write codes for the regulation of violence into law and policy. During the American Civil War, Union forces adopted one of the first military codes on the laws of war. Often referred to as the Lieber Code, after its author, Francis Lieber, these regulations were issued by Abraham Lincoln in 1863 as General Order No. 100, "Instructions for the Government of Armies of the United States in the Field." The code distilled the customs of war that had been developing in the United States and internationally. The tensions of the Civil War made questions of justice central to the fratricidal struggle, not least because the Union sought to pacify the Southern states and reincorporate their populations back into a peaceful and unified nation.

The Lieber Code was a major development in articulating legitimate means in warfare, since no other nation's armed forces had produced a similarly systematic work specifying the internationally accepted rules of war. Sparing noncombatants and limiting unnecessary damage were central features of the code. Its articles specified that unarmed citizens and their property should remain unharmed as much as possible and forbade wanton violence and destruction. The code said it was a mark of uncivilized societies to not provide protections of this kind in war.

The Lieber Code paid close attention to the question of military necessity in warfare and by implication the problem of proportionality. If one believed that only a proportional application of violence in war is just, this raised the question of violence proportional to what? Should the violence used be somehow proportional to the ends sought in the war, to the violence used by the other side, to the expected military advantage to be gained from a specific violent act? The idea of military necessity has been one influential answer to this question. The Lieber Code defined military necessity as those measures which were indispensable for securing the ends of the war but which were not cruel nor wantonly destructive. Any violence that exceeded this military necessity was disproportionate and unjust. However, Lieber's and similar definitions of military necessity contained ambiguities. Determining what violence is necessary in order to obtain the goals of a war is no simple calculation. As a result, these determinations have often been left to military leaders, and it has been common to accept as legitimate any violent act that could plausibly be portrayed as useful in winning the war, thereby equating military necessity with military utility.

Other armed forces around the world, including those of Prussia, France, and Spain, followed the example of the United States in issuing their own detailed codes and manuals on the laws of war. Each of these projects to express and codify the boundaries between legitimate and illegitimate violence in war drew on the long-standing traditions and customs of just conduct in war and the ideas of discrimination and proportionality that were central to them. These codes were not binding international treaties meant to constrain state action, but they drew on ideas of humanity that their authors believed had universal validity. Advocates of this body of limitations on the violence of war, like Lieber, drew on an Enlightenment tradition that believed these restraints were naturally apparent through the application of reason—that to be truly human, civilized peoples had abandoned savage and inhumane practices such as aggressive warfare and indiscriminate violence and destruction, practices attributed to wild beasts and animalistic urges. In this way, military codes concerning the laws of war reflected broader transnational norms about justice that noncombatants and other unthreatening individuals and groups should be spared from violence. This taboo against attacking the unthreatening, this ideal of discrimination and noncombatant immunity, helped to reinforce the justice of self-defense, the protection of victims, and proportionality as well. If attacking the unthreatening is wrong, then defense against those attacks and protection of their victims have a compelling case for legitimacy, with the proviso that disproportionate responses risk aggravating the original harm.

As states were recording the customs of war in national codes and manuals, many of those same states were negotiating the first international agreements addressing just conduct in warfare. These new treaties between states were binding legal agreements once signed and ratified, although few international mechanisms existed to enforce them. In 1864, many of the leading states of Europe signed the first Geneva Convention on the treatment of the sick and wounded in warfare. Drawing on the tradition of sparing the unthreatening from harm, the convention specified that all wounded and sick soldiers should be cared for by all sides in a conflict and that the medical personnel who cared for them should be treated as neutrals and left unmolested. Even though the convention did not include any general statements of the principle of discrimination, it was a landmark agreement in that it established the first international treaty providing a legal basis for protecting noncombatants and by implication made it clear that enemies could not be exterminated regardless of their roles. Admittedly, the convention addressed a rather narrow issue, the humane treatment of wounded soldiers and medical personnel, saying nothing about other noncombatants. Another Geneva Convention negotiated a few years later provided similar protections for the sick and wounded at sea. This narrow focus was a common feature of international treaties on the humane conduct of war, a focus which often obscured the underlying principles of justice upon which they were founded. The treaties, being political products of negotiation and compromise, consisted of narrow, technical, and concrete stipulations on which agreement was feasible when consensus on statements of general principles was elusive.

The exigencies of the Civil War prevented the United States from officially participating in the negotiation of the Geneva Convention of 1864, but Americans eventually ratified the treaty, as did a number of Latin American and Asian countries. The 1864 convention was the first of many international agreements that formed the basis of international humanitarian law and it emerged from a broader international humanitarian movement. Led by the International Committee of the Red Cross (ICRC), this movement of nongovernmental organizations and activists advocated for the ideal of humanitarianism, especially in war, of which the 1864 convention was a concrete expression. To this movement, humanitarianism was the duty to relieve human suffering wherever it occurred, and these groups viewed unnecessary suffering in war as an acute injustice.

War and International Law in the Early Twentieth Century

When the United States went to war with Spain in 1898, humanitarianism and questions of justice were not far from the minds of American leaders. In calling for war, President William McKinley did not rely primarily on an appeal to U.S. national interests or a claim of reason of state and a sovereign right to war. Instead, he stressed self-defense and humanitarian motives as the justifications for going to war. In his request to Congress for a declaration of war, McKinley claimed that the most important reason for war was that Spain's fight against Cuban insurrectionists was a menace to peace in the region. However, the threats McKinley sought to defend his country against were hardly dramatic, more akin to parochial interests than existential menace. The president cited the proximity of the island and the active trade conducted with its inhabitants, which put American citizens in "constant danger" and threatened American property and trading ships. The weakness of his claims to self-defense may have been why McKinley argued that another important reason for U.S. intervention was to end the barbarities and horrible misery on the island. Americans widely shared the view that the harsh tactics the Spanish had used to fight the insurgents, including the establishment of concentration camps to control the Cuban population, were a grave injustice. With the American peace movement in disarray and the widespread popularity of the war, pacifist voices questioning the justice of the conflict were not very prominent.

However, the issue of sparing noncombatants from harm did attract significant attention. Beyond offering the atrocities against Cubans as a major justification for going to war, fighting in the Philippines sparked controversy over the killing of noncombatants. In defeating Spain, the United States had occupied the Philippine Islands. When the United States decided to keep the Philippines as a colony instead of granting its independence like it did with Cuba, Filipinos rose up in resistance and a second war broke out between American forces and local guerrillas. Allegations that the U.S. Army was killing prisoners and torturing Filipino guerrillas spurred questioning and public criticism of these harsh tactics. The U.S. Senate conducted an investigation, and a series of courts-martial convicted a handful of American officers for the mistreatment of Filipino noncombatants, including one general, Jacob H. Smith, who was found guilty of ordering the indiscriminate killing of Filipino men on the island of Samar. Although historians have since debated the extent of the harm inflicted on Filipino noncombatants by U.S. forces, Americans at the time did not ignore the problem of noncombatant immunity.[5]

As the United States was fighting guerrillas in the Philippines, the first of two international peace conferences held in The Hague considered additional agreements to limit legitimate weapons and means of warfare and to further peaceful settlement of international disputes. The negotiations resulted in the Hague Conventions of 1899 and a revision and expansion of those conventions in 1907. The Hague Conventions, along with the Geneva Conventions, became the main body of the laws of war and international humanitarian law in the twentieth century. These treaties served as international expressions of what states could accept as right and just in warfare. The United States joined the major European powers in officially participating in the peace conferences and signing the conventions, as did a number of other non-European states including Iran, Mexico, Japan, and Turkey. President Theodore Roosevelt had even been the one to propose the second conference in 1907.

The Hague Conventions specifically forbade certain weapons deemed to inflict useless suffering or unnecessary deaths, such as poison, asphyxiating gases, and bullets designed to expand or flatten in the human body and cause excessive injury. The conventions also banned certain practices like pillaging or the punishing of spies without a trial. Like the Geneva Conventions, the Hague agreements contained few explicit statements of the principles underlying the specific provisions of the treaties. Instead of vague generalities with the potential for unpredictable applications, governments agreed to narrow restrictions for which they could more clearly foresee any disadvantages for their armed forces or advantages to the enemies. These narrow specifications reflected broader principles but also constrained those principles by limiting the scope of their application.

The provisions in the Hague Conventions reflecting the norm of noncombatant immunity demonstrated this challenge in articulating underlying principles clearly. Inclusion of a general statement of the principle of noncombatant protection was complicated by disputes among government representatives over a number of controversial issues surrounding the idea. A particularly contentious issue was how to treat irregular partisan and guerrilla fighters. These partisans and guerrillas were indisputably armed combatants, but their ability to blend into the general population offered them protections as noncombatants to which they had no right. Despite including a general principle—"The right of belligerents to adopt means of injuring the enemy is not unlimited"—the protection of noncombatants was expressed in the conventions through specific, and often narrow, regulations on which the concerned states could agree. The Hague agreements contained a number of provisions to protect soldiers who were no longer combatants or a threat to their opponents because they had been captured or wounded. Articles stated that prisoners of war must be "humanely treated" and prohibited declarations that no quarter would be given. The conventions also reaffirmed the Geneva agreements on the humane treatment of the sick and wounded on land and at sea. A limited aspect of noncombatant immunity was also expressed through restrictions on attacks against communities. The bombardment of towns, villages, and habitations or buildings which were not defended was prohibited and the requirement imposed that all necessary steps be taken "to spare as much as possible edifices devoted to religion, art, science, and charity, hospitals, and places where the sick and wounded are collected, provided they are not used at the same time for military purposes."

Beyond regulating the methods of combat, the Hague treaties also sought to provide a method for settling disputes among states without a resort to war. Challenging the notion that warfare was a legitimate form of conflict resolution, the agreements established various international mechanisms for arbitration. The right of sovereigns to go to war was increasingly being scrutinized by an international community intent on avoiding war's terrible costs. The accords reflected and bolstered a broader international movement, composed of pacifists and nonpacifists, which advocated for arbitration as an alternative to war.

World War I

International arbitration did not turn out to be the panacea hoped for and the Hague laws did not prevent the violence of the First World War from becoming a human catastrophe. The belligerents violated many of the Hague provisions, including the use of poison gas. In a bloody stalemate of trench warfare, the Great War killed eight-and-a-half million men in uniform and wounded twenty-one million more. An estimated six-and-a-half million noncombatants died, and naval blockades spread famine throughout the German Empire. Faced with this tragedy of unprecedented human destruction, many rethought the dangers of relying on warfare as a normal means to resolve international conflicts. Pacifists spoke up strongly in the United States and elsewhere and their arguments resonated in the following years. As one example, the platform of the Woman's Peace Party, founded and led by Jane Addams, called war the "sum of all villainies." It decried war's waste and cruelty; the death, maiming, and poverty it fostered; and its destruction of home and peaceful industry. The platform called for the abolition of war and the substitution of law in its place as well as the replacement of armed force with economic pressure and nonintercourse.[6] Sentiments questioning the institution of war ran so strongly that once Woodrow Wilson reversed his opposition to American involvement in the conflict he adopted a pseudo-pacifist justification for the war: it would be a war to end war.

Following the terrible destruction of the First World War, momentum increased to curtail war and limit the grounds on which it could be justified. By promoting the idea of collective security, the League of Nations constituted a serious institutional challenge to states' sovereign rights to war. Membership in the League obligated states to submit their disputes to some form of nonviolent resolution, whether arbitration, judicial settlement, or decision by the League Council. Despite Woodrow Wilson's enthusiastic advocacy for the League, the United States failed to join the world organization largely out of a popular desire to avoid entanglements in the disputes of other nations, but the country did not turn its back to the problem of war and instead pursued an experiment in outlawing war categorically. In 1928, the United States and the leading powers of Europe negotiated the Kellogg-Briand Pact, in which state signatories renounced war as an instrument of national policy. Many, including the U.S. Senate, interpreted the treaty as allowing a continued right of self-defense for states, and the agreement was eventually joined by most of the established states in the world.

In addition to raising questions about the justice of utilizing war to settle interstate disputes and further state interests, the First World War brought a re-examination of methods seen as too horrible and inhumane for legitimate use in warfare. Using the Hague Conventions as their standard, the European victors in the war attempted to organize the first international trials for war crimes since the defeat of Napoleon a century earlier. Among the grave injustices the trials sought to redress were the massacres and forced deportations of Armenians by the Ottoman Empire, which killed approximately one million people. Britain, France, and Russia condemned the atrocities against the Armenians as "crimes against humanity," coining the term and suggesting that widespread harm to civilians was more than simply an injustice of war but also a broader outrage against universal values. However, some governments like the United States opposed trying anyone for "crimes against humanity," claiming that such actions were violations of morality but not law. Such opposition and additional political and procedural issues prevented the international trials from ever being held.[7]

The aftermath of the Great War also saw further legal efforts to restrict inhumane weapons and other means of combat. The extensive use of gas warfare spurred the international community to negotiate the 1925 Geneva Protocol banning the use of gas and bacteriological warfare. The agreement reinforced the Hague provisions against gas and other weapons that caused useless suffering and unnecessary deaths. In 1929, states signed the Geneva Convention on the Treatment of Prisoners of War, which expanded and clarified Hague regulations, reaffirming protections for captive soldiers no longer in combat. With the introduction of bombardment from aircraft during the First World War, fears that new aerial technologies would bring widespread indiscriminate killing of civilians prompted unsuccessful attempts to formulate international law regulating aerial bombardment. Jurists and technical advisors met at The Hague in the winter of 1922–1923 to draft a set of rules for air warfare. One of the draft articles prohibited the terrorizing of civilian populations, destroying private property not of a military character, and injuring noncombatants. However, governments were reluctant to constrain unnecessarily their future use of a new military technology, the potential uses of which were barely understood.

World War II and Its Legacy

The international agreements that followed the First World War represented a trend toward increased scrutiny by the international community of the questions of wartime justice. A trend had begun in which international institutions were narrowing the legitimate justifications for war down to national self-defense and were more fully articulating noncombatant immunity and the elimination of unnecessary suffering in war as norms in international affairs. The Second World War marked another major step in this trend, and one in which the United States played a leading role. The horrors of the Second World War shocked much of the world into greater attention to both the problems of war and of inhumanity in it.

However, that was not how the war began for the United States, which remained disillusioned by the failure of the First World War and its peace settlements to bring lasting tranquility. As had been the case in the First World War, the United States was reluctant to enter the conflict that broke out in Europe in 1939. Arguments for justice did not propel the country into the fight. The Japanese surprise attack on Pearl Harbor did. With such a clear case for self-defense as the justification for fighting another terribly destructive world war, the United States experienced much less political division over the perceived justice of the war. Pacifist protests, while not entirely absent, were much more muted and isolated than they had been during the First World War. This quiescence was despite the even higher human costs of a war that killed approximately sixty million people worldwide, most of them civilians.

Outrage at Japanese and German aggression and atrocities, however, ensured that questions of justice would not be neglected. Although some called it "victors' justice," the Allies, led by the United States, held international war crimes trials to bring German and Japanese leaders and other perpetrators to account. Although the tribunals consisted of judges from the various Allied powers, Americans led the prosecution at the Nuremberg trial of the major German war criminals and the Tokyo war crimes trials were established by U.S. authority. These trials broadened the notion of international crime beyond what had been thought of as war crimes, those illegitimate methods and means of warfare which violated the laws of war expressed by the Hague and Geneva Conventions. Not only did defendants face charges for these conventional war crimes but the tribunals also charged them with aggressive, unprovoked warfare, labeled "crimes against peace," at the insistence of U.S. leaders. Basing the charges on the Kellogg-Briand Pact, the tribunals prosecuted the Japanese for the surprise attack on Pearl Harbor and their invasions of China and tried the Germans for a conspiracy to start the war in Europe.

The tribunals also sought a reckoning for the atrocities that went beyond conventional war crimes. Added to the list of charges were "crimes against humanity." Revelations of German concentration camps, forced deportations, slave labor, and the extermination of millions of Jews in what would later be known as the Holocaust shocked the world. But international law had scant precedents for holding officials accountable for harm to their own subjects, even if the harm occurred in the course of a war. Many of the victims of the Holocaust and other German atrocities were inhabitants of German-controlled territories and not citizens of countries that were fighting the Axis powers. The postwar tribunals revived the idea of crimes against humanity. This notion suggested that some actions are so terrible and unjust—namely, the massacre of defenseless populations—that there exists a universal right to prohibit them. This time American resistance to the idea did not prevail, and the international war crimes trials following the Second World War left a durable legacy.

This legacy was embodied in the United Nations and in the further elaboration of international humanitarian law that followed the war. As a successor to the failed League of Nations, the United Nations had as a primary purpose the prevention of aggressive warfare among states. The very first provision in the UN charter states that the organization's purpose is to take collective measures to prevent and remove threats to the peace and suppress acts of aggression. Article 51 guarantees that nothing in the charter impairs the "inherent right" of self-defense against armed attacks. The leading world powers after the war—the United States, the Soviet Union, the United Kingdom, France, and China—each held veto power over UN collective security actions, which left any one of them as the sole arbiter of whom to punish for aggression. As a consequence, the organization was a weak restraint on aggression by the great powers themselves. Nevertheless, the United Nations as an institution, like the Nuremberg and Tokyo war crimes trials, reflected the strengthening international norm that self-defense was virtually the only remaining legitimate justification for war.

The United Nations also acted to write the crime of genocide into international law. Recognizing the horrible injustice of exterminating entire groups of people, like the Holocaust perpetrated against European Jews, the United Nations negotiated the 1948 Convention on the Prevention and Punishment of the Crime of Genocide. The convention outlawed the intentional destruction of national, racial, or religious groups, whether in peacetime or in war, reinforcing the international norm that civilian populations should not be indiscriminately killed. The Genocide Convention was part of an important shift in how a growing segment of the international community was characterizing the questions of wartime justice, and global morality more generally. The United Nations was helping to define a set of human rights, ratifying the Universal Declaration of Human Rights one day after it passed the Genocide Convention. These rights were meant to apply to all people universally regardless of the government or laws under which they lived. These universal rights challenged the notion of state sovereignty, suggesting that a broader conception of justice existed than that which national laws might embody. As one of these supposedly universal rights, protection from genocide, while meeting very little moral opposition, did encounter objections based on this potential conflict with state sovereignty. The U.S. Senate refused to ratify the Genocide Convention out of concerns that the law would usurp American domestic law and be applied against white Americans' treatment of African Americans in the South. The treaty would wait for U.S. ratification until 1988.[8] Despite resistance to the idea of translating human rights into international law, activists for justice in war in the second half of the twentieth century increasingly defined their advocacy in terms of human rights instead of in the older mode of humanitarianism.

Another response to the human suffering inflicted by the Second World War was a major revision of the Geneva Conventions. The International Committee of the Red Cross proposed this undertaking as a way to mitigate the types of crimes the Germans and the Japanese had committed, and U.S. negotiators actively participated in the 1949 Geneva conference that drafted the new conventions. The conference updated the conventions on the treatment of the sick and wounded on land and at sea and the convention on prisoners of war and produced one entirely new convention on the "Protection of Civilian Persons in Time of War." The new convention was primarily concerned with the repression of civilian populations in occupied areas and consisted of requirements for their humane management. It offered a variety of protections against collective punishment, pillaging, inhumane internment, and other forms of arbitrary violence toward civilians who have found themselves at the mercy of an occupying army. Other innovations addressed the problem of the international community's previous refusal to offer protections to irregular and partisan fighters. The primary change to the prisoner of war convention was language that defined a legitimate combatant more precisely and acknowledged that resistance fighters who conformed to a few simple practices deserved the same protections under the convention as regular soldiers.

One omission in the treaties pointed to the reality that the agreements were products of political compromise as opposed to clear expressions of high-minded ideals. The conventions were largely mute on the significant threat to noncombatants of indiscriminate violence from increasingly destructive weapons. At the 1949 Geneva conference, the Americans and the British opposed the inclusion of restrictions on bombing and blocked the Soviet Union's attempts to use the treaty to outlaw atomic weapons.[9] The United States and Britain had conducted the heaviest strategic bombing campaigns during the Second World War, targeting industry and urban areas behind enemy lines and killing many civilians. These campaigns culminated in fire bombing attacks that burned most of Germany's and Japan's major cities and the dropping of atomic bombs on Hiroshima and Nagasaki, killing more than 100,000, mostly civilians. With such large noncombatant death tolls, Americans searched for a way to distinguish the carnage they had inflicted through strategic bombing from the crimes of the Germans and the Japanese. One solution that gained prominence in the decade after the war was the notion that unintended harm to noncombatants, what would later be referred to as "collateral damage," was tragic but justifiable. Only the intentional killing of people uninvolved in the fighting of wars remained generally condemned as inhumane and indefensible.[10]

The Cold War

The international response to the horrors of the Second World War through the international war crimes tribunals, the United Nations, and the revision of the Geneva Conventions significantly strengthened the regime of international humanitarian law and embodied new international norms, placing greater constraints on states in going to war and how they fought those wars. These institutions would play an important role in regulating war's violence in the twentieth century and into the twenty-first. However, these new humanitarian institutions encountered immediate challenges in the emerging Cold War struggle between the United States and the Soviet Union, which brought a resurgence of the realist views of war and justice that had been so prevalent in the nineteenth century.

The Korean War illustrated how difficult finding anything approaching international consensus on questions of justice in war could be in the midst of Cold War tensions. Remarkably, the Korean War was fought as a collective security action by a United Nations coalition that claimed it was fighting against North Korean aggression. The United Nations justified its war on behalf of South Korea as self-defense against an unwarranted attack by another sovereign state and discounted the idea that the war was a civil war within a country that had been divided at the end of the Second World War. But this would be the first and last time during the Cold War that the United Nations would be mobilized to back a war against aggression, and it only occurred in Korea because the USSR failed to exercise its veto power in the UN Security Council, a mistake it and the other veto-holding powers would not make again. Even with UN sanction, the United States and South Korea did most of the fighting for their side, and claims that the war was a fight against aggression and to uphold the principle of self-defense did not prevent it from becoming deeply unpopular among the American public.

Instead of embracing idealistic crusades against aggression or for the prevention of crimes against humanity, American foreign policy leaders increasingly defined their decisions on war and peace in the Cold War in terms of national interests. The reasoning normally offered for this stance was that the Soviet Union was ruthlessly pursuing its interests in the international arena and that the United States had to maintain a similar focus if it were to meet the Soviet challenge. Building on the writings of E. H. Carr from the 1930s, American scholars and diplomats like Hans Morgenthau, George Kennan, and later Henry Kissinger advocated this type of "realistic" approach to foreign policy, criticizing idealistic and utopian endeavors that sought to bring universal justice to an anarchic international system governed by power. The realists raised tough questions for the tradition of just war. If national self-defense was to be the only justification for going to war and aggressive war was to be condemned as a crime, how did one define and identify aggression? Couldn't any national interest be couched in terms that suggested it was being pursued out of some broad notion of self-defense? The United Nations never got very far in answering these questions, abandoning plans to codify an official definition of aggression. The International Committee of the Red Cross advocated the strict separation of the question of the justice of going to war from the question of just means in war and focused its efforts on regulating violence and advocating for noncombatant immunity even as international agreement on how to define aggression and self-defense remained elusive.

Lack of a widely accepted definition did not stop President Lyndon Johnson from accusing North Vietnam of aggression against South Vietnam when he sent American armed forces to fight in Southeast Asia. Heated controversy over the Vietnam War brought debates about justice and pacifism back to the center of American political discussion and challenged the Cold War policies and alleged national interests that had carried the country into the war. The Vietnam War generated widespread public opposition and an active antiwar movement that led to teach-ins at universities, large protest marches, and draft resistance. The antiwar movement questioned the reasons for fighting as well as the means by which the war was fought. Many rejected Johnson's claim that South Vietnam was an independent state under attack from a communist North Vietnam covertly supplying an insurgency. Instead, they viewed authoritarian South Vietnam as a U.S. puppet regime, the conflict as a civil war within the Vietnamese nation, and the United States as an imperialist aggressor in Southeast Asia.

Protestors also challenged the justness of the American conduct of the war. They expressed outrage at the destruction inflicted on the country, especially the civilian casualties, and questioned whether such a human cost could be worth American aims there. Atrocities like the My Lai massacre, in which American soldiers gunned down approximately 500 Vietnamese villagers—almost all of them women, children, and old men—further undermined the war's legitimacy. Widespread bombing and use of the chemical incendiary napalm also spurred opposition. One speaker from the peace organization Women Strike for Peace decried napalm, saying the U.S. secretary of defense "would not go out in the street and pour acid on a little child. . . . He would be horrified at the very thought of it. And yet he can let his airplanes go out there and pour it on these Vietnamese children!"[11] American officials answered these criticisms by claiming that napalm and other American weapons were being directed only against combatants and other military targets and that any harm to noncombatants was unintended, which, these officials charged, contrasted with the intentional terrorist attacks against civilians perpetrated by the Viet Cong.

Controversy over Vietnam propelled not only protest in the streets but also a resurgence of attention to the just war tradition among scholars and intellectuals as well as a modern theory of just war. The political theorist Michael Walzer's 1977 book *Just and Unjust Wars* was a critical early work in this revival of just war thinking, but his was only one of many contributions to a lively scholarship on just war and its critics in the late twentieth and early twenty-first centuries. Even among its advocates, the specific form that just war theory has taken varies, but generally the theory is divided into two branches, one concerning just cause and often referred to by the Latin phrase *jus ad bellum*, which translates as "the right to war," and the other branch concerning just conduct and called *jus in bello* ("right in war"). In addressing *jus ad bellum*, theorists usually advance six criteria for a war to be just: just cause, right intention, legitimate authority of the polity undertaking the war, last resort, probability of success, and the proportionality of the goals of the war to its costs. *Jus in bello* comprises the principles of noncombatant immunity (also known as "discrimination") and proportionality, often balanced with ideas of military necessity.

As scholars were translating the complicated history of the just war tradition into a formal theory, the Geneva Conventions were undergoing another important round of revision which finally provided clear expression of the principle of noncombatant immunity in international law. The 1977 Additional Protocols to the Geneva Conventions provided a sweeping update and expansion to international humanitarian law. They effectively combined the Geneva and Hague treaties into a more unified legal code. Additional Protocol I updated the laws of war concerning international wars while Additional Protocol II expanded a portion of that law to civil wars and internal conflicts. One of the new agreements' most significant aspects was the detailed provisions on the protection of civilians from war's violence. The protocols defined limits on targeting that stressed prohibitions on intentional attacks against noncombatants and nonmilitary targets. Although the United States refused to ratify the Additional Protocols in the 1980s, the U.S. armed forces have since come to acknowledge that provisions of the Additional Protocols have become customary international law and therefore binding for the United States.[12]

Significantly, the preamble of Protocol II referred to human rights, offering basic protections to everyone. This reference reflected the growing importance of thinking about the questions of justice in war in terms of a universal set of human rights. The human rights movement of the 1970s was fueled by disillusionment around the world with nationalism and communism. Universal rights for individuals substituted for the promises that nationalist and communist policies had failed to deliver.[13] In the United States, with many concerned that an amoral pursuit of narrow national interests had brought the failed policies of the Vietnam War, President Jimmy Carter promised to bring values back into American foreign policy and prioritize the support of human rights around the world. For Americans, support of universal rights had the added advantage of undermining Soviet rule in Eastern Europe. The 1975 Helsinki Accords, negotiated among the United States, USSR, and other European nations, included pledges to respect human rights and fundamental freedoms and to cooperate in economic, scientific, and cultural endeavors. Although not legally binding, the Helsinki human rights provisions were monitored by a transnational network of nongovernmental organizations, including the new organization Human Rights Watch, which along with other groups made noncombatant immunity and the protection of civilians human rights issues as they reported on civilian casualties and other war atrocities around the world. Nevertheless, universal notions of human rights were not without opposition. Since Europeans and the United States had played such a dominant role in articulating human rights and establishing human rights institutions, many challenged their universal nature and argued they were Western notions that neglected other cultural traditions.

Although questions of justice were attracting more attention with the rise of the human rights movement, distinguishing wars for self-defense from aggressive wars to further national interests was not any easier to do at the end of the Cold War. The American invasions of Grenada in 1983 and Panama in 1989 illustrated how small a threat might turn into a claim of self-defense. In justifying the invasions, American presidents offered only hypothetical threats to American citizens or small-scale attacks on Americans in those countries—unspecified dangers to 1,000 Americans, mostly medical students, living in Grenada at the time of a violent coup by Cuban-backed insurgents and vague threats by the Panamanian leader Manuel Noriega against Americans followed by the killing of an American soldier and harming of several others in Panama. Since the United States also sought to prevent the spread of leftist influence in Latin America while protecting its access to the Panama Canal and had long fought to maintain its dominance in the Caribbean and Central America, realist and pacifist critics of these invasions questioned the importance of the self-defense justifications in actually motivating U.S. leaders.

Contrast these American claims of self-defense with Iraq's invasion of Kuwait in 1991, which the United States condemned as aggression and went to war to reverse. Saddam Hussein accused Kuwait of aggression and conducting an economic war against Iraq through a policy of driving down oil prices. Although even more tenuous a claim of self-defense than the ones American leaders used in Grenada and Panama, all three justifications treated the idea of self-defense in war as a capacious concept. While the United Nations rejected Iraq's unpersuasive claims and supported Kuwait's unambiguous claims of self-defense by endorsing a U.S.-led coalition to end Iraqi occupation of Kuwait, much ambiguity has remained in defining self-defense. A narrowing of the idea of just cause down to self-defense does not necessarily promise to place many restrictions on states resorting to war.

Post-Cold War Trends

With the end of the Cold War, three trends shaped the questions of justice and war as the twentieth century ended and the twenty-first century opened: humanitarian intervention and the responsibility to protect, international tribunals for war crimes and crimes against humanity, and the response to terrorism. Humanitarian crises in Somalia, Yugoslavia, and Rwanda, brought on by terrible civil wars in the 1990s, increased political pressure in the United States, and in the international community more broadly, to consider military interventions to protect basic human rights, such as stopping mass harm to noncombatants and preventing genocide. The global norm condemning genocide had grown so influential by the end of the twentieth century that the international community proved reluctant, as in Rwanda, to call mass atrocities "genocide" because of the popular pressure the label could bring for a forceful response.

The United Nations and the International Commission on Intervention and State Sovereignty in the 2000s began promulgating the responsibility to protect (R2P) principle, which set an expectation that the international community should intervene to stop mass atrocities and genocide if a state fails to prevent them. The principle met a mixed response early on. While states including the United States have often added humanitarian justifications to their proclaimed reasons for going to war, such as the U.S. argument that Saddam Hussein's violence against his own people gave additional justification for the 2003 American invasion of Iraq, the United States and the international community for years refrained from sending armed forces to Darfur or Syria to end the humanitarian crises there.[14]

The end of the Cold War also allowed a resumption of international tribunals, similar to the Nuremberg and Tokyo tribunals, which held individuals, including heads of state, criminally accountable for violations of international law. In the absence of superpower conflict that had previously hampered international cooperation, tribunals were established for war crimes committed in Yugoslavia, Rwanda, and Sierra Leone. In 1998 the international community adopted the Rome Statute that established a permanent international criminal court with a mandate to try the most serious violations of international law. This reintroduction of international war crimes tribunals provided an important legal mechanism through which the global community could confront the questions of justice in war and actively enforce norms.

At the same time, the growing prominence of terrorism as a central security concern of the international community in the early twenty-first century raised questions about terrorism's relationship to war. Increasingly states defined terrorism as intentional attacks on noncombatants and therefore as a grave injustice, but leaders were left asking whether terrorist attacks justified going to war as a response. Since the usual mode of terrorism has been isolated attacks by small groups, even if occasionally the attacks inflict extensive casualties as in the 9/11 attacks, many have argued that terrorism is a form of crime, or violence at the substate level, that calls for a police rather than a military response.

President George W. Bush rejected this argument after 9/11 and went to war in Afghanistan against the Taliban government, which he accused of harboring the Al-Qaeda perpetrators of the 9/11 attacks. In his statements on national security policy, what would come to be known as the Bush Doctrine, President Bush said the United States was exercising its right to self-defense in taking military action against terrorism, but his claim can be seen as again utilizing a very broad definition of self-defense and raises the question of whether war is a disproportionate response. In contrast during the 1990s, President Bill Clinton initiated a series of international retaliatory measures for terrorist attacks short of war, including cruise missile strikes against Al-Qaeda training camps and economic sanctions against the Taliban government in Afghanistan. Certainly, the 9/11 attacks were on a much greater scale than the overseas embassy bombings and attack on the USS *Cole* that Clinton confronted, but his actions illustrate alternatives to responding to terrorism with war, alternatives which Americans have continued to debate.

The danger of post-9/11 terrorism against the United States has also raised questions over the justice and legality of other measures used to combat the threat. The Bush administration's "enhancement" of interrogation methods employed against terrorism suspects provoked charges in the international community and among Americans that the United States was using torture. Critics charged that the use of the simulated drowning technique known as "waterboarding" as well as the abuses against U.S.-held prisoners of war at Abu Ghraib constituted torture and violated international humanitarian law. The indefinite detention of terrorist suspects at Guantanamo Bay likewise fostered challenges to the justice and legality of U.S. methods for combating terrorism. These terrorist suspects were not treated as prisoners of war, and yet they have also not been given trials as criminals. The question of whether the struggle against terrorism is a fight against criminals or a war is far from resolved.

The history of Americans' engagement with questions of war and justice in the modern world is a history of struggle over the fundamental problem of human violence. The threat of violence is a basic human fear; violence is an always-available tool for human endeavor, and war is the most dramatic and destructive expression of human violence. How to control the violence of war, both its initiation and conduct, has been a major preoccupation of Americans and the broader international community. The gross human costs and destructiveness of war may make the idea of placing limits on war's violence seem absurd, but the question of when killing and destruction are legitimate has been intertwined with the very definition of modern warfare. Illegitimate and unjust forms of social violence are labeled insurrection, terrorism, and genocide while war is the name that respectable violence takes, thereby forcing us to answer the question of when war's violence is just.[15] The international laws of war and humanitarian law and just war theory may seem like obscure and esoteric subjects, but they, like the critiques realists and pacifists provide, are the responses to these difficult questions of violence, power, and justice in a diverse and contentious international community.

Discussion Questions

1. What are the critiques of the just war tradition that Americans advocating for realist and pacifist approaches to the questions of justice in war have offered?

2. What role has law played for Americans in confronting questions of justice in war?

3. How have American approaches toward the questions of justice in war evolved over time and how do they compare to the approaches of Europeans and other peoples around the world?

Notes

1 This chapter draws throughout on the works of Geoffrey Best, *Humanity in Warfare* (New York: Columbia University Press, 1980); John Fabian Witt, *Lincoln's Code: The Laws of War in American History* (New York: Free Press, 2012); Gary Jonathan Bass, *Stay the Hand of Vengeance: The Politics of War Crimes Tribunals* (Princeton, NJ: Princeton University Press, 2000). The websites of the International Committee of the Red Cross (www.icrc.org) and the Avalon Project of the Yale University Law Library (avalon.law.yale.edu) are also invaluable resources for texts and background materials on the laws of war.

2 Vesselin Popovski, Gregory M. Reichberg, and Nicholas Turner, eds., *World Religions and Norms of War* (New York: United Nations University Press, 2009), 306, 309–311.

3 Gregory M. Reichberg, "Norms of War in Roman Catholic Christianity," in ibid., 142–165.

4 Stephen C. Neff, *War and the Law of Nations: A General History* (New York: Cambridge University Press, 2005).

5 Paul A. Kramer, *The Blood of Government: Race, Empire, the United States, and the Philippines* (Chapel Hill: University of North Carolina Press, 2006); Brian McAllister Linn, *The U.S. Army and Counterinsurgency in the Philippine War, 1899–1902* (Chapel Hill: University of North Carolina Press, 1989).

6 *Year Book of the Woman's Peace Party*, 1916, https://catalog.hathitrust.org/Record/002132390

7 Bass, *Stay the Hand of Vengeance*, 106–146.

8 Lawrence J. LeBlanc, *The United States and the Genocide Convention* (Durham, NC: Duke University Press, 1991), 235–238.

9   Raymund T. Yingling and Robert W. Ginnane, "The Geneva Conventions of 1949," *American Journal of International Law* 46, no. 3 (July 1951): 427.

10 Sahr Conway-Lanz, *Collateral Damage: Americans, Noncombatant Immunity, and Atrocity after World War II* (New York: Routledge, 2006).

11 Tom Wells, *The War Within: America's Battle over Vietnam* (Berkeley: University of California Press, 1994), 84.

12 *Operational Law Handbook* (Charlottesville, VA: International and Operational Law Department, Judge Advocate General's Legal Center and School, 2009), 14.

13 Samuel Moyn, *The Last Utopia: Human Rights in History* (Cambridge, MA: Belknap Press, 2010).

14 Alex J. Bellamy, *The Responsibility to Protect: The Global Effort to End Mass Atrocities* (Cambridge, MA: Polity, 2009).

15 Ian Clark, *Waging War: A New Philosophical Introduction* (New York: Oxford University Press, 2015).

Further Reading

Geoffrey Best. *Humanity in Warfare*. New York: Columbia University Press, 1980.

Michael Walzer. *Just and Unjust Wars: A Moral Argument with Historical Illustrations*. New York: Basic Books, 1977.

John Fabian Witt. *Lincoln's Code: The Laws of War in American History*. New York: Free Press, 2012.

2

American Empire

STEFAN AUNE

> We have traversed a trackless desert of
> seven hundred miles to establish in the
> heart of the continent an empire which
> must grow in importance until we shall
> be known and acknowledged by all the
> world.
> —Milton DeLano, Mayor of Denver, to
> William Tecumseh Sherman, 1867

I vividly remember sitting in a hotel room in 2003 watching news coverage of the first air strikes on Baghdad. The dark skyline would suddenly erupt in light, explosions illuminating the city they were demolishing. Here was American power fully and terribly on display. Operation Iraqi Freedom was fought half a world away, but it felt closer. An unprecedented level of media access broadcast the war into American homes and those images fed the controversy that accompanied the violence.[1] The Iraq War provoked some of the largest global antiwar resistance in history but led to a simultaneous outpouring of hawkish patriotism. In the months leading up to and during the war it seemed as if the words "empire" and "imperialism" were everywhere, hurled as a critique or claimed as a national duty.[2] The *New York Times* announced, "American Empire: Get Used to It."[3] Protestors shouted, "No blood for oil!" while commentators like Robert Kaplan, Charles Krauthammer, and Dinesh D'Souza happily embraced American empire as a solution to the world's problems. Drawing a comparison to British imperialism, writer Max Boot argued that "Afghanistan and other troubled lands today cry out for the sort of enlightened foreign administration once provided by self-confident Englishmen in jodhpurs and pith helmets."[4] Even writers wary of the Bush administration's aggressive unilateralism believed that the United States should embrace its superpower role. Joseph Nye called attention to the need for "soft power" and a U.S. foreign policy that would dominate the world through attraction rather than coercion.[5] Critics, unabashed imperialists, and those in between were all engaged in a discussion about empire and the United States' place in the world. These were not new debates.

In 2003 "empire" may have been on the tip of everyone's tongue, but President George W. Bush was quick to reject the term. In a speech at the U.S. Military Academy he argued that "America has no empire to extend or utopia to establish." A few months later, he told a gathering of veterans at the White House that America had "no territorial ambitions." "We do not seek an empire. Our nation is committed to freedom for ourselves and for others."[6] However, in the aftermath of the Bush administration's declaration of a war on terror, the number of countries in which the United States inserted or based troops rose dramatically through "aggressive campaigns of coercion and financial enticement." The Pentagon boasted the ability to unleash overwhelming military force anywhere in the world thanks to an international infrastructure of military bases, a network the president was intent on expanding and strengthening.[7] Whether or not Bush wanted to call this an "empire," it was clear that U.S. power was truly global and that he was willing to use that power to enforce the administration's political vision.

Empire has not always been a concept that American presidents denied, particularly presidents who have presided over the expansion of borders. Thomas Jefferson regularly championed what he called the "Empire of Liberty," the idea that the United States had an obligation to expand its boundaries as an alternative to European political influence.[8] Other presidents invoked the practice (if not the word) when speaking of the country's territorial ambitions. President James Polk was influenced by the idea of "manifest destiny" in his push for war with Mexico.[9] Manifest destiny rendered U.S. territorial acquisitions divinely ordained, allowing politicians to avoid unpleasant comparisons to European imperialism.[10] As the United States acquired overseas colonies at the turn of the century Theodore Roosevelt wrote that "expansion is the cause of peace" when he advocated that the country maintain its occupation of the Philippines "so that one more fair spot of the world's surface shall have been snatched from the forces of darkness."[11] Indeed, despite Bush's claim to the contrary the United States has continually added new territories and spheres of influence throughout its history. From the moment of the country's creation continental expansion into land held by Native nations has been ongoing. Colonies or territory in Mexico, Hawaii, Cuba, Guam, Puerto Rico, and the Philippines have been or continue to be held by the United States, gained through wars, occupation, and annexation. And though less visible, a global network of military bases, islands on every continent, permits this "archipelago empire" to project power anywhere.[12] If we want to make empire visible, following the movements of its military is a good place to start.

"Empire" and "imperialism" seem to come to the forefront of public discussion every time the United States is engaged in a controversial war or occupation.[13] This was true in Iraq and Afghanistan, just as it was in Nicaragua, Vietnam, Korea, Haiti, the Philippines, Mexico, and in the Black Hills of what is now South Dakota. Military violence is one of the more visible aspects of imperial power. But what is "empire"? Both critics and proponents seem to have a sense that empire is big, powerful, and expansive, but more precise descriptions are harder to come by. Likely associations probably include the British Empire and the similarly accented villains from Star Wars, but the idea of an American Empire may be new for some readers. You may be resistant to the idea, or simply have never thought about U.S. history in those terms. You would not be alone.

As the United States grew (at the expense of Native peoples, Mexicans, Hawaiians, and others) "empire" began to invite comparisons to the imperialism of Britain, Spain, and France, an anxiety that increased as the country began to acquire overseas colonies at the end of the nineteenth century. By the twentieth century "empire" and "imperialism" were dirty words, more often used by critics rather than proponents of foreign policy. For a long time U.S. academics rejected the terms altogether. William Appleman Williams declared in the 1950s that "one of the central themes in scholarship on US history is that there is no American empire."[14] He was referring to an idea called "American exceptionalism," the belief that the political and social development of the United States is unique, free of the injustices associated with other empires throughout history. Working against this idea, Williams argued that the United States was an empire that blended economic control with territorial expansion, an argument that rose to prominence in the mid-twentieth century.[15] During the Cold War, imperialism was a critique hurled back and forth between the United States and the Soviet Union. Most recently, the war on terror has revived ideas of empire in U.S. political discourse, with both negative and positive connotations.[16] Empire seems to play a central role in the way that America is imagined, whether as decidedly anti-imperial or as the last empire standing.

A simple and consistent definition of "empire" would inevitably fail to account for the varied ways in which the United States has impacted the rest of the world. It is far more useful to treat empire as a toolkit, a way of looking at American history that focuses on a set of related questions. First, we can explore questions of power, whether expressed through political, economic, or military means. Empires wield power in asymmetrical ways, controlling other political entities and dictating economic and cultural flows. Power also includes another keyword, "sovereignty," which describes the authority exercised by a state, something which an empire often imposes at the expense of competing or indigenous sovereignties. Second, we can focus on space. Empire is a spatial designation, referring to the acquisition and occupation of territories, the spread of influence, and the expansion of borders. Empire can be local, regional, continental, and global, often all at once. Here we might also think of colonialism, the imperial practice of establishing control over distant (or not so distant) territories in pursuit of land and resources. Finally, empires seek to mobilize difference, including racial, gender, sexual, national, and class differences. The United States is no exception, and categories of difference have been crucial in justifying and promoting the expansion of control throughout the world.[17]

Power, space, and difference, while not comprehensive, offer a useful framework for analysis of U.S. history. Ultimately these different approaches to the study of empire are tools from our toolkit, ways to analyze and understand how power functions globally. Empire can be approached in economic, cultural, and political terms, but nothing highlights the contours of empire like military power. The U.S. military has been at the center of successive waves of territorial expansion, both continental and overseas, and today maintains a powerful worldwide network of military bases. This chapter contends that analyzing U.S. history as an imperial history helps to illuminate a militarized empire that often seems hidden from view. By examining three crucial historical periods—continental expansion, overseas territorial acquisitions at the end of the nineteenth century, and the modern network of worldwide military bases—militarism is shown as central to understanding the steady growth of U.S. territory, power, and influence over its history.

Settler-Colonialism and Continental Expansion

U.S. history is typically imagined as an east-west story told from the perspective of settlers who moved across the continent in covered wagons. However, what if we shift our viewpoint and face east from Indian Country?[18] From this perspective settlement looks more like an invasion. Historian Ned Blackhawk calls this the sobering challenge of U.S. history—"reconciling the dispossession of millions with the making of America."[19] The United States may have emerged from conflict with Europe's empires, but it donned the imperial mantle in relation to Native people as the new nation's borders expanded. For the United States the history of empire is inseparable from the concept of settler-colonialism. In contrast to more extractive forms of colonialism premised on the acquisition of resources or the exploitation of labor (for example, many European colonies in Africa), settler-colonialism is a project of replacement, one that seeks the elimination of Native peoples. Land is central to this process. Settlers attempt to found new political institutions, create borders, and establish claims to territory. This makes the colonial process "a structure, not an event."[20] This eminently quotable formulation is a useful way to think about colonialism as a system rather than a discrete historical period.

Colonialism in the United States was not an episode of history that ended hundreds of years ago. It is an ongoing process and set of institutions that continually infringe on the pre-existing sovereignty of Native people, sovereignty they never relinquished in the many treaties signed with the United States. A recent example is the debates over the Keystone XL and Dakota Access oil pipelines, which the Rosebud Sioux and the Standing Rock Sioux nations have vigorously opposed, the Rosebud Sioux declaring the routing of the pipeline through their territory as an "act of war."[21] The structural nature of settler-colonialism means that any discussion of U.S. empire in the twentieth or twenty-first-century needs to acknowledge ongoing colonialism as the precondition for the existence of an expansive and powerful U.S. state. Historians have to avoid what Vine Deloria Jr. calls "the cameo theory of history" wherein "indigenous peoples make dramatic entrances, stay briefly on the stage, and then fade out."[22]

The American Revolution may have been a rebellion against a colonial empire, but upon independence the United States began a process of territorial expansion, the latest in a series of empires that had sought to acquire land in the "new world." This framing only makes sense if we acknowledge that North America was home to hundreds of Native nations and peoples with their own claims to political sovereignty rather than the vast emptiness it was often depicted as being. Indeed, many Native nations viewed American settlers as the greater threat and fought alongside the British during the war. Mohawk leader Joseph Brant argued that his people had to "defend their Land and Liberty against the Rebels, who in great measure begin this rebellion to be sole masters of this continent."[23] This support for the British would be betrayed in the war's aftermath. The Treaty of Paris, which ended the Revolutionary War in 1783, ceded Native-held land to the United States that was not the British government's to give away, provoking anger from Native peoples living on that land.[24]

The new nation's conflicts with Native people over land would only increase in the ensuing years, largely driven by the belief in "manifest destiny," a term coined in an 1845 speech by writer John L. Sullivan. He believed it was "our manifest destiny to overspread the continent allotted by Providence for the free development of our yearly multiplying millions."[25] This process of continental expansion dramatically increased the size of the United States while having a catastrophic effect on Native people.

U.S. claims to land involved more than just physical acts like settlement and war. They also involved symbolic and cultural assertions of discovery and ownership that ignored the presence of Native peoples.[26] Typically these claims were fundamentally opposed to the reality on the ground, particularly on land that Britain, France, and Spain claimed in the interior of the continent in the seventeenth, eighteenth, and early nineteenth centuries.[27] For example, on the first map printed of the newly independent United States, the states of Connecticut, Virginia, North and South Carolina, Georgia, and Florida had borders extending west to the Mississippi River, far beyond their present boundaries.[28] The political authority of eastern states certainly did not extend that far, but they still asserted ownership of that space on a map. That land may have been imagined as U.S. territory, but on the ground much of it remained Native space.

Native nations and peoples were not passive victims of the colonial process. They resisted, allied, advised, and traded with the United States. Powerful polities such as the Haudensoasaune Confederacy and the Cherokee Nation played key roles in the American Revolution and during the decades when the United States was a young nation. Conflicts with Tecumseh's pan-Native confederacy and wars with southeastern Native groups like the Creeks and Seminoles occupied the early years of the nineteenth century. Indeed, aside from the Civil War and the Mexican-American War the U.S. military spent much of the nineteenth century focused on wars with Native people. Even the Mexican-American war, a conflict for empire in its own right that dramatically expanded the borders of the United States, was influenced by Native political actors. Historians now understand that Native fighters fundamentally impacted the results of the war, as their raids and attacks had already weakened northern Mexico. Some scholars have even argued that the Comanche carved out their own empire on the southern plains that not only stalled European imperialism but actively reversed it, halting Spain's northward advance and dominating the southern great plains.[29] The Comanche were not the only Native nation to impede and interrupt European colonialism, and they are an example of how important it is to view Native peoples as active and powerful participants in U.S. history. In the second half of the nineteenth century, Native resistance to settler-colonialism would intensify as the U.S. military pushed west, leading to a series of conflicts that exercise an enduring influence on the American imagination as the "Indian Wars."

In the aftermath of the Civil War the U.S. military overcame sectional differences by defining itself in opposition to Native peoples along the frontier.[30] Increasing waves of settlement, spurred on by the 1862 Homestead Act that made land in the West available, provoked a series of conflicts as settlers, soldiers, and explorers encroached on Native lands. These campaigns against Native peoples occurred during the emergence of a modernizing U.S. military. Civil War generals represented an old guard that increasingly conflicted with younger officers interested in industrializing the military and updating the education and training of soldiers.[31] What this means is that the coalescing institutions of the modern U.S. military were forged in a period of settler-colonial conflict. Officers and soldiers had to adjust to irregular warfare that confounded their training, heavily rooted in the European tradition of what they called "civilized war."[32] The "savage" and "Indian country" became enduring military tropes, recycled in future wars in the Philippines, Vietnam, Iraq, and elsewhere. Indians became the quintessential enemies of U.S. expansion no matter where the military happened to find itself. During the Iraq War, a prominent military theorist warned that "if the government of Iraq collapses . . . you've got Fort Apache in the middle of Indian country, but the Indians have mortars now."[33] Statements like this are indicative of how the beliefs that motivate U.S. empire travel across time and space. They help us to see continuity between different periods of U.S. expansion. The ability to recognize these continuities is one of the most useful aspects of using empire as an analytical tool. The U.S. military seems to fight and refight the Indian Wars everywhere it goes. This was certainly true in the next stage of U.S. imperial expansion at the turn of the century.

Imperial Paternalism

As the nineteenth century ended prominent historians and politicians worried that the end of continental expansion put the U.S. political experiment in peril. Frederick Jackson Turner's influential frontier thesis proposed that the U.S. egalitarian political culture was due to the availability of "free land" in the West that had provided a space for American democracy to flourish. Turner, declaring the frontier closed in 1893, feared this marked an end to the democratizing effect of settler-colonialism on U.S. society. Turner made little mention of the Native people that occupied this supposedly free land or the military conflicts that had enabled expansion. In contrast, his fellow historian (and future president) Theodore Roosevelt argued in his own writing that conflicts with the "weaker race" had helped to forge the American people into a superior civilization. Roosevelt would maintain this emphasis on masculinity and racial superiority throughout his political career, championing what he called "the strenuous life" and advocating overseas militarism as a necessary alternative to the now-closed frontier. Roosevelt's vision of aggressive expansion, or "peace by the sword," would play out in the early years of the twentieth century.[34] In just a few decades the U.S. military would move from one of the worst massacres of the Indian Wars, the slaughter of hundreds of Lakota at Wounded Knee in 1890, to the annexation of Hawaii in 1893, followed by the War of 1898 and subsequent occupations of Cuba, Guam, Puerto Rico, and the Philippines. It was a period of transition, but also of continuity, as the ideological justifications for settler-colonialism were transformed into a doctrine of paternalism that justified overseas expansion.

According to Roosevelt and other proponents of U.S. expansion only war and occupation could bring about the uplift of those they deemed unable to govern themselves. Ideas about racial and gender difference helped to shape these paternalistic attitudes. Roosevelt invoked this ideology in his criticism of the anti-imperialists who questioned the occupation of the Philippines which followed the defeat of Spain in the War of 1898. In a speech titled "The Strenuous Life" he argued:

> I have scant patience with those who fear to undertake the task of governing the Philippines, . . . [or] shrink from it because of the expense and trouble; but I have even scanter patience with those who make a pretense of humanitarianism to hide and cover their timidity, and who cant about "liberty" and "the consent of the governed" in order to excuse themselves from their unwillingness

to play the part of men. Their doctrine, if carried out, would make it incumbent upon us to leave the Apaches of Arizona to work out their own salvation, and to decline to interfere on a single Indian reservation. Their doctrines condemn your forefathers and mine for ever having settled in these United States.[35]

Roosevelt's statement encapsulates the doctrine of paternalism and its connection to settler-colonialism. He views the occupation of the Philippines as a duty, similar to what poet Rudyard Kipling famously called "The White Man's Burden" in his 1899 poem. He scorns "timidity" and talks about the duties of real men, which was representative of the patriarchal gender politics of the period.[36] Finally, Roosevelt views the occupation of the Philippines as a continuation of continental settler-colonialism, arguing that governing the Philippines is just as necessary as the conquest of the Apache people, both of which will lead to their "salvation." Roosevelt was not alone in thinking that the United States had an obligation to govern over "uncivilized" races. Senator Albert Beveridge similarly argued in 1900 that God "made us adepts in government that we may administer government among savage and senile peoples."[37] Many U.S. politicians in this period believed that white men had a particular genius for government. This combination of racial and gender superiority was a potent ideology, a set of beliefs that worked to justify empire.

There was plenty of resistance to the War of 1898 and the imperialist aspirations of politicians like Roosevelt and Beveridge. Many Americans worried that gaining control of foreign territories threatened democracy. In an 1898 broadside published by the Anti-Imperialist League, John G. Carlisle warned that the war could "change the very essence of our national character," converting the government into a "war-making, tax-consuming, land-grabbing, and office-distributing machine."[38] Anti-imperialists viewed foreign occupations as antithetical to the country's political institutions. They argued that the United States was in danger of the same degeneration experienced by other empires throughout history, including the Spanish Empire they had recently defeated. Opponents of the war regularly criticized the acquisition of overseas colonies as a betrayal of the belief in government by consent rather than force. However, they often reproduced the same sort of racialized paternalism found in the arguments of pro-imperialist writers. In the same broadside quoted above, Samuel Gompers, founder of the American Federation of Labor (AFL), worried that "if these new islands are to become ours . . . can we hope to close the flood-gates of immigration from the hordes of Chinese and the semi-savage races coming from what will then be part of our own country?"[39] Officials like Gompers used the same paternalistic view of race to argue against, rather than in favor of, imperialism. For them imperialism represented a threat of contamination, not only a dilution of U.S. political principles but of the racial and cultural makeup of the country itself.[40] Ideas about white racial superiority informed both sides of the debate over American expansion. Ultimately, the United States would commit to a

FIGURE 2.1 "School Begins," by Louis Dalrymple (1899). Library of Congress Prints and Photographs Division.

long-term occupation of the Philippines without transforming it into a state or territory as Gompers feared. Paternalism won out over racial isolationism as the United States pursued Roosevelt's vision of empire.

The racial and gender paternalism of the early twentieth century was not confined to political and academic discourse. It made its way into popular forms of media where visual representations regularly depicted people in the new U.S. colonies as backward, primitive, and unfit for self-government.[41] Political cartoons from the period often depicted Cuba, the Philippines, Puerto Rico, and other colonial possessions as unruly children looked after by a patient Uncle Sam.

In the 1899 cartoon "School Begins" by Louis Dalrymple a schoolmaster Uncle Sam looks over his classroom (Figure 2.1). The front row is occupied by Cuba, Puerto Rico, Hawaii, and the Philippines, who are depicted in caricature as sullen and unwilling to learn. Behind them a group of students, representing recently admitted states, quietly read their books. In a corner a Native student, wrapped in a blanket, reads an upside-down alphabet book while a Chinese boy stands just outside the door. An African American child cleans a window on the edge of the room. The chalkboard bears the message "The consent of the governed is a good thing in theory, but very rare in fact."[42] This cartoon and others like it made the case for empire by depicting U.S. control as a necessary step in the education of nonwhite colonized peoples. The Native student's isolation and inability to correctly hold a book is either a critique of the failures of the reservation system or a representation of the presumed inferiority of Native peoples, or perhaps both, while the black student's menial labor and separation within the classroom speaks volumes about the racism of legalized segregation under the Jim Crow system.[43] The cartoon draws a clear connection between settler-colonialism and antiblack racism to the white supremacy of the newly global U.S. empire. This racial paternalism denied the self-determination of those deemed unable to successfully govern themselves.

The War of 1898 resulted in the Treaty of Paris, which ceded Spanish colonial territories to the United States, including the Philippines. U.S. acquisition and subsequent occupation of the Philippines betrayed Filipino hopes for independence. War between the U.S. military and the Filipino revolutionary army, which had previously worked to end Spanish colonial rule, began soon after U.S. occupation and for decades Filipinos would fight for self-determination through military and political means. From the beginning, U.S. claims to authority in the Philippines were driven by the belief that Filipino people were incapable of self-government.[44] President William McKinley, when questioned on his policy in the Philippines, argued that "we could not leave them to themselves—they were unfit for self-government . . . there was nothing left for us to do but to take them all, and to educate the Filipinos, and uplift and civilize and Christianize them, and by God's grace do the very best we could by them."[45] As the United States settled into an occupation that would last until the Second World War, with an even longer military presence, McKinley's policy of "uplift" was used to deny Filipino demands for self-government. Filipinos were portrayed as uncivilized and backward to postpone the transfer of political authority.

Much of this discourse was based on racialized comparisons of Filipinos to Native people. For example, George Anderson, a commander on the island of Luzon, wrote of Filipinos that "they are rank barbarians, not much above our better class of Indians."[46] Similarly, Brig. General Theodore Schwan wrote that the Filipinos "are in identically the same position as the Indians of our country have been for many years, and in my opinion must be subdued in much the same way, by such convincing conquest as shall make them realize fully the futility of armed resistance."[47] These sorts of references were frequent and widespread, and should come as no surprise given that most high-ranking officers serving in the Philippines had also seen action in campaigns against Native people.[48]

Imperial paternalism can be used to analyze numerous other interventions, wars, and occupations throughout U.S. history. Although the explicitly racial paternalism of the occupation of the Philippines has become less visible, the United States has continued to enforce its political vision throughout the twentieth and twenty-first centuries. Historically, one of the central tenets of U.S. foreign policy has been a negative attitude toward revolution and social change in other countries. Analyzing U.S. history as an imperial history reveals these tensions between democracy and empire. Efforts to foster stable governments and economic development have sometimes clashed with negative attitudes toward the political self-determination of others. This was particularly true during the twentieth-century process of decolonization and revolution, as European colonies gave way to newly independent nations that were often wary of Western political and economic influence.[49] At the same time, Central and South America has functioned as a workshop for different imperial practices—military, economic, and political.[50] In places like Haiti, Guatemala, El Salvador, Chile, Nicaragua, and elsewhere the U.S. sponsored military coups, fought counterinsurgency wars, and sought to manipulate economies. Political and economic interests often worked hand in hand. The nineteen-year occupation of Haiti that began in 1915 installed a new government and forced the adoption of a new constitution more favorable to foreign investment, a pattern seen in other countries throughout the twentieth century.[51] Economics and the promotion of global capitalism was a key element in later interventions, such as the U.S.-sponsored coups in Guatemala in 1954 and Chile in 1973. Historians have noted the existence of a U.S. "market empire" that may not involve territorial control but certainly involves the promotion of U.S. interests through the dominance of economic forces.[52]

U.S. interventions intensified during the Cold War. Although typically conceived as a global conflict between the United States and the Soviet Union, countries like Nicaragua and El Salvador became battlegrounds where Cold War struggles influenced national politics.[53] Foreign interference took an imperial form as democratically elected governments were opposed on ideological grounds, leading to decades of brutal violence. The United States was often willing to support repressive and violent dictatorships if they were anticommunist.[54] It is important to avoid reducing complex situations to simple explanations, but paternalism is a highly useful lens through which to analyze the many instances of political and economic intervention that have resulted in near-constant foreign involvement for U.S. governmental and military forces. These interventions have been justified in various ways, but whether viewed positively or negatively they represent a willingness to regulate and control politics and economics on a global scale. Much of this global reach is enabled by U.S. military bases spread throughout the world. We have seen how settler-colonialism is a useful tool for analyzing the continental expansion of the United States and how paternalism helps to make sense of the ways foreign interventions and occupations have been justified. In the final section the military itself becomes our tool of analysis. Thinking spatially and geographically we can ask a simple question—where is the U.S. military?

Empire of Bases

In the twenty-first century, nothing is more indicative of U.S. empire than the global reach of the U.S. military. Much of this power comes from its approximately 800 military bases located in around eighty countries, accounting for about 95 percent of the world's foreign military bases.[55] No other country comes close to the U.S. level of worldwide military control. Great Britain, France, and

Russia each have a few foreign bases, while Japan, South Korea, India, Chile, Turkey, and Israel each have one. The United States probably has more military bases than any other empire in history, yet most Americans remain largely ignorant of their numbers and location.[56] The history of these bases is an imperial history, tied to war, occupation, and military expansion. Wherever the U.S. military has gone bases have usually followed, giving the United States an ongoing presence long after the war or occupation is over.

The creation of bases has accompanied each wave of U.S. expansion. Military forts enabled continental conquest—255 in total—which functioned as foreign bases on land that was often still controlled by Native peoples. These forts operated as the military outposts of settler-colonialism and were targeted by Native peoples as violations of territorial integrity.[57] The War of 1898 and subsequent occupation of overseas colonies resulted in a global basing system, and by 1938 the United States had fourteen military bases outside its continental borders in Puerto Rico, Cuba, Panama, the Virgin Islands, Hawaii, Midway, Wake, Guam, the Philippines, Shanghai, the Aleutians, American Samoa, and Johnston Island. By the end of the Second World War there were 30,000 installations in approximately 100 countries, a massive buildup in military power to which scholars have attributed the rise of U.S. global hegemony. The number would decrease significantly after the end of the Second World War, falling to 2,000 by 1948 and declining throughout the century as the country demobilized and resistance to the U.S. military presence forced the closure of some bases. The explosion of foreign bases during World War II would be followed by surges during the Korean War, the War in Vietnam, and the Wars in Afghanistan and Iraq, showing that wars and occupations continue to expand U.S. territory, even if the form of those acquisitions has shifted since the days of settler-colonialism and annexation.[58] The contemporary number, which hovers around 800 to 900, is still an impressive network that places the military within striking distance of every spot on the globe.[59] Historian Bruce Cumings calls the modern form of U.S. empire an "archipelago empire," small islands of U.S. control from which power can be projected anywhere in the world. It has become increasingly difficult to tell where the boundaries of the United States begin and where they end.

The archipelago empire has not proliferated without local and international resistance. Military base infringement on national sovereignty has provoked opposition from some local communities, who not only object to their role in war-making but also criticize the effects of pollution and environmental degradation, as well as crime and sexual violence.[60] Long-term resistance has confronted some of the longest-held military bases, in places like the Philippines, South Korea, and the Japanese island of Okinawa.[61] For most U.S. citizens these bases are either invisible or accepted as a natural part of our national security apparatus. David Vine argues that Americans "consider the situation normal and accept that US military installations exist in staggering numbers in other countries, on other peoples' land. On the other hand, the idea that there would be foreign bases on US soil is unthinkable."[62] Proponents of U.S. military bases argue that they enhance national security and foreign policy, allowing America to impose a military-backed political stability on an unstable world.[63] This sort of military power is enthusiastically embraced by advocates of U.S. empire. Niall Ferguson notes that "if military power is the sine qua non of empire, then it is hard to imagine how anyone could deny the imperial character of the United States today." U.S. military base commanders control territories "beyond the wildest imaginings of their Roman predecessors."[64] For advocates of these bases military strength translates into power and security, maintaining U.S. global supremacy.

Nevertheless, the role of bases in national security has not escaped questioning. Some analysts view U.S. military bases as endangering, rather than protecting, national security. Former CIA consultant Chalmers Johnson argues that the bases encourage heavy-handed military responses to problems that ultimately increase, rather than decrease, foreign or terrorist threats to the United States.[65] They also act as a drain on finances and resources, both of which must be pumped into the network of military bases to keep it functional.[66] The contested role that military bases play in U.S. foreign policy will continue to generate debate, affected by changes in the global political landscape and the form that future wars take. In the meantime the bases function as a global network of empire, outposts of American military power that have been at the forefront of U.S. expansion since the earliest days of settler-colonialism. As a marine stationed in Iraq explained in 2003, "This is like cowboys and Indians."[67] And as long as the world is imagined as "Indian country," dangerous territory threatening the United States from all sides, the justifications for an empire of bases will remain intact.

Discussion Questions

1. How does the narrative of U.S. history change if we put the experiences of Native people at the center of the story?
2. What are the differences between continental expansion, an overseas colony, and a foreign military base? How can each be understood as an element of empire?
3. What are some of the political implications in calling the United States an empire? Why might some be resistant to that characterization?

Notes

1   To avoid repetition, I will use "U.S." and "American" interchangeably but ask the reader to be aware of the problems inherent in using a hemispheric name to describe a country.
2   This chapter will use "empire" and "imperialism" as related terms, with imperialism describing the practices of empire. They have not always been used interchangeably, with "imperialism" often functioning as a criticism or negative description. For a brief

history of the usage of both terms in U.S. history, see Shelley Streeby, "Empire," in *Keywords for American Cultural Studies*, ed. Bruce Burgett and Glenn Hendler (New York: New York University Press, 2007). In the twenty-first century "empire" has been increasingly linked to the process of globalization, particularly in the influential work of Michael Hardt and Antonio Negri.

3   David Harvey, *The New Imperialism* (Oxford: Oxford University Press, 2003), 3–4.

4   Niall Ferguson, *Colossus: The Price of America's Empire* (New York: Penguin Press, 2004), 4–5.

5   Joseph Nye, "Lessons in Imperialism," *Financial Times*, June 16, 2002, 1.

6   Harvey, *The New Imperialism*, 4; Michael Ignatieff, "The American Empire: The Burden," *New York Times*, January 5, 2003.

7   Catherine Lutz, ed., *The Bases of Empire: The Global Struggle against US Military Posts* (New York: New York University Press, 2009), 36, 47–48.

8   Douglas Brinkley and Gail Feigenbaum, "Thomas Jefferson's Empire of Liberty," *American History* 38, no. 3 (August 2003): 78.

9   Brian DeLay, *War of a Thousand Deserts: Indian Raids and the US-Mexican War* (New Haven, CT: Yale University Press, 2008), 219.

10 Burgett and Hendler, *Keywords for American Cultural Studies*, 97.

11 Theodore Roosevelt, "Expansion and Peace," *The Independent* 51 (December 21, 1899): 3404.

12 Bruce Cumings, "Is America an Imperial Power?," *Current History* 102, no. 667 (November 2003): 358.

13 Paul A. Kramer, "Power and Connection: Imperial Histories of the United States in the World," *The American Historical Review* 116, no. 5 (December 2011): 1349.

14 William Appleman Williams, "The Frontier Thesis and American Foreign Policy," *Pacific Historical Review* 24, no. 4 (1955): 1.

15 An excellent example of this scholarship can be found in Walter LaFeber, *The New Empire: An Interpretation of American Expansion, 1860–1898* (Ithaca, NY: Cornell University Press, 1963).

16 Burgett and Hendler, *Keywords for American Cultural Studies*, 97.

17 These categories are drawn, in part, from a much longer and more comprehensive analysis of "empire" as an analytical tool in Kramer, "Power and Connection." For an exploration of the spatial characteristics of empire, see Philip Deloria, "From Nation to Neighborhood: Land, Policy, Culture, Colonialism, and Empire in U.S.-Indian Relations," in *The Cultural Turn in US History: Past, Present, and Future*, ed. James W. Cook, Lawrence B. Glickman, and Michael O'Malley (Chicago: University of Chicago Press, 2008). Further discussion of the role that difference plays in the formation of empire can be found in Amy Kaplan and Donald E. Pease, eds., *Cultures of United States Imperialism* (Durham, NC: Duke University Press, 1993).

18 Daniel K. Richter, *Facing East from Indian Country: A Native History of Early America* (Cambridge, MA: Harvard University Press, 2001).

19 Ned Blackhawk, *Violence over the Land: Indians and Empires in the Early American West* (Cambridge, MA: Harvard University Press, 2006), 3.

20 Patrick Wolfe, *Settler Colonialism and the Transformation of Anthropology: The Politics and Poetics of an Ethnographic Event* (London: Cassell, 1999), 2.

21 "House Vote in Favor of the Keystone XL Pipeline an Act of War," *Lakota Voice*, November 15, 2014, http://www.lakotavoice.com/2014/11/15/house-vote-in-favor-of-the-keystone-xl-pipeline-an-act-of-war/.

22 Pekka Hämäläinen, *The Comanche Empire* (New Haven, CT: Yale University Press, 2008), 6.

23 Alan Taylor, *The Divided Ground: Indians, Settlers and the Northern Borderland of the American Revolution* (New York: Knopf, 2006), 80.

24 Gregory Evans Dowd, *A Spirited Resistance: The North American Indian Struggle for Unity, 1745–1815* (Baltimore: Johns Hopkins University Press, 1992), 93–94.

25 Bruce Cumings, *Dominion from Sea to Sea: Pacific Ascendancy and American Power* (New Haven, CT: Yale University Press, 2009), 63.

26 Jean M. O'Brien, *Firsting and Lasting: Writing Indians out of Existence in New England* (Minneapolis: University of Minnesota Press, 2010), 2.

27 Michael J. Witgen, *An Infinity of Nations: How the Native New World Shaped Early North America* (Philadelphia: University of Pennsylvania Press, 2012), 116.

28 "Abel Buell Map of US," Geography and Map Reading Room, Library of Congress, http://www.loc.gov/rr/geogmap/buellmap.html.

29 Hämäläinen, *Comanche Empire*, 3–9; Brian DeLay, introduction to *War of a Thousand Deserts*.

30 Cecilia Elizabeth O'Leary, *To Die For: The Paradox of American Patriotism* (Princeton, NJ: Princeton University Press, 1999), 116.

31 A discussion of this history is found in T. R. Brereton, *Educating the U.S. Army: Arthur L. Wagner and Reform, 1875–1905* (Lincoln: University of Nebraska Press, 2000).

32 Robert M. Utley, *Frontier Regulars: The United States Army and the Indian, 1866–1891* (New York: Macmillan, 1974), 44.

33 Stephen W. Silliman, "The 'Old West' in the Middle East: US Military Metaphors in Real and Imagined Indian Country," *American Anthropologist* 110, no. 2 (June 2008): 240.

34 Richard Slotkin, *Gunfighter Nation: The Myth of the Frontier in Twentieth-Century America* (New York: Atheneum, 1992), 48–53.

35 Qtd. in ibid., 53

36 Kristin L. Hoganson, *Fighting for American Manhood: How Gender Politics Provoked the Spanish-American and Philippine-American Wars* (New Haven, CT: Yale University Press, 1998), 3–4.

37 Qtd. in ibid., 22.

38 "Anti-Imperialist Broadside #2" (Anti-Imperialist League, Washington, DC), Library of Congress, Carl Schurz Papers, 1842–1983, Box 204, Reel 112.

39 Ibid.

40 For more on the relationship between the foreign and the domestic, see Amy Kaplan, *The Anarchy of Empire in the Making of US Culture* (Cambridge, MA: Harvard University Press, 2002), 6.

41 Mary Renda offers a useful description of paternalism in Renda, *Taking Haiti: Military Occupation and the Culture of US Imperialism, 1915–1940* (Chapel Hill: University of North Carolina Press, 2001), 15.

42 Louis Dalrymple, "School Begins," still image, 1899, Library of Congress Prints and Photographs Division, http://www.loc.gov/pictures/item/2012647459.

43 "Jim Crow" refers to the system of legal and social segregation that operated in the United States in the eighteenth and nineteenth centuries. For more, see Leon F. Litwack, *Trouble in Mind: Black Southerners in the Age of Jim Crow* (New York: Knopf, 1998).

44 Paul Kramer, *The Blood of Government: Race, Empire, the United States, and the Philippines* (Chapel Hill: University of North Carolina Press, 2006), 5.

45 General James Rusling, "Interview with President William McKinley" (repr. from *The Christian Advocate*, January 22, 1903, 17), in *The Philippines Reader*, ed. Daniel Schirmer and Stephen Rosskamm Shalom (Boston: South End Press, 1987), 22–23.

46 Qtd. in Glenn Anthony May, *Battle for Batangas: A Philippine Province at War* (New Haven, CT: Yale University Press, 1991), 147.

47 Andrew J. Birtle, *US Army Counterinsurgency and Contingency Operations Doctrine, 1860–1941* (Washington, DC: Center of Military History, United States Army, 1998), 112.

48 Peter W. Stanley, ed., *Reappraising an Empire: New Perspectives on Philippine-American History* (Cambridge, MA: Harvard University Press, 1984), 34.

49 Jeremi Suri, *Power and Protest: Global Revolution and the Rise of Detente* (Cambridge, MA: Harvard University Press, 2003), 131.

50 See Michael H. Hunt, *Ideology and U.S. Foreign Policy* (New Haven, CT: Yale University Press, 1987); Greg Grandin, *Empire's Workshop: Latin America, the United States, and the Rise of the New Imperialism* (New York: Metropolitan/Owl Books, 2007), 2.

51 Renda, *Taking Haiti*, 10.

52 Victoria de Grazia, *Irresistible Empire: America's Advance through Twentieth-Century Europe* (Cambridge, MA: Belknap Press, 2005), 3.

53 In places like El Salvador U.S. support for military death squads and paramilitary forces resulted in civilian massacres. See Mark Danner, *The Massacre at El Mozote: A Parable of the Cold War* (New York: Vintage Books, 1994).

54 Mahmood Mamdani, *Good Muslim, Bad Muslim: America, the Cold War, and the Roots of Terror* (New York: Pantheon Books, 2004), 188.

55 The exact number of bases is very difficult to determine. For further discussion, see David Vine, "Where in the World Is the US Military?," *Politico*, http://www.politico.com/magazine/story/2015/06/us-military-bases-around-the-world-119321.html.

56 David Vine, "The United States Probably Has More Foreign Military Bases Than Any Other People, Nation, or Empire in History," *The Nation*, http://www.thenation.com/article/the-united-states-probably-has-more-foreign-military-bases-than-any-other-people-nation-or-empire-in-history/.

57 For example, the Lakota war to defend the Powder River country during 1866–1868.

58 Catherine Lutz, *The Bases of Empire*, 10–14.

59 Ibid., 10.

60 Ibid., 30.

61 Ibid., 35–37.

62 David Vine, "The United States Probably Has."

63 Catherine Lutz, *The Bases of Empire*, 10.

64 Niall Ferguson, *Colossus*, 17.

65 Chalmers Johnson, "The Sorrows of Empire: Imperialism, Militarism and the End of the Republic," *Sigur Center Asia Papers* 19 (2004): 6.

66 Chalmers Johnson, *The Sorrows of Empire: Militarism, Secrecy, and the End of the Republic* (New York: Metropolitan Books, 2004), 306–308.

67 Qtd. in Silliman, "The 'Old West' in the Middle East," 240.

Further Reading

Amy Kaplan and Donald E. Pease, eds. *Cultures of United States Imperialism* (New Americanists). Durham, NC: Duke University Press, 1993.

Paul A. Kramer. "Power and Connection: Imperial Histories of the United States in the World." *The American Historical Review* 116, no. 5 (December 2011): 1348–1391.

Walter LaFeber. *The New Empire: An Interpretation of American Expansion, 1860–1898*. Ithaca, NY: Cornell University Press, 1963.

3

Domestic Politics and Antiwar Activism

NICK WITHAM

Since the War of 1898, American military conflict has taken place overseas, often at a great distance from the contiguous United States. Nonetheless, domestic politics has played a key role in shaping Americans' understandings of war and its relationship to national identity. In charting the role of antiwar protest in U.S. foreign relations from 1898 to the present, this chapter focuses on six case studies: debates about American imperialism during the Spanish-American and Philippine-American Wars, the question of neutrality in response to the Second World War, African American civil rights and the Cold War, opposition to the War in Vietnam, activism against Ronald Reagan's anticommunist interventions in Central America, and antiwar responses to the global "War on Terror." Doing so seeks to answer three fundamental questions. First, what traditions of thought and culture have opponents of war drawn on and how have they understood the relationship between their dissent and their patriotism? Second, to what extent has antiwar activism been articulated in terms of the "national interest" and/or "solidarity" with communities outside of the United States? Third, how have political responses on the home front shaped and constrained the ability of the American state to wage war?

In examining the changing answers to these questions provided by antiwar activists over the course of more than a century, the chapter advances two core arguments. First, "antiwar" activism as a category should encompass not only movements that aimed to end U.S. involvement in specific overseas conflicts but also those opposed to the nation's pursuit of foreign relations writ large, thus labeling themselves as "anti-interventionist" or "antimilitarist." Only by integrating these movements into the history of antiwar activism do we get a full sense of the manifold oppositions that U.S. foreign policy faced in the twentieth century and beyond. The chapter's second argument is that protest on the home front has played a vital role in shaping American responses to war, not least when we integrate the perspectives of African American and female activists, who have often viewed U.S. militarism through the important lenses of race and gender. Ultimately, then, an understanding of the rich and complex tradition of domestic opposition to America's wars allows for a fuller appreciation of the manner in which modern war has been shaped by social forces from the "bottom up" as well as by military and political forces from the "top down."

Anti-Imperialism and the Aftermath of 1898

The "splendid little war" waged against the Spanish Empire between April and August 1898 allowed the United States to emerge as an imperial power with control over Cuba, Puerto Rico, and the Philippines.[1] The war also gave rise to a significant strain of American anti-imperialism, not least because, even after victory against the Spanish had been declared, the United States remained entangled in a violent and controversial three-year conflict with insurgent Filipino republicans.[2] The domestic debates about the proper function of U.S. foreign policy that took place during the Spanish-American and Philippine-American Wars highlighted not only deep divisions among political elites over the morality and practicalities of U.S. imperialism but also the manner in which gender and race played decisive roles in shaping antiwar sentiment.

It was the U.S. ambassador to Great Britain, John Hay, who coined the term "splendid little war" in a congratulatory letter to Theodore Roosevelt, the U.S. Army colonel who led his "Rough Riders" to a famous victory at the battle of San Juan Hill, Cuba, on July 1, 1898. For Hay, the war was an example of how the United States ought to engage with the world. It had "begun with the highest of motives," he suggested, was being "carried on with magnificent spirit," and would be concluded "with that fine good nature, which is, after all, the distinguishing trait of the American character."[3] However, not all Americans agreed that U.S. conduct during its conflicts with Spain and the Philippines epitomized the nation's highest ideals. Opposition to U.S. expansionism came to a head in Boston in November 1898 with the formation of the Anti-Imperialist League (AIL), which initially aimed to prevent Congress from approving the peace treaty with Spain that would lead to the military occupation of Cuba, the acquisition of Puerto Rico, and the purchase for $20 million of the Philippines. Senator George Frisbie Hoar of Massachusetts, for example, believed that "free government" could not be installed in the Philippines by the United States and was joined in this assumption by lawyers, clergy, and academics who saw American military intervention as an abrogation of moral and legal norms.[4] After the

AIL failed to stop the signing of the peace treaty, the movement continued to register its dissent from U.S. imperial policy and developed a nationwide network committed to promoting what they saw as the archetypal American value of peaceful "liberty," defined in opposition to "empire," which was viewed as ambitious, militant, and aggressive.[5]

Another key figure in the rise of anti-imperialism was William Jennings Bryan, a Nebraska politician with a very different constituency from the northeasterners involved in the AIL. He rose to prominence as a leader in the populist movement, which drew on the support of militant midwestern and southern farmers and called for better representation of agrarian communities in the American political system. By 1900, when Bryan ran as the Democratic Party's nominee for president for the second time, he was a zealous anti-imperialist, casting his opposition to the war with the Philippines in populist terms: "If we have an imperial policy, we must have a great standing army as its natural and necessary complement. The spirit which will justify the forcible annexation of the Philippine Islands will justify the seizure of other islands and the domination of other people, and with wars of conquest we can expect a certain, if not rapid, growth of our military establishment."[6] Bryan thus saw with startling clarity how American imperialism might lead to the rapid expansion of the nation's military capacity and the untethering of this capacity from the moorings of democratic control. As American war-making powers expanded throughout the twentieth century, he was proved correct, and his rhetoric was echoed by antiwar activists on a number of occasions.

Both the Spanish-American and Philippine-American Wars were framed by their proponents as opportunities to prove "American manhood" and as "race wars" waged against inferior and uncivilized foreigners.[7] Unsurprisingly, then, the cause of anti-imperialism was taken up by feminist and African American activists, who highlighted the links between their domestic oppression and the underpinning philosophies of U.S. imperialism. Women played significant roles in the AIL and often focused on the masculinist violence unleashed by U.S. forces against their opponents in the Philippines.[8] In a similar vein, African Americans campaigned against the "racial arrogance" of U.S. imperialism, and antilynching activists such as Ida B. Wells viewed their campaign as a form of anti-imperialism due to the links between violence at home and its international counterpart.[9]

For the AIL, opposition to war and imperialism was driven by a calculation of national interest as well as the values of American exceptionalism, which posited that the United States was a unique nation based on its dedication to liberty and democracy. Indeed, these explicitly nationalist frames of reference help to explain why both women and African Americans were treated with "ambivalence" and held at arm's length by the group. Indeed, in many cases even Progressive anti-imperialists resorted to racist and sexist arguments against their nation's turn toward empire.[10] It must also be recognized that the anti-imperialist movement as a whole was ultimately ineffective in achieving its primary aim of preventing the United States from establishing itself as an imperial power. Nonetheless, the AIL's influence, along with Bryan's success in channeling opposition to war in the Philippines as a key plank in the platform of the Democratic Party, demonstrates that anti-imperialism was a mainstream position by the turn of the twentieth century and that domestic concerns played a vital role in shaping Americans' views of war.

Neutrality and the Second World War

Domestic dissent emerged in response to U.S. military intervention in the First World War, with radical intellectual Randolph Bourne echoing a common sentiment by arguing at its close in 1918, "war is essentially the health of the state" and that involvement in military conflict, whether at home or abroad, fundamentally tarnished the nation's moral fabric.[11] However, for the next illuminating domestic debate about the nation's global role during the course of the twentieth century, we should look to the conflict that took place between supporters of military intervention and advocates of neutrality during the early years of the Second World War. The key question for those involved was whether or not the United States should return to its pre-1917 tradition of nonintervention in European wars or, alternatively, come to the aid of the Allied Powers in their clash with Nazi Germany and Imperial Japan. The December 7, 1941, Japanese attack on Pearl Harbor rendered U.S. intervention in the war unavoidable, and the genocidal atrocities committed by the Nazis as part of the Holocaust subsequently shored up the moral case for participation in what is often termed the twentieth century's "good war."[12] Nevertheless, it is important to remember that U.S. public opinion was bitterly divided over the question of intervention between 1939 and 1941 and that advocates of neutrality, often pejoratively labeled "isolationists" during and after the war, played a central role in structuring the terms of this discussion.[13]

As the Nazis moved westward through Europe in 1939 and 1940, the war dominated the political agenda in the United States. President Franklin D. Roosevelt wanted to use both economic and military power to aid the allies. In these efforts, his administration was supported by a range of organizations, such as the Committee to Defend America by Aiding the Allies, which was created in May 1940, grew to include over eight hundred chapters by December 1941, and sought to sway public opinion by promoting U.S. support for the Allied powers.[14] Building on this support, Roosevelt signed the Lend-Lease Act in March 1941, which committed the United States to supplying the Allies with food, oil, and munitions. A range of anti-interventionist viewpoints came to the fore in opposition to these developments, arguing that intervention in the Second World War would betray the national interest and do irreparable harm to America's standing in the world.

One such advocate of neutrality was the historian and public intellectual Charles A. Beard, a staunch critic of U.S. foreign policy throughout the 1930s and author of books with provocative titles such as *The Devil Theory of War* (1936). Beard's primary critique of interventionism was that it diverted the attention of the Roosevelt administration away from solving the economic problems caused by the Great Depression.[15] At the same time, the Nye Committee (a Senate investigation into the arms industry led by North Dakota senator Gerald Nye) argued that American munitions manufacturers were war profiteers, thus playing into significant public support for neutrality.[16] Taken together, these developments highlight the doggedness of anti-interventionist arguments from the left of the political spectrum, which suggested that the U.S. national interest was best served by a focus on domestic rather than international problems.

However, neutrality was also a popular idea among conservative Americans. Perhaps the most famous representative of this group was Charles A. Lindbergh, an aviator who traveled widely in Europe during the 1930s and used this experience to argue against intervention in the Second World War. For Lindbergh, the idea of the national interest was also key, but, unlike Beard, he aligned with the America First Committee (AFC), a conservative pressure group founded in 1940 that was dedicated to the proposition that the United States should invest funds in creating "an impregnable defense for America" rather than supporting the Allies.[17] This emphasis on "preparedness" was also based on a critique of New Deal liberalism, which was viewed by many conservatives as inherently un-American because of its emphasis on government intervention in the economy and the creation of a welfare state. Such arguments often tended toward nativism and anti-Semitism, as when Lindbergh argued in Des Moines, Iowa, in September 1941 that Jewish Americans were key proponents of intervention and that "their greatest danger to this country lies in their large ownership and influence in our motion pictures, our press, our radio, and our government."[18]

Conservative advocates of neutrality also feared the impact of conscription. For example, Gerald L. K. Smith, a far right clergyman, justified his opposition to intervention with reference to the protection of the heterosexual nuclear family, placing particular emphasis on the values of Christian motherhood in his vitriolic campaigns against the Roosevelt administration. While most anti-interventionists went into retreat after Pearl Harbor, those who had emphasized a family-oriented ideology insisted in the aftermath of the Allied victory that the United Nations (founded in 1945) would "perpetuate and exacerbate war's detrimental effects on family life."[19] Another anti-interventionist trope that survived American entry into the Second World War was opposition to the power of the Soviet Union. Lindbergh and Smith were joined in the conservative anti-interventionist ranks by Republican politicians such as Robert A. Taft and the U.S. ambassador to Great Britain, Joseph P. Kennedy, in arguing that the greatest danger to the world was not Nazi Germany but Soviet Russia and that intervention would, in the long term, increase the likelihood of successful communist revolutions in Europe. As the historian Justus D. Doenecke has argued, in this view of world politics lay "the seeds of much Cold War thinking."[20]

Rather like the anti-imperialism of the 1890s, the arguments in favor of neutrality put forward during the period between 1939 and 1941 were shaped by a range of domestic responses to the question of military intervention abroad. Similarly, it is difficult to conclude that the anti-interventionist movement was a success. After all, the United States entered the Second World War and eventually fought alongside the USSR to defeat Germany and Japan. Nonetheless, the movement fed into an intense debate about the future of U.S. foreign policy. Moreover, some of its themes remained persistent and relevant in the postwar world. For these reasons, then, it is vital to remember that the triumphant American internationalism that emerged from the war faced significant challenges on the home front.

Black Internationalism and the Cold War

After the Allied victory in the Second World War, U.S. policymakers quickly adopted the mantle of global leadership in the Cold War. This new struggle against the USSR and its communist satellites was not a military conflict in the conventional sense and was waged in primarily ideological terms. When conflict did break out, it usually took place via proxies in various parts of the developing world. Nonetheless, a range of movements developed in opposition to the anticommunist foreign policies pursued by the Truman, Eisenhower, and Kennedy administrations, perhaps most notably among African American activists who sought to use the rhetoric of the Cold War to highlight the racial inequalities experienced in the Jim Crow South, where segregation, political disenfranchisement, and racial violence were common experiences. If the United States was so keen to promote freedom and democracy abroad, these dissenters asked, why did it tolerate the continuation of segregation and other forms of racial discrimination at home? Black activists, including the poet Claude McKay, the historian and sociologist W.E.B. Du Bois, the journalist Claudia Jones, and the internationally renowned performer Paul Robeson, demanded answers to this question; they saw U.S. foreign policy as inherently linked to the worldwide project of white supremacy. Despite not engaging in conventional antiwar activism and instead using the rhetoric of the Cold War to highlight ongoing racial inequality in the United States, their contributions were nonetheless essential to the landscape of postwar opposition to U.S. foreign policy.

In certain cases, African Americans actively supported the USSR, and the Soviets won significant propaganda victories within some communities by lending their support to anticolonial movements in Africa and Asia.[21] More often, though, black activists were drawn into a nonaligned stance of international solidarity with people of color elsewhere in the world, based on the identification of a shared history of racial oppression. In this analysis, African Americans were an "internal colony" comparable to those societies suffering under the discriminatory policies of European settler-colonialism.[22] Black internationalists of all stripes came together at the 1955 Bandung Conference in Indonesia, which stressed economic cooperation among Asian and African states and condemned both Soviet and American foreign policy as imperialistic. After attending the conference, the American novelist Richard Wright noted that "the despised, the insulted, the hurt, the dispossessed—in short, the underdogs of the human race—were meeting. Here was class and racial and religious consciousness on a global scale. . . . This meeting of the rejected was in itself a kind of judgment upon the Western world!"[23] Bandung demonstrated that even as the U.S. government attempted to paint black internationalists as Soviet dupes, their opposition to the Cold War was multifaceted and defied simplistic ideological classification.

Three of the most significant sites of inspiration for black internationalists were India, South Africa, and Cuba. African American activists became centrally concerned with Indian politics during the Second World War, speaking out against British colonialism on the subcontinent in an effort to pressure the U.S. government into backing the independence movement led by Mahatma Gandhi.[24] After independence came on August 15, 1947, India became a bulwark for what the historian Nico Slate has called "colored cosmopolitanism," a set of ideas that identified connections between the Indian and American freedom struggles in order to pressure the U.S. government into resolving the problems of racial inequality in the South.[25] As a consequence, figures such as Du Bois and Robeson became widely popular among Indian leftists, and mainstream civil rights organizations such as the NAACP regularly sent delegations to the subcontinent to explore the racial dynamics of Indian society. While the civil rights leader Martin Luther King Jr.'s debt to philosophies of Gandhian nonviolence is well-known today, these alternative transnational links were also vital in developing a black internationalist consciousness that opposed the politics of the Cold War.

South Africa was another important postwar ally for the United States, which led to a strategic alliance between the two countries that provided American access to vast supplies of manganese, chrome, and uranium that served as important resources for the armaments industry. However, after the 1948 election of the South African National Party, which created the system of apartheid that strictly segregated white and black citizens and would remain in place until 1994, the alliance became linked in the minds of many African Americans to the racial similarities between the two countries.[26] As they became more outspoken on the hypocrisy of American support for South Africa, antiapartheid activists found themselves subject to travel restrictions and other forms of state repression that limited their willingness to speak out. Nonetheless, the existence of this black internationalist critique, and the speed with which it was stifled by state power, highlighted "the inherent fragility" of Cold War racial norms on both sides of the Atlantic.[27]

The success in 1959 of the Cuban Revolution in overthrowing the U.S.-backed regime of Fulgencio Batista provided another important inspiration for black internationalists. The new president of Cuba, Fidel Castro, wanted to play a leadership role in the decolonized world and, as a part of this mission, made an iconic visit to the Harlem neighborhood of New York City as part of a 1960 delegation to the United Nations. Castro refused to stay in the midtown hotel usually favored by Cuban diplomats and instead gave his patronage to the African American–run Hotel Theresa. Black activists were consequently inspired by Castro, and by the Cuban Revolution's advocacy of socialism. They were also curious about exaggerated claims that racism had been eliminated on the island, and those who could do so consequently traveled to Cuba as political tourists.[28] In making these trips, African Americans imagined themselves to be part of a "counterhegemonic axis that included Mississippi, Harlem and Havana," challenging Cold War foreign policy while at the same time finding inspiration for their domestic activism.[29]

Black internationalism was therefore an important feature on the landscape of U.S. foreign relations during the Cold War. Indeed, conscious efforts by activists to compare race relations in America and the decolonizing world gave rise to a discourse of "Cold War civil rights" that would play an important role in pressuring the U.S. government and judiciary into implementing noteworthy measures for racial equality during the 1950s and 1960s, such as the Supreme Court decision in *Brown v. Board of Education* (1954) and the Civil and Voting Rights Acts of 1964 and 1965.[30] In these ways, African American protest against the racial logic of the Cold War bore significant fruit, even if most black internationalists would have preferred a more radical solution to the problems caused by white supremacy, both at home and abroad. While they did not espouse conventionally "antiwar" viewpoints, these activists highlighted the hypocrisies of American interaction with the Third World, and their critique of the links between U.S. foreign relations and white supremacy would prove influential among subsequent activist generations, especially during the Vietnam era. Once again, the domestic and the international proved to be fundamentally entwined.

The Anti-Vietnam War Movement

The most intense and disruptive domestic debate over U.S. foreign policy during the twentieth century took place during the late 1960s and early 1970s, focused on the War in Vietnam. U.S. presidents since Franklin D. Roosevelt had involved their administrations in the knotty process of Vietnamese decolonization, which led to the country's division into North Vietnam, supported by the USSR and China, and South Vietnam, which was backed by the United States. However, the intensity of American involvement dramatically increased after the August 1964 Gulf of Tonkin incident, which allowed President Lyndon B. Johnson to pass a resolution officially authorizing the use of U.S. military force. Between 1965 and 1968, both the number of U.S. troops on the ground and the number of U.S. bombs dropped on North Vietnam rose considerably. Johnson thus "Americanized" the war and justified intervention by suggesting that South Vietnam was a bulwark against the spread of communism throughout Asia.[31]

Previously, during the 1950s and early 1960s, a large-scale movement against the proliferation of nuclear weapons and the attendant "military-industrial complex" had emerged in the United States. While public opinion was generally acquiescent to administration policy in Southeast Asia at the start of the conflict, the dissent engendered by the movement in opposition to nuclear weapons fed into the more immediate issue of the War in Vietnam.[32] Antiwar sentiment emerged as soon as 1965, then, but became significantly more widespread in the aftermath of the Tet Offensive (a series of surprise attacks launched by the North Vietnamese on January 30, 1968), which led several public figures to oppose the war, such as Democratic politicians Robert F. Kennedy and Eugene McCarthy, as well as CBS news anchor Walter Cronkite.[33] When Richard Nixon was elected later that year, it was on a platform that promised the American people "Peace with Honor"; however, the new president's failure to end the war quickly only undermined public confidence.

Vietnam therefore became a public ordeal for America, with the emergence of a massive and diverse peace movement that called attention to the inherent military and political problems presented by the war. The largest antiwar demonstration was organized by the National Mobilization Committee to End the War in Vietnam (known as "the Mobe") and took place in Washington, DC, on November 15, 1969, with a crowd of at least 500,000 marching for peace.[34] Wall Street bankers, mainstream journalists, and politicians of both parties also voiced opposition to the war. Historian Robert Buzzanco has called these groups "ruling class anti-imperialists," who developed "a critique of specific policies of imperial overstretch rather than an overarching condemnation of the U.S. imperial system itself" and believed that U.S. standing in the world would best be served by a rapid withdrawal of military force.[35]

A considerable amount of antiwar sentiment went much further than this. The student New Left, which emerged on campuses around the country and centered on the organization Students for a Democratic Society (SDS), argued that the war demonstrated that foreign policy was not democratically accountable. For example, when radical historian and New Left activist Staughton Lynd spoke in May 1965 at an SDS-organized protest at the University of California–Berkeley, he claimed that the Johnson administration would not permit "the majority of the people in (America) to have a responsible discussion and to determine (their) own foreign policy."[36] College campuses throughout the United States played host to protests, thus creating confrontation between students, university officials, and local law enforcement. These confrontations were

sometimes counterproductive and led to a negative image of the peace movement as privileged middle-class students who did not respect their countrymen
fighting abroad.[37] However, when the authorities responded disproportionately—as they did at Kent State University on May 4, 1970, where four protestors were shot dead and nine others injured—their overreactions turned public
opinion even further against the war.

Vietnam also raised important questions about race and citizenship. When
Martin Luther King Jr. spoke out against the war for the first time in a 1967
sermon, he drew attention to the social and racial inequalities of the conflict:
"We have been repeatedly faced with the cruel irony of watching Negro and
white boys on TV screens as they kill and die together for a nation that has been
unable to seat them together in the same schools. . . . I could not be silent in the
face of such cruel manipulation of the poor."[38] This theme was pushed further
by radical African American opponents of the war. One example was Eldridge
Cleaver, a member of the Black Panther Party who traveled to North Vietnam
in 1969 as part of an anti-imperialist delegation and returned home to argue
that African Americans should reject their status as U.S. citizens and adopt a
stance of radical solidarity with the Vietnamese communists.[39] Similarly, radical Mexican American activists in the Chicano movement opposed the war and
rejected the impulse to view military service as a key marker of assimilation into
U.S. society.[40] Both of these examples show that the politics of solidarity played
a key role in the anti–Vietnam War movement.

Opposition to the war also emerged from within the military, with soldiers
resisting deployment or, once in Southeast Asia, refusing to fight.[41] Vietnam
Veterans Against the War (VVAW), founded in 1967, had 30,000 members by
1973. It drew veterans and active GIs into the antiwar movement and organized
high-profile demonstrations, such as a 1971 televised event at which hundreds
of veterans threw their service medals onto the steps of the U.S. Capitol. The
same year, VVAW representative John Kerry appeared before the Senate Committee on Foreign Affairs and argued, "When thirty years from now our brothers go down the street without a leg, without an arm, or a face, and small boys
ask why, we will be able to say 'Vietnam' and not mean a desert, not a filthy
obscene memory, but mean instead where America finally turned and where soldiers like us helped it in the turning."[42] VVAW's patriotic approach to activism
consequently helped to draw support from working-class communities, who
mistrusted antiwar sentiment associated with students and the counterculture.[43]
In a context where millions of Americans feared conscription, draft resistance
also formed an important method of protest, involving attempts to render the
legal enforcement of conscription futile because of the sheer number of refus-
als to submit to the draft. As the historian Michael S. Foley has shown, draft
resisters justified their actions via appeals to American patriotism and felt that
acts of civil disobedience aimed at ending the draft were more effective than the
organization of antiwar demonstrations.[44]

While considerable debate has taken place between historians about the precise impact of antiwar protest during the Vietnam era, the general consensus is that policymakers in both the Johnson and Nixon administrations had their ability to wage war constrained by public opinion, particularly after the Tet Offensive.[45] While the views of radical dissenters such as the Black Panthers were easily dismissed by most Americans, opposition among GIs, veterans, and high-profile public figures undoubtedly shifted the public away from support for the war. Once again, then, Americans' perceptions of military intervention abroad were shaped by the politics of the home front in a range of significant ways, and the memory of Vietnam would linger long after the fall of Saigon to the North Vietnamese on April 30, 1975.

The Central America Solidarity Movement in the "Age of Reagan"

After Ronald Reagan's inauguration as president in 1981, his administration went about implementing a foreign policy that sought to actively confront the global threat of Soviet-inspired communism and therefore defeat the "Vietnam syndrome" that had supposedly infected the American body politic. Reagan's foreign policy team saw Central America as an essential testing ground for its new doctrine.[46] The 1979 overthrow of the Somoza regime in Nicaragua by the Sandinista National Liberation Front (FSLN) was, in the eyes of the administration, the most obvious example of the threat posed by Soviet- and Cuban-inspired revolution in Central America. The United States consequently intervened to provide economic and military support for the Contras, a group of right-wing Nicaraguans intent on overthrowing the FSLN. Guerrilla movements in El Salvador, Guatemala, and Honduras were also perceived as a danger to U.S. strategic and business interests, as well as to American territorial integrity, with Reagan regularly making addresses to the nation connecting these indicators to the existence of a communist conspiracy throughout the Americas.[47]

It was in this context that the Central America solidarity movement emerged, encouraging diplomatic solutions based upon the rule of international law in opposition to the Reagan administration's tactics of covert military intervention and intersecting with the emerging international discourse of "human rights."[48] Groups such as the Nicaragua Network and Committee in Solidarity with the People of El Salvador (CISPES) were formed by those with leftist political sympathies, many of whom had been involved in the anti-Vietnam War movement. In the aftermath of Reagan's invasion of Grenada in 1983 and under the assumption that a similar attack on Nicaragua was imminent, the nationwide Pledge of Resistance movement was established in 1984 in order to gather the signatures of U.S. citizens vowing to commit acts of civil disobedience in the event of such an offensive. Drawing 100,000 signatories from across the nation by 1989, the Pledge drew in a much smaller number of participants than the large Vietnam-era demonstrations but nonetheless highlighted the breadth of domestic support for the movement.[49]

Solidarity activists developed a variety of transnational methods to forge connections with Central American communities affected by conflict and political repression. The sanctuary movement, for example, developed out of the various religious congregations involved in the struggle for solidarity. It aimed to help refugees facing political repression in El Salvador, Guatemala, and Honduras enter the United States and to provide them with shelter, social services, and legal advocacy. Those involved in sanctuary believed that the church should stand as a place of refuge from poverty and political terror, and therefore pledged to maintain the confidentiality of those they helped, even in the face of arrest and prosecution. At the same time, a range of female activists, intellectuals, and filmmakers linked anti-interventionism and feminism to critique the patriarchal structures that dominated women in both North and Central America, as exemplified in the activism of organizations like MADRE and in documentary films such as *When the Mountains Tremble* (Pamela Yates and Thomas Newton Sigel, 1983), which told the story of Rigoberta Menchú, an indigenous Guatemalan peasant-turned-guerrilla who subsequently became a winner of the Nobel Peace Prize.[50] These new forms of feminist anti-interventionism chimed with the emergence of groups such as Women's Pentagon Action, a feminist antinuclear collective that launched a critique of Reagan's resurgent Cold War militarism.[51] As in the Vietnam era, then, anti-interventionist activism overlapped with a larger peace movement in important ways.

Activists sought to characterize the revolutionary upheaval that was affecting the region as primarily indigenous. This argument was meant to challenge Reagan's claim that a Soviet- or Cuban-inspired global plot constituted the motivating force behind the region's instability.[52] As the historian Van Gosse has shown, the movement also sought to resist the administration's attempt to "refight" the War in Vietnam in the Western Hemisphere. Activists campaigned against escalation of U.S. involvement in the region and sought to end all aid to counter-revolutionary forces there, a struggle that was pithily summarized in a CISPES slogan of the time: "El Salvador is Spanish for Vietnam."[53]

Religion played a key role in the movement. The adoption of Central America solidarity as a key issue by various congregations appealed to large numbers of individuals not commonly associated with radical or reform politics, and went a long way to disarming anticommunist criticism of the movement. For example, in 1983 William Sloane Coffin, an influential clergyman and activist, spoke out against U.S. policy in Central America by arguing, "If we the people of the United States don't stop this killing south of the border, we shall never again be able to lift our heads and criticize the Soviets for what they are doing south of their border."[54] The doctrines of liberation theology, which emerged as a political force in the region during the 1970s, were more radical. Molding the symbols of the liturgy to a tangible anti-imperialist political project, left-wing Catholics stood in solidarity with the poor and disenfranchised of Central America.[55] Popular cultural forms also became broadly aligned with the cause of the movement during the 1980s; novels such as Robert Stone's *A Flag for Sunrise* (1981) and films such as Oliver Stone's *Salvador* (1986) dramatized the politics of Central American solidarity, establishing an informal yet prominent cultural front in the struggle against U.S. interventionism.[56]

The avoidance of an all-out military intervention in Nicaragua and the passage of the Boland Amendments by Congress between 1982 and 1984 that limited U.S. government assistance to the Contras both point to the structural constraints placed on the Reagan administration by public opinion mobilized in the cause of anti-interventionism. So does the enormous scale of the controversy around the Iran-Contra affair in 1986 and 1987, when it became public that administration insiders had sold weapons to Iran in return for the release of hostages, with the profits channeled to right-wing forces in Central America.[57] However, Central America solidarity activists were nowhere near as influential as their Vietnam-era counterparts. By the mid-1990s very few of those with whom they sympathized held positions of power or influence in the region, a fact that represented a victory for the administrations of Reagan and George H. W. Bush, his vice president and successor in the White House. Viewed another way, then, the experience of anti-interventionist activists in the 1980s was one of stopping an outright war but not of stopping the covert operations that meant the United States was never truly "at peace" with Central American national liberation movements.

Opposition to the "War on Terror"

When the Cold War ended in 1989, the United States emerged as the only super-power in a supposedly "unipolar" world. Humanitarian interventions by United Nations forces in Somalia and Yugoslavia under the presidencies of George H. W. Bush and Bill Clinton led many Americans to believe that their nation had learned to intervene multilaterally in order to protect human rights. However, the September 11, 2001, attacks on the World Trade Center and the Pentagon, perpetrated by the Islamist terror network Al-Qaeda, decisively shifted the course of American foreign policy. Under the banner of a global "War on Terror," the administration of George W. Bush sent U.S. forces to invade Afghanistan in October 2001, thus ousting the Taliban regime, which had provided support for Al-Qaeda. Bush and his neoconservative foreign policy advisors went on to launch a pre-emptive invasion of Iraq in March 2003 to topple the country's brutal dictator, Saddam Hussein, who, they argued, had a highly developed program for the creation of weapons of mass destruction. Domestically, the administration responded to the attacks by introducing the PATRIOT Act in 2001, which dramatically expanded the national security state's surveillance capabilities. Furthermore, the Justice Department began a program of indefinite detention of suspected terrorists, with hundreds being interned at the U.S. base at Guantanamo Bay and other so-called "black sites" across the world.[58]

In the immediate aftermath of 9/11, much of American society was intolerant of political dissent. As the novelist David Foster Wallace observed, in many communities there developed a "weird accretive pressure" to hang flags outside houses, to the extent that those who refrained were mistrusted.[59] Indeed, even journalists who had been ardent left-wing opponents of U.S. military intervention during the Cold War, such as Christopher Hitchens and Paul Berman, changed their views to become supporters of the invasions of Afghanistan and Iraq.[60] Nonetheless, opposition to the War on Terror did emerge. When a use-of-force resolution was passed by both houses of Congress on September 14, 2001, to authorize military strikes on Afghanistan, Barbara Lee, the Democratic representative for Oakland, California, was the only member to vote in opposition. "I am convinced that military action will not prevent further acts of international terrorism against the United States," she argued, and went on to conclude with a warning: "As we act, let us not become the evil that we deplore."[61] When a similar resolution was proposed in October 2002, Congress sanctioned the invasion of Iraq, albeit less overwhelmingly. One notable dissenter was Illinois state senator Barack Obama, who suggested that while he was not opposed to all wars, "What I am opposed to is a dumb war. What I am opposed to is a rash war. What I am opposed to is the cynical attempt by Richard Perle and Paul Wolfowitz [two prominent neoconservatives in the Bush administration] and other armchair, weekend warriors . . . to shove their own ideological agendas down our throats, irrespective of the costs in lives lost and in hardships borne."[62] In making this case, Obama not only voiced opposition to the war but also to the foreign policy ideology that underpinned the Bush administration's view of America's role in the world.

On the streets, opposition to the invasion of Iraq was more vociferous. A series of antiwar groups formed, from the explicitly left-wing International ANSWER (Act Now to Stop the War and End Racism) to the more broad-based coalition United for Peace and Justice. Networks such as MoveOn.org capitalized on the organizational power of the internet and email, and there were strong links between the antiwar movement of 2002–2003 and the alter-globalization movement that had developed during the 1990s in opposition to the policies of the World Trade Organization and other international bodies.[63] Building on the feminist peace activism of the 1980s, CODE PINK was formed to challenge the masculinist terms in which U.S. military intervention was justified, and Cindy Sheehan, whose son was killed while serving in Iraq, emerged as a prominent antiwar spokesperson.[64]

These groups combined to participate in several massive antiwar demonstrations. For example, 500,000 people marched in the streets of New York on

February 15, 2003, with an estimated 2.5 million marching in other cities across the country. The protests were not isolated to the United States; a million activists marched in London while in Spain an estimated 5.7 percent of the population protested the war.[65] These figures dwarfed those of comparable antiwar protests from the Vietnam era and led *New York Times* journalist Patrick E. Tyler to suggest that "there may still be two superpowers on the planet: the United States and world public opinion."[66]

However, the protests demonstrated a series of limitations. Their lack of racial diversity led Barbara Epstein to decry the "whiteness of the anti-war movement."[67] Moreover, peace activists struggled to forge internationalist bonds of solidarity with the people of the Middle East.[68] Antiwar protestors also faced tremendous difficulty in building a movement that lasted beyond the marches of 2003, at least in part because of the absence of conscription.[69] By the presidential election of 2008, a moment at which Bush's wars were almost universally unpopular, there was no visible antiwar movement to speak of. While Obama's antiwar stance in relation to Iraq helped him to victory against the Republican candidate John McCain, he was not an antiwar president, nor an anti-interventionist or antimilitarist one. Once in office he oversaw a "surge" of military force in Afghanistan and managed the roll-out of unmanned drone strikes across the Middle East, while nevertheless struggling to end indefinite detention at Guantanamo Bay. If the War in Iraq formally ended in ignominy for the United States, the broader War on Terror continues almost unabated.

To understand the significance of domestic politics and antiwar activism for the history of U.S. foreign relations since 1898, it is worth returning to the three questions that have animated this chapter. First, what traditions of thought and culture have opponents of war drawn on, and how have they understood the relationship between their dissent and their patriotism? In many cases, antiwar activists argued that *they* were the real patriots. This was true of the AIL in 1898, of the AFC in 1941, of SDS in 1965, and of Pledge of Resistance in 1984. Dissenters also used American ideals of liberty and equality to critique the realities of U.S. foreign policy, as was the case for African Americans activists throughout the period under examination. However, the thought and culture that inspired peace protestors often originated from far beyond the United States. Whether it was Latin American, Asian, or African politics that activists referred to, they demonstrated that internationalism was often just as significant as patriotism in the formation of their ideas.

Second, to what extent has antiwar activism been articulated in terms of the "national interest" and/or "solidarity" with communities outside of the United States? American war-making has often been justified in practical rather than moral terms, and, as such, its opponents have regularly pointed out that conflict might actually be against the national interest. This was especially true of politicians and other elite actors who found themselves voting against, or otherwise opposing, U.S. interventions overseas. However, ordinary Americans—be they workers, women, or ethnic minorities—often found that they could generate as much sympathy for their cause by pointing out the similarities between their domestic experiences and those communities directly impacted by American war-making, whether in the Philippines, Vietnam, El Salvador, or Iraq. These were moral arguments about the equality and vulnerability of all people in the face of war and oppression that demanded the end of an entire war-making system, a view that usually sat in tension with more limited and practical arguments against individual wars.

Finally, how have political responses on the home front shaped and constrained the ability of the American state to wage war? As we have seen, the record of movements in opposition to U.S. foreign policy has been mixed. While most historians agree that anti-Vietnam War activism helped bring that war to an end, in the other cases examined, the record is primarily one of failure. Policymakers proved adept at learning the lessons of previously unpopular foreign interventions, and opposition movements, while vibrant, often lacked the unity and singularity of purpose necessary to make major inroads. The United States has therefore continued to wage wars, and the persistence of opposition to these wars has been matched by the malleability of American power to circumvent the opposition it has encountered. Nonetheless, from the War of 1898 to the War on Terror, U.S. policymakers formed their strategies with domestic constituencies in mind, and antiwar activists played a vocal and important role in the process of foreign policy deliberation.

Put simply, then, as U.S. war-making powers expanded during the twentieth and twenty-first centuries, so too did opposition to those powers in the form of antiwar, anti-interventionist, and antimilitarist activism. Any explanation of what it has meant for America to be at war therefore needs to take account of what it has meant for Americans to be opposed to war, and how this dissent was shaped by the politics of the home front.

Discussion Questions

1. What traditions of thought and culture have opponents of war drawn on, and how have they understood the relationship between their dissent and their patriotism?
2. To what extent has antiwar activism been articulated in the terms of the "national interest" and/or "solidarity" with communities outside of the United States?
3. How have political responses on the home front shaped and constrained the ability of the American state to wage war?
4. In what ways have antiwar, anti-interventionist, and antimilitarist movements been comparable and how have they contrasted since 1898?

Notes

1   On the War of 1898, see Louis A. Pérez Jr., *The War of 1898: The United States and Cuba in History and Historiography* (Chapel Hill: University of North Carolina Press, 1998).

2   On the Philippine-American War, see David Silbey, *A War of Frontier and Empire: The Philippine-American War, 1899–1902* (New York: Hill and Wang, 2007).

3   John Hay to Theodore Roosevelt (July 27, 1898), in *The Encyclopaedia of the Spanish-American and Philippine-American Wars*, vol. 1, ed. Spencer C. Tucker (Santa Barbara, CA: ABC Clio, 2009), 888.

4   For a detailed discussion of the AIL and its key protagonists, see Robert L. Beisner, *Twelve against Empire: The Anti-Imperialists, 1989–1900* (New York: McGraw-Hill, 1968).

5   Michael Patrick Cullinane, *Liberty and American Anti-Imperialism, 1898–1909* (New York: Palgrave MacMillan, 2012), 21.

6   William Jennings Bryan, "The Paralyzing Influence of Imperialism" (July 6, 1900), in *Wartime Dissent in America: A History and Anthology*, ed. Robert Mann (New York: Palgrave MacMillan, 2010), 68.

7   On masculinity, see Kristin L. Hoganson, *Fighting for American Manhood: How Gender Politics Provoked the Spanish-American and Philippine-American Wars* (New Haven, CT: Yale University Press, 1998); on race, see Paul A. Kramer, "Race Making and Colonial Violence in the U.S. Empire: The Philippine-American War as Race War," *Diplomatic History* 30, no. 2 (April 2006): 169–210.

8   Erin L. Murphy, "Women's Anti-Imperialism, 'The White Man's Burden,' and the Philippine-American War," *Gender and Society* 23, no. 2 (April 2009): 257–260.

9   Hazel V. Carby, "'On the Threshold of Woman's Era': Lynching, Empire, and Sexuality in Black Feminist Theory," *Critical Inquiry* 12, no. 1 (Autumn 1985): 265.

10   Murphy, "Women's Anti-Imperialism," 262–263.

11   Randolph Bourne, "The State," in *War and the Intellectuals: Essays by Randolph S. Bourne*, ed. Carl Resek (New York: Harper and Row, 1964), 71.

12   For a useful discussion of the idea of the Second World War as the "good war," see Adam Kirsch, "The Battle for History," *New York Times Book Review*, May 29, 2011, 10–11.

13   For an important discussion of these terms, see Brooke L. Blower, "From Isolationism to Neutrality: A New Framework for Understanding American Political Culture, 1919–1941," *Diplomatic History* 38, no. 4 (April 2014): 345–376.

14   Andrew Johnstone, *Against Immediate Evil: American Internationalists and the Four Freedoms on the Eve of World War II* (Ithaca, NY: Cornell University Press, 2014), 4–6.

15   Clyde W. Barrow, "The Diversionary Thesis and the Dialectic of Imperialism: Charles A. Beard's Theory of American Foreign Policy Revisited," *Studies in American Political Development* 11, no. 3 (Fall 1987): 251.

16   Ibid., 62.

17   Qtd. in John A. Thompson, "Another Look at the Downfall of 'Fortress America,'" *Journal of American Studies* 26, no. 3 (December 1992): 399.

18   The speech is quoted at length in "Lindbergh Sees a 'Plot for War,'" *New York Times*, September 12, 1941, 2.

19   Laura McEnaney, "He-Men and Christian Mothers: The America First Movement and the Gendered Meanings of Patriotism and Isolationism," *Diplomatic History* 18, no. 1 (January 1994): 54.

20   Justus D. Doenecke, "Rehearsal for Cold War: United States Anti-Interventionists and the Soviet Union, 1939–1941," *International Journal of Politics, Culture and Society* 7, no. 3 (Spring 1994): 387.

21 Gerald Horne, "Race from Power: U.S. Foreign Policy and the General Crisis of White Supremacy," in *Window on Freedom: Race, Civil Rights and Foreign Affairs, 1945–1988*, ed. Brenda Gayle Plummer (Chapel Hill: University of North Carolina Press, 2003), 53.

22 On the concept of internal colonialism, see Ramón A. Gutiérrez, "Internal Colonialism: An American Theory of Race," *Du Bois Review* 1, no. 2 (September 2004): 281–295.

23 Richard Wright, *The Color Curtain: A Report on the Bandung Conference* (New York: World Publishing, 1956), 12.

24 Penny M. von Eschen, *Race against Empire: Black Americans and Anticolonialism, 1937–1957* (Ithaca, NY: Cornell University Press, 1997), 30–31.

25 Nico Slate, *Colored Cosmopolitanism: The Shared Struggle for Freedom in the United States and India* (Cambridge, MA: Harvard University Press, 2012), 162–163.

26 Thomas Borstelmann, *The Cold War and the Color Line: American Race Relations in the Global Arena* (Cambridge, MA: Harvard University Press, 2001), 72–73.

27 Nicholas Grant, "Crossing the Black Atlantic: The Global Antiapartheid Movement and the Racial Politics of the Cold War," *Radical History Review* 119 (Spring 2014): 87.

28 Cynthia Young, "Havana Up in Harlem: LeRoi Jones, Harold Cruse and the Making of a Cultural Revolution," *Science and Society* 65, no. 2 (Spring 2001): 12–38.

29 John A. Gronbeck-Tedesco, "The Left in Transition: The Cuban Revolution in U.S. Third World Politics," *Journal of Latin American Studies* 40, no. 4 (November 2008): 665.

30 Mary L. Dudziak, *Cold War Civil Rights: Race and the Image of American Democracy* (Princeton, NJ: Princeton University Press, 2001).

31 Fredrik Logevall, *Choosing War: The Lost Chance for Peace and the Escalation of War in Vietnam* (Berkeley: University of California Press, 1999).

32 Paul Boyer, "Activism to Apathy: The American People and Nuclear Weapons, 1963–1980," *Journal of American History* 70, no. 4 (March 1984): 835–843.

33 On the domestic impact of the Tet Offensive, see David F. Schmitz, *The Tet Offensive: Politics, War, and Public Opinion* (Lanham, MD: Rowman & Littlefield, 2005).

34 Penny Lewis, *Hardhats, Hippies, and Hawks: The Vietnam Antiwar Movement as Myth and Memory* (Ithaca, NY: Cornell University Press, 2013), 133.

35 Robert Buzzanco, "Ruling-Class Anti-Imperialism in the Era of the Vietnam War," in *Empire's Twin: U.S. Anti-Imperialism from the Founding Era to the Age of Terrorism*, ed. Ian Tyrell and Jay Sexton (Ithaca, NY: Cornell University Press, 2015), 216.

36 Lynd's speech is excerpted in Vietnam Day Committee, eds., *We Accuse: A Powerful Statement of the New Political Anger in America* (Berkeley, CA: Diablo Press, 1965), 154.

37 On the public image of antiwar protestors, see Jerry Lembcke, *The Spitting Image: Myth, Memory and the Legacy of Vietnam* (New York: New York University Press, 1998).

38 Martin Luther King Jr., "Beyond Vietnam: A Time to Break the Silence, April 4, 1967," *American Rhetoric*, March 10, 2010, http://www.americanrhetoric.com /speeches/mlkatimetobreaksilence.htm.

39 Judy Tzu-Chun Wu, *Radicals on the Road: Internationalism, Orientalism, and Feminism during the Vietnam Era* (Ithaca, NY: Cornell University Press, 2013), 121.

40 Lorena Oropoeza, *¡Raza Sí! ¡Guerra No! Chicano Protest and Patriotism during the Viet Nam War Era* (Berkeley: University of California Press, 2005).

41 David Cortright, *Soldiers in Revolt: GI Resistance during the Vietnam War* (Boston: Haymarket Books, 2005).

42 John Kerry, "Vietnam Veterans against the War Statement," in *Takin' It to the Streets: A Sixties Reader*, ed. Wini Breines and Alexander Bloom (New York: Oxford University Press, 1995), 222.

43 Lewis, *Hardhats, Hippies, and Hawks*, 128–130.

44 Michael S. Foley, *Confronting the War Machine: Draft Resistance during the Vietnam War* (Chapel Hill: University of North Carolina Press, 2003), 14.

45 Andrew Preston, "The Irony of Protest: Vietnam and the Path to Permanent War," in *Reframing 1968: American Politics, Protest and Identity*, ed. Martin Halliwell and Nick Witham (Edinburgh: University of Edinburgh Press, 2018), 71.

46 On the "Vietnam syndrome," see Alexander Bloom, "'The Mainspring in This Country Has Been Broken': America's Battered Sense of Self and the Emergence of the Vietnam Syndrome," in *Four Decades On: Vietnam, the United States, and the Legacies of the Second Indochina War*, ed. Scott Laderman and Edwin A. Martini (Durham, NC: Duke University Press), 58–83.

47 James M. Scott, *Deciding to Intervene: The Reagan Doctrine and American Foreign Policy* (Durham, NC: Duke University Press, 1996), 152–192.

48 For a discussion of human rights and the movement, see Christian Smith, *Resisting Reagan: The U.S. Central America Peace Movement* (Chicago: University of Chicago Press, 1996). For the broader context of human rights and U.S. foreign relations, see Barbara J. Keys, *Reclaiming American Virtue: The Human Rights Revolution of the 1970s* (Cambridge, MA: Harvard University Press, 2014); Mark Philip Bradley, *The World Reimagined: Americans and Human Rights in the Twentieth Century* (New York: Cambridge University Press, 2016).

49 For the original pledge, see Jim Wallis, "A Pledge of Resistance," *Sojourner*, August 10, 1984, 10–11.

50 Nick Witham, "U.S. Feminists and Central America in the 'Age of Reagan': The Overlapping Contexts of Activism, Intellectual Culture and Documentary Filmmaking," *Journal of American Studies* 48, no. 1 (February 2014): 199–221.

51 Wesley G. Phelps, "Women's Pentagon Action: The Persistence of Radicalism and Direct-Action Civil Disobedience in the Age of Reagan," *Peace and Change* 39, no. 3 (July 2014): 339–365. For more on 1980s antinuclear activism, see Robert Surbrug Jr., *Beyond Vietnam: The Politics of Protest in Massachusetts, 1974–1990* (Amherst: University of Massachusetts Press, 2009).

52 Héctor Perla Jr., "Si Nicaragua Venció, El Salvador Vencerá: Central American Agency in the Creation of the U.S.-Central American Peace and Solidarity Movement," *Latin American Research Review* 43, no. 2 (2008): 136–158.

53 Van Gosse, "'El Salvador Is Spanish for Vietnam': A New Immigrant Left and the Politics of Solidarity," in *The Immigrant Left in the United States*, ed. Paul Buhle and Dan Georgakas (Albany: State University of New York Press, 1996).

54 William Sloane Coffin, "Ahab and Naboth" (July 3, 1983), in *The Collected Sermons of William Sloane Coffin: Volume II, the Riverside Years*, ed. Martin E. Marty (Louisville, KY: Westminster John Knox Press, 2008), 51.

55 Sharon Erickson Nepstad, *Convictions of the Soul: Religion, Culture and Agency in the Central America Solidarity Movement* (Oxford: Oxford University Press, 2004), vii–viii.

56 For a fuller discussion of this cultural activism, see Nick Witham, *The Cultural Left and the Reagan Era: U.S. Protest and Central American Revolution* (London: I.B. Tauris, 2015).

57 Roger Peace, *A Call to Conscience: The Anti-Contra War Campaign* (Amherst: University of Massachusetts Press, 2012), 3–5.

58   Timothy Naftali, "George W. Bush and the 'War on Terror,'" in *The Presidency of George W. Bush: A First Historical Assessment*, ed. Julian E. Zelizer (Princeton, NJ: Princeton University Press, 2010), 59–87.

59   David Foster Wallace, "The View from Mrs Thompson's," *Rolling Stone*, October 25, 2001, 93.

60   On these liberal interventionists, see Richard Seymour, *The Liberal Defense of Murder* (London: Verso, 2008); Maria Ryan, "Bush's 'Useful Idiots': 9/11, the Liberal Hawks and the Cooption of the 'War on Terror,'" *Journal of American Studies* 45, no. 4 (November 2011): 667–693.

61   Barbara Lee, "War against Afghanistan" (September 14, 2001), in *Wartime Dissent in America: A History and Anthology*, ed. Robert Mann (New York: Palgrave MacMillan, 2010), 168.

62   Barack Obama, "Speech against the Iraq War" (October 2, 2002), *National Public Radio*, January 20, 2009, http://www.npr.org/templates/story/story.php?storyId =99591469.

63   On the links between the antiwar and alter-globalization movements, see T. V. Reed, "Globalization and the 21st-Century Peace Movement," in *Peace Movements and Pacifism after 9/11*, ed. Shin Chiba and Thomas J. Schoenbaum (Northampton, MA: Edward Elgar, 2008).

64   Richard Seymour, *American Insurgents: A Brief History of American Anti-Imperialism* (Chicago: Haymarket Books, 2012), 187.

65   Joris Verhulst, "February 15, 2003: The World Says No to War," in *The World Says No to War: Demonstrations against the War on Iraq*, ed. Stefaan Walgrave, Dieter Rucht, and Sidney Tarnow (Minneapolis: University of Minnesota Press, 2010), 16–17.

66   Patrick E. Tyler, "A New Power in the Streets: A Message to Bush Not to Rush to War," *New York Times*, February 17, 2003, A1.

67   Barbara Epstein, "Notes on the Antiwar Movement," *Monthly Review* 55, no. 3 (July/August 2003): 111.

68   This point is discussed in Alexander Cockburn, "Whatever Happened to the Anti-War Movement?," *New Left Review* 46 (July–August 2007): 29–38.

69   Epstein, "Notes on the Antiwar Movement," 113.

Further Reading

Robert Mann, ed. *Wartime Dissent in America: A History and Anthology*. New York: Palgrave MacMillan, 2010.

Richard Seymour. *American Insurgents: A Brief History of American Anti-Imperialism*. Chicago: Haymarket Books, 2012.

Ian Tyrell and Jay Sexton, eds. *Empire's Twin: U.S. Anti-Imperialism from the Founding Era to the Age of Terrorism*. Ithaca, NY: Cornell University Press, 2015.

The Military-
Industrial Complex

MARK R. WILSON

Are governments and societies corrupted by the economics of war and defense? This question may be an ancient one, but it has seemed especially important to Americans since the early Cold War era. By the 1950s, the United States was spending enormous resources on weapons, year after year, even when its military forces were not engaged in major combat operations. In January 1961, President Dwight D. Eisenhower used his farewell address to caution Americans against the potential dangers of what he dubbed the "military-industrial complex." Just a few years later, as the Vietnam War raged, critics of that conflict seized on Eisenhower's phrase as they sought explanations for what they saw as the tragic failures of the United States, abroad and at home.

Half a century later, the phrase "military-industrial complex" may be less commonly heard, but it is hardly gone. In recent years we have been introduced to new variants of the phrase, including the "medical-industrial complex" and the "prison-industrial complex." These new "complexes" are important, but their ascendance should not blind us to the continuing significance of the original one. The United States, as it maintains the most powerful military forces in the twenty-first-century world, continues to spend enormous resources on defense. These outlays, which had dipped during the post Cold War decade of the 1990s, grew significantly in the opening years of the twenty-first century, as the United States responded to the 9/11 attacks with military operations in Afghanistan and Iraq, as well as larger investments in "homeland security." In other words, Eisenhower's military-industrial complex appears to be an enduring and resilient institution. It still carries very high costs; it affects the lives of millions of people (and has the potential to affect the lives of billions), at home and abroad. For all of these reasons, today's students of war and society have good reason to give it their attention.

What is meant by the phrase "military-industrial complex"? To some extent, it serves simply as a lively synonym for the defense sector or the armaments industry. That is, it refers to the networks of producers, sellers, promoters, and consumers of the goods and services required by armed forces. Thus the companies and workers making things like submarines and missiles are part of the military-industrial complex, as are the military agencies purchasing them. But "military-industrial complex" is not just a value-neutral synonym for defense sector. More often than not, it is a pejorative term, meant to imply that the modern defense sector, at least as it has developed in the United States since 1945, is a dangerous monster that benefits special interests while harming the public good. In his 1961 farewell address, Eisenhower pointed to both of these definitions—the more neutral one and the more negative. No radical pacifist, Eisenhower regarded the defense sector as necessary. At the same time, he warned that it might become too powerful, too wasteful, and too damaging to the best traditions of American capitalism and democracy. Since the 1960s, this warned-of "military-industrial complex," which Eisenhower suggested was a possible future evil to be avoided, is what is most often suggested by those who use the term.

However it may be defined, the military-industrial complex, despite its importance, is not very well understood by scholars and the public.[1] This chapter offers a short introduction to its history, beginning in 1961, with President Eisenhower's famous address. It then moves backward in time, to consider the long-run development of military-industrial relations leading up to the Cold War era. The second half of the chapter moves past 1961, to consider how the military-industrial complex observed by Eisenhower has changed over time, into the early twenty-first century. Throughout, the aim is to avoid repeating conventional wisdom and myths, in favor of pointing to tough questions that still require better answers.

Readers will be challenged to think about the ways in which the U.S. military-industrial complex (used here to refer to the defense sector) has changed over time, especially in terms of the shifting balances within it, between public and private capacities. Throughout American history, the military has been supplied by a complex mix of public, private, and, some might suggest, semiprivate entities, including for-profit weapons manufacturers, merchants, and service providers, as well as government-owned factories and in-house enterprises. Never in American history has the military-industrial complex been fully private—or public. However, there have been some significant shifts in the public-private balance, including those that have occurred in recent decades. If we consider the very long run of U.S. history, today's military-industrial complex, as it has developed in the half century since Eisenhower's farewell address, looks remarkably privatized. So, to the extent that the evils of the military-industrial complex are attributed to improper private gain at public expense, we seem to have good reason today to heed Eisenhower's call to be vigilant, to do more to understand and monitor the defense sector.

Origins of the Term and Its Immediate Historical Context: The Early Cold War Era

Although Eisenhower's warning about the military-industrial complex has resonated long after 1961, we should understand it as the product of a specific historical context. When he gave the speech, the Cold War was only a little more than a decade old. During the first years of this dangerous struggle, which saw the first Soviet atomic bomb test in 1949 and the outbreak of the Korean War in 1950, the White House was occupied by Harry S. Truman. But it was Eisenhower, not Truman, who faced the troubling reality that he could not protect Americans from annihilation. In this sense, Eisenhower was the first U.S. president since Abraham Lincoln to grapple with an existential threat to national survival. This threat was made obvious in 1957, when the Soviet Union succeeded in launching into orbit *Sputnik*, the first man-made satellite. *Sputnik* signaled to Americans not just the broad danger of possibly falling behind their Cold War enemy in the field of science and technology but the more specific and immediate danger of an attack from long-distance missiles. The same rockets that launched *Sputnik*, that is, could be used to deliver unstoppable atomic weapons.

This unprecedented threat from abroad worried Eisenhower, who, even as he called for bilateral disarmament and peace, believed that the Cold War context forced the United States to break from tradition by maintaining substantial armed forces during what was ostensibly peacetime. These forces included not just hundreds of thousands of soldiers and sailors on active duty but also, as Eisenhower explained in his 1961 address, the "military-industrial complex." During the early Cold War, Eisenhower said, the United States had been "compelled to create a permanent armaments industry of vast proportions," which included hundreds of research laboratories and weapons production facilities. All of these were necessary, Eisenhower believed, given the geopolitical situation that had developed since 1945. However, Eisenhower also believed that Americans must monitor the military-industrial complex with extreme vigilance, so that it did not gain "unwarranted influence." The giant new defense sector must not be allowed to throw the U.S. economy and government out of "balance" (a word Eisenhower used many times in his 1961 address), by destroying "our liberties and democratic processes" in the name of national security.

That the most famous critique of the military-industrial complex was delivered by a former U.S. military commander strikes some people as ironic, or even implausible. However, Eisenhower's concerns were genuine, and they were informed by personal experience. In the years leading up to the address, he had often found himself in the position of trying to rein in what he saw as excessive requests for new weapons. Every year, the navy, the air force, and the army could be counted on to submit inflated budget requests, with ever-higher "needs" for new aircraft carriers, bombers, tanks, and missiles. From his perspective in the White House, committed to finding a reasonable balance between the nation's legitimate needs for guns as well as butter (to use a term employed at the time by economists discussing the balance between consumer and military spending), Eisenhower felt that Congress and the military services, along with other powerful people in America, erred on the side of asking for too many guns.

For Eisenhower, as for many other critics of the military-industrial complex, including pacifists, fiscal conservatives, and left-leaning social scientists, the excessive calls for more weapons seemed to come from three distinct groups. One was the military establishment itself. Military officers from all three main branches (army, navy, and air force), along with many civilian officials at the Pentagon, claimed that they needed more new weapons to keep the country safe. (Interservice rivalries also contributed to this problem, as each of the branches sought to outdo one another and protect or expand its own budget.) A second major player was Congress. For many members of Congress, the years of the Second World War and the early Cold War were a time when military contracts translated into hundreds or thousands of jobs in their districts. Most members were reluctant to see these jobs disappear; they also wanted their districts or states to receive a share of new defense spending. The result during Eisenhower's presidency was that Congress often authorized larger defense budgets than the White House sought. There was a partisan dimension to this dynamic: especially after Sputnik, many Democrats (who regained control of both houses of Congress after the 1954 elections) claimed that Eisenhower and his fellow Republicans had failed to provide the country with adequate security. Finally, sitting on the third point on what would later be called the "iron triangle" of the military-industrial complex, were military contractors who lobbied Congress and the Pentagon for more business. These contractors were potentially the greatest beneficiaries of the military-industrial complex, since they had the ability (at least if all went well) to reap large dollar profits from defense orders. During his years as president, Eisenhower was disappointed in all three of these groups, which, in his view, were putting selfish concerns ahead of the national interest. His deep frustration with all three—contractors, Congress, and his own military—informed his 1961 critique.[2]

Eisenhower's perspective was shaped not just by his time in the White House in the 1950s but also by earlier encounters with the defense sector. In the 1920s and 1930s, he had been part of a team of military officers that had worked on planning for mobilizing the American economy for another potential world war. In this sense, Eisenhower himself participated in the building of the military-industrial complex. However, during the interwar years, when he was working on mobilization planning, U.S. military budgets were small; most military contractors had small work forces and were struggling to survive. The nation's number-two private builder of navy submarines, the Lake Torpedo Boat Company, went out of business in 1924. Eisenhower's memories of this background provided him with a solid historical understanding of the development of the military-industrial complex since the 1910s. Informed by this knowledge of the past, he stressed in his address that the Second World War and the early Cold War years constituted a major historical turning point, a sharp break with tradition. This was in some ways an accurate assessment, but it also overlooked or obscured some of the most important long-run factors in the development of the military-industrial complex.

In his address, Eisenhower claimed that before the Second World War, "the United States had no armaments industry." Strictly speaking, this was false. Since its birth in the 1780s, the United States had maintained a respectable army and navy, both of which were outfitted mainly by domestic industries. (These included the military's in-house operations, such as its navy yards and armories, as well as private contractors, including companies still known today, such as Du Pont and Colt.) What is true is that before the Second World War, the U.S. defense sector was quite small relative to the size of the whole economy. In Eisenhower's day, between the Korean and Vietnam Wars, defense spending amounted to nearly 10 percent of gross domestic product (GDP). In contrast, for most of U.S. history before the Second World War, except during wars, only about 1 percent of GDP went to defense. So Eisenhower was correct to imply that the Cold War defense sector was huge in historical terms, even if he went too far by claiming that there was no peacetime arms industry in earlier decades.

Hidden behind Eisenhower's hyperbolic claim about the absence of military industry in early U.S. history was a subtextual point, hard to recognize today, about the rise of the private, for-profit side of the defense sector. As Eisenhower knew from personal experience, before the Second World War, much of the materiel consumed by American armed forces in peacetime was produced not by for-profit contractors but rather by the military's own in-house production facilities, including shipyards and arsenals. Because most of this in-house capacity has disappeared since Eisenhower's 1961 address, it is easy to forget. But as we survey the long-run development of the military-industrial complex, it is worth keeping in mind that the second half of the twentieth century was remarkable not just in terms of how the U.S. defense sector grew in size but also in terms of how it became more privatized.

Before Eisenhower: Long-Run Developments, 1780s–1950s

During the first century of U.S. history, starting with the nation's founding in the 1780s, Americans built a national military that was active and robust, even if it remained second-rate, in global terms. Thanks to the Atlantic Ocean, the U.S. Army did not have to compete directly with the land forces of the great

European powers, including France and Prussia. To be sure, Britain's Royal Navy, easily the best in the world, did present serious potential security problems. But after the War of 1812, the United States avoided direct military conflict with Britain. In many ways, the Royal Navy actually offered Americans benefits by providing security and stability to international commerce. Meanwhile, the United States, which was far more populous than Canada or Mexico, became the most formidable military power in the Americas. This was most obvious in the late 1840s, during the Mexican-American War, which ended with the United States seizing huge amounts of formerly Mexican territory in the trans-Mississippi West.

To arm and equip its soldiers and sailors, the early United States, imitating European powers such as France and Britain, built an impressive public-private military manufacturing system. This system did not exist in the 1790s, when the government paid private contractors to deliver small arms and warships. But after 1800, and particularly after the War of 1812, which exposed the shortcomings of the nation's infant defense sector, American civilian and military officials relied largely on the government's in-house production facilities. Among these were several naval shipyards, which had been opened at the turn of the nineteenth century, in Boston, New York, Philadelphia, Portsmouth (New Hampshire), and Norfolk (Virginia). These navy-run shipyards would produce most of the nation's new warships until late in the century. Meanwhile, the U.S. Army also built and maintained its own network of armories and arsenals, which supplied small arms and ammunition. One of the most important of these installations was the Springfield (Massachusetts) Armory, which, along with a smaller sister facility in Harpers Ferry, Virginia, would manage by the 1850s to turn out truly world-class rifle muskets. More than their counterparts elsewhere in the world, these army-run small arms plants succeeded in pioneering the use of interchangeable parts.[3]

Although the military's in-house production facilities supplied the peacetime armed forces with much of their finished equipment and weaponry, the American defense sector of the nineteenth century also relied on for-profit contractors. This was certainly true in wartime, when military demand temporarily overwhelmed the capacities of the in-house plants. During the Civil War, for example, only about 20 percent of the materiel consumed by the Union armies came from government installations; the rest was purchased directly from contractors. Even in peacetime, private contractors were important. Naval shipyards and army armories did not make every single component they needed but instead contracted with private suppliers, including local mills, machinists, and engineers, who offered the military high-performance products. Thus in mid-nineteenth century New England, in the region around the Springfield Armory, there developed an innovative industrial cluster (akin to Silicon Valley of the late twentieth century), in which public and private establishments interacted successfully to build state-of-the-art weapons. Meanwhile, on the western frontier, the army relied largely on contractors, including long-distance wagon transport companies that employed hundreds of oxen and mules, to supply its far-flung network of forts.[4]

Perhaps in part because this early American defense sector contained a now-unfamiliar mix of public and private industrial establishments, many historians of the military-industrial complex have located its origins a bit later in time. At the end of the nineteenth century, as the United States started to build a world-class steel navy, it began to rely more heavily on contractors, including private shipyards and steel mills. Among these were some companies, including the Newport News Shipbuilding and Drydock Company and the Bethlehem Steel Company, that would remain among the nation's most important military contractors through much of the twentieth century. These firms not only built most of the new warships but also supplied many of their high-tech components, including dense armor plate, powerful new engines, and self-propelled torpedoes. Designing and building this new generation of weapons in a competitive global environment required the navy and its contractors to push the technological state of the art, using more scientific research and experimentation. For all these reasons, the naval shipbuilding program in the age of Teddy Roosevelt is understood by some as the first true precursor to the Cold War military-industrial complex.[5]

The intermingling of business and the military grew during the First World War, many historians have suggested, as corporate leaders went to Washington to help direct the big war mobilization of 1917–1918. One important new agency on the home front was the War Industries Board, populated by so-called dollar-a-year men, corporate executives who remained on their companies' payrolls during their temporary work on war mobilization. In the Second World War, corporate executives led a similar emergency mobilization agency called the War Production Board. Both agencies have been criticized by students of the military-industrial complex, who have suggested that such arrangements inevitably allow the selfish interests of for-profit companies to be confused with the public's legitimate national security needs.

The First World War also brought new levels of public concern about "profiteering" (a word that became popular at that time) and the potentially dangerous consequences, for international security, of industrial capitalism. Questions about the legitimacy of war profits were, of course, nothing new. They had been raised around the world since ancient times; Americans had struggled with these issues during the Revolutionary War, during the Civil War, and, more recently, during congressional investigations of alleged malfeasance in the navy shipbuilding program at the end of the nineteenth century. But during the First World War, the sheer size of the dollar profits of major American military contractors (who supplied Britain and France as well as the United States), including Bethlehem Steel and Du Pont, was hard to ignore. Not just during the First World War, but throughout the 1920s and 1930s, public resentment of so-called war profiteers, who enriched themselves while ordinary soldiers risked life and limb, became an important political force. One important expression of this critique, in the mid-1930s, was the Nye Committee, a special U.S. Senate panel, which carried out a sweeping investigation of the arms industry. At times, the Nye Committee, like many other people around the world during this era, suggested that for-profit weapons manufacturers and arms dealers were partly to blame for the catastrophe of the First World War. Their economic self-interest, it was alleged, led them to lobby national governments to build up their arsenals. Thus the Nye Committee, along with many veterans groups, pacifists, socialists, and others in the early twentieth century, voiced a powerful critique of the problems that came from the admixture of capitalism and war. Much of what they said would be revived a generation later, by Cold War–era critics of the military-industrial complex.[6]

While the history of First World War–era attacks on profiteering is relatively well-known, far less well remembered is the fact that during this period the United States created a more nationalized defense sector, in which public ownership and oversight became quite strong. This style of military economy was part of the broader Progressive and New Deal reform efforts, which saw the national government grow in scope and power. In what sense did the U.S. defense sector become more nationalized, or "progressive"? The most obvious signs of this shift appeared in the Navy Department, which during the First World War was led by Josephus Daniels, a spirited Progressive (and white supremacist) from North Carolina. Daniels and his allies were suspicious of the big steel companies and other private contractors, who, they alleged, were systematically overcharging the government. Daniels's solution was to have the U.S. Navy make more of its ships and weapons in its own in-house facilities. In the 1920s and 1930s, Congress approved a new shipbuilding formula, which demanded that half of all new warships be constructed in the navy's in-house yards. Meanwhile, the army continued to supply many of its peacetime needs from its own in-house arsenals. So when the Nye Committee called in the mid-1930s for a wholesale nationalization of most of the U.S. arms industry, this demand was in fact less radical than it appears to us today. During the first half of the twentieth century, the U.S. military-industrial sector was largely government owned and military managed—more so than it had been at the turn of the century, when the navy had relied more heavily on private contractors to build and outfit its new steel ships.

This early twentieth-century reversion, back to the earlier nineteenth-century practice of having much of the military's normal requirements furnished from government-owned, government-operated facilities, raises some interesting questions about the history of the military-industrial complex. For one thing, it challenges the notion that there was a linear path of development, in which for-profit businesses became more and more dominant over time. It also suggests that we should not believe that the military-industrial complex must come in only one particular form. Instead, the record of the past suggests that even if we confine ourselves to the case of the United States, the military has interacted with the nation's capitalist economy in a variety of different ways, which include different balances of public and private capacities and knowledge. In these terms, it may make sense to understand the U.S. mobilization for the Second World War not so much as the catalyst for the version of the "military-industrial complex" that was so much discussed in the 1960s by Eisenhower and by critics of the Vietnam War but rather as the final expression of an earlier, more nationalized and highly regulated form of military economy.

To be sure, during the Second World War, there were plenty of for-profit companies involved in military production. Indeed, as the war mobilization grew until it absorbed about 40 percent of the nation's economic output, most American manufacturers were drawn into war production. Specialty military contractors like Newport News and Boeing for the first time became truly large companies with tens of thousands of employees instead of the hundreds they had employed before 1940. Meanwhile, the nation's biggest and most profitable industrial corporations, such as General Motors and Du Pont, switched out of civilian production, becoming leaders of the military-industrial effort. As noted above, some corporate executives also helped to lead the industrial mobilization in Washington, at temporary agencies such as the War Production Board. So to the extent that the military-industrial complex is defined by deep interactions between the military establishment and industrial corporations, it was certainly flourishing during the Second World War.

Still, despite all the contracting on the home front, the economic mobilization was largely directed by public officials, including military officers and their agencies. Most of the many billions of dollars' worth of new war plants built for the Second World War were operated by contractors, but they were owned by the U.S. government. By 1945, the government owned something close to 20 percent of the nation's entire industrial capacity. The navy's in-house shipyards, along with other government-owned, government-operated war plants continued to be important suppliers to the armed forces. Military agencies served as top managers of the industrial mobilization, by overseeing all the contracts and delivering many components to the prime contractors who assembled finished weapons. The military also developed a powerful apparatus for price and profit control, which helped keep contractor profits down to levels considerably lower than they had been during the First World War. So the military-industrial complex of the early 1940s, such as it was, was a defense sector in which public ownership, oversight, regulation, and in-house production were all at historically high levels.[7]

The period immediately following the Second World War, during the Truman presidency (1945–1953), was critically important in the development of the military-industrial complex. During the first part of this period, from 1945 to 1947, there was a truly deep-cutting postwar demobilization, during which defense spending quickly dipped down to about 7 percent of GDP. Military contractors expected these cuts and slashed payrolls accordingly, while attempting to increase sales to civilian markets. Briefly, at least, this appeared to be a thoroughgoing postwar retrenchment, comparable to the ones that the United States had undertaken after the Civil War and the First World War. However, the Truman years ended up seeing major increases in military spending, which ushered in the military-industrial complex. One of the most important reasons for this was the Korean War of 1950–1953, during which the Truman administration and Congress dramatically boosted military spending, not just for the war itself but for more general purposes as well. They were reacting not just to the North Korean invasion but also to events a year earlier, in 1949, when the Soviet Union had its first successful test of an atomic weapon. Also in 1949, communists took power in China. In light of all these developments, champions of higher defense spending won the day.

One difficult question about these important Truman-era developments concerns the influence of the defense lobby in the late 1940s and early 1950s on the choice of policymakers to ramp up military outlays. On the one hand, it seems clear that unique geopolitical developments—that is, the growing Cold War, including the Korean War—were the most important causes of the swelling of the military-industrial complex. However, as Eisenhower and others suggested, it was also the case that self-interested parties, including defense contractors and members of Congress, may have exaggerated geopolitical dangers in order to boost revenues or jobs. As early as the late 1940s, the aerospace industry did mount organized public relations and lobbying campaigns, warning Americans that more weapons were needed to keep the country safe.[8] That these efforts continued into the 1950s bothered Eisenhower and helped inspire his farewell address. Meanwhile, there were increasing criticisms, including those voiced by sociologist C. Wright Mills in his influential book *The Power Elite* (1956), of the problem of the revolving door. Many military officers, when they retired, joined aerospace companies, where they received high salaries, presumably in return for sharing their expertise about military requirements. Meanwhile, corporate executives went to Washington, just as they had during the world wars, to serve in high positions at the new Defense Department (created in 1947). For example, Eisenhower's choice as secretary of defense, Charles E. Wilson, was a longtime executive at General Motors.

Did the defense lobby and its revolving door cause Congress and the Pentagon to spend more on weapons than was justified, even given the exceptional geopolitical context of the early Cold War years? If the answer to this question is yes, as many critics of the military-industrial complex have suggested, we are left with difficult questions: what was, in fact, a rational and optimal level of defense spending after 1945, and how much of the excess above that optimal level should be attributed to domestic political factors as opposed to Americans' perceptions (or misperceptions) of global threats? These questions have been explored already by several historians and political scientists but remain ripe for further study by a new generation of scholars.[9]

The most important new weapons of the 1950s, ballistic missiles, illustrate some of the most beneficial products of the military-industrial complex, as well as its most terrifying aspects. By the early 1960s, crash programs by all three major branches of the U.S. military had succeeded in fielding ballistic missile systems, both land and submarine based, which became the core of the U.S. strategic (nuclear) weapons force. These weapons were the products of the military-industrial complex in its fully developed early Cold War form—a vast, lavishly funded network of contractors, military agencies, nonprofit think tanks, and universities.[10] All of this talent and money was devoted to building weapons that, if used, would kill tens of millions of people in a matter of a few hours, if not end human civilization entirely. This was, on one level, the military-industrial complex at its most perverse.

But the military-industrial complex of the missile age also seemed to come with some benefits, including positive technological spinoff effects. This is not to suggest that only war and military spending can cause major technological advancements; often, the military has benefited from technologies developed in the civilian sector, for civilian purposes. However, there can be no doubt the military-industrial complex of the Cold War era accelerated some important technological advancements, which ended up being enjoyed by civilians. One of the best examples is the field of computing. The microprocessors at the heart of modern digital computers, for example, were developed to a large extent by scientists and engineers under Defense Department contracts. Silicon Valley owed much of its early growth to military orders. Although the military was hardly the only catalyst for technological change after 1945, it was an important one. This was especially the case around the time of Eisenhower's address, when military spending on research and development (R&D) reached over 1 percent of GDP. Military contracts, including projects sponsored by the Defense Department's Advanced Research Projects Agency (ARPA/DARPA), founded in 1958, helped to create many of the technological wonders now taken for granted, from global positioning satellite (GPS) systems to the internet.[11]

The successful transfer of such "dual-use technologies" to the civilian economy may be understood as part of another relatively positive aspect of the record of the Cold War military-industrial complex: its failure to become the kind of overwhelming force, warned about by Eisenhower, that could totally dominate American society and government. As the political scientist Paul Seabury observed at the time, although the United States had a military-industrial complex, the Soviet Union *was* a military-industrial complex.[12] In the 1940s and 1950s, many critics feared that the United States might become a "garrison state," in which all other priorities and activities became subsumed by the focus on military preparedness. Historians and political scientists disagree about the extent to which this problem was successfully avoided. However, the growth and dynamism of the civilian economy, as well as the sharp decline after the Vietnam War in the relative importance of defense spending in the larger national economy, suggests that the post-1945 American garrison state, or national security state, was less than omnipotent.[13]

Since Eisenhower: Privatization, 1960s–present

As the declining economic importance of the defense sector after the 1960s suggests, we need to understand the military-industrial complex not as a historical constant, impervious to change since it was called out by Eisenhower in 1961. Nor was it, as some have suggested, an unstoppable snowball, which could only grow in size and influence, over time, despite Eisenhower's prophetic warning. (Such is the implication of one of the most comprehensive filmic treatments of the military-industrial complex in recent years, the 2005 documentary film *Why We Fight* directed by Eugene Jarecki.) Rather, we need to understand the post-1961 military-industrial complex as a dynamic institution that underwent major structural changes, with many of its elements proving to be vulnerable rather than omnipotent.

Indeed, only weeks after Eisenhower delivered his 1961 address, the military-industrial complex found itself faced with a powerful would-be reformer: Defense Secretary Robert S. McNamara. A former Ford Motor Company executive, McNamara would serve for seven full years, under Presidents John F. Kennedy and Lyndon B. Johnson. During this period, McNamara and his team of top civilians at the Defense Department shook up the military establishment, including the military-industrial complex, in more ways than one. Devoted to efficiency and cost-cutting, which they believed they could achieve sensibly through logical and mathematical analysis, McNamara and his team started by taking authority away from the military branches. With more power in the hands of civilians in the Defense Department, military acquisition was overhauled. McNamara and his team dramatically moved away from cost-plus-fixed-fee contracts, in favor of more fixed price orders and competitive bidding. They encouraged "total package procurement," which required contractors to take more responsibility at the outset, starting with a rigid contract covering all costs, for all phases of the development of a weapon, from design to prototyping to production to delivery. Meanwhile, they also carried out a remarkable (but poorly remembered) privatization of the defense sector by selling off government-owned assets and closing down many of the military's long-standing in-house production facilities. All of these reforms destabilized the military-industrial complex during the 1960s, mostly in the direction of making it more like what one might expect to find in a competitive civilian market. These major reforms were underway before the escalation of the War in Vietnam but continued as that conflict became more serious. Here was a historically unusual situation: a major cost-cutting and privatizing reform effort across the defense sector, pursued simultaneously with a major new mobilization for war.

The McNamara reforms had mixed results. Although they were widely resisted and criticized, especially as the Vietnam War worsened, McNamara's efficiency initiatives had lasting influence in Washington, not just in the Defense Department, but across the whole government. However, more than a few of McNamara's defense acquisition practices had poor results, in part because they were so demanding and strict. The Defense Department used total package procurement in its orders for C-5 aircraft, built by Lockheed. In the case of the C-5, as in other weapons ordered under the "total package" scheme, there were massive cost overruns. Because these relatively strict contracts contained penalties for such overruns, the Defense Department was soon faced with the prospect of having Lockheed, one of its biggest suppliers, go bankrupt. Indeed, thanks to the C-5 order, along with other difficulties on the civilian side of its business, Lockheed, by the beginning of the 1970s, was failing. It survived only because of a major federal bailout. This story may serve as an example of the resilience of the dysfunctional military-industrial complex that was so often denounced by critics during the Vietnam War, but it also pointed to the power of McNamara's reforms to transform the defense sector, sometimes in ways that frightened contractors.[14]

As the story of Lockheed's C-5 suggests, McNamara and his team seem to have succeeded, at least in the short term, in limiting contractor profits. Most studies of this issue suggest that from the late 1950s to the late 1960s, the profit margins of military contractors, whether measured by return on investment or by simple ratios of earnings to revenues, declined. Although such figures should have cheered critics of the military-industrial complex, they were rarely incorporated into popular accounts of the defense sector, which assumed that it was both noncompetitive and highly profitable.[15] Meanwhile, McNamara's successors at the Defense Department, including Secretary of Defense Melvin Laird and his deputy David Packard, worked in the early 1970s to find ways to boost the profits of their suppliers. This was not simply because they wanted to avoid more cases of bankrupt contractors in the mode of Lockheed but because they believed that the increasingly privatized defense sector, with more private capital at risk, deserved greater rewards. As the government sold off more of the defense plant that it had acquired during the Second World War and the Korean War, it required the private sector to invest more in production equipment and factories. After the Vietnam War, Pentagon officials, along with the companies themselves, reasoned that higher dollar profits would be required to incentivize and reward this new investment. Thus it was public policy, and not just contractor trickery, that led the Defense Department to adjust upward their tolerance for contractor profits, at least as measured in crude earnings to sales ratios or in total dollar terms.

Meanwhile, many critics of the military-industrial complex, far from endorsing the view that contractors needed higher profits, emphasized that the defense sector was rife with waste. Certainly this was true during the Vietnam War, when a leading congressional critic, Senator William Proxmire of Wisconsin, issued his published condemnation of the Pentagon, entitled *Report from Wasteland: America's Military-Industrial Complex* (1970).[16] By the mid-1970s, following the post–Vietnam War drawdown, which involved substantial cuts to the defense budget, such criticisms became less common. They revived, however, in the 1980s, during the new defense buildup carried out by the administration of President Ronald Reagan. Criticizing their predecessors for having cut military budgets too sharply after the Vietnam War, Reagan and his advisors shifted the terms of the Cold War, with a more aggressive military posture that challenged the Soviet Union. (Some believe that this hastened the demise of the Soviet Empire, while others believe other factors were more important.) Predictably, the new surge in defense spending in the early 1980s brought with it some new concerns about the alleged evils of the military-industrial complex. During the Reagan years, the press presented the public with a steady diet of reports of scandalous waste, including purchases by the military of $500 hammers and $2,000 toilet seats.

The 1980s scandals were politically complex, in the sense that they pointed to at least two distinct villains. One of these was the private sector, which evidently was willing to overcharge the Pentagon to pad its profits. But at least equally guilty, it seemed, was the government. For critics of the military-industrial complex, this story of multiple villains was familiar; it had been a standard part of the Vietnam War critiques, including Proxmire's, which blamed Pentagon waste along with contractor profiteering. This perspective was in some sense more balanced than the one offered in the 1930s by the Nye Committee, which focused on the evils of the for-profit companies. Half a century later, government bureaucracy was identified as a major problem. Indeed, while the 1980s scandals certainly reinforced the suspicions of the more anticorporate critics of the military-industrial complex, in many ways the media coverage of the 1980s scandals, along with the Reagan administration's handling of them, was more generous to the contractors than it was to the Pentagon. This result fit with the broader political context of the day, which saw increased condemnations of government incompetence and overreach in a variety of fields, from taxation to industrial regulation.[17]

The rising defense budgets of the early 1980s suggested again the ways in which the military-industrial complex was fostered not just by contractors and the Pentagon but also by Congress. Again, in accounts that described the defense sector as driven by an "iron triangle," Congress always figured as one of the key pieces of the triad. And for good reason: most members of Congress fought hard to prevent the loss of existing defense installations or jobs in their districts and states; many jockeyed to find ways to deliver to their constituents a share of the spending on new programs. Meanwhile, even members of Congress whose districts lacked any prospect of significant future defense spending might in theory be influenced by the defense lobby, which, like other lobbies, had money to contribute to the campaign chests of agreeable representatives.

These political dynamics surrounding Congress's interactions with the defense sector raise important questions about whether the legislative branch has contributed to systematic overspending on defense. To most critics of the military-industrial complex, the answer to the question is obvious. However, among political scientists, this question has been the subject of a serious debate. Several scholars have used statistical analysis of data (mostly from the 1980s and 1990s) that speak to the relationship between congressional voting behavior and the geography of defense installations, spending, and contracting. Using these data, some researchers have questioned traditional assumptions about the links between the geography of defense spending and the willingness of members of Congress to vote for higher or lower defense budgets. They have suggested that perhaps we need to understand that legislators' voting on defense budgets is driven not just by local economic interests or lobbying but perhaps at least as much by party affiliations or ideology. However, other scholars, using similar techniques with different or additional data, have suggested that the traditional critique of the military-industrial complex, which holds that members of Congress contribute to bloated budgets by acting selfishly to protect defense jobs in their districts, remains closer to the truth.[18]

We will benefit from further investigations of these questions about Congress, some of which should complement the statistical studies with more qualitative research using the records of individual legislators, lobbying groups, and Pentagon offices. Is it the case that over the course of the Cold War, Congress became bolder, and more powerful, in its attempts to influence not just the size of the aggregate defense budget but also the nation's choices about how to arm itself? In other words, can we do more to trace the history of a growing political struggle between Congress and the Pentagon over specific weapons programs? Future studies of this question may dig deeper into the record of Cold War naval shipbuilding, where, it seems, Congress insisted on a fleet that contained more nuclear ships (that is, ships driven by nuclear power plants) than the Defense Department wanted. Other investigators may revisit well-known cases, such as that of the B-1 bomber, which was killed under the Carter administration only to be revived (albeit briefly) in the 1980s or, better yet, still underdocumented stories from which we still have much to discover.

As they write a fuller, richer history of the military-industrial complex, future investigators may need to wean themselves from the most simplistic version of its traditional critiques, by recognizing that actors in the defense sector can be vulnerable. While many unnecessary or obsolete weapons are built, some weapons programs are actually canceled, sometimes before production begins. This was true even during the height of the Cold War, when the Defense Department cancelled the "Dyna-Soar" project (a space glider-bomber), under development at Boeing, one of its most important contractors, in the early 1960s.

More recently, in 2002, at the beginning of the post-9/11 defense buildup, Secretary of Defense Donald Rumsfeld cancelled the army's "Crusader" mobile artillery system.[19] Such examples suggest that although the military-industrial complex may be powerful, even top defense contractors and their congressional champions have struggled, and sometimes even lost outright, in the ongoing chase after limited resources. Whereas some critics have alleged that the defense sector is monopolistic and devoid of competition, in truth military contractors, like their counterparts in other industries, understand themselves as insecure firms, fighting with one another for shares in a market with irregular demand.

It is not just specific weapons programs that can be vulnerable but also leading military contractors. This was true even during the early Cold War, when defense dollars were abundant. This presumably favorable environment could not save the Curtiss-Wright Corporation, which, as one of the nation's very biggest military contractors of the late 1930s and Second World War, presumably was in an excellent position to prosper after 1945. However, Curtiss-Wright failed to satisfy its military customers; soon, this soured relationship caused the company to drop out of the ranks of important aerospace prime contractors.[20] More recently, the vulnerability of individual firms was evident in the wave of defense sector consolidations during the 1990s, as post–Cold War cutbacks put more financial pressure on contractors. The result was a dramatic new concentration in the industry, as several dozen firms were folded into a handful of bigger ones in a matter of just a few years. Whereas the Vietnam War–era critics of the military-industrial complex often complained that the defense sector was too monopolistic (or, more precisely, oligopolistic) in the 1960s, thirty years later, it appeared to have become far more so. By the beginning of the twenty-first century, the military's biggest weapon systems were built by only a very small group of companies, including Lockheed Martin, Boeing, General Dynamics, Raytheon, and Northrop Grumman.[21]

The last years of the twentieth century brought not only more consolidation but also the continuation and even acceleration of trends that had been evident from the Vietnam War era, including globalization and privatization. During the McNamara years, as we have seen, there were important new steps in the direction of privatization, as the military shed in-house production facilities and other installations. This continued after the 1960s. But it was joined by new forms of privatization. For example, the post-1945 military had for many years owned and operated much of the housing used by military families, along with long-distance logistics operations, health care services, and a variety of other activities that went beyond combat on the battlefield. After the Vietnam War, when the military transitioned from a draft-based manpower system to the All-Volunteer Force, and particularly after the end of the Cold War, as the Clinton administration pursued new reforms to government operations, many more of the military's in-house installations and operations were privatized. By the 1990s, this was true even in the fields of health care and housing.[22]

By the early twenty-first century, as the United States engaged in new conflicts in Iraq and Afghanistan, one of the most striking new developments in the theaters of war was the rising ratio of contractors to military personnel. This change was most obvious in the field of security services, which saw the rise of new for-profit companies, such as Blackwater, which supplied men with guns. Whereas formerly such security was provided by regular military personnel, now the job of guarding embassies and other installations was handled by contractors. For some, this was simply a logical effort to benefit from the agility and long-term cost savings that might be gained from contracting out. But the increased U.S. reliance on for-profit security companies was also widely questioned by critics, who suggested that it might reduce the ability of regular military commanders to control the use of force, among other potential problems.[23]

Somewhat less well publicized but actually more significant in the changing balance between regular military personnel and contractors was a new reliance on private providers of logistical services. In the past, in-house military enterprises had handled a good deal of the work of transporting military personnel and their equipment, along with everyday base services, including cooking and cleaning. This logistical support work became more privatized in the early 1990s, when the Pentagon started to award large new comprehensive contracts for services at overseas military bases. The pioneer contractor in this field was Brown & Root/Kellogg Brown & Root (KBR), which soon became a subsidiary of Halliburton, a leading firm in the oil industry. KBR, along with other companies such as DynCorp, the Supreme Group, and the Fluor Corporation, now handled much of the work that in previous generations had been done by the military itself. Here was yet another example of the shifting balance between private and public in the military-industrial complex. The new contracts were denounced by some critics, many of whom called attention to the fact that the first big logistics contracts with KBR were awarded during the tenure of Secretary of Defense Richard B. ("Dick") Cheney, who then, soon after leaving office, became the chief executive officer of Halliburton. (By the early 2000s, when the logistics contracts became even larger in order to support operations in Afghanistan and Iraq, Cheney was the nation's vice president.) The Cheney-Halliburton case seemed to some critics an important example of the "revolving door" problem, of government officials moving in and out of jobs with defense contractors. This had always been a concern of military-industrial complex watchdogs, including Eisenhower himself. But the increasing reliance on contractors, now for security and logistical services along with weapon systems, seemed to make the problem even more serious.[24]

This new defense sector, the one that emerged by the fiftieth anniversary of Eisenhower's 1961 address, was not only far more privatized than the one that had existed during the early Cold War but also more globalized. On one level, it was more heavily reliant on global supply chains; over time, it appears, the

Pentagon, like the U.S. economy as a whole, started to rely more heavily on foreign sources of weapons and components. Meanwhile, the defense sector came to rely heavily on sales to foreign governments, just as it had done (in its much smaller form) in the 1930s, during the trials of the Great Depression. By the late 1960s, if not before, the United States was contributing mightily to the global proliferation of conventional weapons, by selling large quantities of arms to its allies, or would-be allies, all around the world. This trend harkened back to the era of the First World War, when many critics of the arms industry focused its global impact, involving international cartels and cross-border sales. A generation or two after the Vietnam War, this global character of the military-industrial complex attracted more attention, not just from monitors of U.S. arms exports but also in popular treatments, such as those developed by Hollywood. In films such as *Lord of War* (2005) and *War Dogs* (2016), audiences were encouraged to consider the evils not just of the traditional military-industrial complex at the domestic level but rather of a global network of producers, customers, and dealers.[25]

By the beginning of the twenty-first century, Americans encountered a military-industrial complex that was not simply the same thing that Eisenhower had described in 1961, nor simply an expanded or shrunken version of what it had been. Instead, its structure, economics, and politics had been substantially transformed since the early Cold War, just as they had been altered from the birth of the Republic through the Second World War. Until now, students of war and society have done too little to appreciate and study this interesting record of transformation and change. In the future, as the military-industrial complex continues to evolve, as it continues to shift into new technologies such as robots (including drones) and cyberwarfare, in tandem with changing domestic and global political contexts, we will have even more need for fresh perspectives on the subject.

Discussion Questions

1. To what extent were Eisenhower's worst fears realized? That is, to what extent has American capitalism and democracy been twisted to serve the special interests of defense contractors and their allies in Congress and the Pentagon?

2. How might we begin to measure the net balance between the negative effects of the military-industrial complex, such as overinvestment in wasteful weapons, with its more positive aspects, such as the encouragement of technological innovation?

3. What should we understand as the ideal mix of private and public in the defense sector? To what extent should the military retain or build its own in-house capacities for weapons design and production, as opposed to contracting out to for-profit firms?

Notes

1 To be sure, there are a handful of outstanding works, including some fine overviews with ample references to some of the best books and articles on the subject. See especially Alex Roland, *The Military-Industrial Complex* (Washington, DC: American Historical Association, 2001); Alex Roland, "The Military-Industrial Complex: Lobby and Trope," in *The Long War: A New History of U.S. National Security Policy since World War II*, ed. Andrew J. Bacevich (New York: Columbia University Press, 2007), 335–370; Benjamin Franklin Cooling, "The Military-Industrial Complex," in *A Companion to American Military History*, ed. James C. Bradford (Malden, MA: Wiley-Blackwell, 2010), 966–988; James Ledbetter, *Unwarranted Influence: Dwight D. Eisenhower and the Military-Industrial Complex* (New Haven, CT: Yale University Press, 2011); Mark R. Wilson, "Farewell to Progressivism: The Second World War and the Privatization of the 'Military-Industrial Complex,'" in *Capital Gains: Business and Politics in Twentieth-Century America*, ed. Richard R. John and Kim Phillips-Fein (Philadelphia: University of Pennsylvania Press, 2017), 80–94, 256–261.

2 Ledbetter, *Unwarranted Influence*, 106–131; Dolores E. Janiewski, "Eisenhower's Paradoxical Relationship with the 'Military-Industrial Complex,'" *Presidential Studies Quarterly* 41 (December 2011): 667–692; Roland, "Military-Industrial Complex: Lobby and Trope," 336–340.

3 Merritt Roe Smith, *Harpers Ferry Armory and the New Technology: The Challenge of Change* (Ithaca, NY: Cornell University Press, 1977); Cooling, "Military-Industrial Complex," 971.

4 Paul A. C. Koistinen, *Beating Plowshares into Swords: The Political Economy of American Warfare, 1606–1865* (Lawrence: University Press of Kansas, 1996); Mark R. Wilson, *The Business of Civil War: Military Mobilization and the State, 1861–1865* (Baltimore: Johns Hopkins University Press, 2006).

5 Benjamin Franklin Cooling, *Gray Steel and Blue Water Navy: The Formative Years of America's Military-Industrial Complex, 1881–1917* (Hamden, CT: Archon, 1979); Thomas J. Misa, *A Nation of Steel: The Making of Modern America, 1865–1925* (Baltimore: Johns Hopkins University Press, 1995); Thomas R. Heinrich, *Ships for the Seven Seas: Philadelphia Shipbuilding in the Age of Industrial Capitalism* (Baltimore: Johns Hopkins University Press, 1997); Katherine C. Epstein, *Torpedo: Inventing the Military-Industrial Complex in the United States and Great Britain* (Cambridge, MA: Harvard University Press, 2014).

6 Stuart D. Brandes, *Warhogs: A History of War Profits in America* (Lexington: University Press of Kentucky, 1997).

7 Mark R. Wilson, *Destructive Creation: American Business and the Winning of World War II* (Philadelphia: University of Pennsylvania Press, 2016).

8 Karen S. Miller, *The Voice of Business: Hill & Knowlton and Postwar Public Relations* (Chapel Hill: University of North Carolina Press, 1999).

9 Among the many valuable studies of this subject is Michael J. Hogan, *A Cross of Iron: Harry S. Truman and the Origins of the National Security State, 1945–1954* (New York: Cambridge University Press, 1998).

10 Stuart W. Leslie, *The Cold War and American Science: The Military-Industrial-Academic Complex at Stanford and MIT* (New York: Columbia University Press, 1993).

11 Roland, *Military-Industrial Complex*, 12; Janet Abbate, *Inventing the Internet* (Cambridge, MA: MIT Press, 1999); Christophe Lécuyer, *Making Silicon Valley: Innovation and the Growth of High Tech* (Cambridge, MA: MIT Press, 2007); Alex Roland, *War and Technology: A Very Short Introduction* (New York: Oxford University Press, 2016).

12 Roland, *Military-Industrial Complex*, 61.

13 Michael S. Sherry, *In the Shadow of War: The United States since the 1930s* (New Haven, CT: Yale University Press, 1995); Aaron L. Friedberg, *In the Shadow of the Garrison State: America's Antistatism and Its Cold War Grand Strategy* (Princeton, NJ: Princeton University Press, 2000); Bacevich, *Long War*; Hugh Rockoff, *America's Economic Way of War: War and the US Economy from the Spanish-American War to the Persian Gulf War* (New York: Cambridge University Press, 2012), 273; Jacques S. Gansler, *Democracy's Arsenal: Creating a Twenty-First Century Defense Industry* (Cambridge, MA: MIT Press, 2011), 21.

14 Walter S. Poole, *Adapting to Flexible Response, 1960–1968* (Washington, DC: Office of the Secretary of Defense, 2013).

15 Roland, "Military-Industrial Complex: Lobby and Trope," 348–351.

16 William Proxmire, *Report from Wasteland: America's Military-Industrial Complex* (New York: Praeger, 1970); Roland, "Military-Industrial Complex: Lobby and Trope," 344–345.

17 Daniel Wirls, *Buildup: The Politics of Defense in the Reagan Era* (Ithaca, NY: Cornell University Press, 1992).

18 Kenneth R. Mayer, *The Political Economy of Defense Contracting* (New Haven, CT: Yale University Press, 1991); Rebecca U. Thorpe, *The American Warfare State: The Domestic Politics of Military Spending* (Chicago: University of Chicago Press, 2014).

19 Christopher M. Jones and Kevin P. Marsh, "The Politics of Weapons Procurement: Why Some Programs Survive and Others Die," *Defense & Security Analysis* 27, no. 4 (2011): 359–373; Nicholas Michael Sambaluk, *The Other Space Race: Eisenhower and the Quest for Aerospace Security* (Annapolis, MD: Naval Institute Press, 2015).

20 Eugene Gholz, "The Curtiss-Wright Corporation and Cold War-Era Defense Procurement: A Challenge to Military-Industrial Complex Theory," *Journal of Cold War Studies* 2 (Winter 2000): 35–75.

21 Gansler, *Democracy's Arsenal*, 32–40.

22 Jennifer Mittelstadt, *The Rise of the Military Welfare State* (Cambridge, MA: Harvard University Press, 2015).

23 P. W. Singer, *Corporate Warriors: The Rise of the Privatized Military Industry* (Ithaca, NY: Cornell University Press, 2003); Deborah D. Avant, *The Market for Force: The Consequences of Privatizing Security* (New York: Cambridge University Press, 2005).

24 Pratap Chatterjee, *Halliburton's Army: How a Well-Connected Texas Oil Company Revolutionized the Way America Makes War* (New York: Nation Books, 2009); David Vine, *Base Nation: How U.S. Military Bases Abroad Harm America and the World* (New York: Metropolitan Books, 2015); T. Christian Miller, *Blood Money: Wasted Billions, Lost Lives, and Corporate Greed in Iraq* (New York: Little, Brown, 2006); Christopher Kinsey and Malcolm Hugh Patterson, eds., *Contractors and War: The Transformation of United States' Expeditionary Operations* (Palo Alto, CA: Stanford University Press, 2012); Andrew J. Bacevich, *Breach of Trust: How Americans Failed Their Soldiers and Their Country* (New York: Henry Holt, 2013), 126–129.

25 These films were directed, respectively, by Andrew Nicholl and Todd Philips.

Further Reading

James Ledbetter. *Unwarranted Influence: Dwight D. Eisenhower and the Military-Industrial Complex*. New Haven, CT: Yale University Press, 2011.

Alex Roland. *The Military-Industrial Complex*. Washington, DC: American Historical Association, 2001.

Harvey M. Sapolsky, Eugene Gholz, and Caitlin Talmadge. *US Defense Politics: The Origins of Security Policy*, 2nd ed. New York: Routledge, 2014.

5

Military Demographics

JENNIFER MITTELSTADT

Who Serves When Not All Serve?

In 1967, at the height of the War in Vietnam, the American system of conscription—commonly referred to as the draft—faced mounting criticism: which Americans were being sent to fight in the jungles of Southeast Asia? Citing disproportionate numbers of African Americans killed in action and high proportions of working class and poor men taking the places of middle-class, college-bound young men, critics including civil rights movement leader Martin Luther King Jr. and young senator Bobby Kennedy (D-NY), pronounced the draft unfair and undemocratic. President Lyndon Johnson, who by then had sent over one million men to the unpopular war in Vietnam, responded by creating an Advisory Commission on the Selective Service Administration to investigate charges of the draft's inequities. In fact, the American system of conscription, created during World War I with the Selective Service Act (1917), and then reactivated for the Second World War and again for the Cold War period, had over time developed special exemptions, exemptions that allowed some American young men to avoid the draft while capturing others in its net. While there were obvious exemptions for physical limitations, developmental disabilities, and criminal backgrounds, men could also be excused from military service for enrolling in college or graduate school, pursuing the ministry, or working in a profession considered essential for defense, like applied science.[1] The commission's final report, titled pointedly In Pursuit of Equity, asked plainly about the fairness of this patchwork of obligation that knitted some Americans to military service and severed others: "Who serves," it asked, "when not all serve?"[2]

The Vietnam War caused a crisis of military manpower legitimacy, but it was not the first time the nation had wrestled with questions about who should serve in the American military. At the beginning of the twentieth century, as U.S. presidents, Congress, and secretaries of war pressed the United States onto the world stage, they made new decisions about how to man an expanding military force and who would serve in the nation's growing foreign engagements. At root, military manning touched on fundamental questions facing a democratic society. What were the obligations of citizens to the state, especially in an increasingly militarized nation? Who could or should serve in the armed forces? And how should the nation organize and structure its military in order to meet those goals?

The U.S. government changed its answer to these questions over the course of the twentieth century. While the century dawned with a small professional military of volunteers, both the First and Second World Wars swelled the military and reconfigured military manpower policy, necessitating the nation's first fully national drafts. Rather than reverting to a system of volunteer service, however, the draft continued after the Second World War, as the nation maintained a large standing military during the Cold War battle against the Soviet Union. Thus the military never reverted to its tiny early twentieth-century size. Millions of men were drafted in the 1950s and 1960s, and as the nation pursued a new war in Vietnam in the mid to late 1960s and early 1970s, those numbers grew. At the close of the Vietnam War, however, the United States dramatically altered its military manpower scheme. In 1973 the United States abandoned the draft and created the modern All-Volunteer Force. No longer would citizens feel the press of military obligation that had drawn in millions in the First and Second World Wars, the War in Korea, and the Vietnam War. Only those who chose to serve would join the military. Even during times of war, service would constitute a choice, not a duty.

These two issues—wartime mobilizations and the toggling between conscription versus volunteer service—determined "who served" over the course of the twentieth century, generating notable variation and inequalities in military service. As this chapter explains, military demographics were more representative of the spectrum of social classes, races, and ethnicities in the larger American society during war and during the decades when the nation relied upon the draft. Thus, from the First through the Second World Wars and the early Cold War era, and even, surprisingly, on through Vietnam, the military was generally speaking a relatively fair reflection of American society at large. The military was less representative in class, race, and ethnic terms in the last quarter of the century, however, when the draft gave way to the All-Volunteer Force and America fought wars with recruits rather than conscripts.

This chapter describes the groups of Americans who served in the U.S. military over the course of the twentieth century and how they changed over time. Over the decades, military service broadened in some respects but narrowed in others. During the first three-quarters of the twentieth century, when large-scale wars and conscription obtained, the military drew in large numbers and a wide cross-section of Americans—people of varied racial, ethnic, and class backgrounds entered the military. From the new 1917 Selective Service Act through the Second World War, and even into the Cold War era and through the conflict in Vietnam, the armed forces preserved much of this class, regional, ethnic, and racial diversity and representation. By contrast, the twentieth century would close with a different military—the All-Volunteer Force—and a narrowed class composition of military personnel. Paradoxically, the volunteer force that narrowed class representation and reduced the representation of white Americans broadened representation among women and later among gays and lesbians, who both answered the military's needs for volunteer personnel in an increasingly scarce manpower pool and also sought military service as a mark of equal citizenship. The question "who serves?" thus had two different answers. Both answers, though, changed not only the face of the military but also its structure and function, and its connections to American citizenship and democracy.

From the First World War to the War in Vietnam

The twentieth century dawned with a small professional military in the United States, one that had only once, during the unprecedentedly massive Civil War, relied upon a draft initiated by the federal government. That experiment with conscription had harkened back to earlier hierarchical traditions of military service that allowed propertied men of the nation to avoid military service through the purchase of substitutes—usually poor men who for a price took their place. The harrowing draft riots in New York City in 1863 signaled the growing danger of systematic discrimination in favor of the middle and upper classes in military service that would have to be addressed in any following large-scale mobilization.[3] In these uprisings, the angry immigrant white working classes of New York rose up to attack the draft offices and military installations and even African Americans—in their minds symbols of the war they had been drafted to fight. While the riots garnered understandable attention, their ferocity suggested that huge numbers of men had been caught in the draft's net. In fact, 94 percent of Civil War soldiers volunteered. Still, the inequities of the draft enraged that remaining 6 percent and their peers.[4]

Fifty years later, when nationalist struggles in Europe drew the United States into a worldwide military conflict—then called the Great War—President Woodrow Wilson initiated a reformed system of conscription to avoid such violence—the modern Selective Service Act. The Selective Service attempted to use modern scientific and systematic methods of statecraft to avoid the obvious inequities of the Civil War era. It issued standards of age, health, religious, and moral criteria, and prohibited the substitutions and buyouts that the Civil War allowed. Even so, some wealthy and middle-class young men could still gain exemptions. And as a result large numbers of the working class and the poor still served as in earlier times. Nonetheless, so widespread and so large was the mobilization that 3.5 million served during World War I—one-quarter of all American men aged eighteen to thirty-one, 67 percent of whom were drafted. This breadth and scope meant that that significant portions of the native-born white middle classes also served.[5]

For the first time in American history, recent immigrants were heavy represented, particularly those who had recently arrived during the great wave of immigration beginning in the 1880s. Italians, Poles, and Bohemians joined Syrians, Hungarians, and Russian Jews in World War I to comprise one-fifth of the armed forces.[6] At first, the Selective Service only allowed certain immigrants to serve, however. "Enemy aliens"—recent immigrants from Germany, for example—were barred. Those who were already naturalized or those who had "declared" officially their intention to become citizens could join the military. Immigrants who had not declared—called "nondeclarants"—who constituted the bulk of the immigrant population—were initially rejected. But in major cities, the decision to leave them off the Selective Service rolls meant that native-born men were drafted in larger numbers, causing resentment and outcry. Eventually, therefore, the military accepted nondeclarants. No matter their status, the armed forces utilized the wide swath of immigrants who joined as a model and symbol of American democracy and unity. The army created a special unit of immigrant soldiers to display their skill and patriotism to native-born Americans.[7]

Although the United States demobilized after the First World War, its continued economic growth and international influence positioned it as an important world power by the eve of a second great worldwide conflagration in the early 1940s. When the United States began mobilizing for possible war in 1940, it began the single largest and most representative military mobilization in U.S. history. The enormous scale of the war quintupled the mobilization of the First World War, drawing fifteen-and-a-half million American men into the military. Five-and-a-half million men joined as volunteers, while ten million more men were pulled in through the wide net of the draft, totaling 56 percent of all eligible American men, more than twice the percentage of the First World War.

The result was a military force unlike any other in the country's history. The massive mobilization forced the white middle classes to join in significant numbers. Even wealthy men—men from blue-blood families at Harvard, celebrities from Hollywood, and professional baseball players—were drawn into the military, serving alongside the usual working class. The Second World War drew in a cross-section of native-born citizens alongside a high percentage of immigrants, mostly naturalized or second-generation Americans.[8] Italians and Jews from New York and New Jersey fought alongside Poles from Chicago, Boston Irish, Cajuns from Louisiana, and "hillbillies" from Appalachia. Lewis Hershey, who headed the Selective Service during the Second World War, called the multiethnic draft "an excellent force for the solidification and unification of the nation." The army's own manuals from World War II celebrated the armed forces' diversity during the war: "America is a composite nation embracing many distinct elements. The average unit," the army explained, consisted of "men of many nationalities. The Irish, the Swede, the Pole the Jew, the Italian."[9] When the army hired Hollywood director Frank Capra to make the "Why We Fight" movies for its troops and the public, they showcased American defense of diversity and inclusiveness as a purpose of the war.[10] To be sure, many soldiers recalled ethnic prejudice in their units—the war was no ethnic utopia, and the epithets were not rare. But many men also recalled the true amalgam of men; their many letters home testified to the welcome diversity of the Second World War experience.[11]

The same spirit of patriotic mixing was not allowed for some groups, including Japanese Americans and African Americans, who served under very different conditions than their white ethnic compatriots. Nonwhites' participation in the war highlighted the ways in which military service represented not only a burden to be shared equally among citizens but also a privilege for which marginalized Americans had to fight.

Both Japanese Americans and African Americans fought in historically unprecedented numbers in the Second World War. Even as many of their family members were placed in internment camps, and even though they were suspected as "enemy aliens," thousands of *Nisei*, second-generation Japanese Americans, volunteered to fight.[12] And whereas in the First World War only 350,000 African Americans served, the Second World War brought three times as many into the services—over 1.1 million. But unlike their white fellow citizens, whose ethnically diverse origins were welcomed and celebrated, Japanese Americans and African Americans' participation was deemed controversial in the segregated society of the time.[13] As a result, the military forbade both Japanese Americans and African Americans from joining the multiethnic units that Americans of European extraction shared.

The case of African American servicemen places in sharp relief the racially discriminatory nature of some military service. Following prejudicial practices from civilian life, the military restricted African Americans' service, channeling them into segregated components and keeping them from public view.[14] And while some units fought in combat roles, notably the Tuskegee Airmen, the 761st Tank Battalion, the 92nd Infantry Division, and the 452nd Anti-Aircraft Artillery Battalion, most African Americans in the U.S. military were confined to logistics and operations support roles. African Americans in the navy were confined to the Seabees, building ports and docks or laboring as stevedores, loading and unloading and cleaning ships. In the army they joined transportation and construction units, delivering materiel, building fortifications and posts, and cooking and cleaning.[15]

Discriminatory treatment propelled a vigorous debate among African Americans themselves as to whether they should volunteer, accede to the draft, or refuse to participate in the war. How, after all, might they justify fighting the racist Nazi regime when they themselves endured the violence and bigotry of second-class citizenship? Many leading African Americans came down on the side of joining, arguing that they should use their selfless military service to the nation in order to stake a claim to their full citizenship rights and responsibilities. A. Phillip Randolph, the powerful union and civil rights leader, tied military service during the war to the campaign for equal civil rights. The influential African American newspaper the *Pittsburgh Courier* articulated the argument as the "Double V Strategy"—victory in Europe for the United States and victory at home for African American civil rights. African Americans' story in the Second World War illustrated how "fairness" in military service could mean more than sharing the burden to serve; it could also mean claiming the right to serve.[16]

After the Second World War, the United States maintained its relatively broad representation, both reinstating the draft after a brief one-year hiatus and ending military segregation in 1948. Policymakers argued that Cold War competition with the Soviet Union necessitated a large standing military. While the armed forces declined from its massive wartime size, it nevertheless remained remarkably large for a peacetime force. Young men eager to serve in the military on their own terms, rather than being subject to the local draft board, volunteered in significant numbers. Army personnel numbered approximately one-and-a-half million, about half of whom still represented draftees. The Korean War temporarily swelled manpower to over five-and-a-half million volunteers and draftees, but afterward the number settled at around two-and-a-half million on active duty.[17]

Because the United States maintained a large armed force with a draft in the postwar era, much of the broad representation and increased social mixing that characterized the Second World War experience persisted. In the 1950s and 1960s, the military represented perhaps the only place in American life where a true social leveling occurred—an upending of the usual authority of the upper and middle classes over the working class. Working-class, middle-class, and occasionally even upper-class Americans could all be drawn into the military through the draft, ending up in a cross-sectioned enlisted corps that treated all equally. "Such an enforced leveling of the classes," renowned military sociologist Charles Moskos noted in his landmark study *The American Enlisted Man*, "has no parallel in any other existing institution in American society."[18] And in an age and a nation purportedly devoted to democracy, Moskos and other Americans viewed the leveling as not only ideal but essential, both to the success of the military and the nation.

The Vietnam War challenged these precepts of representation and social leveling in the American military. Unlike the first two world wars and the Korean conflict, the War in Vietnam never gained the approval of a large majority of Americans, particularly draft age men. Antiwar protest emerged among some students and pacifists as early as 1965, just as President Johnson escalated the war, and continued to grow year by year. By 1967, civil rights organizations and some Catholic left groups had joined the opposition. And by 1968, majority public opinion ran against the war. That year, the dramatic North Vietnamese Tet Offensive—coordinated attacks across South Vietnam—demonstrated the power and persistence of Ho Chi Minh's forces; it was also the year with the highest American casualty rate: 14,592 service personnel perished.[19] Though not all Americans joined in antiwar protests, polls showed that a majority of whites and African Americans, of the working class and middle class, all opposed the war.[20]

Although the U.S. military continued to operate within roughly the same system of conscription that had characterized the period from the Second World War through the early 1960s, the war's unpopularity meant that many men avoided the draft, particularly those with the resources and personal and professional connections to do so. Using draft exemptions based on mental and physical health, education or vocation, and conscientious objection, a larger proportion of white middle-class men avoided military service in a way that they did not and could not during the Second World War.[21] As a result, in the period from 1965 through 1969, during the escalation of the Vietnam War, middle-class men were underrepresented, and the burden of war—especially in combat units—was borne by the working class, white and African American.[22] The Vietnam War also represented the first time a large number of Puerto Rican men, approximately 45,000, served. "We know," protested Dennis Mora, "that Negroes and Puerto Ricans are being drafted and end up in the worst of the fighting."[23] Working-class Americans of all types sensed the inequalities of the draft acutely: "You bet your goddam dollar I'm bitter," one firefighter whose son died in Vietnam admitted. "The college types, the professors ... their sons don't end up in the swamps over there. . . . They're deferred, because they're in school. Or they got sent to safe places. Or they get out with all those letters they have from doctors."[24]

In 1969, as both the war and opposition to it raged on, Nixon altered the Selective Service System to help defuse charges of unfair representation. He created a draft "lottery." Rather than allowing the Selective Service to "channel" manpower and "select" and "defer" men into or out of the military based on education or profession, conscription would be truly random.[25] Like the daily lottery, an official reached into a jar and chose at random a capsule containing a number that corresponded to a day of the year. The first number picked, 258, corresponded to the 258th day of the year, September 14, and the selective service then called up all men of appropriate age with that birthdate. The lottery equalized somewhat the burden of military service. But the deferments for education promised prior to the lottery system were grandfathered until 1971, so for two more years the working class was still overrepresented.[26]

Still, for all the perceived inequities of military service during the Vietnam conflict, the military of that period was significantly more representative of broader American demographics than most understood. About 40 percent of eligible draft age men served, nearly twelve million total. With the end of education exemptions in 1969 and the advent of the national draft lottery, middle-class white men were pulled back into the military in larger numbers. Conscription in 1970 produced a military with 28.2 percent of the total force (regular military and National Guard or reserve) having attended college, a good marker of middle-class status. And the military became more racially representative as well. About 14 percent of military personnel were African American, above but very close to their proportion in the general population, which hovered around 12 percent.[27]

The Era of the All-Volunteer Force

Although few perceived it at the time, the relative equity of the Vietnam-era draft became more apparent after the end of that war, when the nation's leaders, in the president's words, "buried the draft."[28] In December 1972, the Selective Service called up its very last military conscript—never since has a citizen been drafted. The U.S. military transformed into a purely volunteer force, referred to as the All-Volunteer Force (AVF).

The AVF reflected the unpopularity of the Vietnam War and its draft, but it also reflected the growing popularity of the ideas of an increasingly influential group of free market economists led by University of Chicago professor Milton Friedman. They rejected the long-held premise of conscription—that military service functioned as a fundamental duty of American democratic citizenship, arguing the opposite: that the compulsory nature of the draft was antithetical to an American concept of liberty. Military service, they contended, could only be a free choice, not a compelled duty to the nation.[29] Severing the duty of service from the rights of citizenship, the new volunteer force asked the question, when none were forced, who would serve and why would they serve?

Military leaders, especially in the U.S. Army, which had historically relied most heavily on the draft for filling its ranks, faced these questions with considerable worry. Surely some Americans would join for patriotic purposes, but the military's own surveys demonstrated that number was small. A bigger advertising budget allocated by Congress would reach out to potential recruits through television, magazines, and newspapers, to remind them of the military.[30] But for the bulk of recruitment and retention, the military turned to bread and butter: raising pay and increasing and expanding military benefits.[31]

Military benefits and social services provided a potent tool for enlistment and retention, since American society did not at the time—and still does not—provide generous universal social benefits to all citizens in the manner of many European nations. On the eve of the transition to the volunteer force, Charles Moskos's sociology colleague and frequent coauthor, the University of Chicago's Morris Janowitz, predicted, "The military establishment" would have to accept that it would function as "more of a welfare state than civilian society" in order to survive within the constraints of a volunteer force.[32] And it did, rapidly expanding traditional military benefits like family housing, the post exchange (PX), the commissary, and travel expenses from solely officers and career personnel to all ranks, even the lowliest army privates. The military also created vast new programs that touched on nearly every aspect of life: education, child care, counseling, finance, and legal aid.[33] In 1985, the military revived the GI Bill, providing eligible recruits with funding for postsecondary education after their service. The military reasoned that these special military social welfare services would convince recruits to join and then cement their loyalty to the volunteer force.[34] Indeed, with the volunteer force manpower costs came to account for a huge proportion—sometimes exceeding 50 percent—of the Defense Department budget.[35]

If the higher pay and robust benefits provided the answer to why many Americans would choose to serve, they also hinted at the answer to the question who would serve. The working classes and the near poor were more likely to find military life attractive, faced as they were with a lack of decent pay or a strong, universal government safety net. Their lower levels of education and training left them in poorly paid, often irregular jobs, usually without good benefits. By 1975, two years into the era of the volunteer force, the demographics had already changed markedly from the draft era preceding it: the services were less middle class, more working class and lower income, and less educated. The new volunteer force did not come close to the representativeness of the Second World War era, of course, when massive mobilization and conscription had produced widespread participation and engaged men from across the class and race spectrum. But it did not even approximate the representativeness of the Vietnam era either. While the draft in 1970 produced a military between a fourth and a third of whose members had college experience, the new volunteer force counted only 5.3 percent of its new enlistments with college training.[36] The volunteer force drew Americans clustered toward the bottom of the income scale rather than the middle. The Department of Defense denied accusations from observers that the new volunteer force constituted a "poor man's" military.[37] But the numbers called that claim into question, especially in the largest branch of the services, the U.S. Army. In 1975, while only 5 percent of American families had very low incomes under $2,900 per year, the percentage of army enlistees from such families nearly doubled that. And while 40 percent of American families earned under $10,999/year, 53 percent of army enlistees' families did. In 1976, the numbers of recruits from officially designated "low-income families" grew sharply, from 16 percent whose households earned less than $5,000 a year to 30.2 percent.[38] A defense manpower task force reluctantly conceded, "Enlistees in the Army come from a somewhat less favored socio-economic background."[39]

Military sociologists who had long studied military manning underscored the transformation of the army into a less educated, working-class institution with the end of the draft. "I am most impressed by what I do not often find," Charles Moskos explained to Congress, "urban and suburban white soldiers of middle class origins."[40] "The volunteer Army is going contrary to the national trend, recruiting lesser-educated people when in society as a whole more people [are] finishing high school."[41] One of his young colleagues, David Segal, put the class inequities of the new volunteer force more bluntly, noting that "under the current all-volunteer format, the college graduate is almost extinct." Since college attendance was a close proxy for middle-class status, the data suggested that the middle class had virtually vanished from the volunteer army.[42]

As the white middle class departed the military in the volunteer era, the African American working classes began to join in larger numbers than ever before. By the 1970s, with a segregated military over two decades removed, African Americans found a more meritocratic system, which, though not without discrimination, nevertheless offered one of the sole venues in America where, as Moskos put it, "whites are regularly bossed around by blacks." The military offered a path to social and economic security and mobility, a fact testified to by African American recruits' higher educational achievement, in general, compared to white recruits.[43] The numbers of African Americans in the army grew enormously. Under the draft in 1970, black soldiers had constituted about 14 percent of enlisted entrants into the army, in fairly direct proportion to their representation in the population. By 1977, they constituted 30 percent of new entrants into the enlisted ranks.[44] Their representation in the officer corps increased 500 percent.[45] High enlistment rates combined with their similarly high re-enlistment rates so that African Americans constituted nearly one-fourth of the total army by 1977 and one-third by 1980.[46] In the ranks of E_1-E_3, comprising the lowest-ranking soldiers and first-time recruits, nearly 37 percent were African American.[47] In some of the ground maneuver combat divisions, it was "not uncommon to find units that are 50 percent black."[48]

Latinos also joined the volunteer force in larger numbers. When the era of the volunteer force commenced, only about 2 percent of the services were "Hispanic" (the designation used by the military at that time for a wide swath of Spanish-speaking people from Puerto Rico and the Caribbean, Mexico, and Latin America). Beginning in the mid-1980s, however, the numbers of Mexicans, Puerto Ricans, and other Latin Americans rose, with the U.S. Marine Corps and U.S. Navy garnering the largest proportion. By 2006 Latinos comprised 13 percent of military personnel, just below their proportion of the overall population.[49]

Professor Moskos and his military sociology colleagues raised questions about the demographic shifts occurring with the new volunteer force, specifically about "the nonrepresentation of the white middle class." They worried that the American middle class would soon find itself isolated from the military, resulting in a worrisome "distrust and lack of interest" from this "large segment of civilian society," arguably the most politically influential American demographic at the time.[50] Some military officials also worried about this development. For example, in separate discussions, both Donald Rumsfeld, who in late 1974 was serving as the military assistant to President Ford in the White House and would soon become secretary of defense in 1975, and Army Secretary Bo Calloway discussed what a less socially representative volunteer force might mean.[51] In a "perfect" world, Calloway conceded, "a representative army . . . would have exactly the same percentage of rich and poor, black and white, of north and south, of all the demographics, exactly the same as America is." While perfect representation was impossible to achieve, the military should, he believed, come close if it could, as it had during the draft era.[52]

Yet the military and political leaders forgot these hopes very quickly. The military rightfully endorsed the high number of African Americans serving in its ranks. Secretary of the Army Bo Calloway called the U.S. Army "the best opportunity for a minority, particularly blacks, to really be able to proceed entirely on their merits with absolute equality."[53] But the military began to deny the facts about the growing numbers of lower-income and less educated white soldiers in its ranks. The Defense Department and the services refused to collect any data on the income levels of their personnel. Supporters of the volunteer force began to insist that the military was a "middle class" institution, drawing on Americans' broad cultural and social affiliation with the middle class but denying the evidence accumulating of the working-class origins of most soldiers.[54]

By the early 1980s, the debate over the gap between military personnel and civilians faded. With the election of Ronald Reagan and his enormous financial and political investment in the military and the Cold War, discussions about the class and racial background of volunteers virtually died.[55] Reagan's Military Manpower Task Force in 1982 reported to him that "the social origins of those who freely choose to accept the burdens and benefits of military service should not be a recruiting criterion." The Department of Defense would therefore make "no attempt to identify recruits by social origin."[56]

If the all-volunteer service drifted from broad and equal representation along the lines of class and race, it moved toward greater representation of the American population in another way—the incorporation of women. It was a remarkable change. The First World War marked the first formal incorporation of women into military service, when regular army and navy nurses served overseas in Europe and the U.S. Navy and Marines allowed women to enlist in roles other than nursing.[57] The Second World War's massive mobilization forced the nation to create much larger and more well-defined roles for women. The women's components—Women's Army Corps (WACs) and its Women Airforce (WASPs) and the Navy's Women Accepted for Voluntary Emergency Service (WAVEs)—took in around half a million women.[58] Operating in gender-segregated units, under their own distinct chains of command, the women's corps persisted after the Second World War through the Cold War era and Vietnam.

The volunteer force permanently altered the pattern and scope of women's participation in the military and revealed, in ways similar to the experience of African Americans, how military service operated as an opportunity to claim full citizenship for groups historically excluded. In 1978, the military abolished the separate auxiliaries for women and lifted the cap on women, with dramatic results on their enlistment. On the eve of the volunteer force, women constituted 1.3 percent of active-duty enlisted personnel, about 12,000 total. By 1978, that number had increased over four times to over 50,000, with women constituting 6.6 percent of enlisted personnel.[59] By 1980 they were nearly 9 percent of the army.[60] And by the end of the century they numbered around 15 percent of the total force. African American women joined the new volunteer force, especially the army, in unprecedented numbers. Fully half of all women in the army were African American.[61] Both white and nonwhite women sought access to military service as a privilege that offered the opportunity to claim equal citizenship in an institution that had previously excluded them.

Gay men and women also sought fair access to military service in the late twentieth century. Gay and lesbian Americans had always served in the military—an estimated 650,000 served in the Second World War alone.[62] But they did so in relatively secrecy, because the military had banned homosexuality and monitored it closely since World War II.[63] With the advent of the gay rights movement in the 1970s, some gay and lesbian service members began to challenge their exclusion and claim their identities as gay active-duty personnel or veterans. In the 1980s most active-duty personnel who did so were discharged—some court-martialed. But the activism of gay and lesbian soldiers, sailors, airmen, and marines—and their civilian allies—pressured the military to alter its ban. In 1993, the Defense Department issued the "Don't Ask, Don't Tell" rule, allowing gay and lesbian citizens to serve if they neither acted on their homosexuality nor discussed it openly. A difficult compromise that resulted in more, not fewer, discharges, it refueled agitation among gay and lesbian service people and advocates and made visible a gay and lesbian tradition of military service that had for decades been repressed.[64] Continued pressure led to a complete reversal of the ban on homosexuality in 2011.

Military manpower specialists and military sociologists, as well as many politicians and women's rights advocates, generally welcomed especially the gendered changes in the all-volunteer military.[65] They noted how women's participation reflected wider advancement of women's rights and opportunities in American life. They also documented the essentialness of female personnel to the viability of the volunteer force: women's numbers closed the recruitment gap created with the end of the draft, and their higher education levels and lower disciplinary problems increased military readiness. "Women are an integral part of the Army," insisted army chief of staff Bernard Rogers five years after the switch to the volunteer force. They were not "part-time soldiers—here in peace, gone in war." Military leaders knew women were in the military to stay.[66]

Yet not everyone welcomed gender inclusion. In the 1980s and 1990s, critics of women in the military, who ranged from recent active-duty officers like Jim Webb (a U.S. Navy officer who became secretary of the navy, senator from Virginia, and candidate for the presidency) to conservative religious women like Phyllis Schlafly of the influential Eagle Forum and Elaine Donnelly of the Center for Military Readiness charged women with endangering the military, either by reducing military readiness or by burdening the military with "social issues" like child care.[67] *Time* magazine published articles questioning, "If Mom's a GI, Who Babysits?"[68] And former officers asked sarcastically if "we turn the army into a baby-sitting service" to accommodate female soldiers.[69] In the early 1980s, the army felt such pressure from without and within its ranks that it put a "pause" on its recruitment of women.[70]

Resistance to women in and with the military recurred in the early 1990s. After the Persian Gulf War, news reports followed the lead of Elaine Donnelly, who issued yet another round of criticisms of women in the military. Media in the Gulf Region reported on the so-called Love Boat, the USS *Acadia*, a navy vessel purportedly afloat with record numbers of pregnant servicewomen. Though the report later proved entirely erroneous, it fueled doubts about women's commitment to the military and their readiness.[71] Indeed, the military's difficulty accepting women became even more evident in the navy's sexual harassment scandal known as Tailhook, in which female naval personnel were groped and insulted by hundreds of navy officers at a convention.[72] More than anything, the persistence of extensive sexual violence in the military, most recently in the early 2000s during the Wars in Iraq and Afghanistan, reveals that female personnel in the military have not been fully accepted. It remains to be seen whether women's historic formal entrance into combat units beginning in 2013 reduces resistance to women's military service.

Just as female military personnel have faced opposition from within the military, so, too, have women *married* to military personnel, the "dependents" of the volunteer force. A rarely cited but vitally important change in the military's demographics in the late twentieth century has consisted of the transformation of the military from a bastion of single males into an institution of families. For most of the nation's two centuries, "the military (the army) met its manpower goals by accepting only single male soldiers."[73] Throughout the eighteenth and early nineteenth centuries, the military refused married men or simply looked the other way, ignoring their families' existence and letting the subsequent hardship act as a discouragement. U.S. law beginning in 1847 banned soldiers with wives from enlisting. In the army, policies strongly discouraged marriage and were aimed at reducing the number of military families. To the degree that military families did exist, most were families of senior officers.[74] In the army, soldiers joked: "If the army wanted you to have a wife, it would have issued you one."

While the enormous mobilization of the Second World War necessitated for the first time the enlistment of married men in all ranks, it was the switch to the all-volunteer service that cemented the transformation of the military into an institution of families. The volunteer system pushed the numbers higher than ever before because of the new kinds of recruits who joined. Unlike the draft-era force, which relied on a relatively small cadre of career soldiers augmented by large numbers of young, one-term draftees, the volunteer force hinged on a much larger cohort of older career personnel. These personnel had to be highly trained, too, as the military switched to a more technologically sophisticated mode of war; the high costs of training personnel produced heavy pressure to retain them.[75] The new emphasis on producing career personnel, or at least multiple enlistments, reinforced the demographic trend toward marriage and family since as they aged, soldiers, sailors, airmen, and marines were more likely to marry. In addition, military personnel in the volunteer era were in general more likely to marry than the general population. Whereas first-termers of the draft-era military had been unlikely to be married or have children, first-termers in the volunteer military married early and more often. Nearly one-third of personnel in the lowest ranks (E1–E4) had "dependents," as wives and children were called in the early 1970s. By 1977, six of ten members of the armed forces were married, with over 80 percent of the officer corps married and about 50 percent of enlisted personnel.[76] By 1983, there were one-and-a-half times as many family members as actual military personnel.[77] Army posts and air force and naval bases teemed with wives and children, swelling the surrounding schools, overflowing the available military housing, and lending a new atmosphere to the once severe, masculinized everyday life of the military. In the late twentieth century, military service became as never before "a family affair."[78]

Just as the incorporation of female personnel occasioned resistance from within the military, so, too, did the rise of the family-friendly military among some military leaders. During the 1991 war in the Persian Gulf, Operation Desert Storm/Desert Shield, the army castigated army wives in its after action report, calling them "overly demanding" and "overly dependent," relying too much on the army's family support programs. In the 1990s, the army undertook a campaign to assert influence over wives, through an Army Family Team Building program, and made increasing efforts to encourage these women to rely on themselves, rather than the army, when in need. Some members of the other services expressed similar doubts about wives. In 1993, the commandant of the United States Marine Corps announced that he was prohibiting recruitment of any more married marines, since wives and marriage "detracted from readiness." While the Defense Department quickly forced the commandant to retract his statement, the flare-up revealed the military's ambivalence over the vast numbers of families who populated the late twentieth-century volunteer force.[79]

By the end of the twentieth century and beginning of the twenty-first, the altered face of the military produced an armed force in some ways more different from the civilian world and in others more similar. In matters of class background, compared to the more distant wartime and draft military of earlier decades, the All-Volunteer Force was composed decisively of less affluent Americans, and in that way did not represent the nation's population. In matters of family, gender, and sexuality, however, the story was different. The military had moved toward greater representation, though not without considerable friction.

The Consequences of Demographic Change in Military Service

Over the course of the twentieth century, the country changed how it filled military ranks and, as a result, altered the people within it. The armed forces—increasingly small, comprising mostly working-class volunteers and their hundreds of thousands of family members—was isolated within an ever more encompassing military system. At the end of the twentieth century, fewer than 1 percent of Americans were active-duty members of the armed forces. Many lived on or near large military installations, distinct from and sometimes great distances from civilian communities. Even the comprehensive military benefits offered to lure and retain soldiers stood out as differentiated from and generally better than those similar civilians had access to. All of this accentuated what scholars of the military have, over time, dubbed the "military-civilian divide"—a growing and problematic gap between American civilians and military personnel.[80]

In many ways the military and military personnel did draw away from the civilian world after the end of the draft. In order to build and maintain the volunteer force and its large and generous structure of social support for the military, military leadership and regular military personnel alike crafted public arguments concerning the distinctions between soldiers, sailors, airmen, and marines, on the one hand, and civilians on the other. Army leaders insisted that "a soldier is different from a civilian. . . . There is no counterpart to a soldier."[81] One secretary of defense argued it was "insulting and demeaning to compare a combat soldier . . . to a 'nine to five' civilian."[82] Many draftees of the First and Second World Wars and Cold War era saw themselves as "working stiffs," drawn temporarily into a universally shared military experience, and afterward felt affiliations with both the worlds of war and the services and also with civilian working life. By contrast, in the volunteer military it was not uncommon to hear degradation of civilian's jobs and roles in society as merely "nine to five" work, "easy" or lacking significant contribution to the nation.[83] A well-documented turn among military officers toward conservative evangelical Christianity in the late 1970s through the 1990s sharpened in-group/out-group distinctions among military personnel.[84] In the U.S. Marine Corps, for example, one journalist documented marines describing how civilians "lived dirty" while they "lived clean."[85] The volunteer force encouraged an "exceptional" status awarded to the member of the military, one that rarely fully flourished and never dominated under the draft, when any male citizen might also be, or have been, a soldier, sailor, airman, or marine.

While some military personnel and leaders have accentuated the gaps between the military and civilian worlds, they alone did not create them. The model of a volunteer military itself produced much of the distance between service personnel and civilians. As today's military personnel point out, with such a small number of Americans in the military, and with so few from the middle classes, most civilians know little of the lives led by servicemen and servicewomen and their families. During the Wars in Iraq and Afghanistan, some civilians placed yellow ribbons on their cars reminding others to "remember the troops." Or they thanked personnel "for their service" in airports or parking lots when they came across them. But symbols and words were not the same as serving, and some military personnel even took offense, as it suggested that Americans could simply delegate their wars to others rather than sharing the burden themselves.[86] There is no doubt that the volunteer force took in fewer Americans than the military of the draft era, leaving only a small minority of Americans with any direct experience with or understanding of the military. It was significant that the military became more working class, with a virtually absent middle class, especially an absent white middle class. The military-civilian gap was a gap of class, and to some degree race, in which war and the armed forces had become largely a working-class affair.

Though these profound changes went largely unnoticed by Americans, a quiet debate persisted about military personnel in relation to the civilian population in an era when fewer from a narrower cross-section served and when there was no conscription. Beginning in 2003 with the onset of the War in Iraq, some Americans raised the question of whether the nation should return to the draft. That same year and every year afterward through 2015, Congressman Charles Rangel (D-NY) introduced legislation to reinstate the draft. "When I served [in the military during the draft era]," Rangel pointed out, "the entire nation shared the sacrifice" of war.[87] A similar concern had been expressed by Moskos forty years earlier: was it dangerous in a democracy to have civilians so disconnected from the military, especially during a time of war? Was it dangerous to have a military that maintained a sharp differentiation from civilians? What was a fair, democratic way to maintain a military without, as one former army colonel put it, "breaching the trust" of civilians, military personnel, or the nation's democratic values?[88] The questions remained largely unanswered, as proposals for the draft did not advance, and most Americans, with no direct stakes in the answers, continued their lives outside of war and the military.

Discussion Questions

1. How and why did the population performing military service change over time in the United States?
2. When was the representation of the American population in the military broadest and why? When was it narrowest and why?

3. Why did some leaders see military representation as a vital issue while others did not?
4. Why has the fully representative incorporation of some groups been resisted?

Notes

1 Amy Rutenberg, "Service by Other Means: Changing Perceptions of Military Service and Masculinity, 1940–1973," in *Gender and the Long Postwar: Reconsiderations of the United States and the Two Germanys, 1945–1979*, ed. Karen Hagemann and Sonya Michel (Baltimore: Woodrow Wilson Center Press/Johns Hopkins University Press, 2014), 165–184.
2 National Advisory Commission on the Selective Service, *Report of the National Advisory Commission on the Selective Service—In Pursuit of Equity: Who Serves When Not All Serve?* (Washington, DC: U.S. Government Printing Office, 1967).
3 On the Civil War draft riots, see Iver Bernstein, *The New York City Draft Riots: Their Significance for American Society and Politics in the Age of the Civil War* (New York: Oxford University Press, 1990).
4 Natalie Gentile Ford, *American All! Foreign-Born Soldiers in World War I* (College Station: Texas A&M University Press, 2001), 51.
5 Mitchell Yockelson, "They Answered the Call: Military Service in the United States Army during World War I, 1917–1919," *Prologue Magazine* (National Archives) 30, no. 3 (Fall 1998), http://www.archives.gov/publications/prologue/1998/fall/military-service-in-world-war-one.html; Ford, *American All!*, 51.
6 Thomas Bruscino, *A Nation Forged in War: How World War II Taught Americans How to Get Along* (Knoxville: University of Tennessee Press, 2010), 52.
7 Ibid., 5.
8 Ibid., 58. Only 112,000 total "aliens" fought in World War II.
9 Ibid., 58, 59.
10 Ibid., 60.
11 Ibid., 78, 79.
12 Lyn Crost, *Honor by Fire: Japanese Americans at War in Europe and the Pacific* (New York: Presidio Press, 1994); Bill Yenne, *Rising Sons: The Japanese American GIs Who Fought for the United States in World War II* (New York: St. Martin's Press, 2007).
13 "African American" (Collection Description and History), The Institute on World War II and the Human Experience, Florida State University, http://ww2.fsu.edu/African-American; Alexander Bielakowski, *African American Troops in World War II* (London: Osprey Press, 2010); Kimberly Phillips, *War! What Is It Good For? Black Freedom Struggles and the US Military from World War II to Iraq* (Chapel Hill: University of North Carolina Press, 2012); Neil A. Wynn, *The African American Experience during World War II* (Lanham, MD: Rowman & Littlefield, 2010).
14 Phillips, *War!*; Wynn, *The African American Experience*.
15 Wynn, *The African American Experience*, 5. African Americans had also been confined largely to such roles in World War I. See Chad L. Williams, *Torchbearers of Democracy: African American Soldiers in the World War I Era* (Chapel Hill: University of North Carolina Press, 2010), 111–112.
16 Phillips, *War!*; Wynn, *The African American Experience*.
17 Richard Holmes, ed., "US Military Service and Casualties in Major Wars and Conflicts, 1775–1991," in *Oxford Companion to Military History* (New York: Oxford University Press, 2001), 849.

18 Charles Moskos, *The American Enlisted Man* (New York: Russell Sage, 1970), 76.

19 Christian Appy, *Working-Class War: American Combat Soldiers and Vietnam* (Chapel Hill: University of North Carolina Press, 1993), 29.

20 Penny Lewis, *Hardhats, Hippies, and Hawks: The Vietnam Antiwar Movement as Myth and Memory* (Ithaca, NY: Cornell University Press, 2013).

21 Appy, *Working-Class War*, 28–29.

22 Ibid.

23 Qtd. in Richard Moser, *The New Winter Soldiers: GI and Veteran Dissent during the Vietnam Era* (New Brunswick, NJ: Rutgers University Press, 1996), 70.

24 Appy, *Working-Class War*, 42.

25 On military manpower and Selective Service channeling, see Amy J. Rutenberg, "Drafting for Domesticity: American Deferment Policy during the Cold War, 1948–1965," *Cold War History* 13 (2013): 20.

26 Appy, *Working-Class War*, 29.

27 Defense Manpower Commission, *Defense Manpower: The Keystone of National Security* (Report to the President and the Congress, April 1976) (Washington, DC: U.S. Government Printing Office, 1976), 162; Office of the Assistant Secretary Of Defense (Manpower, Reserve Affairs, and Logistics), *America's Volunteers: A Report on the All Volunteer Armed Forces* (Washington, DC: U.S. Department of Defense, 1978), 38.

28 Jennifer Mittelstadt, *The Rise of the Military Welfare State* (Cambridge, MA: Harvard University Press, 2015), 1–16.

29 *The Report of the President's Commission on an All-Volunteer Armed Force* (Washington, DC: U.S. Government Printing Office, 1970).

30 Beth Bailey, *America's Army: Making the All Volunteer Force* (Cambridge, MA: Harvard University Press, 2009).

31 Mittelstadt, *Rise of the Military Welfare State*, 17–45.

32 Morris Janowitz, "A New Role for the Military Forces," *Current*, June 1972, 45.

33 Mittelstadt, *Rise of the Military Welfare State*, chaps. 1, 3, 4, 5.

34 Volunteer military forces in European countries provide far fewer distinct military benefits because all citizens, including soldiers, have access to universal social welfare.

35 Mittelstadt, *Rise of the Military Welfare State*, 3.

36 Defense Manpower Commission, *Defense Manpower*, 159. Charles Moskos cited a figure of less than 5 percent before Congress in 1978. "Status of the All-Volunteer Armed Force," U.S. Congress, Senate, Hearings before the Subcommittee on Manpower and Personnel of the Committee on Armed Services, 95th Congress, 2nd sess., June 20, 1978, 39.

37 "Study Finds No Poor-Man's Army," *Army Times*, January 12, 1976, 15.

38 Adam Yarmolinsky and Gregory D. Foster, *Paradoxes of Power: The Military Establishment in the Eighties* (Bloomington: Indiana University Press, 1983), 75; Jay Fingan, "DoD: All-Vol Forces Reflect National Image," *Army Times*, March 14, 1977, 25.

39 Defense Manpower Commission, *Defense Manpower*, 2:11; Office of the Assistant Secretary Of Defense, *America's Volunteers*, 44; Jay Finegan, "More EM Recruits Coming from Low-Income Families," *Army Times*, January 23, 1978, 29.

40 Charles Moskos, qtd. in "Status of the All-Volunteer Armed Force," 40. See also Yarmolinsky and Foster, *Paradoxes of Power*, 74.

41 Charles Moskos, qtd. in "Status of the All-Volunteer Armed Force," 39.

42 David R. Segal, "Military Organization and Personnel Accession: What Changed with the AVF . . . and What Didn't," in *Conscripts and Volunteers: Military Requirements, Social Justice, and the All-Volunteer Force*, ed. Robert Fullinwider (Totowa, NJ: Rowman and Allanheld, 1983), 10.

43 The African Americans who joined the military, on average, outscored their white peers. Charles Moskos, qtd. in "Status of the All-Volunteer Armed Force," 40.

44 Defense Manpower Commission, *Defense Manpower*, 162; Office of the Assistant Secretary Of Defense, *America's Volunteers*, 38.

45 Defense Manpower Commission, *Defense Manpower*, 162.

46 "An Analysis and Evaluation of the U.S. Army: The Beard Study," prepared by Jerry Reed, appendix, U.S. Congress, Senate, "Status of the All-Volunteer Armed Force," Hearings Subcommittee on Manpower and Personnel of the Committee on Armed Services, 95th Congress, 2nd sess., June 20, 1978, 146.

47 George Davis, "Blacks in the Military: Opportunity or Refuge?," *Black Enterprise* 10, no. 12 (July 1980): 23.

48 Mady Wechsler Segal, "Women's Roles in the U.S. Armed Forces: An Evaluation of Evidence and Arguments for Policy Decisions," in Fullinwider, *Conscripts and Volunteers*, 83, 11.

49 Mady Wechler Segal and David Segal, "Latinos Claim Larger Share of Military Personnel" (Figure 1), *Population Reference Bureau*, October 2007, http://www.prb.org/Publications/Articles/2007/HispanicsUSMilitary.aspx.

50 Wechsler Segal, "Women's Roles in the U.S. Armed Forces," 21.

51 Donald Rumsfeld, memo to Bo Calloway, November 15, 1974, in Bernard Rostker, *I Want You! The Evolution of the All-Volunteer Force* (Santa Monica, CA: RAND Corporation, 2006).

52 Howard H. Calloway, former secretary of the army, interview by Major Robert Griffith, United States Army, Center for Military History, September 23, 1983, Denver, CO, Series II, Box 14, Folder 9, Oral Histories, All Volunteer Army Collection, U.S. Army Military History Institute at Carlisle Barracks, Pennsylvania, 9.

53 Ibid.

54 "Study Finds No Poor-Man's Army," 15.

55 Mittelstadt, *Rise of the Military Welfare State*, 94–119, 148–170.

56 Military Manpower Task Force, *A Report to the President on the Status and Prospects of the All-Volunteer Force* (Washington, DC: U.S. Government Printing Office, November 1982), 2:11.

57 Kimberly Jensen, *Mobilizing Minerva: American Women in the First World War* (Urbana: University of Illinois Press, 2008).

58 Leisa Meyer, *Creating G.I. Jane: Sexuality and Power in the Women's Army Corps during World War II* (New York: Columbia University Press, 1996).

59 Office of the Assistant Secretary of Defense, *America's Volunteers*, 70.

60 "Fact Sheet on Women's Leadership," *Rutgers Institute for Women's Leadership*, 2010, http://iwl.rutgers.edu/research_njwc.html.

61 Women pressed against the gendered limits of the military, moving beyond the few military occupational specialties (MOSs) allowed to them by the military in the 1970s and 1980s to enter traditionally male MOSs. Increasingly, they also played critical roles in combat, whether in air crews or gun crews, and also served as medics or intelligence personnel attached to combat units.

62 Steve Estes, *Ask and Tell: Gay and Lesbian Veterans Speak Out* (Chapel Hill: University of North Carolina Press, 2009), 5.

63 For gay men and women in World War II, see *Alan Berube, Coming Out under Fire: The History of Gay Men and Women in World War II* (New York: Free Press, 1990).

64 Estes, *Ask and Tell*.

65 Bailey, *America's Army*, 162–164.

66 Ibid., 163.

67 A good account of this resistance can be found in Carol Burke, *Camp All-American, GI Jane and the High and Tight: Gender, Folklore, and Changing Military Culture* (Boston: Beacon Press, 2004), chap. 8.

68 "Army Husband: If Mom's a G.I., Who Babysits?," *Time*, April 16, 1979, 82.

69 James Webb, "Women in the Armed Forces," *Newsweek*, February 18, 1980, 42.

70 Bailey, *America's Army*, 171.

71 Mittelstadt, *Rise of the Military Welfare State*, 179.

72 On Tailhook, see Jean Zimmerman, *Tailspin: Women at War in the Wake of Tailhook* (New York: Doubleday, 1995); Burke, *Camp All-American*, chap. 8.

73 Sondra Albano, "Military Recognition of Family Concerns: Revolutionary War to 1993," *Armed Forces and Society* 20, no. 2 (Winter 1994): 284.

74 Ibid., 284–285, 286.

75 David R. Segal, *Recruiting for Uncle Sam* (Lawrence: University Press of Kansas, 1989); Charles Moskos, John Allen Williams, and David R. Segal, *The Postmodern Military: Armed Forces after the Cold War* (New York: Oxford University Press, 2000).

76 Sar Levitan and Karen Cleary Aldeman, *Warriors at Work: The Volunteer Armed Force* (Beverly Hills, CA: Sage Publications, 1977), 56.

77 U.S. Army Chief of Staff, *The Army Family* (white paper), 1983, 5, http://www.dtic .mil/dtic/tr/fulltext/u2/a143245.pdf.

78 Elizabeth Wickenden, *The Military Program and Social Welfare* (New York: National Committee on Social Work in Defense Mobilization, 1955).

79 Mittelstadt, *Rise of the Military Welfare State*, 178.

80 There is a substantial literature on the military-civilian gap. For some examples, see Andrew Bacevich, *Breach of Trust: How Americans Failed Their Soldiers and Their Country* (New York: Metropolitan Books, 2013); Peter Feaver and Richard Kohn, eds., *Soldiers and Civilians: The Civil-Military Gap and American National Security* (Cambridge, MA: MIT Press, 2001); Bruce Flemming, *Bridging the Military-Civilian Divide: What Each Side Must Know about the Other and about Itself* (Washington, DC: Potomac Books, 2010); Thomas S. Szayna et al., *The Civil-Military Gap in the United States: Does It Exist, Why, and Does It Matter?* (Santa Monica, CA: RAND Corporation, 2007).

81 Larry Carney, "Rogers Will Try to Halt Erosion of Benefits," *Army Times*, January 17, 1977, 3.

82 Donald Rumsfeld, *The Report of the Third Quadrennial Review of Military Compensation* (Washington, DC: Department of Defense, 1976), 12.

83 Mittelstadt, *Rise of the Military Welfare State*, 63–67.

84 Anne Loveland, *American Evangelicals and the US Military, 1942–1993* (Baton Rouge: Louisiana State University Press, 1996); Mittelstadt, *Rise of the Military Welfare State*, 148–170.

85 Tom Ricks, *Making the Corps* (New York: Touchstone Books, 1998).

86 Matt Richtel, "Please Don't Thank Me for My Service," *New York Times*, February 21, 2015, http://www.nytimes.com/2015/02/22/sunday-review/please-dont-thank-me -for-my-service.html?_r=0; Stanton Coerr, "Three Reasons to Stop Thanking Me for My Military Service," *The Federalist*, July 16, 2015, http://thefederalist.com/2015 /07/16/3-reasons-to-stop-thanking-me-for-my-military-service/; Camillo Mac Bica, "Don't Thank Me for My Service," *Truthout*, June 3, 2012, http://www.truth-out.org /opinion/item/9320-dont-thank-me-for-my-service. A Google search of "don't thank me for my service" will turn up not only articles but also dozens of online forums about this issue among military personnel. Also, David Finkel's *Thank You for Your*

Service (New York: Farrar, Strauss, and Giroux, 2013) provides an-depth portrait of recent veterans' relationship to the civilian world upon returning from the Wars in Iraq and Afghanistan, highlighting, if not explicitly, the gap between military personnel and civilians.

87 Qtd. in Martin Matishak, "Rangel: Reinstate the Draft," *The Hill*, March 19, 2015, http://thehill.com/policy/ defense/236365-rangel-renews-call-for-war-tax-national-draft.

88 See Bacevich, *Breach of Trust*; E. J. Dionne, Kayla Meltzer Drogosz, and Robert E. Litan, eds., *United We Serve: National Service and the Future of Citizenship* (Washington, DC: Brookings Institution, 2003); James Fallows, "The Tragedy of the American Military," *The Atlantic*, January/February 2015, http://www.theatlantic.com /magazine/archive/2015/01/the-tragedy-of-the-american-military/383516/.

Further Reading

Christian Appy. *Working-Class War: American Combat Soldiers and Vietnam*. Chapel Hill: University of North Carolina Press, 1993.

Andrew Bacevich. *Breach of Trust: How Americans Failed Their Soldiers and Their Country*. New York: Metropolitan Books, 2013.

Beth Bailey. *America's Army: Making the All Volunteer Force*. Cambridge, MA: Harvard University Press, 2009.

Kimberly Phillips. *War! What Is It Good For? Black Freedom Struggles and the US Military from World War II to Iraq*. Chapel Hill: University of North Carolina Press, 2012.

6

Combat

CHRISTOPHER HAMNER

Scholarly examinations of the relationship between war and society frequently place heavier emphasis on "society." Historians in the field often focus on the way that societies think about military institutions and how the presence of those institutions influence culture, the economy, and public memory. For decades, traditional military histories—of the maps, arrows, and great generals variety—usually excluded any consideration of the larger societal context of battles. Contemporary studies of war and society often reverse the equation, focusing attention on societal dynamics and avoiding deep examination of the battlefield.

But no examination of the complex relationship between war and society can be complete without a careful consideration of combat itself. To be sure, battle represents only a tiny fraction of military history as a whole. Even during wartime, only a small proportion of troops are engaged in active combat, and usually only for part of the time. But the preparation for combat animates an enormous part of a society's military activities. Raising and equipping armies, the diplomatic machinations revolving around war and deterrence, the efforts to constrain and control military forces, the processes of reflecting on war and commemorating it—all intersect at some point with the necessity of putting soldiers onto a battlefield where bullets are flying.

Combat is just as difficult to study as it is critical to understand. Those difficulties stem from a number of factors. One is its very nature: battle is chaotic, terrifying, and violent, qualities that language cannot easily capture. Combat veterans frequently suggest that combat is intrinsically indescribable; its violence and emotional power simply cannot be put into words. One American GI of the Second World War, unsatisfied with his attempts to portray the

essence of combat in his letters home, compared writing about combat to taking a photograph of a skidding, roaring racecar zooming past at high speed. The
mute, motionless print expresses "no snarl, no roar, no smell of exhaust, oil and
rubber, no sense of blinding speed." Like those whose understanding of battle
comes only through reading about it, the viewer of such a picture catches only a
washed-out glimpse of the event itself. The eyewitness can only mumble, "Hey,
you had to be there..."[1]

Another factor that makes battle difficult to study is its overwhelming confusion. Battles consist of tens of thousands of individual actions, all occurring
in the midst of cacophonous noise, smothering smoke, and often overpower-
ing physiological sensations. In the effort to make sense of the confusion and
chaos of battle, military historians often impose a narrative, with a discernible
cause-and-effect structure, on its complicated and interconnected events. Those
narratives are familiar to anyone who has read a traditional account of a famous
battle. One general's disastrous decisions led to his troops being butchered; the
brave stand of some other small group of soldiers in the face of seemingly insur-
mountable odds saved the position and thus the victory. Imposing such a clear-
cut cause-and-effect understanding is a natural tendency for historians. But it is
also a tendency at odds with the descriptions of participants involved in actual
battle. From the perspective of the individual soldier caught in the maelstrom,
combat has the effect of dramatically narrowing the field of view. As an American soldier of the Civil War put it, "The extent of the battle seen by the common soldier is that only which comes within range of the raised sights of his
musket."[2] Even generals, whom we might expect to have a better view of a battle
as a whole, struggle to understand what is happening. Arthur Wellesley, Duke
of Wellington (the British commander who defeated Napoleon at Waterloo
in 1815) wrote that describing a battle was like describing all of the encounters
that comprise an enormous, formal ball, in that "no individual can recollect the
order in which, or the exact moment at which, they occurred, which makes all
the difference as to their value or importance."[3] The impossibility of capturing
all of the disparate events that contribute to a battle adds another layer of difficulty for scholars attempting to study combat in a rigorous and systematic way.

There is one other huge challenge to scholars seeking to study battle: unlike
other human activities, combat kills many of its participants. Many of the voices
scholars would most like to hear never have the chance to record their thoughts
and experiences. Taken together, these problems make battle slippery and confusing—an extraordinarily difficult phenomenon for historians to describe.

And yet this complex, slippery phenomenon has been a fixture of human
interactions for millennia. The fact that writing about combat presents special
challenges for scholars does not release historians from the responsibility of
attempting to understand and depict it in all its complexity. And despite all of
the difficulties, it is possible to make some broad statements about the essence
of combat. Battle is defined in part by broad continuities: there are features

of armed combat that remain nearly unchanging no matter the time, place, or context. Danger is ever-present, as are fear, trauma, and chaos. The necessity of death and the unavoidability of killing have shaped every battlefield from the ancient Greeks to the twenty-first century. Common human responses to battle appear strikingly similar over time as well, since so many of those responses are biologically hardwired. Whether at Bunker Hill in 1776, Shiloh in 1862, Iwo Jima in 1945, or Fallujah in 2004, there are some important broad similarities in the individual soldier's experience of combat, no matter when or where it occurred. The *nature* of warfare is unchanging. As the eminent British military historian John Keegan put it, "What battles have in common is human: the behavior of men struggling to reconcile the instinct for self-preservation, their sense of honor and the achievement of some aim over which other men are ready to kill them."[4]

Yet there are many changes evident in battle, as well, because the *character* of war evolves constantly. Scholars and soldiers who have studied battle as a human experience cannot help but note the ways that battle has changed over time. Some of those evolutions are dramatic and obvious. There have been many prominent evolutions in the technology of war, for example; the shoulder arms carried by foot soldiers provide one straightforward example. The Continental soldier of the late eighteenth century carried a single-shot musket known informally as the "Brown Bess." Limited in accuracy and slow to load and fire, the individual soldier of the War of Independence could shoot to a range of about forty yards two or three times a minute. American soldiers in the twenty-first century, in contrast, can fire sixty rounds a minute much more accurately at distances up to twenty times greater. An eighteenth-century Continental soldier would hardly recognize the immense firepower wielded by his twenty-first-century successor, the destructive equivalent of an entire infantry company in the War of Independence. The appearance of armored tanks, manned and unmanned aircraft, improved communications, night vision headsets, vastly more accurate and more destructive artillery—all are obvious ways that the character of combat has changed over the past two-and-a-half centuries.

These elements, continuity and change, coexist in the study of battle. From the perspective of the individual soldier, there is a universal element in warfare that stems from its most basic nature: combat always involves the smothering presence of fear, the unavoidable necessity of killing, and a kind of sensory overload and overwhelming confusion found in very few other human activities. While the Continental soldier of the War of Independence would not recognize much of the sophisticated equipment carried by his successor in the U.S. Army of the twenty-first century, both soldiers would find the trembling hands as they reloaded their weapons all too familiar.

Technological changes in the hardware of war exert a profound influence on the character of battle at any one point in time. Some of those changes are straightforward and easy to identify. Cavalry troops on horseback were a common sight on battlefields for centuries, until largely disappearing at the end of the nineteenth century; it is a rare combatant in the twenty-first century who spots a mounted soldier in battle. Prior to the twentieth century, of course, foot soldiers never contended with the roar of armored, motorized tanks or the silent, invisible threat of buried landmines. And before 1914, ground troops only occasionally had reason to look up at the sky during battle—nearly all of the activity and danger occurred on the surface of the earth. By the middle of the twentieth century, however, savvy infantrymen learned to scan the skies regularly to identify enemy aircraft or locate the support of friendly planes. And though American troops of the twenty-first century no longer worry about hostile aircraft in combat (no American ground soldier has been killed by an enemy plane since 1953) the advent of unmanned, remotely piloted drones for surveillance and attack represents yet another evolution in the character of combat. The way that battles are fought—and the tactics that soldiers employ in fighting them—are in no small part a product of the state of military technology at a given time. Over the past two centuries, this combination of technology and tactics has dramatically reshaped the experience of combat for the individual soldier. One particularly important change is at the center of this chapter's analysis of battle.

One of the most pronounced differences in combat from the eighteenth century to the twenty-first is the tactical change created by the introduction of more accurate, rapid-firing weapons. Until the twentieth century, armies usually marched into battle in tightly packed lines of soldiers. Those formations, known as *linear tactics* from the orderly lines of soldiers marching in lockstep, are familiar to anyone who has seen an artist's rendition of a Civil War battlefield (Figure 6.1). The modern imagination often recoils from this image. The vision of lines of men marching into battle at a slow, deliberate pace, wearing brightly colored uniforms, with drums beating and banners flying, violates everything we imagine we know about the importance of stealth and cover. To march out in the open, with troops standing upright and aligned in neat rows as they stride forward, seems a nearly suicidal way of fighting.

And indeed the casualties on the linear battlefield were sometimes catastrophic. Soldiers grouped into tight formations, advancing at a slow and steady pace and announcing their presence with drums, shouts, and brightly colored uniforms, made extremely appealing targets for their opponents. The grim determination of Union troops at the 1862 Battle of Fredericksburg provides an infamous example of the horrific casualties soldiers sometimes suffered in linear formations. Confederate soldiers had massed in a defensive line behind a stone wall atop a bluff known as Marye's Heights; Union commanders ordered their troops to assault and capture the position. With brigades arrayed in lines, marching uphill over a quarter mile of open ground with banners flying in the crisp December air, the Union soldiers provided easy targets for enemy cannon and for more than three thousand Confederate riflemen. One out of every four soldiers in the first wave was wounded or killed. Successive assaults fared even

FIGURE 6.1 A stylized artist's representation of Union and Confederate soldiers deployed in lines at the 1864 Battle of Franklin. "The Battle of Franklin." Copyright 1891 by Kurz and Allison Art Publishers, Chicago IL.

worse; in some brigades, fully half the men were hit attempting to breach the defenders' line. In all, fourteen separate assaults tried to climb the crest. Not a single Union soldier reached the wall; a few troops came within forty yards, but most were struck more than a hundred yards away by the withering Confederate fire. Between six and eight thousand Northern troops were wounded or killed in the futile attempt.

Though the modern imagination flinches at the idea of troops marching methodically into battle in the open and then standing, exposed, during a fire-fight, it is useful to keep two things in mind. The first is that this experience—fighting from tightly packed lines out in the open—has been the overwhelming rule, rather than the exception, throughout thousands of years of organized warfare. What we often imagine as "real combat" (troops scattered, close to the ground, disguised with camouflage, stealthily picking their way across a seemingly deserted battlefield toward a hidden enemy) is the exception. Fighting in that fashion is relatively new to human conflict. Only in the past century or so have armies adopted these modern tactics. For millennia before the early twentieth century, armies employed linear tactics; indeed, there is a relatively unbroken connection between the tactics of the Greek phalanx and the formations utilized by the Union and Confederate armies during the Civil War two thousand years later.

The second, related notion to bear in mind is that these linear formations did not persist so long because they were ineffective. Quite the opposite: linear tactics proved keenly effective, often devastatingly so, on hundreds and hundreds of battlefields leading up to the twentieth century. Students learning about the American War of Independence often boggle at the British redcoats, whose distinctive red uniforms and close-packed formations appear to violate every commonsense principle of war. It seems obvious that the American militiamen, using "Indian tactics" adopted from their Native American foes and firing from behind trees, rocks, and fences rather than marching out in the open, would quickly send the plodding Redcoats running.

But in fact the opposite is true. The British regular troops had developed a fearsome reputation based on their iron discipline and their steady performance in combat. Those who faced the British formations described a terrifying experience, staring at an unyielding mass of men that continued to bear down on their own positions, seemingly undeterred by the loss of soldiers to bullets and cannonballs. And the American patriot militia suffered from the opposite reputation—poorly disciplined and unable or unwilling to stand their ground for any predictable period of time. (George Washington himself was constantly infuriated by the unreliable performance of the militia, which he held to be worse than useless.)[5] It was not until the patriots developed their own European-style army—one with professional discipline and which marched into battle out in the open in the traditional European linear formations—that they were able to meet the British regulars on a more or less even footing. The fact that Union and Confederate forces continued to employ variations on European linear tactics during the American Civil War eight decades after the War of Independence provides further evidence of the effectiveness of those formations.

The persistence and effectiveness of the linear tactical system stemmed in part from the weapons available to the armies. From the invention of gunpowder to the late nineteenth century, linear tactics helped compensate for some of the inherent shortcomings in the technology of war. Until the late nineteenth century, the individual infantryman's weapon was a single-shot musket—cumbersome to wield, slow to load, and generally inaccurate—sometimes wildly so. Over time, gradual improvements in the technology of the soldier's musket extended its range, increased its accuracy, and improved its reliability. Those improvements in technology, while steady, generally occurred gradually. The Brown Bess musket carried by the Continental soldiers of the War of Independence was similar enough to be recognizable in its design and operation to the Springfield and Enfield muskets carried by the soldiers of the Union and Confederate armies eighty years later.

The most important invention in the shoulder arms of the nineteenth century was nearly invisible to the casual observer. The inside of the barrel of the Brown Bess musket was smooth—thus its classification as a "smoothbore" musket. The round ball ammunition those smoothbores fired was extremely inaccurate. Like a baseball pitcher's knuckleball, the bullet emerged from the muzzle of the weapon without any spin—and, like a knuckleball, the bullets themselves were buffeted by wind and did not follow predictable trajectories. Professional officers of the eighteenth century estimated that their soldiers' muskets were accurate only to about forty yards.

The linear tactics favored by European (and later American) armies helped compensate for both the slow rate of fire and the inaccuracy of the smoothbore musket. Organizing men into lines helped mass their fire. Rather than have individual soldiers take aim at specific targets (a nearly pointless effort with an inaccurate smoothbore), entire companies of soldiers would fire in the same direction at once. The resulting volley of fire unleashed hundreds of musket balls at an opponent. Though no individual soldier was particularly accurate, at least some of the bullets in a volley would find their targets. In between volleys, groups of soldiers rushed to load and fire their cumbersome weapons together. Linear tactics remained workable into the nineteenth century in part because they helped overcome the intrinsic limitations of the weapons themselves.

Technology offered another, different solution to the problem of inaccurate shoulder arms. European gunsmiths had discovered a way to improve the accuracy of muskets in the fifteenth century. Airborne projectiles that spin as they travel are steadier and vastly more accurate; imagine a quarterback throwing a football in a perfect spiral. The way to impart the critical spin was to *rifle* the musket—to cut long, spiral grooves in the barrel that would give the bullet a twist as it traveled toward the muzzle. That knowledge had been around for centuries, but a variety of factors prevented its adoption on a mass scale until the middle of the nineteenth century. Early rifled barrels had to be individually smithed, a time-consuming and costly process. And loading a rifled musket required a foot soldier to ram a tight-fitting projectile down a long barrel, a difficult, dangerous, and time-consuming task amid the maelstrom of battle. The persistence of smoothbore muskets into the early nineteenth century helps explain why linear tactics remained viable for so long.

But weapons technology alone cannot explain the presence and persistence of linear tactics in battle for thousands of years. Linear formations, with large numbers of soldiers grouped into close quarters, also helped armies manage their troops amid the chaos and confusion of combat. In combat, armies struggle to exert some control over their soldiers and to issue the commands and instructions that keep them fighting in an organized, concerted way. Before the advent of wireless communications technology in the twentieth century, armies relied primarily on commands that soldiers could hear (shouts, drums, and bugles) and see, like the large flags that troops carried into battle. Those rudimentary communications technologies had many obvious shortcomings, their extremely limited range being perhaps the most important. Packing soldiers into linear formations maximized the effectiveness of shouted commands and regimental banners, helping armies exert some degree of control over their troops.

Noting the persistence of linear tactics over the seventeenth, eighteenth, and nineteenth centuries is not to suggest that combat remained the same for soldiers engaged in the fighting. Combat evolved over time even within the linear system, in both subtle and not-so-subtle ways. Battles grew longer. During the War of Independence, the fighting might last an hour or two; by the Civil War, battles often raged all day—or, in a few cases, over multiple days. The size of the battlefield expanded, as well; battles that might involve eight thousand soldiers fighting on a piece of ground little bigger than a square mile during the War of Independence grew to involve more than a hundred thousand fighting across fields more than ten times as large by the time of the Civil War. For the participants, that meant more noise, more confusion, more suffering, and more death. But the underlying character of the fighting—what it required them to do and to endure—changed much less dramatically. Combat evolved fairly slowly from the seventeenth century to the mid-nineteenth century; as time passed, battle became larger, more intense, and more deadly, but a Continental soldier from the 1770s would recognize the basic tactics of Civil War battlefields even if the scale of the fighting would have shocked him.

A much more dramatic break appeared in the twentieth century. To an outside observer, combat in the twentieth century *looked* very different from the kinds of battles that dominated the eighteenth and nineteenth centuries. American soldiers of those earlier conflicts would have found the battlefields of the twentieth century thoroughly alien.

Technological innovations contributed to these evolutions. The introduction and refinement of automatic weapons was a particularly important change. Unlike the single-shot muskets carried by soldiers in the sixteenth, seventeenth, eighteenth, and early nineteenth centuries, these new weapons fired bursts of multiple bullets at once, without requiring the soldier to stop and load each round individually. The effect was dramatic: by the time of the Great War in 1914, a three-man team operating a machine gun could fire as many bullets in a minute as an entire thousand-man Napoleonic infantry regiment a hundred years earlier. Technological advances affected artillery as well: new cannons could fire at much greater distances and much more accurately, and new high-explosive shells meant that twentieth-century artillery rounds packed a much deadlier punch than earlier eighteenth- and nineteenth-century projectiles.

Taken together, these changes in weapons technology wrought massive changes in the character of ground combat. The geometric increase in the volume of fire that armies could generate altered the landscape of battle profoundly. As a German veteran of the Western Front during the Great War memorably put it, the new technologies had unleashed a "storm of steel" on the battlefield.[6] The sheer increase in the number of projectiles in the air rendered the battlefields of the twentieth century supremely lethal. Armies of the seventeenth, eighteenth, and nineteenth centuries had managed to fight in the open, albeit with heavy and sometimes catastrophic losses. The deadly new storm of steel made the old ways of fighting—particularly linear formations maneuvering on exposed ground—suicidally ineffective.

The trench fighting of the Great War was a product of that tactical confusion. Unable to advance successfully across open battlefields and lacking an alternative to the linear formations they had employed for hundreds if not thousands of years, armies burrowed underground. Digging into the earth's surface reduced troops' exposure to the deadly projectiles in the storm of steel. But armies dug into trenches could not take the offensive. When attackers did emerge from the trenches to assault an enemy position, the defenders' automatic weapons and artillery cut them to ribbons. The British soldiers attacking along the Somme in 1916 suffered an astonishing 400,000 casualties in twenty weeks of fighting— nearly 58,000 on the first day alone. In the face of such an imbalance between attackers and defenders, the conflict devolved into a muddy, ghastly stalemate, with soldiers on both sides increasingly reluctant to go "over the top" of their trenches to attack enemy positions.

Battles like the Somme, Verdun, and Passchendaele became infamous for the slaughter that took place there and inflicted millions of casualties over the four years of the Great War. Although generals and armies on both sides experimented with a number of technologies (from poison gas and early airplanes to the first crude armored tanks) in an effort to break the trench stalemate, none of the new hardware could by itself solve the fundamental tactical problem.

The ultimate solution to that problem was not a new piece of military hardware but a new way to fight. If deploying troops out in the open had become too deadly to implement, armies would no longer march their soldiers out in orderly formations. Instead, they dispersed their troops, spreading them out across the battlefield. Soldiers replaced their brightly colored uniforms with drab camouflage to better blend in with their surroundings. Rather than march upright, soldiers went to ground when bullets began flying. Dropping to the ground helped soldiers make use of the "dead space" in the terrain, places that opposing soldiers could not see and which provided some protection from enemy bullets. Instead of massing volleys by regiment, small teams of soldiers worked in concert. One group provided covering fire to keep the defenders' heads down and prevent opponents from firing their own weapons, while another group of friendly soldiers sprinted to a new piece of dead ground. Once there, the two elements reversed roles: the forward soldiers provided suppressive fire while their comrades located a different piece of dead ground and raced to it. This coordinated movement in teams allowed attacking soldiers to take the initiative once again, even amid the deadly firepower of modern weaponry.

The new system of *modern tactics* or *dispersed tactics* enabled large numbers of soldiers to operate effectively on the offensive again for the first time since the advent of automatic weapons. The German army first employed a version of these modern tactics in the last year of the Great War, and other belligerents quickly adopted and refined the new tactical system. The effect was profound and visible within just two decades: where the Great War was characterized by

FIGURE 6.2 Red Army soldiers pick their way across the empty battlefield during the Battle of Stalingrad in 1942. Getty Images.

static positions and trench warfare and dominated by the defensive, the Second World War featured fast and sustained movement as massive armies took to the offensive. The new tactical system also gave rise to one of the most pronounced changes in the character of combat over the past century—the advent of the "empty battlefield," in which soldiers were now spread out and hidden from view, rather than marching in the open wearing brightly colored uniforms and flying banners and flags (Figure 6.2).

Evolutions in military technology, weaponry, and tactics altered combat in dramatic and easily observed ways. But beneath all of these changes in the character of warfare lay an equally profound continuity—the critical importance of motivating soldiers to risk their lives and fight even among the terrifying and deadly circumstances of battle. Armies can only fight if they can deliver soldiers who are willing to fight (or who can be compelled to do so) and to hazard the trauma and danger of the battlefield. The magnitude of that task is difficult to overstate. Performance in combat demands behaviors that violate every biological instinct for self-preservation. As two American military psychologists noted during the Second World War, fighting requires rational humans to do things—like pilot a bomber through a swarm of enemy fighters over a heavily defended target or advance across a fire-strewn beachhead—that are fundamentally irrational.[7]

In combat, the natural biological impulse to seek safety from danger runs headlong into the military's equally unyielding demand that soldiers stay and do their duty. That tension can produce unsettling realizations in troops in battle. As a Union veteran admitted after the Civil War, "The truth is, when bullets are whacking against tree trunks and solid shot are cracking skulls like egg shells, the consuming passion in the breast of the average man is to get out of the way."[8]

Combat, wherever and whenever it occurs, places extraordinary burdens on both individual soldiers and on the units they comprise. The Union soldiers attacking Marye's Heights during the 1862 Battle of Fredericksburg provide a vivid example: What led the soldiers in the first wave to step off and attack such a well-defended position out in the open? What motivated the soldiers in the last assault, looking out over the carnage of the previous, futile assaults and surveying the bleeding, moaning victims of the earlier efforts? In 1945, three marine divisions totaling more than 60,000 men attacked the tiny volcanic island of Iwo Jima in the Pacific. Fanatical resistance by 21,000 Japanese soldiers—nearly all of whom died fighting in their bunkers and caves—cost the Marines 6,000 dead and more than 20,000 wounded as they used flamethrowers and grenades to root out the tenacious defenders. How did those soldiers manage to endure five savage weeks of close-quarter combat in some of the most appalling conditions imaginable?

Military history offers many examples of soldiers performing seemingly impossible acts of bravery. Equally as often, however, soldiers and their units fail to overcome their fears and either panic and flee from battle, refuse to advance in the first place, or surrender (individually or en masse) once in combat. Sometimes there are examples of both terrific steadfastness and uncertain commitment in the very same episode. The first day of the three-day battle at Gettysburg during the American Civil War, for example, found two Union infantry corps (bodies of troops comprising between nine and twelve thousand soldiers) arriving northwest of the Pennsylvania town and attempting to prevent advancing rebel troops from capturing the vital road junction to the southeast. On the left side of the Union line, the First Corps fought extremely well, with one of its battle-tested units demonstrating why it had earned the nickname "the Iron Brigade" in previous fights. On the right side, the less capable Eleventh Corps, commanded by Union General Oliver O. Howard, performed much more poorly, confirming to many its reputation as "Howard's Cowards." The First Corps fought with great determination even after its commander was killed leading his men at the front and ultimately conducted an orderly fighting retreat back through town. The Eleventh Corps, in contrast, shattered during the battle. Its troops ran back through Gettysburg in disarray, dropping their equipment as they fled in panic. One of the corps generals hid in a root cellar for the remainder of the three-day battle to escape capture by the Confederates.

How do soldiers manage to marshal the will to face enemy fire across an open field or steel themselves under the weight of a ferocious artillery barrage? What makes some soldiers and units stand up to the tests of combat while others break and run? These enduring questions of human behavior defy easy answers. Historically, militaries have depended on a variety of motivators to get soldiers to face combat. There is no single, one-size-fits-all motivator that can convince every soldier to withstand the rigors of battle. In most cases, it seems, a combination of factors convinced their soldiers to stay and fight with at least a modicum of commitment.

And sometimes a modicum of commitment to battle is all a soldier can muster. Many serve in battle with limited enthusiasm. During the Second World War, American GIs sometimes spoke longingly of what they called the "million-dollar wound"—that is, an injury severe enough to warrant removal from combat (being shot through the fleshy part of the buttock, for example), but not so serious as to leave a permanent, crippling injury. That soldiers might fantasize about receiving such a nondisfiguring wound as a ticket out of combat even while in battle suggests at least some who are willing to fight but who lack a deep patriotic commitment to the cause.

Nonetheless, history abounds with examples of militaries delivering enough soldiers with sufficient motivation into combat. Every battle is, in some sense, evidence that two sides were able to furnish soldiers willing to suspend their powerful biological instincts long enough to fight. Historically, armies have used a combination of carrots and sticks—rewards for fighting that help *pull* soldiers into the fight and penalties for not fighting that *push* soldiers into battle.

The sticks are often more obvious than the carrots. Throughout history, armies have placed a great deal of emphasis on coercion—threats of direct physical punishment—to compel their soldiers to go forward. (The eighteenth-century Prussian general Frederick the Great highlighted this dynamic in his observation that an effective soldier should be more afraid of his own officers than of the enemy.)[9] The notion that armies would physically threaten their own troops in order to get them to fight is somewhat alien to most twenty-first-century Americans, but in fact the application of physical punishment or the threat to do so has been one of the most consistent ways to motivate troops in combat throughout history. Rallying his troops before an 1864 battle, for example, a Confederate general reminded the men that they were fighting to protect their homes and loved ones, and to preserve personal and familial honor—and then, in case those appeals were insufficient to motivate the soldiers to face swarms of enemy bullets, he brandished his sidearm and threatened to personally "blow the brains out of the first man who left ranks."[10] Fifty years later, an American marine fighting in the First World War heard a sergeant make a similar coercive threat to one of his wavering comrades: "Don't you turn yellow and try to run," the sergeant shouted. "If you do and the Germans don't kill you, I will."[11]

The linear tactics that dominated battlefields before the twentieth century helped facilitate those kinds of motivators. Soldiers who advanced into battle in tightly packed lines could be easily observed by their officers and NCOs. Having comrades at either elbow and marching between lines of friendly troops made it physically difficult to escape battle. Even for the soldier who privately wished to run from the firing line, there was often nowhere to go. The tightly packed formations dramatically limited the foot soldier's options once battle began.

Coercive threats—the stick—have been a part of nearly every American army. But relying solely on the stick is a problematic way to compel soldiers to fight, and armies that brutalize their soldiers into fighting eventually suffer from severe problems with morale. American cultural expectations make excessive use of punishment as a motivator even more difficult. During the Civil War, a Northern nurse asked President Abraham Lincoln why he did not simply execute more soldiers who deserted their units as a deterrent. Lincoln responded that the nation would not tolerate it: "You cannot order men shot by dozens or twenties. People won't stand it, and they ought not stand it."[12] Driving soldiers into battle is not a perfect solution to the problem of motivating troops to endure combat. Whenever possible, military systems prefer committed, motivated soldiers who are not merely fighting to avoid punishment by their own officers. Carrots, the offer of incentives and rewards, provide a useful way for the military to pull soldiers into combat so that they fight at least partially out of genuine commitment—whether that commitment is to an abstract political cause or (as appears far more often the case) something more immediate and tangible.

Those incentives have taken a number of forms in American armies. Occasionally they are tangible—a financial reward, for example—to encourage soldiers to commit to battle. Those kinds of concrete, monetary incentives were once extremely powerful motivators for soldiers to face battle; mercenary armies fought much of the enormously destructive Thirty Years' War in the seventeenth century, for example. In certain circumstances, offering soldiers money in exchange for fighting (or offering the victorious side the chance to pillage the losers, as was common in the Middle Ages) proved an effective way to get soldiers to face the danger and uncertainty of combat.

But as battle became increasingly lethal, the power of those monetary rewards lessened. A mercenary might accept payment for service in combat when there was still a fairly realistic chance to survive the engagement. But no amount of money would convince a reasonable person to face battle when one of every three soldiers might be wounded or killed. A financial reward is simply ineffective amid the storm of steel of the modern battlefield. Money alone cannot motivate soldiers to face those kinds of deadly odds.

But other kinds of incentives proved more reliable tools to get soldiers to stay and fight, even in the absence of explicit punishments. For millennia, armies sent soldiers into battle alongside men they knew and trusted. The armies of the ancient Greeks sent brother into battle alongside brother, and placed fathers next to sons in the phalanx. A similar practice operated in the American armies of the Civil War. Both sides recruited their regiments locally, so that men would serve alongside friends and acquaintances they had known as civilians and—presumably—had some kind of pre-existing relationship with. The process of recruiting soldiers geographically and sending men into battle alongside comrades they already knew gradually receded in the twentieth century. But the practice did not disappear overnight. During the Great War, the British recruited more than a hundred battalions by promising that recruits who signed up with friends and coworkers would serve together, rather than be randomly assigned to units. These "pals battalions" suffered terrible casualties in the fighting of 1916. Those losses fell especially hard on particular towns and localities, leading the British to discontinue the practice in the latter two years of the war.

Though it placed unbearable burdens on some unlucky towns, sending men into battle alongside friends from civilian life provided individuals with a powerful motivator to endure the stress and trauma of battle. Bonds of trust, friendship, and interdependence, commanders agreed, would form more readily among men with pre-existing relationships, making it more difficult to flee the fighting. And within the tightly packed linear formations, the presence of comrades in such close quarters could serve as both stick *and* carrot. A soldier who fled from the battle line (or who ran even before the unit began fighting) knew that he had few options afterward. Running away from a regiment in which all the soldiers knew one another and all hailed from the same town provided a potent incentive to stay and fight. The knowledge that cowardice in battle would be easily observed by comrades (and that letters describing that cowardice under fire would quickly arrive home and destroy a reputation) pushed some reluctant soldiers into battle. And the presence of trusted friends on either side in the firing line helped pull others into the fight. Civil War soldiers referred to the physical, tangible reassurance of friendly troops as the "touch of the elbow," and to judge from their letters and diaries, the presence of that physical reassurance was the single most important thing that helped them withstand the fear and trauma of the battlefield. "The man who can go out alone and fight against overwhelming odds is very rare," noted one nineteenth-century soldier. But "for every one such, there are thousands more who can 'touch the elbow' and go forward to what seems like certain death."[13] Another Civil War veteran concurred, noting that "men fight in masses. To be brave they must be inspired by the feeling of fellowship. Shoulder must touch shoulder."[14]

Many of these motivators—carrots and sticks—functioned effectively within the context of the linear battlefield. (And for good reason: armies evolved those motivators over thousands of years of trial-and-error experience fighting from lines.) The reassuring physical presence of comrades and the knowledge that a refusal to fight would be seen and noted by nearby comrades proved powerful enough to get thousands of often unenthusiastic troops to stay and fight. The advent of dispersed tactics in the twentieth century upended those traditional motivators. The modern system solved the immediate tactical problem, allowing troops to take the offensive even against the storm of steel. But dispersing soldiers across the battlefield, having them go to ground under fire, and camouflaging them from view also drained the traditional combat motivators of most of their power. Soldiers spread out across the battlefield could no longer rely on the "touch of the elbow" to steel their wills; the nearest friendly soldier might be yards away and nearly hidden from sight. Similarly, leaders could no longer monitor their troops' behaviors directly, which made credible coercive threats much more difficult to deliver and enforce. As one British general of the Second World War lamented, "Nothing is easier in jungle or dispersed fighting than for a man to shirk" his duty. If a soldier had "no stomach for advancing," the commander observed, "all he has to do is flop into the undergrowth; in retreat, he can slink out of the rear guard, join up later, and swear he was last to leave."[15]

On the empty battlefield, the time-tested methods of getting soldiers to fight lost much of their power. But the record of the savage world wars of the twentieth century provides overwhelming evidence that military systems successfully met the challenge of finding new ways to motivate soldiers even within the massive new demands of evolving combat. Part of that solution was a dramatic new approach to training soldiers. Preparing soldiers for the linear tactics of the seventeenth, eighteenth, and nineteenth centuries consisted mostly of rote drill. Soldiers spent hours mindlessly practicing the many steps involved in loading and firing their single-shot weapons, and rehearsing the complex choreography necessary to maneuver large blocks of men in the confusion of battle.

Those rote exercises had a number of benefits on the linear battlefield. They drilled critical actions into the muscles of the soldiers, such that they could perform those actions automatically without thinking, even when excited or terrified. Within the linear system, such unthinking action was a benefit. A nineteenth-century soldier who began thinking hard about the defenses he faced at the crest of Marye's Heights and about the options he might pursue to avoid them was far less likely to go along with the assault. To be a good soldier, most commanders of the eighteenth and nineteenth centuries agreed, a man had to first be transformed into a kind of automaton who could act with little thought.

On the empty battlefield, such automatons were nearly useless. Coordinated movement in teams required soldiers to assess a wide range of options and to make intelligent choices under the enormous stress of battle: how to use a particular piece of dead space, when to time a sprint across an open field, whether to attack a position from the front or try to flank it. Where linear combat prized automatons, the modern battlefield required soldiers to exercise an enormous degree of autonomy. New training regimens designed for the Second World War focused not just on drill and marching in unison, though those old traditions remained a part of military training even in the twentieth century. But new, realistic training exercises supplemented the old marching practice. Those exercises subjected soldiers to some of the sights, sounds, and sensations of combat through live-fire drills and lifelike combat exercises and were based on the idea of "battle inoculation"—exposing recruits to a taste of the fear they would feel in combat *before* they arrived in battle. Just as a person inoculated with a particular disease in a controlled exposure might acquire some immunity to that disease, military leaders hoped that soldiers exposed to some elements of battle in training would handle their fears more confidently in actual combat.

The combination of practiced repetitions drilled into the soldier's muscles and realistic training exercises that allowed trainees to rehearse battle situations, first pioneered during World War II, persists into twenty-first-century military training. And for good reason: experience suggests that it works. One marine sergeant aboard a Humvee that survived an intense running firefight through an Iraqi town in 2003 remembered that, in the heat of battle, "It was just like training. I just loaded and fired my weapons from muscle memory. I wasn't even aware what my hands were doing."[16]

The demands of the linear battlefield altered other parts of the combat experience as well. For centuries, Western armies depended on officers and noncommissioned officers (the corporals and sergeants who help the officers administer discipline and who are often thought of as the backbone of a military organization) to lead troops into the maelstrom of combat. High-volume automatic weapons and dispersed tactics did not change the importance of effective leaders in combat. But the different tactical systems changed what troops valued in their leaders. In the eighteenth and nineteenth centuries, the close quarters of combat placed a high value on commanders who could maintain an outward appearance of calm. Soldiers spoke with reverence of "conspicuous gallantry," an officer's ability to remain steady even in the midst of battle. One Union soldier reserved his highest praise for his commander, a man who "seemed to think bullets are of no account"; others praised leaders who strode through a hail of shrapnel as casually as a man might walk through a rainstorm.[17] In the twentieth century, such displays of conspicuous gallantry had become suicidally foolhardy. Soldiers came to favor officers who knew the business of fighting well—who could read a piece of terrain effectively and who did not take pointless chances with the lives of their men. Personal bravery still won praise, but leaders did not necessarily demonstrate it through indifferent exposure to a hail of bullets.

Training and leadership could not transform every wide-eyed recruit into a steely-eyed killer, of course. Nor did it have to. Battle does not require that soldiers be fanatics; it requires only that they meet some threshold of willingness to go forward. Thus an American soldier in Vietnam might carry a cigarette lighter he had personalized with an engraving of the four U's—"The Unwilling, led by the Unqualified, to kill the Unfortunate, and die for the Ungrateful"— yet still engage the enemy and return fire when confronted with actual combat. As many veterans and scholars have noted, once in battle, committed participation in the mission of the group is often the best way to maximize one's personal chances of staying alive. And, as many combat veterans have noted, battle often reduces participants' concerns to that bare essence. As a twenty-one-year-old American soldier in the 2003 invasion of Iraq observed after seeing a disfigured body in battle, "Everything in life is overrated except death."[18]

A final continuity that emerges from any study of battle over time is the nearly universal presence of psychological symptoms, often incapacitating ones, in soldiers who have been exposed to the trauma of combat repeatedly. The persistence of those symptoms in veterans, and the difficulty of diagnosing, treating, and even naming the maladies, forms one last enduring puzzle in the web of human behaviors associated with combat.

Soldiers and scholars have noted the toll that exposure to battle takes on the human psyche since ancient times. Indeed, the *Iliad*, perhaps the first war story in human history, has as its central plot device the refusal of the Greek hero Achilles (veteran of many, many battles) to continue fighting. While Achilles has reason to be angry with his commander, the narrator Homer also suggests that Achilles's previous combat experience has taken a heavy toll on the hero. Achilles, Homer implies, may simply have seen too much war. Generations of soldiers and physicians have noted similar patterns among combat veterans and have struggled to describe, diagnose, and treat the symptoms.

The symptoms of these maladies display some surprising similarities over time. That may be because their roots lie in human biology, and physiology changes more slowly than other dimensions of the human experience. Soldiers in battle describe a number of common physical effects, no matter when and where they fight. A racing heartbeat, dry mouth, trembling limbs, and damp palms are near-universal reactions to the danger of combat. But some symptoms of combat trauma seem to vary by time and circumstance. During the First World War, British veterans of the savage trench warfare on the Western Front often fell prey to bouts of mutism—an inability to speak in patients with no otherwise observable physical problems in the mouth, tongue, jaw, or lips. Other soldiers who had not suffered physical wounds developed limps.

The effort to diagnose, explain, and treat the psychological effects of combat has confounded medical practitioners for generations. Many of the first attempts to explain and treat the symptoms of combat trauma appear hopelessly naïve (sometimes cruelly so) to modern sensibilities. During the Civil War, soldiers in both the Union and Confederate armies suffered trauma upon repeated exposure to the acute strain of battle. In a pre-Freudian age, doctors looked to some tangible cause for the symptoms and named the affliction "soldier's heart." They imagined that physical pressure on that organ (possibly from too-tight knapsack straps on long marches) had somehow led to other symptoms. During the Great War, doctors examining soldiers suffering from post-battle trauma coined the term "shell shock" to explain its roots. Those physicians still believed in a physical cause, though they had turned their attention from the cardiac system to the brain; "shell shock" described the damage that the powerful but invisible blast of pressure from an exploding shell could cause to the brain even when there was no other physical evidence of a wound.

By the Second World War, physicians and psychologists had moved away from a physical explanation for the symptoms. Instead they settled on the term "combat fatigue" to describe GIs who, though they bore no outward signs of damage, nevertheless were unable to face battle again. During the Vietnam era, military doctors developed the diagnosis post-traumatic stress disorder, or PTSD, to describe similar clusters of symptoms. Both diagnoses reflected the belief that combat trauma was at bottom psychological: the damage was not physical but emotional. In an age of psychiatry, the notion that combat trauma could be caused by physical damage done by an invisible shock wave seemed embarrassingly unsophisticated.

Recent experience has brought the twenty-first-century understanding of combat trauma nearly full circle. After more than a decade fighting wars in Iraq and Afghanistan, the American military has had the unwelcome opportunity to study thousands of soldiers wounded by the signature weapon of those conflicts, the improvised explosive device. Modern medical equipment enables doctors to see actual tissue damage in the brains of sufferers. It now seems that the shock waves produced by a nearby explosion can produce combat traumas in ways that military doctors a century ago could only guess at.

Gaining an understanding of combat does not require memorizing hundreds of battle maps, the names of famous commanders, the range and caliber of dozens of weapons, or the casualty rolls of centuries' worth of battles. But to cultivate a thorough understanding of how war affects society, it is crucial to have at least some familiarity with the nature of what soldiers do and endure in combat. The character of battle at any given moment in time—its specific tactics, demands, and effects—exerts a profound effect on the way a society imagines war, prepares for war, wages war, and recovers from war. And the unchanging nature of war-fare—the fear, trauma, and exhilaration that violent struggle produces—leaves deep marks on participants. Due to some interesting and long-standing cultural traditions, American armies have usually been composed mainly of amateurs. Until the advent of the All-Volunteer Force in 1973, American wars were fought largely by temporary soldiers who would bristle at being called "professionals." For them, military service was an often unwelcome interruption in an other-wise peaceful civilian life. Their self-identification as temporary soldiers makes their experiences in battle all the more important to students of the relation-ship between war and society. Those veterans carried the memories of combat, and the visible and invisible scars the experience left, back to civilian life. Those experiences shaped thousands of decisions about war in the home, in the public square, in the voting booth, and in dozens of other venues long after the guns had fallen silent.

Discussion Questions

1. How is the *nature* of war different from the *character* of war?
2. How has the character of combat changed over time?
3. How and why have the ways that soldiers are motivated to face the trauma and danger of battle evolved?

Notes

1 John B. Babcock, *Taught to Kill: An American Boy's War from the Ardennes to Berlin* (Washington, DC: Potomac Books, 2005), 81.
2 Leander Stillwell, *The Story of a Common Soldier of Army Life in the Civil War, 1861–1865* (n.p.: Franklin Hudson, 1920), 38.
3 Arthur Wellesley to John Croker, August 8, 1815 in John Gurwood, *Selections from the Dispatches and General Orders of Field-Marshal the Duke of Wellington* (London: John Murray, 1842), 887.
4 John Keegan, *The Face of Battle* (New York: Viking, 1976), 303.
5 John Shy, *A People Numerous and Armed: Reflections on the Military Struggle for American Independence* (New York: Oxford University Press, 1976), 126.
6 Ernst Jünger, *Storm of Steel* (London: Chatto and Windus, 1929).
7 Roy R. Grinker and John P. Spiegel, *Men under Stress* (Philadelphia: Blakiston, 1945).
8 David Thompson, qtd. in Robert U. Johnson and C. C. Buel, eds., *Battles and Leaders of the Civil War* (New York: Century Co., 1882), 2:662.
9 J.F.C. Fuller, *A Military History of the Western World* (New York: Funk and Wagnalls, 1955), 2:196.
10 Bryan Grimes to wife, September 20, 1864, Grimes Papers, Southern Historical Collection, University of North Carolina, Chapel Hill.
11 Elton E. Mackin, *Suddenly We Didn't Want to Die: Memoirs of a World War I Marine* (Novato, CA: Presidio Press, 1993), 29.
12 Mary Livermore, *My Story of the War: A Woman's Experience* (Hartford, CT: A. D. Worthington & Company, 1890), 559.
13 E. L. Marsh, "Military Discipline," in *War Sketches and Incidents* (Des Moines, IA, 1898), 2:107.
14 William Thompson Lusk, *War Letters of William Thompson Lusk, Captain, Assistant Adjutant-General, United States Volunteers 1861–1863* (New York: Private printing, 1911), 247–248.
15 William Slim, *Defeat into Victory* (New York: David McKay Company, 1961), 451.
16 Brad Colbert, qtd. in Evan Wright, *Generation Kill: Devil Dogs, Captain America, and the New Face of American War* (New York: G. P. Putnam's Sons, 2004), 143.
17 Aldace Freeman Walker to father, September 18, 1864, in *Quite Ready to Be Sent Somewhere: The Civil War Letters of Aldace Freeman Walker*, ed. Tom Ledoux (Victoria, BC: Trafford Publishing, 2002), 300.
18 Jeffrey Carzales, qtd. in Wright, *Generation Kill*, 119.

Further Reading

John Keegan. *The Face of Battle*. New York: Viking, 1976.
James McPherson. *For Cause and Comrades: Why Men Fought in the Civil War*. New York: Oxford University Press, 1997.
Leonard Wong, Thomas A. Kolditz, Raymond A. Millen, and Terrence M. Potter. *Why They Fight: Combat Motivation in the Iraq War*. Carlisle Barracks, PA: Strategic Studies Institute, U.S. Army War College, 2003.

7

Veterans and
Veterans' Issues

WILBUR J. SCOTT

In the spirit of full disclosure, I am both a sociologist and a veteran of the war in Vietnam. Although crafting this essay using my sociological lens, I think the reader might appreciate that both these statuses have stoked my interest in veterans' issues for decades.[1] For example, being a veteran of a war that ended badly for the United States and disastrously for our South Vietnamese allies often has led me to compare my own experiences with those of my father, who served in the Second World War and those of today's men and women who have done their part in Afghanistan and Iraq. This much is apparent: the conduct and outcome of a war affect both veterans' views of their service and the opinions of others about them.

Veterans of each generation also have sought each other out and developed their own formal organizations. People of all walks of life do this sort of thing when they have vital experiences to which they collectively attach social and political significance. Military service is one such experience that lends itself to group formation. Successive wars and conflicts thus produce generations of veterans with bonds of common brotherhood and, since the advent of the All-Volunteer Force (AVF) in 1973, sisterhood.

Similarly, each war/conflict creates its own signature issues and legacies. The modal diagnoses among World War II vets at Veterans Administration (VA) hospitals were alcoholism and standard psychiatric disorders. In those days, there was no official diagnosis for a psychological trauma that persisted after a war's end. A new physicians' reference, the *Diagnostic and Statistical Manual* (DSM-III), remedied this oversight in 1980 by adding post-traumatic stress disorder (PTSD), which quickly became a diagnosis associated with the post-Vietnam experience. In Afghanistan and Iraq, where the modal cause of combat-related deaths is the "improvised explosive device" (IED), PTSD, traumatic amputations, and mild traumatic brain injury (mTBI) are the most commonly associated conditions. An important part of these stories is how such conditions have pushed the boundaries of medical knowledge and practice and how Department of Veterans Affairs (DVA) facilities have had to be reconfigured to accommodate them.[2]

This chapter reviews such issues with an eye toward two related themes: what conceptual schemes are helpful in making theoretical and practical sense of all this and how these issues have evolved in recent wars/conflicts.

What Is a Veteran; How Many Veterans Are There?

The DVA defines a veteran as someone who falls into one of three categories:[3]

1. Those who served in the active-duty military, Coast Guard, uniformed Public Health Service, or uniformed National Oceanic and Atmospheric Administration[4]
2. Reservists and National Guardsmen/women who were called to active duty
3. Those disabled while on active-duty training

Excluded from this definition are current active-duty members, those who were dishonorably discharged from military service, and those whose time on active duty was for training purposes only.

This may seem like a lot of contortions in quest of a definition. However, a certain amount of legalese is necessary, as the definition of veteran defines eligibility for benefits, medical treatment, and, possibly, compensation by the DVA. Certain of these entitlements are extended only to veterans who served in time of war, so it is important also to note the dates of service under which someone has qualified for veteran's status.

Currently the DVA identifies "wartime" veterans as those who served during the following time periods: December 1941 to December 1946 (World War II), July 1950 to January 1955 (Korean War), August 1964 to April 1975 (Vietnam Conflict), August 1990 to January 1991 (Persian Gulf War), and September 2001 to the present (Operation Enduring Freedom, Afghanistan, and Operation Iraqi Freedom).[5] Those whose service falls in the interim periods are classified as "peacetime" veterans.

It may seem surprising, but there is no easy way to know exactly how many veterans there are and when they served. There is no registry that enumerates them and tracks their every move. Hence, the DVA in recent years has sponsored national probability surveys to estimate with precision their numbers and

Table 7.1.

Percent of U.S. Veterans by Period of Service, as Estimated by National Survey of Veterans (NSV), 2001 and 2010[a]

Period of Service	2010 NSV	2001 NSV
Afghanistan/Iraq Wars (since September 2001)	11.7%[b]	—
August 1990 to August 2001[c]	18.7%	13.9%
May 1975 to July 1990	27.2%	27.9%
Vietnam conflict (August 1964 to April 1975)	33.5%	36.1%
February 1955 to July 1964	17.5%	16.9%
Korean War (July 1950 to January 1955)	10.9%	16.9%
January 1947 to June 1950	1.7%	6.7%
World War II (December 1941 to December 1946)	8.6%	20.5%
November 1941 or earlier	0.4%	—[d]
Estimated total number of veterans	22.5 million	25.2 million

[a] Adapted from National Survey of Veterans (NSV), 67. See note 3.
[b] Column percentages sum to more than 100% because some veterans served in more than one period of service.
[c] Includes veterans of the Persian Gulf War.
[d] The 2001 NSV did not contain an item concerning service prior to World War II.

characteristics. The consensus is that there currently are just over nineteen million men and women who meet the preceding definition. This represents about 9 percent of the U.S. population who are eighteen years of age or older.

Best guess estimates of the breakdown by era are summarized in Table 7.1. One might expect the numbers of veterans to be increasing because of the long wars in Afghanistan and Iraq. Actually, the number of U.S. veterans has been declining steadily since 1980, when there were about twenty-eight million. As Table 7.1 shows, in 2001 there were about twenty-five million and in 2010 about twenty-two-and-a-half million veterans.

This decline is occurring for two main reasons. One, the large veteran cohorts of World War II and Korea now are quite old. The veterans of Korea these days are in their eighties and of World War II in their nineties, so both are dying off rapidly with each passing year. For example, the National World War II Museum in New Orleans estimates that, of the sixteen million soldiers, sailors, and marines who served during that war, only about 697,800 of them still are alive and these old-timers are dying at a rate of about 430 a day.[6]

Second, the United States has fought its wars since 1973 with an All-Volunteer Force (AVF). By their nature, AVFs rely on smaller, more highly trained military forces than did previous draft-based militaries made up of massive but less technically sophisticated armies. The growing numbers of younger veterans of Afghanistan and Iraq therefore do not offset the shrinking numbers of the older ones. As Table 7.1 shows, service in World War II and Korea accounted for one-fifth of U.S. veterans in 2010 (8.6 and 10.9 percent, respectively), down from just over a third of veterans in 2001 (20.5 and 16.9 percent). While the percentages at the upper and lower ends of the eras currently are shifting, service in Vietnam accounted for one-third of the U.S. veteran population in both 2001 and 2010. However, most Vietnam veterans now are in their sixties and their percentage of the veteran population will decrease markedly as they continue to age. Within twenty years the U.S. veteran population is expected to be around fifteen million and virtually all of them will be from the wars in the Persian Gulf and Afghanistan/Iraq.[7]

Important Demographics

As we have seen, portions of the veteran population are quite old. The average person in the United States over the age of eighteen is around forty-five years old, but the average veteran is almost sixty. This has implications for the programs and services the DVA must be prepared to provide. For starters, the veteran population has distinctive subgroups. Younger veterans require services and medical care associated with postdeployment issues and combat-related injuries, while older veterans need care and services related to aging. The VA/ DVA has not always been equally ready to provide both kinds of assistance. For example, in the decades following World War II, the VA slowly transformed itself to accommodate the evolving requisites of that war's veterans as they grew older. Suddenly in the 1970s, VA facilities and programs were found wanting when they experienced large influxes of Vietnam veterans with completely different needs.[8]

Some demographics of veterans are affiliated with these age characteristics and the circumstances of younger veterans often stand in contrast to those of their more numerous older comrades. Seven out of ten veterans are married and a majority have children. For most, their children are grown and no longer live at home—obviously a characteristic that holds for older rather than younger veterans. Similarly, a plurality of veterans are not in the labor force, not because they cannot find work but because they are retired. Most veterans own their own homes (again, about 70 percent) and the modal income category among them is $20,000 to $40,000 per year (though 30 percent make more than $60,000 per year).

Other features of the veteran population reflect characteristics of the AVF. Prior to the AVF the primary military organization for women was the Women's Army Corps (WAC), a gender-segregated branch of the army. Formed during World War II (as were other temporary units for women), the idea of U.S. women in uniform initially was met with opposition if not outright derision. However, with the stated purpose to "release a man for combat," the WAC and similar organizations during World War II attracted about 350,000 women who performed noncombat jobs as switchboard operators, bakers, file and postal clerks, secretaries, stenographers, mechanics, stateside pilots, and so forth. The goal was for women to make up 2 percent of the total force, a target never attained even during the high-volunteer days of World War II.

The WAC was retired from service in 1978 and women soldiers were reassigned to a range of noncombat military jobs within a gender-integrated AVF.[9] With the improvement in status and opportunity, the percentage of women in the AVF quickly eclipsed the old 2 percent goal and soon reached nearly 15 percent.[10] Consequently, the proportion of women veterans has grown over the past four decades and women now make up just over 8 percent of all U.S. veterans. This number is projected to double over the next twenty years as older veterans, mostly male, continue to die and the younger generation of veterans becomes more predominant.

Women veterans currently differ from male veterans in several ways.[11] They are on average around forty-five years of age—about fifteen years younger than their male veteran counterparts. They also have higher levels of education and mostly are employed in good jobs. On the downside, their jobs yield lower incomes than do those for males, veterans or otherwise. Women veterans also are more likely than male veterans to be divorced and to have children in the household. Finally, the DVA essentially was designed to care for male veterans, so it often is not attuned to the needs or medical requirements specific to females.

Women veterans also differ from their nonveteran female counterparts in several respects. They are slightly older than nonveteran women, more likely to be married (often to another veteran or service member), better educated (the percentages who have completed some college, are college graduates, or have graduate degrees *all* exceed those of nonveteran women), more likely to be employed full-time, and, in every age category, have household incomes that exceed those of nonveteran women. Clearly, some women veterans have found significant financial advantages in volunteering for military service, as only some of their advantages in education and income are due to age differences from nonveteran females. This would seem especially so for black women, who make up 12 percent of the U.S. female population but account for more than 20 percent of women veterans.

This economic advantage also extends to minority veterans across the board, female and male alike.[12] Black, Hispanic, American Indian, and Asian veterans all are financially better off than nonveterans of the same racial/ethnic category. The personal income levels of the former exceed those of the latter in every category by about 40 percent. The result is that the veteran population, now about 80 percent white, will be more racially and ethnically diverse in the coming decades as the AVF continues to attract significant numbers of minority group volunteers. This trend is one anticipated before the shift to the AVF, though it usually was expressed as a fear—the worry that the AVF would become a refuge for lesser-qualified minorities. What has occurred, to the contrary, is that the AVF consistently has attracted minorities whose qualifications exceed minimum standards.

These trends among women and minorities underscore one of the important differences between a draft-based military and the AVF. In the former, young males mostly in the eighteen-to-twenty-one age group were inducted and most remained in the service only for a limited period of time. Draftees' pay was substandard, even in comparison to low-level civilian occupations, and any advantage to one's subsequent civilian career often was minimal. By its very nature, an AVF must compete with the civilian labor market. Hence, salaries in the AVF are substantially higher than for draft-based militaries and numerous educational opportunities are available both while *in* the military as well as after separation from service. It is typical, therefore, to hear volunteers for the AVF cite both patriotic (*I want to serve my country*) and material (*I want to improve my lot in life*) reasons for signing up.[13]

Veterans as Social Groupings

Sociologists distinguish among the characteristics people have, dividing them into those that are *ascribed* (that is, present at birth—sex, race, age, place, and class of origin) and those that are *achieved* (acquired by virtue of what they do—educational attainment, intragenerational social mobility, being a veteran, and so on). For example, I am many things: a (casual) acquaintance of many, brother, dog handler, father, foodie, (close) friend of a limited few, glasses-wearer, hiker, husband, male, professor, son, (Vietnam) veteran, white (of Scottish-Irish and German descent), to name a few. I have listed these alphabetically rather than in terms of how central each is to my sense of who I am, how much time and effort I invest in each, or how much affinity I feel when encountering someone else with the same characteristic.

One use for such listings is noting the extent to which certain of these characteristics become a basis for associating with others. People sharing virtually any characteristic are a "potential group," meaning it is possible that they might at some point attach significance to it, form bonds with others having that same characteristic, and even engage in collective action to advance causes of concern to them. This is most likely when people have developed intense, distinctive life experiences by virtue of how some characteristic has affected the substance and trajectories of their lives. If wearing glasses, for instance, were a consistent basis for rebuff, discrimination, and deprivation, someone with externally worn corrective lenses eventually might exclaim, "Glasses-wearers of the world, unite! You have nothing to lose but your chains!" and the cry for action would resonate with a mass of bespectacled followers.[14]

Military service in time of war is an especially cogent basis for group formation. The United States historically has relied upon a rather small, professional military during peacetime and expanded into a substantially larger one during times of war.[15] When relying upon a draft to do so, the resulting expansions and contractions first pull large groups of civilians into military ranks during a war and then expel them back into civilian life at the conclusion of the conflict. In the era of the AVF, the small professional force has compensated numerically in time of war by activating reserve and National Guard units and by deploying service members to combat zones multiple times.

There are many similarities all veterans share from their time in the military. In both draft-based militaries and the AVF, training consists of intense resocial-ization to reorganize service members' personalities so they may fill otherwise unaccustomed roles, accept the risk of being killed or injured, and, in some cases, perform unfamiliar acts such as killing other humans. The conclusion of one's time in the military calls for a subsequent resocialization back into hab-its and behaviors consistent with civilian life, although former service members usually are left to do so informally themselves.

Still, there are natural fissures within the ranks of veterans because exactly what they experience while in the military varies considerably. One obvious divide is between former officers and enlisted personnel. However, the charac-teristic producing the most variation is service during wartime versus peacetime. Exactly what this means to veterans and to others in the larger society differs in response to a number of circumstances, not the least of which is the popularity of the war in which they served. Wars and their conduct differ tremendously in scope and detail, making simple classification difficult. However, one way to cat-egorize them, albeit crudely, is on the basis of sentiment concerning "how well the war went." This suggests a continuum labeled at one end "good war" and at the other "bad war."

In the modern American psyche, the good war-bad war distinction reared its ugly head after Vietnam. It was inevitable that veterans and the American pub-lic alike would contrast what went down in Vietnam with the glories of World War II. In the latter, American shores were assaulted in the December 7, 1941, surprise attack on Pearl Harbor by Japanese warplanes. More than 2,000 sail-ors, airmen, and civilians died in the onslaught that day. Hence, the moral right-ness of the war was not in question.[16] The U.S. military—indeed, the whole of American society—mobilized for total war on two fronts: against the Germans and Italians in the European theater and against the Japanese in the Pacific. The United States emerged victorious in 1945 against these militaries to establish itself as the world's premier superpower (along with the Soviet Union, our ally during the war).

In contrast, the pretext for America's introduction of ground troops into South Vietnam was a 1964 incident in which a U.S. destroyer and three North Vietnamese torpedo boats exchanged gunfire off the northern coast of Vietnam, with no American casualties. What began as a defensive measure involving 3,500 Marines in 1965 escalated into offensive operations against the North Vietnam-ese army and indigenous South Vietnamese insurgents. At the peak of the war

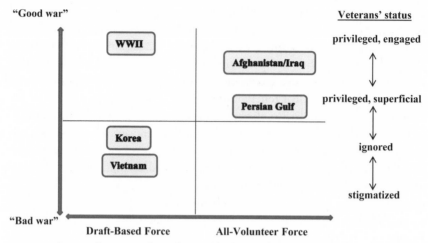

FIGURE 7.1 A veteran's status is often influenced by the "good/bad war" distinction and type of military force.

in 1969, more than 600,000 American troops were in theater. While a more plausible strategic rationale was embedded in Cold War politics, debate over the legitimacy of the U.S. military presence in Vietnam continued throughout a war that culminated in the withdrawal of U.S. troops in 1972 and the total collapse of the South Vietnamese government in 1975.[17]

Figure 7.1 presents a hierarchy of statuses that may be accorded veterans, ranging from "stigmatized" to "ignored" to "privileged but superficial" to "privileged and engaged." The axis that figures most prominently into where veterans fall is the relative goodness/badness of their war. A second relevant difference for recent generations of U.S. veterans may be between those wars/eras relying upon a draft versus the AVF.

Veterans of World War II and of the Vietnam conflict are easy to place in the resulting two-dimensional space. Although both wars utilized draft-based militaries, they fall at opposite ends of the good war/bad war distinction. As victors in the prototypical good war, World War II veterans have been characterized generously as the "greatest generation."[18] No such label has been accorded veterans of the wars in Vietnam or Korea, who are stereotypically thought of as "reviled" and "forgotten," respectively.[19] Many accounts have emphasized the uniqueness of the unpleasantries associated with the Korean and Vietnam conflicts. Ironically, World War II, with its broad-based support, victorious culmination, and largesse in veterans' benefits is the exception rather than the rule in our nation's wars.

The cases of Persian Gulf and Afghanistan/Iraq veterans provide interesting comparisons. Both fall within the "privileged" range. The war in the Persian Gulf went very well; once combat started between military forces on the ground, coalition forces led by the United States routed the Iraqi Army in about one hundred hours! Persian Gulf veterans returned home to acclaim in large part because they provided a resounding answer to the question "Can the AVF actually fight and win a war?" Their status however is limited by the extreme brevity of their war. What kind of war, after all, lasts for only a hundred hours in its combat phase?[20] Nevertheless the Persian Gulf War provides a model for the preferred American way of war—a technically proficient, sufficiently amassed U.S. force smashes a near-peer, conventional military swiftly and decisively. Unfortunately, no other wars in our nation's history match this template and none other in the modern era has shaped up this way.

In defiance of the "swift" and "decisive" criteria, the conflicts in Afghanistan and Iraq already have wound on for more than a dozen years with no satisfactory end in sight. Active-duty, reserve, and National Guard units have all been extensively involved, many deploying to the Middle East multiple times. Polls have shown since 2005 that a majority of Americans have agreed that "the U.S. made a mistake in sending troops to Iraq." The percentage saying so reached a high of 63 percent in 2008 and has since declined somewhat to 57 percent in 2014 and 52 percent in 2015. The percentage saying it was a mistake to send troops to Afghanistan rose from 25 percent in 2005 to 49 percent in 2014, decreasing to 42 percent in 2015.[21] While the American public has expressed substantial reservations about the wars themselves, it nevertheless has heaped adulation on their veterans. Perhaps they appreciate the tremendous burdens shouldered by these troops while the vast majority of us have remained insulated from the impacts of what it has taken to wage these wars.

The gap between the sacrifices borne by the nation and U.S. military has not gone unnoticed. In a critique of this situation, U.S. Army officers General Peter Chiarelli and Major Sean Smith wrote that in "current and future conflicts, we must change this. . . . The U.S. as a Nation . . . has not gone to war since 9/11. Indeed, the Departments of Defense and State and the Central Intelligence Agency are at war while the American people and most of the other institutions of national power have gone about their normal business."[22] Wars employing draft-based militaries have plenty of shortcomings but typically have not merited this criticism.

Veterans as Political Constituencies

Veterans not only have attached significance to their veteran-ness but on occasion have formed large, politically influential veterans' organizations. In the nineteenth century, for example, Union army veterans were honored with grand parades at the end of the Civil War—a good war for the North—but the idea of the federal government having some responsibility for those who served in time of war was unpopular in those days.[23] Paying for care and benefits, the argument went, was the equivalent of treating veterans like mercenaries rather than patriots or, worse yet, of putting them on the dole.

Union veterans however expected more than a handshake and pat on the back.[24] More than two million had served in the Union army and there simply were not enough jobs to go around with their sudden return to civilian life. Further, they saw others who not only had *not* served but had prospered in their absence.[25] So when a former field surgeon founded an organization in 1866 for Union veterans—the Grand Army of the Republic (GAR)—it soon had hundreds of local posts and by 1890 almost half a million members.[26]

The GAR was both a fraternal organization (having clandestine initiation ceremonies, secret passwords, and mysterious handshakes) and an advocacy group. It became a formidable political force as its members increasingly voted as a bloc to secure concessions for veterans. Politicians of both parties pandered to the "veteran vote," but the Republican Party became the GAR's favored of the two parties over the issue of veterans' pensions. When key Democrats in the House of Representatives balked at both the idea and costs of such pensions, the GAR successfully targeted them for defeat in their re-election campaigns and Republicans happily filled their seats. By 1885, "veterans' pensions" was the largest single item in the federal budget and accounted for 18 percent of total expenditures.[27]

In the twentieth century, the two major veterans' organizations have been the American Legion and the Veterans of Foreign Wars (VFW). The VFW began as a very small organization in 1899 for veterans of the 17th Infantry Regiment who served in the War of 1898, also known as the Spanish-American War. In 1913, it expanded its eligibility requirements to include any who served in that war (and, later, any "foreign" war). The Legion was founded by a small group of civilians in 1915 *prior* to the entrance of the United States into the First World War, with the goal of encouraging the country to commit troops to that war. The American Expeditionary Force (AEF) joined the fray in 1917. Veterans returned home in 1919 demoralized by the savagery of the war and by their dismal prospects for employment. As after the Civil War, the discharge of almost three million soldiers all at once greatly complicated their employment picture. World War I veterans did receive a $60 mustering-out bonus, but this gesture did little to relieve their plight.

AEF military officers resurrected the Legion, this time as a veterans' organization, but carried with them the traditional "veterans are patriots, not mercenaries" position. Hence the Legion hierarchy was cool to the idea of cash benefits for veterans. Furthermore, both Republicans and Democrats had undergone a change in thinking. The former, a past champion of veterans' pensions, was moving in the direction of fiscal constraint in government programs, and the latter, with the approaching Great Depression, toward economic policies favoring all citizens, not just veterans. Only the VFW supported the ill-fated 1932 march on Washington, DC, by disgruntled veterans who demanded immediate access to a cash bonus payable to them in 1945. "The next war," some said, "if they want me, they'll have to burn the woods and sift the ashes."[28]

All this changed with World War II. As the war in 1944 was grinding into its final stages, there was concern that the separation from service of some sixteen million soldiers, sailors, airmen, and marines would trigger another Great Depression. In anticipation of this, President Franklin Roosevelt, at the instigation of the Legion, proposed a G.I. Bill of Rights. The G.I. Bill would provide stipends allowing veterans to finish high school or attend college and to obtain loans at reduced interest rates for starting a business or buying a home.

The bill had staunch opposition. John Rankin (D-Miss.), a budgetary conservative and chair of the House Committee on Veterans' Affairs, objected that it would be a "boon for the unmotivated," and Dr. Robert Hutchins, president of the University of Chicago, worried that it would turn colleges and universities into "educational hobo jungles."[29] Nonetheless, with the Legion behind it, Congress passed the bill and President Roosevelt signed it into law on June 22, 1944, more than a year before the war's end.

The G.I. Bill, and its ready availability as veterans returned home, was only the first step. The war's end also witnessed an influx of World War II veterans into politics. By 1950, almost 100 members of Congress were veterans and, in 1952, General Dwight D. Eisenhower was elected president. Still, appropriations for veterans' programs moved by fits and starts until Rep. Olin "Tiger" Teague (D-Tex.), himself a World War II veteran, replaced Rep. Rankin in 1955 as chair of the Committee on Veterans' Affairs. Over the next two decades, veterans' legislation flowed freely. A tag-team known informally as the "Iron Triangle"—veterans' organizations led by the Legion and VFW, Teague's House committee, and top officials at the VA—worked hand-in-hand. Initiatives and interference from outside the triangle were not tolerated.

Thus, when Vietnam veterans began returning home during the late 1960s and early 1970s, there already was in place an elaborate network of programs and services. However, the network catered to World War II veterans, who by then had been home from war for more than twenty-five years and whose wants and needs were no longer tightly connected to their wartime service. As such, Vietnam veterans displayed an array of medical and psychological requirements that the VA was not well equipped or inclined to handle, and tensions between the two generations of veterans flared.

One result was that Vietnam veterans in those years avoided the Legion and VFW in droves and sought out their own leaders and remedies. One such leader was Bobby Muller, a former marine lieutenant who was wounded by enemy gunfire and paralyzed from the waist down. Infuriated by the inattentive care he experienced in an overburdened VA hospital, Muller became an angry and articulate spokesperson for Vietnam veterans. In an interview with me, he explained:

> I caught a bullet through the chest, through both lungs, severed the spinal cord, and right out the back.... I should have died on the hill. That kind of wound. Where I got it. I was incredibly lucky.... From the time I was shot, I never cried.

The hospital ship, the naval hospital, [I never cried]. When I got to Kingsbridge [VA] hospital and saw this was the place I was going to be staying, it so over-whelmed me I broke down and cried. My mother broke down and cried. It was overcrowded. It was smelly. It was filthy. It was disgusting.[30]

Muller went on to found an organization, the Vietnam Veterans of America (VVA), with the motto "Never again will one generation of veterans abandon another."[31] The VVA aggressively took on the disconnect between Vietnam vet-erans' needs and available VA services. A thorn in the side of the Iron Triangle and its insider system for getting things done, Muller soon was the recipient of some stern fatherly advice: "They said, look, long after your [special needs] and all its costs . . . , you'll be happy to fall back on . . . the system we've put together. You know, don't break the f*&^# bank, guys. Don't upset the applecart."[32]

Slowly, the VVA and other Vietnam veterans' organizations devoted to spe-cific war-related needs were able to carve out concessions. The biggest of these was the recognition in 1980 of post-traumatic stress disorder and, later, of Agent Orange–related diseases as worthy of treatment and compensation by the DVA. In addition, Vietnam veterans over the years have moved into the Legion and VFW and, with the passing of World War II veterans, come to dominate those traditional organizations. The contentiousness of the process though left many embittered.

The newest waves of veterans from Afghanistan and Iraq have been benefi-ciaries of how this political history has unfolded. As in the post–World War II era, few politicians have questioned the government's responsibility for treating and compensating veterans who have incurred harm or for providing financial assis-tance as a sign of gratitude. The biggest issue often is cost, but the privileged status accorded veterans of Afghanistan and Iraq usually has muted this debate. In addi-tion, the Iron Triangle has faded to a shadow of its former self. Vietnam veterans found solutions by going around it, and these days, introducing veterans' legisla-tion and currying support for it are likely to come from a wider array of sources.

Finally, while Afghanistan/Iraq veterans to date have not joined the Legion or VFW in large numbers, they have gravitated toward their own organiza-tions such as the Iraq and Afghanistan Veterans of America (IAVA). Founded in 2004 by Paul Reichoff, who served as an infantry platoon leader in Iraq, the IAVA's online website reports that 186,000 eligible veterans have logged in to accept free membership.[33]

The Trauma of War

As noted previously, an important marker among veterans is whether or not one served during wartime. An even more prestigious distinction is having experi-enced combat action. The military after all is the prime institution in society, along with police forces, entrusted with the legitimate use of lethal violence.

Not all veterans, even those with wartime service, actually have participated in life-and-death combat encounters. To have been at "the tip of the spear," and to have done so honorably and courageously, is the ultimate in military service.[34]

Military sociologists have advanced the terms "cold" and "hot" to capture the varieties of military service.[35] Cold military organizations are combat units that are in garrison, support units in secure environments in or out of the combat zone, and sections of combat organizations that by the nature of their work always are removed from the fight. A military organization becomes "hot" when warfare or simply dangerous operations become reality. Hence, even service in a combat unit will fluctuate depending upon whether it is in hot or cold space. Similarly, a service occupation—truck driver, for instance—may ordinarily be cold but become a hot one in a combat area where convoys may be ambushed. The 2010 national survey of veterans reports that 33.9 percent of current veterans have served in a war zone and say they have witnessed, or been party to, the deaths or wounding of others.[36]

A way to measure the intensity of combat is through the characteristics of wartime casualties. Table 7.2 contains casualty figures for the wars discussed in this chapter.[37] Militaries commonly note the numbers of battlefield deaths (KIAs, killed-in-action) and of soldiers incurring nonmortal combat wounds (WIAs, wounded-in-action). However, there are three main killers in war—battlefield deaths, disease, and accidents. In the Civil War, for instance, only about a third of the Union and Confederate war deaths were a result of combat (38.5 and 36.4 percent, respectively). The big killer on the battlefield was disease, principally dysentery, diarrhea, and typhoid fever. The same holds for the Spanish-American War, where malaria was widespread. Recent advances in military medicine have improved sanitary conditions so that accidents have now replaced disease as a significant cause of wartime death. For example, in Vietnam, most noncombat deaths were due to accidents of some sort—for instance, fatalities occurring when fuel vapors caused a helicopter to explode upon takeoff or a weapon discharged unexpectedly while being cleaned.

A second important indicator with particular implications for the medical needs of veterans is the ratio of WIA to KIA. In the nineteenth century, if wounded, the good news was that the soldier was alive; the bad news was that he was alive but now a recipient of inadequate or misguided medical care. Hence, the ratio of WIA to KIA in the Civil War (0.61 to 1) is quite low. In the twentieth century, the ratio has risen steadily with advances in how quickly the wounded can be removed from the battlefield and in the quality of medical care in field hospitals. This is notably true for Vietnam and the Wars in Afghanistan and Iraq (5.22 and 7.69 to 1, respectively). One consequence has been an increase in the numbers who have survived a traumatic amputation. It is not unusual these days to encounter veterans who are double or even triple amputees.

A final measure of intensity is to add deaths from all causes to the number of wounded and then divide by the total number of troops in the theater of

Table 7.2.

U.S. War Casualties[a]

War or Conflict	Number in Theater (in millions)	Total Deaths[b]	Battle Deaths (percentage)	Wounds Not Mortal[c]	Ratio of Wounded in Action to Dead	Dead and Wounded out of Total in Theater (percentage)
Civil War	2.213	364,511[d]	38.5%	224,097	0.61-to-1	26.6%
Spanish-American War	0.261	2,446	15.7%	1,662	0.68-to-1	1.6%
World War I	2.300	116,516	45.8%	204,002	1.75-to-1	13.9%
World War II	8.913	405,399	71.9%	670,846	1.65-to-1	12.1%
Korean War	1.789	36,574	92.2%	103,284	3.06-to-1	14.0%
Vietnam conflict	3.403	58,220	81.4%	303,644	5.22-to-1	10.6%
Persian Gulf War	0.695	383	38.6%	467	1.22-to-1	< 0.01%
OEF/OIF[e]	1.900	6,764	78.7%	52,014	7.69-to-1	3.1%

[a] Casualties are for wars discussed in this chapter. Table entries constructed from data in DeBruyne and Leland (see note 37), Tables 1, 6–9, and 12.

[b] The category of total deaths includes those occurring as a result of hostile action (battle deaths), deaths in theater not a result of hostile action (accidental deaths), and deaths as a result of disease.

[c] Nonlethal injuries as a result of hostile action (wounded in action).

[d] Confederate casualties are estimated at 258,000, with 36.4 percent of those classified as battle deaths.

[e] The official military designations for the Wars in Afghanistan and Iraq are Operation Enduring Freedom (OEF) and Operation Iraqi Freedom (OIF), respectively.

combat. Again, the Civil War was especially life-threatening. In fact, it is still the case that more American soldiers died in the Civil War, Union and Confederate, than in all other U.S. wars combined. Adding the numbers of those killed and wounded, about a fourth of the soldiers in the Union army were casualties in that war (26.6 percent). For the world wars, Korea, and Vietnam, the corresponding figures range from 10 to 14 percent and, for Afghanistan and Iraq, about 3 percent.

These casualty figures reflect many variables, including the type of warfare. The Civil War, World Wars I and II, and Korea all featured near-peer militaries locked in combat. Artillery and bombs thus were the major killers in combat. Vietnam was a hybrid war, in which the South Vietnamese Army and U.S. military took on an invading North Vietnamese Army and South Vietnamese civilian insurgents, both of whom engaged in guerrilla warfare. Here small arms fire was the principal cause of combat deaths. In Afghanistan and Iraq, coalition forces have fought insurgent paramilitary groups relying heavily on hit-and-run tactics. Modal combat injuries or deaths for these wars are the result of IEDs—that is, homemade bombs or leftover artillery shells that are detonated remotely or by pressure plates. The associated concussions for those who survive have added a new diagnosis in the veteran lexicon—mild traumatic brain injury (mTBI).

Veterans sometimes are overwhelmed by the stress produced by all this while still in the war zone and/or by the memories of their experiences once returning home. (The same, of course, applies for civilians who live in a war zone, although for them there is no "going home.") Historically there has been debate over what to call such traumatic stress and about exactly why it occurs.[38] In the Civil War, it was often referred to as "soldier's heart," resulting perhaps from the youth of the soldiers or from a lack of "manliness" among them. In World War I, soldiers frequently were bombarded by artillery during trench warfare, so the condition was termed "shell shock." The long duration of the fighting in World War II, and the observation that soldiers often fought bravely for long periods of time before having problems, led to the designation "combat fatigue." Whatever it was called, however, there often were connotations that "real men" did not exhibit such reactions.

Wars often push the limits of medical knowledge and traumatic reactions provide an apt illustration. Physicians and psychiatrists at first did not know what to make of war trauma and early physicians' desk references—manuals listing officially recognized diseases and disorders—had no entry for it. However, the first one after World War II, the *Diagnostic and Statistical Manual-I* (DSM-I) in 1952, did have an entry labeled "gross stress reaction" (GSR). The diagnosis emphasized that any combat-related impairment should cease once the soldier left the war zone. Thus, veterans by definition could not have it (since they were no longer in the military). Still, many VA psychiatrists in the 1950s observed symptoms among their World War II veteran patients they recognized informally as GSR.

The DSM-II came out in 1967 in the midst of the Vietnam War. Strangely, it did not retain GSR or modify its definition to include delayed or chronic dimensions. As best I can tell, the committee in charge of this manual simply removed it without explanation. The committee did recommend classifying veterans who presented traumatic symptoms as having either an adjustment reaction to adult life or a schizophrenic reaction, undifferentiated type. Dr. Art Blank, the VA's director of psychiatry in those days, later described the situation to me as "dysfunctional and bizarre." Neither treatment associated with these diagnoses was appropriate for traumatic stress and, as after World War II, many VA physicians informally developed their own treatment modalities. The situation was rectified only after Vietnam veterans and sympathetic psychiatrists worked to ensure the DSM-III, published in 1980, included an entry for post-traumatic stress disorder (known simply since then as PTSD).[39]

Though the PTSD diagnosis initially was met with skepticism by many VA administrators and U.S. military leaders, these days both are well equipped to proactively address the issue of war trauma. Still, there remains a stigma attached to receiving the diagnosis. There is the worry, even among the veterans themselves, that the problems are "only in their head" and therefore not real. A highly respected military psychiatrist, Dr. Charles Hoge, has sought to dispel such concerns.[40] Relying on his own extensive clinical evidence and a great deal of reputable research evidence, he has carefully laid out the symptoms required for diagnosis, the physiological and psychological bases for the integrity of the diagnosis, and recommended paths for treatment and eventual post-traumatic growth.

Parting Thoughts

A rather unusual memorial is tidily tucked away in a grove of trees more than 12,000 feet above sea level in mountainous southwestern Colorado. Built more than twenty years ago, it is titled simply *Soldierstone*. Unless one knows exactly where to look for it, a person would be unlikely to stumble across it accidentally. A bumpy four-wheel-drive road gives out a quarter mile to the south of its remote high-country location, and the Colorado Trail, a half mile to the west, is suitable only for those on foot, mountain bikes, or dirt bikes. The closest town, Saguache, a small, dusty place that last saw its better days several decades ago, is more than fifteen miles away and several thousand feet lower in altitude.

It is only in the last couple of years that information about *Soldierstone* and its whereabouts have become available on the internet.[41] The inspiration for the memorial came from retired army Lt. Col. Stuart Allen Beckley, a former Special Forces officer from the Vietnam era. In 1990, he approached a granite shop, Ark Valley Memorial in Rocky Ford, Colorado, that specialized in making headstones and other engravings. According to the owner and head stonecutter, Mike Donelson, Beckley had a detailed plan and statement of intent. He wanted to purchase several tons of specially engraved granite blocks for a memorial that would be a tribute "from American soldiers to unremembered friends, . . . forgotten soldiers from Vietnam, Laos, Cambodia, the Hmong, the Montagnard tribes of Central Vietnam, the Koreans, Thais, French, Germans, Slavs, North Africans, Black Africans and others of all religions and persuasions who were willingly or unwillingly expended during the long wars lost in hopes, proud and vain, for the people of Indochina, 1945 to 1975."[42]

The plan called for a ten-foot-tall, four-sided granite obelisk with three of the sides devoted to Vietnam, Cambodia, and Laos and the fourth side to *Soldierstone* inscriptions. In addition, there were to be thirty-six 300-pound, flat granite panels to be placed in a circle up to fifty meters from the obelisk, each devoted to some group of unremembered friends. Finally, Beckley had chosen a spot for the memorial, a secluded place located on National Forest land atop Sargent's Pass high above Saguache. The National Forest Service officially approved the project with assurances from Beckley that he would keep the project "low profile."

Beckley died of cancer in 1995 before the engravings could be completed and the memorial assembled on Sargent's Pass. However, Donelson with the help of others saw the project through to completion. The memorial remained relatively undiscovered until a mountain biker stumbled onto it in 2013 and posted a video of herself walking from obelisk to panel after panel, expressing with each step awe at what she saw. Since then there has been an increase in visitors seeking it out. Its location though keeps the numbers small. I myself have been there twice and once, with a Special Forces comrade, spent the night without seeing any other person for the twenty-four-hour period.

There is no mention of Beckley on the memorial or any inscription specifically explaining his intentions. With its many inscriptions, viewers are left to draw their own meaning. Rio Grande District forest ranger Mike Blakeman offered this observation of those who do come: "It's a place for solace, it's a place for people to spend some time . . . thinking about some of the lost loved ones—people maybe they were [in] Vietnam with, or any of the other wars we've been in."[43]

All the memorial's features are meticulously designed and deeply thought out. So, Lt. Col. Beckley must have given its location equally reflective consideration. Surely he realized its inaccessibility guaranteed that only a handful of people would ever see it. One is left to wonder therefore why he chose such an out-of-the-way location. Had he found special solace while passing through or camping there one night? Did he return there time after time for this purpose? Was he attracted to the area's name, Sargent's Pass?

Perhaps the location's very remoteness had persuaded him. Consider that it clearly is not a Vietnam veterans' memorial, of which by now there are many. It is a memorial that stretches America's Vietnam war memory to include the broader war in Indochina and the many peoples and soldiers, far beyond those from the United States, whose lives were forever affected by it. Maybe Lt. Col. Beckley had learned from broaching this view with others that only a few of us, the survivors of any war, are willing and able to take this step.

Discussion Questions

1. The demographics of the U.S. veteran population figure prominently into who is a veteran and what his or her defining characteristics are. What are some of these characteristics and of what importance are they? How are these affected by our reliance on an All-Volunteer Force?

2. What is it about "being a veteran" that has led so many veterans over the years to form socially and politically active organizations? What do you see as the implications for a veteran population drawn exclusively from an All-Volunteer Force? Do you see this as problematic?

3. Our understanding of trauma associated with warfare has changed over the years. In the past, "soldiers' heart" to "shell shock" to "combat fatigue" implied that war trauma was an abnormal reaction by soldiers to war (some even suggested it was merely a form of "malingering").

Post-traumatic stress reaction (PTSD) on the other hand denotes a normal reaction (trauma) to an abnormal situation (war). It also clearly applies to civilians in the war zone. What are your thoughts about this change and what are its implications for war policy?

Notes

1 Views expressed in this chapter are those of the author and do not necessarily reflect official policies or positions of the U.S. Air Force Academy, U.S. Air Force, U.S. Department of Defense, or U.S. Government.

2 The first federal agency to administer all veterans-related programs, the Veterans Bureau, was created in 1921. It was redesignated the Veterans Administration (VA) in 1929. The VA was elevated to presidential cabinet status in 1989 and renamed the Department of Veterans Affairs (DVA). I will use the term VA for the period 1929–1988 and DVA for the period 1989 and thereafter.

3 U.S. Department of Veterans Affairs, *National Survey of Veterans, Active Duty Members, Demobilized National Guard and Reserve Members, Family Members, and Surviving Spouses* (Rockville, MD: Westat Corporation, 2010), 51–52.

4 Active duty is defined as full-time military status. This includes some service members in reserve units but does not include full-time National Guard duty. Most of those in the reserves and National Guard are called to active duty for a short period of time each year. In times of military necessity, they also may be activated for much longer periods and deployed to combat zones.

5 War was never officially declared by the U.S. Congress during the war in Vietnam—hence the designation "Vietnam Conflict."

6 National WWII Museum, *WWII Veterans Statistics*, 2016, http://www.nationalww2museum.org/honor/wwii-veterans-statistics.html.

7 Department of Veterans Affairs, Office of the Actuary, *Veteran Population Projection Model—VetPop2014*, 2015, Table 1L, http://www.va.gov/vetdata/docs/Demographics/New_Vetpop_Model/VetPop2014Document.pdf.

8 Wilbur J. Scott, *Vietnam Veterans since the War: The Politics of PTSD, Agent Orange, and the National Memorial* (Norman: University of Oklahoma Press, 2004), 106–116. Originally published as *The Politics of Readjustment: Vietnam Veterans since the War* (Hawthorne, NY: Aldine de Gruyter Press, 1993).

9 The only military specialties closed to women were combat-specific slots. The combat-exclusion clause for women was lifted in 2015 by Secretary of Defense Ashton Carter.

10 The percentage varies considerably by branch of the military—currently around 6 percent for the marines, 15 percent for the army and navy, and 22 percent for the air force.

11 National Center for Veterans Analysis and Statistics, *Profile of Women Veterans: 2013*, http://www.va.gov/vetdata/docs/SpecialReports/Women_Veterans_2013.pdf.

12 National Center for Veterans Analysis and Statistics, *2013 Minority Veterans Report*, http://www.va.gov/vetdata/docs/SpecialReports/Minority_Veterans_2013.pdf.

13 Wilbur J. Scott, David R. McCone, and George R. Mastroianni, "Psychological Contracts in Two U.S. Combat Units in Iraq: What Happens When Expectations and Realities Diverge?," *Sociological Focus* 39 (2006): 304–306.

14 Some readers may recognize this refrain is modeled after words from Karl Marx's 1848 *Communist Manifesto*: "Workers of the world, unite ..."

15 David R. Segal, *Recruiting for Uncle Sam: Citizenship and Military Manpower Policy* (Lawrence: University Press of Kansas, 1989).

16 There was debate after the war about the rightness/wrongness of dropping atomic bombs on the essentially civilian populations of Hiroshima and Nagasaki. The Geneva Convention's Law of Armed Conflict (LOAC) is one of the legacies of this debate. LOAC is designed to restrict the violence in warfare as much as possible to combatants. The bombings of cities as occurred in World War II are not legally permissible under LOAC.

17 The Cold War refers to the era of tensions from 1945 to 1990 between the capitalist core nations—the United States, Western Europe, and Japan—and the communist core countries of the Soviet Union and "Red" China. Both the United States and the Soviet Union had massive nuclear arsenals that precluded direct warfare between them. Wars in Korea and Vietnam thus were viewed as "proxy wars" between the United States and the Soviet Union/Red China.

18 Thomas Brokaw, *The Greatest Generation* (New York: Random House Paperbacks, 2001).

19 Joel Osler Brende and Edwin Randolph Parson, *Vietnam Veterans: The Road to Recovery* (New York: Plenum Press, 1985), chap. 3; Richard Severo and Lewis Milford, *The Wages of War, When Soldiers Come Home—From Valley Forge to Vietnam* (New York: Simon and Schuster, 1989), chap. 7.

20 The brevity of the war should not detract from the gravity of the fact that 383 Americans died during the 1990–1991 war.

21 Andrew Dugan, "Fewer in U.S. View Iraq, Afghanistan Wars as Mistakes," *Gallup*, June 12, 2015, http://www.gallup.com/poll/183575/fewer-view-iraq-afghanistan-wars-mistakes.aspx.

22 Peter W. Chiarelli and Sean W. Smith, "Learning from Our Modern Wars: Imperatives of Preparing for a Dangerous Future," *Military Review* (September/October 2007): 38.

23 Severo and Milford, *Wages of War*, 128–134.

24 Union veterans did receive a one-time $250 payment at the end of the war that was to make up for missed monthly paychecks during the war plus a small bonus. They were also entitled to $75 if they lost a leg and $50 for a lost arm (or they could opt for an artificial limb in lieu of the money). Detractors noted there were plenty of "charlatans and harlots" eager to help them spend their severance and disability payments.

25 The Union army relied upon a draft. However, if drafted, a man did not have to be inducted if he could find someone else to go in his place. Hence, men of means often paid substitutes to serve for them, a practice that skewed the class composition of the army. Incidentally, my great-grandfather served in the Union army with the 4th Indiana Regiment (though he had never set foot in Indiana). According to family lore, he was paid $50 to do so by a gentleman who approached him at Ellis Island in New York City shortly after he arrived as an immigrant from Germany.

26 Former Confederate soldiers formed an organization in 1889, the United Confederate Veterans. The UCV consolidated a number of smaller local groups into a single organization. Its stated purpose was social and fraternal rather than political, but activities such as honoring the Confederacy and Confederate war dead often took on political dimensions.

27 Severo and Milford, *Wages of War*, 176–179.

28 Brende and Parson, *Road to Recovery*, 86.

29 Severo and Milford, *Wages of War*, 286–290.

30 Qtd. in Scott, *Vietnam Veterans since the War*, 95–96.

31 The VVA became the only organization exclusively for Vietnam veterans recognized by Congress. Unlike traditional veterans' organizations, the VVA opened its membership to both Vietnam veterans and their family members.

32 Qtd. in Scott, *Vietnam Veterans since the War*, 114.

33 *Iraq and Afghanistan Veterans of America*, http://iava.org/.

34 The term "tip of the spear" has a different meaning in today's irregular wars. For an analysis, see Wilbur J. Scott, David R. McCone, Robert J. Jackson, Lisa Sayegh, and Joe Don Looney, "The 'Tip of the Spear' Revisited: Evidence from Recent Deployments of U.S. National Guard Troops to Iraq and Afghanistan," *Military Behavioral Health* 1 (2013): 59–67.

35 Joseph L. Soeters, Donna J. Winslow, and Alise Weibull, "Military Culture," in *Handbook of the Sociology of the Military*, ed. Guiseppe Carfario (New York: Kluwer Academic/Plenum Publishers, 2006), 237–254.

36 U.S. Department of Veterans Affairs, *National Survey of Veterans*, 62.

37 Nese E. DeBruyne and Anne Leland, *American War and Military Operations Casualties: Lists and Statistics* (Washington, DC: Congressional Research Service, 2015).

38 Brende and Parson, *Road to Recovery*, chap. 4.

39 Scott, *Vietnam Veterans since the War*, 57–71.

40 Charles W. Hoge, *Once a Warrior, Always a Warrior: Navigating the Transition from Combat to Home—Including Combat Stress, PTSD, and mTBI* (Guilford, CN: Globe Pequot Press, 2010).

41 Grace Hood, *Soldierstone*, http://hiddencolorado.kunc.org/soldierstone/.

42 Ibid.

43 Ibid.

Further Reading

Charles W. Hoge. *Once a Warrior, Always a Warrior: Navigating the Transition from Combat to Home—Including Combat Stress, PTSD, and mTBI*. Guilford, CN: Globe Pequot Press, 2010.

Lewis Milford. *The Wages of War, When Soldiers Come Home—From Valley Forge to Vietnam*. New York: Simon and Schuster, 1989.

Wilbur J. Scott. *Vietnam Veterans since the War: The Politics of PTSD, Agent Orange, and the National Memorial*. Norman: University of Oklahoma Press, 2004.

8

War, Persecution, and Displacement

U.S. Refugee Policy since 1945

JANA K. LIPMAN

Who is a refugee? Do men and women fleeing persecution have a greater right to resettlement in the United States than other migrants? And, if so, how does one define "persecution"? Is a Jewish woman fleeing Nazi Germany in 1939 a refugee? How about a Cuban businessman living in Havana in 1959? Is a Haitian worker who opposed the Duvalier government in the 1970s a refugee? A twenty-first-century Honduran teenager who fears gang warfare in her local community? And how does the United States define the thousands of individuals in Iraq, Afghanistan, and Syria who have been displaced by contemporary wars in the Middle East?

These questions have been at the heart of this country's refugee policy since 1945, and they continue to be salient in contemporary debates over refugee resettlement in the United States. "Refugee" implies that the individual at hand faces persecution or violence and deserves just what the term implies—refuge and its protection.

Deciding who is and who is not a refugee has been anything but straightforward over the past century. Moreover, the answers have not been static, but rather refugee policy has changed over time, in response to U.S. Cold War ideology, massive movements of people, crises on borders, and post-9/11 security concerns.

Wars have always caused violence, destruction, and displacement for combatants *and* for civilian populations. However, as historian Peter Gatrell has argued, World War II marked a watershed in "the making of the modern refugee," which he defined not only by unprecedented displacement but also the development of the United Nations High Commissioner for Refugees (UNHCR), the proliferation of nonprofit relief agencies, and "the refugee regime," which sought to create a legal international framework defining and governing refugees.[1] According to the 1951 UNHCR definition, a refugee is an individual who has a "well-founded fear of being persecuted for reasons of race, religion, nationality, membership of a particular social group or political opinion." The UNHCR and nongovernmental agencies that work with refugees also generally identify themselves as neutral humanitarian organizations that provide protection outside political considerations. While this ideal is rarely met in practice, the United States generally did not even aspire to it. Throughout much of the twentieth century, refugee policy was intimately tied to Cold War politics and immigration restriction. The United States defined most refugee claims through the prism of anticommunism, and as a result, those fleeing communist countries were most likely to be admitted. This practice slowly shifted after 1980, and by the turn of the twenty-first century, the country routinely accepted tens of thousands of migrants per year as refugees. Still, politics and U.S. interests routinely played a role. Immigration historian Roger Daniels estimates that since 1945, the United States has accepted approximately four million migrants under a range of refugee provisions.[2] However, debates over immigration, security, and political interests still define who gains refugee status and who does not.

U.S. refugee policy changed significantly from World War II through the early twenty-first century. By including select "case studies," readers can connect individuals' personal stories with changing political landscapes and resettlement policies. These stories also illustrate the complexity of individuals' lives and histories that do not always fit a simple definition. There are multiple themes that recur, even as refugee policy itself changed and adapted over time—for example, the intersection of U.S. immigration policy with treatment of refugees. Until 1980, the United States did not have a separate policy governing "refugees," and so the executive branch repeatedly admitted large numbers of individuals on its own authority as "parolees." In addition, the U.S. government often designated certain national groups as having strong claims to refugee status while rejecting other national groups as being primarily "economic migrants" or "illegal aliens." This slippage between "refugee," "immigrant," and "illegal alien" privileged certain national groups and underscored the political nature of refugee policy.

Another theme involves racial politics, which became increasingly intertwined with refugee policies throughout the twentieth century. At first, the United States only imagined refugees as being white Europeans fleeing the Iron Curtain, but as the century progressed, those claiming refugee status were far more likely to be Cubans, Vietnamese, Haitians, Central Americans, and Middle Easterners. The fact that after the 1950s, most refugees either had tenuous claims on whiteness, such as Cubans, or were of Asian, Latin American, Middle Eastern, or African descent meant that American racial politics and legacies of discrimination intersected with refugee policy.

There were multiple contradictions in the U.S. media and government's representation of refugees. The dominant iconography represented refugees as undifferentiated, apolitical, helpless victims, needing American support and shelter. This visual image erased the political and military backgrounds of many of these individuals and was meant to generate sympathy and support in the broader population. However, at other times, refugees were positioned as untrustworthy, possibly criminal aliens. While this duality was not unique to the United States, it created a contradictory image of the refugee as both a possible victim and a threat.

Another intersection involved U.S. military engagements in Southeast Asia, Latin America, and later the Middle East, to which a disproportionate number of refugees directly owed their status. Individuals fleeing Cuba, Vietnam, and Iraq were often refugees because of their previous ties to U.S.-backed governments and policies. As a counterpoint, El Salvadorans, Haitians, and Guatemalans often found their lives at risk and sought refuge in the United States *because* of U.S.-backed authoritarian governments which terrorized local communities. In both cases, U.S. military aid and power often created the environment for what became refugee crises.

In dealing with these complicated crosscurrents, the United States developed a refugee resettlement bureaucracy that drew on both government support and voluntary agencies' expertise. By the twenty-first century, refugees entering the United States benefited from the domestic services that grew throughout the Cold War—namely, rights to education, employment, and public benefits for at least their initial resettlement period.

Case Study

Regina Kesler was a Polish Jew, who like tens of thousands of others fled to the Soviet Union with her family during World War II to escape the Nazi occupation. These families and individuals were not imprisoned in Nazi concentration camps but rather survived the war in the Soviet Union. Although often faced with physical deprivation, hard labor, bitter cold, and hunger, they did not face systematic execution or life in a concentration camp. As such, they fell outside the now-common understanding of a Holocaust survivor. After the war Regina and her family returned to Poland with the help of the United Nations. Kesler recalled that their Polish neighbors resented their renewed presence in the community: they "thought we had died and would never return." Antisemitism remained central to postwar Polish politics, and Kesler and her family left again, this time to Sweden and then the United States.[3]

Was Regina a refugee?

Displaced Persons and the Origins of U.S. Refugee Policy

Population displacement due to war of course is nothing new. In the U.S. context, one could potentially use the rubric of "refugees" to understand a broad range of populations, from French and creole planters in Saint Domingue who fled to Louisiana after the Haitian Revolution to American Indians chased west by U.S. military forces to former African American slaves who sought safety in Union camps during the Civil War. For the twentieth century, scholars point to World War I and the collapse of the Ottoman Empire as watershed moments. Along with brutal casualties, the war generated 1.5 million refugees on the Western Front alone as well as massive upheaval in Russia; the Armenian genocide led to close to 250,000 Armenians fleeing to Russia.[4] The end of World War I also marked the emergence of new institutions, such as the League of Nations and its first High Commissioner for Refugees in 1921 and the expansion of the International Committee of the Red Cross's scope to include refugee relief.[5] However, the League of Nations defined a "refugee" quite narrowly in response to the Armenian genocide and the Russian revolution, as a "Russian" or "Armenian" who no longer had "protection of the government."[6] During this era, the United States failed to join the League of Nations, and fears of domestic radicalism during World War I created an impetus for immigration restriction. The 1924 Immigration Act was a victory for exclusionists who for decades had been advocating closing U.S. ports to new migrants. The act established nation-based quotas for the first time, which intentionally limited immigration from southern and eastern European countries.

With the rising power of Nazi Germany in the 1930s, the United States confronted its first major twentieth-century refugee crisis with general, and well-documented, inaction. The United States did not have a separate refugee policy at this time, and therefore, Jews and other Europeans fleeing Nazi Germany had to apply for the scarce spaces designated in the 1924 immigration law. The United States did admit approximately 150,000 Europeans through various channels during the 1930s and 1940s, but these numbers paled in comparison to both the acute need and the high immigration rates in the early twentieth century.[7] Select intellectuals, scientists, and artists such as Marc Chagall and Hannah Arendt managed to gain entry into the United States, but cases like these were few and far between and involved bureaucratic innovation and diplomatic maneuvering outside State Department protocols. For those who lacked resources, connections, or luck, the U.S. State Department routinely denied visa requests and created multiple obstacles to Jewish applicants. In fact, the United States did not even fill its German immigration quota during the 1930s, largely due to anti-Semitism and heightened concerns over "security."[8] Most famously, the United States refused entry to 933 Jews on a German ship, the *St. Louis*, even though a majority of the passengers had started the visa application process in Europe. The individuals on the *St. Louis* were not allowed to disembark in Cuba, their intended first port, or the United States, and instead sailed past Florida and returned to Europe, after which 254 did not survive the war.[9]

At the end of World War II, the U.S. State Department estimated that there were at least twenty to thirty million displaced persons in Europe alone.[10] The United Nations set up numerous camps for displaced persons (DPs) in Germany, Italy, and Austria.[11] DPs included Germans and eastern Europeans, along with Jewish survivors of the war. Recognizing that the unprecedented numbers of DPs could lead to political instability, President Harry Truman supported the 1948 Displaced Persons Act, the first U.S. legislation that prioritized accepting Europeans who had been "victims of nazi or fascist regimes."[12] This legislation also found advocates among mainline Protestant, Catholic, and Jewish organizations who wanted the United States to welcome the war's victims. Between 1948 and 1952, the United States accepted 400,000 DPs, although the law continued to minimize the number of Jewish DPs granted U.S. visas. In total, only 63,000 of the DPs admitted into the United States were categorized as "Jewish."[13] The program was generally recognized as a success by both the U.S. government and the legislation's advocates, and former DPs settled throughout the United States. The DP legislation also set a precedent of delegating resettlement services to voluntary organizations such as the National Catholic Welfare Council, Church World Services, the National Lutheran Council, and the Jewish-affiliated Hebrew Immigrant Aid Society.[14]

The postwar era also saw the emergence of new international organizations, which were charged with defining, managing, protecting, and resettling refugees. First came UNRRA (the UN Relief and Rehabilitation Agency), followed by the International Refugee Organization (IRO), and finally the UN High Commissioner for Refugees (UNHCR). Although the UNHCR was relatively weak and underfunded at its inception in 1950, the 1951 UNHCR Convention's definition of "refugee" remains the guiding international legal framework for refugee claims. There is a formal universalism in the UNHCR language, and the definition focused on individual persecution and included an underlining assumption of anticommunism.[15] While a key player in shaping the parameters of the UNHCR, the United States did not sign the 1951 convention. Instead, the United States viewed the politics of refugees almost exclusively through the lens of the Cold War.

Case Study

A young Vietnamese girl was born in the northern part of South Vietnam. Her father was a security guard for the American consulate. She, her mother, and her siblings lived apart from her father in a small village some distance away with a community of Vietnamese Catholics. She experienced the war directly, and bullets flew through her window, forcing her family to relocate. As the North Vietnamese Army advanced south, her family fled to Saigon. She remembered her older sister picking her up from the second grade. As a young child, she did not realize the danger or rupture in her life, and instead recalls being excited at leaving school early and "going on a vacation." Her brother stayed behind and died in a firefight with the North Vietnamese forces. The rest of the family was able to reunite with her father and together they walked toward Saigon on foot. She wrote that there were people everywhere trying to escape. There was a sense of fear in the air: "They all knew that they would have no future once the Communists took over the Country. They would be jailed and even executed."

Her father's work for the Americans made them all worried. Her family was able to make it onto a U.S. cargo plane on April 28, 1975, two days before the fall of Saigon. The young girl remembers a brief stay in Guam and Camp Pendleton in California before relocating to Oregon under the sponsorship of a Catholic church. "Even though I have been in the United States for thirteen years, I still keep my Vietnamese heritage inside me. I know I always will. No matter what the hardships I encounter, I shall always remember the saying, 'A journey of a thousand miles begins with a single step.'"[16]

Was this girl a refugee?

Cold War Refugees: Hungarians, Cubans, and Vietnamese

During the Cold War, the United States defined "refugees" as those individuals fleeing communist countries. The Cold War was central to U.S. refugee policy. The optics of a person rejecting the Soviet Union, or later other communist countries, and seeking "refuge" in the West provided the United States with an ideological "win" against communism on the world stage. The 1953 Refugee Relief Act created new nonquota spaces for 209,000 "escapees" or "refugees," whom legislators imagined as Europeans who had rejected the communist world.[17] In practice, there was also a great deal of suspicion of possible "escapees." These individuals had to face rigorous security evaluations and could not have a communist affiliation in their past. Given that many were trying to leave communist countries, this ideological purity was often impossible to prove and, in practice, an anomaly as Communist Party membership was often a prerequisite for educational and professional opportunities behind the Iron Curtain. A veneer of suspicion remained that potential refugees might in fact be communists attempting to infiltrate the United States. As a result, despite U.S. Cold War rhetoric, the United States admitted relatively few people as "escapees" and both the language of rescue and security marked the representation of many refugees.

The U.S. response to the 1956 Hungarian Revolution established several new precedents for U.S. refugee policy. In 1956, intellectuals and students challenged Hungary's Stalinist government and pressed for internal reforms and greater autonomy from the Soviet Union. The protesters occupied a broad ideological range, from reformers who wanted to maintain socialism to critics of the communist state who wanted a complete break with the Soviet bloc. The Soviets feared the fracturing of their power in Europe, and when the Hungarian leadership declared its neutrality in the Cold War, the USSR ordered troops to reassert Communist Party and Soviet control in Hungary.[18] Thousands of individuals fled across Hungary's borders, with approximately 180,000 people entering Austria and an additional 20,000 crossing into Yugoslavia. Notably, most of these Hungarians would not have met the UN's definition of a "refugee," as few faced immediate personal persecution or threat.[19] The vast majority saw an opportunity to leave Hungary and its depressed economy, and they sought a new life in the West. While this did not necessarily coincide with the UN's definition, the United States along with Western Europe defined these men and women as anticommunist actors and refugees deserving of aid and support.

Between 1956 and early 1957, the United States accepted 38,000 Hungarians, and this decision cemented "refugees" in the American imagination and public policy as white, anticommunist Europeans. President Eisenhower used a loophole in the McCarren-Walter Act of 1952 to allow the Hungarians to enter as "parolees," shifting authority away from Congress and toward the executive branch. This increased the power of the executive and allowed the U.S. government to act outside the limited quotas outlined in the 1924 Immigration Act. The United States also eschewed the stringent security measures of the early 1950s; the screening process for Hungarians applying for U.S. entry in Austria was superficial and swift. In many ways, Eisenhower used this refugee program to compensate for the lack of U.S. military support for Hungary's revolutionaries. Despite pressure to respond to the Soviet crackdown in Hungary and champion the revolutionaries, the president did not want to risk American lives or escalate the confrontation with the Soviet Union. As a result, while the United States was unwilling to confront the Soviet Union in central Europe, it was willing to save Hungarian refugees and resettle them in America.

Most of the Hungarians first went to a makeshift refugee camp at Camp Kilmer, a defunct U.S. Army base in New Jersey. The U.S. government again relied on a combination of federal dollars and infrastructure alongside voluntary organizations to help resettle these individuals, who were refugees in all but formal legal status. As part of the process, historian Carl Bon Tempo argues that the U.S. government proactively "sold" the Hungarians to the American public as an easily assimilated population, emphasizing traditional gender roles and consumer culture, with well-placed profiles of the Hungarians in *Time, Life,* and *Reader's Digest.*[20] In 1958, Congress passed legislation enabling Hungarians to start the process of applying for U.S. citizenship. In contrast, historian Madeline Hsu notes the greater U.S. reluctance to accept Chinese nationals in the wake of the Chinese Revolution; however, Cold War ideological imperatives did give Chinese intellectuals and professionals a foothold in the United States via the Refugee Relief Act and the president's parole authority. She argues that by admitting a small sliver of the more than 1.5 million refugees in Hong Kong, the United States could promote its liberal credentials and select for the most educated, trained, and ideologically aligned Chinese migrants. In total, the United States accepted roughly 10,000 Chinese via these programs between 1944 and 1960.[21]

The U.S. response to the Hungarian Revolution was a turning point for four reasons. First, the use of the "parole" loophole enabled presidents to admit large numbers of people into the United States, circumventing the restrictionist U.S. immigration laws and Congress in the name of anticommunism. Second, it used the policy and rhetoric of "rescue" to demonstrate its Cold War credentials, particularly when it was unwilling to commit military and political resources abroad. Third, it decreased the scrutiny of individual applicants by simplifying complicated political realities and defining entire national groups as "anticommunist." Finally, it relied on a mix of government and nonprofit agencies to assist with resettlement.

Many of these patterns would repeat themselves with U.S. policies toward Cubans and Vietnamese. The United States staked much of its Cold War credibility on its isolation of Cuba and its military support for South Vietnam. As these military, economic, and political endeavors failed to topple communist governments, the United States developed ad hoc refugee policies to compensate for the failure of its political and military campaigns. Again, we see the use of parole, the emphasis on and assumption of "anticommunism," and the public rhetoric of "rescue." However, Cubans and Vietnamese also posed new challenges for the United States; their numbers far exceeded the Hungarians and their migration was ongoing, rather than a brief one-time affair. These migrants also disrupted the vision of refugees as white and European, and they brought large Latino and Asian populations into the United States. Once in the United States, Cubans and Vietnamese developed organized and effective lobbying groups which became bases for local political power.

The Cuban Revolution followed the Hungarian Revolution by just three years. The revolutionary 26th of July Movement led by Fidel Castro famously challenged, outwitted, and outmaneuvered the U.S.-backed government of Fulgencio Batista, and Batista himself fled the island on January 1, 1959. Although the 26th of July Movement was not immediately identified with communism or the Soviet Union, it clearly challenged the status quo, and wealthy Cubans began to leave Cuba for the United States in the early months of 1959.

Between 1959 and 1962, approximately 250,000 Cubans left the country. The majority of them resettled in the continental United States, although many Cubans also relocated to Spain, Mexico, and Puerto Rico.[22] Most of these Cubans came from wealthy to upper-middle-class backgrounds and identified as white (although their racial status would be more complicated because of language and nationality in the United States). At this point, there were still regular commercial flights between the two countries, and Castro did not oppose the exit of a population which he saw as a threat to his revolution.

As he had done for the Hungarians, President Eisenhower paroled the Cubans into the United States outside of U.S. immigration law and practice. According to historian Maria Cristina García, the Cubans saw themselves as "exiles" waiting to return and reclaim their country, and U.S. policy initially mirrored this idea, assuming Cubans would remain in the United States only until the Castro regime had been overthrown.[23] Like the Hungarians, and unlike earlier programs for Eastern Europeans, Cubans were not subjected to intensive screening or background checks; their presence in the United States was deemed de facto evidence for their desire to live outside a communist country. These individuals did not have to prove an individual "fear of persecution" or meet the UNHCR's stricter definition; rather, the United States viewed all Cubans entering the United States favorably as ideological allies worthy of aid and resettlement. As long as Cubans were willing to proclaim their current anticommunism, officials deemed them eligible for entry.[24] Moreover, the U.S. government along with the Catholic Church also provided services to this new population, which included direct cash assistance, health care, job training, ESL classes, and other social service support.[25] In addition, because most of these Cubans were from Cuba's upper classes, they were disproportionately white despite Cuba's multiracial population, and this also increased their acceptability as future Americans.

Cuban children also emerged as a visible and vulnerable population needing to be saved from communism and revolution. Operation Peter Pan, a program whereby the U.S. government and the Catholic Church worked together to acquire visas and flights for more than 14,000 unaccompanied Cuban children, became particularly symbolic for both Cuba and the United States. This program arguably rescued Cuban youth from a communist education and military service, and they were resettled in a range of foster care settings.[26] This program elevated the humanitarian nature of U.S. resettlement policy and the children themselves became symbols of U.S. benevolence and hope. Carlos Eire's memoir, *Waiting for Snow in Havana: Confessions of a Cuban Boy*, expresses both the pain and hope of the rupture between his childhood in Cuba and his coming of age in the United States. In contrast, the Cuban government viewed this program as institutionalized kidnapping, and it is still a common trope in the state-run media's critique of U.S. refugee policy for Cubans.

The U.S. government eventually recognized that the "exiles" in South Florida were becoming a permanent population. Although the United States had attempted to overthrow Castro with CIA-backed exiles, the result was disaster and humiliation, and Castro's army trounced the exiles at the Bay of Pigs in 1961. While Fidel Castro consolidated his power in the early 1960s, thousands of Cuban men and women continued to leave Cuba and resettle in the United States. In 1965, the U.S. provided daily "Freedom Flights" between Varadero, Cuba, and Miami for thousands of Cubans, and in 1966, Congress passed the Cuban Adjustment Act. This enabled any Cuban who arrived in the United

States to regularize his or her nebulous immigration status and become a permanent resident in just two years. The Cuban Adjustment Act was a singular piece of legislation. In this way, U.S. policy toward Cubans was exceptional, and it has endured throughout the century, only changing with Barack Obama's normalization of relations with Cuba in 2017.

The mid-1960s marked two other significant legal changes. First, the United States passed the 1965 Immigration Act, which overturned the 1924 law, eradicating national quotas and creating a system based on professional skills and family reunification. Unintentionally, this legislation opened the doors for far more legal migration from Latin America and East Asia. Second, the United States also signed the 1967 UNHCR Protocol Relating to the Status of Refugees. Although historians Gil Loescher and John Scanlan argue that the ratification of this protocol was largely symbolic, it did place the United States within the international framework for the first time.

The 1960s also saw the escalation of the U.S. War in Vietnam. This brutal war caused high casualties and displacement within Vietnam for more than a decade. The eventual U.S. loss and abandonment of South Vietnam became etched in popular memory through the images of helicopters lifting off rooftops and former Vietnamese allies clamoring to be rescued. In 1975, the United States admitted over 130,000 Vietnamese, the majority of whom had been in the South Vietnamese military or had connections to the U.S. government. This sudden crisis resembled the mass entry of Hungarians and Cubans. The United States envisioned all of the Vietnamese, as it had those earlier nationalities, as refugees, because they were fleeing a communist government. Unlike the Hungarian or Cuban crises, however, the United States was not just providing refuge to anticommunist migrants; in this case, the U.S. War in Vietnam was the key catalyst which had created this large influx of refugees.

There were also clear distinctions in the programs and reception for the Vietnamese. First and foremost was the war itself. United States advisors had supported the South Vietnamese government since its inception in 1954 and U.S. troops engaged in active warfare between 1964 and 1973. The United States had staked its military and political credibility on supporting the South Vietnamese government, and its rapid collapse signaled U.S. weakness and loss on the world stage. The Vietnam War marked a major turning point in the twentieth century, one that indicated the limits on U.S. global power. As partial compensation for this failure, the government and military argued that the country had a responsibility toward their former Vietnamese allies. Many military, CIA, State Department, and other government agencies had direct ties to these individuals and sought to sponsor specific friends and colleagues.[27] South Vietnamese military personnel and government officials saw their identities transform from allies into refugees almost overnight. As scholar Yen Le Espiritu argues, the United States sought to erase the horrors of the war and hoped that the rescue mission of Vietnamese refugees might recast the country in a more benevolent and humanitarian light.[28] Newspapers across the country depicted the Vietnamese migrants as apolitical, with many photojournalists snapping shots of U.S. politicians with Vietnamese children and highlighting July 4th activities in resettlement camps.[29]

In April 1975, President Gerald Ford established the Inter-Agency Task Force (IATF), which organized the transferal and resettlement of this first generation of Vietnamese refugees. Again, as in the case of the Hungarians, the federal government admitted Vietnamese as "parolees," outside immigration legislation, and not as "refugees." The IATF sent Vietnamese to U.S. military bases in Arkansas, California, Pennsylvania, and Wisconsin, where they took English classes and waited for sponsors, often affiliated with religious voluntary agencies, which would assist them with housing, job placement, and cultural adjustment. Unlike the Cuban program, which focused on Florida, the U.S. government did not want the Vietnamese to establish a singular strong community, as the Cubans had in Miami. Instead, the goal was to settle Vietnamese through individual, rather than group, sponsorships, presumably to reduce the economic burden on any one city or state. However, the Vietnamese soon upended this plan. Like refugees before them, they exercised agency and sought to shape their lives on their own terms. Many reconnected with family and friends, leading to large Vietnamese communities in Orange County, northern Virginia, Houston, and New Orleans.

Unlike the Hungarians and the Cubans, the Vietnamese were the first major refugee population that was decidedly nonwhite. Many Americans resented the presence of Vietnamese refugees in their communities and worried that the United States had fought the Vietnamese as adversaries only to end up with them as neighbors. In seeing all Vietnamese as "the enemy," these Americans did not recognize that most Vietnamese entering the country had been U.S. allies. There was also a xenophobic racism against Vietnamese that built on longstanding anti-Asian politics. Finally, the economic recession in the 1970s led to resentment that federal aid was going to Vietnamese rather than to programs that would benefit U.S. citizens.

Despite this popular critique, the United States government continued to articulate bipartisan support for Vietnamese refugee resettlement. The world community, in turn, also saw the resettlement of Vietnamese as being the fiscal, political, and often moral responsibility of the United States. Although the initial 130,000 Vietnamese were resettled with relative efficiency and success, it was just the beginning of the so-called "boat people crisis" in Southeast Asia. Between 1978 and 1980, more than 350,000 Indochinese left Vietnam, Cambodia, and Laos by boat and by land, and they found themselves seeking asylum in refugee camps in Thailand, Indonesia, Malaysia, the Philippines, and Hong Kong. This exodus continued throughout the 1980s. Again, the UNHCR, the Southeast Asian nations, and the Vietnamese themselves believed the United States had a unique and leading role to play in resolving this crisis. By 1995, the

United States had accepted close to one million Vietnamese who were resettled through voluntary agencies.

The Hungarian, Cuban, and Vietnamese cases collectively defined "refugee" in the United States as those fleeing communism. Although screening increased for Vietnamese boat people after 1989, for most of this era, nationality and anti-communism shaped refugee policy. In addition, the executive branch found flexibility in its parole power, and it acted in response to crises and outside of U.S. immigration law.

Case Study

In 1981, Joseph Denis, a Haitian man who feared the local security forces, decided to seek refuge in the United States. Denis reported that a government police officer had asked to graze his oxen on Denis's land, and when Denis objected and said no, the officer arrested him. Although he was released without charges days later, his house burned down. "It was threatening for me. . . . So I sold some oxen, put the money away and paid for my trip here, $85. I was scared to leave because I was told it was a long dangerous trip, but I could not stay in Haiti anymore." Like many thousands of Haitians, he took his chances in a small boat and, with sixty-one other people, navigated toward Florida. On reaching U.S. shores, the federal government detained Denis at the Krome Detention Center. He was shocked to be imprisoned and became suicidal at times. "I have heard there are Americans who resent my coming here. . . . But to them I say, I cannot go back to Haiti. Don't send me back to Haiti."[30]

Is Denis a refugee?

1980 Refugee Act, the Reagan Administration, and the End of the Cold War

During the 1970s, the ad hoc nature of Vietnamese, Cambodian, and Laotian migration prompted Congress to regularize its policies and reassert its own authority. The 1970s also marked the rise of human rights rhetoric across the political spectrum, and it was a hallmark of President Jimmy Carter's administration. Both liberal and conservative members of Congress saw calls to human rights as beneficial, with liberal-leaning politicians condemning right-wing authoritarian governments, such as Chile and Indonesia, and conservative congressmen denouncing human rights violations in the Soviet Union.[31]

The result was the 1980 Refugee Act championed by Senator Edward Kennedy and Congresswoman Elizabeth Holtzman. President Carter signed the bill into law on March 17, 1980.[32] The law defined a "refugee" in line with the UNHCR's definition for the first time. At least on paper, the United States no longer defined refugees as only those fleeing communist governments but recognized any individual with a "well-founded fear of persecution on account of race, religion, nationality, membership in a particular social group or political opinion." The aim was to codify a more neutral ideological practice and include individuals who might face persecution from a noncommunist yet brutal political regime. However, the law set a ceiling of 50,000 refugees per year, although the president would still be able to parole individuals into the United States if there were "compelling reasons in the public interest."[33] Finally, it provided a clearer mechanism through which individuals *within* the United States could apply for asylum. Potential refugees outside of U.S. borders would apply to enter the United States—at a U.S. embassy or in a refugee camp. An individual already in the United States, whether legally or illegally, was now able to petition for asylum and permanent residence based on a credible fear of persecution in his or her home country. This provision eventually became far more important than its authors anticipated.

Despite congressional intentions, however, it soon became clear that legislation could not predict the crises that would create mass numbers of refugees. In 1980, a half dozen Cubans intentionally crashed the gates of the Peruvian Embassy, and when word got out that the embassy was sheltering those who claimed asylum, 10,000 more Cubans stormed the area. While this could have been a moment in which Fidel Castro and the Cuban state were forced to grapple with their waning legitimacy, Castro flamboyantly turned the tables and managed to refashion internal dissent into a refugee crisis for the United States by opening the port of Mariel, approximately twenty-five miles west of Havana, and allowing what became called the Mariel boatlift. Cuban Americans mobilized and ferried more than 100,000 Cubans in small boats from Mariel to Miami. In order to delegitimize the migrants' rejection of Cuba and the political challenge to his government, Castro also opened Cuba's jails and mental hospitals and brought these individuals to Mariel as well. Cuban Americans who came to rescue their relatives were compelled to take many Cubans they didn't know. In this way, Castro branded all of the Cubans leaving as *escoria*, or scum—unwanted, criminal, and deviant.[34]

The Mariel boatlift overran the recently signed Refugee Act, which allowed for only 50,000 refugees a year and required a careful screening and processing system outside U.S. borders. It underscored the inability of legislation to predict the nature or timing of refugee crises. Notably, the Carter administration did not admit the Cubans as "refugees." Instead of following in Eisenhower and Ford's footsteps and admitting them as "parolees," the government created yet another new legal category: "Cuban-Haitian entrant (status pending)."

Technically "entrants" and not refugees, the Mariel Cubans faced prejudice in both the American media and the Cuban American community. Because of Castro's dramatic language and the inclusion of former prisoners, *marielitos* were often imagined as mostly criminals, an image solidified in popular culture by Al Pacino's portrayal of gangster Tony Montana in *Scarface* (1983). In addition, the Mariel population was younger, with more males, and included a much-higher proportion of black Cubans than earlier generations. According to Maria Cristina García, anywhere from 15 to 40 percent of *marielitos* would be seen as "black" in the United States, compared to only 3 percent of the pre-1980 Cuban American community.[35] In practice, a sizeable proportion of the Cuban *marielitos*, approximately 26,000, did have criminal records, but the vast majority were for "political" crimes—that is, black market dealings or because they were identified as "sexual deviants" or homosexuals.[36] While most found sponsors, gained access to federal benefits, and eventually settled in Florida, the media continued to represent them differently from the older, and presumably more assimilable, generations of Cubans.

The government's blanket acceptance of Cubans as opponents of communism and Castro stood in contrast to its rejection of the vast majority of Haitian migrants. Human rights organizations, Haitian American activists, and the Congressional Black Caucus argued that there were extreme levels of violence and persecution in Haiti under the government of Jean Claude Duvalier, colloquially known as "Baby Doc." During the Mariel boatlift, at least 10,000 Haitians also entered the United States, providing the impetus for the first binational description of refugee status ("Cuban-Haitian entrant"). Haitians who arrived between April and October of 1980 were able to resettle just like their Cuban counterparts. However, Haitians who arrived after October 1980 would no longer be "entrants"; they would be "illegal aliens."

According to the Reagan administration, Haitians were not refugees. They were "economic migrants" violating U.S. immigration law. This hostility against Haitian migrants foreshadowed Reagan's aggressive anticommunist, Cold War stance within the Caribbean. It also highlighted discriminatory practices against black migrants, albeit using the race-neutral language of "economic migrants." The Congressional Black Caucus repeatedly criticized U.S. policies toward Haitians, but after 1980, it became increasingly difficult for Haitians to gain asylum. The United States also entered a bilateral agreement with Haiti, agreeing to return Haitians in direct violation of the UNHCR's policy against *refoulement*. It began an active interdiction policy in 1981 whereby the Coast Guard stopped Haitian boats at sea, performed cursory asylum hearings, and then returned Haitian asylum seekers back to Haiti at a rate of almost 100 percent. Library of Congress research specialist Ruth Wasem documented that of 22,940 Haitians stopped and interrogated by the Coast Guard, only eleven were deemed eligible to apply for asylum.[37] The United States claimed the Haitians were not leaving to escape political persecution but rather were seeking to escape poverty.

This contrast between Cubans and Haitians became even more acute in the 1990s when political upheaval in Haiti and an economic crisis in Cuba caused thousands of individuals from both countries to seek refuge in the United States. After the collapse of the Soviet Union, the Cuban economy was in shambles, and Castro dubbed it the "Special Period." Given the intense economic problems, tens of thousands of Cubans built rafts or *balsas* and headed for the

United States. Simultaneously, a coup against Jean Bertrand Aristide in Haiti led to persecution and attacks against Aristide's former supporters, many of whom were working class or peasants, and they too took to the seas. The U.S. government this time brought the Cubans and Haitians to the U.S. naval base at Guantánamo Bay, hoping that by processing and holding the Cubans and Haitians "outside" the United States, but on a U.S. base, they could manage the crisis. The results again were stark. Nearly all of the Cubans, who almost universally left because of economic hardships and desperation but not individual political persecution, were allowed entrance into the United States. In contrast, the U.S. admitted only one-third of the Haitians, notwithstanding their horrific stories of persecution and fears of violence. By insisting that the division between "refugee" and "economic migrant" fell along these national lines, the United States consistently advantaged Cubans and discriminated against Haitians. U.S. law also failed to consider that economic and political motivations were often closely intertwined.

The U.S. refugee policy in Central America again demonstrated the role of anticommunist politics in refugee policy. Like Vietnam, albeit on a smaller scale, the United States had a heavy military and economic footprint in Central American civil wars. And as in the case of Vietnam, U.S. actions triggered displacement, violence, and refugee streams throughout the 1980s. During the Reagan administration, the president emphasized his Cold War politics in Central America, supporting the Contras in Nicaragua against the revolutionary Sandinista government and backing anticommunist, violent military dictators in Guatemala and El Salvador. The violence and civil wars within Central America resulted in approximately one million migrants traveling to Mexico, and then hundreds of thousands entering the United States illegally. In general, the United States categorized Salvadorans and Guatemalans as "economic migrants" who came to the United States for jobs and better employment, ignoring the violence, fear, and terror in their communities. However, as one Salvadoran testified in front of Congress about government violence, "I fled from bombs, from airplanes. . . . The soldiers came on foot and the airplanes were above us. . . . We saw people massacred and we suffered. We came from the mountains, fleeing. The airplanes were horrid, some had bombs, others shot bullets, others had rockets."[38] Of course, in many cases, both violent political persecution and economic factors motivated men and women to head north to the United States. Disentangling these factors became a matter of semantics and discrimination, again setting up one national group as "real" refugees and another national group as illegal aliens.

In the 1980s, this policy of exclusion and denial of Central American refugee claims led to a grassroots sanctuary movement with ties to liberal politicians who opposed U.S. policies in Central America. The sanctuary movement included grassroots activists, liberal-leaning churches, and later larger organizations such as Amnesty International. Collectively they provided refuge to

Central American migrants seeking shelter, advocated for them, secured legal services for individuals, and defied U.S. immigration law. Individuals who supported the Central American asylum seekers did so in the name of humanitarianism, human rights, and sometimes solidarity, and they denounced the U.S. support for Central American governments and violence that led people to flee their countries in the first place. These advocates gained the support of members of Congress such as Rep. Joseph Moakley and Sen. Edward Kennedy who lobbied to grant protective status to Salvadorans who were in the United States illegally.[39] As historian Stephen Macekura has argued, Salvadorans were both victims of a U.S. ally, preventing them from asserting anticommunist credentials, and part of a larger trajectory of Latino migrants from Central America and Mexico who were deemed economic migrants—or, more harshly, illegal aliens. Again, as nonwhite migrants, they gained far less sympathy than earlier generations of Eastern European, Hungarian, or wealthy Cuban refugees, and instead found themselves categorized with other nonwhite, "nonrefugee" populations, such as Haitians and Mexicans.

Despite the continued politicization of the term "refugee," the 1980 law did open the doors to a large number of people who would not have gained access to the United States before 1980. Along with Cubans, Vietnamese, and Soviet Jews, throughout the 1980s and 1990s, the United States also accepted Hmong, Sudanese, Somali, and other populations which had previously only had a minuscule presence. In many instances, nationals of "special interest" had greater chances of being accepted as refugees. For example, the CIA had trained Hmong men during the War in Vietnam and, as with the Vietnamese, the government felt a special responsibility to them. Likewise, there was a coalition of Jewish Americans and policymakers who pressured the Soviet Union to allow Soviet Jews to emigrate. Arguing that Soviet Jews faced a "presumption of persecution," they advocated for the United States to welcome them on humanitarian grounds. This dovetailed with the country's policy objective of pressuring the Soviet Union to allow its citizens to emigrate. In the end, coalescing with the collapse of the USSR, at least 200,000 Soviet Jews entered the United States.

The 1980 Refugee Law also had the unintended consequence of creating a new stream of refugees via asylum claims. U.S. law distinguishes between refugees, who apply for entry outside of U.S. borders, and asylees, who claim persecution and asylum once they are in the United States. Many individuals who make asylum claims have entered the United States illegally without documentation or have overstayed travel or student visas. They then petition to remain in the United States due to fears of persecution in their home country. In 2009, Chinese nationals submitted the most petitions and also had the highest rate of acceptance of any country. However, there were also numerous petitions coming from Mexicans, Salvadorans, Hondurans, Haitians, Colombians, and Ethiopians; it is also worth noting that while large numbers of Mexicans and Central

Americans made asylum claims, individuals from South Asia, the Middle East, and Africa were granted asylum at greater rates.[40] Even members of the same nationality could face starkly different results depending on the district where they filed their petitions. Jaya Ramji-Nogales, Andrew I. Schoenholtz, and Phillip G. Schrag call this high degree of arbitrariness in asylum cases "refugee roulette."[41] For example, the number of Chinese nationals being granted asylum can vary from 76 percent at some immigration courts to only 7 percent at others.

Since the 1990s, the U.S. immigration system has become harsher, increasingly criminalizing asylum seekers and holding them in detention centers, jails, or jail-like facilities while they wait for their hearings.[42] In a 2009 report, Human Rights First (an activist nongovernmental organization) stated that close to 48,000 asylum seekers had been held in secure facilities between 2003 and 2009.[43]

Despite these problems, the 1990s and early 2000s also saw the expansion of claims individuals could make outside of the traditional political paradigm. For example, gender violence and discrimination over sexuality became grounds for asylum. This allowed women in abusive relationships who feared for their lives if they were deported to their home countries and, in select cases, individuals who faced violence because of sexual orientation to make asylum claims. While the numbers for both of these categories are relatively low, the recognition of gender violence and violence against LGBT individuals has widened the definition of "protection" to include cases which the 1980 law had not imagined.

As a consequence of these policies, large numbers of refugees have resettled in regions with small immigrant and nonwhite communities. In these cases, local governments and voluntary agencies gained expertise in providing refugee aid and services. The Twin Cities in Minnesota became one such site. Minnesota offered relatively generous benefits for new refugees and a supportive infrastructure, and as a result by the 1980s and 1990s communities of Hmong, Tibetan, Karen (a minority group within Myanmar), Somali, and Sudanese refugees became a visible and prominent part of a city that had previously been defined by generations of Scandinavian and German heritage. Other cities saw similar influxes; for example, Lowell, Massachusetts, became a center for the Hmong community, and Fargo, South Dakota, resettled a large number of Sudanese refugees. In this way, refugee populations have reshaped the landscape of many American communities.

Case Study

A Syrian couple lived in the city of Homs, where the husband owned a used clothing store. As the civil war within Syria escalated in 2011, the family experienced the violence firsthand. "We had to move from street to street to avoid the bombs." They decided to flee and seek safety in Jordan. Once in Jordan, they registered with the UNHCR, and they were interviewed at least six times by international and U.S. officials before gaining clearance to come to the United States.

Originally, the family was slated to be resettled in Indiana. However, the governor of Indiana, Mike Pence, did not want to welcome any Syrians into the state on his watch. As a result, the family was diverted to a community within Connecticut. On hearing about the proposed switch, the Syrian father expressed his frustration: "We were depressed. How could that be the freedoms that we hear about? ... You have to imagine that people are in Syria, the bombs are falling on them, they can't live in their homes, they leave, they live in Jordan, and it's still difficult for them. And then they find this opportunity to live a better life and they take it." He and his wife also expressed thankfulness for the support they received in Connecticut.

Are these Syrians refugees?[44]

The futures of individuals seeking refugee status in the United States have largely been determined by their countries of origin and when they have made their refugee claims. Refugees also still face suspicion and scrutiny even when few debate that they are fleeing violent circumstances like the Syrian family just discussed. In this instance, we can see the Syrian family's fear, their doubts due to the popular suspicion of refugees, but eventually also gratitude. However, with the election of President Donald Trump and Vice President Mike Pence, the U.S. government has instituted its most hostile stance against refugees in decades. As such, it is worth pausing to ask and analyze how U.S. refugee policy has collided with military and diplomatic objectives in the recent past.

With the Wars in Iraq and Afghanistan, the United States again must decide who from those countries is and who is not a refugee. Many Iraqi men who translated for the U.S. military or had jobs with contractors during the occupation later faced danger and violence because of their ties to the United States. As in Vietnam, there is a sense of obligation to these workers, and individuals who worked for the U.S. government or a defense contractor are eligible to apply for refugee status. In total, between 2007 and 2013, the United States accepted approximately 84,000 Iraqis (from over 200,000 applicants).

With the Syrian crisis displacing approximately four million people between 2013 and 2016, the United States has chosen a largely passive position, admitting fewer than 1,500 Syrians in 2015 and promising to accept up to 10,000 in 2016. The country worries about admitting individuals who may be security threats, and the extensive background checks can take between one and two years for individuals applying from refugee camps in Jordan, Lebanon, and Turkey. As in previous generations, these fears of security are intertwined with concerns about integrating new minorities, in this case Muslims. In addition, while Syrians and other Middle Easterners may have similar objectives as the United States—that is, the defeat of the ISIS forces or the Assad regime, they are not easily defined as ideological U.S. allies. Unlike the Hungarians, Cubans, and Vietnamese who were represented as symbols of anticommunism, twenty-first-century Middle Eastern refugees do not benefit from the Cold War's superpower competition and, as a result, fall outside these simple binaries.

Concurrent with the growing Syrian crisis, in the summer of 2014, approximately 68,000 undocumented and unaccompanied minors from Central America entered the United States. These individuals were not fleeing guerrilla warfare by both anticommunist and communist revolutionaries but were instead fleeing gang violence stimulated by drug wars and weak states in Mexico and Central America. Children under the age of eighteen and young women constitute a disproportionate number of these individuals. The United States government responded by sending thousands to detention centers in the American Southwest, where these women and children had limited access to lawyers or local communities. Rather than looking for sponsors and resettling them like Cuban or Vietnamese refugees, the U.S. government most often placed them in deportation proceedings, arguing that they were illegal aliens who crossed the border for economic opportunity. Lawyers and advocates have been at work documenting their cases and working to argue that these families too should be seen as refugees; however, most cases remain in limbo and as of 2017 few have received asylum.

During the 2016 campaign, President Trump flamed fears that refugees cause security risks, and he promised to install "extreme vetting." In his first days in office, President Trump issued an executive order to halt all refugee entry into the United States for 120 days. This order was met with mass protests throughout the country as well as legal challenges; however, it effectively changed the terms of debate. President Trump's administration was not interested in parsing who did and did not meet the threshold of refugee status, but rather it sought to temporarily prohibit entry, even to those who had already been through the stringent process and had received formal refugee status. With large-scale migration and displacement due to wars and violence in the Middle East, Central America, and Africa, it is unlikely that the resettlement of refugees will be resolved easily or that the subject will disappear. Instead, the U.S. acceptance or rejection of individuals as refugees will remain salient, and these policies will identify the contours of U.S. foreign relations, immigration policy, and ideology.

Discussion Questions

1. How did the Cold War shape refugee policy? What changed at the end of the Cold War?
2. Why did the United States develop categories and language such as "parolee" or "Cuban-Haitian entrant" to sidestep the word "refugee"?
3. Has the United States been consistent in its refugee policy? Why or why not?
4. If you were developing U.S. refugee policy, what criteria would you use?

Notes

1   Peter Gatrell, *The Making of the Modern Refugee* (New York: Oxford University Press, 2013), 5.

2   Roger Daniels, *Guarding the Golden Door: American Immigration Policy and Immigrants since 1882* (New York: Hill and Wang, 2004), 190.

3   Atina Grossman, *Jews, Germans and Allies: Close Encounters in Occupied Germany* (Princeton, NJ: Princeton University Press, 2007), 161–162; Regina Kesler, *Grit: A Pediatrician's Odyssey from a Soviet Camp to Harvard* (Bloomington, IN: AuthorHouse, 2009).

4   Gattrell, *Making of the Modern Refugee*, 26, 30–31.

5   Gil Loescher, *The UNHCR and World Politics: A Perilous Path* (New York: Oxford University Press, 2001), 21; David Forsythe, *The Humanitarians: The International Committee of the Red Cross* (Cambridge: Cambridge University Press, 2005), 35.

6   Loescher, *UNHCR and World Politics*, 27–28; Carl Bon Tempo, *Americans at the Gate: The United States and Refugees during the Cold War* (Princeton, NJ: Princeton University Press, 2008), 15.

7   Daniels, *Guarding the Golden Door*, 80.

8   Bon Tempo, *Americans at the Gate*, 17–20; Daniels, *Guarding the Golden Door*, 76–78.

9   Daniels, *Guarding the Golden Door*, 79–80.

10 Loescher, *UNHCR and World Politics*, 34; Daniels, *Guarding the Golden Door*, 98.

11 Atina Grossman, *Jews, Germans and Allies: Close Encounters in Occupied Germany* (Princeton, NJ: Princeton University Press, 2007), 1.

12 Bon Tempo, *Americans at the Gate*, 24, 21–26; Gil Loescher and John A. Scanlan, *Calculated Kindness: Refugees and America's Half-Open Door, 1945 to the Present* (New York: Free Press, 1986), 1–24.

13 Daniel, *Guarding the Golden Door*, 110.

14 Ibid., 107, 103–112.

15 Loescher, *UNHCR and World Politics*, 43–46.

16 Sucheng Chan, ed., "A Journey Called Freedom," in *The Vietnamese American 1.5 Generation: Stories of War, Revolution, Flight and New Beginnings* (Philadelphia: Temple University Press, 2006), 116–126.

17 Loescher and Scanlan, *Calculated Kindness*, 27. Carl Bon Tempo expanded on Loescher and Scanlan's Cold War calculus in *Americans at the Gate*, where he demonstrated how U.S. refugee policy was consistently a result of both U.S. domestic and international policy objectives.

18 Bon Tempo, *Americans at the Gate*, 62.

19 Loescher and Scanlan, *Calculated Kindness*, 50–51.

20 Bon Tempo, *Americans at the Gate*, 77–79.

21 Madeline Hsu, *The Good Immigrants: How the Yellow Peril Became the Model Minority* (Princeton, NJ: Princeton University Press, 2015), 133.

22 Maria Cristina Garcia, *Havana, U.S.A.: Cuban Exiles and Cuban Americans in South Florida, 1959–1994* (Berkeley: University of California Press, 1996), 13.

23 Ibid., 22–23.

24 Bon Tempo discusses the screening process, but the main point is that it was standard, and Cubans were generally accepted *en masse*. *Americans at the Gate*, 111–112, 118–121.

25 Garcia, *Havana, U.S.A.*, 23.

26 Ibid., 23–26.

27 Andrew Friedman, *Covert Capital: Landscapes of Desire and the Making of US Empire in the Suburbs of Northern Virginia* (Berkeley: University of California Press, 2013).

28 Yen Le Espiritu, *Body Counts: The Vietnam War and Militarized Refugees* (Berkeley: University of California Press, 2014).

29 Jana K. Lipman, "A Refugee Camp in America: Fort Chaffee and Vietnamese and Cuban Refugees, 1975–1982," *Journal of American Ethnic History* 33, no. 2 (Winter 2014): 57–87; Mimi Thi Nguyen, *The Gift of Freedom: War, Debt, and Other Refugee Passages* (Durham, NC: Duke University Press, 2012).

30 Reginald Stuart, "Out of Miami Detention, Haitian Tests Freedom," *New York Times*, July 30, 1982.

31 Barbara Keys, *Reclaiming American Virtue: The Human Rights Revolution of the 1970s* (Cambridge, MA: Harvard University Press, 2014).

32 Bon Tempo, *Americans at the Gate*, 173–179; Rogers, *Guarding the Golden Door*, 203–204.

33 Rogers, *Guarding the Golden Door*, 204.

34 Garcia, *Havana, U.S.A.*, 60–66.

35 Ibid., 68.

36 Ibid., 64.

37 See Ruth Ellen Wasem, *U.S. Immigration Policy on Haitian Immigrants* (Congressional Research Service Report), January 21, 2005, http://trac.syr.edu/immigration/library/P960.pdf.

38 Qtd. in Stephen Macekura, "For Fear of Persecution: Displaced Salvadorans and U.S. Refugee Policy in the 1980s," *Journal of Policy Historyz* 23, no. 3 (2011): 357–380.

39 Ibid.

40 Ruth Ellen Wasem, *Asylum and "Credible Fear" Issues in U.S. Immigration Policy* (Congressional Research Service Report), April 6, 2011, http://www.rcusa.org/uploads/pdfs/CRS%20Asylum%20and%20Credible%20Fear%20April%202011.pdf, 23–24.

41 Jaya Ramji-Nogales, Andrew I. Schoenholtz, and Phillip G. Schrag, "Refugee Roulette: Disparities in Asylum Adjudication," *Stanford Law Review* 60, no. 2 (November 2007).

42 Ibid., 329–330.

43 "US Detention of Asylum Seekers: Seeking Protection, Finding Prison," *Human Rights First*, April 2009, https://www.humanrightsfirst.org/wp-content/uploads/pdf/090429-RP-hrf-asylum-detention-report.pdf.

44 Liz Robbins, "Syrian Family Diverted from Indiana, Feels 'Welcomed' in Connecticut," *New York Times*, November 20, 2015.

Further Reading

Carl J. Bon Tempo. *Americans at the Gate: The United States and Refugees during the Cold War*. Princeton, NJ: Princeton University Press, 2008.

Yen Le Espiritu. *Body Counts: The Vietnam War and Militarized Refugees*. Berkeley: University of California Press, 2014.

Maria García. *Seeking Refuge: Central American Migration to Mexico, the United States and Canada*. Berkeley: University of California Press, 2006.

Gil Loescher and John A. Scanlan. *Calculated Kindness: Refugees and America's Half-Open Door, 1945 to the Present*. New York: Free Press, 1986.

9

Race and/in War

CHRISTINE KNAUER

War has been an essential and formative element in American history. Since the colonial era, wars have formed and informed race relations and racial hierarchies in the United States. This chapter provides a critical introduction to the historically problematic position of racial minorities in America's wars of the twentieth century. It places special focus on African Americans, who have historically been the largest and most vocal minority in the armed services. It highlights the often contradictory effects of war on racial minorities and race in general from the First World War until today, noting the close links between military service and citizenship with all its civil rights. As such, it promised to be a way for minorities to negotiate or renegotiate their status and rights in a nation that oppressed and discriminated against them.[1] Thus, the war efforts of racial minorities and their experience of war and service must be considered with this strong connection in mind.

Since the 1700s, the military and the U.S. government has struggled with engaging racial minorities in its various war efforts while all too often continuing to uphold racial hierarchies and subordination. War has been a continuous process of inclusion and exclusion. Until the Korean War, Congress, the War Department, and military leadership attempted to delimit the use of blacks and other minorities in the military, as their service threatened to upset established racial hierarchies. "Throughout the South a Negro in uniform symbolized 'a nigger not knowing his place.'"[2] Black soldiers and recruits had always been the most visible and most offensive symbol of African American (male) strength, prowess, and self-confidence. Racial minorities have constantly repositioned and re-evaluated their stance on America's wars. While segregation and racial inequality ruled the United States throughout much of the twentieth century, wartime demanded a more efficient inclusion and use of otherwise oppressed minorities in the war effort. This provided them with unique leverage to fight for more equality and integration in both the military and civilian realms. Thus, being minority soldiers took on new symbolic meaning. On the one hand, they became the most powerful symbols of racial humiliation, degradation, and segregation, as their service often highlighted the inequalities they faced both in service and at home. On the other hand, they acted as symbols of increasing resistance to white oppression and discrimination, representing prowess and inspired to fight against oppression by their service. Of course, racial minorities often have had diverse opinions about American war efforts, but because of the often contradictory symbolic meaning of their service, they also developed a keen sense of race and racism during and through America's wars.

Doubts about whether military service in wartime would help advance the status of a particular minority in society had always existed. So did criticism of the American endeavors in war by minority groups, especially from African Americans. During the Second World War and the Cold War, racial minorities pointed to the limits of American democracy and the persistence of racism at home and abroad. Throughout their military service in wartime, racial minorities fought a double war—one against the enemy abroad and one against the enemy at home. Black Americans' lives in particular were in constant danger whether they were on the battlefields in Europe, Asia, and Africa or in Mississippi, Chicago, or Los Angeles. A look at the situation of racial minorities in America's most recent wars reveals new tendencies and the persistence of old allegiances of racial minorities. The conflicted relationship of blacks with war and military service in wartime has grown since the Second World War and especially in the twenty-first century, as white privilege and black victimization have continued to hold on strong.[3]

The First World War

U.S. involvement in the First World War was rather short but essential to victory over the German *Reich*. American society in general and the African American community in particular did not agree on how to react to the war. The position of African Americans under the reign of President Woodrow Wilson was precarious at best. Deeply racist, Wilson cooperated closely with southerners and helped to uphold racial oppression and segregation. African Americans had ample reasons not to support the president's entrance into the war in April 1917, since they remained marginalized and abandoned by the White House.[4] With his official blessing, Wilson's quotes were used in the silent film *The Birth of a Nation* released in 1915. While a masterpiece of early cinema, the film condoned the Ku Klux Klan, white supremacy, and lynching. It spoke to the mood and conviction of most white Americans.

At the time, racial tensions ran high not only in the South but also in the North. Black migration to the North had always taken place; however, the numbers of African Americans who left the South after 1916 in hope of a better future in industrial centers were unprecedented. Chicago, New York, and Philadelphia, most notably, promised to be safe havens full of jobs and free of segregation and discrimination. The reality was different, as blacks all too often ended up ghettoized and discriminated against. Working-class whites often considered them to be especially threatening competition in the workforce and did not greet them with much excitement. Despite this, for most blacks, life in the North was better than living in the South and the draw of the North despite all its flaws held on strong throughout the first half of the twentieth century.[5]

The African American community was divided on whether to register for the draft. They were torn between the disappointment over their mistreatment at home and the persisting hope that military service and valor could help them attain full citizenship rights and bring an end to segregation. Even W.E.B. Du Bois, the African American civil rights advocate and a vocal critic of American politics, took an accommodationist stance. He advised blacks to "close ranks" and support the war effort. His plea elicited much criticism among African American commentators, especially on the left. A. Philip Randolph, socialist and editor of the *Messenger*, refused to register for the draft and argued that he would "rather make Georgia safe for the Negro" than "make the world safe for democracy."[6]

Still, most African Americans proved willing to join the armed forces and yet again fight for a country that oppressed and mistreated them. On the first registration day under the Selective Service Act of 1917, more than 700,000 African Americans signed up for service. When discussing the draft, white southern politicians had protested the conscription and arming of African Americans vehemently, as there was "no greater menace to the South than this."[7] Although they could not prevent the drafting of blacks, they ensured that racial hierarchies remained embedded in the military. Ultimately, the need for soldiers did not produce significant racial progress. Black draftees had to register their race and were segregated if drafted. They were only allowed to serve as long as the all-black units were not filled up. Although white units desperately needed replacements, army leadership turned blacks away in their insistence on upholding segregation and eliminating African Americans from combat units.[8]

For blacks, this renewed exclusion came as a surprise, since numerous African American soldiers had participated valiantly in combat during the War of 1898. They were lauded for their valor and six black soldiers received the Congressional Medal of Honor, the highest award for bravery. But combat had changed.[9] The focus had shifted from cavalry and infantry combat to artillery and machine gun warfare. Soldiers on all sides fought in trenches for months on end and handled poison gas. Stereotypes of black incompetence and backwardness remained strong and provided an excuse to exclude them from combat. Military leadership contended that African Americans were unable to handle these new realities. The black soldier, they reasoned, did not have "the mental stamina and moral sturdiness to put him in line against German troops who consist of thoroughly trained men of high average education. It is feared that the enemy will concentrate on parts of the line held by inferior troops, break through and get in the rear of high-class troops who will be at a terrible disadvantage."[10] Deemed unqualified if not entirely incompetent and unreliable, African Americans had very limited chances of advancing in military ranks. Although a segregated officer training school for blacks had been established after a long period of protest by activists, there existed a clear dearth of black officers.

Because of this lack of representation in the upper ranks of the military hierarchy, most African Americans continued to serve under white officers, who all too often came from the South. Despite some racially progressive commanders who wanted their black soldiers to succeed in combat roles, the majority of white officers considered segregation to be the only option for structuring military participation. They viewed blacks' inclusion in combat missions as detrimental to victory and something to be avoided at all costs. In a letter to his superior officer, Major J. N. Merrill of the 368th's First Battalion wrote: "Without my presence or that of any other white officer right on the firing line I am absolutely positive that not a single colored officer would have advanced with his men. The cowardice shown by the men was abject." This devastating assessment resulted in the removal of thirty black officers from service for allegedly being "cowardly," "incompetent," and untrustworthy.[11]

Thus, the majority of the 400,000 active African Americans were relegated to service units during the First World War. They built roads, dug out latrines, and transported supplies to the front lines, but they were excluded from combat. Their task abroad was essential for the success of the war effort and extremely dangerous, but it was not highly respected by other soldiers or the general public. Manly valor could only be gained and a real claim to citizenship could only be made by fighting on the battlefield. Since they were placed in service units, traditional military training with guns was reduced to a minimum and their use in combat would then certainly have been a daring move.[12] Their likely failures in combat situations would then be used to bolster the stereotype of black cowardice and incompetence. While the African American community argued that black soldiers' struggles mostly resulted from discrimination and segregation, few whites really cared.

Despite all the mechanisms of exclusion and limitation that the military leadership applied, a few African American units ultimately participated in combat and did so valiantly during the First World War, but not with the American military. The 369th Regiment out of Harlem, New York, was one of four black regiments sent into combat. After a short and violent training stint in the South that left them underprepared, the soldiers made their way to Europe, where they performed manual labor supporting the white troops fighting in the trenches.

When the French were in desperate need of replacements, John J. Pershing, a comparatively progressive general in the U.S. military, agreed to provide a few regiments to support the French troops. For the black soldiers chosen to join the French in combat, this move represented a unique chance to prove themselves valiant and white America wrong. Many white commanders and soldiers feared the possible consequences, especially when black Americans were incorporated with few complications.[13]

Afraid of the empowering experience African Americans could have abroad, the white military leadership attempted to introduce American rules of racial interactions and white supremacy among European allies. The U.S. military even informed the French and British governments on how their citizens were expected to treat African American soldiers in order to not offend the white majority of the American military body. In the memo "Secret Information Concerning Black Troops" to their French counterparts in 1918, the U.S. military instructed the French about race relations and racial hierarchies in the United States: "Although a citizen of the United States, the black man is regarded by the white American as an inferior being [. . .] The vices of the Negro are a constant menace to the American who has to repress them sternly [. . .] Make a point of keeping the native cantonment population from 'spoiling' the Negroes. White Americans become incensed by any public expression of intimacy between white women and black men."[14]

White soldiers defamed African American soldiers to foreign soldiers and civilians alike, warning them that black men had a proclivity to rape white women. Rumors of rape disseminated quickly and informed the French attitude toward black Americans. Given their own racist stereotypes of their colored colonial subjects, the French and British easily accepted these warnings. Still, they learned to respect their African American comrades and benefited greatly from their fighting. Moreover, compared to the hatred and violence they had to face daily at home and on the field at the hands of white Americans, black men experienced their treatment by the French as mostly respectful and equal. The 369th even earned the Croix de Guerre, the highest French commendation, after helping to protect Paris from the advancing Germans.[15]

Returning from the battlefields in Europe, the 369th Infantry, now known as the "Harlem Hellfighters," marched in the victory parade in New York and were cheered on by an interracial crowd.[16] However, the situation soon turned violent, and many black veterans returning from Europe became targets of white hatred. Racial tensions and violence at home had run high throughout the war. The presence of black soldiers in the South often provoked violent opposition among whites. Blacks grew increasingly frustrated with Jim Crow and its constant humiliation. A riot in Houston, Texas, in August 1917 led to the courts-martial of over 150 black soldiers of the 24th Infantry Regiment. Nineteen soldiers were executed and more than fifty received life sentences for their involvement.

After the war, racial violence was again on the rise, overwhelming any possible changes the war and black participation in it might have brought about. Numerous African Americans fell victim to lynchings, extralegal punishments often for trumped-up charges without due process. In the summer and fall of 1919, social tensions between blacks and whites rose to a new boiling point amid the demobilization of the troops and black migration to industrial centers in the South and North. The returning black soldiers, emboldened by their experience abroad, challenged the precarious state of white supremacy and racial hierarchies. In both the North and the South, the growing competition over access to jobs and housing turned violent, resulting in hundreds of deaths on both sides. It seemed that not much changed with the war. The White House and Congress did not put a great deal of effort into improving the situation of African Americans, nor did state governments. However, while Jim Crow and discrimination continued to rule the nation, African Americans grew more impatient and ready to confront the oppressive system. A "new negro" evolved out of the war that was meant to make the world "safe for democracy."[17]

The Second World War

The Second World War amplified African American activism for an integrated armed forces. In 1940, Congress passed the first peacetime draft in American history with the Selective Service Act. It contained a nondiscrimination clause, but the continuance of segregation made nondiscrimination for racial minorities impossible. African Americans in particular kept pushing for change but were incessantly put off. After a meeting with representatives of the African American community, the War Department formulated a seven-point plan to regulate blacks in the military. African Americans would be allowed in all major branches of the military, proportionate to their percentage in the population, which at the time was around 10 percent.

More importantly, the War Department maintained that segregation had proven successful and remained the only option to create a powerful military, despite ample proof that segregation was inefficient, damaging, and extremely expensive. The military, its leadership contended, should not act as "a sociological laboratory; to be effective it must be organized and trained according to the principles which will ensure success. Experiments to meet the wishes and demands of the champions of every race and creed for the solution of their problems are a danger to efficiency, discipline, and morale and would result in ultimate defeat."[18] Furthermore, President Franklin D. Roosevelt continued to confine blacks to segregated labor battalions, excluding them from combat. With the motto "Segregation without discrimination," the armed forces held on to the doctrine of "separate but equal." Despite its claim to equality, this system perpetuated discrimination against and marginalization of the largest minority group in the country. Multiple studies were conducted to investigate how best to utilize African Americans in the war effort and how to increase morale among black soldiers. But the findings did not convince military leadership to end segregation in the ranks of the armed forces.[19]

Civil rights activists and the black press demanded the end of the quota system and segregation in the armed forces even before America's entrance into the war. One of the most dramatic demands came from A. Philip Randolph, the famous black labor leader, who organized a March on Washington Movement in 1941. Tens of thousands of African Americans, Randolph threatened, would march to and through Washington demanding equality in the workplace and integration of the armed forces. The movement's main slogan read, "We loyal Negro-American citizens demand the right to work and fight for our country."[20] The movement paired patriotism with social criticism demanding immediate social change. It put so much pressure on President Roosevelt that on June 25, 1941, he issued Executive Order 8802 prohibiting employment discrimination because of race, creed, color, or national origin in federal agencies and war-related industries. To the chagrin of many, Randolph discontinued the impending march on Washington, although not the movement itself. From then on, it acted as watchdog for the work of the newly founded Fair Employment Practice Committee (FEPC), which monitored the fate and status of African Americans in the affected businesses. Many of the industrial plants were located in or relocated to the South, where segregation and discrimination raged more rampantly than in the rest of the country. White southerners disdained the committee and its effectiveness was often questionable, but it represented a sign that fundamental change was on the horizon.[21]

The White House took additional steps to appease the black community by establishing the Tuskegee aviation school, by making Benjamin Davis the first black general, and by appointing William H. Hastie as a civilian aide to the secretary of war. However, Roosevelt did not order the desegregation of the military, nor did he pass any new ruling on blacks in the armed forces. When the United States entered the Second World War in December 1941 after the Japanese attack on Pearl Harbor, it did so with fully segregated forces.

Nor were only African Americans affected. Although U.S. propaganda called for unity in times of war and allowed ethnic Americans to integrate fully in the armed forces, the call for unity often excluded some racial minorities.[22] Decades before the U.S. entry into the Second World War, racism and nativism led to a list of amendments and rulings that especially affected Asians. In May 1918, congressional amendments to naturalization regulations had permitted noncitizens who had served in the U.S. Army or Navy access to expedited naturalization. However, the new regulation excluded Asians who had fought for the United States in the First World War. In the following years, the Supreme Court and Congress further restricted Asians from immigrating to the United States and applying for citizenship. There were already ample suspicions against the

Japanese and by default Japanese Americans. Pearl Harbor fueled the persecution of people of Japanese descent in the United States.

Suspected of conspiring with the enemy, 120,000 Japanese Americans were interned during the Second World War following President Roosevelt's issuance of Executive Order 9066 on February 19, 1942. They were removed from the West Coast to concentration camps in the Midwest and the South. Nisei, the second-generation Japanese living in the United States, were grudgingly allowed to serve in the military, but only in segregated units as suspicions and exclusion of racial minorities from the war effort held on strong. As racist assumptions about the Japanese permeated American society, U.S. propaganda and the general discourse characterized them as sly, treacherous, and ruthless. In posters, films, and caricatures, the Japanese were depicted as animals, most prominently as rodents, monkeys, and insects. In others, they were represented as brutes going after helpless white females. This image played on white fear of miscegenation and of racial contamination of the allegedly superior white race. Ultimately, these images dehumanized the enemy, lowering American inhibitions "to kill the japs," whether soldiers or civilians, in masses.[23]

The oppressed state of minorities in the United States did not lack for comment by critics at home and enemies abroad. Blacks pointed to the hypocrisies of the self-acclaimed pinnacle of democracy and freedom. Even before 1939, African American press outlets reported on the disenfranchisement and persecution of Jews in Germany. They underlined the parallels between their own fate in the United States and that of European Jews.

Japanese and German propaganda machines also tried to benefit by pointing to the oppressive system that existed in the United States. They attempted to fuel distrust among minorities and intended to erode the unity the United States proclaimed so vigorously. Thus, race relations became a serious liability for the image of the United States abroad. The American government feared that not only the Japanese but other minorities would align with the enemy. The FBI, for instance, diligently investigated African Americans, suspecting treason as a reaction to white supremacy and segregation.

Starting in June 1942, the newly founded Office of War Information (OWI) explained America's reasons for joining the fight and reported on the valiant soldiers who offered their lives in the name of what, in January 1941, President Roosevelt had called the Four Freedoms everyone in the world should enjoy: freedom of speech, freedom of worship, freedom from want, and freedom from fear. African Americans, however, were usually omitted from press reports and newsreels sent to white news outlets. Willing to participate in America's war effort, the African American community expanded its aims by launching the Double V Campaign, vehemently calling for a victory over fascism abroad and Jim Crow at home. They believed these two issues to be firmly related to one another.

First to use the term "Double V," the *Pittsburgh Courier*, one of the most influential black papers at the time, pledged black willingness to fight for the

United States, but it made unmistakably clear that African Americans would "wage a two-pronged attack against our enslavers at home and those abroad who would enslave us. WE HAVE A STAKE IN THIS FIGHT ... WE ARE AMERICANS TOO!"[24] The OWI closely monitored the African American press and its content. While they needed to include blacks in the call for unity to a certain extent, a positive image of black soldiers remained problematic and thus rare throughout the course of the war. African American newspapers did everything in their power to introduce blacks to war reports in order to help improve their public image. Despite the limited information they received from the OWI, tales of black heroics and defiance of segregation increased in the African American press.

During the Second World War, just as in the First World War, the majority of African Americans were confined to service units, where they had to perform menial labor in supply, maintenance, and transportation. Thus, they continued to be excluded from combat positions, "where manhood and citizenship were defined."[25] But the black press and community celebrated the essential character of their work in support units for the war effort. The *Atlanta Daily World*, a black newspaper, reported that "the American Negro soldier is playing a tremendous part in the development of facilities for speedy military action."[26] These reports bolstered racial pride and willingness to stand against white supremacy at home, where African Americans lived and served in a segregated, discriminated, and marginalized state.[27]

Instead of initiating desegregation, the military went out of its way to uphold segregation and to degrade black men and women in any way possible. More than any other minority group, African Americans' presence in the military again raised difficult questions about the functionality of segregation and issues of citizenship that were unsettling to the whole nation and its racial makeup. In accordance with racial hierarchies and white supremacy, which continued to dominate the armed forces, black soldiers would never be allowed to command white soldiers or be superior to white officers. Black chances for advancement remained slim to none.[28]

Like African Americans, Latinos had similar hopes attached to military service in war and peace. During the First and Second World Wars, the American government had actively included Hispanics in the war effort. Although there were Hispanics who served in the military and some even went overseas, the majority worked as agricultural laborers. But their work was essential for the war effort. Thus, the feeling of one's self-worth in and for the nation as well as national belonging grew in the Latino community. Despite this positive experience, Hispanics were considered nonconforming aliens due to their use of the Spanish language as well as their cultural heritage and religion. Even when they and their families had been in the United States for decades, many white Americans eyed them with suspicion and doubted their dedication to the nation.

Hispanics, mostly Mexican Americans, lived predominantly in separate communities and represented cheap competition on the job market. From Texas to California, where the grand majority lived, they were restricted to low-paying jobs. At the same time, based on preconceived racial stereotypes, they were associated with crime. The white press like the *Los Angeles Times* and the *Dallas Morning News* along with politicians spread ideas of uncontrollable lawlessness and violence among Mexican American teenagers and young adults. The Zoot Suit Riots in 1943, violent clashes between white servicemen and mostly Mexican American youths especially in California, exemplified whites' mistrust of Latinos' identity, loyalty, and patriotism. Latinos all too often felt alienated from a nation that treated them like second-class citizens, segregating them in schools and discriminating against them in the work place.

Despite the prevalence of discrimination, most Hispanics supported the U.S. war effort, often with hopes that the Four Freedoms would encompass them. Between 250,000 and 300,000 Hispanics were either drafted or volunteered in the military. Patriotism was certainly a reason for them to join. Many, however, did so out of pure economic necessity and hopes of social advancement. Assigned to all branches, they fought in Europe as well as in the Pacific. Although classified as white by law and allowed in white outfits, Latinos experienced discriminatory treatment similar to the African American experience.[29] But the war nevertheless advanced a stronger claim to national belonging, the end of discrimination, and equal rights among Hispanics. As in the African American community, Latino veterans were at the forefront of the fight for equality in the United States.

In the final months of the conflict, the majority of blacks sent overseas remained relegated to support troops, yet the demands of war made it necessary to reassign thousands of them to combat. In France, Belgium, and Germany, African Americans successfully fought side by side with whites. To do so, many accepted reductions in rank. The experiment born out of desperation proved successful. Their performance in battle was lauded and belied all stereotypes of black cowardice. It also showed that an integrated environment reduced racial animosity and increased efficiency.[30]

Military leadership and most politicians, however, brushed the positive results aside, dissolved the outfits, and the African American combat volunteers had to return to their support units. Rather than focusing on the experiment's success, the press once again covered in detail the alleged deficiencies of the all-black 92nd Division, which was actively involved in combat in Italy. While the African American press showcased black soldiers' success, many white papers, among them even the rather liberal *New York Times*, reported mass panic and failed missions. Military leaders assigned their alleged failure to African American soldiers' racial characteristics, while they predominantly ignored the negative effects of racism and discrimination on their training, combat performance, and military status.

As black successes in combat were downplayed, allegations of crime and rape against black soldiers were raised. These assertions tapped into long-established stereotypes of criminality and the supposed untamed sexual drive of black men that necessitated white control. Southern politicians reiterated these allegations before Congress, further tarnishing the record of black soldiers. A disproportionate number of blacks were court-martialed and received harsh sentences. Furthermore, African Americans were disadvantaged when discharged because of the predominant lack of combat time and received more "blue"—which meant less than honorable—and dishonorable discharges than white soldiers. Their chances on the civilian job market were already bleak, but a negative military record made these chances almost nonexistent. Passed in 1944, the Servicemen's Readjustment Act (better known as the GI Bill of Rights) was meant to provide returning veterans with educational and job opportunities. However, while the bill was not per se racist, its application and the boards that decided on the applicants' fate were.[31] A similarly bad standing in education and on the job market awaited other racial minorities, particularly Hispanics and Native Americans.

Similar to their positive experience in France during and after the First World War, African Americans considered the conditions and odds for blacks in occupied Germany to be better than in the United States. Although the American military tried to establish segregation and the rules of white supremacy in Europe, many black soldiers felt more respected and equal there than anywhere in the United States. Black soldiers dated white locals and immersed themselves in the integrated club scenes that developed in the civilian world. As they were liberators and occupiers in American uniform Europeans usually showed them respect regardless of their skin color.[32]

The war legitimized by the Four Freedoms and the hypocrisy of being excluded from them emboldened blacks in particular to demand their rights and renegotiate their status in the American polity more forcefully. They went to the voting booth in the South and challenged white supremacy. Their bold behavior caused a backlash among white supremacists and segregationists who fought the returning black veterans with verbal attacks as well as physical violence. As was true after the First World War, a black man in uniform returning victorious represented the quintessential assault against white supremacy. The attack on Isaac Woodard, an African American veteran recently released from his outfit, is representative of the violence black veterans experienced. In February 1946, white police officers removed the honorably discharged African American veteran still in uniform from a bus in South Carolina. They clubbed him and threw him into a jail cell overnight without medical attention. Despite being blinded, Woodard was also fined. Numerous African American veterans experienced similar violence at the hands of civilians as well as police officers in the South.[33]

Additionally, public history and memory of the Second World War whitewashed its course, ignoring, humiliating, and emasculating black men and their

war efforts. If African Americans were included in the official stories and histories of the war, be it in Congress or in white newspapers, long-standing racial
stereotypes were invoked. In a speech opposing the prolongment of the FEPC
in June 1946, Senator James Eastland called black soldiers cowards and perpet-
ual rapists. Published in 1950, *Life's Picture History of World War II* included
but one picture of blacks mourning over Roosevelt's death in its collection of
over one thousand. The negative image of black soldiers was perpetuated in an
attempt to humiliate and invalidate their pursuit of equality through service.[34]
But while the representation of African American soldiers remained negative on
a national level, racism and segregation received more international attention.

Indeed, international newspapers reported regularly on racial violence,
especially against veterans, and segregation in the military. Soviet propaganda
exploited the news of African Americans' troubled fates in the struggle of communist Russia for the support of people of color around the world. Special
attention was given to black soldiers' treatment, which represented the most blatant example of the oppressive and untrustworthy system in the United States.
With the Cold War heating up, segregation and discrimination became an even
more serious liability. The international attention that white supremacy and
oppression of minorities received put pressure on the American government to
improve the situation and status of African Americans in the self-declared beacon of democracy. In this climate of violence and growing international attention, African American activists increased the fight against military segregation.
Formed by the war and disappointed by the lack of change despite their dedicated service, African Americans intended once and for all to end the discriminatory practices that not only hindered their progress but also manifested their
inequality and lack of full citizenship and civil rights. Once again, A. Philip
Randolph stood at the forefront of the movement to achieve integration in the
military, relentlessly pressuring the president to act on the persistence of segregation in the armed forces. While in 1941 he had announced a march of tens of
thousands of blacks on Washington, in March 1948 he threatened a mass civil
disobedience campaign of African Americans against military segregation. He
called on black and white youths to refuse to join the military. His call to openly
resist military service had only one goal: to bring an end to the segregation and
discrimination that had impeded and humiliated black soldiers in both war and
peace. The timing of this movement was calculated; 1948 was an election year
and presidential candidates needed the black vote like never before. Republican
presidential candidate Thomas E. Dewey, governor of New York, was respected
by the African American community and was a formidable competitor for their
electoral support. This rapport, along with the call for civil disobedience during
an election, put President Harry S. Truman under great pressure to act on his
earlier promises to do something about military segregation.

While Randolph's short-lived civil disobedience campaign never evolved into
a mass movement, it represented the growing frustration with the segregation of

and discrimination against blacks in the military as well as in society as a whole. The call for draft resistance at a time of national insecurity went far beyond traditional civil rights tactics and left gradualism behind. Activists made clear-cut demands instead of waiting for whites to allow blacks to achieve equality at their liking. Thus, this call for resisting military service, this impatience and forthrightness, shocked not only the white mainstream but also African Americans. While many blacks lauded Randolph for his ferocity, they feared appearing unpatriotic. Despite evidence to the contrary, military service, especially in war, was still considered the safest and surest way to achieve equality and full civil rights. Refusing to serve threatened this method of advancement. However, despite the lack of support, Randolph's radical path proved successful, as President Harry S. Truman felt it necessary to tackle the issue.[35]

On July 26, 1948, President Truman issued Executive Order 9981, introducing "equality of treatment and opportunity for all persons in the Armed Services without regard to race, color, religion, or national origin."[36] The order did not demand desegregation; it did not even mention the terms "desegregation" or "integration." Still, it forced the military to re-evaluate its position on race and the value of segregation.[37] Established by Truman's executive order, the Committee on Equality of Treatment and Opportunity in the Armed Forces, better known as the Fahy Committee, monitored the actions of the different military branches. The air force and navy complied rather straightforwardly with the demands of the newly created committee. The army, the branch with the most African American recruits, on the contrary, withstood the demands to reform its racial structure. Army leadership held on to segregation and argued that only its continuance could guarantee smooth operation of its units in times of war.[38]

The Korean War

Beginning in June 1950, the Korean War put the efficiency of continued segregation to the test. African American reflections on the Korean War diverged and were strongly informed by considerations of the state of race relations and minorities at home and abroad. Although they were entrenched in Cold War rhetoric and patriotism, blacks used the Korean War to criticize American foreign policy, American concepts of race, the notion of black inferiority, and the continued exclusion and segregation of blacks. As was the case in preceding wars, the Korean War became a platform to criticize American domestic and international policy, while also pledging African American support for the American nation. The war against another oppressed race offered an opportunity to severely condemn the United States system of white supremacy that had been effectively dragged into the international spotlight.

Most African Americans supported America's involvement in Korea as a necessary step to halt the seemingly inevitable spread of communism in the world. With some exceptions, the anticommunist discourse was as ingrained in most African American press outlets and among civil rights activists as it was in the majority of the American mainstream. Nonetheless, African American commentators criticized and challenged the American efforts in Korea. Even the most conservative elements of the black press, such as the *Los Angeles Sentinel*, or the civil rights movement, such as the National Urban League, occasionally took a fairly critical stance toward the war and American foreign and domestic policy, especially when it came to questions of race and minority rights. Early on, many black commentators accused the American government of playing into the hands of communism with the continuance of racial segregation and oppression of black people. A segregated army in Korea supplied "Stalin and Communism with the type of propaganda ammunition that will destroy us."[39] The international exposure of the American "race problem" that was pushed onto the international stage through the American military presence throughout the world and especially in Korea, a country populated by another "minority race," was a powerful tool for African American activists.[40]

While the navy and air force sent integrated units to Korea, the army remained segregated. Racism and racial stereotypes deeply rooted in orientalism also clouded the military's assessment of North Korean and later Chinese soldiers. Military officials had underestimated their fighting abilities and stamina and had expected a quick and smooth victory. However, the Asian enemy came well prepared and with ample combat training and techniques. American troops, white and black alike, struggled against enemy soldiers and Korea's environment. They had to withstand heavy combat and were outnumbered and insufficiently equipped. Still, the United States and its allies believed in the innate superiority of the West and the need to "help" allegedly inferior races and cultures to advance. Moreover, throughout the war, there existed disrespect, even disdain, for Asians, friend and foe alike. Like Japanese soldiers during the Second World War, Koreans and Chinese were described as untrustworthy, sly, and ruthless.[41] Hanson W. Baldwin, the military editor of the *New York Times*, compared the North Korean troops to "barbarians as trained, as relentless, as reckless of life, and as skilled in the tactics of the kind of war they fight as the hordes of Genghis Khan."[42]

The black elite, including the National Association for the Advancement of Colored People (NAACP), the biggest and most influential civil rights organization to date, and numerous commentators in the black press, claimed to have a better understanding of and connection with the racial "other," which could be essential for winning the war in Korea and the wider war against communism. However, black rhetoric and statements belied their "sensitivity" toward the "racial other." Rather than speaking about a special bond of "peoples of color" against white oppression, the Korean War discourse in the black press reveals that African Americans felt they were part of the Western/white civilization, which, in their eyes, was clearly superior to that of the Koreans. The latter were often described as "semi-primitive" and seemingly content with their uneducated and economically dire state. The call for interracial cooperation and unity against white supremacy was not reflected in the newspapers or in the soldiers' experiences and statements.[43]

The 24th Infantry Regiment comprised exclusively of African American units was one of the first to be sent into the war. After weeks of defeats, the all-black outfit won the first victory for the UN allies.[44] While the black press celebrated their successes in the otherwise troubled course of the war, long-standing stereotypes of black cowardice and unreliability reoccurred in newspapers and magazines. *Time*, for instance, claimed that African Americans' "Korea battle record was spotty" at best. An article in the *Saturday Evening Post* reported that blacks "fled like rabbits" in the face of the enemy.[45] Under General Douglas MacArthur, commander of the newly created United Nations forces, African Americans were disproportionately court-martialed and received unusually tough sentences for allegedly misbehaving before the enemy. The NAACP sent Thurgood Marshall, founder and head of the NAACP's Legal Defense Fund, to Asia to investigate the allegations. His findings proved irrefutably that racism and persistence of segregation were the root of the problem.[46] However, any failures on the part of black servicemen continued to be explained with deficiencies allegedly inherent to their race.

High numbers of casualties necessitated desegregation. Amid the surprisingly long and costly conflict, the army could no longer fill its need for replacements while upholding segregation. Nevertheless, military officials and subsequently many white papers explained the dissolution of all-black units and their integration by pointing out that black soldiers clearly improved in the presence of whites. Even explanations of desegregation shed a negative light on African American soldiers and their performance in battle. For most blacks, these reasons and the path to integration were just as important as integration itself. They tried to emphasize their valor and abilities, but whites rarely took notice, as clear victories became rarer the more the war dragged on.[47]

In March 1951, the army sent out a group of social scientists to study the progress of integration in its ranks. Based on surveys among soldiers stationed in Asia, the report proved the positive results of integration and helped General Matthew B. Ridgway, General MacArthur's replacement, to push integration forward. By October 1953, the armed forces declared that 95 percent of the military was officially desegregated. Ultimately, Truman's Executive Order 9981 and the Korean War initiated profound and consequential change with regard to race relations and racial equality in one of the most important American institutions within a relatively short period of time.[48] However, much was left undone. The celebratory assertion by the armed forces did not problematize continuing racism, discrimination, and racial conflicts within the military and society as a whole.

The Vietnam War

While the Korean War enforced desegregation in the military for pragmatic reasons, the Vietnam War was truly the first integrated war in which blacks and whites served side by side. African Americans re-enlisted and joined the armed forces in disproportionate numbers after the Korean War. The military offered more equality and career opportunities than any other job field in the civilian world. As a result, many African Americans joined the military for lack of better alternatives. The job market on both sides of the Mason-Dixon Line remained deeply racist and segregated. Moreover, the lack of equality and the persistence of segregation in education defied *Brown v. Board of Education of Topeka*, the Supreme Court decision that had ordered school integration in 1954. Joining the military seemed to promise black advancement more than in the civilian sector.

Even though the military seemed to offer more opportunities than civilian employment, the educational deficiencies perpetuated by the continuing unequal system of education often reduced African American men's chances for advancement in the military quite significantly. The increasing American involvement in Vietnam revealed these problems blatantly. African Americans had a high failure rate on the Armed Forces Qualification Test, which meant that standards needed to be lowered in order to give them a fair chance. Following a report by Assistant Secretary of Labor Daniel Patrick Moynihan, the administration of President Lyndon B. Johnson came to view military service as a way out of poverty for African American urban youth. Secretary of Defense Robert S. McNamara started Project 100,000, which reduced the standards for recruits. The project coincided with the heightened need for combat soldiers in Vietnam.

The result of this move was to suddenly make available a massive source of new recruits in the black community. By 1966 the armed forces required 150,000 men per year, and 40 percent of the men sent into combat through Project 100,000 were African Americans. While more whites were eligible for the draft, ultimately more blacks were enlisted. Blacks' lack of education made deferments unlikely, while white men in college often used their education to evade the draft. Ultimately, conscription disproportionately affected African Americans and more African Americans served in combat than whites. Thus, between 1965 and 1969 more blacks were maimed or died in battle than members of any other ethnic group.[49]

As in earlier wars, the Hispanic experience of the conflict in Vietnam mirrored that of African Americans and working-class whites. Family, patriotism, and tradition played a major role in drawing many Hispanics into joining the military, while educational and socioeconomic reasons further compelled them into military service. As higher education remained rare for Latinos, the great majority were not eligible for deferments and could rarely evade the draft.

Moreover, many volunteered since the military seemed to offer an escape from poverty and the low-paying jobs to which they were reduced. The rare studies that exist show that Latinos were disproportionately represented in combat outfits. Hispanics filled the lower ranks as Latinos rarely became officers. Over the course of the war, their death toll rose significantly, which prompted frustration and protest, especially among younger Hispanics.[50]

The intensification of the Vietnam War in the 1960s also coincided with the rise of the Chicano/Chicana movement. Younger people especially, in cooperation with labor activists, increased their demands for an end to the discrimination and poverty Latinos experienced in the United States. Moreover, their plight at home was seen as intrinsically linked to the fate of the people in war-torn Vietnam. Both systems of colonization, oppression, and exploitation at home and abroad needed to be defeated. Instead of perpetuating oppression abroad by fighting in the name of the United States in Southeast Asia, activists believed that Hispanics, first and foremost, should stand up for la raza and revolutionize the system at home.

Initially, the majority of the African American community supported the Vietnam War. Due to the draft and voluntary enlistment, many black families had relatives in the military, which made support for their deployment something of a necessity. However, the war also coincided with the height of the African American civil rights movement and revealed the fissures in the movement and the limits of cooperating with the administration in Washington. Moderate civil rights organizations like the National Urban League and the NAACP supported Cold War liberalism and anticommunism. They did not want to lose their close alliance with President Johnson, who had helped advance civil rights and established the War on Poverty. Criticism of any military involvement was considered problematic at best and detrimental to the African American cause at worst. Many black press outlets underlined the heroics and martial professionalism of African American soldiers, countering years of stereotyping them as cowards. However, urban unrest and increasingly violent protests further aggravated the situation and spurred a growing white frustration with the black fight for civil rights and equality. Some civil rights leaders were critical of the Johnson administration. For them, Johnson might have been the greatest civil rights advocate of the twentieth century, but over time his "obsession with Vietnam precluded the realization of his goal of further remedying the historical stain of racism."[51]

In contrast, more radical civil rights activist groups like the Student Non-Violent Coordinating Committee (SNCC) and the Black Panthers opposed the war from the start. They believed Jim Crow at home and imperialism abroad were cut from the same cloth, as they resulted from capitalist oppression and needed to be fought together. Black Power activists felt that they had more goals in common with the Viet Cong and their anti-imperialist ideologies. Their new strategies and growing impatience made cooperation with the New Left as well as the traditional civil rights movement increasingly difficult. Indeed, American involvement in Vietnam put an end to cooperation among factions of the civil rights movement. Furthermore, amid urban violence and the Vietnam War, white liberals too began to give up on civil rights and black equality.[52]

Increasingly, the African American community opposed the war. The famous civil rights leader Martin Luther King Jr. initially supported the war effort, but he gradually developed doubts over the war's justness. Reports on civilian casualties and the rising number of blacks killed swayed his attitude and ultimately elicited his strong criticism, a fact that official remembrance of King today all too often ignores.[53] At the Riverside Church in New York City on April 4, 1967, he voiced his staunch opposition to the war and American treatment of the Vietnamese people. King argued that Americans were "strange liberators," considering that the Vietnamese had to "watch as we poison their water, as we kill a million acres of their crops. [. . .] So far we may have killed a million of them— mostly children. They wander into the towns and see thousands of children, homeless, without clothes, running in packs on the streets like animals. They see the children degraded by our soldiers as they beg for food. They see the children selling their sisters to our soldiers, soliciting for their mothers."[54]

Linking America's growing investment in the war with the apparent decrease of the war against poverty at home, King called for the alignment of the peace and the civil rights movements. America needed a "true revolution of values" to reassess its position in the international and national realms.[55] One even needed to advise conscientious objection to future recruits and draftees. White and black commentators alike often criticized King harshly, going so far as to call him unpatriotic and a traitor. Still, his change of heart and the waves of international and domestic news influenced a growing number of African Americans to rethink their position on the war. King's murder in April 1968 destabilized the black community further. Race riots increased across the nation. Younger African Americans especially became more and more disillusioned with the government's domestic and foreign policy.[56]

At home and abroad, African Americans increasingly lost faith in government and the nation. They also began to lose hope in the notion that service would beget change. While the military had promised to be a launchpad to careers for many African Americans, in practice it seemed to use blacks and the working-class poor as cannon fodder in a war that many now believed perpetuated racial oppression at home and abroad. By 1969, many African Americans had grown to view the draft as a racist tool. Quickly, the black power movement made its way to the soldiers in Vietnam. A growing number of black soldiers used music, hairstyles, and handshakes associated with black power and pride. Race pride, voluntary separatism, and a growing sense of militancy took root among many in Vietnam. In particular, younger black recruits raised questions of racial solidarity with Asians.[57] These developments began to worry military officials. They could no longer ignore the growing racial tensions and reacted by establishing the Defense Race Relations Institute in 1971, later renamed as the Defense Equal Opportunity Management Institute (DEOMI).[58] More blacks than before became officers; this created a more stable and trustworthy environment for black servicemen. Hispanics, on the other hand, were not promoted in greater numbers. In 1973, the draft ended, transforming the military into the All-Volunteer Force. As the American economy struggled and unemployment especially in labor-intensive fields was on the rise, many minorities, yet again, saw the military as a way out of their bleak job opportunities and their social struggles. They enlisted and re-enlisted in great numbers after the Vietnam War to escape the dire economic and social reality of the lives of people of color in the United States.[59]

Beyond Vietnam

During and after the Korean War, the military accomplished what many sectors in the United States still lacked in terms of equality and integration. Sociologists Charles Moskos and John Sibley Butler later contended that "indeed, the nature of race relations in the Gulf War had become such a nonstory that media attention shifted to the more topical issue of women in the military."[60] The biggest leap forward of an African American in the military was the ascendance of Colin Powell to chairman of the Joint Chiefs of Staff, the highest position in the American military. "It [the military] was the only place when I was coming out of college, the only institution in all of America—because of Harry Truman—where a young black kid could now dream; the only place, where the color of your guts and the color of your blood was more important than the color of your skin." Powell joined the Army in 1958, three years after the military officially declared complete integration. For him and many others, "the Army was living the democratic ideal ahead of the rest of America." In his autobiographical writings, Powell attributes his success solely to his own hard work and excellent performance. Touting self-reliance, he has made his opposition to affirmative action unmistakably clear. Thus, Powell sends the message that black advancement can only be respected when achieved through an individual's hard work, without outside help, especially not help from the government.[61]

After the Vietnam War, African Americans and minorities in general continued to be overrepresented in the military. A disproportionate number of African Americans served in the military during Operation Desert Shield/Desert Storm, where 24 percent of those in service were African American despite making up only 12 percent of the general population. Discrimination in education and the labor market made the military interesting and often the only option for advancement among blacks and other minorities. It offered an opportunity for education, training, and health care. While the military had tried to exclude blacks from service fifty years earlier, it now began relying on minorities more and more to fight its wars. While some read it as a sign of racial progress, African American patriotism, and dedication to the nation, a growing number of people felt that blacks just continued being cannon fodder in white men's wars.

Black critics of the Persian Gulf War complained that social inequality in the United States forced minorities into the military to have any chance in life. The persistence of discrimination in civilian life forced them to join, even if they might have had other nonmilitary personal aspirations. They contended that the fight against inequality, drugs, and violence at home was far more important than any foreign war.[62] The much-needed resources for improvements at home were now spent on a war in the Persian Gulf that was being fought for questionable reasons. Based on historical experience, a growing number of black critics questioned how and whether African Americans would be rewarded for their disproportionate service.

The response to the brutal beating of African American Rodney King by white police officers in Los Angeles in April 1991 exemplified the argument that the United States needed to focus on issues at home. The question remained what they were doing and defending in the Persian Gulf when "Black people are still targeted, and ultimately victimized, by the hateful and insidious scourge of racism."[63] War was taking place in the United States and it was upon its own citizens. After victory in the Gulf War in 1991, William Gibson, chairman of the board of directors of the NAACP, demanded that blacks needed to fight forcefully for "economic equality" and "political parity" in America after having done so for other countries.[64] Once again, service in wartime was followed by disillusionment as sacrifices in war did not produce the results they desired or were promised. However, they did not have many options since inequality and discrimination in education and on the labor market continued. On the low-wage labor market, employers openly discriminated against people of color. Blacks remained at least twice as likely to be unemployed as whites.[65] Thus, the American military remained a valuable career option for African Americans even if they ideologically opposed its actions.

During Operation Enduring Freedom starting at the end of 2001 and Operation Iraqi Freedom starting in 2003, blacks still made up 25 percent of the armed forces. But for the first time enlistment numbers dropped significantly. According to the Department of Defense, the number of young blacks willing to enlist had dropped by 58 percent. The military and the press took notice, wondering and worrying that the "longstanding relationship with the US military [that] helped them prove their abilities and offered a way to get ahead" was finally disappearing. Indeed, a growing number of African Americans had severed that special bond to the military, as they saw themselves as having other options to advance. Ample job opportunities existed outside the military and the ongoing war in Iraq kept numerous blacks from joining the service.

Moreover, many African Americans mistrusted President George W. Bush and his war aims, even though black officers and politicians played an important part in justifying and shaping the war effort. President Bush's handling of Hurricane Katrina and its aftermath in New Orleans in 2006 appeared to many blacks as a blatant disregard for African American lives at home. A growing number shared a young African American's question: "Why would we go over there and help them [Iraqis], when [the U.S. government] can't help us here?"[66] Doubts over their service for a country that continued to disregard black lives and rights were raised in all factions of the black community.[67]

Nevertheless, in the 2000s and 2010s, more blacks than ever before have become officers in the various branches of the armed forces. In 2014, Michelle Howard became the highest-ranking African American female officer in the U.S. Navy to date. It was one of many firsts she achieved as an African American woman in a male-dominated field with a long history of racial discrimination and segregation. Since June 2016, she has commanded U.S. Naval Forces Europe-Africa. Moreover, she received these promotions under Barack Obama, the first African American president and commander in chief in American history. However, despite all the advances of blacks, the military under Obama continued to struggle to recruit African Americans.

In contrast, Hispanics, the fastest growing "minority" in the United States, have been joining the service in larger numbers than any other racial group. The military actively recruits them in their attempt to fill the dwindling ranks of the All-Volunteer Force. With recruiting campaigns directed at Spanish-speaking people, the armed forces has succeeded in enlisting Hispanics. An especially high number of Latinas also join, thereby changing traditional gender roles in Hispanic families. However, all too often language barriers complicate this endeavor.

At no other time in recent history was the fundamental relationship between military service and citizenship more blatant than in 2015, when Democrats intended to allow unauthorized immigrants to serve in the military in exchange for a green card and an expedited path to citizenship. However, the proposal never went into effect. Anti-immigrant groups feared a mass legalization of immigrants through military service. Representative Mo Brooks, a Republican from Alabama, stated, "There is no military recruitment and retention deficit that justifies supplanting Americans and lawful immigrants with illegal aliens." In his view, American citizens should not have to compete with illegal immigrant for jobs in the military. The opposition had no intention of allowing more immigrants, and especially Hispanics, into the American polity.

Today, Hispanics, African Americans, and poor whites continue to be disproportionately represented among military personnel as their status and chances of advancement have remained much better in the military than in the civilian world. The military thus continues to be in constant flux as it both promises and denies inclusion into the polity. As an institution, it has served both as a means for the perpetuation as well as the exposure of racial inequalities, and at times stood on the forefront of progressive racial politics; yet it has also been a double-edged sword, all too often exploiting minority populations for lofty goals that were not applied at home. The American military both highlights and evades a discourse on race, ethnicity, and class in the U.S. culture to which it is so inevitably tied.[68]

Discussion Questions

1. How did African-Americans understand the relationship between military service and larger efforts to achieve civil rights across the twentieth century? What accounted for shifts in and conflicts among perspectives on these issues?

2. To what extent did the military as an institution facilitate or prevent the advancement of rights and freedom for African-Americans and Latino troops?

3. What factors account for the continued high enlistment rates of African-Americans and Latinx Americans? What do these enlistment rates reveal about the relationship between the military and society?

Notes

1 Judith N. Shklar, *American Citizenship: The Quest for Inclusion* (Cambridge, MA: Harvard University Press, 1991); Kenneth L. Karst, "The Pursuit of Manhood and the Desegregation of the Armed Forces," *UCLA Law Review* 38, no. 499 (February 1991). The majority of books on blacks in the military and war point to the close connection of military service and valor and the claim to civil rights.

2 Harvard Sitkoff, "Racial Militancy and Interracial Violence in the Second World War," *Journal of American History* 58, no. 3 (December 1971): 667.

3 For an overview of blacks in the military, see Bernard C. Nalty, *Strength for the Fight: A History of Black Americans in the Military* (New York: Free Press, 1986); Jack D. Foner, *Blacks and the Military in American History: A New Perspective* (New York: Praeger, 1974); Michael Lee Lanning, *The African-American Soldier: From Crispus Attucks to Colin Powell* (Secaucus, NJ: Carol Publishing Group, 1997); Gerald Astor, *The Right to Fight: A History of African Americans in the Military* (Novato, CA: Presidio Press, 1998).

4 For a recent look at Woodrow Wilson and racism, see Eric S. Yellin, *Racism in the Nation's Service: Government Workers and the Color Line in Woodrow Wilson's America* (Chapel Hill: University of North Carolina Press, 2013).

5 Recent books on black soldiers and the First World War include Chad Williams, *Torchbearers of Democracy: African American Soldiers in the World War I Era* (Chapel Hill: University of North Carolina Press, 2010); Adriane Lentz-Smith, *Freedom Struggles: African Americans and World War I* (Cambridge, MA: Harvard University Press, 2009); William G. Jordan, *Black Newspapers and America's War for Democracy, 1914–1920* (Chapel Hill: University of North Carolina Press, 2001).

6 "Close Ranks," *Crisis* 16 (July 1918): 111; A. Philip Randolph, qtd. in, e.g., Jordan, *Black Newspapers and America's War for Democracy*, 112.

7 Senator James K. Vardaman, Mississippi, qtd. in "Seeing Black Again," *Hartford Courant*, April 14, 1917, 8.

8   James Mennell, "African-Americans and the Selective Service of 1917," *Journal of Negro History* 84, no. 3 (Summer 1999): 275–287.

9   On African Americans in the War of 1898, see Willard Gatewood, *Black Americans and the White Man's Burden, 1898–1903* (Urbana: University of Illinois Press, 1975); Bruce A. Glasrud, *Brothers to the Buffalo Soldiers: Perspectives on the African American Militia and Volunteers, 1865–1917* (Urbana: University of Illinois Press, 2011).

10   Brigadier General Lyte Brown, Director of War Plans Division of the Chief of Staff, qtd. in Ben Wright, "Victory and Defeat: World War I, the Harlem Hellfighters, and a Lost Battle of Civil Rights," *Afro-Americans in New York Life and History* 3, no. 1 (2014): 41.

11   Williams, *Torchbearers of Democracy*, 27–28, 54–55, 128.

12   Ibid., 98–99.

13   Morris J. MacGregor and Bernhard C. Nalty, *Blacks in the Military: Essential Documents* (Wilmington, DE: Scholarly Resources, 1981), 82–83. This collection of primary sources on blacks in the military from the American Revolution to the Vietnam War remains essential for students interested in the topic.

14   Timothy C. Dowling, ed., *Personal Perspectives: World War I* (Santa Barbara, CA: ABC-Clio, 2006), 12–13; Richard Stillman, *Integration of the Negro in the U.S. Armed Forces* (New York: Praeger, 1968), 14.

15   On black soldiers' service in the French Army and their positive experience, see Williams, *Torchbearers of Democracy*, 93–173; Lentz-Smith, *Freedom Struggles*, esp. 109–168; Frank Roberts, *The American Foreign Legion: Black Soldiers of the 93d in World War I* (Annapolis, MD: Naval Institute Press, 2004).

16   Sebastian Jobs, *Welcome Home, Boys!: Military Victory Parades in New York City 1899–1946* (Frankfurt, Germany: Campus, 2012), 41–72.

17   On racial violence, see David F. Krugler, *1919, the Year of Racial Violence: How African Americans Fought Back* (New York: Cambridge University Press, 2014); Herbert Shapiro, *White Violence and Black Response. From Reconstruction to Montgomery* (Amherst: University of Massachusetts Press, 1988); Williams, *Torchbearers of Democracy*, 249–286.

18   Col. Householder, Chief Miscellaneous Division, Tag Dept., in Morris J. MacGregor and Bernhard C. Nalty, *Blacks in the United States Armed Forces: Basic Documents* (Wilmington, DE: Scholarly Resources, 1977), 5:146. This title encompasses a collection of sources on blacks in the military from the American Revolution to the Vietnam War in thirteen volumes.

19   For good overviews of blacks and the Second World War, see Neil Wynn, *The Afro-American and the Second World War* (New York: Holmes & Meier, 1976); Neil Wynn, *The African American Experience during World War II* (Lanham, MD: Rowman & Littlefield, 2010); Kimberley Phillips, *War! What Is It Good for? Black Freedom Struggles and the U.S. Military from World War II to Iraq* (Chapel Hill: University of North Carolina Press, 2012). For a predominantly top-down look at desegregation, see Richard M. Dalfiume, *The Desegregation of the U.S. Armed Forces: Fighting on Two Fronts, 1939–53* (Columbia: University of Missouri Press, 1969); Morris J. MacGregor Jr., *Integration of the Armed Forces, 1940–1965* (Washington, DC: Center of Military History, 1981), http://www.history.army.mil/html /books/050/50-1-1/index.html; Sherrie Mershon and Steven Schlossman, *Foxholes and Color Lines: Desegregating the U.S. Armed Forces* (Baltimore: Johns Hopkins University Press, 1998).

20   A. Philip Randolph, "'Defense Rotten'—Randolph: Let's March on Capital, 10,000 Strong, Urges Leader Porters," *Pittsburgh Courier*, January 25, 1941, 1.

21 On the March on Washington Movement, see Herbert Garfinkel, *When Negroes March: The March on Washington Movement in the Organizational Politics for FEPC* (Glencoe, IL: Free Press, 1959); David Lucander, *Winning the War for Democracy: The March on Washington Movement, 1941–1946* (Urbana: University of Illinois Press, 2014).

22 Robert Fleegler, "'Forget All Differences until the Forces of Freedom Are Triumphant': The World War II-Era Quest for Ethnic and Religious Tolerance," *Journal of American Ethnic History* 27, no. 2 (Winter 2008): 59–84.

23 On Japanese Americans and Japan, see Wendy Ng, *Japanese American Internment during World War II: A History and Reference Guide* (Westport, CT: Greenwood Press, 2002); Peter Irons, *Justice at War: The Story of the Japanese American Internment Cases* (New York: Oxford University Press, 1983); Bill Yenne, *Rising Sons: The Japanese-American GIs Who Fought for the United States in World War II* (New York: MacMillan, 2007); John Dower, *War without Mercy: Race and Power in the Pacific War* (New York: Random House, 1986), esp. 88–105.

24 "The Courier's Double 'V' for a Double Victory Campaign Gains Country-Wide Support," *Pittsburgh Courier*, February 12, 1942, 1.

25 Steve Estes, *I Am a Man! Race, Manhood, and the Civil Rights Movement* (Chapel Hill: University of North Carolina Press, 2005), 13.

26 "Construction Work in Africa Draws Praise," *Atlanta Daily World*, December 17, 1942, 1.

27 Phillips, *War!*, 1–3; Knauer, *Let Us Fight as Free Men* (Philadelphia: University of Pennsylvania Press, 2014), 22–41.

28 Mershon and Schlossman, *Foxholes and Color Lines*, 77–81; also see Ulysses Lee, *The Employment of Negro Troops* (Washington, DC: Center of Military History, 2001), http://www.history.army.mil/html/books/011/11-4/CMH_Pub_110-4-1.pdf.

29 Latinos, military service, and war remain neglected in historical research; however, see Steven Rosales, "The Right to Bear Arms: Enlisting Chicanos in the U.S. Military," in *The Routledge Handbook of the History of Race and the American Military*, ed. Geoffrey W. Jensen (New York: Routledge, 2016), 416–432; Carole E. Christian, "Joining the American Mainstream: Texas's Mexican Americans during World War I," *Southwestern Historical Quarterly* 92, no. 4 (April 1989): 559–595; Richard Griswold del Castillo, ed., *World War II and Mexican American Civil Rights* (Austin: University of Texas Press, 2008); Maggie Rivas-Rodriguez and Emilio Zamora, eds., *Beyond the Latino World War II Hero: The Social and Political Legacy of a Generation* (Austin: University of Texas Press, 2009); Luis Alvarez, *The Power of the Zoot Youth Culture and Resistance during World War II* (Berkeley: University of California Press, 2008).

30 Lee, *The Employment of Negro Troops*, 689–695; Dalfiume, *Desegregation of the U.S. Armed Forces*, 98–101; Mershon and Schlossman, *Foxholes and Color Lines*, 93–134.

31 On the racism of the GI Bill, see Ira Katznelson, *When Affirmative Action Was White: An Untold History of Racial Inequality in Twentieth-Century America* (New York: W. W. Norton, 2005), 136–165. Suzanne Mettler takes a different position; see Mettler, *Soldiers to Citizens: The G.I. Bill and the Making of the Greatest Generation* (New York: Oxford University Press, 2007).

32 Maria Höhn and Martin Klimke, *A Breath of Freedom: The Civil Rights Struggle, African American GIs, and Germany* (New York: Palgrave Macmillan, 2010).

33 On returning veterans to the South and their political activism, see, e.g., Jennifer Brooks, *Defining the Peace: World War II Veterans, Race, and the Remaking of the*

Southern Political Tradition (Chapel Hill: University of North Carolina Press, 2005).

34 Knauer, *Let Us Fight as Free Men*, 42–63.

35 For a more detailed look at Randolph's campaign, see Paula F. Pfeffer, *A Philip Randolph, Pioneer of the Civil Rights Movement* (Baton Rouge: Louisiana State University Press, 1990); Knauer, *Let Us Fight as Free Men*, 64–91.

36 Executive Order 9981, as qtd. in MacGregor and Nalty, *Blacks in the Military*, 239–240.

37 On Truman and Executive Order 9981 see Geoffrey W. Jensen, ed., "The Political, the Personal, and the Cold War: Harry Truman and Executive Order 9981," in *The Routledge Handbook of the History of Race and the American Military*, 357–375.

38 For details on the Fahy Committee and the progress of integration in the armed forces, see MacGregor, *Integration of the Armed Forces*.

39 "Sensible War Strategy" (Editorial), *Black Dispatch*, July 8, 1950.

40 Knauer, *Let Us Fight as Free Men*, 146–157. For a focus on black critics on the left, see Kimberley Phillips, "'Did the Battlefield Kill Jim Crow?': The Cold War Military, Civil Rights, and Black Freedom Struggles," in *Fog of War: The Second World War and the Civil Rights Movement*, ed. Kevin M. Kruse and Stephen Tuck (Oxford: Oxford University Press, 2012), 208–229.

41 On American hubris, orientalism, and the Korean War, see Bruce Cumings, "American Orientalism at War in Korea and the United States: A Hegemony of Racism, Repression, and Amnesia," in *Orientalism and War*, ed. Tarak Barkawi and Keith Stanski (London: C. Hurst & Company, 2014), 39–64; Charles Kraus, "American Orientalism in Korea," *Journal of American-East Asian Relations* 22 (2015): 147–165; Tarak Barkawi, "Orientalism, 'Small Wars,' and Big Consequences in Korea and Iraq," *Arena* 29/30 (2008): 59–80.

42 Hanson W. Baldwin, "The Lesson of Korea," *New York Times*, July 14, 1950, 4.

43 Michael Cullen Green, *Black Yanks in the Pacific: Race in the Making of American Military Empire after World War II* (Ithaca, NY: Cornell University Press, 2010), 124–125; Knauer, *Let Us Fight as Free Men*, 151–161.

44 A reassessment of the performance of black soldiers in Korea by military historians shows that blacks performed poorly due to institutional racism and segregation; see William T. Bowers et al., *Black Soldier, White Army: The 24th Infantry Regiment in Korea* (Washington, DC: Center of Military History, 1996).

45 "National Affairs: Side by Side," *Time*, August 6, 1951; Harold H. Martin, "How Do Our Negro Troops Measure Up," Saturday Evening Post, June 16, 1951, 30–141.

46 Thurgood Marshall, "Summary Justice—The Negro GI in Korea," *Crisis*, May 1951, 297–304, 350–355; "Mr. Marshall Reports," *Crisis*, March 1951, 181.

47 On the Korean War, the black soldiers, and the black community, see David Widener, "Seoul City Sue and the Bugout Blues: Black American Narratives of the Forgotten War," in *Afro Asia: Revolutionary Political & Cultural Connections between African Americans & Asians*, ed. Fred Ho and Bill V. Mullen (Durham, NC: Duke University Press, 2008), 55–87; Knauer, *Let Us Fight as Free Men*, 172–232; Phillips, *War!*, 93–138; Green, *Black Yanks in the Pacific*.

48 Leo Bogart, ed., *Project Clear: Social Research and the Desegregation of the United States Army* (New Brunswick, NJ: Transaction Publishers, 1992); Lee Nichols, Breakthrough on the Color Front (New York: Random House, 1954).

49 On blacks and the Vietnam War, see Phillips, *War!*, 169–253; James E. Westheider, *Fighting on Two Fronts: African Americans and the Vietnam War* (New York: New York University Press, 1997); James E. Westheider, *The African American in Vietnam:*

Brothers in Arms (Lanham, MD: Rowman & Littlefield, 2007); Herman Graham III, *The Brothers' Vietnam War: Black Power, Manhood and the Military Experience* (Gainesville: University of Florida Press, 2003); Lawrence Eldridge, *Chronicles of a Two-Front War: The African American Press and the Vietnam War* (Columbia: University of Missouri Press, 2012).

50 Lorena Oropeza, *Raza Sí!, Guerra No!: Chicano Protest and Patriotism during the Viet Nam War Era* (Chapel Hill: University of North Carolina Press, 2005).

51 Daniel S. Lucks, *Selma to Saigon: The Civil Rights Movement and the Vietnam War* (Lexington: University Press of Kentucky, 2014), 5.

52 Ibid., 184–186.

53 Kevin Bruyneel, "The King's Body: The Martin Luther King Jr. Memorial and the Politics of Collective Memory," *History & Memory* 26, no. 1 (Spring/Summer 2014): 75–106.

54 Martin Luther King Jr., "Beyond Vietnam," *The King Center*, http://kingencyclope dia.stanford.edu/encyclopedia/documentsentry/doc_beyond_vietnam/.

55 Ibid.

56 On King and Vietnam, see Lucks, *Selma to Saigon*, 141–213.

57 Graham, *The Brothers' Vietnam War*, esp. 115.

58 See Say Burgin, "'The Most Progressive and Forward Looking Race Relations Experiment in Existence': Race 'Militancy,' Whiteness, and DRRI in the Early 1970s," *Journal of American Studies* 49 (2015): 557–574.

59 See, e.g., Martin Binkin et al., *Blacks and the Military* (Washington, DC: Brookings Institution, 1982).

60 Charles Moskos and John Sibley Butler, *All That We Can Be: Black Leadership and Racial Integration the Army Way* (New York: Basic Books, 1996), 35.

61 Colin Powell, with Joseph E. Perscio, *My American Journey* (New York: Random House, 1995), 62, 608.

62 "War in the Gulf—The Troops: Blacks Wary of Their Big Role as Troops," *New York Times*, January 25, 1991, A12.

63 Louise James, "What Were Blacks Defending in the Gulf War?," *Philadelphia Tribune*, April 23, 1991, 10A.

64 "Gibson Calls for Blacks to Fight for Justice at Home," *New Pittsburgh Courier*, July 20, 1991, 1.

65 Bart Bonilkowski, Devah Pager, and Bruce Western, "Discrimination in a Low-Wage Labor Market: A Field Experiment," *American Sociological Review* 74 (October 2009): 777–779.

66 All quotes from Joseph Williams and Kevin Baron, "Military Sees Big Decline in Black Enlistees: Iraq War Cited in 58% Drop since 2000," *Boston Globe*, October 7, 2007, http://www.boston.com/news/nation/washington/articles/2007/10/07 /military_sees_big_decline_in_black_enlistees/.

67 Phillips, *War!*, 255–268; Cynthia A. Young, "Black Ops: Black Masculinity and the War on Terror," *American Quarterly* 66 (2014): 35–67.

68 Roberto Lovato, "Latinos in the Age of (In)Security," *NACLA Report on the Americas* 39, no. 3: 26–29.

Further Reading

Geoffrey Jensen, ed., *The Routledge Handbook of the History of Race and the American Military*, (New York: Routledge, 2016).

Christine Knauer, *Let Us Fight as Free Men: Black Soldiers and Civil Rights* (Philadelphia: University of Pennsylvania Press, 2014).

Adriane Lentz-Smith, *Freedom Struggles: African Americans and World War I* (Cambridge: Harvard University Press, 2009).

Kimberley Phillips, *War! What Is It Good for?, Black Freedom Struggles and the U.S. Military from World War II to Iraq* (Chapel Hill: University of North Carolina Press, 2009).

10

Gender, the Military, and War

KARA DIXON VUIC

On the first day of a class I taught titled "War, Gender, and the Military in U.S. History," I received some puzzled looks. I had described the topics we would cover and the questions we would ask, then invited the students to introduce themselves and explain why they had enrolled. One of the students stated rather frankly that he expected the class would be about battles, not women. "I thought this was going to be about shooting people," he explained, eliciting much laughter and some agreement from several of his colleagues. His statement summarized a common misperception about the class. Some students had seemingly overlooked the word "gender" in the course title, while others who had noticed the word assumed it meant "women." Moreover, as women were prohibited from combat roles at the time, many students assumed that women have had little to no active role in war and thought that perhaps a focus on women would give the class an antimilitary approach. Fortunately, the student remained in the class, and over the course of the semester we all discovered the many ways that gender has played an integral part in the U.S. military and its wars.

As this collection makes abundantly clear, the study of war involves much more than the study of battles, or "shooting," as my student put it. (Though, indeed, women have done some of the shooting.) This chapter offers a focused look at the ways that both the experience and waging of war are intimately tied to gender. It is not possible here to exhaustively consider all of the ways gender has worked in twentieth-century wars. However, while moving chronologically through the century, it is possible to focus on telling examples of how gender has both limited and expanded wartime roles, the ways gender has framed wartime decision making, and the intermittent nature of gender change. To analyze these relationships, we must begin with an understanding that the study of gender investigates the ways that societies and cultures have defined women's and men's expected roles and behaviors and thus, in turn, shape how women and men understand their experiences. It is important to remember that gender beliefs vary widely among different groups of people, which means that wartime gender roles are dependent on such related factors as race, class, sexuality, and region. Not everyone adheres to the same ideas about or ascribes the same meanings to gender, but gender does provide context for everyone's wartime work, in some cases affirming their roles as appropriate while providing a means of challenging the status quo in others.

Gender frames the experience of war in many ways. At times, conventional gender ideologies have determined women's and men's wartime roles. From the colonial era onward, Americans have generally held that men were obliged to serve in the military as a fulfillment of their duty to protect the family and the nation. Being "a man" for many demanded military service in times of national need and conferred particular benefits.[1] This framing of service as masculine excluded women, most obviously, but also some men from the most respected and valued wartime positions, both in the military and civilian society. And yet women and men have frequently enlisted these very ideologies to justify or rationalize new roles and thereby to push the boundaries that constrain them. Wartime demands have also led military and civilian officials to expand possible avenues of service and open new wartime roles, a process that has simultaneously broadened gender roles. Studying the ways these roles have changed also reveals, however, that change comes in fits and starts. Often, national and military leaders have rationalized the expansion of wartime gender roles by assuring that changes were only for the war's duration and then by instating policies that reversed course at war's end. Still, even as postwar periods frequently saw a retraction of wartime gains, gender roles were considerably broader and more fluid at the end of the twentieth century than they were at the beginning.

Additionally, scholars of foreign policy, diplomacy, and strategy have shown that gender frames wartime rhetoric and justifications, shapes the perspectives and motivations of policymakers, and colors the ways Americans understand both enemies and allies. Similarly, gendered understandings have led U.S. officials to ally with those who conform to American gender norms and to discount others whose gender approaches appear less familiar. Taken together, gendered discussions of war-making and descriptions of American entanglements frequently cast war as an honorable adventure for American men and a means of shoring up conventional gender norms in the public at large. To understand more fully why the United States has gone to war and how it has engaged with other nations, we must consider how gender has influenced war-making and conduct.

A Family Affair in the Early Twentieth Century

At the turn of the twentieth century, public concerns about gender and the family framed political discussions of the nation's international obligations and defined men's and women's wartime obligations. Many feared that industrialization, the growth of big business, and an economic downturn imperiled the nation's manhood by removing workers from physical labor and threatening their ability to provide for their families. At the same time, a growing movement agitating for women's political equality threatened to upturn the conventional divide between masculine politics and the feminine home.[2] For Americans worried that these changes would have detrimental effects on men, women, and the family, the possibility of war in the former Spanish Empire offered a solution.

After the sinking of the USS *Maine*, jingoist political leaders cast intervention in Cuba and the Philippines as a masculine endeavor that would invigorate a weakened public masculinity and allow the nation to assert its strength and dominance. Young men could engage in the kind of manhood-building violence that they had formerly been able to harness on the frontier. Moreover, as a generation of Civil War veterans passed and some began to call for new models of citizenship unconnected to martial values, jingoists saw intervention in the former Spanish Empire as an opportunity for a new generation of veterans to strengthen ties between martial service, politics, and an aggressive foreign policy. The language of gender proved so pervasive and powerful that even anti-imperialists opposed to U.S. intervention invoked a language of manhood to justify their position, although they defined manhood in radically different ways.[3]

Gender also framed the ways political leaders described the U.S. relationship with the world, beginning a long century in which policymakers employed familial language to soften wartime decision making. Asserting that it was the nation's paternalistic duty to "save" Cuba and the Philippines, politicians and propagandists cast Cubans and Filipinos as sensual, helpless women or as backward children in need of masculine protection and guidance. Such language framed U.S. intervention as chivalrous and paternalistic, not self-interested or overreaching. It also framed U.S. involvement in familial terms, making what would be known as the Spanish-American and Philippine-American Wars appear as selfless humanitarian efforts instead of violent colonial endeavors.[4] Even after the wars ended, U.S. government officials invoked rhetoric about family as they deemed white, middle-class American women's presence necessary to steer American men toward proper, respectable sexual behaviors. This domestic understanding even framed other U.S. military occupations in the early twentieth century and shaped the expectations and experiences of the soldiers tasked with their execution.[5]

As the United States moved closer to the First World War, discussions of gender and family roles continued to frame debates about how Americans should respond to the declaration of war. In particular, the war elicited new debates about the relationship between citizenship and gender. As suffragists campaigned for women's right to vote, they challenged contemporary legal precedent that denied women independent standing and decades of cultural belief that considered women to be physically and intellectually inferior to men. In theory, all American men were citizens, but as African American men knew too well, being a man did not necessarily mean one enjoyed equal rights. The war, and military service in particular, provided opportunities for individuals to make claims of equal citizenship that would transform notions of gender and for the military and government to redefine the relationship between military service, citizenship, and gender. At the war's end, Americans found that while the conflict had brought new experiences and some lasting change, gendered ideologies were not so easily manipulated.

Conventional gender notions in many ways limited women's options during the war, even as they provided them with a platform from which to press for change. In the early twentieth century, many Americans believed that women should be submissive, religious, and pious, and organize their lives around domestic responsibilities. Many women challenged these notions, but the idea that they were inherently maternal limited the ways they could acceptably participate in the public sphere. As American entry into the First World War loomed, many women embraced maternal ideologies to advance their cause, as a platform both for opposition and for active participation.

Pacifists such as social reformer Jane Addams, Rep. Jeanette Rankin (R-Mont.), who voted against American entry into the war, and members of the Woman's Peace Party argued that women, due to their biological ability to give life, had an innate affinity for peace and should oppose war.[6] Popular culture echoed the notion in a 1915 "top-ten" hit. "I didn't raise my boy to be a soldier," the song began, nor raise him "To shoot some other mother's darling boy." Indeed, "There'd be no war today," it insisted, "If mothers all would say,/'I didn't raise my boy to be a soldier.'"[7] Not all women agreed, however, and as preparedness efforts began in earnest many women began to insist that, as mothers, they should support the war effort. In part, their stance reflected the official perspective on women's wartime duties. Government and military officials insisted that good patriotic mothers willingly sacrificed their sons to the cause. They did, in fact, raise their boys to be soldiers (Figure 10.1).[8] Even women who were not mothers, the government argued, should support the boys at the front. For example, women should engage in volunteer work such as rolling bandages and knitting socks, tasks that, strictly speaking, were unnecessary, but which adapted mothers' domestic chores for military purposes. Military officials even celebrated motherhood in an effort to make military service more palatable to the public by casting the military as an extended family through homey canteens at the front and Mother's Day celebrations among the American Expeditionary Forces.[9]

FIGURE 10.1 Liberty Loan poster reading "Women! Help America's Sons WIN THE WAR."
Library of Congress, Prints and Photographs Division, https://www.loc.gov/item/93510435/.

Many women fell in line with these expectations, in part because those who opposed the war were consequently branded not only disloyal but also bad mothers and women.[10] As the war came to dominate many aspects of American political culture, even many suffragists who had initially rejected maternal politics as a justification for female citizenship came to believe that contributing to the war effort would demonstrate women's fulfillment of their obligations and the nation's concomitant responsibility to grant them equal rights. President of the National American Woman Suffrage Association (NAWSA) Carrie Chapman Catt, for example, initially rejected the idea that wartime service made one a citizen and marched in a women's peace parade in New York City in August 1914 when the war began. When the United States entered the war, however, Catt and NAWSA supported a hospital in France, organized food drives, sold Liberty Bonds, prepared Red Cross supplies, and featured war volunteers and workers in suffrage parades, all part of a concerted effort to demonstrate women's national service in hopes that it would lead to federal support for woman suffrage.

Other suffragists, primarily the National Woman's Party, refused to trade war work for the ballot and instead continued to lobby for suffrage based on ideals of equality. Yet however much they tried to separate their cause from martial service, the war provided them with a clear rationale and platform. Members began picketing the White House in January 1917, armed with banners that used President Wilson's words to draw attention to the hypocrisy of fighting a war "to make the world safe for democracy" while denying women the vote at home. Even women who rejected growing connections between wartime service and citizenship used the war to advance their cause.[11]

Women who sought active service in the war also saw the conflict as an opportunity to demonstrate their equality with men, to gain professional status and recognition, to prove their loyalty and dedication to the nation, and to have an exciting (and acceptable) adventure that would challenge them in new ways.[12] Still, gender remained a central way for women to understand their work and its meaning. In an era when women's work in or with the military was largely unprecedented and an overseas assignment even more revolutionary, maternal gender ideologies rationalized women's unconventional work and in some ways limited its potential power. Thousands of women worked in France in relief agencies and as recreation workers, but because their work was cast as feminine, domestic support, it provoked little public consternation.[13] The Army Signal Corps, for example, recruited 450 women to work as telephone operators, about half of whom were assigned to Europe. The army's description of them as "hello girls" whose feminine voices boosted the morale of the men who spoke with them helped to destigmatize their unconventional work by defining it as at least partly for the enjoyment of men.[14] Those who engaged in conventionally feminine roles such as nursing were readily accepted by the military, which had established a permanent nurse corps at the beginning of the century. As they endured unprofessional treatment, including sexual harassment, however, women pushed against conventional gender norms and fought (albeit unsuccessfully) to gain the equal rank that they believed would protect them and provide them with authority.[15]

Men's military service did not elicit the same kind of public debate that women's did, but the war did usher in significant changes in the ways Americans thought about military service as an obligation of male citizens. Before the First World War, most middle- and upper-class Americans did not consider enlisted military service a particularly honorable line of work. The introduction of the Selective Service Act in May 1917, however, made all eligible men potential draftees, and the War Department worked to craft a new image of soldiers that would create broad-based support for the war effort. This new image enlisted notions of masculinity to paint soldiers as respectable, honorable, and patriotic men who fulfilled their manly duty to protect their homes and families. Propaganda images even used gendered depictions of Germans as brutish and overly violent as a call to arms for American men to protect the women and children who would presumably suffer at the hands of an unrestrained enemy. Men who failed to register for the draft or who sought to avoid military service were then branded "slackers," unmanly cowards and traitors who deserved public ridicule. These associations between service and manhood took hold rapidly, leading men who were ineligible for service because of age or physical disqualification to assure their masculinity by volunteering for draft boards or serving on local volunteer committees.[16]

This new image of masculine military duty reflected Progressive era concerns about gender, race, and the family. African American men volunteered in great numbers for military service, hoping that faithful service would demonstrate both their national commitment and their manhood. Racial discrimination, however, excluded black men from the growing associations between manhood and martial duty by limiting their service to labor battalions where they performed undesirable and often menial tasks.[17] Notions of gender and race similarly combined as local draft boards granted more exemptions to white, married, middle-class fathers than to any other group in an attempt to prevent the war from separating breadwinners from their dependent wives and children.[18] Official publications and activities for soldiers also bolstered the family by emphasizing clean living and sexual restraint as a man's duty to keep himself "fighting fit," both for the war effort and for his wife and children (or future family) at home.[19] At war's end, veterans' benefits provided assistance and, where necessary, rehabilitation for disabled men so that they could fulfill their manly duty to provide for their families.[20]

Freeing Men to Fight in the Second World War

Although conventional gender notions limited women's participation in the First World War and framed men's in familial terms, wartime needs worked against convention to necessitate gender change in later wars. Labor demands on the home front and military personnel needs combined during the Second World War to open a host of civilian jobs and new military roles to women, even as public and military officials worked hard to minimize their potential for radical change to gender and familial structures.

The Second World War demanded a combined home front and military effort to supply both war material and personnel. As war production increased and the draft pulled millions of men into service, labor leaders looked to women to fill an increasing void. Concurrent with prevailing gender ideals, when labor leaders expanded employment they looked first to single women who commonly worked for wages before settling into a life of marriage and motherhood. Hiring single women did not violate most Americans' beliefs about gender and work, but as labor needs continued to increase, employers turned to middle-class wives and mothers, who according to gendered ideals were not generally supposed to work outside the home. Their work challenged prewar notions of gender, but as the war continued, need outweighed convention. By the end of the war, married women outnumbered single women in the workforce for the first time in the nation's history. Economic need had pushed African American women into the workforce long before the Second World War, but wartime demands similarly opened doors that allowed many women who had worked as domestic servants to find better-paying, though more dangerous, industrial work.[21]

Women workers moved into many kinds of jobs, from those that meshed with public notions of acceptable women's work to those that overtly challenged prewar gendered labor divisions. In recent years, the public has celebrated the war's working women as symbols of female power and ingenuity.[22] Indeed, "Rosie the Riveters" who labored in industrial factories have become the iconic image of American women during the war, even though women who held traditional jobs in clerical and service fields far outnumbered female industrial workers.[23] But if women workers have become cultural icons in the years since the war, they presented a number of problems for government officials at the time.

The Office of War Information and the War Manpower Commission worked together to recruit women into labor positions and to minimize the challenge their work posed to gender ideologies. Recruitment posters assured that even dirty industrial work would not undermine American womanhood by featuring well-coiffed, attractive women who were working to help win the war and eager to relinquish their new roles at its end. One U.S. Employment Service poster, for example, featured a stylish young woman whose hair was carefully styled under a red safety scarf and whose makeup remained unblemished, even as she focused intently on her drill. With its American flag background, the poster valorized women's work as critical to the war effort, while the text imploring women to "do the job HE left behind" implied that women's industrial work was only a temporary need (Figure 10.2).[24] Women's domestic skills even explained their value in unconventional work, as when a government film likened airplane production to dressmaking.[25]

FIGURE 10.2 "Do the job HE left behind." Office of War Information, National Archives and Records Administration, https://research.archives.gov/id/513683.

Employers also worked to limit women's transformation of labor by separating men and women into different jobs and paying the women lower wages. Even this distinction failed to appease many male workers who, fearing women's entrance into new jobs would decrease wages, frequently harassed the women. The men need not have tried so hard. At the war's end, industries quickly replaced women workers with men, moving women out of higher-paying industrial work and into the less secure, lower-paid service sector.[26] The war expanded women's opportunities in the workforce in unprecedented ways, but the war's end brought a return to many conventional limitations on the ways women could participate.

Just as labor demands opened opportunities for women, military personnel needs created new opportunities. In early 1941, Rep. Edith Nourse Rogers (R-Mass.) attempted to form a women's auxiliary corps that would employ civilian women to work with the army, but her efforts were unsuccessful. Women had served in the military in previous wars, and thousands of women wore the uniforms of the Army and Navy Nurse Corps, but most Americans considered masculine traits essential to soldiering. After the attack on Pearl Harbor demonstrated a clear need for women's service, however, military leaders reversed their previous opposition and supported women's integration in new roles.[27] The formation of the Women's Army Auxiliary Corps (WAAC) in May 1942 brought women into the army in a radically new way—as soldiers—but the transition was not easy. Female soldiers challenged the strong ties between soldiering and masculinity that had been solidifying since the First World War and led many public officials to lament that women's soldiering signaled a weakening of American manhood. "What has become of the manhood of America," Rep. Andrew Somers (D-NY) bemoaned, "that we have to call on our women to do what has ever been the duty of men?"[28]

Despite some public hesitancy, the military's personnel needs demanded an expanded use of women. Many women filled noncombatant roles similar to jobs that women commonly held in the civilian labor force, such as clerical work. Men had, of course, filled these positions before the war, but as women moved into them, military officials explained, in language that echoed that of their First World War predecessors, that women were particularly well suited for these roles because of their feminine aptitude for menial work. Women also performed conventionally masculine work as motor pool drivers and radio operators, for example, that more directly challenged public associations between soldiering and masculinity, but military officials ensured that women did not receive the same recognition for that work that men did. Until the WAAC was permanently integrated into the army as the Women's Army Corps (WAC) in 1943, their auxiliary status prevented women from receiving overseas pay; the navy and marines refused to assign women overseas at all.[29] Until June 1944, women officers served only with relative rank, which denied them equal pay and benefits with male officers of the same rank.[30]

The army's need to send as many pilots as possible to combat duty perhaps pushed gender boundaries the furthest. The Women's Airforce Service Pilots (WASPs) employed civilian women to transport planes in the United States, tow targets and simulate combat situations to train male pilots, and serve as a reserve of pilots in the event that the United States was attacked. But even as these women performed critical and unprecedented work, the military limited its potential transformative power by employing them only as civilians, thus denying them military and veterans' benefits. Female pilots purchased their uniforms, paid for their room and board, and even financed the funeral expenses of some of the women who died in flying accidents. Only in 1977, after an extensive lobbying campaign, did the WASPs receive veteran status.[31]

As in the civilian labor industry, official images softened the subversive potential of women's soldiering by assuring the public that even as soldiers, women retained their conventionally feminine good looks and heterosexual appeal. Female soldiers, these images affirmed, performed vital work but issued no real challenge to the military hierarchy. The slogan "Free a man to fight," for example, cast women's noncombat service as both necessary for the war effort and secondary to the combat roles men could fill. Leaders of the women's corps similarly devoted significant attention to female soldiers' appearance. Hoping both to undermine public suspicions that women who joined the military were "mannish" and to assure the public that military women were upstanding and respectable, leaders commissioned fashionable uniforms to highlight women's shapely figures, issued coordinating makeup and nail polish, and strictly regulated women's off-duty hours.[32]

With these limitations on women's service and careful manipulation of their images, the American public came to accept women's martial service as essential to the war effort. As early as 1942, 81 percent of respondents to a Gallup Poll noted that they would prefer the army draft single women over married fathers for noncombatant positions.[33] Similarly, amid a severe nursing shortage in early 1945, polls indicated that 73 percent of the public approved of a potential draft of female nurses.[34] Military need had again changed public opinion about the relationship between gender and military service, if only for the duration.

The Nuclear Family Fights the Cold War

At the end of the Second World War, many Americans quickly settled into familiar patterns of life, marrying, raising families, and enjoying the prosperities wrought by a postwar economic boom. Although the popular image of the wartime generation happily contained behind their white picket fences obscures much, that image quickly assumed great significance in the postwar world. Cold War Americans believed the "nuclear" family to be a key difference between the United States and the Soviet Union as well as a fundamental means of resisting Soviet influence and communist expansion. With dad providing for the family and mom raising the children to be good citizens and capitalists, the suburban family helped Americans feel safe and secure in an uncertain time. Domestic containment thus served as the home front version of political containment.[35] Not all Americans were happy being contained, and indeed, many women and men challenged the limitations that popular culture imposed on them. Nonetheless, Cold War preoccupations with conventional gender and sexual roles meant trouble for those who did not conform, such as the thousands of gay men and women who were fired from federal jobs.[36]

While gender concerns framed life in the United States in the early years of the Cold War, government leaders once again explained and justified foreign engagements by invoking conventional gender roles, using the family to build productive relations with people in occupied and allied countries. The U.S. military utilized the safely contained and conventional American family as a tool to ease its growing presence in Germany and Japan. Worried that American GIs stationed abroad would seek out relationships with local women, the U.S. military deployed the men's wives and families in hopes that a more domestic environment would foster good behavior. These families, especially wives, also became "unofficial ambassadors" for the nation by building friendships and serving as representatives of the wonders of the American way of life. The conventionally gendered family thus exported American gender norms abroad as symbols of the nation and its new international standing.[37]

In similar fashion, gender framed Americans' understandings of German and Japanese people and their nations in ways that legitimized the U.S. presence for policymakers. As U.S. soldiers formed relationships with German women, those relationships encouraged Americans to stop thinking of Germans as Nazis or enemies and instead to view them as feminized victims of the Nazi regime who needed American assistance for recovery.[38] A similar process occurred in the occupation of Japan, where images of Japanese people as children or women suggested the nation and its people were in need of American tutelage. In particular, sexualized images of women depicted the Japanese people as alluring and exotic "geisha allies," readily awaiting the intervention of American forces.[39] Sexualized depictions of Asian women extended to inform American images of another Cold War hotspot—Vietnam.[40]

Characterizations of nations as feminine damsels in distress neatly meshed with American policymakers' preoccupations with asserting their own masculinity. The Cold War's rigid demarcation of proper gender and sexual roles had a significant effect on the presidents and foreign policy officials who waged war in Vietnam. Raised to believe in the public value of martial manhood and fearing the consequences of being charged "soft" on communism, a series of political leaders committed themselves and the nation to an unconventional and unwinnable war.[41] Martial values not only affected the political elite but also shaped the expectations and experiences of the male soldiers called upon to fight. Many soldiers grew up with tales of wartime heroism and adventure, symbolized by the popular actor John Wayne, who tamed the frontier and won the Second World War. Yet as the war proved unconventional in its battles and tactics, and as soldiers themselves engaged in brutal tactics, the heroic warrior image began to fall apart. Not even images of benevolent GIs bringing medicine to villagers and orphans could stop its disintegration, which seemed complete as the military withdrew from Vietnam and the nation witnessed the communist victory two years later.[42]

The Cold War witnessed other challenges to conventional wartime gender roles, brought on in large measure by second-wave feminism. Military officials found themselves needing to recruit women to a historically conservative institution, in the midst of a controversial war, and they embraced a variety of tactics that reflected both progressive and conventional gender ideologies. Army nurse recruiters, for example, pitched the military as an institution that treated women equally to men of the same rank, supported advanced education, and provided unparalleled opportunities for advanced practice. At the same time, recruitment materials continued to lure women with promises that they would meet handsome men and wear fashionably feminine uniforms. The military engaged in similarly contradictory practices as it removed distinctions between women's and men's service but continued to frame women's service as secondary to that of men. For example, both the Army and Navy Nursing Corps gave up their prohibition against male nurses in the 1950s and 1960s, making one of the most traditionally feminine occupations less overtly tied to gender, although high-ranking officials continued to insist that female nurses were especially valuable for their morale-boosting effect. When the army promoted Army Nurse Corps chief Anna Mae Hays as the first female general, it removed the "brass ceiling" that had hindered women's career potential. And yet General William Westmoreland undermined the moment's significance when he announced "a new protocol for congratulating lady generals" and kissed her.[43]

Many women who served in the Vietnam War military as nurses and soldiers, as well as women who worked with civilian organizations like the Red Cross, often did so to escape what they saw as a stifling future of domesticity. Even as they often felt constrained in their career options, women worked within the existing limitations to carve out unconventional lives. They joined the military and went to war in an attempt to escape the limitations imposed on them and to attain the education, advanced job training, and financial independence that would enable a different kind of life from the one they felt looming before them. Despite distancing themselves from the feminist movement, many adopted the language and ideals of feminism to advocate for progressive change and to remove limitations on their military careers.[44] Gender roles and expectations changed radically during the Cold War, but as these examples demonstrate, conventional understandings of war as a masculine and heroic endeavor and characterizations of nations as damsels in distress framed the nation's waging of war even as conventional gender roles broke down in society at large.

Gender in the Volunteer Military

In 1973, the decades-old Selective Service draft system ended, and the military became an all-volunteer service. The ending of the draft meant that, for the first time since the Second World War, American men were not obligated to serve in the military.[45] The draft had not resulted in the service of every American man, of course, or even a majority of men, but it did mean that military service was an obligation, a duty that all men were potentially subject to perform. The transition to the All-Volunteer Force, then, initiated a fundamental change in public conceptions of martial gender roles that continues to shape the military in the twenty-first century.[46]

With the draft no longer there to procure sufficient numbers of men or to serve as a default motivation for men to enlist in hopes of having some control over their assignment, the armed forces expanded their methods of appeal. Adopting a greater range of marketing and advertising methods than before, the military attempted to reach young men on their own terms, to de-emphasize the irritating aspects of military life, and to assure them that they would retain (and even enhance) their independence. While the services did not completely abandon their promise that young men could prove or develop a physical masculinity—as the branch with the most combat positions, the Marine Corps retained its emphasis on elite physical prowess and toughness (Figure 10.3)—they did adopt a variety of appeals that they hoped would attract men interested in a military career for many reasons. In many recruitment appeals, the military became a jobs program, not an obligation. Air force and navy ads, for example, often advertised the branches as a place for men to challenge themselves and master technical skills, while the army cast itself as secure employment for men seeking economic independence. "Be all you can be," a popular jingle challenged beginning in 1980, "find your future in the Army."[47] Still, some conventional appeals to masculinity remained, especially in ads that promised sexual adventure as a part of the military experience.[48]

The end of the draft also ushered in significant changes in how the military approached and thought about women. On a practical level, leaders of the armed services knew that the volunteer force would depend on a greater proportion of women to fill the ranks. To attract these women, the branches employed the language of the feminist movement to market themselves as equal opportunity employers who guaranteed women equal pay, respect, education, and career advancement. Yet, while advertisements promised women equality, conventional concerns about gender continued to appear in the form of assurances that military service would not impede a woman's feminine charm, good looks, or romantic potential. While one army ad visually assured women that

FIGURE 10.3 Marine Corps recruiting ad, which, like many others, highlighted how the Marine Corps advertises itself as a place to develop physical brawn. Richard Spencer Papers [COLL/5233], U.S. Marine Corps Archives and Special Collections, Quantico, VA.

they could challenge themselves in unconventional ways by becoming a pilot or mechanic, for example, another reminded viewers that military women enjoyed ample opportunities to pursue romance.[49]

As the number of uniformed women increased, their roles greatly expanded and thus contributed to an overall relaxing of gender divides in the military. Officials removed many restrictions that had limited the number of military occupational specialties that women could hold. Reserve Officers' Training

Corps programs began accepting women in increasing numbers, and the service academies enrolled women for the first time in 1976. The branches ended the separate women's corps in the late 1970s, a move intended to make women a more integral part of the military and streamline their career opportunities but which proved quite controversial. Several WAC directors, for example, feared that integrated training, assignments, and promotion tracks would fail to protect women's interests in the ways that a separate corps could and that integrating women would lead to renewed suspicions about their gender and sexuality.[50]

Yet, even as the expansion of women's roles and ending of the draft blurred former gender distinctions, other events limited—and even reversed—these changes. The mid- to late 1970s and 1980s witnessed both the cultural revival of conventional notions of masculinity based on physical prowess and a backlash against feminist gains. Despite the armed forces' continued reliance on women to make the volunteer force viable, throughout the 1980s the army and air force retracted their recruitment of women and even closed positions that had previously been open to women.[51] This retraction occurred in the wake of public controversy over the question of women in combat, brought on by the proposed Equal Rights Amendment. Its opponents suggested that equal rights for women would require them to register for Selective Service and serve in combat. For conservatives, the possibility of women being in combat represented an unconscionable breakdown of gender differences. When Congress reinstated registration for Selective Service in July 1980, women were not required to register.[52] The Supreme Court upheld the exclusion of women a year later in *Rostker v. Goldberg*, finding that because women were excluded from combat, they could be excluded from registration.[53]

Despite continued resistance to women's military service, particularly in the combat arms, U.S. entry into several wars in the Middle East in the late twentieth and early twenty-first centuries brought forth revived discussions about the relationship between war and gender. Although still excluded from any military role that presented a high risk of exposure to direct combat, women nonetheless were assigned to positions that placed them in exactly that position. While wartime needs led to some blurring of the lines between combatant and noncombat positions in ways that also removed some distinctions between women's and men's service, the marines and army also relied on presumptions about women's gender as they developed counterinsurgency plans. Because religious customs prohibited American men from searching or engaging Iraqi and Afghani women, military officials created Lioness and Female Engagement Teams, small groups of women tasked with security and community relations dealing with local women. Based on the notion that women conveyed a sense of safety and comfort that transcended racial and national divisions, these women-only programs used some of the most traditional ideas about gender as a wartime tactic.[54] While the wars introduced women to new roles, media coverage often highlighted a very conventional image of wartime women. American political leaders frequently echoed a century's worth of wartime rhetoric that rationalized the nation's intervention in Iraq in part as a noble effort to save Muslim women from oppression.[55]

It is tempting to see the twentieth century as one long, progressive march toward the breakdown of rigidly divided wartime gender roles. Wars in the first half of the twentieth century brought women into uniformed military positions and new labor roles. The changing nature of warfare meant fewer positions in the combat arms and a much higher proportion in support roles, reducing associations between soldiering and physical muscularity. Gradually, the military removed limitations on women's career potential and opened occupational specialties, softening the distinctions between men's and women's military roles. At the end of the century, women remained formally excluded from combat, though assignment practices frequently meant women served in combat, if unofficially. A closer look at the ways gender roles changed, however, reveals that change occurred in fits and starts. Retraction often followed wartime expansion, and frequently the same historical moment witnessed agitation for progress toward breaking down binary gender roles as well as resistance to any deviation from convention.

In December 2015, the Department of Defense announced that it was lifting all combat restrictions on women. On the day of the announcement, I walked into my class on War, Gender, and the U.S. military to find two women—both with military career aspirations—cheering the decision. At the end of a semester in which we had examined how martial and wartime gender roles had changed over time, for them the announcement came as a sign of undeniable progress.

Whether one sees the lifting of combat restrictions as progress or not, it promises to alter significantly the relationship between gender and wartime experiences by ending long-standing and firmly entrenched associations between soldiering and masculinity. And yet it remains to be seen how Americans will redefine—once again—their understandings of the relationship between gender and war. As the demands and methods of war evolve, and as women and men maneuver for their places in these wars, gender will continue to play an important role in wartime and in the military experiences of all who serve.

Discussion Questions

1. How have conventional ideas about women's wartime roles both limited their participation and provided a means by which to argue for their expansion?
2. How have notions of wartime masculine duty changed in the twentieth century?
3. How can understanding gender help to illuminate wartime and postwar decision making?

Notes

1   Linda K. Kerber's *No Constitutional Right to Be Ladies: Women and the Obligations of Citizenship* (New York: Hill and Wang, 1998), especially Chapter 5, is an excellent place to start on the relationship between citizenship and military service. On the relationship between war and gender, see Cynthia Enloe, *Maneuvers: The International Politics of Militarizing Women's Lives* (Berkeley: University of California Press, 2000); Laura Sjoberg, *Gender, War, and Conflict* (Cambridge: Polity, 2014).

2   Gail Bederman, *Manliness and Civilization: A Cultural History of Gender and Race in the United States, 1880–1917* (Chicago: University of Chicago Press, 1996); Kristin L. Hoganson, *Fighting for American Manhood: How Gender Politics Provoked the Spanish-American and Philippine-American Wars* (New Haven, CT: Yale University Press, 2000).

3   Hoganson, *Fighting for American Manhood*; Amy S. Greenberg, *Manifest Manhood and the Antebellum American Empire* (Cambridge: Cambridge University Press, 2005); Sarah Watts, *Rough Rider in the White House: Theodore Roosevelt and the Politics of Desire* (Chicago: University of Chicago Press, 2003); Richard Slotkin, *Gunfighter Nation: The Myth of the Frontier in Twentieth-Century America* (Norman: University of Oklahoma Press, 1998).

4   Hoganson, *Fighting for American Manhood*.

5   Vincente L. Rafael, *White Love and Other Events in Filipino History* (Durham, NC: Duke University Press, 2002); Mary A. Renda, *Taking Haiti: Military Occupation and the Culture of U.S. Imperialism, 1915–1940* (Chapel Hill: University of North Carolina Press, 2001).

6   The Woman's Peace Party was renamed the Women's International League for Peace and Freedom after the war.

7   "I Didn't Raise My Boy to Be a Soldier," music by Al Piantadosi, words by Alfred Bryan (New York: Leo Feist, 1915), http://www.loc.gov/item/2002600251/.

8   Popular culture followed suit with a 1917 revision of the formerly popular association between peace and motherhood: "I Didn't Raise My Boy to Be a Slacker," words and music by Theodore Baker (New York: G. Schirmer, [1917]), https://www.loc.gov/item/2013564426/.

9   Chris Capozzola, *Uncle Sam Wants You: World War I and the Making of the Modern American Citizen* (New York: Oxford University Press, 2008); Kimberley Jensen, *Mobilizing Minerva: American Women in the First World War* (Urbana: University of Illinois Press, 2008); Nancy K. Bristow, *Making Men Moral: Social Engineering during the Great War* (New York: New York University Press, 1996). I take up this subject in my examination of women recreation workers in my forthcoming book, "The Girls Next Door: American Women and Military Entertainment," which will be published by Harvard University Press.

10   Kathleen Kennedy, *Disloyal Mothers and Scurrilous Citizens: Women and Subversion during World War I* (Bloomington: Indiana University Press, 1999).

11   On maternal politics, the peace movement, and the suffrage movement, see Jensen, *Mobilizing Minerva*; Harriet Hyman Alonso, *Peace as a Women's Issue: A History of the U.S. Movement for World Peace and Women's Rights* (Syracuse, NY: Syracuse University Press, 1993); Bernadette Cahill, *Alice Paul, the National Woman's Party and the Vote: The First Civil Rights Struggle of the 20th Century* (Jefferson, NC: McFarland & Company, 2015).

12   Jensen, *Mobilizing Minerva*; Susan Zeiger, *In Uncle Sam's Service: Women Workers with the American Expeditionary Force, 1917–1919* (Ithaca, NY: Cornell University

Press, 1999); Lettie Gavin, *American Women in World War I: They Also Served* (Boulder: University Press of Colorado, 1997).

13   Zeiger, *In Uncle Sam's Service.*

14   Gavin, *American Women in World War I.*

15   By contrast, female physicians, whose work did not conform so readily to the era's gender prescriptions, failed to secure military assignments and contracted their work with other nations or private organizations. See Jensen, *Mobilizing Minerva.*

16   Jennifer Keene, *Doughboys, the Great War, and the Remaking of America* (Baltimore: Johns Hopkins University Press, 2001); Jeanette Keith, *Rich Man's War, Poor Man's Fight: Race, Class, and Power in the Rural South during the First World War* (Chapel Hill: University of North Carolina Press, 2004); Gerald E. Shenk, *"Work or Fight!" Race, Gender, and the Draft in World War One* (New York: Palgrave Macmillan, 2005).
     The association between manhood and service similarly led conscientious objectors and white working-class laborers to emphasize their physical prowess during the Second World War by volunteering for dangerous home front work. See Mark Matthews, *Smoke Jumping on the Western Fire Line: Conscientious Objectors during World War II* (Norman: University of Oklahoma Press, 2006); Matthew Basso, *Meet Joe Copper: Masculinity and Race on Montana's World War II Home Front* (Chicago: University of Chicago Press); Timothy Stewart-Winters, "Not a Soldier, Not a Slacker: Conscientious Objectors and Male Citizenship in the United States during the Second World War," *Gender & History* 19, no. 3 (November 2007): 519–542.

17   Adrian Lentz-Smith, *Freedom Struggles: African Americans and World War I* (Cambridge, MA: Harvard University Press, 2009); Chad L. Williams, *Torchbearers of Democracy: African American Soldiers in the World War I Era* (Chapel Hill: University of North Carolina Press, 2010).

18   Keith, *Rich Man's War, Poor Man's Fight*; Shenk, *"Work or Fight!"*

19   Bristow, *Making Men Moral.*

20   Stephen R. Ortiz, *Beyond the Bonus March and GI Bill: How Veteran Politics Shaped the New Deal Era* (New York: New York University Press, 2010); Beth Linker, *War's Waste: Rehabilitation in World War I America* (Chicago: University of Chicago Press, 2011).

21   Susan Hartmann, *The Home Front and Beyond: American Women in the 1940s* (Boston: Twayne, 1982); Emily Yellin, *Our Mothers' War: American Women at Home and at the Front during World War II* (New York: Free Press, 2004); Leila J. Rupp, *Mobilizing Women for War: German and American Propaganda, 1939–1945* (Princeton, NJ: Princeton University Press, 1978); Karen Tucker Anderson, "Last Hired, First Fired: Black Women Workers during World War II," *The Journal of American History* 69, no. 1 (June 1982): 82–97.

22   See Donna Knaff, *Beyond Rosie the Riveter: Women of World War II in American Popular Graphic Art* (Lawrence: University Press of Kansas, 2010), 171–175.

23   Hartmann, *The Home Front and Beyond*; Doris Weatherford, *American Women and World War II* (History of Women in America) (New York: Facts on File, 1990); Yellin, *Our Mothers' War.*

24   Office of War Information, "Do the Job HE Left Behind," https://research.archives.gov/id/513683.

25   Office of War Information, *Glamour Girls of 1943*, September 1943; Maureen Honey, *Creating Rosie the Riveter: Class, Gender, and Propaganda during World War II* (Amherst: University of Massachusetts Press, 1982); Sherna Berger Gluck, *Rosie the Riveter Revisited: Women, the War, and Social Change* (Boston: G. K. Hall, 1987); Hartmann, *The Home Front and Beyond.*

26 Ruth Milkman, *The Dynamics of Job Segregation by Sex during World War II* (Urbana: University of Illinois Press, 1987); Elizabeth Escobedo, *From Coveralls to Zoot Suits: The Lives of Mexican American Women on the World War II Home Front* (Chapel Hill: University of North Carolina Press, 2013); Megan Taylor Shockley, *"We, Too, Are Americans": African American Women in Detroit and Richmond, 1940–54* (Urbana: University of Illinois Press, 2004); Hartmann, *The Home Front and Beyond*; Honey, *Creating Rosie the Riveter*.

27 Mattie E. Treadwell, *The Women's Army Corps* (The United States Army in World War II, Special Studies) (Washington, DC: Office of the Chief of Military History, 1991), http://www.history.army.mil/books/wwii/wac/index.htm; Leisa D. Meyer, *Creating G.I. Jane: Sexuality and Power in the Women's Army Corps during World War II* (New York: Columbia University Press, 1996).

28 Qtd. in Meyer, *Creating G.I. Jane*, 13.

29 Meyer, *Creating G.I. Jane*; Michaela Hampf, *Release a Man for Combat: The Women's Army Corps during World War II* (Cologne, Germany: Böhlau, 2010); Knaff, *Beyond Rosie the Riveter*; Treadwell, *The Women's Army Corps*; Mary V. Stremlow, *Free a Marine to Fight: Women Marines in World War II* (Washington, DC: Marine Corps Historical Center, 1994); Weatherford, *American Women and World War II*; Yellin, *Our Mothers' War*.

30 Army-Navy Nurses' Act, ch. 38, United States Statutes at Large 61 Stat. 41. See also Janann Sherman, "'They Either Need These Women or They Do Not': Margaret Chase Smith and the Fight for Regular Status for Women in the Military," *Journal of Military History* 54, no. 1 (January 1990): 66–67.

31 Sarah Myers, "'A Weapon Waiting to Be Used': The Women Airforce Service Pilots of World War II" (PhD diss., Texas Tech University, 2014); Molly Merryman, *Clipped Wings: The Rise and Fall of the Women Airforce Service Pilots (WASPs) of World War II* (New York: New York University Press, 1998).

32 Meyer, *Creating G.I. Jane*; Hampf, *Release a Man for Combat*; Knaff, *Beyond Rosie the Riveter*; Melissa McEuen, *Making War, Making Women: Femininity and Duty on the Home Front, 1941–1945* (Athens: University of Georgia Press, 2011).

33 Cited in Weatherford, *American Women and World War II*, 36.

34 Barbara Brooks Tomblin, *G.I. Nightingales: The Army Nurse Corps in World War II* (Lexington: University Press of Kentucky, 1996), 198–203; Weatherford, *American Women and World War II*, 19–20.

35 Elaine Tyler May, *Homeward Bound: American Families in the Cold War Era*, 20th anniv. ed. (New York: Basic Books, 2008).

36 Joanne Meyerowitz, *Not June Cleaver: Women and Gender in Postwar America, 1945–1960* (Philadelphia: Temple University Press, 1994); Joanne Meyerowitz, "Sex, Gender, and the Cold War Language of Reform," in *Rethinking Cold War Culture*, ed. Peter J. Kuznick and James Gilbert (Washington, DC: Smithsonian Institution Press, 2001), 106–123; K. A. Cuordileone, *Manhood and American Political Culture in the Cold War* (New York: Routledge, 2004); David K. Johnson, *The Lavender Scare: The Cold War Persecution of Gays and Lesbians in the Federal Government* (Chicago: University of Chicago Press, 2009).

37 Donna Alvah, *Unofficial Ambassadors: American Military Families Overseas and the Cold War, 1946–1965* (New York: New York University Press, 2007).

38 Maria Höhn, *GIs and Fräuleins: The German-American Encounter in 1950s West Germany* (Chapel Hill: University of North Carolina Press, 2002); Petra Goedde, *GIs and Germans: Culture, Gender and Foreign Relations, 1945–1949* (New Haven, CT: Yale University Press, 2004).

39 Naoko Shibushawa, *America's Geisha Ally: Reimagining the Japanese Enemy* (Cambridge, MA: Harvard University Press, 2010).

40 Heather M. Stur, *Beyond Combat: Women and Gender in the Vietnam War Era* (New York: Cambridge University Press, 2011); Jeffrey A. Keith, "Producing *Miss Saigon*: Imaginings, Realities, and the Sensual Geography of Saigon," *Journal of American-East Asian Relations* 22 (2015): 243–272.

41 Robert Dean, *Imperial Brotherhood: Gender and the Making of Cold War Foreign Policy* (Amherst: University of Massachusetts Press, 2001); Cuordileone, *Manhood and American Political Culture in the Cold War*.

42 Stur, *Beyond Combat*; Susan Jeffords, *Remasculinization of America: Gender and the Vietnam War* (Bloomington: Indiana University Press, 1989); Kimberley L. Phillips, *War! What Is It Good For? Black Freedom Struggles and the U.S. Military from World War II to Iraq* (Chapel Hill: University of North Carolina Press, 2012).

43 Kara Dixon Vuic, *Officer, Nurse, Woman: The Army Nurse Corps in the Vietnam War* (Baltimore: Johns Hopkins University Press, 2010); Charissa J. Threat, *Nursing Civil Rights: Gender and Race in the Army Nurse Corps* (Urbana: University of Illinois Press, 2015).

44 Vuic, *Officer, Nurse, Woman*; Stur, *Beyond Combat*.

45 There was a period of approximately fifteen months between 1947 and 1948 when men were not subject to any draft. The draft that had been established in 1940 ended on March 31, 1947. The Selective Service Act of 1948 was enacted in June 1948.

46 Beth Bailey, *America's Army: Making the All-Volunteer Force* (Cambridge, MA: Belknap Press, 2009); Melissa T. Brown, *Enlisting Masculinity: The Construction of Gender in US Military Recruiting Advertising during the All-Volunteer Force* (New York: Oxford University Press, 2012); David R. Segal, *Recruiting for Uncle Sam: Citizenship and Military Manpower Policy* (Lawrence: University Press of Kansas, 1989).

47 Bailey, *America's Army*, 191–197.

48 Bailey, *America's Army*, 79–83; Brown, *Enlisting Masculinity*.

49 "The Army needs girls as well as generals" and "Some of our best men are women," in Bailey, *America's Army*, images inset.

50 Bailey, *America's Army*, 130–171.

51 Although a complete discussion of the military's regulation of sexuality is beyond the scope of this chapter, concerns about gender often entangled with concerns about homosexuality. Until the 1980s, policies regarding the service of gay men and lesbians were not uniform but contingent on a variety of factors, including contemporary understandings of gendered positions of power as manifested during sexual acts, personnel needs, and commanders' discretion. In 1981, however, the Department of Defense mandated the discharge of service members who engaged or attempted to engage in homosexual sex. The introduction of the 1993 Don't Ask, Don't Tell policy was intended to relax this mandate by requiring only the dismissal of service members who openly declared themselves to be gay or lesbian. The policy held until Congress repealed it in 2010. A thorough history of the military's policies on homosexuality does not yet exist, but those interested should begin by consulting works that take up portions of that history. See Allan Bérubé, *Coming Out under Fire* (New York: Free Press, 1990); Meyer, *Creating G.I. Jane*; Margot Canaday, *The Straight State: Sexuality and Citizenship in Twentieth-Century America* (Princeton, NJ: Princeton University Press, 2009).

52 Bailey, *America's Army*; Jeanne Holm, *Women in the Military: An Unfinished Revolution*, rev. ed. (New York: Presidio Press, 1993).

53 *Rostker v. Goldberg*, 453 U.S. 57 (1981).

54 Elizabeth Mesok, "Affective Technologies of War: US Female Counterinsurgents and the Performance of Gendered Labor," *Radical History Review* 123 (October 2015): 60–86.

55 Kelly Oliver, *Women as Weapons of War: Iraq, Sex, and the Media* (New York: Columbia University Press, 2010); Evelyn Alsultany, *The Arabs and Muslims in the Media: Race and Representation after 9/11* (New York: New York University Press, 2012).

Further Reading

Cynthia Enloe. *Maneuvers: The International Politics of Militarizing Women's Lives*. Berkeley: University of California Press, 2000.

Joshua S. Goldstein. *War and Gender: How Gender Shapes the War System and Vice Versa*. New York: Cambridge University Press, 2003.

Laura Sjoberg. *Gender, War, and Conflict*. Cambridge: Polity, 2014.

11

The Embodiment of War

Bodies for, in, and after War

JOHN M. KINDER

On October 11, 1968, Lewis Puller Jr., son of the most decorated marine in U.S. history, was escaping an enemy ambush near the Vietnamese village of Viem Dong when he tripped a booby-trapped landmine made from a howitzer shell. "As shock began to numb my body," he later wrote, "I could see through a haze of pain that my right thumb and little finger were missing, as was most of my left hand, and I could smell the charred flesh, which extended from my right wrist upward to the elbow." Both legs were gone—vaporized in a "pink mist." Close to death, Puller was medevacked to a naval hospital triage unit in Da Nang and then on to Andrews Air Force Base near Washington, DC. He weighed less than sixty pounds and had to be fed through a tube in his nose.[1]

Puller spent the next two-and-a-half years in a Philadelphia hospital as surgeons and physical therapists attempted to heal what was left of his body. Yet, even after his release, he struggled to put the traumas of war behind him. Paralyzed by depression, Puller "drank [himself] into near oblivion almost every night."[2] He eventually sobered up and wrote a Pulitzer Prize–winning autobiography, but the physical and psychological wounds endured. On May 11, 1991, after several unsuccessful attempts at suicide, Lewis Puller put a gun to his head and pulled the trigger. He was forty-eight years old.

Though certainly dramatic, the story of Puller's body is far from unique. From the Civil War to the War on Terror, the militarization and destruction of the human body has been—and continues to be—the defining feature of armed conflict. Imagined simultaneously as a weapon to be honed, a resource to be marshaled, a problem to be solved, and a memorial to be honored, the body has occupied a central (though frequently overlooked) place in American military history. Not surprisingly, ideas about combatants' bodies have long been fraught with contradictions and uncertainties. For some, the military body is an icon of masculinity and the ultimate embodiment of national ideals. For others, it remains a dangerous symbol of the violence and suffering inherent in all armed conflict. As a result, debates about the training and treatment of American bodies in wartime often have as much to do with ideology—the politics of how and why the nation fights—as with the health and welfare of the troops.

Rather than rehearsing a chronological survey, this chapter offers a tripartite account of the three stages passed through by militarized American bodies in wartime. In stage one, bodies are prepared for war. Over the course of the twentieth century, the military has invested ever-greater resources toward altering soldiers' bodies. Potential recruits and draftees have been systematically selected to meet physiological and psychological standards, their bodies and minds then hardened—through relentless exercise, discipline, social engineering, and surgical intervention—to meet the anticipated strains of combat. Stage two concerns the experiences of combatants' bodies in war. In a century of antipersonnel warfare, where victory has often been determined as much by body counts as by territory won, Americans have gone to great lengths to mitigate the inevitable traumas suffered by combatants' bodies. Despite the tremendous advances in triage, military medicine, wound treatment, and rehabilitation, however, frontline soldiers' bodies rarely emerge from war unscathed. Stage three describes the fate of bodies after war—dead bodies, buried bodies, disabled bodies. Americans have struggled to make sense of postwar bodies, alive and dead, in social policy and popular culture. Even as many Americans revere war injury as a symbol of martial service, the war-injured body remains a potent threat to American victory culture.

Despite the military's boundless optimism about "safe" warfare and computerized prosthetics, the human body will pose a danger for war-makers well into the future. Indeed, thanks to advancements in medicine and other technologies, twenty-first-century American military leaders face an unprecedented ethical challenge: how to conduct war in an age when it's possible to obliterate enemy armies without putting a single American soldier in harm's way.

Bloodless Battle, War without Bodies

At first glance, the history of American warfare can often appear strangely devoid of flesh, sweat, and blood. Prior to the late 1960s, Hollywood usually pumped out what scholar and Second World War veteran Paul Fussell called a "Disney-fied" version of warfare. In the big-screen conflicts of John Wayne and Audie Murphy, deaths are quick, suffering is minimal, and "everyone has all his limbs, his hands and feet and digits, not to mention expressions of courage and cheer."[3] Contemporary video games are little better, despite their promise of blood-and-guts realism. When killed, players' characters miraculously "respawn," their bodies ready to take another round of punishment. Even the Greek poet Homer, often considered the godfather of Western war writing, is notably silent when it comes to the more unromantic aspects of wartime embodiment. Missing in Homer's work, observes psychiatrist Jonathan Shay, are a number of "universal realities of war," including the bodily effects of privation and squalor.[4] In *The Body in Pain* (1985), philosopher Elaine Scarry goes so far as to say that "one can read many pages of a historic or strategic account of a particular military campaign, or listen to many successive installments in a newscast narrative of events in contemporary war, without acknowledging that the purpose of the event described is to alter (to burn, to blast, to shell, cut) human tissue."[5]

How is this possible? Scholars themselves share part of the blame. Traditionally, the field of military history has shied away from the bodily dimensions of war (eating and sleeping, sickness and injury, hunger and health). Memoirs and popular histories notwithstanding, much war writing has privileged a bird's-eye view of the battlefield, surveying the movement of armies and not the intimacies of corporeal existence. Over the past few decades, a growing cohort of medical, military, and disability historians have sought to buck this trend, drawing much-needed attention to the "fearsome physicality" of modern warfare.[6] In *The Smell of Battle, the Taste of Siege* (2015), for example, Mark Smith incorporates insights from the novel field of "sensory history" to describe the "unpleasant economy of pain, taste, touch, smell, sight, and sound" endured by Civil War combatants and civilians. "The looming war," in Smith's retelling, "would injure and pollute eyes, subjecting them to new, confusing sights; expose ears to sounds discordant and inhuman; bombard noses with odors rank, fetid, and impure; treat skin with a new, brutal contempt; and initiate radical changes in taste."[7] Later wars were no less contemptible when it came to abusing combatants' bodies and shattering their senses. With a few notable exceptions, however, historians have tended to relegate ears, noses, and other body parts to the margins of the American war story.

As much as willful omission, the invisibility of bodies is also a product of language. American military discourse is awash in euphemism, to the extent that flesh-and-blood bodies become virtually unrecognizable. In contemporary warspeak, soldiers' deaths are renamed "losses," the killing of civilians "collateral damage." Pressed on the dangers of modern combat, military officials rarely invoke the specter of mass slaughter; rather, they extol the "price" of victory, the "cost" of battle, and the heroics of the "fallen." This process of substitution extends to soldiers themselves, whose flesh-and-blood traumas are subsumed in the collective "damage" suffered by the imagined bodies of entire armies or nations. As media scholar Roger Stahl puts it, "Communications becomes the 'nervous system' to be 'shut down,' supply lines become 'arteries' to be 'ruptured,' reconnaissance are 'eyes' to be 'blinded,' and the leadership a 'head to decapitated.'"[8] Abraham Lincoln famously indulged in this kind of rhetoric in his Second Inaugural Address (1865), challenging the war-weary public to "bind up the nation's wounds."[9] Nations don't have wounds, of course, but that did not matter. The metaphor stuck, and it has been a favorite of politicians and war apologists ever since. More than one hundred fifty years later, the language of modern war remains a force of abstraction, more adept at describing metaphorical bodies than material ones.

Visual culture shares a similar tendency to distract and obscure. In conventional military maps, bodies disappear altogether, the lives and suffering of individual soldiers metaphorically refigured into abstract symbols cast about on an unchanging, two-dimensional plane. Charts and graphs of military "casualties"—a generic term for victims of wartime violence—are no less bloodless, transforming thousands, if not millions of deaths into lines on a page. Since the early nineteenth century, critics of war have sought new ways to visualize war's bodily destruction. In June 2014, for example, *Mother Jones* magazine released a video map by photographer Jerry Redfern meant to convey the scale of the U.S. bombing campaign against Laos from 1964 to 1973. For more than a minute and a half, viewers watch as a flurry of 600,000 red and green dots— each representing a separate bombing run—blanket a digital outline of the country. The effect is poignant and strangely entrancing, made even more so by the musical accompaniment by pianist Peter Rudenko. Yet, for all of its initial power, the video adheres to the same kind of abstraction that makes such bombings possible in the first place: the erasure of bodies in favor of dots on a map.[10]

In the mid-nineteenth century, the invention of photography threatened to transform Americans' perceptions of bodies in wartime. Writing about photographer Matthew Brady's exhibition The Dead of Antietam in October 1862, Oliver Wendell Holmes declared, "Let him who wishes to know what war is look at this series of illustrations. These wrecks of manhood thrown together in careless heaps or ranged in ghastly rows for burial were alive but yesterday."[11] Unlike painting or illustration, photography promised an unbiased window into historical truth. Since that time, war's critics have routinely used photography to debunk military euphemism and spotlight, in theologian Harry Emerson Fosdick's words, war's "plain, stark, ugly meaning."[12] Bodily suffering—especially the suffering of enemies—is a common theme in American war photography. Indeed, critic Susan Sontag observes that "the appetite for pictures showing bodies in pain [is] as keen, almost, as the desire for ones that show bodies naked."[13]

Nevertheless, war photographers have not always made bodies a main priority. Part of the problem was technological. Up until the 1930s, the weight and technical limitations of photographic equipment made it difficult to capture scenes of frontline combat. Moreover, the federal government has often sought to mold public perceptions of bodily destruction. During the First and Second World Wars, censorship agencies eliminated disturbing images of American troops. Americans at home did not begin to see photos of dead GIs until 1943, when *Life* published George Strock's photograph of three recently killed soldiers on Buna Beach in New Guinea. The public response was overwhelmingly positive, and news agencies regularly printed pictures of U.S. war casualties throughout 1944 and 1945.[14] During the Vietnam War, the military loosened press restrictions even further, and photographers shocked audiences with their gruesome images of bodies burned, mangled, or poisoned by modern weaponry.

However, this moment of press freedom was relatively short-lived. Convinced that scenes of slaughter had depressed civilian morale, government regulators in the wake of Vietnam sought to reassert their control over images of bodies in wartime. Starting with the Persian Gulf War of 1990–1991, military officials attempted to restrict photographers' access to the battlefield, and photojournalists complained about a culture of intimidation among officers hostile to the media presence.[15] In December 2009, the Pentagon decided to lift its eighteen-year-old ban against the news media photographing dead soldiers' flag-draped coffins. (Families of the dead still had to give their consent.) Reactions to the policy change were mixed; opponents of the change stressed the need to respect the privacy of the dead, while advocates argued that the public had a right to see the human cost of the nation's foreign policy.[16] Yet, even before the ban was lifted, digital cameras, smart phones, and online file-sharing sites like YouTube had rendered military censorship efforts largely obsolete. Since the start of the post-9/11 War on Terror, American troops themselves have amassed an unprecedented digital archive of war's toll on civilians' and combatants' bodies.[17] The only problem is getting Americans at home to look at them.

One additional factor—perhaps above all others—has made it possible for us to overlook war's relentless churn of human bodies: geographical distance. Since the mid-nineteenth century, the bulk of the population has experienced war from afar. The genocidal campaigns against Native Americans notwithstanding, American wars take place "over there"—out of sight and, very often, out of mind. For the last century and a half, the U.S. public has been sheltered from wartime injury to an extent that would be unimaginable in the rest of the world. The one notable exception was during the Civil War, a conflict notorious for its consumption of young bodies. In *This Republic of Suffering* (2008), historian Drew Gilpin Faust notes, "Bodies were in important ways the measure of the war—of its achievements and impact; and, indeed, bodies became highly visible in Civil War America." Newspapers ran lists of the wounded, both armies used casualties to gauge battlefield success, and frontline reports "rendered the physicality of injury and death all but unavoidable."[18] At war's end, more than 600,000 living bodies had been transformed into corpses—some of which would lie unburied in forests for years.

Prepping Bodies for War

The relationship between bodies and war does not begin on the battlefield. Although many Americans still venerate the republican ideal of the citizen-soldier, the military has long espoused the belief that not all bodies are meant for combat. During the Civil War, military recruiters tended to overlook perceived physical or mental impairments. Starting in 1863, thousands of disabled Union soldiers joined the Veterans Reserve Corps (better known as the "Invalid Corps"), performing light military duty so that nondisabled men could join the fight. By the early twentieth century, however, physical standards had become more exacting. During the First World War, the War Department argued that soldiers' healthy bodies were a vital military resource, as necessary to winning the war as the latest high-tech weaponry. According to the U.S. Army Medical Department, "The significance of the physique of the soldier to the army is everywhere recognized and much effort is expended to select the physically fit. A solder must have a good nervous system, heart and vessels without serious defect, good feet, strong inguinal muscles and fascia, strong bones and ligaments, and well-functioning joints, keen sense organs, and freedom from organic diseases."[19] Unlike in previous conflicts—when, in one observer's words, "any one who was not lame or crippled or blind or clearly diseased, would do to stop a bullet"—the Great War demanded a new kind of soldier with a new kind of body.[20]

Beyond meeting a set of physical standards, American combatants were required to "fall within certain limits of size" and adhere to a strict set of bodily and behavioral norms. The standardization of bodies and behavior—a hallmark of the industrial era in general—was critical to the task of mobilizing millions of soldiers for battle. Experts within the War Department used calculations of body size and requirements in the production of everything from gas masks and uniforms to "standard food rations." Although the duties of soldiers were increasingly specialized, modern fighting men were expected to be virtually interchangeable in terms of size, strength, nutritional needs, and overall health. As a result, civilian draft boards and military personnel were encouraged to take a harsh stand when it came to rejecting or discharging would-be soldiers—especially those who displayed signs of incurable "defects," neurological disorders, or eccentric behavior. Treatment of mentally (and physically) ill soldiers was costly and, in the words of one observer, "interfered with the training of their brighter or better-adjusted comrades." According to a memorandum sent to company commanders, suspect cases included not only patients with recognizable diseases but also a wide range of physical and social deviants: men who had difficulty learning drill or following instructions, delinquents, company "butts," emotionally unstable men (too readily moved to tears or anger), known or suspected homosexuals, epileptics, drug addicts, bed wetters, stammering speakers, and "negligent, untidy, or otherwise seemingly inferior or objectionable individuals."[21] Men who deviated from military standards of normality were, in the eyes of military officials, best weeded out before they donned a uniform.

However, even the fittest enlistees struggled to maintain the military's high standards of physical and mental health. Throughout the First World War, disease, accidents, fatigue, and the temptations of alcohol proved dire threats to the bodies of American troops. In an effort to "conserve" the nation's fighting strength, physicians and Progressive reformers within the Commission on

Training Camp Activities (CTCA) developed an integrated program of physical training, prophylaxis, and social hygiene education.[22] Before their enlistment, draftees were encouraged to prepare for war's rigors by exercising daily and ridding their bodies of internal pollutants.[23] Once in uniform, they were subject to a strict regimen of discipline and drill, their every bodily function monitored to maximize efficiency and unit cohesion. Many of these lessons might seem basic by today's standards. Doughboys in training were instructed to urinate only in designated latrines, brush their teeth at least once daily, carefully inspect their skin for lesions and sores, wash and dry their feet following every march, and avoid standing in a breeze when perspiring or wearing wet clothes. Liquor and "lewd women" were out of bounds; instead, new recruits were encouraged to take up "wholesome" activities such as calisthenics and boxing.[24] The end result of the CTCA's campaign was a new model of martial embodiment: physically fit, sexually pure, socially responsible, and in total control of one's instincts.

During the Second World War, military officials intensified their efforts to screen, monitor, and—in many cases—transform the bodies of would-be GIs. Upon arrival at an army induction center, the typical inductee was stripped to his underwear and marched through a cordon of physicians, each tasked with identifying a specific physical weakness or flaw. "From his feet to his ears, he was poked, pricked, prodded, and measured," writes Christina Jarvis in *The Male Body at War* (2010). "His height, weight, chest size, and other physical statistics were recorded, and blood and urine samples were taken for tests."[25] A dentist made a cursory examination of the inductee's teeth; a psychiatrist asked whether he "liked girls." At the end of it all, each man was assigned one of three designations: fit for service, fit for limited service, or unfit for service. Between November 1940 and October 1945, more than eighteen million men passed through military induction centers—and the test results often proved alarming. In some years, upwards of 40 percent of inductees failed to meet the military's standards of physical and mental fitness, prompting observers to fret about the dangerous decline of national health.[26] Even those accepted might seem slight by today's standards of beefed-up masculinity. The average successful inductee, notes Jarvis, was "68.1 inches tall, weighed 152 pounds, had a chest size of 34 inches at expiration, and was generally free of disease."[27]

Still, the military remained confident that its training programs could whip even the softest civilian into shape. Despite war's obvious dangers, the military had long trumpeted its ability to remake men's bodies for the better. During the First World War, the slogan "The United States Army Builds Men," often accompanied by images of thickly muscled soldiers, was a mainstay of recruitment campaigns. In the interwar years, peace activists routinely mocked such promises, but they could do little to shake the idea that military service offered a sure path to physical improvement—at least in the short run.[28] Indeed, in the decades since the Second World War, the military's promise of bodily transformation has been one of its biggest selling points. Journalist Thomas E. Ricks

FIGURE 11.1 Even in an age of cyberwarfare and high-tech weaponry, the U.S. military continues to view healthy bodies as critical to the nation's capacity to wage war. This photo shows a
group of Marine Corps recruits attempting to complete a physical fitness test on August 29,
2016. Photo by Lance Cpl. Kailey Maraglia; courtesy of the United States Marine Corps, U.S.
Department of Defense, https://www.defense.gov/Photos/Photo
-Gallery?igphoto=2001619884.

describes this process in *Making the Corps* (1997), his chronicle of life at marine
boot camp on Parris Island, South Carolina, in the mid-1990s. Upon arrival,
recruits endure a thirteen-week trial of physical training, strength and endur-
ance tests, and harsh discipline (Figure 11.1). Heads shaved and frequently short
on sleep, they are taught how to march (the marine way), eat (the marine way),
and stand (the marine way). In this world, Ricks notes, "pleasure is suspect, and
pain and sacrifice are good."[29] Those who make it to graduation have been so
hardened by exercise that they are virtually unrecognizable to their friends and
family—and that's the point. As one drill instructor informs them early in their
training, "Every recruit here, whether he is fat or skinny, tall or short, fast or
slow, has the ability to become a United States Marine, if you can develop self-
discipline and spirit."[30]

The various branches of the military continue to publish lengthy standards of
physical and mental fitness. As of June 2016, recruits with authenticated histories of chronic liver disease, anal polyps, or "cretinism" were likely to be rejected,
as were those with abnormal uterine bleeding, penile lesions ("not amenable to
treatment"), or cardiac heart disease. Men below sixty inches (or above eighty
inches) in height can be rejected, as can women who are too tall or too short.[31]
However, in the postdraft military, recruiters have routinely been forced to

adopt more elastic health standards, particularly when it comes to would-be soldiers' waistlines. Although some commentators warn that the U.S. "obesity epidemic" represents a vital threat to national security, the rising importance of cyberwarfare and other forms of sedentary combat have raised new questions about the necessity of uniform military fitness standards.[32] After all, it doesn't take thick biceps or a tight waist to operate a computer or pilot a drone.

Even so, the U.S. military has traditionally classified certain bodies as ineligible for active-duty service, no matter how dire the circumstances. Well into the twentieth century, the armed forces relied upon biased thinking and stereotypes to determine whose bodies were fit for uniform. During the First World War, for example, military screening guidelines warned against men whose "degenerate" bodies (wide hips, narrow shoulders, minimal body hair) seemed to exhibit a dangerous degree of gender nonconformity.[33] By the 1940s, military inspectors openly surveyed recruits' bodies for signs of "sexual deviance" in an effort to weed out homosexual recruits, a practice that both reflected and reinforced discrimination against gays and lesbians in the broader culture.[34] Prior to the second half of the twentieth century, African Americans were largely characterized as unfit for any military duty beyond physical labor. Indeed, Americans' ideas about bodies were so clouded by racism that, during the Second World War, blood banks bowed to racist (and scientifically meritless) demands to segregate "white" and "black" blood plasma.[35]

More than any other group, though, the armed forces' screening and training programs exhibited the greatest institutional bias against the bodies of women. As feminist scholars Monica J. Casper and Lisa J. Moore point out, "Social and cultural beliefs about femininity inscribed onto women's bodies—softness, fragility, and nurturance—are not what make up 'the few, the proud,' and the hard. . . . There exists a widespread ideology that women's bodies do not belong in the military because they are incongruent with the masculinized" hardships of combat.[36] Women's experiences in the most recent U.S. wars have started to erode such attitudes. Nevertheless, critics of gender integration continue to cite women's bodies to justify their exclusion from the battlefield.[37]

Bodies in War

Prior to the twentieth century, the greatest threat to American bodies in wartime was infection and disease. During the Civil War, typhoid, dysentery, yellow fever, and malaria were endemic on both sides. In occupied Cuba, following the War of 1898, tropical illnesses killed seven times as many U.S. troops as wounds on the battlefield.[38] By the start of the twentieth century, advances in sanitation and antiseptic surgery had begun to turn the tide, but progress remained slow. In the First World War, large numbers of American doughboys—the nickname given to members of the American Expeditionary Force—suffered from diarrhea, diphtheria, and scarlet fever. Deadlier still was the

"Spanish flu" (influenza), which killed tens of thousands of U.S. troops—and more than 650,000 civilians—in 1918–1919. Since the introduction of penicillin and other antibiotics in the 1940s, death rates from disease and infection have steadily declined, leading some commentators to wax poetic about the relative "safety" of the modern battlefield.[39] Despite such advances, ill health remains one of war's most persistent legacies. Following the brief U.S. military excursion against Saddam Hussein in 1990–1991, hundreds of thousands of American troops exhibited symptoms of what came to be known as Gulf War syndrome, a chronic disorder caused by exposure to the chemically toxic environment.[40]

On top of disease, combatants have faced a host of bodily dangers, from exploding cannon balls (the Civil War) and poisonous gas (the First World War) to razor-sharp punji sticks (Vietnam) and suicide bombers (the War on Terror). Some war injuries are historically specific, their frequency and character dependent on such factors as fighting conditions, armaments used, military tactics, and the ingenuity of the combatants themselves. During the First World War, for example, the height and angle of descent of falling shrapnel shells resulted in high rates of wounds to the arms, shoulders, face, and upper back. The number of men "blown into unidentifiable fragments" also spiked, a product of new developments in high-explosive munitions.[41]

Similar patterns exist for other wars. In post-9/11 U.S. conflicts, the use of improvised explosive devices (or IEDs) has led to an upsurge of traumatic brain injury (TBI), a form of brain trauma often resulting from a concussive blow to the head. According to a report by the Congressional Research Service, U.S. service members suffered more than 327,000 TBI incidents between 2000 and June 2015. The vast majority—over 82 percent—were categorized as "mild" (or as mTBI), primarily experienced as brief periods of disorientation and memory loss. In more severe cases, symptoms lasted for days and brain imaging scans revealed signs of permanent damage. Many of the worst TBI cases were compounded by penetrating injuries to the dura matter, the protective membrane that surrounds the brain and spinal column.[42]

Starting in the mid-2000s, a number of commentators adopted the term "signature wound" to describe TBI and other forms of injury that—for whatever reason—have come to be associated with specific military conflicts. Writing in *USA Today* in 2005, journalist Gregg Zoroya offered a brief table identifying the "signature damage" of past wars:

Civil War: Amputations from bone-shattering gunshot wounds
World War I: Lung damage from gases
World War II: Effects of radiation among GIs who visited Hiroshima
Korean War: Circulation and joint problems from intense cold
Vietnam War: Illnesses from Agent Orange defoliant
Persian Gulf War: Fatigue, skin rashes, shortness of breath; ailments called
　　"Gulf War syndrome"[43]

As the list suggests, the term "signature wound" does not describe most common forms of wartime injury or even the most significant at the time. During the Civil War, only around 45,000 soldiers survived full or partial limb amputations, a small fraction of the serious wounds suffered by combatants on both sides. Indeed, the term "signature wound" is applied in such a random or haphazard fashion that it betrays its own meaninglessness. (Over the last decade, TBI, post-traumatic stress disorder, wounds to the genitals, and "moral injury" have all taken a turn as the "signature wounds" of the War on Terror.)[44]

Rather, "signature wound" operates as a form of ideology, a concept—in the words of sociologist Jerry Lembcke—with "more cultural clout than diagnostic" utility.[45] Much like other forms of military euphemism, the term functions as a tool of disavowal, allowing its user to insist that each war's violence is wholly unlike anything that has come before. In other words, it lends weight to the pernicious myth that each new war is unique and, as such, current generations bear no ethical responsibility if the latest military adventure does not turn out as planned. (For what it's worth, the term also legitimates a hierarchy of injury in which certain kinds of wounds—and certain kinds of wounded combatants—are afforded greater symbolic worth than others.) Even those who acknowledge the existence of TBI in previous wars, for example, nevertheless insist that its current manifestation is different—now having risen to "signature" status. "Often accompanied by burns, organ damage, and blunt or penetrating injury," wrote Matt Grills in *The American Legion Magazine* in 2008, "this is not the TBI of wars past."[46]

Terms like "signature wound" are problematic for another reason: they mask the banal, unromantic, and ultimately predictable nature of most war injury. The destruction of American bodies in wartime has typically involved the lethal combination of two elements: explosive force and metal. There are exceptions. Over the past one hundred fifty years, American troops have been beaten, gassed, strangled, stabbed, starved, burned, and drowned; they have been eaten by sharks and tortured in POW camps; and they have fallen victim to the "blunders" (training-camp accidents, failed technology, errors of forethought) attendant to all military campaigns.[47]

However, the greatest battlefield threat to American life and limb has been the high-speed projection of chunks of metal—whether in the form of Civil War–era machine-gun bullets, World War II–era exploding shells, or shrapnel from homemade IEDs. Since the introduction of gunpowder-based weapons in the Middle Ages, arms manufacturers have waged a relentless campaign to fine-tune the body-shredding capacity of military weapons. In the aftermath of the Civil War, experts in the field of wound ballistics carried out lengthy experiments on the "explosive effect" of high-velocity projectiles on human flesh. At the time, many wound experts were animated by a desire to create what were euphemistically called "humane" weapons—arms designed to injure opponents while limiting the likelihood of permanent disability or death.[48] But their dream of bloodless war was short-lived. On the killing fields of Passchendaele

FIGURE 11.2 Although some U.S. newspapers downplayed the threat of bodily injury, hundreds of thousands of American troops were wounded on the Western Front during the First World War. This Signal Corps photograph shows wounded doughboys being treated in the ruins of a French church in 1918. Library of Congress, Prints & Photographs Division, LC-USZ62-37482, https://www.loc.gov/item/2016650682/.

and Verdun, the armies of Europe mass produced injury on a scale previously seen only in the pages of science fiction (Figure 11.2).[49]

Indeed, since the emergence of modern war techniques in the nineteenth century, Western militaries have tended to adopt a maximalist approach to bodily destruction, resulting in bigger guns, heightened killing capacities, and more expansive definitions of "legitimate" targets. By the early twentieth century, notes journalist Ben Shephard, "Artillery could now be deployed from miles behind the front line; mounted on recoilless carriages, the guns could keep firing, without tedious resighting, as fast as their crews could reload. Death could come suddenly and without warning from out of the sky."[50] Although writers and military propagandists would continue to tout the relevance of hand-to-hand combat, the weapons that dominated twentieth-century warfare—machine guns, explosive shells, and incendiary bombs, among others—were designed to kill indiscriminately and *en masse*.

For those on the ground, the results of such weapons—and the logic that enabled them—defied language and staggered the senses. In his best-selling memoir, *Kitchener's Mob: The Adventures of an American in the British Army* (1916), James Norman Hall conjures a nightmarish world of mass butchery:

The worst of it was that we could not get away from the sight of the mangled bodies of our comrades. Arms and legs stuck out of the wreckage, and on every side we saw distorted human faces, the faces of men we had known, with whom we had lived and shared hardships and dangers for months past. . . . One thinks of the human body as inviolate, a beautiful and sacred thing. The sight of it dismembered or disemboweled, trampled in the bottom of a trench, smeared with blood and filth, is so revolting as to be hardly endurable.[51]

Some combatants relied upon humor or mental exercises to block out the horror. During the Second World War, Paul Fussell coped by telling himself that "the dead don't know what they look like. . . . The man whose mouth drips blood doesn't know what he's doing, the man with half his skull blown away and his brain oozing on to the ground thinks he still looks OK."[52]

Others shielded their psyches with alcohol and drugs. The writer James Jones, a veteran of Pearl Harbor and Guadalcanal, recalled that the men he was with got "blind asshole drunk every chance we got."[53] Denied booze in their rations, the men of the "greatest generation" distilled liquor from torpedo fluid and drank cocktails made from aftershave; they smoked cigarettes by the pack and—in some cases—turned to harder substances to stay sharp (amphetamines) or ease the pain (morphine).[54] In the Vietnam War, Americans' alcohol of choice was beer; their drug, marijuana, which large numbers of American troops smoked to relieve stress and wage symbolic protest. The military pushed drugs as well, as it had during the Second World War. While politicians at home raged against doped-up troops, notes historian Jeremy Kuzmarov, commanders in the field distributed "amphetamines or 'pep pills' to soldiers serving on long-range reconnaissance missions to prevent them from falling asleep or to help them lose weight."[55]

Nevertheless, the crushing burden of war eventually took a toll on soldiers' mental health. Throughout history, military psychiatrists have assigned a number of names—"nostalgia," "shell-shock," "battlefield fatigue," or "post-traumatic stress disorder" (PTSD)—to describe the psychiatric trauma produced by modern warfare. During the First World War, British journalist Philip Gibbs recalled one shell-shocked youth standing outside a dugout: "His steel hat was at the back of his head, and his mouth slobbered, and two comrades could not hold him still."[56] Psychological injuries were initially associated with the concussive impact of high-velocity shells (hence, "shell shock"); however, the very sight of dead bodies was enough to cause some men to "crack up" (or "break down").[57] Memoirs of U.S. combatants in the Second World War, for example, frequently describe a slow process of psychological brutalization. In *Goodbye, Darkness* (1980), William Manchester's memoir of his experience with the United States Marine Corps on Iwo Jima, the author recalls, "I was in the midst of a satanic madness: I knew it. I wanted to return to sanity: I couldn't."[58] After forty-five days of combat in Nazi-occupied France, many American GIs had regressed to a "vegetative state," according to the psychologists who followed their progress.[59] By the war's end, the deadened look of psychologically traumatized troops had even acquired a name: the thousand-yard stare.

It should be noted that none of war's bodily dangers are unique to ground combat. Over the past century, American service personnel have been sucked out of plummeting airplanes, scalded by exploding boat fuel, crushed on transport ships, and murdered far behind the front lines. Perhaps the only bright side of war's ubiquitous suffering is that it has allowed physicians and scientists a rare opportunity to study the effects of bodily illness, injury, and privation on a mass scale. From the Civil War to the War on Terror, wartime "guinea pigs"—both military and conscientious objectors—have been used to investigate everything from shellshock to the effects of systematic starvation.[60] Indeed, some of the most successful advancements in military medicine—improved triage techniques for sorting wounded troops, antigravity flight suits for World War II–era bombing crews, and others—have stemmed from trial-and-error experiments conducted in times of military conflict.

Even so, it would be a mistake to view such efforts simply in terms of medical "progress." Rather, research aimed at limiting the body's susceptibility to pain (and hunger, stress, shock, fatigue, mental collapse) is frequently deployed toward an additional aim: determining how best to inflict these same bodily hardships on America's enemies.

Bodies after War

In *Soldier Dead* (2005), journalist Michael Sledge conjures a darkly poetic scene of war's aftermath: "When the engines of Mars leave the battlefield, they leave behind vivid reminders of the struggle that took place: scarred land, destroyed and discarded equipment, and the corpses of those who fought and died—millions in the wars of the twentieth century alone."[61] For as long as the United States has fought wars, the production of corpses—the transformation of living bodies into dead ones—has been one of the few constants. Not surprisingly, since the mid-nineteenth century, the United States has invested considerable economic and political resources in locating, identifying, and honoring military corpses. In 1862, the War Department issued General Order No. 33 instructing Union field commanders "to secure, as far as possible, the decent internment" of soldiers killed in battle.[62] The task was easier said than done. Following the Battle of Gettysburg, as Drew Gilpin Faust writes, "an estimated six million pounds of human and animal carcasses lay strewn across the field in the summer heat."[63] Armed with little more than shovels and picks, recovery parties dragged the decomposing corpses from the battlefield and buried them in shallow graves. At the war's end, hundreds of thousands of combatants were exhumed and reburied in cemeteries across the United States (Figure 11.3).

FIGURE 11.3 During the Civil War, retrieving dead bodies from the battlefield was gruesome work. This 1865 stereograph by photographer John Reekie shows men digging up the remnants of Union soldiers several months after the Battle of Cold Harbor in Virginia. Library of Congress, Prints & Photographs Division, LC-DIG-stereo-1s02702, https://www.loc.gov/item/2011649977/.

In later conflicts, the nation's effort to recover military corpses was impaired by an additional obstacle—geography. World War II battlefields, for example, were spread out across thousands of miles. In response, the American Graves Registration Service (AGRS) devised an elaborate system for "processing" the nation's war dead. Collected from makeshift graves, corpses followed a circuitous route to AGRS "collection points," where they were examined, photographed, fingerprinted, and then shipped off to one of 454 "temporary cemeteries." There the corpses remained, most wrapped in a blanket and placed directly in the earth, until the war's end, when more than 260,000 dead troops were disinterred and reburied either in the United States or in a permanent overseas cemetery.[64]

Starting in the Korean War, the military adopted a policy of "concurrent return." Instead of waiting for years, corpses were immediately shipped to a central clearing house, embalmed, and then—pending the wishes of the next of kin—sent back to the United States.[65] As of 2013, the U.S. military had recovered the remains of nearly all of the 6,700 service members killed up to that point in Iraq and Afghanistan. Most passed through the mortuary at Dover Air Force Base in Delaware, where they were ritualistically cleaned, dressed, fitted with appropriate insignia, and photographed for their family members.[66] However, prior to the recent string of desert conflicts, the recovery of corpses remained an inexact science. In Korea, Vietnam, and elsewhere, some bodies simply disappeared—swallowed by jungle muck, consumed by flames, picked apart by animals, or blown to unidentifiable pieces by high-explosive weaponry. As techniques for recovering the war dead have improved, Americans have grown increasingly intolerant of the notion that any body can go "missing in action" (MIA). After the Vietnam War, a vocal coalition of veterans, MIA family members, and political activists waged a decades-long campaign to recover the bodies of U.S. combatants (alive or dead) and to hold accountable those who, in their view, had betrayed the government's obligation to bring all of the troops home.[67]

Although more than a million U.S. combatants have died in military campaigns since 1861, the vast majority of American bodies have returned from war alive, if not always in one piece. Today, thanks to advancements in transportation, wound treatment, and emergency medicine, American troops are able to survive wounds that would have been fatal only a few decades earlier. This is not a new phenomenon. In fact, the trend toward faster, more efficient care has dominated military-medical thinking for more than a century. As one high-ranking officer testified before Congress in 1969, "In World War II, average time from wounded to treatment was 10.5 hours for abdominal wounds. . . . In Vietnam, because of the extensive use of the helicopter ambulance, the average time is 2.8 hours."[68] Ironically, war's disabled survivors pose a greater threat to future military policy than the dead. The cost of treating disabled bodies—an expense that can stretch for decades—far exceeds that of maintaining military cemeteries. As living embodiments of past violence, the bodies of disabled veterans serve as public reminders of wars that many Americans would rather forget. No less important, disabled veterans undermine the clichéd metaphors of "healing" and "closure" so often favored in the wake of unpopular wars. Some bodies simply never heal; some wounds never close—as much as our political narratives or national myths demand that they do so.

Prior to the twentieth century, government measures regarding disabled veterans typically came in two forms: monetary pensions and soldiers' homes. In 1862, Congress authorized the provision of "general pensions" for all service-disabled Union vets. Rates ranged "from thirty dollars per month for high-ranking officers to eight dollars for privates or common sailors," and amputees were granted additional funds to purchase braces or artificial limbs.[69] At the war's end, veterans' groups like the Grand Army of the Republic successfully lobbied to liberalize veterans' benefits further, eventually transforming the pension system into a de facto social safety blanket for former Yankees and their families. Disabled Confederates, it should be noted, were ineligible for federal benefits. As a result, hundreds of thousands of war-injured Southerners were forced to rely on charitable contributions and meager state allowances to make ends meet.

Shortly before the war's end, the federal government launched a second major initiative for compensating disabled vets—the National Home for Disabled Volunteer Soldiers (NHDVS), a network of eight facilities that provided long-term shelter for thousands of sick, disabled, or aged Union vets. Individual branches resembled rural colleges, with living quarters, workshops, care facilities, and well-manicured grounds. When in residence, vets wore uniforms and were expected to follow military regulations. As with the pension scheme, housing ex-soldiers did not come cheap; between 1866 and 1930, the cost of the NHDVS system topped $250 million. However, veterans' advocates maintained it was well worth the price. As J. C. Gobrecht, author of an early book on the network, wrote in 1875, "The Soldiers' Home is a 'living monument'; one upon which the war-worn veteran may gaze with pleasurable emotion as he proudly contemplates it and exclaims: 'I live in the hearts of my countrymen.'"[70]

By the 1890s, however, critics increasingly complained that pensions and soldiers' homes did more harm than good. According to detractors, not only were both programs prohibitively expensive but they also bred a culture of dependency and unmanly idleness. As a result, in the First World War, the United States adopted a new approach to what came to be known as the "problem of the disabled veteran"—rehabilitation. Rehabilitation was an integrated program designed to help disabled veterans reintegrate into postwar society as productive workers. In phase one—physical reconstruction—government health workers attempted to rebuild soldiers' bodies using the latest techniques in orthopedic surgery, physical therapy, and other disciplines. In phase two—vocational rehabilitation—veterans took classes or pursued lengthy jobs-training programs aimed at making them self-supporting.[71]

The ideological core of rehabilitation was the belief that war disability—understood as physical impairment, economic dependency, and idleness—was a temporary condition, one that might be transcended (or at least largely mitigated) with the help of technology and government planning. In the words of one American rehabilitation officer, the program's "ultimate object . . . is the refitting of the disabled soldier to take his place in the world as a useful citizen, trained by the best instructors to make a good living for himself, to restore him to civil life not only sound in body but better equipped mentally to succeed in his calling than before his entrance into the service of his country."[72] In the end, World War I–era rehabilitation programs failed to live up to their supporters' lofty predictions. Of the 330,000 troops eligible for government rehabilitation, only about 128,000 successfully completed their training programs. By the late 1920s, the federal government had spent more than half a billion dollars on veterans' pensions, social relief programs, and medical care, with no end in sight.[73]

Despite these early setbacks, rehabilitation soon became the ideological backbone of federal policies toward disabled veterans. Today, rehabilitationist ideas—about rebuilding war-wounded combatants and refitting them for civilian life—are so commonplace that it is hard to imagine any alternatives. In fact, the less popular the military conflict, the more significant the promise of rehabilitation has become. As anthropologist Zoë H. Wool explains in her recent study of American soldiers severely injured in Afghanistan and Iraq, "Work on the body of the injured soldier—rehabilitative and imaginative alike—is . . .

work to smooth over public visions of war and postwar life in contemporary America, to obscure the violence and pain of war in gestures of hope and gratitude that are nonetheless based on their presence."[74] Put another way: if a rehabilitated double-amputee can run a 5K or start a family, how bad can war injury actually be?

In 2007, journalists published a high-profile exposé documenting mistreatment of patients at Walter Reed Army Medical Center, the premier U.S. military medical facility, located in Washington, DC.[75] Though commentators feigned surprise and outrage, the scandal was by no means exceptional. Since the Civil War, government policies toward disabled veterans have been repeatedly marred by ill planning, indifference, and abuse. Today's disabled veterans face many of the same problems as their twentieth-century forebears: government runaround, bureaucratic red tape, long waits for treatment, and seemingly arbitrary criteria for determining whose disabilities "count." Political leaders bear much of the blame. As journalist Aaron Glantz writes in *The War Comes Home* (2009), "In virtually every generation, politicians repeat again and again that they 'support the troops' even as their policies and budget conditions ensure a difficult homecoming."[76] Other factors play a role as well. In profiling the latest advances in medical prosthetic technology, well-meaning journalists often send the message that no wound is permanently disabling, despite the fact that severely injured soldiers often endure multiple surgeries and years of painful healing. Likewise, many disabled veterans lack the economic resources and political wherewithal to effect long-term structural change. Veterans' groups do what they can, but they face an uphill battle. Even after nearly a century of rehabilitation, the disabled soldier's body raises troubling questions about the human toll of increasingly unpopular—and often failed—U.S. military adventures around the globe.

Future Bodies, Future War

The body remains a problem for American war-makers. For all of the advances in medicine and technology, twenty-first-century combatants fighting in Iraq and Afghanistan are as susceptible to hunger, heat, and thirst as their counterparts in the Second World War. Without immediate treatment, a shell fragment in the carotid artery is just as deadly today as it was when armies fought at Gettysburg and Antietam. In addition, the spectacle of war-damaged bodies is more likely to spark public outrage in 2017 than ever before. Blaming the U.S. defeat in Vietnam on casualty-phobic civilians, military planners embraced philosophies of "risk aversion" and "force protection," often going to great lengths to limit—in the words of historian Andrew Bacevich—"direct American exposure."[77] The Pentagon reckoned—correctly, it turns out—that the post-Vietnam public had little stomach for high rates of U.S. casualties, particularly if the rationale for the war was suspect from the start. As of January 2017, more than fifteen years since the start of the War on Terror, nearly 6,900 American combatants have died fighting in Iraq, Afghanistan, and elsewhere in the Middle East.[78] At that rate, U.S. troops would need to fight—and die—for another century before the death count would approach that of American forces in Vietnam.

However, even as the United States girds itself for a future of lengthy and possibly endless warfare, it is likely that U.S. casualty rates will continue to decline. Since the 1980s, rapid developments in drone technology, imaging systems, and robotics have made it increasingly possible to remove American bodies from the battlefield. In her 2011 essay "War without Humans," writer Barbara Ehrenreich observes, "When American forces invaded Iraq in 2003, no robots accompanied them; by 2008, there were 12,000 participating in the war."[79] "Unmanned systems," to use military parlance, can go places humans can't go (e.g., environments contaminated by toxins), see things humans can't see (e.g., the heat registers of human bodies within a concrete bunker), and complete tasks that humans cannot or simply do not want to complete. Unlike human bodies, they don't get hungry, tired, or afraid—and no one protests at home when they are blasted to pieces a half a world away.[80] In the rare cases when American "boots" do hit the ground, the bodies that wear them will be prosthetically enhanced—their vision extended with night goggles, their torsos hardened by shrapnel-resistant body armor, their nervous systems fine-tuned through implants and pharmacology, their minds plugged in to a vast network of communication. If technologists' predictions are correct, the warrior body of America's twenty-first-century conflicts will have more in common with the Terminator than with World War II's G.I. Joe.

None of this is to predict a painless future. In America's twenty-first-century wars of "remote-control killing" and "high-tech assassins," bodies will continue to be mangled, incinerated, atomized, crushed, blown apart, and permanently scarred.[81] The crucial difference is that, even more so than in previous conflicts, a wildly disproportionate number of those bodies will belong to America's enemies. In a 2015 joint report, Physicians for Social Responsibility, Physicians for Global Survival, and the International Physicians for the Prevention of Nuclear War conservatively estimate that 1.3 million people have died as a result of U.S.-led campaigns in Iraq, Afghanistan, and Pakistan since September 11, 2001.[82] In all of world history, no nation has been capable of inflicting mass death on such a scale while exposing so few of its citizens to the dangers of combat. Going forward, Americans must grapple with the difficult ethical question of whether preserving the bodies of its nation's warriors is worth the price in other people's blood.

Discussion Questions

1. To what extent have the military's attitudes toward bodies—before, during, and after war—evolved over time? What might explain such changes (or lack thereof)?

2. According to the author, what explains the relative absence of "bodies" in the cultural memory of American war? Do you agree with the author's assessment? Can you think of other factors besides the ones mentioned?

3. To what extent do military body standards reflect broader values—about health, race, gender, and so on—in American culture?

Notes

1 Lewis B. Puller Jr., *Fortunate Son: The Autobiography of Lewis B. Puller, Jr.* (New York: Grove Press, 1991), 157, 161, 165.

2 Ibid., 337.

3 Paul Fussell, *Wartime: Understanding and Behavior in the Second World War* (New York: Oxford University Press, 1989), 268, 270.

4 Jonathan Shay, *Achilles in Vietnam: Combat Trauma and the Undoing of Character* (New York: Touchstone, 1994), 121.

5 Elaine Scarry, *The Body in Pain: The Making and Unmaking of the World* (New York: Oxford University Press, 1985), 64.

6 Drew Gilpin Faust, *This Republic of Suffering: Death and the American Civil War* (New York: Vintage, 2008), 267.

7 Mark M. Smith, *The Smell of Battle, the Taste of Siege: A Sensory History of the Civil War* (New York: Oxford University Press, 2015), 135, 2.

8 Roger Stahl, *Militainment, Inc.: War, Media, and Popular Culture* (New York: Routledge, 2009), 27.

9 Abraham Lincoln, "Lincoln's Second Inaugural Address," in *Lincoln's Gettysburg Oration and First and Second Inaugural Addresses* (New York: Duffield and Co., 1907), 46.

10 The video "Bombing Missions over Laos from 1965 to 1973" is embedded as part of Fatama Bhojani's story, "Watch the US Drop 2.5 Million Tons of Bombs on Laos," *Mother Jones*, March 26, 2014, http://www.motherjones.com/politics/2014/03/laos-vietnam-war-us-bombing-uxo. With writer Karen J. Coates, Jerry Redfern further documents the bombing campaign in *Eternal Harvest: The Legacy of American Bombs in Laos* (San Francisco: ThingsAsian Press, 2013).

11 Qtd. in H. Bruce Franklin, "From Realism to Virtual Reality: Images of America's Wars," in *Vietnam and Other American Fantasies* (Amherst: University of Massachusetts Press, 2000), 8.

12 Qtd. in John M. Kinder, *Paying with Their Bodies: American War and the Problem of the Disabled Veteran* (Chicago: University of Chicago Press, 2015), 234.

13 Susan Sontag, *Regarding the Pain of Others* (New York: Picador, 2003), 41.

14 Susan D. Moeller, *Shooting War: Photography and the American Experience of Combat* (New York: Basic Books, 1989), 206–207.

15 Torie Rose Deghett, "The War Photo No One Would Publish," *The Atlantic*, August 8, 2014, http://www.theatlantic.com/international/archive/2014/08/the-war-photo-no-one-would-publish/375762/; for a similar critique of British press coverage of the Persian Gulf War, see John Taylor, "The Body Vanishes: Photojournalism in the Gulf War," *Contemporary British History* 8, no. 2 (1994): 289–304.

16 Elisabeth Bumiller, "U.S. Lifts Photo Ban on Military Coffins," *New York Times*, December 7, 2009, http://www.nytimes.com/2009/02/27/world/americas/27iht-photos.1.20479953.html?_r=0.

17   See Liam Kennedy, "Soldier Photography: Visualising the War in Iraq," *Review of International Studies* 35 (2009): 817–833.

18   Faust, *This Republic of Suffering*, xvi.

19   United States Surgeon-General's Office, *The Medical Department of the United States Army in the World War* (Washington, DC: Government Printing Office, 1927), 15:45. Hereafter noted as MDUSAWW.

20   Woods Hutchinson, "Weighed in the Balance of the War: How Our National Physique Stood the Acid Test in the Draft," *The Red Cross Magazine* 14, no. 4 (1919): 39.

21   MDUSAWW, 10:64–65.

22   Nancy K. Bristow, *Making Men Moral: Social Engineering during the Great War* (New York: New York University Press, 1996).

23   See Committee on Public Information, War Department, "Training the Male Body for War" (No. 9), in *Home Reading Course for Citizen-Soldiers* (Washington, DC: Government Printing Office, 1917).

24   Lincoln C. Andrews, *Fundamentals of Military Service* (Philadelphia: Lippincott, 1916), 378–384.

25   Christina S. Jarvis, *The Male Body at War: American Masculinity during World War II* (DeKalb: Northern Illinois University Press, 2010), 56.

26   Ibid., 57, 60–61.

27   Ibid., 59.

28   Kinder, *Paying with Their Bodies*, 223.

29   Thomas E. Ricks, *Making the Corps* (New York: Scribner, 1997), 43.

30   Ibid., 55.

31   "Medical Conditions That May Prevent You from Joining the Military," *Military.com*, June 14, 2016, http://www.military.com/join-armed-forces/disqualifiers-medical-conditions.html.

32   John Cawley and Johanna Catherine Maclean, "Unfit for Service: The Implications of Rising Obesity for U.S. Military Recruitment" (Working Paper 16408), *National Bureau of Economic Research*, September 2010, http://www.nber.org/papers/w16408; Julie Watson, "Navy Loosens Body Fat Rules to Retain Sailors," *Military Times*, March 7, 2015, http://www.militarytimes.com/story/military/2016/03/06/navy-loosens-body-fat-rules-fitness-tests/81402312/.

33   Margot Canaday, *The Straight State: Sexuality in Citizenship in Twentieth Century America* (Princeton, NJ: Princeton University Press, 2009), 62–64.

34   Allan Bérubé, *Coming Out under Fire: The History of Gay Men and Women in World War Two*, 2nd ed. (Chapel Hill: University of North Carolina Press, 2010).

35   Albert E. Cowdrey, *Fighting for Life: American Military Medicine in World War II* (New York: Free Press, 1994), 170–171.

36   Monica J. Casper and Lisa Jean Moore, *Missing Bodies: The Politics of Visibility* (New York: New York University Press, 2009), 148.

37   Megan MacKenzie, *Beyond the Band of Brothers: The US Military and the Myth That Women Can't Fight* (Cambridge: Cambridge University Press, 2015).

38   Kinder, *Paying with Their Bodies*, 44.

39   Ibid., 22.

40   Robert J. Topmiller and T. Kerby Neill, *Binding Their Wounds: America's Assault on Its Veterans* (Boulder, CO: Paradigm, 2011), 93–115.

41   MDUSAWW, 11:9.

42   Hannah Fischer, *A Guide to U.S. Military Casualty Statistics: Operation Freedom's Sentinel, Operation Inherent Resolve, Operation New Dawn, Operation Iraqi Freedom,*

and Operation Enduring Freedom (Congressional Research Service Report No. RS22452, Washington, DC, 2015), 4, https://fas.org/sgp/crs/natsec/RS22452.pdf.

43 Gregg Zoroya, "Key Iraq Wound: Brain Trauma," *USA Today*, March 4, 2005.

44 Jordan Robertson, "Iraq War's Signature Wound: Brain Injury," *Washington Post*, September 15, 2006; "Silent Wounds: The True Signature Wound of the War on Terror," *Veterans Today*, February 23, 2010; David Zinczenko, "The Signature Wound of the War in Afghanistan Should Be a Signature Cause for Men Anywhere," *Men's Health*, January 3, 2012; David Wood, "The Grunts: Damned If They Kill, Damned If They Don't," *Huffington Post*, March 18, 2014, http://projects.huffingtonpost.com/moral-injury/the-grunts.

45 Jerry Lembcke, *PTSD: Diagnosis and Identity in Post-Empire America* (Lanham, MD: Lexington Books, 2013), 145.

46 Matt Grills, "Traumatic Brain Injury (TBI): Signature Wound of the War," *The American Legion Magazine* (May 2008): 26.

47 Fussell, *Wartime*, 19–35.

48 Kinder, *Paying with Their Bodies*, 36–37.

49 H. Bruce Franklin, *War Stars: The Superweapon and the American Imagination*, rev. exp. ed. (Amherst: University of Massachusetts Press, 2008), 19–53.

50 Ben Shephard, *A War of Nerves: Soldiers and Psychiatrists in the Twentieth Century* (Cambridge, MA: Harvard University Press, 2001), 2.

51 James Norman Hall, *Kitchener's Mob: The Adventures of an American in the British Army* (Boston: Houghton Mifflin, 1916), 168–169.

52 Qtd. in Kenneth D. Rose, *Myth and the Greatest Generation: A Social History of Americans in World War II* (New York: Routledge, 2008), 57.

53 Qtd. in ibid., 38.

54 Michael C. C. Adams, *The Best War Ever: America and World War II*, 2nd ed. (Baltimore: Johns Hopkins University Press, 2015), 70.

55 Jeremy Kuzmarov, *The Myth of the Addicted Army: Vietnam and the Modern War on Drugs* (Amherst: University of Massachusetts Press, 2009), 16–26, 16.

56 Qtd. in John Ellis, *Eye-Deep in Hell: Trench Warfare in World War I* (Baltimore: Johns Hopkins University Press, 1976), 118.

57 "For more on psychological injury in World War I, see Shephard, *A War of Nerves*.

58 Qtd. in Rose, *Myth and the Greatest Generation*, 57.

59 Ibid., 31.

60 Todd Tucker, *The Great Starvation Experiment: Ancel Keys and the Men Who Starved for Science* (Minneapolis: University of Minnesota Press, 2007).

61 Michael Sledge, *Soldier Dead: How We Recover, Identify, Bury, and Honor Our Military Fallen* (New York: Columbia University Press, 2005), 8.

62 Qtd. in ibid., 33.

63 Faust, *This Republic of Suffering*, 69.

64 Jarvis, *The Male Body at War*, 160–163.

65 E.B. Sledge, *With the Old Breed: At Peleliu and Okinawa* (Novato, CA: Presido Press, 2007), 41.

66 James Dao, "Last Inspection: Precise Ritual of Dressing Nation's War Dead," *New York Times*, May 25, 2013, http://www.nytimes.com/2013/05/26/us/intricate-rituals-for-fallen-americans-troops.html?pagewanted=all.

67 H. Bruce Franklin, *M.I.A., or Mythmaking in America* (New Brunswick, NJ: Rutgers University Press, 1993); Michael Joe Allen, *Until the Last Man Comes Home: POWs, MIAs, and the Unending Vietnam War* (Chapel Hill: University of North Carolina Press, 2009).

68 Qtd. in Kinder, *Paying with Their Bodies*, 275.

69 Jaylynn Olsen Padilla, "Army of 'Cripples': North Civil War Amputees, Disability, and Manhood in Victorian America" (PhD diss., University of Delaware, 2007), 85.

70 Qtd. in John M. Kinder, "Architecture of Injury: Disabled Veterans, Federal Policy, and the Built Environment in Late Nineteenth and Early Twentieth Century America," in *Veterans' Policies, Veterans' Politics: New Perspectives on Veterans in the Modern United States*, ed. Stephen R. Ortiz (Gainesville: University Press of Florida, 2012), 70.

71 Beth Linker, *War's Waste: Rehabilitation in World War I America* (Chicago: University of Chicago Press, 2011); Kinder, *Paying with Their Bodies*, 117–148.

72 Robert Blanchard, "Physical Reconstruction and What It Means to the Wounded," in *U.S.A. General Hospital No. 28*, ed. Edward O. Harrs and Sydney B. Flower (Fort Sheridan, IL: 1919), 30.

73 Kinder, *Paying with Their Bodies*, 146, 148.

74 Zoë H. Wool, *After War: The Weight of Life at Walter Reed* (Durham, NC: Duke University Press, 2015), 12–13.

75 Dana Priest and Anne Hull, "Soldiers Face Neglect, Frustration at Army's Top Medical Facility," *Washington Post*, February 18, 2007.

76 Aaron Glantz, *The War Comes Home: Washington's Battle against America's Veterans* (Berkeley: University of California Press, 2009), 208.

77 Andrew Bacevich, *The New American Militarism: How Americans Are Seduced by War* (New York: Oxford University Press, 2005), 57, 58.

78 An updated tally of American casualties statistics for the combined theaters of the War on Terror—Operation Iraqi Freedom, Operation New Dawn, Operation Enduring Freedom, Operation Inherent Resolve, and Operation Freedom's Sentinel—can be found at http://www.defense.gov/casualty.pdf.

79 Barbara Ehrenreich, "War without Humans," *The Nation*, July 11, 2011, http://www.thenation.com/article/war-without-humans/.

80 See Max Boot, *War Made New: Technology, Warfare, and the Course of History 1500 to Today* (New York: Gotham Books, 2006); P. W. Singer, *Wired for War: The Robotics Revolution and Conflict in the 21st Century* (New York: Penguin, 2009).

81 Medea Benjamin, *Drone Warfare: Killing by Remote Control*, rev. ed. (New York: Verso, 2013); Alexander Cockburn, *Kill-Chain: The Rise of High-Tech Assassins* (New York: Henry Holt, 2015).

82 The report's authors argue that the total death count might actually "be in excess of 2 million, whereas a figure below 1 million is extremely unlikely" (15). See Physicians for Social Responsibility, *Body Count: Casualty Figures after 10 Years of the "War on Terror"* (1st intl. ed., trans. Ali Fathollah-Nejad, March 2015), http://www.psr.org/assets/pdfs/body-count.pdf.

Further Reading

Drew Gilpin Faust. *This Republic of Suffering: Death and the American Civil War*. New York: Vintage, 2008.

Christina S. Jarvis. *The Male Body at War: American Masculinity during World War II*. DeKalb: Northern Illinois University Press, 2010.

John M. Kinder. *Paying with Their Bodies: American War and the Problem of the Disabled Veteran*. Chicago: University of Chicago Press, 2015.

Michael Sledge. *Soldier Dead: How We Recover, Identify, Bury, and Honor Our Military Fallen*. New York: Columbia University Press, 2005.

12

War and the Environment

RICHARD P. TUCKER

Battle zones damage the natural world as well as destroying or disrupting human life. Less obviously, military operations have environmental impacts in peacetime too.[1] From its earliest days the American military, like all military forces, has existed in environmental settings and consequences have resulted. This essay tracks several dimensions of that story, including the direct environmental impacts of battle (and its increasing intensity as the technology of destruction has become more powerful), natural resource extraction that has supported military operations (including energy sources), the expansion of military bases and weapons testing, the impact of new weapons, and the military's evolving eco-consciousness. The essay will proceed both thematically and chronologically, tracing these themes through world wars and other conflicts, as well as peacetime, over a century and more.

The Escalating Environmental Impact of Battle

In the preindustrial era the weapons available to fighters were not powerful enough to cause much long-term damage. But in the Civil War of 1861–1865, the first major industrial war, pitched battles and sieges severely damaged many southern forests, farms, and cities. As the war dragged on, the damage intensified in 1864 when the Union Army launched scorched earth campaigns across Georgia's farmland and Virginia's Shenandoah Valley, destroying the crops and livestock that were the survival base of the Confederate Army.[2]

Moving west of the Mississippi after 1865, the federal cavalry adapted these techniques for the white conquest of Native America.[3] This expansion culminated in 1898 in the Spanish-American War. In the Philippines, the first joint army-navy campaign far from North America, the U.S. Navy eliminated the Spanish Navy overnight, but Filipino patriots continued to resist foreign domination, struggling against the American occupation forces for four bloody years. The U.S. Army was trained and organized primarily in small units for the Indian Wars. Unprepared for lengthy campaigns it applied the scorched earth strategy of counterinsurgency, crippling the enemy's resource base until resistance crumbled.

In the First World War the United States did not enter the carnage until 1917. By the time American forces arrived in Europe in the war's final year, they could participate only in areas that had already been ravaged by the forces of European empire. The Second World War was an entirely different matter, though there was no fighting in the United States (except for a brief encounter with Japan in the Aleutian Islands). The Cold War era brought massive changes in the military landscape of the United States (see below), but the impact of fighting on ecosystems was largely in Korea and Vietnam. The environmental history of the Korean War (1950–1953) has not yet been written. The environmental history of the Vietnam War is far better known, as we will review.

Natural Resources Extraction to Support Military Operations

Throughout our history the military has relied on equipment and supplies from an industrializing economy whose demands on natural resources have expanded exponentially. This important dimension of the environmental history of military operations can be traced by looking at key strategic resources.

Metals

Environmental impacts appeared wherever metals were mined and industrial products were produced. Escalating from the First World War onward, the steel industry built ships, weapons, cars, trucks, and more.[4] U.S. Steel had rapidly become the world's largest steel producer after its founding in 1901; by 1914 it produced half of American output. Wartime investment and profits further consolidated its position. A major domestic source of iron was the Mesabi Range in northern Minnesota, a region of enormous open-pit mines that scar a wide landscape. New factories also changed the land, transforming surrounding areas. Steel plants in Pittsburgh and along the south shores of Lake Michigan in Indiana shaped the country's Steel Belt, bringing in new workers who needed housing and public services while producing serious pollution of land and water. Many industrial pollution sites in what is now the Rust Belt began with industrial expansion during this war.

Copper was equally vital for that war, as a conductor of electricity and as casing for ammunition. By 1914 the United States produced 60 percent of the world supply from domestic sources and 20 percent more from international sources. The war's insatiable demand for copper led to severe environmental impacts wherever it was mined. Anaconda Copper was a dominant corporation;

it had risen to national scale in Butte, Montana, site of its vast open-pit mine.[5] Shortly after 1900 Anaconda expanded into the copper belt of Bisbee in southern Arizona, and beyond into Cananea, Sonora, forty miles across the Mexican border, creating mines, smelters, sawmills, ranches, and workers' shantytowns.

During the First World War American corporations accounted for half of total nineteenth-century global production. Copper prices doubled by 1916, funding rapid American expansion into Chile, which holds the world's largest copper deposits at sites in both the northern Atacama Desert and the high Andes of central Chile.[6] Wartime Chile yielded six million tons (equal to half of its entire nineteenth-century production). One great mining complex alone produced net earnings of $140 million for its American owners, one of the great windfall profits of wartime.

The Second World War's total mobilization of human and natural resources further transformed the industrial map of the continent, unavoidably causing environmental damage. Metallurgy was the core of the surge. The steel industry's sources of iron once again included the Mesabi Range of northern Minnesota, where open-pit mines gouged the land. Lead, essential for weapons, was 25 to 50 percent imported, with domestic production mostly located in Kansas, Utah, and Idaho. At the processing plants lead pollution became a serious public health problem. Other critical metals, such as tungsten, molybdenum, and nickel, had to be imported from locations around the world.

Aluminum, a newer industry, saw intensive expansion. Alcoa held a monopoly in the United States, so the history of that giant corporation was a key to the industrial ecology of the war years. This industry centered in the Pacific Northwest, based on the harnessing of the Columbia River, where the Bonneville Dam (1938) and Grand Coulee Dam (1941) were newly completed. "During World War II electricity from the dams went almost totally to defense. National defense, in turn, gave the region the industrial base it so longed for. The dams powered the shipyards of Portland, Vancouver, and Seattle, the aluminum mills the Defense Plant Corporation built across the Northwest, and the factories that turned aluminum into airplanes. They supplied power to the top secret project at Hanford which was producing plutonium for the atomic bomb dropped on Nagasaki. . . . And so aluminum came in 1943 to consume 60 percent of the megawatt-hours the Bonneville Power Authority sold."[7]

Timber

American forests felt the stress of war even more; the examples in this essay are taken primarily from the two world wars. Timber harvesting in the First World War had complex long-term impacts on the forests and their management. High wartime prices and massive government funding brought in new technologies, such as trucks and tracked motor vehicles as well as additional logging roads. The most dramatic damage occurred in the pine belt of the

Southeast, where corporate timber operators owned large tracts of land that had been degraded by the slave system, the Civil War, and the region-wide depression that followed. In the late 1800s southern pine lumber built cities in the eastern United States and Europe; millions of acres were clear-cut. The companies had the logging roads, railroads, sawmills, port facilities (in every major port from Baltimore to Houston), and a skilled labor force to respond aggressively to huge wartime demand.[8]

During the war southern lumbermen faced skyrocketing demand for construction timber to build factories, office buildings, warehouses, shipyards, and military camps. It took 600 million board feet of lumber just to house the expanded army. Big firms introduced new logging locomotives, steam skidders, and other machinery, producing mountains of sawdust and slabs, most of which were burned. They were followed by "peckerwood" sawmill operators, who cut smaller trees to produce second-grade construction lumber.

The First World War also introduced airplanes into the arsenal of industrial warfare. American factories produced 15,000 planes by the war's end, harvesting spruce and fir from the forests of the Northwest, as well as using hardwoods for frames. Though not a major consumer of forest products, this was the beginning of the vast aeronautics industry that would be crucial in the Second World War.

The Second World War continued the trend, using an ever-wider range of forest products:

> When critical shortages developed in other materials—notably the metals—wood . . . was seized as a substitute. Wood boxes and paper were enlisted for agricultural packaging when the burlap supply from India was cut off; tight cooperage took the place of metal drums in many special uses; timber replaced steel in small, fast marine craft such as subchasers and torpedo boats; construction designs were changed to specify timbers rather than steel for the long beams and arches over plant floors, for bridge members, and for river barges and radio towers; experiments were made looking to the use of veneer and plywood in large quantities in place of the then-scarcer light metals in gliders and in trainers and transport planes.[9]

There was a huge program of military camp construction in the early months of the war. It then took 500 board feet to ship each soldier and his equipment to a European war zone, and 50 board feet per month thereafter to keep him fighting. Most of the timber came from the conifer forests of the Northwest, in the form of plywood for military housing, pontoon bridges, ship interiors, packaging, lifeboats, training planes, gliders, and cargo transport planes. By 1944 Douglas fir was needed for the Normandy invasion and for pilings to rebuild virtually every European port. The pilings had to be 60–120 feet long, lengths that could come only from old growth trees. Such great lengths had to be shipped by rail across North America, then formed into huge rafts 25 pieces wide, with 160 more atop, towed by tugs to the Normandy coast. The scale of this effort could only be accomplished in North America.

Rubber

Rubber was also critically important for industrial warfare, especially for motor vehicles. Until the Second World War the only source was natural rubber, processed from the latex of a tree widely scattered within the Amazonian rain forest. Attempts to grow it in dense groves there collapsed because of a tree disease that had coevolved with the tree.[10] But botanical experimenters had found that rubber plantations could be successful in Southeast Asia, where the disease did not occur. American investment in rubber plantations in Southeast Asia began in 1907 in Dutch colonial Sumatra. When urgent wartime demand erupted in late 1914, U.S. Rubber Corporation's workers planted 14,000 acres of trees in the war's first year, a monumental effort of forest clearance. Production continued to rise throughout the war, as fast as labor could be mobilized and trees could grow. War in Europe was devouring rainforests half a world away. The massive wartime investment in new plantations had its payoff on civilian markets after the war, when Goodyear became the largest operation in Southeast Asia, transforming a vast acreage from tropical forest to single-species tree farms.[11]

Imperial wars resumed in 1931, when Japan's military rulers invaded Manchuria, capturing its important industrial complex. Japan then turned its attention to the Dutch East Indies as a source of petroleum and rubber, which might cut off Southeast Asian supplies. By then more than 90 percent of U.S. rubber came from Southeast Asia. Only a qualitative breakthrough in rubber production could alleviate that danger. Fortunately for the war effort, a new type of rubber derived from petroleum became available, transforming the industry. In the 1920s DuPont had succeeded in polymerizing a form of rubber which it called Neoprene. The German chemical industry worked in parallel, as Germany struggled to become independent of imported natural rubber. In a joint effort the German chemicals giant IG Farben and Standard Oil of New Jersey negotiated a contract to develop synthetic rubber. After the Nazi regime took power in 1933, it pushed the work, and IG developed a petroleum-based rubber which it labeled Buna-S. By 1939 IG improved Buna enough to meet military requirements and was able to use it for many wartime purposes.

Before the breakdown of Standard Oil's collaboration with IG Farben, Standard learned the Buna process and shared it with Firestone Tire. Led by these two, American industry succeeded in producing high-quality petroleum-based rubber in 1939. At a cost of $700 million, including a major subsidy from Congress, American companies went into full-scale production of synthetic rubber, reaching almost 700,000 tons in 1944. Without that remarkable effort, the American military machine would not have been able to function. In the postwar world petroleum-based rubber would provide approximately half of world rubber consumption. One consequence of this profound war-caused shift was to reduce pressure on tropical forest ecosystems.

Energy: Fossil Fuels

In the long perspective the energy sources of modern warfare are perhaps the most fundamental element of the military's environmental costs. From the mid-nineteenth century until World War I coal was the essential energy source for both the railroads and the rapidly developing national electric grid.[12] In the First World War soft (bituminous) coal miners achieved record production in 1918, bringing many marginal, low-efficiency mines into production. The inevitable result was severe air, ground, and water pollution; it would be another half century before effective environmental protection laws came into operation.

In that war petroleum emerged as a permanent addition to the energy sources used for fighting. The great navies—British, German, and American—were rapidly switching from coal to oil as fuel, while cars and trucks fought the war on land. From 1915 onward the United States supplied three-fourths of the Allies' petroleum consumption. The booming demand for petroleum was a bonanza for producers. Most supplies still came from wells in Texas and California.[13] But fears of postwar petroleum depletion led the military, civilian agencies, and corporate planners led by Standard Oil and Gulf Oil into an intensive search for new sources outside the United States. The first move beyond American borders was along the Gulf Coast of Mexico. In 1900 the coastal Huasteca area was still largely undeveloped, but a vast reservoir of oil had been discovered there under swamps and lagoons. U.S. oil investments along Mexico's Gulf Coast rose from $85 million in 1914 to $200 million in 1919. Systematic poisoning of the region's delicate ecology accelerated during World War I until it became one of the most severely degraded petroleum regions anywhere.[14] By 1920 major American corporations were also probing for sources in Venezuela, the Middle East, and Southeast Asia.[15]

In the Second World War coal remained the primary fuel for factories and power plants as well as for homes. Wartime industry required a 50 percent increase in coal production from immediate prewar times. Most of the increase took the form of strip mining in West Virginia and western Pennsylvania, keeping costs low by using more heavy machinery and less labor than in the deep mines of earlier years but also creating long-term environmental disasters in the process.

Oil was critical for automotive transport. From 1939 onward, federal agencies were organized in close collaboration with the largest oil corporations to control and manage oil supplies for both American and Allied forces. Between December 1941 and August 1945 80 percent or more of the Allies' needs were supplied from U.S. sources. Even within Los Angeles oil pumping accelerated in locations around the city.[16] Shipping the oil became a problem on the Atlantic Coast, which received 90 percent of its supplies by sea, where tankers were vulnerable to German subs; additional railroad shipment was limited. As a result new pipelines were built, led by the Big Inch from Texas to New York and the Little Inch from Illinois to the East Coast. Together they shipped almost 400 million barrels eastward between 1943 and 1945. All of these new wartime installations helped shape the postwar fossil fuels economy.

Hydropower played an important new role as well, starting with the 1930s dams of the Tennessee Valley Authority. The Bureau of Reclamation and the Corps of Engineers also built dams on the Colorado and Columbia Rivers, which powered military research and weapons plants, creating whole new communities on land that until then had seen only light impacts from human presence.

Base Building, Infrastructure, and Weapons Testing

The work of constructing and maintaining a major military force has always had environmental consequences. American military history is no exception. Military engineers began reshaping the continent's coastlines in the 1600s. One of the most important early naval bases was in Tidewater Virginia, where it guarded Hampton Roads and Chesapeake Bay against Spanish, French, and Dutch ships. Fighting to defeat the British in the War of Independence, the U.S. Army created the Corps of Engineers in 1779 to build coastal forts and harbors to defend against enemy navies. Every step of the conquest and settlement of the continent had environmental consequences. In its early work of domesticating natural environments for military purposes, the corps built a system of naval yards and forts from Charleston, Massachusetts, down the Atlantic Coast and around the Gulf Coast. Constructed of stone and wood, each one required local quarrying and forest clearance. The corps also began taming rivers as the United States moved westward to create a landscape that was both civilian and military.[17] By the time of the Mexican War of 1846, forty-eight forts were completed or under construction, and more were built as the West was won.

When that conquest was complete by the 1890s, American imperial ambitions began reaching beyond Florida into the Caribbean and beyond the West Coast across the Pacific. The navy was becoming a force in the national arsenal, as shipbuilding and maintenance began to transform harbors on the West Coast, starting with San Francisco Bay, reshaping the natural systems of river mouths, bays, and coastlines. The navy's coal-fueled ships required secure port facilities and coaling stations across the Pacific, first at Pearl Harbor in Hawaii, then also at Pago Pago in Samoa and beyond.[18] American military operations ultimately built a worldwide network of several hundred bases, each of them having environmental impacts on lands and waters.[19]

The military mobilization for the First World War was over before any major expansion of military sites was attempted. Later, by early 1940, the War Department managed 2.1 million acres and the Navy Department a half million acres. In the Second World War military operations spread across the country. Suddenly military authorities acquired vast new acreage. By 1945 more than fifty-two million acres were controlled and managed by the military, with civilians largely excluded. In the Cold War years that followed, these locations would undergo enormous accumulations of toxic and radioactive pollutants.[20]

On civilian-controlled lands the Sunbelt emerged across the southern states, as the national labor force moved into many new or expanded military industries.[21] Florida was home to major new army and navy installations.[22] Coastal ecosystems underwent industrial encroachments on harbors, bays, and tidelands. On the West Coast, Los Angeles and its hinterland became a central location for the airplane (and later aerospace) industry, while the navy expanded its operations in San Diego.[23] In San Francisco Bay new artillery was installed at the Golden Gate against the threat of Japanese bombardment. In the East Bay the Kaiser Shipyards were built on extensive wetlands and tidal flats, complemented by the Naval Supply Base in Oakland and the Naval Landing Forces Equipment Depot in Albany, funded by $5 billion in navy contracts. By 1943 military industry employed 80 percent of the region's industrial labor force, bringing in 90,000 workers. In Richmond they built 727 cargo ships. The area also attracted many subcontractors. The swelling population necessitated overnight provision of sprawling urban infrastructure, all of it using construction materials.[24]

The long nuclear legacy of the Second World War rested on an unprecedented collaboration to develop atomic weapons and nuclear power, which was launched as the Manhattan Project. (Uranium ore came from mines in Colorado, northern Canada, Czechoslovakia, and the Belgian Congo.) The project constructed entire small cities on more than thirty sites across the United States, Canada, and the United Kingdom, and provided water, power, consumer goods, public facilities, and transportation networks for each one. By 1945 the project employed 130,000 people. Army engineers managed site planning and construction. One of its central sites was Oak Ridge, in the Blue Ridge Mountains near Knoxville, Tennessee. Its job was to separate U235 from U238 for reactors. This was energy-intensive work, and TVA dams were available for power and cooling. The tightly controlled site occupied 59,000 acres of former woodlands; 1,000 families were moved out.

A more remote site, Los Alamos, New Mexico, was chosen for most work on bomb designs. Its 54,000 acres were taken mostly from the U.S. Forest Service. Los Alamos was another planned community, with water, roads, and housing for 75,000 people.[25] Hanford, Washington, was chosen as the site for building reactors to produce plutonium from uranium. For this crucial work the government initially took 40,000 acres of semiarid farm and ranchland, mostly shrub-steppe vegetation, along fifty miles of the Columbia River; ultimately it spread over 586 square miles. In sixteen months, between April 1943 and July 1944, this complex built more than 500 buildings and brought in 51,000 people. DuPont chemists and engineers were central to planning and building plutonium production facilities.[26]

For all its environmental impacts, the Manhattan Project proved a stunning success when the first atom bomb exploded near Alamogordo, New Mexico, in July 1945. The blast radiated arid land remote from major populations (though Navajos and ranchers who had lived there were displaced).[27] The war ended a month later, when Hiroshima and Nagasaki were obliterated by similar bombs. But there was little respite; the Cold War began almost immediately, and the U.S. military-industrial system was sustained largely intact.

In the early years of the Cold War the air force played the key role in providing delivery systems. The bombs were loaded in B-52s to fly across Canada and the North Pole region to Soviet targets, from new or expanded air bases along the northern borders of the United States. Each base required land that had previously been under civilian or federal control. Many of these sites were decommissioned in the 1990s, but some of the installations remain. An example is Ellsworth Air Force Base, ten miles east of Rapid City, South Dakota, where open range was transformed. Begun in 1941 for B17s, in the early Cold War Ellsworth became a regional headquarters of the Strategic Air Command. Today B-1 bombers are based there.

Intercontinental ballistic missiles followed in the 1960s, another step toward filling in the militarized map of the United States. Next door to Alamogordo, White Sands Missile Range, the largest military site in the country, became the primary missile testing location. White Sands was 3,200 square miles of flat, arid rangeland, nearly the size of Connecticut, with brutally hot summers and harsh winters.[28] Every branch of the Department of Defense tested experimental weapons and delivery systems there over the following years.

Missile installations with their underground silos crisscrossed the Great Plains, including several Minuteman missile sites, eight Titan sites, and eight Atlas sites, in addition to more nuclear-carrying B-52 air bases. Each one involved guarding acreage on farmland or prairie, building silos (including 1,000 Minutemen), expanding the road networks and power lines of the surrounding regions, and building housing and consumer goods centers for workers. This project was led by Boeing, General Motors, and other major corporations, with hundreds of subcontractors. As one commentator writes, "Every dollar spent tied more and more people and companies into the burgeoning national security state. Their development solidified the military-industrial complex, creating a long-term web of dependencies that connected the Air Force, dozens of contractors spread across the nation, and the politicians who sought to protect them."[29] The National Security State was now full-blown, with environmental impacts in every state and every ecological region.

Impact of New Weapons

In the accelerating arms race of modern warfare, each industrial power has put massive resources into developing more and more destructive weapons. In the

Second World War the United States emerged as the leader in this race. But the race was clearly on in the previous war. The First World War has been called "the chemist's war." In 1917 an appalling weapon new to history appeared on the battlefields of northern France—chemical warfare. Germans used mustard gas in the battle of Ypres that July, and British and French industry quickly retaliated. Until then the American chemical industry was far behind its European counterparts in this area, but DuPont and other chemical companies caught up quickly, working with a new federal agency, the Chemical War Service. To manufacture these new weapons, a complex was constructed at the Edgewood Arsenal near Baltimore between November 1917 and November 1918, on a 4,500-acre parcel within the newly acquired 35,000-acre Aberdeen Proving Ground. Almost overnight Edgewood became the most advanced chemical weapons facility in the world and the only facility capable of producing all four of the gas weapons used in the Great War. Military engineers transformed the area into an industrial landscape. An army engineering report read: "This territory before the War was a little wilderness, the home of wild ducks, geese, and game of all kinds. Today it holds a maze of chemical plants, is covered with a network of roads, railroads, pipelines and all that goes with a huge manufacturing plant and proving ground for chemical warfare agents."[30]

In sum, as one expert writes, "The new weapons systems of the Great War such as aircraft, poison gas, submarines, and tanks demonstrate the complete industrial and economic commitment of the various belligerents in addition to the unprecedented scientific and technological expertise applied by scientists, engineers, and physicians who willing served the military needs of the state. Over the course of the next century, both the cultural legacy and environmental impact of chemical weapons use during the Great War continued to evolve."[31]

The Second World War was the time when the ultimate environmentally destructive weapon appeared—the atomic bomb. The war ended after Hiroshima and Nagasaki, but the Soviet and Western Allies almost immediately broke into opposing camps, fueled by the fear of nuclear devastation. In anticipation of a confrontation with the Soviet Union, the United States began testing nuclear weapons in the South Pacific within a year of the bombing of Hiroshima and Nagasaki. In July 1946 Operation Crossroads detonated the first of a series of bombs on Bikini and Eniwetok Islands. As the Soviets entered the nuclear race, the United States then carried out the world's first thermonuclear (hydrogen) bomb test in 1954.[32]

On land within the United States small nuclear bomb explosions were conducted from 1951 until 1992 at the Nevada Test Site, 1,360 square miles of desert and mountains. Radioactive winds routinely blew across much of Nevada and Utah.[33] Even in the 1950s alarm over radioactive fallout from blasts in Nevada began to spread, as civilians downwind began to suffer a range of cancers.[34]

The superpowers came to the brink of an obliterating war in the Cuban Missile Crisis of October 1962. Backing away from the precipice, the United States,

Britain, and the USSR signed the Limited Nuclear Test Ban Treaty in 1963, pledging a permanent end to aboveground nuclear weapons tests. Although the treaty allowed underground nuclear weapons testing to continue, and both the United States and USSR proceeded on that basis, the result was a lessened environmental impact from nuclear weapons testing.

In the Second World War American forces also developed more powerful incendiary weapons. A thickened petroleum gel called napalm allowed a new use of fire as a weapon. Napalm was first developed for incendiary bombs by scientists at MIT and other universities, working with major chemical and oil corporations led by Standard Oil. Napalm was derived from crude oil imported from Venezuela, plus copra (boiled, dried coconut) from various tropical locations for a fatty acid component. Production came on line in early 1943, and 500,000 pounds were manufactured that year; the amount escalated to twelve million pounds in 1945.

Napalm was first used decisively in August 1943 by U.S. forces in Sicily, as they launched the invasion of Italy. Napalm was later dropped on Germany in October of that year in a raid on an aircraft factory; ultimately 20,000 tons of napalm were dropped on German cities and industries. From there it was taken to Japan. More than 16,000 tons were dropped on Japanese cities, incinerating them almost as surely as atom bombs. Manufactured by Dow Chemical, DuPont, and their competitors, napalm was extensively used again in the Korean War, first as strategic weapons against North Korean and Chinese forces, and then on urban-industrial centers and their civilian populations, including Pyongyang. Its use rose exponentially in the War in Vietnam, totaling 388,000 tons between 1963 and 1973, a far greater amount than in all of the Second World War. Most of this incendiary material was used to complement chemical defoliants, burning forests that had shriveled under chemical attacks.[35]

The American War, as the Vietnamese call it, was the great environmental operation of the American military from the early 1960s until 1975.[36] As a massive counterinsurgency campaign, it was designed primarily to separate Viet Cong troops from their civilian supporters and supplies of food and materiel. Environmental warfare emerged there in a new version of chemical warfare. American commanders had collaborated with the British Army, which used defoliants against communist insurgents in the forests of Malaya during the 1950s. In Vietnam the U.S. Air Force launched Operation Ranch Hand in 1962, dropping chemical defoliants on hill forests and farms to deprive insurgent forces of cover and food, as well as to clear areas around military bases and along strategic roads in the lowlands. Over a nine-year period several chemical agents were used, but Agent Orange dominated.[37] Manufactured by the Dow and Monsanto Chemical Corporations, twenty million gallons were dropped on South Vietnam, and additional amounts were sprayed on Laos and Cambodia.

Chemical defoliants elicited a growing international protest, led by the scientific community. By 1970 reports on dioxin, the carcinogenic element in Agent

Orange and other defoliants, were being published, and the antiwar movement placed this issue at the center of the struggle.[38] But reliable scientific information was not easy for the public to obtain, in the face of stonewalling by the strategic command in Washington and its corporate allies. Recent ground-level studies have indicated partial recovery of some areas, but radical changes in vegetation cover remain. After the war ended in 1975, 2.4 million gallons were still in American military hands. Most of that was sent to remote Johnston Atoll in the mid-Pacific for incineration.[39]

The Military's Evolving Eco-Consciousness: The Greening of the Military

In recent years, as American society has become more concerned about environmental deterioration, the military has reflected that trend, in gradual and complicated ways. Throughout the early Cold War years there was little concern for the environmental fallout of rapid military acceleration. Beginning in 1963 that began to change, as Congress passed a series of landmark environmental protection laws which established a legal framework for pollution mitigation. The first Clean Air Act was passed in 1963; it was followed by the pivotal Environmental Protection Act in 1969 and the first Clean Water Act in 1972. There was considerable controversy about whether these laws were applicable to the military, which strongly resisted the cleanup requirements. The Pentagon developed a legal doctrine—sovereign immunity—asserting that if environmental constraints interfered with the military's fundamental responsibility to preserve national security, environmental laws could not be enforced. But public health problems, most obviously cancer, were accelerating. And contamination of groundwater, wetlands, lakes and rivers, estuaries, and grasslands was reaching the headlines. By the 1980s hazardous waste problems on industrial sites around the country, both military and civilian, were becoming too numerous and too severe to ignore.

How could the new cleanup standards be implemented? Where would the enormous cost of cleanup (of both toxic and radioactive sites) come from? Congress finally addressed the funding question in 1980, when it established the so-called Superfund.[40] The National Priorities List of 1982, a comprehensive ranking of severely polluted federal sites, most of them military, implemented the Superfund. The 1984 Defense Environmental Restoration Account was specifically designed to fund cleanup of military installations and lands. In the next few years the military reviewed over 9,800 sites within the United States. More than 2,650 were determined to need cleanup and restoration; the cost was projected to cost several hundred billion dollars. Under President Reagan, only sixteen sites were cleaned up, but the process accelerated in the early 1990s.

As the Cold War rapidly wound down in the late 1980s, the Pentagon faced the prospect of seriously reduced funding, as Congress created Formerly Used Defense Sites, decommissioning bases and turning them over to civilian authorities.[41] By the mid-1990s 70 of 470 major military sites were closed, but the EPA required that each one meet the same standards considered acceptable for any civilian site. This became a major dimension of Superfund investment. The greatest cleanup task of all was the plutonium wastes at Hanford, which were managed by the Department of Defense with Rockwell International as the main corporate contractor. By 1996 $75 billion had already been spent there, with forty more years of work expected.[42]

In 1990 the Pentagon created the Legacy Resource Management Program to preserve the natural and cultural heritage of lands under its administration. Implementation accelerated after the end of the Cold War, but the process continued to be intensely controversial as to how serious or effective the military was. Civilian specialists and citizens groups mounted intensive pressure for faster and more verifiable cleanup of military sites.[43] Giving additional teeth to the law, the 1992 Federal Facilities Compliance Act required the military to meet EPA cleanup standards.[44]

The 1973 Endangered Species Act became a major challenge to managers of military lands but also provided the legislative basis for collaboration between the Pentagon and the Fish and Wildlife Service of the Interior Department. Some military reserves already included wildlife reserves, as far back as the 1930s, when the Army Air Corps and the Fish and Wildlife Service began collaborating.[45] A well-known example is the Rocky Flats Arsenal outside Denver. By prohibiting civilians from access to its lands, Rocky Flats had become a de facto wildlife refuge. In 1986 bald eagles, then an endangered species, roosted there. The Fish and Wildlife Service began conducting wildlife surveys there, identifying over 200 bird species. In 1992 federal legislation created the Rocky Mountain Arsenal National Wildlife Refuge, which has been managed by the Fish and Wildlife Service since then. Toxic cleanup had to be carried out on 5,000 acres; this was completed in 2010.[46]

So the effort to reduce the toxic legacy on military (as well as civilian) sites continued, and so did the public controversy. By the turn of the millennium the American military had a widening range of environmentally innovative work. Its research and development budget, as set by Congress, made possible long-range planning. Anticipating the post–fossil fuel era ahead, the army designed solar and wind energy systems for land sites, and the navy began using solar energy systems. The air force launched research on alternative fuels for its planes, to complement high-octane jet fuel.

Ongoing Wars in the Middle East and Afghanistan

Meanwhile, international operations have continued for the American military, in wars across the Mideast and western Asia.[47] These efforts have resulted in their own environmental impacts. The Persian Gulf War (1991), the ongoing warfare in Iraq (beginning in 2003), and the struggle in Afghanistan have done severe damage to cities, farmlands, forests, grazing lands, deserts, and wet-lands.[48] As long as fighting continues and it is extremely dangerous to conduct postconflict environmental surveys on the ground, some conclusions have to remain tentative. And since many armed forces have contributed to the damage, it can be difficult to specify which force has been responsible for which impact.

The Persian Gulf War took place after a decade of war between Iraq and Iran and a subsequent Iraqi invasion of Kuwait in 1990 to gain control of its vast petroleum supplies. The United States retaliated in early 1991, forcing the Iraqi Army to retreat back to Baghdad. In the course of the campaign the American Air Force bombed power plants and the electricity grid, damaging Iraq's urban water supplies and sewage management, as well as rural irrigation flow, leading to waterlogging and increased salination.[49] The thousands of military vehicles involved in the Iraqi retreat and the American pursuit also damaged deserts, resulting in more destructive sandstorms and threats to oases that supported migratory camel herds.

A decade later the American military returned to Iraq, overwhelming Saddam Hussein's regime with unprecedented high-tech weaponry. Once again the attack damaged water storage on the Euphrates and Tigris Rivers and the power stations that distributed water for urban public health. This resulted in severe urban environmental pollution in greater Baghdad, Basra, and other cities, as toxic garbage accumulated.[50] The countryside suffered as well, including irrigation in the fertile plains of the Tigris-Euphrates basin, where canals and irrigation channels were damaged by military movements. Many have been repaired by now, despite continuing political breakdown and sectarian violence.

The ongoing war for control of Afghanistan began with the Soviet invasion in 1979, which lasted for a decade, causing serious damage to irrigated farming systems and urban life.[51] After the collapse of the Soviet Union, a decade of turmoil followed, including the rise of the Taliban. American forces were involved behind the scenes until September 11, 2001; that December the U.S. Air Force launched a campaign to cripple Al-Qaeda, bombing its bases in the mountains of eastern Afghanistan. American and NATO armies followed on the ground, conducting a counterinsurgency campaign that remains unresolved.

The environmental costs of thirty-seven years of fighting have been heavy. Much cropland depends on irrigation systems, many of which have been destroyed. Pistachio groves in the north have been severely reduced. On the wide semiarid pastoral lands the herds of sheep have been decimated and juniper shrubbery reduced for firewood. The eastern mountain forests along the Pakistan border have been seriously deforested from 1980 onward from fighting and wildfires. Massive illegal firewood cutting, trucked to markets in Pakistan, has made the situation even worse. Farther west, in the wetlands of the Helmand River Basin, dams built since the 1950s are only partially functioning.[52] A multiyear drought from 2003 to 2009, followed by floods in 2010, added further misery.[53] American and NATO military forces have made efforts to rebuild

Afghan infrastructure in a follow-up stage of counterinsurgency, in collaboration with international civilian agencies and many voluntary organizations. But their work is severely compromised by the continuing turmoil across the country. A trend of ecological degradation continues in a war-torn land that can hardly afford the additional stress.

And so the tension continues, between the perennial environmental costs of military operations—which steadily intensify as the destructive power and efficiency of weapons accelerates—and the increasing efforts of military planners and managers to mitigate those costs. It is difficult to be sure what the environmental costs have been in any particular case, because they are so complex and systemic. We are still struggling to comprehend the full legacy of the Vietnam War, and the closer we come to understanding recent and ongoing wars, the more difficult it is, since it is a risky task to study the impacts on the ground. But one thing is evident: the environmental dimensions of war and the preparation for war must not be ignored.

Discussion Questions

1. In your mind, what should be included in the list of *environmental* dimensions / impacts of military operations?
2. Which environmental consequences of World Wars I and II had the most lasting legacies? How did the conditions of the Cold War influence those changes?
3. Which factors contributed to the rise of military environmentalism, and how has the American military responded to the great environmental challenge?

Notes

1 The history of the American military includes both environmental *settings* (typically the work of military geographers) and environmental *impacts* (the work of environmental historians). Now a new field of study is emerging, often called warfare ecology or the political ecology of war. See Gary E. Machlis and Thor Hanson, "Warfare Ecology," *Bioscience* 58, no. 8 (September 2008): 729–736. For global perspectives, see Richard P. Tucker, "War and the Environment," in *Blackwell Companion to Global Environmental History*, ed. J. R. McNeill and Erin Stewart (Oxford: Blackwell, 2012); J. R. McNeill, "Woods and Warfare in World History," *Environmental History* 9, no. 3 (July 2004): 388–410. For the impact on natural resources, see Ronald H. Huisken, "The Consumption of Raw Materials for Military Purposes," *Ambio* 4, no. 5/6 (1975): 229–233. See also the website environmentandwar.com.
2 Lisa M. Brady, *War upon the Land: Military Strategy and the Transformation of Southern Landscapes during the American Civil War* (Athens: University of Georgia Press, 2012).

3   Robert M. Utley, *Frontier Regulars: The United States Army and the Indian, 1866–1891*
    (Bloomington: Indiana University Press, 1973); Andrew C. Isenberg, *The Destruction
    of the Bison* (Cambridge: Cambridge University Press, 2000). For a broad perspective
    on those years, see Paul A. C. Koistinen, "The Political Economy of Warfare in Amer-
    ica, 1865–1914," in *Anticipating Total War: The German and American Experiences,
    1871–1914*, ed. Manfred F. Boemeke, Roger Chickering, and Stig Förster (Cambridge:
    Cambridge University Press, 1999), 57–76.

4   Paul A. C. Koistinen, *Mobilizing for Modern War: The Political Economy of American
    Warfare, 1865–1919* (Lawrence: University Press of Kansas, 1997).

5   Timothy LeCain, *Mass Destruction: The Men and Giant Mines That Wired America
    and Scarred the Planet* (New Brunswick, NJ: Rutgers University Press, 2009).

6   For details of the environmental damage, see Thomas M. Klubock, *Contested Com-
    munities: Class, Gender, and Politics in Chile's El Teniente Copper Mine, 1904–1951*
    (Durham, NC: Duke University Press, 1998).

7   Richard White, *The Organic Machine* (New York: Hill and Wang, 1995), 72–73.

8   Thomas D. Clark, *The Greening of the South* (Lexington: University Press of Ken-
    tucky, 1984), 24–35.

9   David Novick, Melvin Anshen, and W. C. Truppner, *Wartime Production Controls*
    (New York: Columbia University Press, 1949), 205–206.

10 Greg Grandin, *Fordlandia* (New York: Metropolitan Books, 2009).

11 Richard P. Tucker, *Insatiable Appetite: The United States and the Ecological Degrada-
    tion of the Tropical World* (Berkeley: University of California Press, 2000), chap. 5.

12 Thomas P. Hughes, *Networks of Power: Electrification in Western Society, 1880–1930*
    (Baltimore: Johns Hopkins University Press, 1983); Christopher Jones, *Routes of
    Power: Energy and Modern America* (Cambridge: Harvard University Press, 2014);
    Peter A. Shulman, *Coal and Empire: The Birth of Energy Security in Industrial
    America* (Baltimore: Johns Hopkins University Press, 2015).

13 Brian Black, *Crude Reality: Petroleum in World History* (Lanham, MD: Rowman &
    Littlefield, 2012); Daniel Yergin, *The Prize: The Epic Quest for Oil, Money, and Power*
    (New York: Simon and Schuster, 1991); Paul Sabin, *Crude Politics: The California Oil
    Market, 1900–1940* (Berkeley: University of California Press, 2005).

14 Myrna Santiago, *The Ecology of Oil: Environment, Labor, and the Mexican Revolution,
    1900–1938* (Cambridge: Cambridge University Press, 2006).

15 Yergin, *The Prize*.

16 Sarah Elkind, "The Nature and Business of War: Drilling for Oil in Wartime Los
    Angeles," in *Cities and Nature in the American West*, ed. Char Miller (Reno: Univer-
    sity of Nevada Press, 2010), 205–224.

17 Francis Paul Prucha, *The Sword of the Republic: The United States Army on the Fron-
    tier, 1783–1846* (Bloomington: Indiana University Press, 1968).

18 Shulman, *Coal and Empire*, 125–137.

19 For an overview, see J. R. McNeill and David S. Painter, "The Global Environmental
    Footprint of the U.S. Military, 1789–2003," in *War and the Environment*, ed. Charles
    Closmann (College Station: Texas A&M University Press, 2009), chap. 2.

20 Jean Mansavage, "For Lands Sake: Military Acquisition and Use of Property for
    National Defense during World War II," in *The Nature of War: American Environ-
    ments and World War II*, ed. Thomas Robertson et al., in preparation.

21 Roger W. Lotchin, ed., *The Martial Metropolis: U.S. Cities in War and Peace* (New
    York: Praeger, 1984); Roger W. Lotchin, "The Origins of the Sunbelt-Frostbelt Strug-
    gle: Defense Spending and City Building," in *Searching for the Sunbelt*, ed. Raymond
    A. Mohl (Knoxville: University of Tennessee Press, 1990), 47–68.

22 Ann Markusen, Peter Hall, Scott Campbell, and Sabina Deitrick, *The Rise of the Gunbelt: The Military Remapping of Industrial America* (New York: Oxford University Press, 1991).

23 Roger W. Lotchin, *The Bad City in the Good War: San Francisco, Los Angeles, Oakland, and San Diego* (Bloomington: Indiana University Press, 2003).

24 Matthew M. Booker, *Down by the Bay: San Francisco's History between the Tides* (Berkeley: University of California Press, 2013).

25 Valerie Kuletz, *The Tainted Desert: Environmental Ruin in the American West* (New York: Routledge, 1998), 48ff.

26 Kate Brown, *Plutopia: Nuclear Families, Atomic Cities, and the Great Soviet and American Plutonium Disasters* (New York: Oxford University Press, 2013).

27 Ryan Edgington, *Range Wars: The Environmental Contest for White Sands Missile Range* (Lincoln: University of Nebraska Press, 2014).

28 Ibid., 6.

29 Gretchen Heefner, *The Missile Next Door: The Minuteman in the American Heartland* (Cambridge, MA: Harvard University Press, 2012), 25.

30 Gerard Fitzgerald, "The Chemists' War: Edgewood Arsenal, World War I and the Birth of a Militarized Environment," in *Environmental Histories of World War I*, ed. Tait Keller, J. R. McNeill, Martin Schmid, and Richard P. Tucker, in preparation, 2.

31 Ibid., 1.

32 Stewart Firth, *Nuclear Playground* (Honolulu: University of Hawaii Press, 1987). For the long-term environmental impacts of all nuclear bomb tests in the Pacific, see Mark D. Merlin, "Environmental Impacts of Nuclear Testing in Remote Oceania, 1946–1996," in *Environmental Histories of the Cold War*, ed. John R. McNeill and Corinna R. Unger (Cambridge: Cambridge University Press, 2010).

33 Kuletz, *Tainted Desert*; Bruce Hevly and John M. Findlay, eds., *The Atomic West* (Seattle: University of Washington Press, 1998); Leisl Carr Childers, "Incident at Galisteo: The 1955 Teapot Series and the Mental Landscape of Contamination," in *Proving Grounds: Militarized Landscapes, Weapons Testing, and the Environmental Impact of U.S. Bases*, ed. Edwin A. Martini (Seattle: University of Washington Press, 2015), 75–110.

34 Robert A. Divine, *Blowing in the Wind: The Nuclear Test Ban Debate, 1954–1960* (New York: Oxford University Press, 1978), 262–280. For the cancer impact, see Terry Tempest Williams, *Refuge: An Unnatural History of Family and Place* (New York: Vintage, 1991).

35 Robert M. Neer, *Napalm: An American Biography* (Cambridge, MA: Harvard University Press, 2013).

36 For background, see David A. Biggs, *Quagmire: Nation-Building and Nature in the Mekong Delta* (Seattle: University of Washington Press, 2010).

37 Edwin Martini, *Agent Orange: History, Science, and the Politics of Uncertainty* (Amherst: University of Massachusetts Press, 2012), chap. 4.

38 David Zierler, *The Invention of Ecocide* (Athens: University of Georgia Press, 2011).

39 A very influential early evaluation can be found in Arthur H. Westing, ed., *Ecological Consequences of the Second Indochina War* (Stockholm: Almqvist and Wiksell, 1976). An important recent study is Martini, *Proving Grounds*, chap. 4.

40 John A. Hird, *Superfund: The Political Economy of Environmental Risk* (Baltimore: Johns Hopkins University Press, 1994).

41 Robert F. Durant, *The Greening of the U.S. Military: Environmental Policy, National Security, and Organizational Change* (Washington, DC: Georgetown University Press, 2007).

42 Glenn Zorpette, "Hanford's Nuclear Wasteland," *Scientific American* (May 1996): 88–97.

43 One important group was the National Toxic Campaign Fund, which published *The U.S. Military's Toxic Legacy* in 1991, charging the Department of Defense with suppressing data on cleanup of many hazardous sites.

44 For implementation, see Kenneth N. Hansen, *The Greening of Pentagon Brownfields* (Lanham, MD: Lexington Books, 2004).

45 Jean A. Mansavage, *Natural Defense: U.S. Air Force Origins of the Department of Defense Natural Resources Conservation Program* (Washington, DC: Air Force History and Museums Program, 2014); David G. Havlick, "Restoration and Meaning on Former Military Lands in the United States," in Martini, *Proving Grounds*, 265–287.

46 Peter Coates, Tim Cole, Marianna Dudley, and Chris Pearson, "Defending Nation, Defending Nature? Militarized Landscapes and Military Environmentalism in Britain, France, and the United States," *Environmental History* 16 (July 2011): 456–491.

47 For a severe critique, see Barry Sanders, *The Green Zone: The Environmental Costs of Militarism* (Oakland, CA: AK Press, 2009).

48 See the Costs of War Project's website: Watson.brown.edu/costsofwar/.

49 For the impact of the regional conflict from 1980 to 2003, see United Nations Environment Programme, *Desk Study on the Environment in Iraq* (Nairobi: UNEP, 2003), 65ff.

50 For damage to the urban environment in Baghdad and other Iraqi cities in the initial campaign, see United Nations Environment Programme, *UNEP in Iraq: Post-Conflict Assessment, Clean-Up and Reconstruction* (Nairobi: UNEP, 2007).

51 T. A. Formoli et al., "Impacts of the Afghan-Soviet War on Afghanistan's Environment," *Environmental Conservation* 22, no. 1 (Spring 1995): 66–69.

52 The most reliable sources include United Nations Environment Programme, *Afghanistan: Post-Conflict Environmental Assessment* (Nairobi: UNEP, 2003); United Nations Environment Programme, *UNEP in Afghanistan* (Nairobi: UNEP, 2007).

53 For a vivid ground-level account of these years, see Christian Parenti, *Tropic of Chaos: Climate Change and the New Geography of Violence* (New York: Nation Books, 2011), chap. 9 ("Drugs, Drought, and Jihad: Environmental History of the Afghanistan War").

Further Reading

Lisa M. Brady. *War upon the Land: Military Strategy and the Transformation of Southern Landscapes during the American Civil War*. Athens: University of Georgia Press, 2012.

Edwin A. Martini, ed. *Proving Grounds: Militarized Landscapes, Weapons Testing, and the Environmental Impact of U.S. Bases*. Seattle: University of Washington Press, 2015.

J. R. McNeill and Corinna R. Unger, eds., *Environmental Histories of the Cold War*. Cambridge: Cambridge University Press, 2010.

Richard P. Tucker and Edmund Russell, eds. *Natural Enemy, Natural Ally: Toward an Environmental History of War*. Corvallis: Oregon State University Press, 2004.

13

Communications Media, the U.S. Military, and the War Brought Home

SUSAN L. CARRUTHERS

What images do we associate with the media in wartime? In all likelihood, we envision journalists thrust into unfamiliar terrain, awkwardly attired in brand new flak jackets and helmets, whether writing for newspapers, filming for television broadcasts, making audio recordings for radio programs, or capturing photographic images to help civilians at a safe remove make sense of armed conflict. Imagined in this way, journalists and soldiers stand in stark contrast. Indeed, the media and the military are often regarded, and often regard one another, as antagonistic professions driven by irreconcilable imperatives. Where journalists are committed to publicity, the armed forces remain fiercely dedicated to secrecy; news organizations crave sensation and scoops, while the military strives to keep tactical intelligence under wraps. These are well-worn notions. Although many scholars now challenge the associated claim that news media make the pursuit of victory harder by relentlessly showcasing war's human costs—a charge that gathered force after the War in Vietnam—it still remains commonplace to consider "the media" as external to the military. War reporting thus appears something done *to*, not by, uniformed personnel.[1]

There is a less familiar path. Instead of focusing on the commercial mass media that supplies representations of war to distant audiences, "media" can more broadly include the shifting technologies that allow servicemen and women to stay in touch with loved ones back home. A key contention here is that military personnel themselves have long served as primary producers of stories about war through their everyday interactions with family members and friends. The media that matter in wartime, then, aren't restricted to professional news agencies. Just as important to students of war and society (and arguably more important) are the channels of communication that enable deployed personnel to remain connected with those left behind when servicemen and women are dispatched on active duty overseas. Evolving communications and transportation technologies have transformed the means, ease, and speed with which messages—whether written on paper, recorded on vinyl or tape, or rendered as code—bridge geographical distance.

Contact with home occupies a special place in the lives of men and women at war. In U.S. popular culture, images of "mail call"—as fatigued soldiers clamor for the daily distribution of letters from home—have formed a sentimental staple of wartime iconography from the birth of photojournalism in the Civil War to Hollywood combat films. Since 2011, the Smithsonian National Postal Museum in Washington, DC, has devoted a permanent exhibit to the phenomenon of how soldiers receive and dispatch letters, tapes, and parcels. If mail from home reminds those in uniform that they're fondly remembered and that a familiar world exists eagerly awaiting their return, communications *from* the front have also profoundly shaped civilians' perceptions of war. Often, both soldiers and civilians share a belief that the words of those in uniform—derived from a vantage point inaccessible to civilians—carry greater truth value than any journalistic report.[2]

When this faith is shown to be misplaced, indignation can erupt. In October 2003, the *New York Times* registered outrage that U.S. army officers had instructed junior servicemen in Iraq to dispatch pro forma letters to their families with a view to republication in local hometown newspapers. These missives, printed in no less than eleven papers, described American efforts to rebuild Kirkuk. In identical language, the soldiers' letters all depicted Iraqi children "in their broken English shouting, 'Thank you, Mister.'" The *Times* response to this propaganda initiative typifies feelings of violation expressed by many U.S. news outlets: "Letters home from the war front are some of the revered aspects of history, a treasury of soldiers' impressions and firsthand narratives that hold a value apart from the individual lives put firmly on the battle line. It's all the more disturbing, then, that an apparently orchestrated campaign of letter writing has arisen among some of the American forces in Iraq to highlight what are alleged to be overlooked success stories."[3] In other words, those officers responsible for producing the template had done more than breach a bond of trust between senders and family members perplexed to receive these syntactically correct and implausibly upbeat letters. They had also corroded the epistolary authority vested in soldiers as war's most unimpeachable witnesses—its own form of sacrilege.[4]

Behind such criticism hovers a larger lament—namely, that the era of the soldier-scribe is fast approaching its end. Over the past decade, an increasingly widespread observation holds that men and women in uniform, along with just about everyone else, rarely write "old-fashioned letters" any more, turning instead to the multiple possibilities for speedier communication offered by cell phones and the internet. Historians, archivists, and others who look forward to looking back anticipate a regrettable dearth of intimate primary sources from the Wars in Iraq and Afghanistan. Scholars of new media, by contrast, have dissected soldiers' novel incarnations as bloggers, videographers, and instant pundits, often construing the blogging-tweeting-uploading soldier in more positive terms. The term "citizen journalist," they point out, need not imply civilian status.[5]

A fresh approach to the military and new media is appropriate. Whereas most academic interest has thus far concentrated on the circulation of photographic and video imagery by uniformed personnel, focusing interest on soldiers' communication with home in a digital age can give insight into how affective ties are regulated and leveraged by commanding officers and how both the military and civilians understand the relationship between "over there" and "over here" in an era of protracted war and serial redeployments. What does it mean to be and stay connected in a hypercommunicative, putatively post-epistolary age? Drawing on a wide range of sources from armed services' websites to the specialized literature of military psychiatry, and from popular culture to veterans' memoirs, this essay explores how U.S. service personnel use Facebook, Skype, instant messaging, and email—alongside "regular" mail—to maintain intimate relationships while deployed in Iraq and Afghanistan. While it's easy to fixate on the "newness" of digital media, it can be fruitful to identify precisely what is and is not novel about present-day forms of communication. I suggest that, while new media create distinctive challenges and opportunities for deployed personnel and their loved ones, wartime exchanges between soldiers and civilians have long blurred any sharp distinction between the realms of public and private. Staying in touch—in centuries past, as in the present—fulfills functions both intimate and social, marital and martial.

Staying Connected: Technologies and Practices of Communication

It was hard when Lt. Col. Brad Summers left his family for 11 months to serve with the Army in Iraq.

But one thing his wife, Crista, always thought about when her husband would talk to her and their three boys about five times per week was how lucky they were that they got that much.

"I'd think of Vietnam" and all the other wars, where men and women were unable to even hear the voices of their loved ones, much less see them on a computer screen as her family did using Skype, an online video telecommunications tool.

So began an Associated Press story widely circulated in U.S. newspapers in November 2009.[6] With its upbeat emphasis on the ability of today's soldiers to be virtually present in their stateside homes, this report typifies much discussion of new media's superiority over old-fashioned letter writing. Journalists and digital media scholars alike often conjure an abrupt rupture between the "digital age" and everything that preceded it. Soldiers, it's easily imagined, put pen to paper for centuries before the emergence of the internet in the 1990s radically, and irrevocably, reshaped modes of communication for the better. Thanks to Skype, instant messaging, and social media sites like Facebook, active-duty personnel can remain connected with civilian society as never before, drawing emotional support from bonds that are easily sustained irrespective of geographical distance and duration of deployment. Before the digital age, claims media scholar Lisa Ellen Silvestri, soldiers at war were "exempt from home-front relational commitments." "War" and "society," in this account, were almost hermetically sealed and self-contained realms.[7]

Close attention to the past, however, reveals more complex and shifting communication practices over time. Although literate soldiers have dispatched missives home from the front in every war in U.S. history, speed of delivery has fluctuated considerably rather than simply getting ever faster over time. The physical form in which mail is dispatched has also undergone some variation. Postcards were widely adopted by American soldiers sent overseas during the First World War, only in part because their small dimensions made them easier to transport in bulk. Whether embellished with touristic scenes or preformulated messages that could be checked ("I am well," "The weather is fine," and so on), postcards let servicemen signal their survival to folks back home, even if they curbed more expressive outpourings. Ostensibly a boon to doughboys with shaky or nonexistent literacy, these cards were also easier for officers to monitor than lengthier epistles. Mail to and from the Western Front took some time to cross the Atlantic by steamship. But the impressive volume of letters dispatched from the states to members of the Allied Expeditionary Force—thirty-five million letters sent abroad between July 1, 1917, and June 30, 1918—indicates that American soldiers were hardly cut off from familial attachments by their deployment abroad in perilous circumstances.[8]

The connective tissue binding uniformed personnel overseas to loved ones at home thickened considerably during the Second World War. Within months of U.S. entry into the war in December 1941, the military and civilian postal services were deluged by such a vast quantity of letters and parcels to and from uniformed Americans that they introduced "V-mail" in an attempt to streamline transmission. Senders of V-mail wrote letters on a single preprinted sheet which was then photographed and shrunk onto 16mm microfilm. A single reel, weighing just five ounces, could contain about 1,500 letters, considerably reducing the amount of cargo space required to transport mail overseas. When the reels reached their destination, individual V-mails were printed—reduced in size to a quarter of the letter's original dimensions—and delivered to their addressees. Yet despite this innovation, the United States Post Office handled a staggering thirty-eight *billion* pieces of mail in 1945 alone.[9]

Besides V-mail, the Second World War saw experiments with soldiers recording messages onto phonograph discs which were mailed to their loved ones and played on standard record players, by then a fixture of many more affluent American homes. Already in the 1940s, the military establishment recognized that hearing a spoken message might represent a qualitative improvement over the written word. Although the technology was (by present-day standards) cumbersome, these phonograph recordings marked the start of a decades-long search to improve the means by which soldiers could verbally address, and then actually converse with, spouses, parents, and children at home. By the time of the Vietnam War, American GIs were able to chat with family members from time to time—albeit with much preplanning along with a good deal of delay and interference—thanks to a system known as MARS, the Military Affiliate Radio System—a telephone hookup completed via a third-party amateur radio operator.[10] More commonplace was the practice of exchanging messages recorded onto tape. Over the course of the war, cassette players became cheaper and more widely owned, sold at reduced rates in army PXs "in country." But for soldiers and families without personal access to these new gadgets, welfare agencies like the United Service Organizations, the YMCA, and American Red Cross provided free recording facilities, along with airmail dispatch of tapes to and from service personnel in Vietnam. In the mid-1960s, these "living letters" seemed the very latest thing to Americans who already regarded themselves as inhabiting the "electronic age."[11] In May 1968, the *Boston Globe* ran a lengthy feature about how one army surgeon—"amid the heat, stench and destruction of Vietnam"—read *Stuart Little* to his three sons in Concord, Massachusetts, with the tape recorder providing "his lifeline with home."[12]

Since the 1970s, the communications revolution has proceeded speedily but also fitfully. Despite experimentation with MARS during the Vietnam War, active-duty personnel deployed overseas did not enjoy the use of telephones until the invasion of Panama (codenamed "Operation Just Cause") in 1989. Even then, access was haphazard and calls made through official channels were costly, prompting some soldiers to resort to public pay phones in Panamanian supermarkets. Enlisted men were frustrated by limited access to military telephones and the high charge per minute. The military establishment, meanwhile, delivered a mixed verdict on its phone service in Panama and concurrent peacekeeping operations elsewhere. Some officers resented the ways in which their role as the mediator of communication between "home" and "away" was being usurped, circumvented, or undermined by the access enlisted men and women enjoyed to unsupervised phone calls. In these officers' judgment, long-distance conversation was apt to fuel the circulation of rumors. Unconfirmed news, sometimes about matters as grave as combat fatalities, traveled via informal grapevines instead of approved channels. Rather than improving esprit, access to phones could have just the opposite effect. If conversations were stilted or angry, or when servicemen or women failed to call home with the regularity their partners desired, phone calls could depress morale—a mercurial military commodity. Officers regretfully noted that, in less communicative couples, spouses tended to blame a partner's silence on the military's inadequate provision of phones, not individuals' intermittent reluctance to use them. As a result, relations between spouses living on bases in the United States and rear detachment officers tended to deteriorate along with the marriages.[13]

The growth of the internet, a development which has unfolded alongside the "War on Terror," provoked considerably more controversy within the military establishment. Despite digital media's advantages in terms of rapid delivery and convenience—no need for paper, writing implements, postage stamps, or congressional approval to waive mailing charges for military personnel— electronic communication posed sharp questions about operational security, or OPSEC in military shorthand. Who might be eavesdropping on servicemen and women's online correspondence, and what malign use might they make of nuggets plucked from the ether? But while the Pentagon feared "the enemy" might mine servicemen and women's email and social media activity for valuable intelligence, senior commanders also fretted about their own dwindling ability to keep tabs on what information deployed personnel divulged in communications with an increasingly diffuse home front—an increasingly obsolescent concept as "here" and "there" became detached from grid coordinates.[14]

New digital platforms for sharing text, photo, and video content with an ever-expanding online audience, rather than a single addressee, caused the armed services particular alarm. In part, this anxiety arose in anticipation of inadvertent leaks—or, worse yet, purposeful "whistle-blowing"—by active-duty personnel letting slip sensitive details about particular units' locations and activities. Undoubtedly, though, the Department of Defense worried (and continues to worry) about more than OPSEC narrowly defined. Whether dealing with professional journalists reporting on the military or with what uniformed personnel themselves communicate to the world beyond "the wire," the armed services seek to protect the *reputation* of the American military and the image of war-making as a noble profession governed by rules aimed at minimizing human harm. Ideally, servicemen and women should appear committed to their mission—neither inappropriately jocular about, nor gratified by, the business of inflicting bodily harm, as suggested by a series of leaked photographs showing military personnel posing with maimed corpses in Afghanistan.[15] At the same time, active-duty personnel—stoic warriors who execute orders with consummate professionalism—must appear neither critical of the underlying purposes served by war nor unduly perturbed by the grave toll it takes on human life. This high-wire stunt isn't easily sustained.

Fears about differently damaging kinds of online content prompted the U.S. military to adopt a highly restrictive approach to internet use. In the early 2000s, the Department of Defense (DOD) limited and monitored access to computers by military personnel, introducing guidelines that required bloggers-in-uniform to gain their commanding officer's permission before posting new content.[16] When restrictive measures failed to curb the internet's popularity, the armed services attempted to create a parallel military intranet, along with a social media site akin to Facebook, for the exclusive use of uniformed personnel and their families. Another initiative to combine the internet's potential for immediacy with heightened security of transmission took the form of Motomail. Short for "motivational mail," this United States Marine Corps service permitted family members to log onto a secure site and write to marines on active duty in Iraq. With the content encrypted, these communications were emailed to nine bases in Iraq, where specially customized printers then produced hard copies of the letters, sealed into secure "tear-strip" envelopes. The only human contact with these hybrid communications—snailmail crossed with email—came in the process of delivery. Marines received their Motomail just like any other letter distributed at mail call. But unlike items entrusted to the USPS, which might take weeks to reach remote locations, Motomail was guaranteed to arrive the same day. This service, which lasted from 2004 until it fell victim to DOD budget cuts in 2013, was briefly copied by the army with a variant branded "Hooahmail."[17]

Over the past half decade, American service personnel have been granted greater latitude to connect via Facebook, Instagram, Skype, and the many other constantly mutating ways in which civilians routinely communicate with one another. With internet stations a fixture of U.S. military bases overseas, including in Iraq and Afghanistan, communications technologies have moved far beyond earlier eras' heavy (if not total) reliance on surface mail to sustain emotional bonds between those at war and those at home. But some cautionary notes are nevertheless in order. First, the mere existence of these connective technologies doesn't invariably translate into reliable, round-the-clock access to them for deployed personnel. Nor does the availability of networked computers guarantee that men and women at war *necessarily* stay in closer contact with home. Where there's a way, there's not necessarily a will. The exhausting, intermittently terrifying, and tedious nature of life at war can deplete the necessary energy for the kind of ceaseless interaction that's become a round-the-clock feature of life in the digital age. Waiting in line for access to a computer station, and awareness that others are impatiently massing behind a keyboard, may be too frustrating to endure regularly. Prearranging calls or videoconferences can be equally difficult. Deployed personnel don't always know in advance when they'll be free from operational duties. And they may also be well aware that failure to call at an agreed time is liable to occasion worry at home.[18] For these reasons and others discussed below, "old-fashioned" letter writing persists among at least some deployed personnel. And old-fashioned letters take just as long, if not longer, to reach their recipients as mail sent during the Second World War.

Public Privacy and Published Intimacies

As postal service promotional campaigns and military deployment manuals both point out, there's something special about letters. Fragile yet durable, letters provide the recipient with a physical token from the sender: paper a love one has touched, familiar handwriting, perhaps also the imprint of a lipsticked kiss or a lingering scent. "They provide service members with something tangible to carry with them throughout the deployment," the DOD *Military Deployment Guide* points out.[19] They may bear traces of the physical and emotional conditions of production—water stains, coffee splashes, teardrops—as well as markings of the journey between "there" and "here." To receive a letter is to be simultaneously brought close to the sender and yet reminded of physical separation. So, at any rate, letters can be fondly conceived. It does, however, require a particular sensibility to cherish letters as sentimental substitutes for the missing sender, and not all wartime correspondents necessarily share such understandings. Thus one National Guardsman noted that his attempts to bring his wife into closer contact with his environs in Iraq—by sprinkling sand in his letters—had gone awry, widening rather than closing the gap between home and away. "After several letters, she asked him to take greater care when sending mail because, she told him, the 'dirt makes a mess when I open your letters.' He was sending the sand in hopes she would save it, but never told her that was what he was doing. 'I guess I thought she'd know to keep it for me.'"[20]

Digital media, by contrast, offer immediacy at the expense of tactility. The lost personal touch is more than compensated, for many users, by what's gained—an ability to connect in "real time," to see and be seen, to share both text and images, and talk—not necessarily to just one person at a time. Whereas letters are necessarily more monologic, the interval between communications often so long and unpredictable as to hinder meaningful back-and-forth, Facebook status updates, instant messaging, and video conferencing allow for different kinds of interaction. Although disembodied, online activity may yield a more satisfying and lifelike substitution for in-person encounters than older communications technologies. Among other things, deployed parents can now remain visually and aurally alive to their children—not someone whose presence is restricted to words on a page or the voice on an audiocassette. Indeed, Skype enables military personnel and their loved ones vicariously to experience the full gamut of human experience. As numerous press stories have pointed out over the past decade, American servicemen in Iraq and Afghanistan have "virtually" attended their babies' births courtesy of Skype's admission into the labor ward. By way of unforeseen corollary, however, one military spouse witnessed her husband's death via Skype, spending two hours—while the connection remained live—attempting to alert personnel on his base in Afghanistan to her partner's fatal mid-sentence collapse.

Digital technologies foster certain kinds of sharing that simultaneity permits. But the intimate uses, pleasures, and frustrations of digital communication have attracted less scholarly attention than the widespread sharing and networking—with audiences both intended and otherwise—that social media encourage. In recent years, much has been written about U.S. soldiers in Iraq and Afghanistan as videographers and photojournalists. Their graphic self-representations, enthusiasts argue, provide civilians a more textured sense of war as lived experience than anything offered hitherto by conventional journalism. But while some civilian commentators welcome the "grunt's eye view" of soldiers' blogs, photos, and videos as a boon to civilians' understanding of what deployed personnel do, and of how they make sense of what they're doing in Iraq and Afghanistan, others understand new media in less valorizing terms. Critics point to the military establishment's appropriation of new media to boost recruitment and, more broadly, reassert authority over a "narrative" it insists on rendering in the singular. In the United States and beyond, some scholars lament the capabilities of new communications media to promote "digital militarism." As soldier-selfies and domesticated images of conflict pervade not just video games but the larger image-world of the internet, the business of war-making—the primary enterprise of armed forces—loses its lethal charge. The line between soldiering and tourism blurs, with civilians becoming habituated to a state of permanent mobilization without taking stock of how abnormal this normalization of militarism is.[21]

Despite their divergent value judgments, academic analysts typically stress the newness of new media in making public what was once more exclusively intimate. But this emphasis misses crucial, and more continuous, dimensions of wartime communication. Letters from the front have rarely—if ever—been private. At least until the Vietnam War, a military censor obtrusively monitored what was exchanged between sender and recipient. For enlisted men, "the censor" didn't hover as an impersonal abstraction. He was the unit's commanding officer, and to subalterns' chagrin, superiors weren't always discreet about what they read. Indeed, some officers were callous enough to laugh publicly with one another over some of the mail, deriving amusement from inadvertent malapropisms and effusive endearments.[22] Cruel amusement was not the intentional point of censorship, however. Monitoring mail served two formal functions. Surveillance of enlisted men's letters not only allowed officers to delete any information that might compromise security but also yielded insights into the state of subordinates' morale—a different, but equally valuable form of intelligence.

Officers have not been alone in valuing letters as a source of renewable energy for war-making. As long as soldiers have received mail from home, they have doubtless also shared the content of these missives with buddies by reading letters aloud or passing them around. Mail can thus build morale—and strengthen emotional ties—in more ways than one. Paradoxically, no genre of letter has perhaps done more to solidify bonds between fighting men than the terse note from home that breaks off a romantic relationship—the "Dear John." Construed as notifications of betrayal by faithless wives or girlfriends, these communications gained unique cultural prominence during the Vietnam War. According to contemporary press reports, such letters had never before been sent in such profusion. Wives and girlfriends in earlier wars, advice columnists chided female readers, had been courteous enough to wait until their soldier spouses or fiancés returned to confront them with news of a relationship's breakdown. For commentators eager to blame GIs' demoralization (and ultimately defeat) on a perfidious home front, the "Dear John" phenomenon emblematized civilian America's treacherous abandonment of its men at war in Vietnam. In at least one instance, a breakup letter was introduced into an American serviceman's court-martial as evidence of temporarily insanity at the time its recipient killed four Vietnamese. The psychiatrist who testified on this marine's behalf also noted that, among the many specimen letters he had amassed in Vietnam, was a "tape recording sent in by a girl who showed herself to be a true child of our technological age; she tape recorded an amorous session with the new boyfriend for the benefit of the old boyfriend."[23]

Readers familiar with *Jarhead*, Anthony Swofford's memoir of his 1991 Persian Gulf War service with the Marine Corps (or Sam Mendes's cinematic adaptation) will know that the "Dear John" outlived the Vietnam War along with male rituals of shaming-by-sharing that cement bonds between soldiers on the rubble of failed romance, uniting men in shared hatred of women. "Near the regimental mess hall there is a Wall of Shame, where jarheads post photos of unfaithful women, women who've gone bad on debts or stolen some poor jarhead's car and all of his clothes or simply informed him that the ride has ended." Warming to his theme, Swofford describes forty or more photos "affixed with duct tape" to a six-foot-tall post, and annotated with scabrous captions detailing the marines' sentiments towards their exes. "I look at more of the pictures and I think of the poor jarheads who've left their platoon tents and walked the slow desert walk to the chow hall, but rather than receiving the chow they've proudly displayed the narrative of their cuckoldry. It is not necessarily a bad thing to be able to tell the story of your woman's betrayal."[24] Some military personnel continue to hold that sentiment. The internet now provides a much more efficient mechanism to display and deride images of women (rarely men) who have purportedly wronged active-duty personnel. One website, *The Brigade*, invites users to "post 'tasteful' pix of unfaithful Jody who's sent you a dear john," with a forum to share comments. Those more drawn to romantic melodrama might turn instead to Nicholas Sparks's Iraq War weepie, *Dear John* (made into a movie by Lasse Hallstrom), for a very different rendering of the theme, in which the lovelorn protagonists continue to write pages-long letters—until the arrival of the eponymous missive.[25]

As the breakup example shows, far from being a private matter between a single sender and a solitary recipient, wartime correspondence can serve multiple public functions. Throughout the twentieth century, belligerent states promoted correspondence between soldiers and civilians both to boost soldiers morale and amplify civilians' patriotic commitment to the war effort. During the Second World War, both Nazi Germany and the Soviet Union encouraged letter writing as a responsibility of citizens mobilized for total war. The Wehrmacht entreated its personnel to regard letters home as a "spiritual vitamin" to reinvigorate flagging civilian esprit. "The homeland suffers from characterological anaemia," one official publication informed soldiers. "In his letters and during leave time the soldier is to act like a blood donor, restoring the belief and willpower of his relations." For its part, the Soviet state placed more emphasis on the "dialysis" civilian correspondence could perform for the Red Army.[26] Similarly, U.S. citizens—women, most particularly—received constant reminders, whether from newspapers, magazines, Hollywood, or the Office of War Information, that soldiers craved "'the three L's'—laughs, lookers and letters." Film historian Thomas Doherty notes that "the movies could deliver two out of the three and make kith and kin feel mighty guilty about not mailing off the third."[27]

Irrespective of ideological hue, states oriented to waging total war not only encouraged mass letter writing but promoted wider publication of letters to, and especially from, the front. Radio broadcasts, small-town newspapers, and printed anthologies all provided a wider audience for missives that may originally have been intended for one addressee alone or, in some cases, fabricated specifically for propagandistic purposes. In the United States, practices common during the Second World War have not disappeared in the digital age. Soldiers' dispatches home continue to be widely recirculated by media new and old, as furor over the army's "faked" letter from Kirkuk attests. A particularly durable public-private genre is the soldier's last letter: whether a consciously crafted final testament to be read only in the event of death, or a letter made all the more poignant because the writer did not anticipate that their words would be the last communication with home.[28] If soldiers' letters in general constitute "ammunition" to fire up the home front, these dispatches aim most directly at the heart. One cannot, after all, argue with the dead. And though servicemen and women's final words can fuel both pro- and antiwar sentiment, the intent of those publishing them is generally to recycle grief into renewed patriotic commitment. Loss of life functions as an implicit (if not more explicit) argument for sustaining the war to redeem the deaths of those whose final words have been immortalized in print.[29]

Meanwhile, numerous American schools, churches, youth clubs, libraries, and other volunteer organizations continue to organize letter-writing campaigns, hoping to foster awareness among civilians of the conditions, sacrifices, and service of deployed personnel while raising the spirits of men and women on duty overseas. Commenting on the boost that her army specialist son received from letters via the hometown library in which he had worked as a teenager, one mother noted: "It gives them a greater incentive to complete their mission. . . . To get letters from back home, from your hometown, is a thrill—letters from children especially, because they are so sincere and open."[30] Her words tap a familiar vein of wartime sentimentality, redolent of J. D. Salinger's vignettes of soldiers' correspondence with children, in which the child's unchecked curiosity and naïve candor hold out a redemptive possibility amid war's lies, suffering, and squalor.[31] Updating these communicative practices for the digital age, deployed personnel have also been brought into classroom conversation—live from Iraq and Afghanistan—through the agency of Skype, in patriotic "troop supporting" programs.

Surveillance and Self-Restraint

Valorized as the raw unfiltered stuff of war, frontline dispatches are far from unmediated. No matter how personal the contents of a letter to or from a soldier may appear, wartime correspondence is a practice surrounded by external parties looking to regulate and oversee its form and content. Communication with home is an intensely disciplined activity—a claim that remains true in the digital age. What differs are some of the forms that regulation assumes. Individual commanding officers no longer read mail with black ink in one hand and a sharp knife in the other; they certainly don't sit at the elbow of every serviceman or woman who IMs or calls home. But military personnel are constantly reminded that their mail *may* be scrutinized and that their online activity is not private. Harder to censor it may be, but internet use, by leaving ineradicable traces of the user, is in many ways easier to monitor and cache than communications written on paper and sent by mail. Old-style censorship, after all, rested on the vigilance and dedication of officers—not all of whom took their role as censor with complete seriousness.

Military personnel can be—and have been—disciplined as a result of surveilled online activity. In 2006, toward the end of the long era when gay men and women were legally debarred from service, internet correspondence with a male partner was used to "out" air force major Mike Almy while he was on active duty in Iraq. In this case, Almy's private relationship was deemed to constitute a separable offense. Public remarks of an unabashedly political nature can also get service personnel in trouble. Unlike American civilians, members of the armed forces do not enjoy an unfettered right to free speech protected by the First Amendment. Bound by the Uniform Code of Military Justice (UCMJ), service personnel undertake on oath not to participate in overt political advocacy, engage in hate speech, issue racial slurs, or disrespect their commander in chief.

For egregiously violating the latter stipulation, marine sergeant Gary Stein was discharged after making an inflammatory post about Barack Obama on Facebook, announcing that he would not obey certain orders the president might issue and superimposing the latter's face on a poster for *Jackass: The Movie*. Marines now find themselves in the curious situation of being able to "like" a presidential candidate's Facebook page while being forbidden from posting any comments about their preferred politicians—based on the questionable assertion that "liking" does not constitute expression of an opinion.[32]

Stein's case attracted considerable civilian attention. But heavy-handed forms of constraint, suppression, and punishment are not the most pervasive ways in which the military shapes expression. As Michel Foucault pointed out decades ago, the most effective forms of discipline are those that subjects internalize unselfconsciously and constantly reproduce in the minutiae of daily life, not those generated by fear of transgression and its draconian punishment. Pursuing this insight means that we should redirect our attention away from repression to the "positive" forms of advice issued to military personnel and their loved ones about how best to communicate with one another and with online audiences more broadly.

Military manuals, training seminars, and magazines brim with reminders about appropriate use of social networking sites—or how "not to be a 'twidiot.'"[33] Each branch of the armed forces and reserves produces comprehensive deployment manuals together with numerous publications and training materials that offer, among other things, prescriptive guidance about what to say and, crucially, *not* say in communications with home—whether in letters, emails, phone calls, videoconferences, blogs, or Facebook posts. In these guidelines, OPSEC looms less large than cautionary reminders about not causing loved ones to worry. If, as the Department of Defense maintains, the "greatest morale builder for deployed service members is communication with home," then both military personnel and their loved ones require instruction in the arts of suppression required to ensure that communication fulfills an appropriately "beneficial and uplifting" function rather than exacerbating the distress of separation.[34]

Much of this advice appears aimed squarely at the home front in an effort to limit both the information and emotional moods reaching deployed personnel from back home. Military initiatives to protect combat troops from potentially injurious outside influences have received far less scholarly attention than the obverse—attempts to police and control communications leaving an area of operations. Yet senior commanders are, and have been, highly sensitive to what is communicated *to* frontline forces from home—whether major domestic developments that might corrode troops' morale or more quotidian "bad news" from home. During the Vietnam War, senior officers wanted to suppress news of Martin Luther King Jr.'s assassination, fearing that this shocking development would aggravate already inflamed relations between black GIs and white officers.[35] Given this sensitivity to anything and everything that might depress morale or foster indiscipline, it's perhaps no surprise that the armed services should seek to induce habits of self-restraint among family members, spouses, and loved ones communicating with men and women deployed in Iraq and Afghanistan.

Today's military duly issues copious advice about the need to remain upbeat in everyday communications, to avoid self-pity, and to repress any doubts about the durability of a relationship until the partner returns. But the issuing of highly prescriptive advice is hardly a new phenomenon. Women in the past were similarly bombarded with instructions—often by self-appointed civilian authorities like magazine columnists and agony aunts—about what to say and send (or desist from saying or sending) to soldiers overseas. In February 1918, for example, the *Ladies Home Journal* printed a full-page article, "His Letter to His Sister," ostensibly penned by a doughboy to his naïve sibling at home. "Dear Sis," it began, "I want to be frank with you and say cut out the sob stuff in your letters! And look here, honey, tell mother the same, when you get a chance. . . . I hate to think of you and mother working yourselves up into a state over me, what I have to go through, and so on, churning yourselves into hysteria."[36] Stoicism was the order of the day, on home and fighting fronts alike.

Despite the fact that women now comprise some 15 percent of the U.S. military, the imaginary target of these lessons in epistolary etiquette remains implicitly gendered—a young wife struggling to run a home and raise a family unaided. A dominant motif concerns the need to strike an appropriate balance between undue pessimism and improbable optimism, between revealing too little and divulging too much. In other words, the military spouse must adopt a cheerful disposition without faking high spirits so relentlessly as to trigger anxiety about what turbulence might lie concealed behind this mask. The DOD *Deployment Guide* advises: "Service members know that things do not run smoothly even when they are at home. The more 'everything is great' letters they get, the more service members are likely to worry about what might be omitted from their letters. Service members might also misconstrue those letters to suggest that they are not needed at home anymore." Be plausible, in other words. Disclose just enough of home life's lumpy texture without lapsing into negativity, since conveying "every little problem or irritation in a letter" is as undesirable as excessive avoidance. "These letters can make service members feel guilty about being away and not being able to help support their families at home." Include the good and the bad, the joys and frustrations, "always making clear how much the service member is missed, but that the situation is tenable, can be managed, and will make them stronger."[37]

Military manuals concern themselves not only with the factual content of communication but also with appropriate verbal registers. Advice-givers stress clarity. Ambiguity, they warn, fosters anxiety. "Neither service member nor family members should have to read between the lines or spend time worrying over what something means or implies." Service personnel and their interlocutors are also cautioned against sarcasm and humor. "When speaking with someone face-to-face, tone of voice and facial expressions can clearly convey when one is being sarcastic or when one is kidding around. It is not so easy to convey those things in writing."[38] But since anger, on the other hand, is so readily communicable, its damage so difficult to repair at a remove, heavy emphasis is laid on repressing rage. Military personnel and family members alike are warned against contact on "a particularly bad day," turning to a journal as an alternative place to "vent." Since digital media encourage precipitate haste—in composition and transmission alike—these injunctions apply with particular force to use of the internet. "Be careful using this method of communication for an emotionally laden message," cautions an army readiness manual. "It's better to compose [an email], park it for a few hours, review it for clarity and kindness, and then send it."[39]

As this profusion of pointers, cautions, and prohibitions surrounding service personnel's communication suggests, the military understands ties with home as critical to morale in both positive and negative ways. If it's true that a letter, text, call, or video-chat can make a soldier's day, reinforcing a positive sense of self, "miscommunications," "bad calls," and distressing news can have a corrosive effect on esprit. At worst, harmful interactions can take a lethal toll. Recent studies by military psychiatrists in both the United Kingdom and United States emphasize negative family interactions as a more frequent precipitant of suicide by deployed personnel than proximate sources of stress or trauma.[40]

Communication between deployed forces and the home front as a "mixed blessing" is not a novel theme of the digital age. Anything that can stimulate morale can presumably also depress it when absent or unreliably supplied. "Mail call" is bound to leave some soldiers empty-handed, in receipt of upsetting news from home, or more painfully conscious of the gulf between "here" and "there" than before. Family ties can provide positive reinforcement of individual feelings of well-being but can also threaten to weaken a soldier's solidarity with his immediate military "primary group." Edward Shils and Morris Janowitz's classic 1948 analysis of "Cohesion and Disintegration in the Wehrmacht in World War II" noted the double-edged character of communication between home and front. What family ties added to and subtracted from fighting men's psychic reserves was in constant flux. By the final months of the Second World War, "all telegrams to soldiers at the front had to be passed by [Nazi] party officials in order to insure that no distracting news reached the soldiers."[41] Unlike their American counterparts, German soldiers had to worry not only about whether they themselves would make it back alive but whether their homes would still be standing and family members unscathed by the time troops were finally demobilized. As the war dragged on and Allied bombing of German cities intensified, the prospect of returning to an unaltered home front became ever less tenable. Not surprisingly, soldiers who deserted or surrendered were frequently those who had been in recent contact with their families.

Distressing news caused some men to lose hope in their ability to protect loved ones, making them prone to surrender to the advancing Red Army, while others ran away to improve the odds of being able to defend their homes and families.

The capacity of new media to transpose deployed servicemen and women into their vacated domestic lives with greater immediacy and three-dimensionality amplifies this double-edged family effect. "Home" is more vividly present in the space of war than ever before, or as a U.S. Army War College study put it, the family has shifted "from an abstract to a concrete concept." This development has had deleterious consequences for both individuals and unit cohesion.[42] Service personnel in Iraq and Afghanistan must negotiate the competing expectations and norms of home life and deployment with much greater speed—and a superior capacity to compartmentalize—than was required of soldiers in conflicts past. This can present an impossible challenge. To put the issue starkly: how does an individual read bedtime stories to an infant via Skype at one moment and go out on patrol the next, primed for the possibility of killing or being killed?

This example is, for illustrative purposes, an extreme one. Not all deployed personnel confront danger frontally or relentlessly. But the larger point remains. Today's servicemen and women face centrifugal demands to be both here and there—at war and at home—and hence to switch effortlessly between behaviors befitting a soldier, partner, or parent. This balancing act requires those at war to become ever more expert in habits of suppression, keeping from home "unspeakable" things that the serviceman or woman may have seen, felt, or done. New media's demand for instant and repeat performances of "normality" in deeply abnormal circumstances begs questions as to what becomes of unspoken experience. How or when does the repressed return? For many service personnel in the here-and-now, though, the issue isn't one of post-traumatic deferral but immediate familial avoidance. The impossibility of the juggling act leads some deployed personnel to withdraw altogether from contact with home.[43] Only by avoiding cellphones and the internet is it possible to achieve a bearable degree of separation between here and there, a distinction constantly challenged by technologies that collapse not only space and time but boundaries between roles that rest on fundamentally incompatible values.

Taking Love to Make War

The United States military today faces twin crises: soaring incidences of suicide and unprecedented rates of divorce among its personnel. In 2012, U.S. servicemen and women in Afghanistan were twice as likely to take their own lives as to be killed by enemy forces. Suicide and divorce alike pose a frontal challenge to the military's understanding of its relationship with family— as an abstraction and as the bedrock of military organization and individual social support. That the military itself constitutes a "family" is a fundamental conceit of the U.S. armed services. This self-understanding may strike civilians, and indeed some service personnel, as problematic, given that military personnel are more likely to experience rape, get divorced, or take their own lives than their civilian counterparts. But "family" nevertheless constitutes the military's preferred metaphor for itself as a kinship network. At the same time, a practical commitment to—and advocacy of—marriage and family has underpinned the U.S. military's reconstitution as an all-volunteer service in the wake of the Vietnam War. For the military, families are domesticating agencies in both senses of that term. They provide married military personnel with a foundation of emotional well-being, while the presence of spouses and children on base is intended to check "indiscipline" otherwise rampant in an organization comprising primarily men in their late teens and early twenties. Since the 1970s, the U.S. military has incentivized marriage and promoted parenthood. The lure of superior accommodation and resources to assist families operates in tandem with the more intangible, but no less pervasive, force of heteronormative expectation.[44]

It consequently comes as no surprise that the military should respond to the current crisis of suicide as a manifestation primarily of family dysfunction that needs to be fixed by better training and care of "dependents," along with remedial steps to bolster healthy relationships. If the majority of suicides are triggered by negative intrusions of home into the lives of deployed personnel, then the appropriate response is necessarily to make families more functional to ensure that home/front interactions remain a source of positive support. Cultivating this kind of "resilience" is one goal of initiatives such as the Comprehensive Soldier Fitness program. As the military is well aware, it takes love to make war. But sustaining love—stretched thin by distance and danger—isn't always easy.

From a civilian perspective, however, the diagnosis of the military's current malady and its prescribed cure may look far less self-evident. Perhaps chronic rates of suicide among active-duty personnel and veterans are less the result of dysfunctional military families than the chronic dysfunction of war itself, exacerbated over the past decade by serial redeployments. This proposition upturns a cherished nostrum of military service, widely echoed in American civil society—namely, that war enlarges individual capabilities, producing men and women strengthened by the experience. Hence, introducing a special issue of *Newsweek* devoted to fallen soldiers' letters, editor Jon Meacham writes: "What emerges from the following pages is the sense that the fallen are better men, and women.... What is constant in war is the humanity of the warrior."[45] But while Meacham's recuperative impulse is understandable—reassuring loved ones that lives were not lost in vain—such claims about war's ennobling effects also obscure harder truths. Military service may have made these individuals more selfless, courageous beings, but it also ended their lives. If war enhances some capabilities, it nevertheless exacts a terrible toll on all those caught up in it. Often the change that frontline service produces is not for the better.

Mental and bodily injuries sustained in war can, and frequently do, damage lives irreparably. Suffering, in short, more commonly degrades human potential than enlarging it.

Discussion Questions

1. Why, and with what justification, are frontline military personnel often considered, both by themselves and by civilians, as the most authoritative witnesses to war? What forms does this privileged claim to knowledge assume?

2. Consider how organizational and personal pressures interact to shape what, and how, military personnel and their loved ones communicate with one another in wartime. Does self-censorship offer a better explanation than formal restraints on speech for what remains unsaid between deployed personnel and civilians back home?

3. How have social media (like Facebook), digital technology, and cell phones altered the ways in which frontline military personnel communicate with family members and friends? Do these changes represent a fundamental break with patterns of wartime communication prevalent before the 2000s or is there more continuity than change in how "Home" and "Front" interact in the twenty-first century?

Notes

1 For an overview of these debates, see Susan L. Carruthers, *The Media at War* (Basingstoke, UK: Palgrave Macmillan, 2011), and for a vigorous rebuttal of the case that the media "lost the war" in Vietnam, see Daniel Hallin, *The "Uncensored War": The Media and Vietnam* (New York: Oxford University Press, 1989).

2 Smithsonian National Postal Museum, "History of America's Military Mail," *Mail Call*, http://postalmuseum.si.edu/mailcall/index.html; Yuval Noah Harari, "Armchairs, Coffee, and Authority: Eye-Witnesses and Flesh-Witnesses Speak about War, 1100–2000," *Journal of Military History* 74, no. 1 (January 2012): 53–78.

3 "Fighting the War at Home," *New York Times*, October 15, 2003.

4 Soldiers' letters (selectively chosen, of course) have long been printed in American newspapers while the United States has been at war. These dispatches from the front are invested with particular authority: not only the "I was there" imprimatur of the eyewitness but the "I fought there" authority of what Harari calls the "flesh witness." Edited anthologies of soldiers' correspondence form a distinct subgenre of war literature. For representative examples, see Mina Curtiss, ed., *Letters Home* (Boston: Little, Brown, 1944); Annette Tapert, ed., *Lines of Battle: Letters from American Servicemen, 1941–1945* (New York: Times Books, 1987); United States Postal Service, *Letters from the Sand: The Letters of Desert Storm and Other Wars* (Washington, DC: USPS, 1991); Andrew Carroll, ed., *War Letters: Extraordinary Correspondence from American Wars* (New York: Scribner, 2001); Bill Adler, ed., *Letters from Vietnam* (New York: Presidio Press, 2003).

5   Melissa Wall, "The Taming of the Warblogs: Citizen Journalism and the War in Iraq," in *Citizen Journalism: Global Perspectives*, ed. S. Allen and E. Thorsen (New York: Peter Lang, 2009).

6   "Army Lieutenant Colonel Visits Henderson Students," *The Eagle Post*, November 4, 2009, http://www.theeaglepost.us/community/article_8ac59c5c-abb5-5b1b-a586-b32c66efd1d4.html.

7   Lisa Ellen Silvestri, *Friended at the Front: Social Media in the American War Zone* (Lawrence: University Press of Kansas, 2015), 15. For an argument stressing continuity, despite changing technologies of delivery, see Seth Shapiro and Lee Humphreys, "Echoing Old and New Media: Comparing Military Blogs to Civil War Letters," *New Media & Society* 15, no. 7 (2013): 1151–1167.

8   Cary Nelson, "Only Death Can Part Us: Messages on Wartime Cards," *Iowa Journal of Cultural Studies* 8 (Spring 2006): 25–43; on First World War correspondence more broadly, see Martha Hanna, "War Letters: Communication between Front and Home Front," *International Encyclopedia of the First World War, 1914–18 Online,* http://encyclopedia.1914-1918-online.net/article/war_letters_communication_between_front_and_home_front.

9   This figure represents the total volume of mail, without distinction as to whether the sender was a member of the armed forces or a civilian. Judy Barrett Litoff and David C. Smith, "'Will He Get My Letter?' Popular Representations of Mail and Morale during World War II," *Journal of Popular Culture* 23, no. 4 (Spring 1990): 24. For a firsthand appreciation of the emotional significance of wartime correspondence, see Frank F. Mathias, *GI Jive: An Army Bandsman in World War II*, chap. 3 ("Mail Call") (Lexington: University Press of Kentucky, 1982).

10 Louise Hickman Lione, "Word from Home via MARS," *Baltimore Sun*, May 1, 1966, D3; Morton G. Ender, "G.I. Phone Home: The Use of Telecommunications by the Soldiers of Operation Just Cause," *Armed Forces & Society* 21, no. 3 (Spring 1995): 435–453.

11 Richard J. H. Johnson, "Vietnam Getting More USO Clubs," *New York Times*, September 25, 1966, 11.

12 Robert Taylor, "Tapes: This War's Cherished Link between Home and Vietnam," *Boston Globe*, May 19, 1968, A3.

13 Ender, "G.I. Phone Home"; Larry W. Applewhite and David R. Segal, "Telephone Use by Peacekeeping Troops in the Sinai," *Armed Forces & Society* 17, no. 1 (Fall 1990): 117–126.

14 Silvestri, *Friended at the Front*, 6.

15 Susan L. Carruthers, "Why Can't We See Insurgents? Enmity, Invisibility and Counterinsurgency in Iraq and Afghanistan," *Photography & Culture* 8, no. 2 (July 2015): 191–211.

16 Tatum H. Lyle, "A Soldier's Blog: Balancing Service Members' Personal Rights vs. National Security Interests," *Federal Communications Law Journal* 59, no. 3 (June 2007).

17 Hope Hodge Seck, "The End of MotoMail," *Marine Corps Times*, September 23, 2013, 3.

18 Ramon Hinojosa, Melanie Sberna Hinojosa, and Robin S. Högnäs, "Problems with Veteran-Family Communication during Operation Enduring Freedom/Operation Iraqi Freedom Military Deployment," *Military Medicine* 177 (February 2012): 191–197; Talya Greene, Joshua Buckman, Christopher Dandeker, and Surg. Cdr. Neil Greenberg, "How Communication with Families Can Both Help and Hinder Service Members' Mental Health and Occupational Effectiveness on Deployment," *Military Medicine* 175 (October 2010): 745–749.

19 Department of Defense, *Military Deployment Guide: Preparing You and Your Family for the Road Ahead* (Washington, DC: Department of Defense, 2011), 131, www.first.army.mil/divEast/documents/pdf/DeploymentGuide.pdf.

20 Hinojosa et al, "Problems with Veteran-Family Communication," 194.

21 Adi Kuntsman and Rebecca L. Stein, *Digital Militarism: Israel's Occupation in the Social Media Age* (Stanford, CA: Stanford University Press, 2015). It should be stressed, though, that the line between soldiering and tourism has long been an extremely fuzzy one. See Scott Laderman, *Tours of Vietnam: War, Travel Guides, and Memory* (Durham, NC: Duke University Press, 2009); Vernadette Vicuña Gonzalez, *Securing Paradise: Tourism and Militarism in Hawai'i and the Philippines* (Durham, NC: Duke University Press, 2013); Debbie Lisle, *Holidays in the Danger Zone: Entanglements of War and Tourism* (Minneapolis: University of Minnesota Press, 2016); Vernadette Vicuña Gonzalez and Jana K. Lipman, eds., "Tours of Duty and Tours of Leisure," *American Quarterly* 68, no. 3 (special issue, September 2016).

22 Ann Pfau, "Postal Censorship and Military Intelligence during World War II," paper presented at the Winton M. Blount Postal History Symposium, Smithsonian National Postal Museum, September 27, 2008, https://postalmuseum.si.edu/symposium2008/pfau-postal_censorship.pdf.

23 Peter S. Kindsvatter, *American Soldiers: Ground Combat in the World Wars, Korea and Vietnam* (Lawrence: University Press of Kansas, 2003), 110; Ann Pfau, "Allotment Annies and Other Wayward Wives: Wartime Concerns about Female Disloyalty and the Problem of the Returned Veteran," in *The United States and the Second World War: New Perspectives on Diplomacy, War, and the Home Front*, ed. G. Kurt Piehler and Sidney Nash (New York: Fordham University Press, 2010), 104–106; Emanuel Tanay, "The Dear John Syndrome during the Vietnam War," *Diseases of the Nervous System* 37, no. 3 (March 1976): 165.

24 Anthony Swofford, *Jarhead: A Marine's Chronicle of the Gulf War and Other Battles* (New York: Scribner, 2003), 91, 92.

25 Nicholas Sparks, *Dear John* (New York: Grand Central Publishing, 2009). For the comments section, see http://thebrigade.thechive.com/dear-john/.

26 Qtd. by Jochen Hellbeck, "The Diaries of Fritzes and Letters of Gretchens: Personal Writings From the German-Soviet War and Their Readers," *Kritika: Explorations in Russian and Eurasian History* 10, no. 3 (2009): 578, 586.

27 Thomas Doherty, *Projections of War: Hollywood, American Culture and World War II* (New York: Columbia University Press, 1999), 180.

28 Hellbeck, "Diaries of Fritzes."

29 Jon Meacham, "The War in the Words of the Dead," *Newsweek*, special issue, April 1, 2007, http://www.newsweek.com/war-words-dead-97551; Pamela Colloff, "Letters Home," *Texas Monthly* 32, no. 7 (July 2004).

30 Qtd. by Chip Marshall, "Salute to Soldiers," *American Libraries* 35 (November 2004): 10.

31 J. D. Salinger, "A Boy in France," *Saturday Evening Post*, March 31, 1945; Salinger, "For Esmé—With Love and Squalor," *New Yorker*, April 8, 1950.

32 "Marine's Facebook Rants Earn Ticket out of Military," *USA Today*, April 13, 2012, 8; Silvestri, *Friended at the Front*, 18, 30.

33 Jason Meshaw, "Don't Be a Social Media Twidiot," *The Mobility Forum*, September/October 2009, 14–15; Karen Schmitt, "About FACE: Social Media in the Military Environment," *Defense Transportation Journal* 65 (June 2009): 8–16; SSgt. Patrick D. Ward, "Social Media Postings: Should Marine Leaders Monitor Their Marines?," *Marine Corps Gazette*, November 2011, 81–83.

34 "Someone Blogged, Maintaining OPSEC in Social Networking Realm," *SCOPE* 43, no. 6 (June 2012): 4–5; Office of Reserve Affairs, Army National Guard, *Personal & Family Readiness Toolkit*, 3rd ed., May 2007, 34, http://www.nationalguard.mil /Portals/31/Documents/ARNGpdfs/familyresources/Family-Readiness-Toolkit.pdf.

35 Carruthers, *Media at War*, 119.

36 "His Letter to His Sister: The Man Who Was Drafted Tells Her Some Truths," *Ladies' Home Journal*, February 1918, 35.

37 DOD, *Military Deployment Guide*, 132.

38 Ibid., 132, 133.

39 U.S. Army, *Deployment Readiness Handbook for DA Civilians and Family Members*, 2010, 21, https://www.myarmyonesource.com/cmsresources/Army%20 OneSource/Media/PDFs/Family%20Programs%20and%20Services/Family%20 Programs/Deployment%20Readiness/Operation%20READY/DEPLOY_READY_ CIVILIAN_FAMILY_links.pdf.

40 Christine Lehmann, "Soldiers Say Combat Stress Second to Personal Stress," *Psychiatric News* 39, no. 8 (April 16, 2004): 25; Susan W. Durham, "In Their Own Words: Staying Connected in a Combat Environment," *Military Medicine* 175, no. 8 (August 2010): 554–559; Greene et al., "How Communication with Families Can Both Help and Hinder"; Hinojosa et al., "Problems with Veteran-Family Communication"; Kathleen Mulligan et al., "Effects of Home on the Mental Health of British Forces Serving in Iraq and Afghanistan," *British Journal of Psychiatry* 201 (April 26, 2012): 1–6; Pat Matthews-Juarez, Paul D. Juarez, and Roosevelt T. Faulkner, "Social Media and Military Families: A Perspective," *Journal of Human Behavior in the Social Environment* 23 (2013): 769–776.

41 Edward A. Shils and Morris Janowitz, "Cohesion and Disintegration in the Wehrmacht in World War II," *Public Opinion Quarterly* 12, no. 2 (Summer 1948): 290; Greene et al., "How Communication with Families Can Both Help and Hinder," 747.

42 Durham, "In Their Own Words," 558; Leonard Wong and Stephen Gerras, "CU @ the FOB: How the Forward Operating Base Is Changing the Life of Combat Soldiers," *Strategic Studies Institute*, March 2006, https://ssi.armywarcollege.edu /pdffiles/PUB645.pdf

43 Durham, "In Their Own Words," 558; Silvestri, *Friended at the Front*.

44 On these phenomena and the All-Volunteer Force's instrumentalization of "love" and "family," see Kenneth T. MacLeish, *Making War at Fort Hood: Life and Uncertainty in a Military Community* (Princeton, NJ: Princeton University Press, 2013); Beth Bailey, *America's Army: Making the All-Volunteer Force* (Cambridge, MA: Belknap Press, 2009).

45 Meacham, "The War in the Words of the Dead."

Further Reading

Andrew Carroll, ed. *War Letters: Extraordinary Correspondence from American Wars*. New York: Scribner, 2001.

Judy Barrett Litoff and David C. Smith. "'Will He Get My Letter?' Popular Representations of Mail and Morale during World War II." *Journal of Popular Culture* 23, no. 4 (Spring 1990): 21–43.

Lisa Ellen Silvestri, *Friended at the Front: Social Media in the American War Zone* (Lawrence: University Press of Kansas, 2015).

Smithsonian National Postal Museum, "History of America's Military Mail," *Mail Call*, http://postalmuseum.si.edu/mailcall/index.html.

14

War in Visual Culture

BONNIE M. MILLER

Mass audiences engage with visions of war through the filter of spectacle—produced to invoke an affective response and viewed at a safe distance from the actual violence or destruction. The visual culture of American warfare has grown exponentially over the last 250 years, and as such, war has come to be made to fit the contours of image. The September 11, 2001, terrorist attacks provide an exemplary case of a hostile attack whose meaning was shaped by its transformation into a global media phenomenon. Film director Robert Altman noted the extent to which visual representation informed reality, suggesting that the "movies set the pattern" and the terrorists "copied the movies." Just days after 9/11, German composer Karlheinz Stockhausen described the disaster as "the greatest work of art that is possible in the whole cosmos."[1] Such observations reflect the aesthetic power of the disaster itself and its all-consuming effect on American visual culture, as the indelible images of the planes crashing into the World Trade Center and its aftermath were reshown for weeks after the fact. Most Americans experienced 9/11 through these shocking images, not through direct experience, and indeed, the visual production of 9/11 played out like a film script.

Visual images instruct us how to see and how to think. Whereas the roots, causes, and effects of wars can be complex, images have the potential to simplify and encapsulate—capturing glimpses in time or key moments deemed important enough to be reimagined. Accurate or not, the effects of war images can, at times, be irrevocable and enduring, making them important agents in shaping how military events are understood, judged, and remembered. Of those images that public audiences collectively witness, each viewer brings to the "act of looking" his or her own cultural knowledge and ways of seeing. But what war pictures viewers get to look at and how they see them is also contingent upon many historical factors.

Tracking the evolution of what domestic audiences choose to see, how they see it, what the government allows them to see, and what meaning they ascertain from it, in effect, functions as a barometer of public perceptions of and participation in U.S. military affairs. These indicators wax and wane in different political and cultural climates and as new technologies become available, but what has not wavered is the resolve to capture war as an aspect of human experience in visual form. In fact, one can trace the historical development of media technologies through the progression of visual engagement with American wars, both domestic and global. What began during the early Republic as an effort to find new and better ways to create visual representations of war ultimately became a struggle about how to contain them. Visual containment manifests in different forms: controlling perspective (what can be viewed in the making of images), controlling content (what is allowed to be shown and what is censored), controlling narrative (dictating how images get contextualized), and controlling distribution and access (determining audience).

Though image production had been critical to the propaganda campaigns of nineteenth-century wars, the government's role in harnessing and regulating those images was unsystematic. By the First World War, it had become clear to political and military leaders that images are indeed as powerful and dangerous as other weapons in the military arsenal; to make war, the U.S. government would not only have to limit image production for purposes of military censorship but also actively generate a visual narrative to shape public perceptions of war. While war pictures can be an effective mobilizer, they can also expose war's destructive impacts. As technologies advanced both for making war and documenting the results, government leaders recognized the political necessity of controlling what is seen and how it is seen. But even as leaders strive to dictate the terms by which state actions are understood, they are impeded by the increasingly global flow of communication as well as by the efforts of media interests, resistors, opponents, and participants to disrupt their authority and present alternative perspectives.

This chapter examines broad cultural trends in the visual production of American warfare over time, tracing the forms and images that have been used to support and resist U.S. wars since its inception as a nation. Although "seeing" war-related images may give viewers greater visual proximity to the operations and impacts of U.S. military conflicts, war pictures have as much potential to distort and misrepresent as they do to clarify and expose; it all depends on what content makes it into the "frame" as well as the context by which images are shown and circulated.

Reading War Images: Reframing the Frame of the Frame

Scores of painters, sketch artists, photographers, and engravers have sought to document the major historic conflicts of the modern era with their art, offering future generations a visual vantage point on past events. Some endeavored to get close to the front lines at great personal risk. But inevitably, these images offer historians a limited and highly subjective view. Every artist brings to his or her work a certain national orientation, political perspective, and/or set of cultural understandings that consciously or subconsciously guide the selection and presentation of content that enters into the "frame" of the image. As the image then gets circulated, via publication, exhibit, documentary, broadcast, website, or other means, producers place it within discursive contexts that provide another level of framing to circumscribe its potential meaning for viewers (in other words, providing a "frame" to the picture or "framing the frame"). Framing, therefore, exists at multiple levels: in the content itself of the initial image, and then in how the image is embedded within other media contexts; the viewer experiences the image itself but rarely free of textual or sequential narration.

Government leaders, to build support for their policies, may try to dictate the visual narrative by encoding images within ideological frameworks of nationalism, moral righteousness, and patriotic duty. In some cases, mass audiences come to associate these images with certain beliefs and values. But the challenge for political and military leaders is not just to articulate these meanings effectively and broadly but also to sustain them within an increasingly unwieldy narrative. Once an image enters public circulation, it is vulnerable to reappropriation, particularly as it circulates in new contexts and as events evolve. An image of war dead presented in one context as heroic sacrifice, for example, can be leveraged elsewhere to challenge the merits of U.S. military policy. Frames break down and get reconstructed, which makes the visual containment of the artist's initial intended meaning a persistent problem. When an image breaks frame, its meaning can completely change.[2]

Compounding the problem of visual containment is the fact that images often have multiple frames that may not align with one another. Viewers may encounter an image, for instance, embedded in a political frame, created as propaganda to justify the goals of the political-military-industrial-economic complex. This same image might also be framed for entertainment purposes. The extensive visual and popular cultures of war (theatrical productions, war films, video games, TV shows, and so on) transform complex political conflicts into dramatic and action-packed storylines of good and evil. Driven by profit, these cultural diversions enfold actual military events within fictionalized narratives that advertently or inadvertently impact popular perceptions of actual military policies and personnel, often simplifying or misrepresenting complex perspectives, glorifying or romanticizing participants, demonizing opponents, or igniting passions for belligerent responses.

Likewise, image-makers might situate their work in a documentary frame, claiming to provide visual footage for the sake of historical documentation or edification. News broadcasters might pledge to report earnestly on military developments while relaying these accounts in a sensationalistic narrative mode, thus serving the commercial function of boosting ratings. For example, when newscasters after 9/11 reported under the constant guise of "breaking news" on terror alerts and security threats, as with the reporting of powdered anthrax in government mail, they exploited public fears and anxieties to keep viewers tuned in. Determining how viewers find meaning in war images, therefore, cannot be inferred by reading the image alone; rather, the cultural historian must analyze the image in relation to its "frames"—how and where the image was presented, to whom, and for what purpose, while acknowledging that the image remains susceptible to being co-opted and reframed at any time.

One of the most critical functions of visual media in wartime is to circulate a coherent and reproducible image of the enemy. Such images serve to crystallize and articulate American values in relation to those of the "enemy," consolidating sentiments of nationalism, democracy, and capitalism. As image-makers bring enemies into focus, they draw upon culturally available categories of social difference to construct their visual portraits, exercising familiar stereotypical resonances. Most notably, constructions of race, gender, and sexuality function as visual languages to encode the difference between "us" and "them," to define patriotism and heroism (typically in gendered terms), to demonize enemies (often as sexual predators or racialized beasts), and to demarcate colonial subjects or occupied governments as in need of U.S. support (often as juvenile or racial subordinates). For example, prowar propagandists have typically personified American militarism through images of masculine brawn and likewise disparaged critics of war or those who opt out of military service through images of feminine debility. These visual vocabularies emerge from already existing domestic norms of social difference and get reaffirmed through the contexts of war.

1776–1917: Making War Visible to Americans on the Home Front

Seeing is a powerful form of knowledge, and from the nation's beginnings, artists have sought out visual interventions to break down the distance between the home front and battlefields of war. Early image production was fraught with limitations in its capacity to depict war accurately, but the enterprise nonetheless ignited fascination with war imagery as a means of recording human experience. The period roughly coinciding with the nineteenth century saw a dramatic rise in the mass consumption of war-related media through the development of new visual technologies, genres, and practices; war became a form of popular spectatorship.

The American Revolution inspired a group of artists to portray glorious battle scenes and military portraits using the genre of historical painting. John Trumbull, one of its most well-known arbiters, had apprenticed with famous

FIGURE 14.1 John Trumbull's *The Death of General Warren at the Battle of Bunker's Hill, 17 June 1775*. Courtesy of the Museum of Fine Arts, Boston.

Anglo-American painter Benjamin West and in 1786 began producing a series of Revolutionary War paintings. Having planned thirteen in total, he completed six by the end of the eighteenth century and finished two more in the early nineteenth century. Trumbull explained in a letter to Thomas Jefferson that his intent was "to preserve and diffuse the memory of the noblest series of actions which have ever presented themselves in the history of man." Some of Trumbull's most famous works include *The Death of General Warren at the Battle of Bunker's Hill, 17 June 1775* and *The Death of General Montgomery in the Attack on Quebec, 31 December 1775*. Trumbull did indeed observe the Battle of Bunker Hill, but from a safe distance and through field glasses, so his vantage point prevented him from being a true eyewitness (Figure 14.1). Even so, his purpose was hardly objective. He made clear in his letter to Jefferson that his intentions were of a patriotic nature rather than as a historian, glorifying the new nation's heroes and celebrating its triumphant victory through his art. In this way, while these paintings left indelible scenes of great battles and heroic martyrdom, their visual function was more about historical mythmaking and solidifying nationalism than accurate documentation.[3]

Each passing conflict in the nineteenth century fueled the cultural demand for more and better wartime imagery. The Mexican-American War, for example, became the most recorded event in history in its time. Replacing older methods of engraving and etching, the development of lithography allowed a thriving printmaking industry to vastly increase the number of Mexican War prints available for public consumption. From actual eyewitness renderings of battles

BATTLE OF BUENA VISTA.
VIEW OF THE BATTLE GROUND AND BATTLE OF "THE ANGOSTURA" FOUGHT NEAR BUENA VISTA, MEXICO FEBRUARY 23RD 1847. (LOOKING S. WEST.)

FIGURE 14.2 H. R. Robinson lithograph, *Battle of Buena Vista: View of the Battle-Ground and Battle of 'The Angostura' Fought near Buena Vista, Mexico, February 23rd 1847. (Looking S. West)*. Courtesy of the Library of Congress, Prints and Photographic Division, LC-DIG-pga-02525.

to compositions based on eyewitness accounts, their degree of verisimilitude varied significantly. An aide-de-camp to General Zachary Taylor by the name of Major Joseph Horace Eaton, for instance, provided a series of sketches that became the basis of a famous print of the Battle of Buena Vista on February 23, 1847 (Figure 14.2). Eaton derived his sketches based on multiple eyewitness accounts and his firsthand experience as an army topographer. While there is some evidence of tactical accuracy in the print, its grandiose panoramic viewpoint, warm use of color, topographical perspective, and orderly military formations romanticize and sanitize it. Such prints offered idealistic visions of war, as neat configurations of militias facing each other in battle, with no evidence of fear, bloodshed, or chaos. In this case, the aerial view further minimizes viewers' encounters with individual soldiers struggling in the fight.[4] Despite this unrealistic perspective, the circulation of lithographs and other prints during and after the Mexican War provided a basis for Americans to visualize the battles and celebrate American victories.

The Mexican War was also the earliest U.S. military conflict to be affected by the breakthrough of photography, although to a very limited extent. By the Civil War, however, the medium of photography was ripe to make that war more visible to Americans than any before it. For the first time in American history, civilians far from the battlefields could bear direct visual witness to its human cost, forcing Americans north and south to confront mass war death in a whole new way. With over 600,000 soldiers dead, the prevailing rituals of Christian death and funeral rites had to be adapted and in some cases abandoned due to death on such an unprecedented scale.[5] Seeing those bodies in photographs gave Americans on the home front a connection to the dead left behind, but photographs also provided a special connection to the living. Many soldiers felt great personal urgency to have their likenesses permanently recorded, to be sent home to loved ones as tokens of remembrance in case they did not survive the war. As a result, thousands of professional photographers traveled with both the Union and Confederate armies. Using a cumbersome wet plate process to compose their views, which required a portable darkroom and optimal conditions, including complete immobility of the subject to attain clarity, photographers mostly took portraits, which comprised the majority of photographs taken during the war. The Bostwick brothers, for example, followed the Army of the Potomac for two years, taking photographs of soldiers on the outskirts of the battlefields.

Beyond the portraits, the most prevalent photographic subjects during the Civil War were landscapes (churches, farmhouses, battlefields, encampments, and so on), as well as ammunition and artillery. Because these inanimate subjects were perfectly still, they best served the limitations of the medium—as did dead bodies. Matthew Brady, Alexander Gardner, and their corps of artist-photographers produced over 10,000 plates, some of which documented the war dead. After the major battles, Brady, Gardner, and others published collections of these photographs as well as exhibiting them before American audiences, with startling impact. In 1862, the *New York Times* wrote of Brady's exhibition of the dead at Antietam: "If he has not brought bodies and laid them in our dooryards and along the streets, he has done something very like it. . . . You will see hushed reverent groups standing around these weird copies of carnage, bending down to look in the pale faces of the dead, chained by the strange spell that dwells in dead men's eyes."[6]

In spite of its limitations during these early years, photography afforded Americans a firsthand look at the devastation of the horrific war, making it seem closer and more "real." The *New York Times* review observed how these images deeply affected and mesmerized viewers. Photographs like Gardner's *The Dead of Antietam* or *A Harvest of Death*, Gettysburg confronted Americans with gruesome images of death and devastation. Seeing an image of a dozen or so dead bodies had to have been a shocking sight, and yet no photograph could encapsulate the estimated six million pounds of human and animal remains lying wasted on the battlefield at Gettysburg during that hot July.[7] The technology did not allow for photographers to capture on film the chaos and terror of the battles themselves, instead leaving records of small glimpses into the bloody results. Left out of the picture was the totality of the carnage as well as the raw emotion felt by the soldiers enduring those long, arduous battles, facing disease, privation, and unimaginable loss. For this reason, historian Alan Trachtenberg asks whether this body of photographs actually show "war."[8]

Civil War photography shifted the visual narrative of America at war from romance to realism; as the nation came to terms with the extent of death and destruction wrought from the civil conflict, the images shattered illusions of glory and dominance for both sides. When the war first began, the North and South both expected the war to be swift and decisive, and both sides had the mistaken expectation that their side would easily triumph. As the realities of the war set in, photographers helped to reframe the nation's expectations about its duration and cost. Rather than depict patriotic renderings of symbolic sacrifice, photographers displayed dead bodies lying on the battlefields as anonymous scattered corpses—no names, no heroic stories, no closure. Still, this new mode of realism didn't necessarily make the images *realistic* in the sense of providing a true visual recording of actual war events. As already noted, Civil War photographs were inevitably limited in what they could convey, leaving much of the experience of that war out of the visual frame. Moreover, because of the need to pose subjects, photographers often had to compose the shots ahead of time. By staging photographic scenes of war, the photographers were not simply capturing historical moments; they were creating samples to conform to the visions and perceptions of war experience they wanted their viewers to see.

But the mode of visual storytelling had indeed shifted. Gardner describes the dead at Gettysburg in his textual accompaniment to his photograph Field Where General Reynolds Fell, Gettysburg (July, 1863) (Figure 14.3):

> Some of the dead presented an aspect which showed that they had suffered severely just previous to dissolution, but these were few in number compared with those who wore a calm and resigned expression, as though they had passed away in the act of prayer. Others had a smile on their faces, and looked as if they were in the act of speaking. Some lay stretched on their backs, as if friendly hands had prepared them for burial. . . . The faces of all were pale, as though cut in marble, and as the wind swept across the battlefield it waved the hair, and gave the bodies such an appearance of life that a spectator could hardly help thinking they were about to rise to continue the fight.[9]

In his descriptions of pale, marble-cut faces and smiling corpses, Gardner infused a majestic beauty into the subjects lying dead and dying in his frame. Reassuring his viewers that most soldiers did not suffer in death and were now in God's grace, he dignified them and instructed viewers to see their legacy as enduring. Viewers searched those photographs for glimmers of recognition of loved ones, but the national trauma of the war cut deep and it took many years after the fact before the nation was ready to re-engage with the war photographs. American poet Oliver Wendell Holmes, whose son was injured in the war, claimed that the stereograph cards showing photographs from Antietam

FIGURE 14.3 Alexander Gardner, *Field Where General Reynolds Fell, Gettysburg (July, 1863).*
Reprinted from *Gardner's Photographic Sketchbook of the American Civil War 1861–1865* (New
York: Delano Greenidge Editions, 2001), Plate 37.

were so painful to look at that he felt the need to lock them away in a drawer.[10]
In fact, although Brady petitioned Congress in 1869 to purchase the Civil War
photographic archive, they refused to act. It took him nearly a decade to persuade Congress to acquire the collection in the interest of historical preservation, causing them to fade from public view for nearly a generation.[11]

The publication of political cartoons in nineteenth-century broadsides,
prints, newspapers, and illustrated periodicals became another visual tool
for representing the politics of war. Unlike the objective claims of eyewitness
sketch artists and photographers, political cartoonists overtly conveyed their
bias through their works, offering political commentaries on military affairs.
Their visual mode was largely figurative, drawing upon familiar symbols and
iconography to reflect upon the meaning of U.S. actions. Wartime matters not
only inspired the cartoonist's pen but also boosted media consumption more
broadly. Newspaper circulation increased considerably during the Civil War,
as more Americans turned to newspapers to follow daily events and get word
on the fate of their enlisted kin.[12] During and after the Civil War, a burgeoning market for illustrated newspapers and periodicals revolutionized American
publishing; by the Spanish-American War of 1898, the reading public came
in contact with wartime events through an array of visual media, encapsulat-
ing a new mode of spectatorship of war. Many newspapers that had only rarely

FIGURE 14.4 W. Charles, *A Boxing Match, or Another Bloody Nose for JOHN BULL*. Courtesy of the Library of Congress, Prints and Photographic Division, LC-USZ62-5214.

incorporated cartoons and illustrations before the war with Spain turned to the power of images to frame their war coverage.[13]

A recurring visual trope in nineteenth-century cartoon art was the representation of war as a fistfight in which a brawny America gave his opponent an earnest thrashing. During the War of 1812, William Charles of Philadelphia etched in watercolor a cartoon depicting President James Madison beating up King George III. Charles embodied the president and king, respectively, in the figures of Brother Jonathan and John Bull, stock characters that were often used in American and British editorial cartoons to represent the two nations. Brother Jonathan personified the entrepreneurial New Englander and would gradually evolve into the figure of Uncle Sam while John Bull, the creation of Scottish satirist John Arbuthnot, epitomized the English farmer. In the cartoon, George's black eye and hemorrhaging nose clearly denote who has the upper hand and symbolize U.S. naval supremacy in the war (Figure 14.4). King George III says: "Stop . . . Brother Jonathan, or I shall fall with the loss of blood—I thought to have been too heavy for you—But I must acknowledge your superior skill—Two blows to my one—And so well directed too! Mercy, mercy on me, how does this happen!!!" Madison retorts, "Ha-Ah Johnny! You thought yourself a '**Boxer**' did you—I'll let you know we are an '**Enterprize**'ing Nation and ready to meet you with equal force any day." In line with the conventions of cartooning of that period, the image is burdened with considerable text in order to convey its meaning. By 1898, the amount of text in most cartoons diminished,

FIGURE 14.5 C. G. Bush, "Next!," *New York World*, July 18, 1898, 7.

giving greater primacy to the pictures themselves. Still, this iconographic theme of war as a personal fistfight persisted.

In C. G. Bush's cartoon in the *New York World* (Figure 14.5), after significant land and naval victories had made Spanish surrender imminent, Uncle Sam proclaimed his worth by physically obliterating Spain before representatives of the world's leading powers. "Next!" reads the caption, a veiled threat to the other world powers that the United States had become a serious contender on the international stage. The United States acquired its first overseas colonies after defeating the Spanish in the War of 1898, facilitating a more aggressive role in the global competition for resources, labor, and power. Yet national consensus was lacking, and a wave of anti-imperialist sentiment surfaced. This cartoonist took a position within that debate, equating President William McKinley's foreign policies with manly vigor, confidence, and authority. While these two cartoons differ in pictorial convention and historical context, one can see a familiar thread in the visual glorification of American militarism: rising U.S. supremacy coded in terms of masculine bravado and physical prowess.

By the First World War, the new mandate of visual containment had already begun to take sway. The U.S. government's first systematic attempt to institutionalize the production of war propaganda came when President Woodrow Wilson named Kansas newspaper editor George Creel the head of the newly minted Committee on Public Information, an agency tasked with creating prowar posters, paintings, billboards, music, movies, speeches, and pamphlets to stir support for the war. In order to reach a broad audience, including the growing population of new immigrants, Creel created three divisions—news, film, and pictorial publicity. Whereas in previous wars journalists and other media producers were the ones generating war-related content, which may or may not have aligned with the administration's foreign policy goals, in the First World War the government began actively producing and disseminating its own media content to foster patriotic sentiment and rationalize U.S. military actions in the war.

In addition to creating its own propaganda, the U.S. government actively targeted potential war detractors, a practice spearheaded by Postmaster General Albert S. Burleson. One of Burleson's targets was *The Masses*, a radical socialist magazine edited by Max Eastman and Floyd Dell. Eastman and Dell mobilized both editorial and pictorial strategies to impart their antiwar sentiments, and in 1916, they published Robert Minor's cartoon titled "At Last a Perfect Soldier" (Figure 14.6). This example shows how critics of U.S. foreign policies have also employed the cartoon medium as a vehicle of resistance as well as challenged the links drawn between masculinity and militarism. In this cartoon, Minor represents the soldier as a gargantuan, headless specimen, as he stands before a jubilant army medical examiner eager to enlist him. He suggests here that U.S. military culture defines the ideal soldier as physically commanding but intellectually mindless. If he were to think through his actions, he might ask questions or defy orders he deems unethical. Because cartoons offered a pithy statement at a quick glance, they had great subversive potential. After the passage of the Espionage Act of 1917, the government shut down the magazine and indicted the editors of *The Masses* on the grounds that they had obstructed enlistment.[14] Given the inundation of prowar propaganda circulating in public space and the quick shutdown of critical media sources such as *The Masses*, which sought to present alternative viewpoints, American viewers were largely presented with a singular perspective on the war.

Three key innovations revolutionized visual access to war during the early twentieth century: the rising popularity of newsreels (motion picture coverage), the development of aerial photography (providing a new angle of vision), and the advance of photojournalistic technologies. The artist-photographer-editor

FIGURE 14.6 Robert Minor,
"At Last a Perfect Soldier!,"
The Masses, July 1916.

still dictated what would and would not be seen, but visual imperatives had changed. By World War I, soldiers could bring their own handheld cameras, extending image production beyond the hands of the professionals. Kodak's Vest Pocket Camera was specifically marketed as "The Soldier's Kodak Camera."[15] Despite limitations in what professional photojournalists could photograph and publish, soldiers could now take and send pictures of day-to-day life on the front in their letters home to friends and families. What is more, the reality effect of visual perspective afforded by the rise of photography and film equated actual vision with the representational field, creating greater intimacy of visualization to aid in breaking down the distance between the home front and the battlefield.

Moreover, American popular and military cultures had become increasingly intertwined. As demand increased for more authentic war images, the cultural production of war became more spectacular, more realistic, and in some cases more gruesome. By 1898, American viewers could watch Cuban war plays at the theater, motion picture footage of war-related events at vaudeville houses, or a mock destruction of the USS *Maine* twice a day at the Omaha World's Fair. During World War I, though photographs from the front were censored to American viewers, a glut of prowar posters and paraphernalia circulated publicly. Popular Hollywood celebrities Douglas Fairbanks, Mary Pickford, and Charlie Chaplin became the face of campaigns to encourage the buying of war bonds. Though the relationship between war and cinema in World War I was still nascent (D. W. Griffith was the only American filmmaker authorized to take footage at the front), the genre of war films would thrive by the Second World War. Over time the convergence of what James Der Derian calls MIME-NET, or the military-industrial-media-entertainment network, had gradually solidified in the cultural production of war.[16]

Making War Invisible: The Drive toward Visual Containment

The Second World War provided cause for war images to circulate on an unprecedented scale, through newspapers, magazines, poster campaigns, newsreels, photographs, museum exhibits, government films, and Hollywood movies. Due to rigid censorship of war reporting and broad compliance with government directives, the prevailing image of war dominating American popular culture during the war years cultivated patriotic conviction and a sense of brotherly camaraderie. To mobilize support on the home front, the Office of War Information (OWI) hired artists to create colored posters that circulated nationwide in post offices, train stations, department stores, factories, and schools, promoting values of conservation, enlistment, workplace productivity, and vigilance. Employing techniques from art, fashion, and advertising, these eye-catching posters depicted glamorous nurses and housewives, manly American GIs, and efficient U.S. workers making sacrifices in service to their country.[17] The Office for Emergency Management of the OWI, for example, produced a poster series titled "If You Question It—Report It," which urged Americans to be on guard against attempts by the enemy to sabotage American communities and workplaces (Figure 14.7). OWI poster campaigns, as illustrated here, made a point of distinguishing the threat posed by fascist leaders Adolf Hitler and Benito Mussolini and the German and Italian people more generally. In imagining the nation's enemies, Hitler's recognizable likeness embodied the German threat while the Japanese were represented more holistically, as a subhuman, savage race of apes, rats, and insects bent on destroying the American way of life. "The only good Jap is a dead Jap" became a popular wartime saying.[18] The racial distinction in these posters (as in motion pictures) helped to justify the internment of the West Coast Japanese-American community for the duration of the war, a policy that did not extend to German or Italian Americans.

During World War II, the U.S. government suppressed the publication of material that might subvert the war effort, which meant that Americans were not allowed to see images of war's physical and psychological impacts on its own soldiers or on enemy populations. What is more, the Bureau of Motion Pictures (BMP), a department of the OWI, provided a manual to Hollywood studios with guidelines for how to support the war effort and intervened in the writing of screenplays to bolster morale-building content and excise objectionable material. Elmer Davis, director of the OWI, recognized the power of

FIGURE 14.7 Office for Emergency Management of the Office of War Information, Photo-mechanical Print, c1943–1945. Courtesy of the National Archives, College Park, MD, 44-PA-1059.

film to mobilize the public: "The easiest way to inject a propaganda idea into most people's minds is to let it go in through the medium of an entertainment picture when they do not realize that they are being propagandized."[19] Motion pictures, though fictitious, told stories that drew upon actual war events and referenced real-life political and military figures. This "realistic" framework enabled filmmakers to embed interpretations of the war's history, causes, aims, and impacts into emotionally compelling, action-packed storylines. The Oscar-nominated film *Wake Island* (1942), for example, stirred patriotic sentiment through emotive scenes of American military and civilian lives lost during Japan's attack on this small Pacific island after Pearl Harbor, helping to justify President Franklin D. Roosevelt's decision to bring the United States into the world war.[20] A *New York Times* movie review wrote, "Except for the use of fictional names and a very slight contrivance of plot, it might be a literal document of the manner in which the Wake detachment of Marines fought and died in the finest tradition of their tough and indomitable corps."[21]

With Hollywood taking its cues, the BMP had great influence in shaping a unifying image of the Second World War on screen. After the hard times of the 1930s, this visual paradigm fulfilled a vital cultural need for optimism, unity, and reinvigoration; as historian Andrew Huebner argued, these "images of the positive, heroic serviceman fitted into and advanced a much wider story of American recovery, strength, and masculinity in the aftermath of the Depression."[22] Still, this mythic portrait was not easily sustained as the death toll continued to rise and many veterans returned home physically and mentally strained. By 1945, the OWI perceived a growing sense of public disillusionment with the war's sanitized presentation and a more complex and grim visual portrait of the war began to emerge.[23]

Motion pictures can be a powerful medium to project ideologies of war because the cinematic apparatus allows for an aura of realism and a suspension of disbelief, despite the fictionalization of content. The genre of war films that boomed during and after World War II largely promoted the image of "the good war" with nationalistic and patriotic themes. But did these war films project what World War II was really like? Ron Kovic, in his memoir *Born on the Fourth of July* (1976), felt deceived by them. He claimed that a major source of inspiration for him to join the United States Marine Corps during the Vietnam War was watching World War II films, such as Audie Murphy's story in *To Hell and Back* (1955) and John Wayne's *The Sands of Iwo Jima* (1949). He enlisted to fight in Vietnam but returned home paralyzed, disillusioned, and emotionally scarred, ultimately turning against the war.[24]

In contrast to the boom of World War II films, Hollywood was remarkably silent on Vietnam during the war years, with only one commercial film released during the war dealing directly with the conflict: John Wayne's *The Green Berets* (1968). In fact, most war films released during the Vietnam War focused on World War II and continued the tradition of celebrating the U.S. military and its moral capacities.[25] Amid the cinematic silence, American audiences watched the Vietnam War unfold daily on the news, marking a new level of televised intimacy with war. Unlike the novelty of watching short World War II newsreels in movie houses of the 1940s, viewing television news coverage of the Vietnam War was a more mundane, daily event. The social experience of coming

FIGURE 14.8 Nick Ut photograph, Kim Phúc running from a Napalm attack near Trang Bang, June 8, 1972. Courtesy of Nick Ut/AP Photo.

into contact with these prolonged broadcasts lost its luster over time, as did its hyperpatriotic framing, particularly with the absence of prowar Vietnam films.

The news media had considerable freedom and access in its war reporting during the Vietnam War, and, ultimately, this visual proximity contributed to public weariness with the war effort. Photojournalists and news broadcasters chose not to glorify events or conceal its ugliness. It isn't surprising that *seeing* images, like that of Nick Ut's Pulitzer Prize–winning photograph of Kim Phúc running from a napalm attack near Trang Bang on June 8, 1972, invited a moral repositioning regarding U.S. involvement for many viewers (Figure 14.8).[26] The napalm had burned through her clothes and left her deeply scarred. In the photograph, the young girl's face projects her intense pain and vulnerability, as she came to represent the suffering of innocent Vietnamese civilians due to U.S. military attacks. Americans of the Civil War generation saw images of war death, too, a sight that many struggled to process and accept, but the images disseminated during the War in Vietnam were qualitatively different. Photographic technologies and practices allowed for greater capture of movement and emotion in war scenes. As opposed to the stillness of a corpse, one can see the enduring horror on this young girl's face and the others in the scene as they fled for their lives after the napalm attack. This type of action shot, capturing war's torments to the living, crystallized debates about the ethics of U.S. military actions into the irrevocable symbol of the screaming, naked child. Despite the frontal nudity, Ut did not shirk from photographing the nine-year-old Kim Phúc; rather, he saw the power in capturing that moment, a strategy that resonated with the nation's long history of casting distressed women and children at the center of U.S. propaganda campaigns because they were particularly effective in stirring empathy and rousing action.[27] Broadly circulated, the iconic image became one of the defining images of the Vietnam War.

As many journalists and broadcasters became increasingly critical of U.S. actions amid the circulation of such emotive and divisive imagery, the tide of public opinion shifted against U.S. military intervention in Vietnam. The rise of television allowed for a new form of media coverage that literally brought the war into American living rooms; as viewers watched actual war footage and saw its impacts on the landscape, combatants, and civilian populations, newscasters voiced over their analysis, effectively instructing viewers in how to interpret what they were seeing. Political and military analysts learned a crucial lesson from this experience. The rise in popular disenchantment with the Vietnam War compelled government leaders to bolster media censorship policies moving forward. The British, too, were stirred by this lesson and began imposing regulations on media access through the practice of embedded reporting during the Falklands crisis in 1982. Rather than restrict access entirely, the military allowed "embedded" journalists to travel along with certain transports provided they agreed to report on and show only what the government approved, including not showing any pictures of war dead. In this way, the government dictated what reporters could and could not see as well as what they could make public. Soon after, President Ronald Reagan similarly excluded the media from his initial invasion of Grenada, and this practice would continue into the twenty-first century with the Wars in Iraq and Afghanistan under George W. Bush.[28]

Since the Vietnam era, the visual narratives of wars have been constituted as much by what is left out of the frame as by what makes it in.[29] For example, when President George H. W. Bush invaded Panama in 1989, an operation that cost thousands of Panamanian lives, American news media justified the U.S. action by demonizing the Panamanian president General Manuel Noriega as a threat to American national security and to the Panama Canal. The fact that the U.S. government had been supporting Noriega's administration for decades was left out of the story. Restrictions placed on journalists prevented them from formulating an alternative version of events. Instead, the U.S. government was able to dictate accounts of why the invasion was necessary and how it was carried out; Pentagon press briefings made no mention of the death and destruction created by U.S. intervention. Images of the horrific scenes on the city streets of Panama were simply not taken, and if they were, they could not be shown. Because of embedded reporting and other censorship policies, Americans have seen far fewer images of ensuing conflicts in more recent wars, and some argue this diminished visual engagement has contributed to a larger cultural "epidemic of disconnection" to U.S. foreign affairs, to borrow the phrase coined by journalists Bob Woodward and Tom Brokaw.

In view of the media's critical treatment of the War in Vietnam, the U.S. government chose to restrict journalistic access to key military sites during the Persian Gulf War of 1991. Reporters were excluded from areas where combat fighting or bombing was taking place. That same year, the Pentagon also banned the taking and publication of photographs of the flag-draped coffins of returning American servicemen and women. The intent was to suppress any images of military or civilian death in fear that they might fuel political protest.[30] In place of images of the war dead, new night vision technologies during the Gulf War enabled television broadcasters to showcase visual content in the form of aerial bombardments. In what Anthony McCosker calls an "aesthetic of disappearance," this new vantage point suppressed rather than sharpened visual engagement, presenting war as a pyrotechnics show that masked the actual impact of the bombings for people on the ground.[31] Given the overall absence of war images to show, news broadcasters instead filled airtime with "talk," with retired generals and military analysts contemplating strategies and outcomes.[32] Seeing war as bursts of light in the night sky hindered visual clarity, forcing viewers to rely on the observations and analyses of second-hand accounts.

The spectacle of the September 11, 2001, attacks had a powerful effect on American visual culture. Newscasts of the planes hitting the World Trade Towers and their subsequent collapse replayed on television for months afterward, but this was not the only set of images to pierce the American consciousness. In the days and weeks after 9/11, portraits of the missing blanketed New York City. Pictures of the victims ultimately found a home in the Memorial Exhibition of the 9/11 Memorial Museum at Ground Zero, allowing museumgoers to learn the stories and gaze into the eyes of the diverse set of victims who perished that day. Another image that left its mark became known as the "Falling Man." Newspaper accounts estimate that on 9/11, between fifty and two hundred people jumped from the towers to their deaths. Associated Press photojournalist Richard Drew captured the moment on camera for one unidentified male victim mid-flight. Pictured against the colossal backdrop of the towers, the man descends head first in vertical formation, just seconds away from his inevitable demise. Nationwide press broadly published the photograph, but it provoked a backlash from many viewers who saw it as exploiting this man's privacy and tragic plight. Unlike images of falling buildings, Drew's photograph made visible the human tragedy in a way that was too painful for many viewers to process in the immediate aftermath of the attacks.[33] Jonathan Safran Foer found a way to reclaim the visual power of the "Falling Man" image in his novel, *Extremely Loud and Incredibly Close* (2005).[34] It tells the story of a young boy's journey toward healing after losing his father on 9/11 and ends with a visual flip-book containing a series of screenshots of a man jumping. But rather than replicating the man's fall to his death, Foer reverses the order of the images to have the man ascend back up, recreating the boy's daydream of reversing the events and loss surrounding 9/11 and his father's death.

Hollywood once again self-imposed a regime of censorship after 9/11 when Jack Valenti, head of the Motion Picture Association of America, urged Hollywood filmmakers not to make films portraying Islamic terrorists, to prevent repercussions they might elicit against the American Muslim community. Some independent filmmakers refused to disengage politically, most notably Michael Moore, who used the medium to censure the government's response to 9/11 and the War on Terror in his highly profitable documentary *Fahrenheit 9/11* (2004). Moore held the Bush administration accountable for ignoring crucial intelligence that could have prevented the September 11th attacks and for manufacturing the subsequent invasion of Iraq to advance the interests of the oil and defense industries. Within a few years after 9/11, Hollywood filmmakers rejoined the public dialogue, producing 9/11-based films like *United 93* (2006) and *World Trade Center* (2006), as well as movies chronicling the ongoing Wars in Iraq and Afghanistan, some of which overtly criticized U.S. involvement, such as *The Hurt Locker* (2008) and *Green Zone* (2010). Some media analysts point to Osama bin Laden's death as the point of closure on this period of self-imposed silence, creating a "double negative" within the spectacle that "canceled out the power of invisibility."[35]

Contrary to cinema, television networks embraced the politics of the War on Terror, producing shows such as *24, Homeland, The Grid, The Agency,* and *Threat Matrix.*[36] With its split-screen visuals and "real-time" exposition, *24* showcased sensationalistic terrorism scenarios within a format akin to the twenty-four-hour media coverage after 9/11. Jack Bauer worked against the clock to foil serious terrorist threats, thus rationalizing the fear of terrorists infiltrating American communities and legitimating the idea of an imminent terrorist attack. Just as the treatment of detainees at Abu Ghraib and Guantanamo Bay came under public scrutiny, *24*'s storylines of Bauer extracting key information from terrorists through coercive interrogation techniques overtly sanctioned the practice and rationalized it as a necessary ethical overstep to save American lives. Although framed as entertainment, shows like *24* participated directly in debates about controversial issues related to U.S. military affairs while dramatizing seemingly "real" threats to the nation.[37]

Like the film industry, the fine arts similarly produced few images in the wake of 9/11, creating what Thomas Stubblefield called a "spectacle of absence."[38] After a few years, a number of artists began producing work to counter state-institutionalized war narratives and resist the culture of invisibility. Nina Berman, in her photo essay *Purple Hearts: Back from Iraq,* published in 2004, focused her camera on wounded veterans who had served during the first eighteen months of the War in Iraq. She photographed veterans who had returned with "nonhostile" injuries, which meant that because of the circumstances surrounding their injuries, they were omitted from Pentagon casualty reports despite having

FIGURE 14.9 Nina Berman photograph, Pfc. Alan Jermaine Lewis from the *Purple Hearts* series, 2003. Courtesy of Nina Berman/NOOR.

to live with some form of permanent disability. She sought, in essence, to give visual expression to the soldiers whose injuries the Pentagon had subsequently effaced. In one photograph, she depicts Pfc. Alan Jermaine Lewis, a twenty-three-year-old machine gunner who was injured in Baghdad in 2003 when his Humvee hit a land mine (Figure 14.9). He lost both legs, his face was burned, and his arm was severely broken. Berman depicts him looking adrift as he sits on his bed alone, with one prosthetic removed; the caption reads, "Death has always been around." Berman shares her own perspective in a statement accompanying the public exhibition of the photographs in 2007:

> I seek them out in their hometowns, after they have been discharged from
> military hospitals. I photograph them alone, mainly in their rooms, which to
> me feel like little cages. I strip them of patriotic colors and heroic postures. I
> see them alienated and dispossessed, left empty handed amid dreams of glory
> and escape. While their physical wounds are profound, it is their psychological

condition that is my primary focus. . . . Meeting so many severely disabled young men and women was deeply disturbing to me. I felt complicit because they had fought in my name. And I felt the divide of privilege because I did not have to make a similar sacrifice.[39]

Berman used the art of photography as a means of making their psychological and physical pain visible to American audiences and forcing viewers to come to terms with their part in it. The pain projected on their injured bodies and desolate faces articulates their sense of abandonment and loss.

Even though restricted access and self-imposed censorship may have suppressed certain perspectives on U.S. wars, the visual field has hardly been a void. The visual production of war instead transformed into new forms and contexts and has remained a strategic weapon for state-sponsored mobilization and recruitment campaigns. The Pentagon allowed news outlets to show images in support of the U.S. military that were carefully calculated to prevent public backlash: blissful family reunions, soldiers in training, and military camaraderie. At the same time, selective release of other images, such as pictures of horrific acts committed by the enemy, were permitted to circulate because they functioned to intensify feelings of public outrage and rationalize military action. There have also been numerous staged moments when the U.S. government has manufactured spectacular performances of American military and moral supremacy. The televised "shock and awe" campaign initiating the invasion of Iraq in 2003, for example, depicted war as distant flashes of light, a virtual fireworks show, with no visual indication of human cost. Writes Allen Feldman, "Shock and awe is more than a military tactic; it is simultaneously an exercise in war as visual culture for the consumption of the televisual audience."[40] In a rare instance, CNN displayed images of the pyrotechnic bombings without any voice-over, allowing viewers to see the military operation without commentary and from the safety of their own homes: is this what war looks like?[41]

In stark contrast to the increasingly invisible violence of the Wars in Iraq and Afghanistan was the scandalous release of photographs of physical and sexual abuse of detainees at the Abu Ghraib prison. The U.S. military imprisoned thousands of Iraqis without due process and used methods that were both legally and morally suspect while interrogating some of them to extract information about future terrorist attacks. In 2004, Spc. Joseph Darby gave photographic evidence of torture to the army's Criminal Investigation Command, prompting a criminal investigation. News sources later publicized some of these images and websites, like Salon, offered access to 279 photographs and 19 videos of the abusive treatment. The images were categorized, captioned, and narrated to direct viewing. Despite official denials, the existence of such photographs proved that torture occurs in U.S. military practice, whether sanctioned or not.

These images were never intended for public distribution, so why were they taken at all? Susan Sontag reflected that "the horror of what is shown in the photographs cannot be separated from the horror that the photographs were taken."[42] Some of the photographs were agents of terror themselves, allegedly taken to induce prisoners to talk or face the humiliation and sexual shame of having the photographs shown to their families. But they were not intended for public consumption; when online news outlets like Salon got hold of them, they broke the initial frame of the images and reframed them as a critique of American military abuses. They presented these images of smiling American guards, giving thumbs-ups to the camera in juxtaposition to their suffering victims, as trophies, a means for the guards to mark their own identities and power over their vanquished subjects.

Especially with instances of terrorism, the element of performance is critical to its effectiveness. As Elaine Scarry has stated, "It is not accidental that in the torturers' idiom the room in which the brutality occurs was called the 'production room' in the Philippines, the 'cinema room' in South Vietnam, and the 'blue lit stage' in Chile."[43] Faisal Devji similarly writes how "collective witnessing" is essential for martyred acts, like videotapes of suicide bombings, to have the desired impact: "Martyrdom achieves meaning only by being witnessed in the mass media."[44] As spectators, viewers turn into participants, sharing in the act of seeing the events. Whether engravings of colonial public executions, photographs of public lynchings, or films of abused prisoners, the power of torture lies in its public performance. It must be seen on a mass scale for its purpose to instill fear to be truly realized, so the pain and suffering of the victim gains meaning through public display.

Media analysts have offered conflicting perspectives on the response to these iconic images. Political scientist Stephen Cimbala claimed that the release of the photos in 2004 was hardly shocking to the American public, considering the climate of American popular culture, as Americans had become accustomed to "acts of demonstrative public lewdness, crassness, and barbarism" as well as intense levels of violence and gruesomeness.[45] Even if Americans had become desensitized to violence and obscenity, seeing evidence of U.S. military personnel orchestrating and documenting these abusive acts, and with such casual delight, seemed to cross a line. Military historian Joanna Bourke in *The Guardian* made parallels between the photographs and modes of sadomasochistic pornography, calling attention to the fact that the abuse was specifically performed before the camera and seemed a source of sadistic pleasure for the guards. To Bourke, the cultural experience of seeing these images for viewers was akin to participating in the "pornographic gaze."[46] For American viewers to be able to bear witness to the sexual humiliation of the detainees may have, to a certain extent, made them feel complicit in the abuse. Perhaps this feeling contributed to the sense of public outrage, compelling the Bush administration to scramble to contain the imagery. Media theorist Richard Grusin had a different theory.

He argued that the reason the images were deeply cutting to the American consciousness had more to do with how the images mirrored everyday media practices rather than because of their abusive content. Grusin claimed that Americans may have felt disturbingly connected to the images because of their raw quality—as low-resolution, amateur photographs—that circulated via social media in the same way that many Americans share pictures of friends and family. To Grusin, *how* the images circulated within a particular media context was just as important as the content of the images themselves in understanding the public response.[47]

The leak of photographs from the Abu Ghraib prison represented a moment when the U.S. government's efforts at visual containment broke down. That the photographs were presented as a forbidden behind-the-scenes view of U.S. military actions primed them to have an even more pronounced effect. The Obama administration endeavored to contain the extent of the image archive released to the public, supporting the passage of The Detainee Photographic Records Protection Act of 2009, which called for the suppression of any photographs related to treatment of detainees taken between September 11, 2001, and January 22, 2009. Its express purpose was to limit further disclosure of these images. Thus, despite Obama's assurances of promoting transparency, his record was inconsistent, reflecting the ongoing struggle to fix the boundaries of acceptable visibility of war. He lifted the eighteen-year ban on photographs of American coffins from war-related deaths and released memos that admitted to government authorization of coercive interrogations. Yet in addition to seeking further restrictions on the diffusion of the Abu Ghraib archive, as did his predecessor, he also chose not to release photographs taken of Osama Bin Laden's death, fearing their gruesomeness could prove incendiary and fuel anti-Americanism in the world.[48]

The difficult decisions Obama had to make raises an important issue: what public purpose does seeing images like that of Bin Laden's death or of the torture at Abu Ghraib serve? Does this visibility create knowledge and understanding or does it transform viewers into voyeurs of sights best left unseen?[49] There is no simple answer, but one's perspective must take into account not just the content of the images themselves but also how and why they are framed or reframed in different media contexts, which, as has been shown, critically affect their meaning.

From the eighteenth century into the twenty-first, evolving visual forms and cultural practices have both expanded and limited visual perspectives on American warfare. Images remain fundamental to rationalize U.S. military actions; as Dora Apel writes, "This official framing of war is not passive, but part of the war machinery, producing and enforcing a particular reality while actively excluding any alternative views."[50] Image-making is not only key to military mobilization but also to the operations of war itself. Take, for example, the rise in drone attacks over the last decade. These unmanned, missile-bearing aircraft have cameras, listening devices, and sensors that are linked to global telecommunications systems, enabling operators from safe distances to track their targets and detonate missiles remotely. In this way, visual technologies remain critical to military surveillance, operations, and intelligence efforts.

The rise in war-related media over the last 250 years has had a reciprocal effect: visual imagery functions to excite interest in militarism just as war stimulates the production and consumption of visual culture. As visual technologies, like war-simulating video games (such as PlayStation's "Modern Warfare" series), have grown more technically sophisticated and interactive, viewing war imagery gets closer to seeming "real." The merger of real and virtual war is clearly evident in the military-developed video game America's Army as a highly successful recruitment tool.[51] These technologies meet a psychological need within American culture to understand the enigma of war, but at the same time they glorify it, fulfilling the thirst for spectacle rather than the need for true understanding. The emergence of a new film genre, what Doug Davis calls techno thrillers, depicts U.S. national security at risk for a nuclear terrorist attack. The plots straddle fact and fantasy, creating fictive scenarios of pending threats that seem completely plausible.[52] Consumption of such media impacts how Americans perceive potential threats to the nation, and fear is a powerful agent for politicians to leverage in mustering support for U.S. military actions.

In 1995, President Bill Clinton began declassifying top-secret satellite imagery, an initiative that set the groundwork eight years later for Secretary of State Colin Powell to use satellite images showing "undeniable proof" of Iraq's program for weapons of mass destruction before the UN Security Council. This instance exemplifies how images themselves have become weaponized. The U.S. State Department chooses to release satellite intelligence when there is strategic incentive, but as evidenced by the failure to find weapons of mass destruction in Iraq, images inherently convey a partial story.[53] Images (like weapons) need to be discharged to be effective. To the untrained eye, the abstraction of satellite imagery is subject to interpretation, and in the case of the 2003 invasion, Powell's authority gave legitimacy to his reading of the evidence. Meaning lies in how images get framed or reframed, which in turn shapes their capacity to be effective agents of military mobilization.

It required specialized skill and equipment during the nineteenth century to produce paintings, photographs, or cartoons. But with the invention of handheld cameras and later digital cameras and cell phones, anyone with access could document war and its impacts. Thanks to the internet, dissemination is now instantaneous on a global scale, removing the need for television networks or printing capabilities to achieve broad circulation. The irony is that despite these technological advances, Americans' perspective on the military conflicts fought in their name has become seemingly less visible. But is visual transparency necessarily productive or beneficial? On the one hand, if Americans were granted unfettered access to images of warfare—especially given the mass killing power of modern weaponry—is sustained support for war even possible? For example, after the public watched visual footage of the corpses of U.S. soldiers desecrated by Somali militants in 1993 (the so-called Black Hawk Down encounter) in what was supposed to be a peaceful humanitarian mission to provide food relief, President Bill Clinton felt immediate public pressure to withdraw U.S. troops from the region, which he did. On the other hand, if images, such as those taken on the streets of Mogadishu in Somalia, had been suppressed from public view, would Americans simply "turn it off" in their minds and ignore the actions of the U.S. military, making inevitable the "epidemic of disconnection"?

In 1999, the chairman of the Joint Chiefs of Staff, army general Henry Shelton, suggested that a good litmus test for measuring public support is the "Dover Test," referencing Dover Air Force Base, the port of entry for returning coffins containing the bodies of American casualties. If the public can remain steadfast after seeing these images, he claimed, then they recognize that sacrifice, while still tragic, is warranted in that context. While the Dover Test is hardly an accurate measure of public opinion, one wonders about its implications in light of the Pentagon's policy of suppressing such photographs between 1991 and 2009. American culture invests considerable power in the idea of "seeing as believing," which positions images to have substantial influence if framed effectively, as we saw in 2003; consequently, government leaders since the Vietnam War have felt greater urgency to limit the visual field. Rather than embracing images as a means of inviting public dialogue and reflection about the merits of U.S. military actions, including its human cost, the goal of visual containment has been to remove potential visual triggers, like the photographs that warrant the so-called Dover Test in the first place. Keeping Americans in the dark, so to speak, may seem politically expedient, but is sure to end in failure; in this internet age, the tendencies toward democratizing image production and distribution via global pathways is too strong a force for any policy of containment to succeed. And with fewer images available, the ones that do surface, whether state-sanctioned or not, like those leaked from the Abu Ghraib prison, stand to have more piercing impact.

Discussion Questions

1. How did the evolution of media technologies shape the content and dissemination of war images in different periods of American history?
2. Why is the context in which an image circulates (its "frame") important in shaping the meaning it holds for viewers? What does it mean to say it "breaks" frame?
3. Given the experiences of Vietnam and other wars, is the U.S. government justified in its policies of censoring the production and circulation of war imagery?

Notes

1 Jeffrey Melnick, *9/11 Culture: America under Construction* (Chichester, UK: Wiley-Blackwell, 2009), 50–51; Thomas Stubblefield, *9/11 and the Visual Culture of Disaster* (Bloomington: Indiana University Press, 2015), 3.

2 On breaking frames, see Judith Butler, *Frames of War: When Is Life Grievable?* (London: Verso, 2009).

3 Frances Pohl, *Framing America: A Social History of American Art* (New York: Thames & Hudson, 2002), 78–80.

4 Martha Sandweiss, Rick Stewart, and Ben Huseman, *Eyewitness to War: Prints and Daguerreotypes of the Mexican War, 1846–1848* (Fort Worth, TX: Amon Carter Museum, 1989), 3–10.

5 Drew Gilpin Faust, *This Republic of Suffering: Death and the American Civil War* (New York: Vintage Books, 2008): xvi–xvii, 3–31.

6 Shirley Samuels, *Facing America: Iconography and the Civil War* (New York: Oxford University Press, 2004), 71, 74.

7 Faust, *This Republic of Suffering*, 69.

8 Alan Trachtenberg, *Reading American Photographs: Images as History* (New York: Hill and Wang, 1989), 74.

9 Alexander Gardner, *Gardner's Photographic Sketchbook of the American Civil War, 1861–1865* (New York: Delano Greenidge Editions, 2001), 1:82.

10 Jan Zita Grover, "The First Living-Room War: The Civil War in the Illustrated Press," *Afterimage* 11 (February 1984): 10.

11 Trachtenberg, *Reading American Photographs*, 77.

12 Alice Fahs, *The Imagined Civil War: Popular Literature of the North and South, 1861–1865* (Chapel Hill: University of North Carolina Press, 2001), 19.

13 See Bonnie M. Miller, *From Liberation to Conquest: The Visual and Popular Cultures of the Spanish-American War of 1898* (Amherst: University of Massachusetts Press, 2011).

14 David Lubin, *Flags and Faces: The Visual Culture of America's First World War* (Oakland: University of California Press, 2015), 1–5.

15 Anthony McCosker, *Intensive Media: Aversive Affect and Visual Culture* (Hampshire, UK: Palgrave Macmillan, 2013), 32.

16 James Der Derian, *Virtuous War: Mapping the Military-Industrial-Media-Entertainment Network* (Boulder, CO: Westview Press, 2001).

17 William L. Bird Jr. and Harry R. Rubenstein, *Design for Victory: World War II Posters on the American Home Front* (New York: Princeton Architectural Press, 1998); Derek Nelson, *The Posters That Won the War* (New York: Crestline Books, 1991).

18 John W. Dower, *War without Mercy: Race and Power in the Pacific War* (New York: Pantheon Books, 1986), 79.

19 Qtd. in Clayton R. Koppes and Gregory D. Black, *Hollywood Goes to War: How Politics, Profits, and Propaganda Shaped World War II Movies* (New York: Free Press, 1987), 64. See also Thomas Doherty, *Projections of War: Hollywood, American Culture, and World War II* (New York: Columbia University Press, 1993).

20 Jeanine Basinger, *The World War II Combat Film: Anatomy of a Genre* (New York: Columbia University Press, 1986), 28–34.

21 Bosley Crowther, "The Screen: 'Wake Island,' a Stirring Tribute to the United States Marines, with Brian Donlevy in the Cast, at the Rivoli Theatre," *New York Times*, September 2, 1942.

22 Andrew J. Huebner, *The Warrior Image: Soldiers in American Culture from the Second World War to the Vietnam Era* (Chapel Hill: University of North Carolina Press, 2008), 49.

23 George H. Roeder Jr., *The Censored War: American Visual Experience during World War II* (New Haven, CT: Yale University Press, 1993), 7–25.

24 Ron Kovic, *Born on the Fourth of July* (New York: Akashic Books, 2005), 64–65.

25 Linda Dittmar and Gene Michaud, "America's Vietnam War Films: Marching toward Denial," in *From Hanoi to Hollywood: The Vietnam War in American Film*, ed. Linda Dittmar and Gene Michaud (New Brunswick, NJ: Rutgers University Press, 2000), 2–10.

26 See discussion in Robert Hariman and John Louis Lucaites, "Public Identity and Collective Memory in U.S. Iconic Photography: The Image of 'Accidental Napalm,'" in *Visual Rhetoric: A Reader in Communication and American Culture*, ed. Lester Olson, Cara Finnegan, and Diane Hope (Los Angeles: Sage Publications, 2008), 175–198.

27 See discussion of the trope of the feminized victim in Miller, *From Liberation to Conquest*, 26–33.

28 Daniel Hallin, *Uncensored War: The Media and Vietnam* (New York: Oxford University Press, 1986), 4.

29 Butler, *Frames of War*, 64–73.

30 The ban on publicly releasing photographs of flag-draped coffins was initially limited to Dover Air Force Base, the largest port of entry for returning casualties. In 2003 Bush extended this policy to include all military bases. Despite some public backlash, the Republican-controlled Senate backed Bush's decision and defeated a Democratic measure to order the release of the pictures. In 2004, however, the courts ordered the Pentagon to release more than 300 images from honor guard ceremonies that had been previously withheld after a website (www.thememoryhole.org) filed against them for violating the Freedom of Information Act.

31 McCosker, *Intensive Media*, 35.

32 Patricia Mellencamp, "Fearful Thoughts: U.S. Television since 9/11 and the Wars in Iraq," in *Rethinking Global Security: Media, Popular Culture, and the "War on Terror,"* ed. Andrew Martin and Patrice Petro (New Brunswick, NJ: Rutgers University Press, 2006), 121.

33 Graley Herren, "Flying Man and Falling Man: Remembering and Forgetting 9/11," in *Transatlantic Literature and Culture after 9/11: The Wrong Side of Paradise*, ed. Kristine Miller (New York: Palgrave Macmillan, 2014), 159–176; Peter Howe, "Richard Drew," *The Digital Journalist*, 2001, http://digitaljournalist.org/issue0110/drew.htm.

34 Jonathan Safran Foer, *Extremely Loud and Incredibly Close* (Boston: Mariner Books, 2005).

35 Stubblefield, *9/11 and the Visual Culture of Disaster*, 181.

36 James Castonguay, "Intermedia and the War on Terror," in Martin and Petro, *Rethinking Global Security*, 152–153.

37 Rebecca Adelman, *Beyond the Checkpoint: Visual Practices in America's Global War on Terror* (Amherst: University of Massachusetts Press, 2014), 141–144.

38 Stubblefield, *9/11 and the Visual Culture of Disaster*, 10.

39 Qtd. in Marcia Vetrocq, "Rules of Engagement," *Art in America* (June/July 2008): 174–175.

40 Allen Feldman, "On the Actuarial Gaze: From 9/11 to Abu Ghraib," in *The Visual Culture Reader*, 3rd ed., ed. Nicholas Mirzoeff (London: Routledge, 2013), 173.

41 Mellencamp, "Fearful Thoughts," 130.

42 Susan Sontag, "Regarding the Torture of Others, *New York Times*, May 23, 2004.

43 Elaine Scarry, *The Body in Pain: The Making and Unmaking of the World* (New York: Oxford University Press, 1985), 28.

44 Faisal Devji, "Media and Martyrdom," in Mirzoeff, *Visual Culture Reader*, 224.

45   Stephen Cimbala, "Abu Ghraib Reveals U.S. Culture," *Centre Daily Times*, May 17, 2004, A6.

46   Joanna Bourke, "Torture as Pornography," *The Guardian*, May 7, 2004.

47   Richard Grusin, *Premediation: Affect and Mediality After 9/11* (Basingstoke, England: Palgrave Macmillan, 2010), 65.

48   Dora Apel, *War Culture and the Contest of Images* (New Brunswick, NJ: Rutgers University Press, 2012), 179; Adelman, *Beyond the Checkpoint,* 26–27.

49   Rebecca Adelman, for example, made the strategic choice not to reproduce such images in her study of the visual culture of the Global War on Terror; she notes that "this lack will draw attention to the visual cravings we have for such images, so that we might query those scopophilic desires more sharply and understand their objects better." *Beyond the Checkpoint,* 16.

50   Apel, *War Culture and the Contest of Images,* 152.

51   Ibid., 177–178.

52   Doug Davis references the films *Sum of All Fears* (2002) and *Peacemaker* (1997). "Future-War Storytelling: National Security and Popular Film," in Martin and Petro, *Rethinking Global Security,* 15–17.

53   See Lisa Parks, "Planet Patrol: Satellite Imagery, Acts of Knowledge, and Global Security," in Martin and Petro, *Rethinking Global Security,* 134–135.

Further Reading

Dora Apel. *War Culture and the Contest of Images.* New Brunswick, NJ: Rutgers University Press, 2012.

Judith Butler. *Frames of War: When Is Life Grievable?* London: Verso, 2009.

Andrew Martin and Patrice Petro, eds. *Rethinking Global Security: Media, Popular Culture, and the "War on Terror."* New Brunswick, NJ: Rutgers University Press, 2006.

Alan Trachtenberg. *Reading American Photographs: Images as History.* New York: Hill and Wang, 1989.

15

War and Film

SCOTT LADERMAN

If it's true that money never lies, what decades of huge box-office earnings demonstrate is that war makes for compelling cinema. And the critics clearly agree. The list of Oscar nominees since 1927, when the newly formed Academy of Motion Picture Arts and Sciences began offering its award for Best Picture, makes this glaringly apparent. Indeed, the very first movie ever to receive the honor, the combat-centered romance *Wings* (1927), was set in the United States and France during the First World War. Two years later, the World War I classic *All Quiet on the Western Front* (1929) won the top prize, and the trend of war-film contenders would continue through the decades, from *Casablanca* (1943) and *The Caine Mutiny* (1954) to *M*A*S*H* (1970), *The Killing Fields* (1984), and *Saving Private Ryan* (1998), among many others. This is not surprising. War is of course about violence—and years of box office attest to Americans' fascination with big-screen gore—but also emotion and human drama. This is a potent combination. If filmmakers love larger-than-life visuals and deep emotional resonance, it is little wonder that war movies have proved such a popular genre.

Broadly speaking, films about war have performed at least three major and usually simultaneous purposes since their genesis in the late nineteenth century. While highly mediated and often misleading, they have appeared to serve as visual records of what transpired. They have been employed as seductive instruments of state and nonstate propaganda. And they have functioned as sources of entertainment, at times in an effort to keep home or battlefront morale high.

Many of the productions have been fictional. Some have been—or have purported to be—nonfictional. What they all have had in common is their use of war for visual or dramatic effect. And while not always successful, they have frequently worked to either buttress or subvert Washington's war-making apparatus and the social consent on which it has relied throughout the long twentieth century.

All Quiet on the Western Front and the First World War

The motion pictures created by the Edison Manufacturing Company and the American Mutoscope & Biograph Company offer a case in point.[1] Produced between 1898 and 1901, when the United States was at war in Cuba and the Philippines, the two companies recorded a number of wartime developments, from troop and ship movements to parades, Cuban *reconcentrados* (rural noncombatants who were forcibly relocated into fortified camps and more populated areas), and the "blanket-tossing" of personnel. In addition to chronicling elements of the American experience, the Edison Company also staged combat re-enactments and dramatic fictional tales in an effort to generate public support for American policy, which, with the formation of the Anti-Imperialist League, was proving surprisingly contentious. In one of these wartime stories, *Love and War* (1899), which the company called an "illustrated song" or a "song picture in six scenes"—as a silent movie, it was supposed to be set to musical accompaniment—a young man the Edison catalog dubs "a hero" is wounded in battle, meets a Red Cross nurse with whom he falls in love, and "returns home triumphantly" as a recently promoted officer to his once anxious but now ecstatic parents.[2] Although aurally silent, the film's visual imagery suggests no criticism of the controversial empire-building in which the United States was then engaged. Instead, viewers were presented with a maudlin story of individual survival, familial concern, and joyful reconciliation. The triumph of the soldier was inseparable from the war in which he was fighting. If he was a hero, it was not because he heroically saved others; he did no such thing. Rather, it had to be because he sacrificed in furtherance of a just cause. *Love and War*, in other words, serves as an early demonstration of the ways that seemingly innocent narratives of men and women in combat could in fact pack a powerful political punch.

Hollywood would prove masterful at delivering such punches. Eric Johnston, who as head of the Motion Picture Association of America from 1946 to 1963 was arguably the most commanding figure in American cinema, clearly recognized the influence the studios wielded in molding popular sentiment. "It is no exaggeration to say that the modern motion picture industry sets the styles for half the world," he wrote. "There is not one of us who isn't aware that the motion picture industry is the most powerful medium for the influencing of people that man has ever built."[3] The reason is simple. Movies captivate people, drawing them into stories in which they tend to identify with sympathetic protagonists, making the protagonists' struggles seem like their own. When it comes to war films, this can work both ways. Films that portray U.S. militarism in positive terms can elicit support for U.S. foreign policy, just as films that portray such militarism negatively can induce popular opposition. Not everyone

FIGURE 15.1 Paul Bäumer (Lew Ayres), left, horrified that he killed a French soldier (Raymond Griffith), in *All Quiet on the Western Front* (1930).

views films identically, of course, so there can be significant variance in how such films are received. But, in general, reception tends to be fairly consistent; consider, for example, the consensus over whether Michael Moore's *Fahrenheit 9/11* (2004) was hostile to the George W. Bush administration.

Sometimes Hollywood works in strange ways, transforming those once considered the "bad guys" into "good guys." Take the case of the aforementioned *All Quiet on the Western Front*, a critical and commercial success that won the Academy Award for Best Picture in 1930. Based on the 1929 novel by Erich Maria Remarque, a German veteran who originally published his work in the Berlin-based newspaper *Vossische Zeitung*, the film—the product of an American studio, Universal, and an American (albeit a Moldovan-born Jewish immigrant) director, Lewis Milestone—follows the exploits and hardships endured by a unit of German soldiers during the First World War. Although the Germans were, of course, the adversaries, it proved difficult for Americans to watch the film without identifying with its protagonists. It certainly helped that they spoke fluent, American-accented English. But more pertinently, the film probably succeeded because its audience had by that time increasingly come to identify with its antiwar perspective. The millions of lives lost through 1919, as well as suspicions that "merchants of death" seeking enormous profits had manipulated the United States into war, made a deep impression on the country. Many Americans had grown wary of foreign entanglements, and "isolationist" sentiment was on the rise. *All Quiet* spoke to this unease (Figure 15.1).

The young German men fighting in the war begin as gung-ho types intent on defending the fatherland. They enthusiastically enlist after hyperpatriotic regalement from their secondary school teacher, who offers confident assurances of a "quick war" with "few losses." To join the German military would make their fathers proud and bring honor to the country, this elderly teacher says. But it does not take long for the boys—and they really were just boys—to be disabused of war's romance. The constant death, the brutal suffering, and the incessant noise quickly sober them up. The teacher would later be taken to task. The film's chief protagonist, Paul Bäumer, visits him while on leave after suffering a combat injury. But first, before returning to the school, a war-jaded Paul is counseled by his father's friend—a man who spent the entire war away from the front and was now sitting comfortably in a tavern—that he and other civilians had suffered even more than the men in battle. Yet "we must carry on," the friend says of the German forces, while patronizingly lecturing Paul about what "you boys . . . must do before you can come home."

By the time Paul reaches his former school, he has had enough. He explodes at his onetime teacher, rejecting his jingoistic entreaties to "save the fatherland." "I heard you in here reciting that same old stuff—making more iron men, more young heroes," he fumes. "You still think it's beautiful and sweet to die for your country, don't you? Oh, we used to think you knew. But the first bombardment taught us better. It's dirty and painful to die for your country. When it comes to dying for your country, it's better not to die at all. There are millions out there dying for their countries, and what good is it?" This creates a stir among the young boys in the classroom. "Paul!" the teacher jumps in. But Paul does not back down. "You asked me to tell them how much they're needed out there," he continues. "He tells you, 'Go out and die.' Oh, but if you'll pardon me, it's easier to say go out and die than it is to do it." The students, horrified at this point by the disjuncture between the propaganda they've been fed and the testimony of someone who has served, lash out with accusations of cowardice. But Paul was done with appeals to patriotism and national duty. "We live in the trenches out there," he says of what the war means to him now. "We fight. We try not to be killed. Sometimes we are. That's all." The classroom scene is one of the most powerful in American film history, suggesting that war's realities appear far different to those who fight than those who simply order or encourage them to do so.

All Quiet was indisputably an antiwar film. It was, moreover, internationalist in perspective, adopting not a German or an American (or a British or a French) point of view but rather one of working-class, denationalized people. It speaks to broad, popular themes, such as transnational solidarity and suspicion of wealthy elites. No Americans appear on screen, but the United States is implicitly condemned along with all the major European powers. Indeed, the movie offers a penetrating critique of World War I in its nonexplanation of why the war happened. The nonexplanation unfolds as the German troops are sitting under a tree, happily chatting amongst themselves, after an unusually fulfilling meal. None can confidently explain the origins of the war. One of the young men suggests that "it must be doing somebody some good." His comrades then join in, arguing that every "full-grown emperor"—like generals, one interjects—has needed a war to make him famous and that manufacturers have used the conflicts to "get rich." "I think it's more a kind of fever," another soldier says. "Nobody wants it in particular, and then, all at once, there it is. We didn't want it. The English didn't want it. And here we are fighting."

That wars are started by elites and that working people are the ones made to suffer—a sentiment that echoed much of the radical commentary of the early twentieth century—is suggested when Kat, a crusty yet affecting member of the unit who is deeply admired by his comrades, offers a final word on the subject. "I'll tell you how it should all be done," he begins. "Whenever there's a big war coming on you should rope off a big field. And on the big day you should take all the kings and their cabinets and their generals, put 'em in the center dressed in their underpants and let 'em fight it out with clubs. The best country wins." All the troops agree.

But, in real life, not all Germans felt similarly. Joseph Goebbels, who would soon serve as head of the Reich Ministry of Public Enlightenment and Propaganda for the Nazi regime, notably led a group of storm troopers in disrupting the Berlin screening of *All Quiet* in 1930. Releasing stink bombs, sneezing powder, and an army of white mice into the theater, Goebbels and his crew of Nazi thugs screamed "Judenfilm!" while savagely beating several members of the audience they took for Jews. In the days that followed, Goebbels led nighttime rallies and torch-lit parades in furious opposition to the film. Mobs went on the offensive across Germany and Austria. In Vienna, 1,500 police defended the Apollo Theater against several thousand rioting Nazis. The Weimar government ultimately crumbled; it yanked *All Quiet*'s exhibition license, claiming the film was "endangering Germany's reputation."[4] Clearly movies are not just celluloid distractions. They have the power to rouse, persuade, and mobilize—and to incite.

From World War II to Samuel Fuller's Cold War

If the Great War inspired, in *All Quiet on the Western Front*, one of the great antiwar novels and films, Hollywood adopted a very different tone when the next global conflagration erupted. Then again, World War II was a very different kind of war. While nothing like the mythologized "good war" of later popular memory—think Tom Brokaw's *The Greatest Generation* or Michael Bay's *Pearl Harbor* (2001)—the conflict did present Americans with an undeniable enemy and thus a more compelling purpose.[5] Germany and Japan both engaged in aggressive, brutal expansion, overseeing the deaths of millions in Europe, Africa, and Asia. After the 1941 attack on Pearl Harbor, American opinion shifted decisively in favor of intervention. Whereas "isolationists" such as Senator Gerald Nye may have charged the American film industry with "drug[ging] the reason of the American people" and "rous[ing] the war fever," Hollywood was in fact quite lethargic in attempting to mobilize the nation, releasing only a relative handful of anti-Nazi films—most notably *Confessions of a Nazi Spy* (1939), *The Great Dictator* (1940), and *The Mortal Storm* (1940)—during the fascists' rise and expansion in the 1930s and early 1940s.[6] After the 1941 Japanese attack on the Territory of Hawaii, however, Hollywood did its part to firm up home front morale, churning out pictures that demonized the nation's adversaries while celebrating its fighting men. Operating under conditions of wartime censorship, the industry made films such as *Bataan* (1943), *Guadalcanal Diary*

(1943), and *Thirty Seconds over Tokyo* (1944) that assumed the war's justice and portrayed their American protagonists as heroic individuals making great sacrifices for the nation.

Yet it was not simply a matter of celebrating the courage and commitment of U.S. troops. With Washington, which collaborated closely with Hollywood, embracing motion pictures as a tremendous propaganda tool, dozens of films sought to convince the American public that the embattled peoples of Britain, the Soviet Union, and China were its ideological kin. Theatergoers may not have needed much coaxing to envision the British as their natural brothers-in-arms, making *Mrs. Miniver* (1942) and other pro-British films a relatively easy sell, but the Soviets—dedicated communists led by a brutal despot who had once signed a nonaggression pact with Nazi Germany—and the Chinese, whom most Americans considered racial inferiors, were another matter.[7] Pictures such as *Mission to Moscow* (1943), *Tender Comrade* (1943), *Song of Russia* (1944), *China Girl* (1942), and *Flying Tigers* (1942) thus assumed outsize importance.[8]

The ideological single-mindedness of the Second World War would morph into stark anticommunism in the 1950s. With the onset of the Cold War, filmmakers came under pressure to ensure that their productions fell in line. The House Un-American Activities Committee, Joseph McCarthy, and the blacklist helped see to that. Dissent led to danger and amounted to disloyalty, so Congress (which investigated actors and auteurs alike) and the studios (which signed their paychecks and funded their films) did everything they could to ensure that the nation's cinematic fare stayed on-message. This meant now presenting the Soviet Union and its revolutionary brethren as devious and ruthless national security threats to a democratic, freedom-loving United States. Yet even as most filmmakers adhered to the first part of that formulation, some were reluctant to subscribe to the second. They in fact challenged what they saw as grave injustices in American society. Such was the case with the screenwriter, director, and producer Samuel Fuller. His *China Gate* (1957), a deeply anticommunist film about the unfolding war in Vietnam, contained a searing indictment of white American racism.[9] Combat films have occasionally been good at this sort of thing. While before the sixties they generally stuck to what Godfrey Hodgson called the "liberal consensus," which shielded filmmakers from questions about their patriotism and loyalty, the movies could still manage to level criticisms along the Cold War's margins.[10] This could mean implicitly denouncing some Americans as contemptible racists, or, in the case of another Fuller production, it could mean showing Americans committing war crimes. That other Fuller production was *The Steel Helmet*, a low-budget 1951 picture whose critical and commercial success set off a competition by the major studios to sign its flamboyant auteur (Figure 15.2).

The Steel Helmet, which Fuller wrote, produced, and directed, is widely credited with being the first American film about the Korean War. Fuller knew

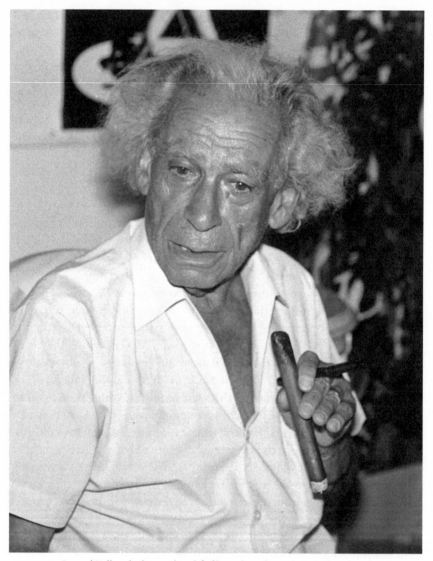

FIGURE 15.2 Samuel Fuller, the larger-than-life filmmaker who wrote, produced, and directed *The Steel Helmet* (1951).

combat well. He had served in Africa and Europe as a U.S. Army infantryman in World War II, an experience that left him with the Bronze Star, the Silver Star, and the Purple Heart. *The Steel Helmet* originated with the diary entries he recorded in the field.[11] True, the Second World War and the Korean War were quite dissimilar, but Fuller's objective in *The Steel Helmet* had less to do with revealing the nature of the Korean struggle than it did with highlighting what he considered the universal experience of American grunts. Fuller thus dedicated his film to the United States Infantry. Years later, he would release his

World War II epic, *The Big Red One* (1980), which was about the 16th Infantry Regiment, 1st Infantry Division. His respect for the men who took up arms for their country was considerable. We often think about the imperative to respect the troops in spite of how we may feel about the war as a late-twentieth-century phenomenon, but in Hollywood its roots in fact run deep.

The Steel Helmet presents a brief snapshot of the Korean War through the eyes of a diverse group of American personnel. These include Sgt. Zack (Gene Evans), whom we first see bound by the wrists after the rest of his unit has been slaughtered; a young Korean boy, Short Round (William Chun), who finds and assists Zack and then accompanies him through the countryside; a black American medic, Cpl. Thompson (James Edwards), who was briefly imprisoned by the Korean revolutionaries after the rest of his platoon was cut down; and a motley patrol of Americans under the command of the inexperienced Lt. Driscoll (Steve Brodie). They all manage to find each other and, together, fight to survive amid the creeping threat posed by what Baldy (Richard Monahan), one of the soldiers, calls the "million Reds out there."

While *The Steel Helmet* has many of the hallmarks of a classic war film—action sequences and explosions, fraternal bonding, tragic outcomes—Fuller manages to deviate from some of film history's more conventional combat scripts. Most obviously, he complicates Cold War representations of the United States as an indisputable force for good. This becomes clear with the touchy issue of race. Zack, the film's white protagonist, at the very least appears racially insensitive, telling Short Round to "eat rice" when he wants him to lay flat on the ground or calling his old war buddy Sgt. Tanaka (Richard Loo) "Buddhahead." But it is an English-speaking Korean revolutionary (Harold Fong) whom the Americans capture that levels the sharpest critique of the nation's unfinished work.

To Cpl. Thompson, for instance, the imprisoned Korean expresses bewilderment. "I just don't understand you," he says before launching into a discursion on segregation. "You can't eat with 'em unless there's a war. Even then it's difficult. Isn't that so?" Thompson concedes the point. But when the Korean says that "you pay for a ticket, but you even have to sit in the back of a public bus," Thompson makes it apparent that he views the prisoner's concern as a mere contrivance. "A hundred years ago I couldn't even ride a bus. At least now I can sit in the back. Maybe in fifty years I'll sit in the middle. Someday even up front. There's some things you just can't rush, buster." The prisoner finds this explanation absurd, denouncing Thompson as "a stupid man" before disgustedly spitting in his direction.

Unable to persuade the African American medic to despise the United States, he goes to work on the Japanese American soldier. "You've got the same kind of eyes I have," the Korean tells Tanaka, noting that "they hate us because of our eyes." When he then asks the veteran of World War II's famed 442nd Regiment whether serving the United States makes him "feel like a traitor," Tanaka parries his feigned brothers-under-the-skin routine. But the Korean is relentless. "They threw Japanese Americans into prison camps in the last war, didn't they?" he asks. "Perhaps even your parents? Perhaps even you?" The look on the American's face suggests a deep sense of betrayal, as do the first words that leave his mouth. "You rang the bell that time," he tells his captive. "They did."

But, rest assured, Tanaka won't fall for the Korean's "slop[piness] as a con artist." When the prisoner says that "they call you dirty Jap rats and yet you fight for them," Tanaka offers a forceful response. "I'm not a dirty Jap rat," he snaps. "I'm an American. And if we get pushed around back home, well, that's our business. But we don't like it when we get pushed around by . . ." Tanaka forces himself to stop, leaving the thought unfinished, worried that he might "forget the articles of war and snap those rabbit teeth of yours out one at a time." This adherence to the law distinguishes him—and, by implication, the United States—from the nation's enemies. "In our country we have rules. Even about war," Tanaka says at one point.

Those rules are at the heart of perhaps the film's most controversial scene. If Americans liked to conceive of themselves as Cold War champions of democracy and human rights, the unsavory tactics of the U.S. military—the actual tactics, not those spun in the celluloid fantasies churned out before 1950—undermined this belief. That Americans in fact violated the laws of war during the Korean conflict is incontestable.[12] Such violations included the bombing and napalming of Korean population centers and the intentional destruction of the infrastructure on which civilians relied. And they certainly included the atrocities—publicized decades later in the United States—at No Gun Ri, where American forces massacred perhaps hundreds of defenseless refugees. Whether such transgressions would appear on the big screen was another matter, however. Showing war crimes is a narrative concession to reality that has become more commonplace in recent decades, even within films about World War II—America's "best war ever"—such as *Fury* (2014).[13] But at the dawn of the Cold War, when anticommunist paranoia led many Americans to conclude that Hollywood was a Kremlin-serving fifth column, such representations could be costly. When the script for the Howard Hughes picture *One Minute to Zero* (1952) showed American artillery fire directed at Korean refugees because their group had been infiltrated by communists, for example, the army withdrew its support for the film.[14] In the case of *The Steel Helmet*, Zack commits an indisputable war crime: he shoots the Korean prisoner of war when he mocks Short Round, who moments earlier had been killed by a sniper's bullet. But, in Fuller's production, Zack was immediately condemned by Lt. Driscoll: "It's a good thing this army isn't made up of fat-headed slobs like you that think this war's run by idiots. Just because those little rats kill our prisoners is no reason we have to do the same thing. No matter how sentimental or personal you get you're supposed to be in the United States Infantry. Soldier? You're no soldier. You're just a big, dumb, stupid, selfish, fatheaded sergeant. And if it takes me twenty years, I'll see that you're shot for killing a prisoner of war. Understand?" Zack realizes the gravity of the situation. "If you die, I'll kill you!" he shouts at the wounded prisoner. But it's no use. The Korean succumbs to his wounds.

Viewers are meant to excuse the crime, however. After all, the prisoner was a despicable communist furthering the expansionist aims of the Soviet Union. We know this because of the hints Fuller dropped along the way. When a sniper's rifle was recovered early in the film, for example, Zack took a look and spewed that it was "made in Russia." Later, when interrogating the prisoner, he asked him, "Where's the rest of your Russians?"[15] This was not a straight war, Fuller was suggesting. It was an anti-imperialist crusade against a "North Korean" enemy intent on furthering the international communist conspiracy. And ruthlessness was required in such a campaign. Even Pvt. Bronte (Robert Hutton), whose World War II conscientious objection was consistent with his priestly ambitions, eventually saw the light. As *The Steel Helmet* reaches its climax, with a massive Korean onslaught against the temple billeting the Americans, Bronte's pacifism dissipates. "When a man lives in a house and it's endangered, and he wants to keep on living in it, he should fight for it," Bronte says moments before being felled by a communist bullet. His final breaths were not unhappy. He perished contentedly behind a machine gun, rapturously delivering a fusillade into the approaching Red enemy.

John Wayne Goes to Vietnam

If the conflict in Korea was a bloody affair to which Americans did their best not to pay attention, the Vietnam War forced them to confront American militarism head on. More than any other conflict in history, the antirevolutionary campaign in Southeast Asia shattered both the nation's perceived moral rectitude and its increasingly shaky veneer of invincibility. A number of films in the 1950s and 1960s tried to capture the growing U.S. involvement in Vietnam, from *A Yank in Indo-China* (1952) and *The Quiet American* (1958) to *The Ugly American* (1963), *Brushfire* (1962), and Sam Fuller's *China Gate*.[16] No wartime motion picture, however, enjoyed more commercial success than John Wayne's *The Green Berets* (1968). Wayne was, of course, one of the best-known actors in the world. He was also an outspoken champion of American militarism. The collapsing support for the War in Vietnam alarmed him. While Wayne was by no means alone in his distress, he did enjoy an advantage over his like-minded compatriots—the tremendous influence he exercised in Hollywood. The Duke, as he was often known, thus sought to counter the war's unpopularity by producing, directing, and starring in a picture that demonstrated its absolute necessity. *The Green Berets*, which was nominally based on a best-selling novel by Robin Moore and which tapped into a widespread fascination with the U.S. Army's most elite forces, was the result (Figure 15.3).[17]

FIGURE 15.3 In *The Green Berets* (1968), Col. Mike Kirby (John Wayne) and his men work to save Hamchunk (Craig Jue), a young Vietnamese boy who symbolically represents the entire Vietnamese people.

Wayne was hardly coy about his objectives. In late 1965 he wrote to the White House about his vision, telling Lyndon Johnson that it was "extremely important that not only the people of the United States but those all over the world should know why it is necessary for us to be [in Vietnam]." The "most effective way to accomplish this," he stressed to the president, "is through the motion picture medium." Wayne was certainly correct about the unsurpassed power of film, and he wanted to exploit that power. He would thus make the "kind of picture" that might "inspire a patriotic attitude on the part of fellow Americans" while "help[ing] our cause throughout the world," he assured Johnson. In particular, he told the president's press secretary, Bill Moyers, several weeks later, the movie would illustrate that "if we abandon these people, there will be a blood bath of over two million souls."[18]

This allusion to what became known as the "bloodbath theory" is important. The basic idea behind the bloodbath theory was that it was morally necessary for the United States—which was by this time in fact responsible for thousands of Vietnamese deaths—to persist in its war effort because, if U.S. forces withdrew, there would be a communist-led slaughter of those countless Vietnamese who supported or had assisted the Americans. The brilliance behind the formulation was its reversal of the war's moral calculus. The war's opponents were transformed into selfish hypocrites unconcerned with the fate of ordinary Vietnamese, while the United States emerged as the only thing standing between the sanctity of innocent life and near-certain genocide. The champions of American militarism could thus claim to be on the side of morality and justice.

The alleged reality of the bloodbath theory was suggested in the film's opening moments. When a journalist attending an open house at Ft. Bragg referred to the war as "ruthless," Sgt. McGee (Raymond St. Jacques) of the Green Berets offered a heartfelt, emotional response. The moral stakes in Vietnam could not be higher, he insisted. "As soldiers . . . we could understand the killing of the military. But the extermination of a civilian leadership, the intentional murder and torture of innocent women and children," these were beyond the pale. "Let me put it in terms we all can understand," McGee continued.

> If this same thing happened here in the United States, every mayor in every city would be murdered. Every teacher that you've ever known would be tortured and killed. Every professor you've ever heard of, every governor, every senator, every member of the House of Representatives and their combined families— all would be tortured and killed. And the like number kidnapped. But in spite of this, there's always some little fellow out there willing to stand up and take the place of those who've been decimated. They need us, Ms. Sutton [one of the journalists at the open house], and they want us.

The response certainly packed an emotional punch, setting the tone for what was to follow. But the bloodbath theory remained notional until much later in the film.

It was only when Wayne and his men descend on an indigenous village in the Vietnamese highlands that the theory was shown to be material reality. The residents of the village had occasionally availed themselves of the medical services beneficently provided by McGee and the Special Forces, and they had requested that the Americans "protect" them from the Vietnamese revolutionaries. They hate "the Cong," the village chief had told John Wayne. But for having accepted the Americans' munificence, the villagers would be made to suffer. What viewers see when the Green Berets arrive is a catalog of horrors. Bodies dangle from the villagers' homes or appear splayed across the ground. The chief, now dead, has his hands bound behind him and is fastened to a pole. Fires consume the humble village dwellings. And a little girl—a sweet, innocent little girl—has been abused and killed. Such barbarity was typical, Wayne suggests to a journalist once skeptical about the war's necessity: "It's pretty hard to talk to anyone about this country 'til they've come over here and seen it. The last village that I visited, they didn't kill the chief. They tied him to a tree and brought his teenage daughters out in front of him and disemboweled them. Then forty of them abused his wife. And then they took a steel rod, broke every bone in her body. Somewhere during the process she died." This, viewers were meant to believe, was the reality of the Vietnam War—which it was, with one important difference. It was the United States, not the National Liberation Front, who became most closely associated with these sorts of atrocities.[19] Whether American audiences bought Wayne's vision is unclear. The film was undoubtedly a commercial success, which perhaps says something about Americans, and it did have its occasional defenders—several Special Forces officers and the arch-segregationist senator Strom Thurmond, for example.

But the critics were overwhelmingly hostile.[20] "*The Green Berets*," wrote Renata Adler in what must register as one of the most scathing reviews in American history, "is a film so unspeakable, so stupid, so rotten and false in every detail that it passes through being fun, through being funny, through being camp, through everything and becomes an invitation to grieve, not for our soldiers or for Vietnam (the film could not be more false or do a greater disservice to either of them) but for what has happened to the fantasy-making apparatus in this country. Simplicities of the right, simplicities of the left, but this one is beyond the possible. It is vile and insane. On top of that"—and here one marvels at the poetic sensibility in this coup-de-grace—"it is dull."[21]

Three Kings and the Challenge to American Revanchism

If the Vietnam War soured the American public on American militarism—a phenomenon that people took to calling the "Vietnam syndrome"—Washington hoped that the 1991 Persian Gulf War might restore their faith in the exercise of American power.[22] President Ronald Reagan had tried in the 1980s to smite at least a fair portion of the public's newly perceived aversion to armed intervention. Overwhelming the tiny island nation of Grenada did not strike most people as particularly heroic, however, and the U.S. support for atrocities and terror in Central America did not exactly scream U.S. moral supremacy.

If Reagan, who of course first captured the public's attention as a handsome big-screen star in the late 1930s, proved unsuccessful in restoring the Cold War consensus, it was not because Hollywood refused to go along. Imperial ideology was woven into much of the era's cinematic output. From *Uncommon Valor* (1983) to Chuck Norris's *Missing in Action* series (1984, 1985, 1988), the industry churned out film after film that sought to transform the American experience in Vietnam from one of great tragedy into ultimate victory. But these efforts failed to pull the nation out of its doldrums. Even Sylvester Stallone, who triumphantly took on the communists as both a decorated warrior (John J. Rambo) and a working-class boxer (Rocky Balboa), proved not up to the task.

But this was hardly for want of trying. After the eponymous hero of *Rambo: First Blood Part II* (1985) learns that he will be returning to Southeast Asia for a covert operation involving "recon for POWs in 'Nam," he asks a question whose answer could have come straight from the real-life president's lips: "Sir, do we get to win this time?" The response from Rambo's onetime commanding officer was vintage Reagan. "This time it's up to you," Col. Trautman (Richard Crenna) says, echoing the president's remarkable statement a year earlier that the United States had worked assiduously to *not* win in Vietnam.[23]

Rambo was hardly alone in seeking to rekindle a normally revanchist nation's spirits. The film's appearance was in fact sandwiched between several Hollywood technospectacles—*Firefox* (1982), *Top Gun* (1986), and *Iron Eagle* (1986)—that tried, but ultimately failed, to do the same. By the close of the decade, the shadow cast by the War in Vietnam still appeared to be hanging over the nation. But the Iraqi invasion of Kuwait in 1990 provided an opportunity. Iraq was ruled by a vicious dictator—albeit a dictator who had long enjoyed the favor of the United States—and repulsing Iraqi bellicosity could at least superficially be characterized as just. So George Bush, who succeeded Reagan as president, insisted on going to war. There would be none of that namby-pamby diplomacy that John Wayne and others on the political right found so distasteful. Saddam Hussein was essentially "Hitler revisited," Bush declared in conjuring the presumed moral clarity of the Second World War, and his "naked aggression" must not stand.[24]

Either fortunately or unfortunately, there would not be time for Hollywood to contemporaneously weigh in on the American campaign. The conflict, while enormously destructive, was over in a matter of weeks—and Americans had been glued to a highly mediated version of it on their television sets, which for the first time delivered carefully selected footage from the Middle East twenty-four hours a day. True, the years that followed the March 1991 ceasefire would witness periodic U.S. bombings and the perpetuation of a brutal sanctions regime.[25] But as far as Hollywood was concerned, cinematic representations would have to be retrospective, with the industry offering only a relative handful of motion pictures in the twelve years before the words *"Iraq"* and *"war"* came to signify something quite different to most Americans. The most highly regarded of these films appeared eight years after President Bush triumphantly declared victory with the resounding cry—more a wish than a definitive boast—"By god, we've kicked the Vietnam syndrome once and for all!"[26]

Three Kings (1999) is among the most sophisticated productions of the post–Cold War era. Appearing on dozens of top-ten lists after it came out, it received widespread praise and won numerous awards. Yet despite being one of the best-reviewed pictures of 1999, *Three Kings* somehow failed to garner even a single Academy Award nomination. This may be a function of its politics; the film was, one critic intoned, "the most caustic antiwar movie of this generation."[27] The snub by the academy outraged reporter Saul Halpert. "Tell me [the total

Oscars blackout] wasn't political," he wrote in an impassioned February 2000 piece for the *Los Angeles Times*. "In the Hollywood fairyland of make-believe, the weird and the supernatural are frequently honored. But sometimes reality just doesn't cut it. How sad."[28]

Written and directed by acclaimed filmmaker David O. Russell and starring George Clooney, Mark Wahlberg, Ice Cube, Spike Jonze, and Cliff Curtis, *Three Kings* offers a blistering critique of what has sometimes been called the Gulf War. And like the best American war films, it uses the cinematic appeal of big-screen violence to suggest something deeper about the United States. The plot involves four American soldiers—one of them, Conrad Vig (Jonze), dies along the way—who attempt to steal millions of dollars in gold bullion that Iraq pilfered from Kuwait.[29] Through a convoluted series of events, the foursome becomes embroiled in the effort by Saddam Hussein's regime at the end of the war to brutally suppress a popular Shiite uprising. Disgusted by the Baathist terror but also stranded and relatively helpless, the Americans agree to assist a group of Shiite men, women, and children flee Iraq for Iran. They encounter challenges along the way, some of which are presented quite humorously, but the Americans do ultimately succeed in delivering the refugees to safety.

Three Kings is an unusually complex big studio production that operates on a number of levels. On one, it addresses Americans' lingering unease with the Persian Gulf War and its unsatisfying and bloody resolution. The picture begins just after the war has ended, and viewers almost immediately confront the question of its purpose. When Special Forces lifer Archie Gates (Clooney) is caught shirking his media-minder duties by having sex with a journalist (Judy Greer), he is scolded by his commanding officer. But Gates does not take it meekly. He dismisses his sexual dalliance by suggesting that the whole war was a charade. "I don't even know what we did here," he complains to the officer, Col. Horn (Mykelti Williamson). "Just tell me what we did here, Ron!" Horn's response suggests the persistent ideological hold of the earlier war in Vietnam. "What do you want to do?" he shouts at Gates. "Occupy Iraq and do Vietnam all over again? Is that what you want? Is that your brilliant idea?" It is not—though, unbeknownst to Russell, the humanitarian nightmare of occupation would of course become a reality several years later—yet the exchange points to the way that the loss in Vietnam framed the continuing unease with the Gulf War's unsettled end. There were other reminders, too. When an Iraqi soldier executes an Iraqi mother with a point-blank shot to the side of the head, Russell's presentation of the ghastly atrocity mirrors the iconic imagery of Nguyen Ngoc Loan executing an alleged National Liberation Front prisoner on a Saigon street in 1968 (Figures 15.4 and 15.5).

That filmmaker Russell did not see the Iraq war as the just cause claimed by the United States is suggested when Troy Barlow (Wahlberg), having been captured by Iraq, is being interrogated and tortured by a surprisingly sympathetic

FIGURE 15.4 A scene in *Three Kings* (1998), in which an Iraqi soldier executes an Iraqi civilian.

FIGURE 15.5 Eddie Adams's Pulitzer Prize–winning photograph of Nguyen Ngoc Loan, a Republic of Vietnam police official, executing Nguyen Van Lem in Saigon on February 1, 1968.

member of the Iraqi armed forces (Saïd Taghmaoui). Barlow, having developed a strange rapport with the U.S.-trained Said, spouts platitudes about the nobility of the American mission. The United States is "saving Kuwait," he claims. We need to "stabilize the region," he adds robotically. "You invaded another country. You can't do that," he also says. Whether Barlow truly believes these utterances is unclear. What *is* clear is that he has no other frame of reference for why he finds himself in the Iraqi desert. Said, who just days earlier had suffered the maiming of his wife and death of his infant son by an American bomb, is apoplectic. He props open Barlow's mouth with a CD case and forces crude oil down his throat, spewing, "This is your fucking stability, my main man."

That the war was about oil is treated as patently obvious. "It's the oil, stupid, not the people," Russell told the *New York Times*. "We don't care about the people or democracy, O.K.?" This is why he focused so much of the film on the repression of the Shiites. "When I made the movie," Russell said, "I felt the abandonment of the Iraqi people at the war's end further pointed to the hypocrisy of our intervention."[30] The moral vacuity of the campaign is articulated by Clooney's character. "Bush told the people to rise up against Saddam,"

Gates tells his three confused compatriots, who have just witnessed Iraqi soldiers destroy a truck delivering milk to starving yet rebellious villagers. "They
thought they'd have our support. They don't. Now they're getting slaughtered."

On a second discursive level, *Three Kings* critiques the emotional and moral
detachment in how Americans too often think of war—what it entails, what
it looks like, how it is reported. Among media scholars, the 1991 campaign is
notable for the remarkable disjuncture between the war's brutal realities and its
antiseptic representation to the American public. Characterized by a constant
stream of favorable military-supplied images, "pool" reporting that discouraged
critical analysis, fawning tributes to the alleged accuracy of American weaponry,
and concerted efforts to elide the war's more controversial elements, the corporate media's image of what transpired essentially amounted to what *Newsweek*
magazine called the "bloodless unreality of [a] Nintendo-game air war."[31] Even
American ground forces were largely shielded from the violence, *Three Kings*
suggests. When Barlow fells an armed Iraqi at the beginning of the film—Russell leaves it ambiguous whether the Iraqi was posing a threat—Vig congratu-
lates him for shooting "a raghead" before confessing that he "didn't think [he]'d
get to see anybody shot in this war." And with the Iraqi having just died a painful death before a visibly disgusted Barlow, other Americans race to have their
photograph taken with the blood-soaked corpse.

For U.S. troops, *Three Kings* intimated, the war may have seemed more like
a fraternity party than a harrowing combat experience. Early in the film we see
the men and women in uniform singing, dancing, and boozing it up in the desert. Indeed, the reservists in *Three Kings* lament their failure to "see any action."
Russell thus shows his audience what that "action" in fact entailed: the charred
and disfigured bodies of those killed by American bombs or "buried . . . alive,"
a cow blown to pieces by an American cluster munition, Iraqi civilians slaughtered by the forces of Saddam Hussein, and the horrific effects of bullets entering the human body. Russell wanted to "resensitize people to violence," Clooney told the *Guardian*. "He used to say to us: 'every bullet counts.' He said that
every day."[32]

On yet a third discursive level, *Three Kings* builds on the work of Sam Fuller
in the 1950s by providing one of the more penetrating critiques of American
racism in recent decades. That it comes couched in a strangely humorous film
about the United States in Iraq only highlights Russell's place as one of this era's
most talented auteurs. *Three Kings*, moreover, transcends the black-white binary
that has historically dominated most American discussions of race. This is not
to suggest, however, that Russell ignores antiblack racism. When the Americans
enter an Iraqi bunker containing electronic goods looted from Kuwait, the savage beating of Rodney King by Los Angeles police officers conspicuously plays
on a television being watched by the Iraqis. In another scene, Vig and Chief
Elgin (Ice Cube)—a white Texas redneck and black "ring of Jesus" Christian,
respectively—argue about whether blacks make good quarterbacks. And later,

when Captain Said is interrogating Barlow, he points to Michael Jackson's "chopped up face" to level a glaring criticism of the United States. "A black man made the skin white and the hair straight, and you know why?" he asks in imperfect English. "Your sick fucking country make the black man hate hisself just like you hate the Arab and the children you bomb over here." ("I don't hate children," Barlow icily responds.)

Said's charge about "hat[ing] the Arab" touches on one of the most powerful elements of *Three Kings*: its blistering condemnation of cross-cultural anti-Arab racism, on the one hand, and its touching demonstration of Arab humanity, on the other. In the wake of the Iraqi invasion of Kuwait, Arab Americans faced racist hostility.[33] Such anti-Arab racism would only deepen in the subsequent decades. There were numerous attacks on Muslims and Arab Americans in the wake of September 11, 2001, for instance, while right-wing evangelists, authors, and radio and television hosts competed to outdo one another in denouncing Arabs as "non-humans" (Michael Savage) or dismissing Islam as "not a religion" but a "worldwide political movement . . . meant to subjugate all people under Islamic law" (Pat Robertson).[34] *Three Kings* powerfully attacks this American affliction.

In one of the more brilliant exchanges on racism to ever appear on film, Elgin objects early in the movie to the use of the terms "dune coon" and "sand nigger" to refer to Arabs, as both build on racial epithets widely used against blacks. The "cap'n uses those terms," Vig points out in defending his employment of the former. Barlow, explaining to Elgin that Vig's "got no high school [and is] from a group home in Dallas," intercedes. "Look, the point is, Conrad, that 'towel-head' and 'camel jockey' are perfectly good substitutes." "Exactly," Elgin agrees. In other words, at a time when the United States was using the multiracial composition of its armed forces to create a positive image of American power, anti-Arab racism was still perfectly acceptable; it crossed the line, however, when its lexicon echoed that used to denigrate African Americans.[35]

Vig, viewers see, is like countless Americans in the difficulty he experiences when trying to distinguish between Arabs—or, for that matter, between Arabs and Persians.[36] In the exchange with Elgin and Barlow, he apologizes for his use of "dune coon" by confessing to confusion over "all this pro-Saudi, anti-Iraqi-type language and all that." And in a later scene, when he, Gates, and Elgin are escorting the refugees through the desert, Vig responds affirmatively when asked by Amir (Curtis) whether he wants "to kill every Arab." "That's what I was trained to do," he says. "No, that was not our training," Elgin jumps in. "We've got Arab allies, man." Nevertheless, we see in *Three Kings* the way that too many Americans proved unable to see Arabs as anything other than an amorphous, indistinguishable mass. For the American troops in the film, the term "Abdul" became the Gulf War equivalent of the Korean and Vietnam Wars' "gook." War requires "othering," and *Three Kings* powerfully shows us how such othering played out in the Middle East.

Unlike most Hollywood cinema, which for years represented Arabs as little more than terrorists, *Three Kings* humanized the Iraqi people.[37] They appear on screen as parents, spouses, and children with the same aspirations and concerns as Americans, and, we see, they love their families just as much as Americans do. When a young girl witnesses her mother being executed, she and her father are devastated. When another mother is reunited with her children, she throws out her arms as they run toward her and embraces them tightly. Even Barlow's torturer, Captain Said, appears sympathetic. He expresses shame at the "bad shit" that happened in Kuwait, and viewers recoil when Russell vividly portrays the death of his sleeping one-year-old son by an American bomb. We see and feel Said's pain. "[*Three Kings*] shows the Arab and the Muslim and their complexity, with feelings and normal aspirations," said Hala Maksoud of the American-Arab Anti-Discrimination Committee. "We're happy that for once we are not stereotyped by Hollywood." In *Three Kings* the Americans come to the realization that "we all belong to the human family," added Hussam Ayloush of the Council on American-Islamic Relations.[38] This was quite a departure from earlier Hollywood fare.

"War Films" in the Post-9/11 Era

Such tributes to global humanity would prove short-lived, however. The attacks of September 11, 2001, saw to that. Millions of Americans continued to harbor anti-Arab and anti-Muslim feelings (with Arabs and Muslims often spoken of synonymously), and in the early twenty-first century they demonstrated little compunction in expressing their bigotry. Donald Trump, when campaigning during the 2016 presidential election, perhaps did more than any other individual to popularize Islamophobic sentiment, infamously calling for a "total and complete shutdown of Muslims entering the United States," but Trump was well within the American mainstream. Tens of millions of his compatriots clearly sympathized with his views.[39] Hollywood, meanwhile, largely moved away from more traditional films featuring infantry units and conventional military campaigns. The American wars in the broader Middle East proved deeply unpopular, and the receding number of battlefield pictures perhaps reflected this souring mood.

But "war films" did not in fact disappear. They simply changed. As the meaning of war expanded with the so-called war on terror, so too did the meaning of a war film. CIA or FBI agents taking on Islamists became a common plot line—*Body of Lies* (2008), *Zero Dark Thirty* (2012), and *The Kingdom* (2007) may be the most notable examples—as did military figures engaged in more solitary or unusual tasks, such as those at the center of *The Hurt Locker* (2008), *Green Zone* (2010), and *American Sniper* (2014).

In recent years there have likewise been a number of "war" films that featured hardly any combat at all. We might ask, for instance, whether *Rendition* (2007) belongs in the genre. A critically acclaimed portrait of the abduction and detention of individuals the United States suspected of Islamist ties, the film is not set on a traditional battlefield. Yet it explores a widespread (and widely denounced) practice in Washington's "War on Terror." Such pictures might make us wonder where exactly one draws the line when "war" is increasingly fought using unconventional means, from cyberattacks to covert operations and drone strikes. Indeed, how to identify a "war film" became increasingly difficult as the twenty-first century progressed, with nearly every facet of American life said to have potentially significant consequences for U.S. national security.

War was no longer marked by the trench battles of *All Quiet on the Western Front*. It extended beyond the anticommunist violence of *The Steel Helmet* and *The Green Berets*. It rarely involved acts of state surrender such as the one in *Three Kings*. Hollywood wars in the new millennium were more often than not about Islamist terror and the U.S. effort to combat it. To be sure, such efforts included the employment of military force, but it also meant that every American was a potential combatant. Vigilance was essential, and consumption was patriotic resistance. Even a vacation with Mickey Mouse could qualify as a blow against terror, President George W. Bush declared.[40] All of which begs the question: In this new American Century, with its global parameters and uncertain combatants, would Hollywood's Clark Griswold (Chevy Chase) replace its John Rambo as the ultimate warrior for the American way?

Discussion Questions

1. What is a "war film"?
2. What political purposes can war films serve?
3. How have war films evolved since the late nineteenth century?

Notes

1 For more on these films, see the important Spanish-American War in Motion Pictures Collection maintained by the Library of Congress, including articles and essays compiled by the archivists, at www.loc.gov/collections/spanish-american-war-in -motion-pictures/.
2 Library of Congress, *Love and War*, www.loc.gov/item/98501279/.
3 Eric Johnston, qtd. in Lary May, *The Big Tomorrow: Hollywood and the Politics of the American Way* (Chicago: University of Chicago Press, 2000), 176.
4 Thomas Doherty, *Hollywood and Hitler, 1933–1939* (New York: Columbia University Press, 2013), 4, 7–8.
5 Tom Brokaw, *The Greatest Generation* (New York: Random House, 1998). For a more complicated portrait of World War II, see, e.g., Michael C. C. Adams, *The Best War Ever: America and World War II* (Baltimore: Johns Hopkins University Press, 1994).
6 Clayton R. Koppes and Gregory D. Black, *Hollywood Goes to War: Patriotism, Movies, and the Second World War from* Ninotchka *to* Mrs. Miniver (London: Tauris Parke Paperbacks, 2000), 40. For an incisive analysis of Hollywood, fascism, and

the Second World War, see Doherty, *Hollywood and Hitler*. For a controversial take, see Ben Urwand, *The Collaboration: Hollywood's Pact with Hitler* (Cambridge, MA: Belknap Press, 2013).

7 See, e.g., M. Todd Bennett, *One World, Big Screen: Hollywood, the Allies, and World War II* (Chapel Hill: University of North Carolina Press, 2012). This is not to say that ideological work was not necessary with respect to Britain. Bennett noted that, among other reasons for the American public's caution, many believed that British propagandists had "hoodwinked" the United States into the First World War and that, beginning in 1939, they were attempting to do the same with the Second (5).

8 For more on Hollywood and World War II, see, among many other works, Bernard F. Dick, *The Star-Spangled Screen: The American World War II Film* (Lexington: University Press of Kentucky, 1985); Thomas Doherty, *Projections of War: Hollywood, American Culture, and World War II*, rev. ed. (New York: Columbia University Press, 1999); Robert L. McLaughlin and Sally E. Parry, *We'll Always Have the Movies: American Cinema during World War II* (Lexington: University Press of Kentucky, 2006).

9 For more on *China Gate*, see Scott Laderman, "Hollywood's Vietnam, 1929–1964: Scripting Intervention, Spotlighting Injustice," *Pacific Historical Review* 78, no. 4 (November 2009): 582, 589–593.

10 The "liberal consensus" was an ideological predisposition characterized by hostility to communism and support for capitalist growth; see Godfrey Hodgson, *America in Our Time* (Garden City, NY: Doubleday, 1976), 67–98.

11 For more on the autobiographical origins of *The Steel Helmet*, see Lisa Dombrowski, *The Films of Samuel Fuller: If You Die, I'll Kill You!* (Middletown, CT: Wesleyan University Press, 2008), 39–51.

12 "Over a period of three years or so, we killed off—what—20 percent of the population," General Curtis LeMay, who headed the Strategic Air Command from 1948 to 1957, revealingly noted in a 1984 interview. LeMay, qtd. in Blaine Harden, "The U.S. War Crime North Korea Won't Forget," *Washington Post*, March 24, 2015, https://www.washingtonpost.com/opinions/the-us-war-crime-north-korea-wont-forget/2015/03/20/fb525694-ce80-11e4-8c54-ffb5ba6f2f69_story.html.

13 Adams, *The Best War Ever*.

14 Lawrence H. Suid, *Guts and Glory: The Making of the American Military Image in Film*, rev. ed. (Lexington: University Press of Kentucky, 2002), 137–138. Suid claims that "the controversial scene could be justified under the rules of engagement," but, he writes, "the Army did not want to become associated with a film that showed its men killing innocent civilians" (138).

15 "I'm not Russian," the prisoner responds. "I'm a North Korean communist."

16 For more on these largely forgotten Vietnam War films released before 1964, see Laderman, "Hollywood's Vietnam, 1929–1964."

17 Robin Moore, *The Green Berets* (New York: Crown Publishers, 1965).

18 Wayne, qtd. in Suid, *Guts and Glory*, 248.

19 Nick Turse, *Kill Anything That Moves: The Real American War in Vietnam* (New York: Metropolitan Books/Henry Holt, 2013).

20 Suid, *Guts and Glory*, 254–256.

21 Renata Adler, "Screen: 'Green Berets' as Viewed by John Wayne," *New York Times*, June 20, 1968.

22 On the Vietnam syndrome, see Alexander Bloom, "'The Mainspring in This Country Has Been Broken': America's Battered Sense of Self and the Emergence of the Vietnam Syndrome," in *Four Decades On: Vietnam, the United States, and the Legacies of*

the Second Indochina War, ed. Scott Laderman and Edwin A. Martini (Durham, NC: Duke University Press, 2013), 58–83.

23 "The President's News Conference," April 4, 1984, *Public Papers of the Presidents of the United States: Ronald Reagan, 1984* (Washington, DC: Government Printing Office, 1986), 1:467.

24 George Bush, "Remarks at a Fundraising Luncheon for Gubernatorial Candidate Clayton Williams in Dallas, Texas," October 15, 1990, *Public Papers of the Presidents of the United States: George Bush, 1990*, https://bush41library.tamu.edu/archives/public-papers/2328; Bush, "Remarks at the Annual Convention of the National Religious Broadcasters," January 28, 1991, *Public Papers of the Presidents of the United States: George Bush, 1991*, http://www.presidency.ucsb.edu/ws/?pid=19250. On the rhetorical use of World War II in more recent U.S. foreign policy, see David Hoogland Noon, "Operation Enduring Analogy: World War II, the War on Terror, and the Uses of Historical Memory," *Rhetoric and Public Affairs* 7, no. 3 (Fall 2004): 339–365.

25 See, e.g., Hans C. von Sponeck, *A Different Kind of War: The U.N. Sanctions Regime in Iraq* (New York: Berghahn Books, 2006). Von Sponeck served as the UN humanitarian coordinator in Baghdad from 1998 to 2000, when he resigned in protest.

26 George Bush, "Remarks to the American Legislative Exchange Council," March 1, 1991, *Public Papers of the Presidents of the United States: George Bush, 1991*, (Washington DC: Government Printing Office, 1991), 1:197.

27 David Edelstein, "One Film, Two Wars, 'Three Kings,'" *New York Times*, April 6, 2003.

28 Saul Halpert, "The Academy Voters Can't Deal with Reality of 'Three Kings,'" *Los Angeles Times*, February 28, 2000.

29 There was some controversy over who deserved the writing credit for *Three Kings*. The most basic idea for the film—a heist that unfolds during the Persian Gulf War—originated with John Ridley, an acclaimed screenwriter who later won an Oscar for *12 Years a Slave* (2013). According to James Chapman and Nicholas Cull, however, David O. Russell deserves the lion's share of the credit for transforming that basic idea into what audiences saw on the big screen. James Chapman and Nicholas J. Cull, *Projecting Empire: Imperialism and Popular Cinema* (London: I. B. Tauris, 2009), 208–209.

30 Edelstein, "One Film, Two Wars, 'Three Kings.'"

31 Tom Morganthau with Douglas Waller, Bill Turque, Ginny Carroll, and Andrew Murr, "The Military's New Image," *Newsweek*, March 11, 1991, 50.

32 Andrew Pulver, "Exploding the Myth of Desert Storm," *Guardian* [London], March 1, 2000.

33 For a number of examples, see Douglas Kellner, *The Persian Gulf TV War* (Boulder, CO: Westview Press, 1992), 248–249.

34 On violence against Arabs, Muslims, and Sikhs (whom many Americans assumed were Arabs or Muslims), see the American-Arab Anti-Discrimination Committee, "The Condition of Arab Americans Post 9/11," November 21, 2001, http://www.adc.org/2001/11/the-condition-of-arab-americans-post-9-11/; Claudette Shwiry Hamad, ed., "Appendix: Hate-Based Incidents, September 11–October 10, 2001," in *Arab American Institute Foundation Report to the United States Commission on Civil Rights*, October 11, 2001, http://www.kingfahdweb.com/library/general/arab-american.pdf. On Michael Savage, see Anatol Lieven, *America Right or Wrong: An Anatomy of American Nationalism*, 2nd ed. (New York: Oxford University Press, 2012), 117. On Pat Robertson, see Steve Rendall, Isabel Macdonald, Veronica Cassidy, and Dina Marguerite Jacir, *Smearcasting: How Islamophobes Spread Fear, Bigotry, and Misinformation* (New York: Fairness and Accuracy In Reporting, October 2008), 11.

35 On military multiculturalism, see Melani McAlister, *Epic Encounters: Culture, Media, and U.S. Interests in the Middle East since 1945*, rev. ed. (Berkeley: University of California Press, 2005), 235–265.

36 Vig at one point asks two Iraqi brothers whether they think "America is Satan." Iranian leaders and activists have of course often referred to the United States as the "Great Satan" since the 1979 revolution.

37 On Hollywood and Arabs, see especially Jack G. Shaheen, *Reel Bad Arabs: How Hollywood Vilifies a People* (New York: Olive Branch Press, 2001); Tim John Semmerling, *"Evil" Arabs in American Popular Film: Orientalist Fear* (Austin: University of Texas Press, 2006).

38 David Finnigan, "Arab-Americans Cheer '3 Kings,'" *Hollywood Reporter*, October 1, 1999.

39 Mona Chalabi, "How Anti-Muslim Are Americans? Data Points to Extent of Islamophobia," *Guardian*, December 8, 2015, http://www.theguardian.com/us-news/2015/dec/08/muslims-us-islam-islamophobia-data-polls.

40 On George W. Bush's call to "fight terror" by "get[ting] down to Disney World in Florida" or "tak[ing] your families and enjoy[ing] life the way we want it to be enjoyed," see George W. Bush, "Remarks to Airline Employees in Chicago, Illinois," September 27, 2001, *Public Papers of the Presidents of the United States: George W. Bush, 2001* (Washington, DC: Government Printing Office, 2003), 1171–1172.

Further Reading

Robert T. Eberwein, ed. *The War Film*. New Brunswick, NJ: Rutgers University Press, 2005.

Peter C. Rollins and John E. O'Connor, eds. *Why We Fought: America's Wars in Film and History*. Lexington: University Press of Kentucky, 2008.

Lawrence H. Suid. *Guts and Glory: The Making of the American Military Image in Film*, rev. ed. Lexington: University Press of Kentucky, 2002.

War and Memory

G. KURT PIEHLER

A generation ago, a reader on U.S. military history would not have contained a chapter on memory. Historians' acknowledgment of "memory studies" as a worthwhile field of study represents an act of both humility and frustration over how individuals remember the past. It has required historians to face the reality that most Americans do not gain their knowledge about the past from books written by historians. Instead, they watch movies, read novels, participate in historical re-enactments, march in Fourth of July parades, visit memorials such as the Vietnam Veterans Memorial or preserved battlefields like Gettysburg National Historic Park, and listen to family members' stories about their participation in historical events. By studying memory, scholars have learned a great deal about how Americans think about not only the past but also how they think about the future.

Why remember past wars? In part, the memory of war can serve as inspiration. Branches of the armed forces maintain official history programs staffed by professional historians who are active-duty officers or civilians, and studying past conflicts is a primary way in which future leaders learn tactics and strategy. Alongside this shared *history*, however, is a shared *remembrance* of the past that inculcates a shared institutional memory through a range of rituals and customs. For instance, since the War of 1812 cadets at the U.S. Military Academy in West Point, New York, have worn a distinctive gray uniform to mark the victory of General Winfield Scott at the Battle of Lundy Lane in 1814. Decades after the Second World War, Marines Corps veteran John W. Berglund described the emphasis placed on learning the past exploits of the corps, which took on an almost mythical dimension: "And the Marine Corps has a devout belief in boot camp, that this is what really makes a Marine. And when they get there, you see some corporal, who's eighteen years old, and after a little while, you'd think he was on John Paul Jones' ship, the *Bonhomme Richard*. He was there at the battle with the Serapis, because he's salty and he's telling you all these things."[1]

How Americans remember past wars has played a crucial role in understanding the development of nationalism within the United States. Not only does the commemoration of war offer narratives that have been used by political, military, and cultural elites to explain the origins of the nation and its historical trajectory, they have also served to define who is a full citizen of the Republic and who is excluded. Efforts to shape one overarching memory of the past have seldom been successful; there are dissenting traditions because elites will squabble.[2] As well, groups whose historical contributions have often been written out of the American past resist that marginalization. Marginalized groups within American society have often used their military service to assert their claims to full citizenship. In the aftermath of the American Civil War, for example, African Americans and their allies asserted that military service entitled them to full rights of freedom, as well as the right to the vote. More recently, gay and lesbian servicemen and women challenged policies that forced them to hide their identities when in uniform while stressing their record of service in times of war.

In studying the question of memory, it is important to recognize the different forms it can take within American society. For instance, combatants and civilians have often carried individual memories of their participation in war that they pass down to family, friends, fellow veterans, and sometimes to a wider public through stories, letters, photographs, diaries, orations, memoirs, and oral histories. In the early Republic, parades and ceremonies on such civic holidays as the Fourth of July and later Memorial Day served as important vessels of memory. After the Civil War, monuments and cemeteries became favored as ways to preserve memory. Memories can also be conveyed and fostered by literary works, motion pictures, and television productions. Mass media has enabled ceremonies that once could only be attended by thousands to be broadcast over radio, television, and the internet to millions.

Historians disagree on whether the terms "collected" or "collective memory" are problematic because they imply a single shared memory and do not recognize that even when some memories are dominant there have always been dissenting memories. For instance, by the late nineteenth century white Americans increasingly commemorated the Civil War as predominantly a struggle to preserve the Union. In doing so, they minimized the conflict as a means to bring freedom to African Americans. However, significant dissenting traditions existed, most notably in the African American communities among such leaders as Frederick Douglass and W.E.B. Du Bois.

Scholars who focus on embracing memory studies have recognized that popular memory has often clashed with historical scholarship, occasionally sparking controversy at the highest levels. In 1995, the Smithsonian Institution canceled an exhibit at the National Air and Space Museum marking the fiftieth anniversary of the use of nuclear weapons in the Second World War after vocal opposition spearheaded by several national veterans organizations and congressional conservatives. Opponents of the exhibit rejected claims that historians and professional curators had greater authority regarding how the events that led to the end of the Second World War should be represented. Critics maintained that historians had distorted the past by challenging the wisdom of using atomic bombs against two Japanese cities filled with military targets and also with civilians. They insisted that if President Harry S. Truman had not ordered the use of nuclear weapons, U.S. forces would have suffered staggering casualties in the planned invasion of Japan.[3] However, history and memory do not always stand in opposition Journalists and historians, most notably Cornelius Ryan and Stephen E. Ambrose, played a crucial role in forging a memory of Operation Overlord, the cross-channel invasion of Europe on June 6, 1944, as the pivotal moment in the Second World War, eclipsing the much larger land offensives launched by the Soviet Union.[4] These examples show some of the varied ways Americans remember war and how these remembrances matter even today.

By exploring these issues through a narrower focus on how cemeteries, holidays, and monuments have shaped the memory of war, it is possible to illustrate how efforts to commemorate past wars have represented an important part of a wider effort at state-building and the growing centralization of power in the hands of the federal government after the American Civil War. It can also be fruitful to pay particular attention to the special meanings that have been attached to memorializing and properly burying the war dead.

Contested Memory of the Civil War

In the twenty-first century, national leaders promise, and American people expect, that servicemen and women will receive proper burial in either a national or private cemetery. However, this has not always been the case and the federal government did not maintain cemeteries for the war dead of the American Revolution and the War of 1812. Moreover, until the Civil War, the federal government delegated virtually all memorial-building, even the Washington Monument in the District of Columbia, to private organizations. Not only did the federal government show no interest in preserving battlefields from the American Revolution or the War of 1812 but Congress even rejected calls to purchase George Washington's home at Mount Vernon. States' rights opponents questioned whether the United States had constitutional authority to preserve historic homes and other sites.[5]

The American Civil War represented a watershed in how Americans commemorated war by establishing national cemeteries for the war dead. In contrast to earlier conflicts, in 1862, President Abraham Lincoln announced that the federal government assumed responsibility for maintaining permanent cemeteries for Union soldiers who died in the war. Even before Robert E. Lee's surrender in April 1865, Lincoln dedicated the Gettysburg National Cemetery, which was established by the state of Pennsylvania in 1864. In the most famous speech of his career, which came to be known as the Gettysburg Address, Lincoln declared that the "hallowed dead" not only deserved a proper burial but that their graves served as an enduring reminder to the living of the need to finish the uncompleted task of bringing a new birth of freedom to the nation. After the war ended, the United States Army created a permanent network of cemeteries, generally near the sites of major battles or military hospitals.[6]

Not all the war dead were treated equally. After the war ended, the federal government excluded Confederate war dead from national cemeteries. To fill the void, Ladies Memorial Associations (LMA) raised private funds to create permanent cemeteries for those who died fighting the Union. During Reconstruction, many former Confederates were disenfranchised and the LMAs provided an avenue to celebrate not only the past but also to rally white resistance against federal efforts to ensure African Americans could exercise the rights of citizenship granted by the Fourteenth and Fifteenth Amendments to the U.S. Constitution.[7]

The Civil War was also the first conflict in which a significant number of officers and soldiers joined broad-based veterans' organizations after the fighting stopped—the Grand Army of the Republic (GAR) for Union veterans and the United Confederate Veterans for those who served the Confederacy. Veterans' organizations served many purposes, but one of their most crucial roles was to preserve collective memories among former comrades, and also to promote wider public memory by sponsoring memorials, holidays, and other forms of public commemoration. Veterans' organization often funded public memorials and also lobbied for public funds to build them. In the closing decades of the nineteenth century the GAR led a successful campaign that secured generous pensions for Union veterans.[8]

The GAR also played a central role in promoting observance of Memorial Day (May 30) to honor the war dead. This holiday, while initially associated with commemorating the sacrifice of only the Union war dead, would in the twentieth century develop into a federal holiday that commemorated the war dead from all America's wars. It is also known as Decoration Day, and a central ritual of this holiday highlights veterans, family members, and others mourners placing flowers on the graves of fallen soldiers.

Memorializing the fallen was a contested idea during the decades following the defeat of the Confederacy in 1865. For instance, during Reconstruction the GAR and federal authorities explicitly mandated that the Confederate war dead interned in Arlington Cemetery would not have their graves decorated. In the South, African Americans principally observed Memorial Day, a holiday that white southerners ignored. Instead, white southerners forged an alternative holiday, Confederate Memorial Day, which commemorated those who fought against the Union.

As well, the Civil War sparked an unprecedented wave of monument-building that established a pattern that continued after the War of 1898 and the First World War. Communities across the nation erected monuments in their town squares or in front of courthouses commemorating the service of the common soldier. In many cases, towns in the North and South purchased commercially produced bronze statues. Battlefields also became major sites of memorialization as regimental associations, state governments, and other groups erected commemorative monuments. In 1890, the federal government began purchasing battlefields and making them into National Military Parks, first administered by the U.S. Army but then transferred to the National Park Service in 1933.

Memory is often contested, and in the case of the Civil War there have been strong divisions in how this war should be remembered. For African Americans and former abolitionists, the Civil War remained pre-eminently a fight for liberty and is remembered as the struggle that not only preserved the Union but also brought an end to slavery.[9] Many white southerners, who developed the ideology of the "Lost Cause," contested the centrality of slavery to the Civil War, discounting it as the decisive factor in causing the war. Moreover, Lost Cause advocates portrayed slavery as a benevolent institution, minimizing the brutality inherent in its foundation. When slavery was commemorated in Lost Cause memorials, white southerners portrayed it as a paternalistic institution and stressed the loyalty of the black "Mammy" who stayed behind and the body servants who accompanied their masters to war. The Lost Cause narrative thus sought to valorize those who fought for the Confederacy and asserted that the federal government had caused the war by infringing on states' rights.[10]

Another important shift that emerged in the late nineteenth century and continued into the twentieth was the new willingness of many white northerners to recognize the valor of former Confederates. In fact, the terms used to define the conflict speak volumes about the attitudes toward race and identity prominent at the time. Initially, the federal government deemed the conflict as the "War of the Rebellion," which was replaced by the "Civil War," followed in the 1920s by white southerners and northerners increasingly using "War between the States." Neo-Confederates in the twentieth century even favored the pejorative "War of Northern Aggression."

Veterans were not the only group to assert a special claim over the memory of past wars. Beginning with the formation of the Sons of the American Revolution in 1889, a host of organizations claimed that ancestry gave them a special role as custodians of the past. The most influential of these societies, the Daughters of the American Revolution (DAR), not only preserved historic sites, documents, and material objects associated with the founders but also sought to shape public policy on a range of issues. Founders of the DAR society deliberately restricted their organization to women who had ancestral links to a member of the Revolutionary War generation. However, ancestry alone would not qualify an individual for membership in the society; only those deemed worthy of membership were accepted, generally favoring women from affluent backgrounds.[11]

Moreover, the organization was racially segregated. Despite the significant participation of African Americans in the American Revolution, the society only admitted its first black member in the 1980s. But even while admitting black members, the DAR also changed membership requirements that made it more difficult for potential black members to join. Those seeking membership were required to produce marriage certificates for their ancestors and descendants connected with the Revolutionary War. For African Americans whose marriages were unsanctioned legally, producing such evidence was impossible.[12]

Veterans and hereditary organizations have asserted a distinct role in public life as a result of their connection with war and military service. The GAR, DAR, Colonial Dames of America, and kindred groups supported efforts ranging from inculcating patriotic instruction into public schools to greater veneration of the American flag and even to helping assimilate recent immigrants into the United States. These groups supported military preparedness, allied with the decision of the United States to go to war with Spain in 1898, and supported engagement in empire-building in the Philippines; for instance, the DAR assisted in screening nurses to be deployed in the War of 1898.[13]

The War of 1898 contributed to a continuing effort by many white southerners and white northerners to recast the memory of the Civil War to promote reconciliation. In commemorating this brief three-month war, President William T. McKinley and his successors stressed the ability of northerners and southerners to fight together in order to liberate Cuba. The decision to open Arlington National Cemetery to the war dead repatriated from Cuba, Puerto Rico, and the Philippines contributed to recasting this graveyard associated with the Civil War into one that promoted national unity. The National Society of the Colonial Dames of America erected a memorial at Arlington commemorating the War of 1898, which was dedicated on Memorial Day 1902. Not only did Arlington in this period acquire the fallen from the War of 1898 but President McKinley and his successor Theodore Roosevelt also created, in the interest of national reconciliation, a Confederate section of the cemetery. This ended the long-standing policy that permitted only the burial of Union soldiers there.[14]

American expansionism paralleled the emergence of legalized Jim Crow segregation and widespread black disenfranchisement throughout the former Confederacy. The memorialization of 1898 was premised on national unity centered on white supremacy, and either ignored or stereotyped African Americans' role in past wars. For instance, the memorial sponsored by the Daughters of the Confederacy at Arlington National Cemetery included a frieze that celebrated martial virtues of Confederates and featured images of the faithful Mammy and loyal bondsman who followed his master into battle. Although efforts to build a monument in Washington, DC, to the black mammy would be derailed by protests from Civil Rights organizations, the United Daughters of the Confederacy did erect a faithful slave memorial in Harper's Ferry, West Virginia in 1931.[15]

The War of 1898 proved a harbinger of expanded overseas involvement. Although the United States remained ostensibly neutral when the war engulfed Europe in 1914, there existed considerable support for France and Great Britain. The French government proved adept at exploiting these sympathies by stressing the legacy of the French role in the American Revolution, particularly the service of Marquis de Lafayette in Washington's army. In several communities across the nation, the French government, along with supporters in the United States, organized "Lafayette Days" to commemorate Franco-American friendship. In the case of Great Britain, efforts to forge closer ties with the United States required forgetting painful memories related to the American Revolution and War of 1812. President Woodrow Wilson and other elites embraced a vision that stressed the common political and cultural ties between the two countries. This view of Britain was strongly contested by a significant number of Irish Americans, who opposed the U.S. entry into a war that they believed only sustained an imperial power that continued to oppose Irish independence.

The Shifting Memory of the World Wars

The First World War witnessed an unmistakable shift in America's role in the world. After considerable debate, the United States declared war against Germany and deployed over two million men to fight alongside French and British troops on the Western Front. Often categorized as a total war, World War I required the mobilization of all aspects of the American economy and society, including the implementation of censorship and the passage of the Sedition Act, used to jail antiwar activists. An officially sanctioned propaganda arm created prose and visual arts that fostered mobilization but also shaped the memory of the war.

The signing of the Armistice with Germany on November 11, 1918, did not end the dissent and the divisions within the United States fostered by America's first European land war. During peace negotiations, President Woodrow Wilson gained support for the establishment of a new international organization, the League of Nations; he envisioned it as establishing a peaceful world order premised on the principles of collective security. After a heated national debate, the U.S. Senate failed to muster the two-thirds vote necessary to ratify the Treaty of Versailles. The success of the Bolshevik Revolution in Russia and the fear of contagion of communism only served to further the disillusionment felt by many Americans with regard to the legacy of the war.

How to define a war that saw such fundamental divisions over its legacy proved difficult in the 1920s and 1930s. However, far from seeking to forget the conflict, the First World War generation constructed monuments and forged new rituals to remember it. Except for the Civil War, no other conflict in American history has spawned so many monuments. Even before departing from France, while awaiting transport home, soldiers gathered in Paris to form the American Legion in 1919, which emerged as the largest and most influential veterans organization of the interwar years. It lobbied aggressively for veterans benefits for members but also put forth a vision of Americanism that claimed to offer a middle path between German militarism and Bolshevism. In practice, the national organization's opposition to radicalism led it to support immigration restrictions, purges of radical professors, and alliances with like-minded organizations. It also remained a strong patron of memorialization efforts for the First World War.[16]

Virtually every effort to commemorate the First World War provoked controversy over such basic issues as where the war dead should be buried, what type of memorial should be built to commemorate the conflict, and what role veterans should play as agents of memory. One of the first significant debates over the commemoration of the First World War centered on where to bury the dead. During the War of 1898, the United States repatriated all the war dead from overseas battlefields. Most families opted to bury their sons or daughters in either hometown cemeteries or at Arlington National Cemetery. During the First World War, the War Department promised to continue this policy and bring home all the war dead after the fighting ended; after the Armistice of November 11, 1918, a broad coalition of nationalists emerged that urged the War Department to reverse this position and ban repatriation. The American Field of Honor Association argued that a fallen soldier should be buried on the field of battle and rest perpetually with his comrades. Supporters of creating permanent overseas cemeteries combined with grand war memorials saw them as powerful symbols of American power and prestige. Nationalists supporting overseas cemeteries included such diverse figures as the famous capitalist Cornelius Vanderbilt and the American Federation of Labor president, Samuel Gompers. American Expeditionary Force commander, General John J. Pershing, weighed in on the debate, lending his support for overseas cemeteries and sought to have the United States follow the precedents established by the British government that prohibited all repatriation of the war dead to any part of the empire. The French government expressed reservations to the United States government over the impact of repatriating bodies from a country ravaged by war.[17]

Opposition from American parents and widows derailed these attempts to nationalize all the war dead. Supported by funeral directors, "Bring Back the Dead" Leagues lobbied for repatriation of the fallen back to the United States. Ultimately, the War Department allowed next-of-kin to elect to decide whether the body of a deceased soldier would be buried in a permanent overseas cemetery or returned to the United States. Only 30 percent of families opted for overseas burial; most wanted their sons or husbands repatriated.

The decision to nationalize the war dead was exemplified by the decision to honor one anonymous soldier with an elaborate state funeral and special place of burial. In doing so the United States was following precedents established by other allies. In the United Kingdom, the Unknown Warrior was entombed in Westminster Abbey and, in France, under the Arc de Triomphe. Although some American politicians called for burying the Unknown Soldier in the Capitol Rotunda, in the end, Arlington National Cemetery became his final resting place. This had important implications for remaking what had once been exclusively a Civil War graveyard into the nation's pre-eminent cemetery. The ceremonies for the American unknown were elaborate. After selection from among several unidentified bodies in France, the Unknown Soldier was transported to the United States, where he lay in state in the Rotunda of the Capitol, before an elaborate burial service at Arlington National Cemetery.

President Warren G. Harding, while speaking at the funeral service held on the third anniversary of the Armistice, November 11, 1921, stressed the representative character of the Unknown Soldier, noting he could be from any section of the country, any economic class, and could be native-born or a recent immigrant. The ceremonies held at Arlington National Cemetery were presided over by Episcopal bishop and former chaplain of the American Expeditionary Force Charles Brent and had a strong Protestant flavor; no speaker at the funeral suggested he was anything but a Christian, except one. The one deviation for the Protestant ethos would be the role granted Chief Plenty Coups of the Crow Nation offering a prayer to the Great Spirit.

The entombment of the Unknown Soldier on November 11 contributed to efforts by the American Legion to make this anniversary of the Armistice into a widely celebrated holiday. During the entombment of the Unknown Soldier, many Americans heeded the call by President Harding for two minutes of silence on the eleventh hour of the eleventh day to mark the actual end of hostilities. The unfinished tomb became a place of pilgrimage, especially for veterans and national leaders on Armistice Day (Figure 16.1). But not all Americans treated the tomb with reverence: some tourists inadvertently ate their picnic lunches on the tomb. Even more ominous, the American Legion protested to the War Department and the White House that juvenile delinquents were desecrating the tomb by playing card games on it. To the dismay of the U.S. Army, which did not want to spare the personnel, President Calvin Coolidge ordered soldiers to regularly guard the tomb. Despite initial misgivings about assigning soldiers to guard the tomb, the army over time embraced this responsibility and developed an elaborate ceremony to mark the changing of the guard.

Creation of permanent cemeteries and monuments in Great Britain and the European continent took the American Battle Monuments Commission (ABMC) over a decade to complete. On some of the most basic decisions, a consensus proved difficult to achieve. Until the First World War, most war memorials carried little religious symbolism; for instance, the U.S. Army

FIGURE 16.1 President Harry S Truman lays a wreath at the Tomb of the Unknown Soldier in Arlington National Cemetery on Armistice Day, November 11, 1946. © National Park Service, Abbie Rowe. Courtesy of Harry S Truman Library, accession no. 73-2574.

Quartermaster General used a headstone that contained no religious imagery to mark the graves of Union soldiers. Initial plans for the gravestones by the U.S. Quartermaster Corps called for a flat headstone similar to the ones used in American national cemeteries and those used by Britain's Imperial War Graves Commission. The Quartermaster Corps sought to create uniform headstones in order to symbolize shared sacrifice and unity in death. In a significant departure in American memorialization, public pressure from several quarters, including the American Legion, led to the adoption of the free-standing cross, with Stars of David monuments placed over the graves of Jewish soldiers.

This pressure also led to changes in the cemeteries themselves. During the first wave of national cemeteries built after the Civil War, the dominant building was a lodge to house the graveyard's superintendent and serve as a place to offer hospitality to visitors. In the overseas cemeteries, the ABMC created Gothic or neoclassical-style chapels that were officially declared to be nonsectarian but included Christian iconography (Figure 16.2). The Jewish Welfare Board raised the question of how a chapel could be deemed nonsectarian if it included such overt Christian symbols as the cross. At first the ABMC ignored these protests, although Jewish groups were more successful in keeping sectarian

FIGURE 16.2 *Flanders Field American Cemetery & Memorial, Chapel, Wortegemseweg 117, Ware-gem, West Flanders, Belgium* (Paul Philippe Cret, architect). Photograph by Jason W. McNatt, 2000. Library of Congress Prints and Photographs Division, Historic American Landscapes Survey, https://www.loc.gov/item/us0012/.

religious symbols off the Tomb of the Unknown Soldier, which was completed and dedicated in 1932.[18]

The issues around the war dead fostered continued controversy even before the 1920s drew to a close. After considerable lobbying by Gold Star Mothers whose sons were buried in ABMC cemeteries, the U.S. Congress provided these women and war widows who had not remarried an all-expense-paid pilgrimage to Europe (Figure 16.3). Although the pilgrimage drew bipartisan support and even the parsimonious President Calvin Coolidge signed the legislation into law, civil rights organizations soon mounted a campaign against the decision of the War Department to segregate the pilgrimages by race after the War Department decided that white and black mothers would form separate delegations, with the former sailing to Europe on ocean liners and the latter on merchant vessels.[19]

Army segregation of the pilgrimage mirrored the segregation experienced by the black troops who died in the war. But black leaders asserted that there should be an equality of treatment for all mothers who sacrificed their sons in war. Unable to convince the War Department and President Herbert Hoover to end segregation, black leaders called on black Gold Star Mothers to boycott the pilgrimage. For many mothers, this proved a wrenching decision since the pilgrimage afforded them the only opportunity to visit the graves of their sons. Some mothers joined the protest and declined the invitation. Other mothers

FIGURE 16.3 Visitors at the Suresnes Cemetery, Paris, in the late 1920s. © unknown. Courtesy of Harry S Truman Library, accession no 70-3169.

decided to participate, and a small cadre of black civil servants and Colonel Benjamin O. Davis sought to provide exemplary treatment for mothers despite the significant institutional racism the pilgrims encountered. For instance, when they gathered in New York City for the voyage, black mothers did not stay in a first-class hotel, and while granted passage on Pullman cars by the government, southern railroads still often refused to honor their tickets.[20]

The wave of monument-building in the immediate aftermath of the Armistice, which continued through the late 1930s, was not confined to federally sponsored monuments. In the 1920s, many communities quickly commissioned and dedicated memorials to the First World War. Among the most popular soldier memorials was the mass-produced sculpture *Spirit of the American Doughboy*, created by E. M. Viquesney.[21] Many big cities developed more grandiose plans to commemorate the conflict, although a good number never gained enough political or financial support. For instance, a cadre of New York sculptors erected a massive temporary victory arch in Madison Square Park for troops to parade underneath, although funding never materialized to make it a permanent memorial.

Not all citizens favored monuments of stone and granite to preserve the memory of the First World War. Many Progressive reformers argued that living memorials were also important; utilitarian projects such as new roads, hospitals, parks, playgrounds, and communities were built as war memorials across the nation. Artists and sculptors challenged the living memorial as an inappropriate form of memorialization, arguing that these utilitarian monuments were materialistic and self-serving; one critic asked whether we should issue mittens in place of medals for acts of bravery. Opponents of living monuments asserted that works of art embodied in a good memorial satisfied man's desire for the spiritual while serving as a respite from crass materialism.

Efforts to memorialize the war took place in a backdrop of doubt among many Americans wondering whether the cost in lives and treasure had been worth it. In one of the great flowerings of American literature, lost generation writers such as John Dos Passos and Ernest Hemingway questioned the impact of modern warfare on such martial values as sacrifice, bravery, and valor. Peace activists built very few peace monuments during the interwar years, but some pacifists sought to reinterpret war memorials to the First World War, which caused alarm in some circles; for instance, the pacifist John Haynes Holmes wrote a play that depicted the Unknown Soldier as rising from the dead and denouncing war. Army military intelligence even expressed concern that pacifists were misinterpreting war memorials.

American monuments and cemeteries would not be finished until the early 1930s, and the dedication ceremonies reflected the shifts in public opinion taking place. In the case of the French public, there was animosity toward the United States because of its insistence that war loans be repaid. For Americans, even many who fought in the war, many expressed the sentiment they had saved Europe once but were not going to do it again. As the international situation worsened, some veterans even argued that it was time to repatriate the Americans buried overseas. After the outbreak of the Second World War interest in commemorating the First World War slackened and Armistice Day ceremonies in many communities lapsed.

Memories can certainly shift and forms of commemoration change over time. For instance, the outbreak of the Second World War forced a re-evaluation of the First World War. No longer could the First World War be viewed as the definitive war to end all wars. In 1954, the U.S. Congress recast Armistice Day, conceived as a holiday unique to the First World War's dead, as Veterans Day, which would honor those who fought in all of America's wars. In 1942, the American Legion, looking to avoid the fate of the Grand Army of the Republic, which was destined for oblivion when the last Civil War veteran died, decided to open up its membership to veterans of the Second World War. An Unknown Soldier from the Second World War was entombed near his comrade in Arlington Cemetery, followed by another from the Korean War, the first hot war of the Cold War, a few years later.

The Second World War did not produce the same wave of memorial-building that had followed the Civil War, the War of 1898, or the First World War. In the 1940s and 1950s, most communities opted to either update their First World War memorials by adding the names of those who served in the Second World War or favored building a range of living memorials, including community centers, hospitals, schools, parks, and highways. Although there were some efforts to make V-J

Day a distinctive national holiday, Congress never made it a federal holiday and only two states, Arkansas and Rhode Island, established it as a state holiday.

At the same time, political controversy hindered left-leaning veterans who sought to establish an alternative to the American Legion, the American Veterans Committee, which never gained the same traction in part because of a successful campaign by conservatives claiming it was a leftist organization infiltrated by communists. As in the case of earlier wars, most veterans did not affiliate with a veterans organization, but those who did join ended up joining American Legion and the Veterans of Foreign Wars. Both organization would be solicitious about ensuring the federal government provided generous benefits to veterans of the world wars.

Explaining this relative lack of interest in memorialization can partly be traced to the importance of other vessels of memory. The postwar years saw a steady stream of novels, motion pictures, television dramas, comedies, and documentaries focusing on the Second World War.[22] But the decline of interest in memorialization can also be traced to the consensus that emerged after the war on the moral necessity of defeating Nazi Germany and Imperial Japan. In contrast to most American wars, a significant revisionist movement never emerged questioning the wisdom of entering the Second World War.

The overseas cemeteries and monuments built by the ABMC were one of the most significant memorialization efforts in the twenty years after the Second World War ended. The ABMC followed precedents established during the First World War; bodies were buried in isolated graves and smaller cemeteries were consolidated into larger ones. Despite an extensive network of military cemeteries throughout the Pacific and Asia, ultimately only two ABMC cemeteries were established in this region—reflecting the chasm between the United States and Asia both culturally and politically. The permanent cemeteries established were in the former American colony of the Philippines and on the Territory of Hawaii. The ABMC created a more extensive network of cemeteries for the European Theater marking the progression of the war, with burial grounds in Great Britain, Tunisia, Italy, France, Belgium, and the Netherlands.

Korea and Vietnam

Despite the creation of the United Nations and a host of multilateral organizations that sought to restructure the international order, the Grand Alliance between the United States, the Soviet Union, and Great Britain quickly fractured after V-J Day. The emergence of the Cold War between the United States and the Soviet Union dampened interest in building memorials to the Second World War. Moreover, World War II memorials would be recast by national leaders to encourage Americans to remain vigilant against the threat of Communism. For instance, ABMC cemeteries became important sites for rituals that highlighted the transatlantic ties undergirded by the North Atlantic Treaty

Organization (NATO) established in 1949. American and European politicians often used the cemeteries as backdrops to deliver speeches on such holidays as Memorial Day and Veterans Day; many of these speeches emphasized the need for the West to remain united against the threat posed by the Soviet Union.[23]

The outbreak of the Korean War in 1950 led the Truman Administration to cancel plans to entomb an unknown soldier from the Second World War next to his counterpart from the First World War. The Korean War was a relatively brief, but costly, war that was fought not as a result of a congressional declaration of war but because of a United Nations Security Council resolution calling on collective action from member nations to halt aggression against South Korea. Although the war engendered only a small antiwar movement, Americans' support for this land war in Asia remained muted. The lackluster support for the war was reflected in the decision of where to bury the American dead. Although many countries that fought under the United Nations mandate buried their war dead in the United Nations cemetery in the Republic of Korea, the United States opted to repatriate all war dead even before the signing of the armistice in 1953. American ambivalence over this conflict was reflected in the controversy regarding how it should be commemorated on the gravestones of the war dead. Should this conflict be characterized as a war or something else? Initially, the United States government did not engrave the term "war" on the official headstones issued for the graves of the war dead.

The Korean War produced even fewer memorials. Until the 1990s, the most significant monument-making was undertaken by the Republic of Korea, which built a series of memorials in their country commemorating America's role in the conflict. The aftermath of the war witnessed a brief flurry of novels and motion pictures but this soon tapered off. Moreover, the most significant films, aesthetically and in terms of box-office success, remained ambivalent about the war. Movies such as *Pork Chop Hill* depicted an American unit decimated in a pointless assault while peace negotiators haggled only a few miles away, and the *Manchurian Candidate* portrayed a group of American POWs brainwashed by their captors, with one of them trained to become an assassin used to disrupt the American electoral system.

Some wars are reimagined even as others are forgotten. The modern civil rights movement that flowered in the Second World War sparked a reassessment of the American Civil War. Black intellectuals had long stood against the grain to assert that slavery must be seen as central to the Civil War and the Reconstruction era that followed. These ideas became mainstream historical interpretation and also influenced the commemoration of the war. For instance, there existed a successful effort to begin to redress the lack of memorials commemorating the service of African American troops. Despite the hundreds of memorials to Civil War veterans, few depicted images of black troops, with the notable exception of the Augustus Saint-Gaudens monument in Boston to the Massachusetts 54th and their white commander. In Washington, DC, the

African American Civil War Memorial dedicated in 1998 would be among the most significant memorials to address this imbalance.[24]

Opponents of the civil rights movement, especially in the South, made widespread use of the Confederate battle flag in demonstrations. In 1956, the state of Georgia even redesigned its state flag to include the battle flag. To demonstrate his opposition to the federal efforts to enforce court-ordered desegregation, Governor George Wallace raised the Confederate flag over the Alabama capitol dome. Neo-Confederate sentiment remained significant even after the success of the civil rights movement in breaking down Jim Crow segregation and ending pervasive black disenfranchisement.

If the civil rights movement divided the nation, the Vietnam War further tore at the national fabric. In contrast to the Korean War, the United States entered this conflict in Indochina without the sanction of the United Nations. American involvement in Vietnam stretched back to the Second World War and the beginning of the Cold War, but it escalated dramatically in the early 1960s. Initially the war provoked only muted debate in Congress, and only two U.S. senators voted against the Gulf of Tonkin Resolution in 1964 authorizing President Lyndon B. Johnson to take military action against North Vietnam. Dissent grew, especially after the Tet Offensive of 1968, which influenced Johnson's decision not to seek re-election. Although the antiwar movement never elected a peace president, Richard M. Nixon orchestrated a withdrawal of American forces after efforts to find a military solution by expanding the war into Cambodia failed. A negotiated peace agreement officially ended the conflict in 1973 but the settlement did not hold. Two years later North Vietnam launched a successful offensive defeating the South Vietnamese regime the U.S. had supported for the past two decades.

The Vietnam War was not the first time that America had to wrestle with defeat. After the Civil War white southerners had to grapple with not only complete military defeat but also a social order reshaped by the end of black chattel slavery. The War of 1812 could hardly be considered a victorious war, especially given the fact the enemy was able to burn the White House and Capitol to the ground. Initially, many Americans followed the advice President Gerald R. Ford offered in an address at Tulane University in April 1975, when he declared that America's role in Vietnam had ended and it was time for Americans to put this war behind them.

Defeat in Vietnam coincided with the bicentennial of the American Revolution and many Americans focused on an earlier war that offered a more triumphal narrative that could be celebrated. The apex of these events took place on July 4, 1976, and included a gathering of historic sailing ships in New York Harbor followed by fireworks that evening. President Ford presided over Operation Sail in New York Harbor and spoke at public events at Valley Forge and at Independence Hall in Philadelphia (Figure 16.4). One of the highlights of the bicentennial celebration was the state visit only a few days after Independence Day of

FIGURE 16.4 President Gerald R. Ford speaks at Independence Hall in Philadelphia on July 4, 1976, in a ceremonial event to mark the bicentennial of the American Revolution. Courtesy Gerald R. Ford Presidential Library and Museum, image BO513-07A.

FIGURE 16.5 *Vietnam Veterans Memorial, Washington, D.C. View from Below Grade* (Maya Ying Lin, architect). Artwork by Paul Stevenson Oles, 1981. Library of Congress Prints and Photographs Division, https://www.loc.gov/item/2004666093/.

Queen Elizabeth II of Great Britain to the United States, including a state dinner at the White House on July 7, 1976. The queen's visit highlighted the close ties between the former mother country and the United States, representing a high point of reconciliation between the two former adversaries.

Americans did not forget Vietnam, and it generated a wave of remembrance. The aftermath of Vietnam witnessed a revival of public interest in building war memorials. Only five years after American helicopters evacuated the American Embassy in Saigon, Congress in 1980 authorized the erection of a national monument on the National Mall. Impetus for the Vietnam Veterans Memorial stemmed not from a federal agency but from a private group of veterans who formed a nonprofit organization that successfully lobbied Congress for authority to build a national memorial on the Washington Mall. Except for the donation of land, the Vietnam Veterans Memorial was funded through private philanthropy. The Vietnam Veterans Memorial Fund organized a national competition for a suitable design for the memorial that included the names of the 58,000 servicemen and servicewomen who lost their lives in one of America's longest wars.[25]

Maya Lin, an architectural student at Yale University, won the competition and her innovative modernist design represented a significant departure from the classical forms that had dominated most monuments, especially in Washington, DC (Figure 16.5). Many former hawks who had supported American

FIGURE 16.6 *Vietnam Memorial Soldiers by Frederick Hart, Washington, D.C.* Photograph by Carol M. Highsmith, 2006. Library of Congress Prints and Photographs Division, https://www.loc.gov/item/2010630680/.

involvement in the war viewed the use of black marble as an aesthetic that symbolized shame and defeat. Equally disconcerting for critics was the absence of traditional symbols—an American flag or any sculptural representation of a soldier who fought in Vietnam.

The most significant barrier to completing the memorial was the opposition of Secretary of the Interior James Watts, who demanded changes to the memorial that included the erection of flagpole and the addition of a sculptural representation of an American soldier who fought in Vietnam. In a compromise, Frederick Hart would be commissioned by the Vietnam Veterans Memorial Fund to create the "Three Soldiers" statue (Figure 16.6). Adding a statue of three male soldiers appeased some critics of Lin's design, but it provoked a significant new debate over representation. Could a monument only depicting male figures adequately represent the women who served in Vietnam? Women veterans of the Vietnam War disagreed and began a movement to erect a statue on the grounds of the Vietnam Veterans Memorial to commemorate their service and their fallen (Figure 16.7).

Plans for the Vietnam Women's Memorial also met significant resistance because of questions about whether the National Mall had become too crowded. John Carter Brown, who chaired the Commission of Fine Arts, in questioning the wisdom of erecting another monument on the mall, wondered where this

FIGURE 16.7 *The Vietnam Women's Memorial, the First Memorial Placed in the Nation's Capital Honoring Women's Military Service Is on the Grounds of the Vietnam Veterans Memorial in Washington, D.C.* Photograph by Carol M. Highsmith. Library of Congress Prints and Photographs Division, https://www.loc.gov/item/2011631447/.

trend would stop, noting there were demands to erect a memorial to war dogs. Ultimately, women veterans prevailed, with Congress in 1988 overruling the Commission of Fine Arts, and a sculpture depicting two women nurses coming to the aid of a wounded male soldier was dedicated in 1993.[26]

Despite the significant controversy that surrounded its design, the Vietnam Veterans Memorial emerged as one of the most visited sites in Washington, DC. Soon after the monument was dedicated mourners began leaving behind a range of objects to commemorate those who died in Vietnam (Figure 16.8). The National Park Service charged with maintaining the memorial has faithfully collected and preserved them. Collectively these objects, ranging from photographs, letters, articles of clothing, and even alcohol, suggest the deep resonance of the Vietnam Memorial with the many who visit it.[27] As well, the Vietnam War Memorial inspired a raft of memorials in different parts of the United States to the Vietnam War that often embraced the modernism of Maya Lin's design. Like the wall, fewer memorials to Vietnam were lily white and they often offered representation of soldiers from different racial identities to underscore the diversity of those who fought in Indochina.

The success of the memorial played an important part in spurring efforts to build national memorials to the Korean War and the Second World War. Private

FIGURE 16.8 Memorial Day, Vietnam Memorial, Washington, D.C. Photograph by Carol M. Highsmith, May 29, 2006. Carol M. Highsmith's America, Library of Congress Prints and Photographs Division, Library of Congress control no. 2010630875.

philanthropy paid for the costs of construction for the Korean and World War II memorials, but while a nonprofit organization built the Vietnam Veterans Memorial, the ABMC took control over the memorial efforts for the Korean War and World War II. In both cases, the memorials represented a return to earlier patterns of memorialization. For instance, the Korean War Memorial centered on rendering men in bronze in battle dress representing different branches of the armed forces engaged in combat. The neoclassical design of the World War II memorial harkened back to designs favored by the ABMC used for the overseas cemeteries built in the late 1940s in Europe and the Pacific. Widely criticized on aesthetic grounds, an act of Congress overrode the objections by the Commission of Fine Arts to the design and authorized its construction.[28]

Reconciliation remained a strong impetus for the efforts to commemorate Vietnam and other conflicts. Many Americans portrayed monuments as not only preserving memory but also enabling healing, even though not all Americans wanted healing. During the 1980s a counter-narrative emerged within such sources of memory as motion pictures and memoirs that increasingly sought to identify the causes of America's failures in Vietnam; betrayal by the home front and political leaders emerged as a dominant theme.[29] For instance, many Vietnam veterans and their supporters demonized Jane Fonda for her decision to visit North Vietnam in 1972. The myth that soldiers returning to Vietnam were abused by antiwar protesters and even spat upon gained deep resonance in popular culture. But as Jerry Lembcke convincingly demonstrates in *Spitting Image:*

Myth, Memory, and the Legacy of Vietnam, there is no evidence for returning Vietnam veterans being greeted by abusive protesters. In fact, Lembcke argues, the antiwar movement sought to reach out to returning soldiers and persuade them to join the opposition to the war. A small but vocal group of returning veterans did form Vietnam Veterans against the War. Eventually, memories of the significant antiwar activism among Vietnam servicemen were largely forgotten.[30]

Memory in an Age of Terrorism

On September 11, 2011, terrorists with the support of the Afghan government attacked the World Trade Center in New York City and the Pentagon in Washington, DC. The United States responded to these attacks by initiating a war sanctioned by the United Nations and NATO against Afghanistan. Although the U.S.-led forces quickly toppled the Taliban government and installed a new regime, it did not win a decisive victory. In 2003, after considerable debate, the United States invaded Iraq without the support of the United Nations. As in Afghanistan, the conventional war against the regime of Saddam Hussein ended after only a few weeks, but the campaign to secure the country took years.

The attacks of September 11 produced a significant wave of memorialization, including the dedication of a major memorial on the site of the World Trade Center. Many communities in New York, New Jersey, and Connecticut built smaller memorials to those killed in the attacks.[31] Another memorial is located in rural Pennsylvania on the site where a hijacked plane crashed after passengers resisted their hijackers; today it is part of the National Park system. But the ongoing nature of the Wars in Afghanistan and Iraq have discouraged efforts to memorialize these wars in granite and stone. Moreover, a professional army that represents less than 1 percent of the population has carried on the struggle in Afghanistan and Iraq; in sharp contrast the world wars and the conflicts in Korea and Vietnam were fought by mass armies raised primarily by conscription. When the Wars in Afghanistan and Iraq come to a complete conclusion will Americans build war memorials to mark them? How has the changing relationship between soldier and society impacted the way Americans remember war?

Studying history to predict the future is at best an imprecise tool. Similarly, what is important to one generation is not always as meaningful to the next. The Americans that went to fight in the "war to end all wars" in 1917 were convinced that battles such as Chateau-Thierry and Argonne Forest would become household names for the ages. Despite building thousands of war memorials, the American memory of the First World War faded with the passing of the World War I generation. By sharp contrast, the American Civil War offers every indication that the conflict between the states will remain pivotal for defining the American national identity for decades to come.

This essay began by discussing the limits of historians in influencing memory, but their role should not be totally discounted. Over the course of the late nineteenth and twentieth centuries, a small band of historians documented the experiences of African American soldiers in the Civil War and laid the groundwork for their rediscovery by a wider public after the modern civil rights movement. Historians play an important role in remembering when many Americans forget or have at best a hazy recollection of the past. In studying military history you are in a small way keeping alive the memory of the men and women who fought in America's wars since the founding of the Republic.

Discussion Questions

1. Why do efforts to memorialize war change over time?
2. What are the different ways Americans seek to preserve the memory of war?
3. Why do Americans remember some wars and forget others?

Acknowledgment

The author would like to acknowledge the editorial assistance of Eleanor Clark, Megan Quinn, and Susan Contente.

Notes

1 John W. Berglund, interview by G. Kurt Piehler and Scott Carroll, April 9, 1998, New Brunswick, NJ, Rutgers Oral History Archives, http://oralhistory.rutgers.edu/interviewees/30-interview-html-text/720-berglund-john.

2 John Bodnar, Remaking America: *Public Memory, Commemoration, and Patriotism in the Twentieth Century* (Princeton, NJ: Princeton University Press, 1992).

3 Edward T. Linenthal and Tom Engelhardt, eds., *History Wars: The Enola Gay and Other Battles for the American Past* (New York: Metropolitan Books, 1996); Michael J. Hogan, ed., *Hiroshima in History and Memory* (New York: Cambridge University Press, 1996).

4 Michael Dolski, *D-Day Remembering: The Normandy Landing in American Collective Memory* (Knoxville: University of Tennessee Press, 2016).

5 The saga of the Washington Monument is examined in Kirk Savage, "The Self-Made Monument: George Washington and the Fight to Erect a National Memorial," *Winterthur Portfolio* 22 (Winter 1987): 225–242. On the preservation of Mount Vernon, see Patricia West, *Domesticating History: The Political Origins of America's House Museums* (Washington, DC: Smithsonian Institution Press, 1999), 1–37.

6 Garry Wills, *Lincoln at Gettysburg: The Words That Remade America* (New York: Simon and Schuster, 1992).

7 William Blair, *Cities of the Dead: Contesting the Memory of the Civil War in the South, 1865–1914* (Chapel Hill: University of North Carolina Press, 2004).

8 Stuart McConnell, *Glorious Contentment: The Grand Army of the Republic, 1865–1900* (Chapel Hill: University of North Carolina Press, 1992); Gaines M. Foster: *Ghosts of*

the Confederacy: Defeat, the Lost Cause, and the Emergence of the New South, 1865 to 1913 (New York: Oxford University Press, 1987).

9 David W. Blight, *Race and Reunion: The Civil War in American Memory* (Cambridge, MA: Harvard University Press, 2001); Caroline E. Janney, *Remembering the Civil War: Reunion and the Limits of Reconciliation* (Chapel Hill: University of North Carolina Press, 2013).

10 There is an extensive scholarship on the ideology of the Lost Cause; see, e.g., C. Vann Woodward, *Origins of the New South, 1877–1913* (History of the South Series vol. 9) (Baton Rouge: Louisiana State University Press, 1951); Rollin G. Osterweis, *The Myth of the Lost Cause, 1865–1900* (Hamden, CT: Archon Books, 1973); Charles Reagan Wilson, *Baptized in Blood: The Religion of the Lost Cause, 1865–1920* (Athens: University of Georgia Press, 1980); Gary W. Gallagher and Alan T. Nolan, eds., *The Myth of the Lost Cause and Civil War History* (Bloomington: Indiana University Press, 2000).

11 Carolyn Strange, "Sisterhood of Blood: The Will to Descend and the Formation of the Daughters of the American Revolution," *Journal of Women's History* 26, no. 3 (Fall 2014): 105–128; Wallace Evan Davies, *Patriotism on Parade: The Story of Veterans' and Hereditary Organizations in America, 1783–1900* (Cambridge, MA: Harvard University Press, 1955).

12 Kristin Ann Hass, *Sacrificing Soldiers on the National Mall* (Berkeley: University of California Press, 2013), 62–71.

13 Cecilia Elizabeth O'Leary, *To Die For: The Paradox of American Patriotism* (Princeton, NJ: Princeton University Press, 1999).

14 Micki McElya, *The Politics of Mourning: Death and Honor in Arlington National Cemetery* (Cambridge, MA: Harvard University Press, 2016), 137–169.

15 Micki McElya, "Commemorating the Color Line: The National Mammy Monument Controversy of the 1920s," in *Monuments to the Lost Cause: Women, Art, and Landscape of Southern Memory*, ed. Cynthia Mills and Pamela Simpson (Knoxville: University of Tennessee Press, 2003), 203–218.

16 William Pencak, *For God and Country: The American Legion, 1919–1941* (Boston: Northeastern University Press, 1989); Kirsten Marie Delegard, *Battling Miss Bolsheviki: The Origins of Female Conservatism in the United States* (Philadelphia: University of Pennsylvania Press, 2012).

17 Lisa Budreau, *Bodies of War: World War I and the Politics of Commemoration in America, 1919–1933* (New York: New York University Press, 2010).

18 G. Kurt Piehler, "The American Memory of War," in *The American Experience of War*, ed. Georg Schild (Paderborn, Germany: Schoeningh, 2010), 217–234.

19 G. Kurt Piehler, "The War Dead and the Gold Star: American Commemoration of the First World War," in *Commemorations: The Politics of National Identity*, ed. John R. Gillis (Princeton, NJ: Princeton University Press, 1994), 165–185.

20 Rebecca Jo Plant and Frances M. Clarke, "'The Crowning Insult': Federal Segregation and the Gold Star Mother and Widow Pilgrimages of the Early 1930s," *Journal of American History* 102, no. 2 (September 2015): 406–432.

21 Steven Trout, *On the Battlefield of Memory: The First World War and American Remembrance, 1919–1941* (Tuscaloosa: University of Alabama Press, 2010), 107–156.

22 Lawrence H. Suid, *Guts and Glory: The Making of the American Military Image in Film*, rev. ed. (Lexington: University Press of Kentucky, 2002), 55–209; John Bodnar, *The "Good War" in Modern Memory* (Baltimore: Johns Hopkins University Press, 2010), 130–165.

23 Sam Edwards, *Allies in Memory: World War II and the Politics of Transatlantic Commemoration, c. 1941–2001* (Cambridge, UK: Cambridge University Press, 2015).

24 Kirk Savage, *Standing Soldiers, Kneeling Slaves: Race, War, and Monument in Nineteenth-Century America* (Princeton, NJ: Princeton University Press, 1997).

25 Patrick Hagopian, *The Vietnam War in American Memory: Veterans, Memorials, and the Politics of Healing* (Amherst: University of Massachusetts Press, 2009).

26 Susan Lyn Eastman, *The American War in Viet Nam: Cultural Memories at the Turn of the Century* (Knoxville: University of Tennessee Press, 2017).

27 Kristin Ann Hass, *Carried to the Wall: American Memory and the Vietnam Veterans Memorial* (Berkeley: University of California Press, 1998).

28 Kirk Savage, *Monument Wars: Washington, D.C., the National Mall, and the Transformation of the Memorial Landscape* (Berkeley: University of California Press, 2009), 266, 298–306.

29 Susan Jeffords, *The Remasculinization of America: Gender and the Vietnam War* (Bloomington: Indiana University Press, 1989).

30 Jerry Lembcke, *The Spitting Image: Myth, Memory, and the Legacy of Vietnam* (New York: New York University Press, 1998).

31 Carrie Rowe Malanga, "New Jersey September 11th Memorials" (D. Litt. thesis, Drew University, 2005).

Further Reading

Lisa Budreau. *Bodies of War: World War I and the Politics of Commemoration in America, 1919–1933.* New York: New York University Press, 2010.

Micki McElya. *The Politics of Mourning: Death and Honor in Arlington National Cemetery.* Cambridge, MA: Harvard University Press, 2016.

G. Kurt Piehler. *Remembering War the American Way.* Washington, DC: Smithsonian Institution Press, 2004.

17

Timeline

Major Events in U.S. Military
History, 1890–2017

KATHERINE ELLISON AND
WILLIAM WATSON

Wounded Knee (1890)

On December 29, 1890, the U.S. Army's 7th Calvary killed upwards of 150 Sioux Indians near Wounded Knee Creek in southwestern South Dakota. The incident occurred due to increased tension between the Sioux Indians and the U.S. government regarding the Ghost Dance spiritual movement, which advocated for Native Americans to return to traditional ways and practice the ghost dance as a remedy for their defeat and confinement to government-sanctioned reservations.

In an effort to both control and assimilate Native Americans, the U.S. government had pushed a series of efforts to alter the native lifestyle, including outlawing the practice of traditional spiritual dances, creating Indian boarding schools, and passing the Dawes Severalty Act of 1887 and future amendments to restrict natives to individual homesteads and, later, reservations. These actions increased pressure among tribes and from the government. In mid-December 1890, the well-known Sioux chief Sitting Bull was wrongfully arrested as a ghost dancer and killed in the process, resulting in the heightened tension that led to the Wounded Knee massacre. The massacre at Wounded Knee marked the last major battle of the Indian Wars of the late nineteenth century.

Turner's Frontier Thesis (1893)

On July 12, 1893, noted historian Frederick Jackson Turner presented a lecture entitled "The Significance of the Frontier in American History" before a crowd in Chicago, Illinois. Turner argued that American expansion and success were explained by the availability of the vast swath of land to the west, known as the frontier, upon which American settlers advanced. Turner credited American strength and values such as individualism for the ability to take on the frontier, free from centralized government, resulting in a unique American past and character. However, by 1890, the frontier was largely settled, according to the U.S. Census Bureau. Turner concluded that this was the end of one era in American history and foreshadowed a questionable future without the presence of such free lands. Turner's frontier thesis, though insignificant at the time, gave rise to modern historical studies of the American West.

Annexation of Hawaii (1893)

The Hawaiian Islands served as a valuable source of sugar cane, a strategic provisioning stop for U.S. ships, and an important area of Protestant missionary work prior to annexation. In an effort to secure U.S. interests in the islands, a treaty of friendship between the United States and Hawaii was negotiated in 1849, followed by a trade agreement in 1875.

The Hawaiian queen Liliuokalani moved to create a stronger government during the 1890s and was deposed by U.S. planter Samuel Dole in 1893, escalating efforts to annex Hawaii in order to avoid higher tariffs on sugar. After the success of the Spanish-American War in 1898 and a general warming toward imperialism by Americans, President William McKinley was convinced to annex Hawaii that same year.

The War of 1898 (1898)

Often noted as being a "splendid little war," the Spanish-American War began in 1898 and lasted less than one year. The war took place primarily in Cuba, which is less than 100 miles from Florida and was then under Spanish control. The precipitating factors that led to an outbreak of fighting included the protection of U.S. business interests on the island, the cruelty of Cuba's governor general Valeriano "The Butcher" Weyler, yellow journalism, and jingoism. The event that led to a U.S. declaration of war, however, was the explosion of the battleship USS *Maine* in Havana Harbor. Sent to show a willingness to protect U.S. business interests at all costs, the Maine exploded without warning on the night of February 15, killing 266 crew members. U.S. newspapers reported that the incident had been caused by Spanish saboteurs and was therefore an act of war, though the actual cause of the explosion remains unclear. President William McKinley asked Congress for a declaration of war on April 11.

The U.S. military was largely unprepared for war. Working with uniforms and weapons from the American Civil War, soldiers fought with rusted rifles and suffered heatstroke in Cuba's tropical climate. However, the short duration of the war, generally low death toll, and significant territorial gains made the war a success in the eyes of many Americans. The conflict convinced Americans that warfare could not only be good but also that it was a reasonable method for imperialistic expansion.

Jingoism (1898)

A popular concept in the United States during the 1890s, jingoism refers to extreme patriotism or nationalism that produces a hawkish foreign policy more inclined to war than negotiation. Commonly connected to both the U.S. annexation of Hawaii and the Spanish-American War, jingoism stems from the belief that American values are so exceptional that they must be shared with or forced upon others, sometimes through war.

Dollar Diplomacy (1909–1913)

Dollar diplomacy was a type of foreign policy first utilized extensively by President William Howard Taft and his secretary of state Philander Knox from 1909 to 1913. According to the tenets of Taft's dollar diplomacy, the point of U.S. involvement abroad was to create economic stability that would, in turn, promote American business interests. The insertion of U.S. banking and business interests into an unstable region served to create a necessary reliance on the United States, not only stabilizing the economy under U.S. standards but, in theory, also stabilizing the government and preventing it from opposing U.S. interests in the future, thereby promoting peace on U.S. terms.

Missionary Diplomacy (1913–1921)

According to President Woodrow Wilson's missionary diplomacy policy of 1913–1921, the United States would deny recognition to any Latin American country hostile to U.S. interests and the aims of American democracy. Wilson believed that democracy was the most moral and ethical form of government and that it was the essential duty of the United States to promote these values abroad.

World War I Beginning (1914)

On June 28, 1914, the heir to the Austrian throne, Archduke Franz Ferdinand, was assassinated in Sarajevo, Serbia, along with his wife, Sophie, while making a military inspection. The assassin, a member of a Serbian nationalist group known as the "Black Hand," sought to kill Ferdinand under the assumption that the Austrian-Hungarian government would then be more conducive to liberating the Slavic peoples within its borders.

The assassination triggered a chain reaction among a secret alliance of ethnic and political partnerships across Europe and Asia. Austria-Hungary declared war on Serbia, Russia came to Serbia's aid, and Germany to Austria's aid, and so on, creating the "Great War" that would later be known as the First World War or World War I. The two sides became known as the Allies and the Central Powers.

After internal pressures from America's immigrant population, growing financial interests in France and Great Britain, and the Zimmerman Telegram, the United States joined the war on the side of the Allies with Wilson's request for a declaration of war on April 2, 1917.

Espionage Act of 1917 (1917)

President Woodrow Wilson signed the Espionage Act of 1917, which regulated American citizens' actions and words during the First World War, into law on June 15, 1917. Intended to prevent the unlawful exchange of pertinent U.S. defense information with the enemy or foreign countries, the act controversially restricted Americans' freedom of speech as well. Prior to the bill's passage, Congress removed those parameters that censored the press, over Wilson's objections. However, a set of additional amendments to the law, known as the "Sedition Act," passed in 1918, made any speech, both spoken and written, advocating dissension against the U.S. government, its flag, or the war punishable by up to twenty years in prison. The sedition portion of the act was repealed in 1920, leaving the remaining Espionage Act in place to be utilized and amended until the present day.

Zimmerman Telegram (1917)

The Zimmerman Telegram was a coded diplomatic message sent during World War I by German foreign secretary Arthur Zimmerman to the German ambassador to Mexico, Heinrich von Eckardt, in January 1917. The German Imperial Government decided to resume unrestricted submarine warfare in the North Atlantic beginning in February of that year and fully expected that this policy would draw the United States into the war. As a way of tempering this expectation, Zimmerman instructed Eckardt to approach his Mexican counterparts and offer an alliance between Mexico and the German Empire. Eckardt was authorized to offer German support to Mexico in order to regain lands ceded to the United States after the Mexican-American War. In return, Imperial Germany expected to wrap up the war in Europe before any substantial American presence could influence the outcome of the Great War. However, the message was intercepted and decoded by British intelligence agents, who subsequently shared it with the American government, and the telegram produced a result opposite to the sender's intent. The U.S. Congress declared war on Imperial Germany in April 1917, a decision that significantly contributed to the Allied victory in 1918.

World War I Conclusion (1918)

Facing growing mutiny from within and a continuing Allied assault, Germany sought a ceasefire by the fall of 1918. On November 11, 1918, World War I finally came to an end when armistice documents were signed in Rethondes, France. Under the terms of the armistice agreement, Germany was required to leave Belgium, France, Alsace-Lorraine, the west bank of the Rhine, Africa, and Eastern Europe, while also repatriating all prisoners of war and giving the Allies a majority of its war goods and equipment. The Allies maintained their blockade of Germany as well.

Despite President Woodrow Wilson's efforts to come to peaceable terms of armistice agreeable to both sides and, later, a mutually agreeable treaty, the Allies who had suffered far more in the war than the United States sought retribution from Germany and asked for strict terms.

Wilson's Fourteen Points Speech (1918)

On January 8, 1918, President Woodrow Wilson delivered his "Fourteen Points" speech before Congress. Meant to address war aims and principles of peace, the address noted fourteen distinct principles necessary for removing all provocations to war. Included within Wilson's speech were such items as open peace covenants, freedom of navigation on the high seas, trade equality, and the creation of a partnership of nations to promote the terms of peace and independence. Though the address was noteworthy for its suggestion of such things as the League of Nations, which made it his most memorable speech, Wilson's Fourteen Points were not fully adopted as part of the Treaty of Versailles. Instead, the Allies sought retribution from Germany and the other Central Powers nations, which created a lingering tension with the peoples of those nations and economic hardship that would later contribute to the start of the Second World War.

Signing of the Treaty of Versailles (1918)

Created at the Paris Peace Conference in January of 1919 to lay out the terms of the peace after World War I, the Treaty of Versailles was the product of negotiation between the "Big Four" allied powers—the United Kingdom, France, Italy, and the United States. Throughout the negotiations, President Woodrow Wilson had secured his League of Nations as part of the agreement but was strongly against the call for reparations and redistribution of territory that the other Allies demanded.

Upon returning to the United States in July, Wilson faced positive reviews of the treaty from the states; however, the Senate strongly opposed the treaty, citing the article containing the League of Nations. The Senate believed that, as written, the treaty ceded the war-making powers of the United States to the League. After numerous reservations were attached to the treaty, the Senate voted on ratification, which failed by just seven votes. As a result, the United States never signed the Treaty of Versailles.

League of Nations Created (1918)

The League of Nations, an international collective security body, was created at the end of World War I with the Covenant of the League, included within the Treaty of Versailles. Originally President Woodrow Wilson's idea and one of his Fourteen Points, the League was to be made up of five permanent members, four rotating members, and an International Court of Justice. Functionally, the League would serve to protect the territorial independence of member nations while arbitrating peace and negotiating terms for sanctions when peace broke down. Because it was directly related to the Treaty of Versailles, the United States never joined the League, and it was therefore far less efficient in its actual operation and later hindered by its connection with problems associated with the treaty itself. After World War II, a much more effective organization, the United Nations, was created as the replacement for the League.

U.S. Isolationism (1919–1939)

Throughout the 1920s and 1930s, the United States experienced a political shift toward isolationism. Prior to World War I the United States had enjoyed de facto isolation due to its protection on either side by oceans. However, the Great War increased U.S. involvement in global affairs. Isolationists argued that World War I had led to an unnecessary number of American deaths and that warfare was unnecessarily promoted by manufacturers of war materials in order to make a profit. Isolationists also argued against the United States joining the League of Nations for fear that it would lead to U.S. involvement in future European wars. Isolationists across the political spectrum pushed such ideas as the Stimson Doctrine and later neutrality acts. Their opponents, interventionists or internationalists, also lacked a strong political bond, making it difficult to break through these isolationist ideas until World War II.

Global Great Depression (1929–1941)

World War I left many of the nations that had fought in disrepair. With the destruction of manufacturing and industry, these nations were also in economic decline. Faced with a dramatic shift in international balances of power, nations strenuously sought to re-establish hard value to their currency by relying upon the gold standard once again. Unfortunately, this made their economic systems less flexible and less able to rebound from further blows to the system, such as the U.S. stock market crash in 1929. Ultimately, the U.S. crash, financial difficulties in France and the United Kingdom, along with German economic issues, created a global depression as countries turned inward instead of coordinating their trade, manufacturing, and financial institutions across the globe. The rise of isolationist ideas also contributed to a concerted effort to avoid international relationships that may have resolved the Depression sooner; instead, the Great Depression lingered through the 1930s until World War II manufacturing helped struggling economies rebound.

Neutrality Acts (1935, 1937, 1939)

The Neutrality Acts were a series of U.S. laws passed under the Roosevelt administration in the 1930s, during the buildup to World War II in Europe and Asia. Passed under a heightened period of isolationism, the Neutrality Acts would slowly shift the United States toward intervention in the war without actually being involved in World War II itself. The first Neutrality Act, in 1935, served its title in prohibiting the export of any arms, munitions, or implements of war to belligerent nations and warning Americans against traveling to such war zones. Extended to 1937, the first Neutrality Act also banned U.S. loans to belligerent nations. In 1937 another Neutrality Act was passed in response to the outbreak of war in Spain, strengthening restrictions on Americans' involvement with belligerent nations and tightening export policies to those nations. An important addition to this act was the "cash-and-carry" provision, which allowed those countries who could pay for goods not considered implements of war, such as oil, with hard currency and carry them on their own ships to buy from the United States. In 1939, a final Neutrality Act extended the terms of cash and carry to all goods and lifted the arms embargo. The United States could now openly produce war goods for sale to those countries at war if they paid for and carried them on their own.

Manhattan Project Established (1939)

The Manhattan Project resulted in the only successful atomic bomb effort during World War II. After pressure from scientists, including Albert Einstein, Roosevelt established a committee to study uranium and its possible use in weaponry in 1939. By 1942, the project, which received nearly $2 billion of government funding, was well underway and seeking to weaponize nuclear technology before the Germans, who were conducting similar research. The project's secrecy prevented political and financial controversies, and scientists, engineers, and the military worked fervently in remote locations around the country until the bomb was complete.

Attack on Pearl Harbor (1941)

The southern end of the Hawaiian Island of Oahu houses Naval Station Pearl Harbor. In 1941, the base housed the majority of the Pacific military commands because of the growing threat that Japan posed. On December 7, 1941, the Imperial Government of Japan launched a secret attack on the Pearl Harbor base utilizing both bombers and submarines. Japan attacked Pearl Harbor in retribution for the U.S. total embargo on all oil and scrap metal to Japan, which it was unable to produce itself but needed for the war. Over 3,000 American lives were lost in the attack.

World War II Begins for the United States (1941)

After slowly manipulating the American mindset toward supporting U.S. involvement in World War II through his series of "fireside chats," along with the provisions of the Neutrality Acts and the Lend-Lease Program, President Franklin Roosevelt found the rationale for entering into World War II on December 7, 1941, with the Japanese attack on Pearl Harbor in Hawaii. Sometimes referred to as a "back door to the war," Pearl Harbor allowed the United States to go to war as a defensive, rather than offensive, measure, which garnered public support for the war and joining with the Allies. On December 8, 1941, Congress approved a request by Roosevelt to declare war on the Imperial Government of Japan unanimously. Further unanimous Senate votes subsequently declared war against Germany and Italy, the remaining major Axis nations, on December 11, 1941.

Japanese Internment Begins in the United States (1942)

In February of 1942, just two months after the Japanese attack on Pearl Harbor, President Franklin Roosevelt issued Executive Order 9066, effectively relocating all persons of Japanese ancestry outside predefined military zones along the Pacific Coast. As a preventative for espionage and to protect those of Japanese ancestry from dangerous anti-Japanese sentiment, Roosevelt's order removed more than 117,000 Japanese and Japanese-Americans from their homes to relocation centers or internment camps that were beyond the military zones toward the interior of the country. Japanese internment continued throughout the duration of the war, and as the war came to a close, the camps were dispersed. Many who had been interred did not return to their homes but relocated elsewhere.

Testing of First Atomic Bomb (1945)

In the early morning hours of July 16, 1945, the first full-scale test of an atomic fission bomb took place in a remote part of the Alamogordo Air Base in New

Mexico. The bomb was exploded on a steel platform above the desert, exerting power greater than 15,000 tons of TNT—more power than expected. President Harry S. Truman was notified of the event at the Potsdam Conference near Berlin, Germany. This test detonation convinced U.S. scientists, military leaders, and politicians that nuclear weapons were viable. Two nuclear bombs were used against the Japanese Empire that same year, ending the war. The emergence of nuclear weapons, however, contributed to distrust between the United States and Soviet Union and to the resulting Cold War.

Use of Atom Bomb on Japan (1945)

The United States deployed atomic weapons against the people of Japan over the cities of Hiroshima on August 6, 1945, and Nagasaki on August 9, 1945. Much debate surrounds the authorization and aftermath of these attacks. U.S. political and military leaders believed that in order to end the war against Japan, either an invasion or atomic attack was necessary. President Harry S. Truman, however, reasoned that, based on the number of casualties that the United States endured in taking the Japanese island of Okinawa, using atomic weapons in lieu of invading the Japanese home islands would save American lives, and for this reason approved the use of nuclear weapons. These attacks alone, however, were not the sole cause of the Imperial Japanese decision to conditionally surrender. Also contributing was the Soviet invasion of Japanese-controlled Manchuria just after midnight on August 9 (prior to the second bombing), the accumulated destruction by conventional allied bombing of most major Japanese cities, and an offer allowing the Japanese emperor to remain as a part of any surrender to the United States.

World War II Ends (1945)

The end of the Second World War is as difficult to define as the beginning. However, two key dates marked the closure of certain theaters of war that involved the United States. Allied victory in Europe (VE Day) was formalized in Berlin on May 8, 1945. Adolf Hitler had committed suicide beneath the ruins of the German capital just over a week prior, and it was left to his successors to accept defeat. In the aftermath of German surrender, Europe, Germany, and Berlin were all divided along east-west lines among the most prominent allies. The eastern portions of the aforementioned lands were occupied and controlled by the Soviet Union, and the western portions likewise by a combination of British, French, and American forces. Allied victory in the Pacific (VJ Day) occurred on September 2, 1945, when the Imperial Japanese government signed a conditional surrender aboard the battleship USS *Missouri*. Afterward, General Douglas MacArthur was named supreme allied commander in Japan, which remained under American occupation until 1951.

Creation of United Nations (1945)

The United Nations was formally created on October 24, 1945, when the United Nations Charter was ratified by a majority of signatories, including the United States, France, Britain, and the Soviet Union. An organization promoted by President Franklin Roosevelt, the United Nations was created to maintain international peace and security along with mutual respect and equality across member countries. Members were also obligated to work together to deal with international issues of human rights. A reincarnation of the failed League of Nations, the UN carried more military weight behind its actions when peace negotiations broke down, though the general concept was similar. Earlier plans for the concepts behind the UN had been discussed in the Atlantic Charter, at the Dumbarton Oaks Conference in Washington, and in Yalta.

Beginning of the Cold War (1945)

The Cold War began sometime during the negotiations at the end of World War II, though there is no exact date. Unlike traditional wars, the Cold War represented a conflict of economic and ideological systems. As World War II came to a close, tensions between the United States and the Soviet Union began to rise. Reasons behind this tension included disagreements over dispersal and control of territory and goods at Yalta and Potsdam, deviation on the use of the atomic bomb on Japan versus ground assault and what that meant for the Soviet Union, general distrust between the U.S. government and that of the Soviet Union, and finally the Soviet Union's unwavering policy of promoting communism. In 1947 the United States actively shifted its relationship with the Soviet Union from one of allegiance to one of "containment," signifying a final push toward the Cold War.

National Security Act of 1947 (1947)

The National Security Act signed into law on July 26, 1947, completely reorganized the foreign policy and military establishments in the U.S. government. It created a National Security Council, the Central Intelligence Agency, a National Securities Resources Board, and a National Military Establishment headed by the secretary of defense, along with several subdivisions, including the Joint Chiefs of Staff. The purpose of this reorganization was to modernize what President Harry S. Truman saw as an antiquated defense system by unifying the military under a civilian chief and streamlining intelligence collection by splitting it between a foreign (CIA) and domestic (FBI) agency. The National Security Act is recognized as the premier legislation of the Cold War era, establishing policy parameters for more than forty years of legislation and showcasing the U.S. position as a world leader.

Truman Doctrine and Marshall Plan (1947, 1948)

The Truman Doctrine of 1947 advocated for the United States to give economic, political, or military aid to any democratic country under threat
from another authoritarian force, whether internal or external. This assistance veered away from traditional U.S. nonsupport in situations that did
not directly involve the United States to one of active intervention and was
in direct response to the communist threat toward Greece and Turkey. The
Economic Cooperation Act or Marshall Plan of 1948 subsequently funded
economic interventions under the Truman Doctrine as it sought to provide
the finances to rebuild European nations under threat of communist exploitation while also supporting new markets for American goods. The Marshall
Plan also legitimized foreign aid programs, a key part of modern American
foreign policy.

Integration of the Armed Forces (1948)

Throughout World War II, African American men and women served the U.S.
military honorably in many capacities while still facing discrimination. Many
believed, however, that their service would help achieve greater civil rights and
an end to Jim Crow segregation. This did not occur, however, and many returning African American veterans were frustrated by the racism that they faced. As
a result of pressure from African Americans, on July 26, 1948, President Harry S.
Truman signed Executive Order 9981 desegregating the U.S. military. The order
declared there would be an equality of treatment and opportunity in the service
without regard to race, color, religion, or national origin. Once a soldier himself,
Truman understood the necessity to be able to trust and protect your fellow
comrades and commanders without distraction by race or other hindrances.
Though Truman's order faced internal complaints, the military was fully integrated by the end of the Korean War in 1953.

National Security Council Memorandum No. 68 (1950)

Created by a request for review of current national security strategies, NSC-68
was produced on April 7, 1950. A lengthy document outlining the hostile threat
from the Soviet Union and how to best strategize for what was shaping up to be
a protracted Cold War, NSC-68 advocated a massive buildup of traditional and
nuclear weapons as well as an increase in the size of the military. Though met
with criticism by some who disagreed with the document's underlying basis that
the Soviet Union was set on world domination, the plans laid out in NSC-68
quickly came to fruition after the invasion of South Korea by communist forces
in the summer of 1950. President Harry S. Truman nearly tripled defense spending from 1950 through 1953 in response.

McCarthyism (1950)

In February of 1950, Senator Joseph McCarthy (R-Wis.) gave a speech claiming there were over 200 known members of the Communist Party working within the State Department and formulating foreign policy. This speech gave rise to McCarthyism, or the use of false accusations of treason or subversion to restrict political voices of dissent. McCarthyism was at its peak during the 1950s when McCarthy oversaw congressional hearings investigating Hollywood personalities and during the Army-McCarthy hearings, in which government officials were questioned on their loyalty. Though tied to the Cold War and Red Scare of the 1950s, McCarthyism is still possible today.

The Korean War (1950–1953)

After World War II, Korea was partitioned at the 38th parallel, with a communist government ruling the northern part of the peninsula and a non-communist government in the south. In 1950, North Korea invaded South Korea with the aim of uniting the country under communist rule. The United States, under the auspices of the United Nations, intervened to repel the North Korean advance, while China joined the North Koreans. The war, which was marked by brutally cold temperatures and fighting by the first integrated U.S. military units, ended in a truce in 1953 that re-established a partition at the 38th parallel and a demilitarized zone separating North and South Korea. Today, that truce—rather than a treaty agreement ending the war—remains in effect, and the U.S. military maintains a substantial presence in South Korea.

Vietnam War Begins (1956)

The beginning of U.S. involvement in Vietnam is difficult to pinpoint. In the wake of the Japanese occupation of Southeast Asia during World War II, Truman sent American troops from the Pacific to Vietnam in 1945 in an effort to support the re-establishment of French colonial rule. French forces, which had been financed by the U.S. government, were forced out of Vietnam after their defeat at the Battle of Dien Bien Phu in 1954. At that point, the UN intervened in Vietnamese affairs, setting up a national election in 1956 in an attempt to unify the country under one government. The election never happened, and Vietnam remained divided between the north and south. For the next seven years, both Eisenhower and Kennedy steadily increased the number of American military advisors and soldiers in South Vietnam in support of a non-communist government opposed to the government in North Vietnam. With the assassination of Kennedy in November 1963, Lyndon Johnson became the fourth American president to try to solve the riddle of Vietnam.

Suez Crisis (1956)

In October 1956, Israeli, British, and French forces invaded the Sinai Peninsula of Egypt in order to gain control of the Suez Canal. They were ultimately forced to withdraw from the area because of pressure from the international community, led by the Soviet and American governments acting through the newly formed United Nations.

The Suez Crisis of 1956 was the result of three interconnected factors in North Africa and the Middle East after World War II. The first was decolonialization, which diminished the power and influence of former colonial giants France and Great Britain, the latter of which held the Suez Canal until the early 1950s. The British were supplanted in Egypt by a charismatic leader, Gamel Abdel Nassar, who represented the second factor, Arab nationalism. Nassar came to power in Egypt via coup d'etat in 1952 and as president promoted a policy of nationalizing the Suez Canal in order to pay for infrastructure projects, most notably the Aswan Dam. The final factor complicating the crisis was the Soviet and U.S. effort to de-escalate the situation and thus gain favor from emerging third world nations in their global rivalry during the Cold War.

Military Industrial Complex (1961)

Military-industrial complex is a broad concept that describes the cooperative relationship between the national defense departments in the American government and private companies operating in a capitalist economy. By aligning their interests, both sectors have gained in power and influence. This relationship took on greater significance during World War II and became the policy de jure during the Cold War. The term "military-industrial complex" was coined by President Eisenhower in his farewell speech in January 1961. "A vital element in keeping the peace is our military establishment," Eisenhower said. "Yet we must not fail to comprehend its grave implications. Our toil, resources and livelihood are all involved; so is the very structure of our society. In the councils of government, we must guard against the acquisition of unwarranted influence, whether sought or unsought, by the military-industrial complex. The potential for the disastrous rise of misplaced power exists, and will persist. We must never let the weight of this combination endanger our liberties or democratic processes."

Space Race Begins (1961)

The "space race" refers to the Cold War–era competition between the American and Soviet governments to develop rocket booster and communications technology. The technologies necessary for space travel also had military applications. Rocket booster technology was important for the concurrent development of nuclear weapons, especially intercontinental ballistic missiles (ICBMs).

Improved communications were necessary to grow and maintain global aware-ness and intelligence. As well, the scientific achievements on both sides were points of national pride. A brief list of "firsts" include the first satellite in orbit (Sputnik I, USSR), first human in space (Yuri Gagarin, USSR), first spacewalk (Alexey Leonov, USSR), and first human on the moon (Neil Armstrong, USA).

The space race led to relative parity in rocket booster technology, which formed the foundation of the so-called mutually assured destruction (MAD) balance of the later Cold War. It also contributed to the present geopolitical landscape, including the creation of the internet and global positioning systems, with instant access to wide varieties of data.

Bay of Pigs (1961)

The Bay of Pigs was a failed invasion of Cuba by U.S.-backed exiles who sought to overthrow Fidel Castro's government in April 1961. Previously, Fidel and his brother Raul had led a guerrilla war against the corrupt Cuban president Ful-gencio Batista, who himself had come to power through a military coup in 1952. When the revolution was over and Batista fled the island, the Castro brothers co-opted a broad-based revolution of peasants, middle-class business people, and academics into a new communist dictatorship under Fidel's leadership.

The invasion itself was a disaster. President Kennedy felt the need to back up his aggressive campaign rhetoric against Castro, and the CIA had been train-ing some exiles for just such an opportunity. However, Kennedy's desire for the invasion to appear independent of U.S. support hampered planning and execu-tion. Drawing lessons from previous U.S. interventions in Latin America, Cas-tro and his forces anticipated the invasion and easily repulsed the invaders and embarrassed the Kennedy administration on the world stage.

Cuban Missile Crisis (1962)

In 1961, the governments of Turkey and the United States began positioning nuclear-tipped Jupiter missiles in Turkey, within range of the majority of the Soviet population. This action, combined with the failed Bay of Pigs invasion in April 1961, created a window of cooperation between Nikita Khrushchev's Soviet Union and Fidel Castro's Cuba. Khrushchev and Castro agreed to deploy Soviet-made medium- and intermediate-range missiles in Cuba, within reach of a substantial portion of the American population. President John F. Kennedy and his Executive Committee (EXCOMM) believed that while some missiles were already in Cuba, the accompanying warheads were in transit. This decision created a ticking-clock narrative during which time Washington and Moscow negotiated the removal of missiles in both Turkey and Cuba.

The crisis created multiple opportunities for escalation, including an Ameri-can quarantine of Cuban waters, which Khrushchev labeled "piracy," the shooting down of an American spy plane, and an American naval attack on a nuclear torpedo–armed Soviet submarine off the shores of Cuba.

Publicly, Kennedy promised not to support another invasion of Cuba in return for the removal of Soviet missiles from the island, while privately agreeing to remove the Jupiter missiles from Turkey. Broadly understood as the most dangerous thirteen days of the Cold War, the Cuban Missile Crisis serves as a cautionary tale in confrontational diplomacy.

Gulf of Tonkin Resolution (1964)

The Gulf of Tonkin Resolution was a joint resolution passed with overwhelming support by the U.S. Congress (House, 416–0; Senate, 88–2) granting undefined war powers to President Lyndon B. Johnson in Southeast Asia. The resolution was a response to two reported sea battles between the USS *Maddox* and vessels from the North Vietnamese Navy on August 2nd and 4th, 1964. At the time, Congress acted on the supposition that both incidents were initiated by the North Vietnamese Navy in an attempt to engage a U.S. warship. However, whether the two incidents occurred as reported remains much debated.

The resolution included the following complementary positions:

1. Congress approves and supports the determination of the President, as Commander in Chief, to take all necessary measures to repel any armed attack against the forces of the United States and to prevent further aggression
2. The United States regards as vital to its national interest and to world peace the maintenance of international peace and security in southeast Asia.

This rationale allowed President Johnson to act without congressional oversight or a declaration of war in the name of American national security in Southeast Asia and enabled the escalation of U.S. involvement in Vietnam.

Vietnam War Escalation (1964)

Beginning in 1964, U.S. involvement in Vietnam accelerated under President Lyndon B. Johnson. Johnson initially increased aerial warfare against North Vietnam, which he argued necessitated an increase in ground troops to protect the airfields. By 1968, more than 500,000 U.S. troops were in Vietnam. The civil war between the Army of the Republic of Vietnam (ARVN, representing South Vietnam) and the National Liberation Front (NLF, also called Viet Cong) had by now expanded to include the combined American armed forces against the Army of North Vietnam (NVA).

Draft Lottery Instituted (1969)

The draft of young American men into the U.S. military during the Vietnam War was administered by the Selective Service System, which was first created to recruit manpower for World War I. In total, over 1.8 million men were drafted between 1964 and 1973. According to federal law, male citizens between the ages of eighteen and twenty-five were required to register for potential conscription. In 1967, the age range was extended to men up to thirty-five years old. However, many men were able to avoid the draft through a system of deferments that protected married men with families, college students, and those with medical conditions. Wealthier Americans could afford to avoid service by attending college or seeking a disqualifying diagnosis from a doctor; poorer Americans could not. As a result, the pool of draftees was disproportionally representative of poor, working-class, and rural Americans. The average age of an American soldier in Vietnam was nineteen years old (as opposed to an average age of twenty-six during World War II). In order to maintain the number of soldiers required to carry on the war in Vietnam, the U.S. government abandoned the deferment system in December 1969 in favor of a lottery that assigned numbers to draft-eligible men based on their birthdays. A low number meant a high likelihood of being drafted.

Secret Bombing of Cambodia (1965–1973)

The secret bombing of Cambodia, which shares a border with Vietnam, began under President Johnson in 1965 and was expanded under President Nixon, using code names such as Operation Menu and Operation Freedom Deal and intended to disrupt NVA and NLF operations on both sides of the border. The bombing efforts intensified under Nixon and continued until August 1973. Secrecy was maintained because it was illegal for American forces to bomb within Cambodian national borders. Moreover, any publicity about illegal bombing would only drive up domestic pressure from the antiwar movement. The North Vietnamese government also did not want to publicize the bombing, which would reveal their cross-border operations, including traveling and maintaining sections of the Ho Chi Minh Trail, on which the NVA moved supplies to support the war effort in South Vietnam.

SALT Talks (1969)

The Strategic Arms Limitation Treaty was the result of negotiations between the Soviet and American governments that began in 1969. The treaty limited nuclear proliferation, which had accelerated after the end of World War II. By 1967 there were six nuclear-armed nation states: the United States, the Soviet Union, Great Britain, France, China, and Israel, and the standing arsenal of just one of the superpowers had enough destructive power to eliminate all life on earth many times over. An additional treaty between the American and Soviet governments, called the Anti-Ballistic Missile Treaty (ABM), was signed in 1972. The ABM Treaty limited research and development of an antiballistic missile program, which, if successful, would disrupt the terrifyingly stable equilibrium of mutually assured destruction (MAD). If either the United States or Soviet Union were close to implementing a workable defense against the other's nuclear arsenal, it would be in the best interest of the other to strike before completion, resulting in a nuclear holocaust. The SALT I Treaty expired in 1985 and was not renewed. The ABM Treaty expired in 2002 and was not renewed.

All-Volunteer Force (1973)

Nixon ended the draft lottery system in 1972 and created the All-Volunteer Force that has served the United States military since 1973. Nixon ended the draft not only to tamp down the antiwar movement but also because of his policy advisors' skepticicm regarding compulsory military service. Policymakers also reasoned that an all-volunteer service would improve morale and therefore the effective fighting capability of the armed forces.

Paris Peace Accords (1973)

The Paris Peace Accords officially ended U.S. military activity in Vietnam and allowed for a temporary cease-fire between North and South Vietnam. The negotiations began in 1968, during the presidential campaign, and continued through five more years of air, naval, and ground operations. The two chief negotiators were Secretary of State Dr. Henry Kissinger and North Vietnamese general and diplomat Le Duc Tho. Despite the lengthy negotiations, the Nixon administration eventually accepted terms that did not significantly differ from those that the Vietnamese had offered in 1968. For their efforts, Kissinger and Tho were awarded the 1973 Nobel Peace Prize. Tho refused to accept the award, and the U.S. Senate did not ratify the treaty.

Fall of Saigon (1975)

The armed forces of North Vietnam captured Saigon, the capital of South Vietnam, in April 1975. Without a significant American military presence in the South, the NVA and NLF easily defeated their ARVN counterparts in the aftermath of the Paris Peace Accords and unified Vietnam by force. As the NVA and NLF forces encircled and overran the city, there was a rapid evacuation of American personnel and South Vietnamese supporters who were working in Saigon. This led to one of the most iconic photos in history, in which a line of people wait desperately on a rooftop, hoping to be rescued by helicopter and flown to the safety of the American Navy operating off the coast.

Iran Hostage Crisis (1979)

The Iran Hostage Crisis began in November 1979 and was a result of the broader Iranian Revolution that started earlier in the year. On the morning of November 4, 1979, a large and diverse group of Iranians gathered outside the U.S. Embassy in Tehran to protest long-standing American involvement in Iranian affairs. Marines guarding the embassy compound refused to shoot the protesters, which emboldened many in the crowd. The protesters swelled and overran the walls of the compound before entering the embassy building and taking hundreds of people hostage. Many of those captured were released, leaving fifty-two white male Americans as the remaining hostages. The hostage-takers announced three conditions for releasing their victims. First, they sought the return of the shah to Iran, who had fled the country and was receiving cancer treatment in the United States, to face justice at the hands of the Islamic revolutionaries. Second, they demanded that the American government apologize for interfering in Iranian affairs. Finally, they demanded that the United States unfreeze all Iranian assets that had been held since the crisis began. The Iran Hostage Crisis appeared as further evidence of U.S. post-Vietnam weakness, particularly after a rescue mission ended in disaster in April 1980. For 444 days, the hostage crisis was the lead story for most news outlets and was impossible to ignore in the United States. The negotiations for release took place under the Carter administration, but as a final insult to his presidency, the hostages were not released until inauguration day in January 1981, just after newly elected president Ronald Reagan took the oath of office.

Strategic Defense Initiative (1983)

The Strategic Defense Initiative, also called "Star Wars," was a proposed ballistic missile defense program that President Ronald Reagan announced in March 1983. The concept was a layered defense of the United States that included spy satellites to monitor missile launches; GPS satellites to track incoming missiles; and space-based battle stations equipped with kinetic energy guns, nuclear-powered X-ray lasers, and huge orbiting mirrors. Had it been completed before the expiration of the ABM Treaty (see previous SALT Talks entry), SDI would have violated the treaty's terms. However, the feasibility of SDI was openly derided by scientists who equated the proposed attempt to defend against a ballistic missile with trying to shoot a bullet with another bullet. However, the announcement of research into such a defensive system drove leaders in the Soviet Union to reconsider how much of their limited economic resources were being spent on national defense and the Cold War.

U.S. Invasion of Grenada (1983)

Grenada is an island in the Caribbean Sea, situated north of Venezuela on the northern coast of South America. The people of Grenada gained their independence from the British Empire in the mid-1970s, only to be ruled by leftist dictator Maurice Bishop, who came to power in a 1979 coup. Bishop was killed and replaced by another leftist group in 1983. The Reagan administration responded to this turmoil by authorizing an invasion of Grenada that returned a democratic government to the island within weeks. The administration framed the intervention as an example of the Reagan Doctrine, which opposed any foreign communist government and supported political opponents of communism even if those opponents were not democratic themselves. The administration also justified the invasion as necessary to protect some 600 American medical students in Grenada, for fear of another hostage crisis.

Iran-Contra Affair (1987)

The Iran-Contra Affair was a complicated web of illegal activity involving the United States, the Middle East, and Central America. In Central America, the Reagan administration was eager to support the Contras in their war against the leftist Sandinistas in Nicaragua. However, the U.S. Congress disagreed with this policy and passed the Boland Amendments, which made it illegal to fund the Contras. Meanwhile, in Lebanon, several Americans were taken hostage by pro-Iranian Islamists in the wake of the Iranian Revolution and hostage crisis. In order to encourage Iranian officials to pressure their supporters to release the hostages, the administration authorized the sale of weapons to Iran, via Israel. The cost of these weapons was inflated, and the bloated profits were redirected to support the Nicaraguan Contras. The policy began to unravel when more hostages were taken to replace those released; administration officials were spotted with Iranian counterparts; and a CIA pilot was shot down, captured, and interrogated in Central America. Reagan went on national television and told the American people that he did not sell arms for hostages. When confronted with evidence that his statement was false, Reagan was put in the position of admitting he was either knowingly lying or too incompetent to know what his staff was doing without his knowledge. Reagan addressed the nation a second time and chose to admit incompetence.

Invasion of Panama (1989)

The U.S. invasion of Panama in December 1989, called Operation Just Cause, was authorized by the George H. W. Bush administration to remove Panamanian president Manuel Noriega from power. Prior to the invasion, Noriega had been playing both sides of the drug war. Noriega was a paid intelligence asset of the CIA, including the period when Bush was director of the CIA. Simultaneously, he allowed Panamanian banks to launder drug money and took a cut for himself. Noriega managed to survive two coup attempts, but he could not stand up to an American military intervention. The Panama invasion provided a testing ground for many of the weapons and press strategies that were successfully implemented during the 1991 Gulf War.

Persian Gulf War (1991)

The 1991 Gulf War, called Operation Desert Storm, successfully liberated the nation of Kuwait from an Iraqi military occupation that began in 1990. Iraqi president Saddam Hussein ordered the invasion of Kuwait in order to gain access to significant oil reserves and to avoid paying a debt owed to the Kuwaiti government, which supported Iraq in their decade-long war against Iran in the 1980s. The U.S. presence in the region began as Operation Desert Shield, which protected Saudi Arabia from a fate similar to Kuwait's. Reporters from numerous news outlets were embedded with American forces and offered first-hand accounts of battle. U.S. military spokespeople shared footage of precision bombings, night vision battle scenes, and other impressive technical innovations. As a result of this media coverage, Americans broadly supported the war, and the quick victory reinforced claims of renewed American supremacy in the Cold War's waning days.

Liberal Interventionism (1992–2000)

For nearly fifty years after World War II, U.S. foreign policy could be summed up in one word: containment. In the wake of the end of the Cold War, U.S. foreign policy took on many forms. Among the new ideologies were interventionism, abstention, pragmatism, and internationalism. President Clinton dabbled in each of these options. His administration committed troops in missions that sought to stop famine in Somalia, support United Nations peacekeeping missions in the Balkans, and restore democratic government to Haiti, but notably the Clinton administation refused to stop the Rwandan genocide of 1994. Clinton's interventions were controversial, with many Americans believing that they were outside the national interest.

Adoption of "Don't Ask, Don't Tell" (1994)

In 1994, the Clinton administration adopted "Don't Ask, Don't Tell" (DADT) as its official policy relating to gay, lesbian, and bisexual Americans serving in the armed forces. The policy replaced the previous practice of investigating and punishing servicemen and women for suspected or witnessed homosexual behavior, and was continued under subsequent administrations until 2011. The policy barred personnel from either disclosing sexual orientation or discriminating against people whom they suspected of being gay, lesbian, or bisexual. The policy received criticism on many fronts and faced multiple legal challenges in court. DADT was finally repealed in 2011 when President Obama, Secretary of Defense Leon Panetta, and Chairman of the Joint Chiefs of Staff Admiral Mike Mullen all concluded that repeal would not negatively impact military readiness.

Desert Fox Strikes (1998)

After the 1991 Gulf War, the United Nations imposed strict sanctions on the Iraqi government in an effort to compel President Saddam Hussein to abandon his chemical, biological, and nuclear weapons programs. Hussein refused to fully cooperate with UN weapons inspections, however, and these sanctions, combined with the destruction that the 1991 war had caused, devastated Iraq and contributed to tens of thousands of civilian deaths. In 1998, after Hussein expelled UN inspectors, the Clinton administration responded with several days of aerial and naval bombardment.

Operation Allied Force (1999)

Throughout the 1990s, the states of the former Yugoslavia had been mired in ethnic conflict and civil war that included an ethnic cleansing campaign against Croatian Muslims led by Serbian president Slobodan Milosevic. When efforts to negotiate an end to this violence failed, NATO undertook the first military mission in its forty-year history, an aerial bombing of Serbian targets that successfully compelled Milosevic to surrender. The Serbian air war was cited by proponents of liberal interventionism as evidence that the United States and its allies could effectively deploy military power to ensure human rights.

The September 11, 2001, Terrorist Attacks (2001)

On September 11, 2001, nineteen hijackers affiliated with the Al-Qaeda terrorist network, which had been formed by Osama Bin Laden in 1988, hijacked four U.S. airliners. The hijackers subsequently crashed two of those aircraft into the World Trade Center towers in Manhattan and a third into the Pentagon, in Arlington, Virginia. The fourth plane, which investigators assume the hijackers intended to use in order to attack either the Capitol or the White House, crashed in rural Pennsylvania after the passengers and crew attacked the hijackers. The scale and spectacle of the attacks made them the most significant acts of terrorism in U.S. history and generated a political and military response that includes the Wars in Afghanistan and Iraq.

The Afghanistan War and Surge (2001–)

The Afghan surge of 2008 responded to an eroding security situation in Afghanistan under Operation Enduring Freedom, which began after the attacks of September 11, 2001. After initially being driven into hiding early in the war, by 2006 Taliban and Al-Qaeda fighters had renewed an insurgency campaign within Afghanistan. By this time, U.S. armed forces were involved in two wars in Iraq and Afghanistan. The Iraq War and surge took precedent, which limited the availability of troops for the Afghan theater. But in 2008, an additional 10,000 troops were deployed in an effort to regain and maintain control of the country. The Obama administration conducted a lengthy review of U.S. policy in Afghanistan in 2009, and ultimately contributed additional troops to stage a counterinsurgency campaign against the Taliban.

The Iraq War (2003–2011)

The Iraq War began as Operation Iraqi Freedom in March 2003, and continues to the present, though American forces left Iraq in 2011 under an agreement negotiated by the George W. Bush administration. U.S. forces invaded Iraq to remove Saddam Hussein from power after the president accused him of manufacturing and stockpiling weapons of mass destruction. Evidence supporting that claim has been significantly criticized. U.S. forces quickly took control of the country and after a few years began to draw down troop numbers. However, an insurgency and civil war broke out during the American occupation, and in 2007 President Bush ordered a renewed effort in Iraq, labeled by the White House as "The New Way Forward," but commonly called the "surge." Embracing a new strategy that emphasized counterinsurgency, the majority of surge troops deployed to Baghdad to maintain security in the Iraqi capital in an effort to support the fledgling democratic government.

Women in Combat Roles (2001–2015)

Regardless of their official position in the armed forces, women have been a part of every war in American history, as soldiers, spies, servants, medical personnel, administrators, pilots, trainers, and much more. In the twenty-first century, women serve in many forward-deployed operations, including air and naval combat missions as well as convoys that are often exposed to hostile fire and improvised explosive devices. Until Secretary of Defense Leon Panetta issued an order to the contrary in 2013, however, women had been banned from military units specifically designated as combat units, and significant debate and research regarding women's capabilities and their likely impact on mission success occurred in the military, in Congress, and among the public. In 2015, the first two female soldiers graduated from the U.S. Army's elite Ranger School.

Later that year, the Department of Defense removed all restrictions on women's military roles.

Drone Wars (2007–)

"Drones" is the shorthand term for unmanned aerial vehicles (UAVs) or unmanned combat aerial vehicles (UCAVs). In the U.S. armed forces, drones are used for multiple purposes, including reconnaissance and surveillance as well as bombing and targeted killing. The technology has developed rapidly in the twenty-first century, and President Barack Obama increasingly relied upon drones to conduct targeted killings in the Middle East, Afghanistan, and Pakistan, as well as in other areas. Proponents of drones defend them as a way of limiting troop exposure to hostile situations and as an economical way of striking enemies with a reusable weapon. Conversely, critics claim that drones increase civilian casualties and create a sense of helplessness and hatred in survivors and their countrymen. Drones are also another weapon that can be used against Americans as easily as for them.

Obama "Ends" Iraq War (2011)

Barack Obama campaigned for president in 2008 by touting his opposition to the Iraq War, but once in office he was committed to improving the situation. One of Obama's priorities was to negotiate an agreement with the Iraqi government regarding the immunity of U.S. personnel in the country from prosecution. When these negotiations proved unproductive, the Obama administration complied with an earlier agreement between the second Bush administration and the Iraqi government to remove American armed forces by the end of 2011. However, several thousand U.S. troops, government employees, and private contractors continue to operate out of the U.S. Embassy in Baghdad.

Libya Intervention (2011)

The 2011 Arab Spring led to a rapid change of authority in Tunisia and Egypt, Libya's neighbors to the west and east, respectively. In Libya, long-time dictator Moammar Gadhafi attacked protesters and rebels militarily, leading to a civil war. Beginning in March 2011, the UN instituted a no-fly zone over Libya, with the majority of the enforcement and air strikes carried out by French and U.S. armed forces. Gadhafi was captured and killed in October 2011. In September 2012, the American consulate in Benghazi, Libya, was attacked, resulting in multiple casualties, including U.S. Ambassador Chris Stevens. A new Libyan civil war commenced after 2014 and continues to the present.

Syrian Civil War (2011)

The Arab Spring spread to Syria in March 2011, leading to an ongoing civil war among several factions. Initially, protests against the government of President Bashar al-Assad were peaceful. However, the Assad regime responded violently, following the precedent set by his father, former Syrian president Hafez al-Assad, in the 1970s and 1980s. During both regimes, tens of thousands of Islamist rebels were killed by Syrian armed forces. The new Assad regime labeled all opponents of his authority terrorists, lumping together such disparate groups as moderate intellectuals, economic reformers, and armed insurgency groups like ISIS and Al-Qaeda. The Assad government, with the military, political, and financial backing of Russia and Iran, has carried out a brutal campaign to eliminate dissent that continues to the present.

Acknowledgments

This book has been a long time in the making. It is the product, in one sense, of more than a decade of friendship that has been defined by sustained conversations about how we could best study and teach about the intersections of warfare, militarism, and U.S. culture. Those discussions—whether they have been held over email or over cocktails—have always been entertaining, enlightening, and encouraging. The transition from those conversations to a volume that explores how the military and the operations that it undertakes intersect with U.S. culture, however, has required support from numerous quarters.

First and foremost, we are grateful to our contributors. We set out to recruit the best scholars on war and society in U.S. culture—the historians whose work has inspired us and that we have found useful in the classroom—and we were gratified by our authors' eagerness to join in this project. That they have responded so amenably to our edits and queries is a testament to their collegiality. Editing their work has been a pleasure, one from which we have learned much.

At Rutgers University Press, Leslie Mitchner has been a steadfast ally—providing us all of the support we needed, answering all of our questions, giving each chapter a thorough reading that generated questions and suggestions that made the arguments stronger and the writing clearer, and graciously hurrying us along when necessary. She also arranged for two thorough and extraordinarily helpful outside readers, both of whom offered comments that reinforced our faith in the project but also prompted us to expand the book's arguments. We are also grateful to the production staff at Rutgers, including Jennifer Blanc-Tal, as well as Milton Chambers, whose copyediting made our prose more readable.

This book would never have come to fruition had we not had the support of our colleagues. At Skidmore College, that includes Erica Bastress-Dukehart, Dan Nathan, Tillman Nechtman, and Greg Pfitzer. At Washington and

Jefferson College, it includes Patrick Caffrey, Victoria List, Tom Mainwaring, and Jennifer Sweatman. At Western Michigan University, colleagues in the Department of History and in Extended University Programs provided generous encouragement for this project.

The most important thanks, as always, go to our families. Special thanks to all who sustain us—Mary Anne Kieran, Kathleen Kieran, Susan Gilmore, Anne Litchfield, Shari Martini, Ed Martini Jr., Gracen Martini-Zeller, Kyan Martini-Zeller, Bill Zeller, and Gennis Zeller. The greatest thanks, however, continue to be reserved for the extraordinary women who have been our partners, Emma Gilmore Kieran and Genanne Zeller. Without their love, support, and encouragement, none of this would have happened, and we are humbled each day when we remember how lucky we both are that such amazing people have chosen to spend their lives with us.

Notes on Contributors

STEFAN AUNE is a doctoral candidate in the Department of American Culture at the University of Michigan. His dissertation project, titled "Indian Wars Everywhere: Resonances of Colonial Violence in the U.S. Military," traces the influence of continental settler-colonialism on broader dynamics of U.S. empire.

SUSAN L. CARRUTHERS is professor of U.S./world history at Rutgers University-Newark, where she has taught since 2002. She is the author of several books, including *The Media at War* and *The Good Occupation: American Soldiers and the Hazards of Peace.*

SAHR CONWAY-LANZ is a historian in the Manuscript Division of the Library of Congress and author of *Collateral Damage: Americans, Noncombatant Immunity, and Atrocity after World War II.*

KATHERINE ELLISON is the director of the Osher Lifelong Learning Institute at Saginaw Valley State University. She holds a doctorate in history from Western Michigan University, specializing in executive power and warfare.

CHRISTOPHER HAMNER is associate professor of history at George Mason University in Fairfax, Virginia, and a specialist in U.S. military history. An honors graduate of Dartmouth College, he received his PhD from the University of North Carolina. His 2011 book, *Enduring Battle: American Soldiers in Three Wars, 1776–1945*, explores the ways that evolving military technologies and tactics affected individual soldiers' willingness to withstand the trauma and terror of combat. He has been a fellow at Harvard University's John M. Olin Institute for Strategic Studies and the U.S. Army's Center for Military History. From 2014 to 2016 he served as a Visiting Professor at the U.S. Army War College in Carlisle, Pennsylvania, teaching courses on military planning, strategy, and operations.

DAVID KIERAN is assistant professor of history at Washington & Jefferson College. He is the author of *Forever Vietnam: How a Divisive War Changed American Public Memory* and the editor of *The War of My Generation: Youth Culture and the War on Terror* (Rutgers University Press, 2015).

JOHN M. KINDER is associate professor of American studies and history at Oklahoma State University and is the author of *Paying with Their Bodies: American War and the Problem of the Disabled Veteran*. He is currently finishing a book about the history of zoos during World War II.

CHRISTINE KNAUER is a historian affiliated with Eberhard Karls University, Tuebingen, Germany, where she received her PhD. Her dissertation on African Americans and the racial integration of the American military was published under the title *Let Us Fight as Free Men: Black Soldiers and Civil Rights*. She is currently working on a book on lynching narratives in the U.S. South.

SCOTT LADERMAN is professor of history at the University of Minnesota, Duluth. He is the author of *Empire in Waves: A Political History of Surfing* and *Tours of Vietnam: War, Travel Guides, and Memory*.

JANA K. LIPMAN is associate professor in the History Department at Tulane University. She is the author of *Guantánamo: A Working-Class History between Empire and Revolution*; her work has also appeared in *American Quarterly*, *Immigrants and Minorities*, the *Journal of Asian American Studies*, the *Journal of American Ethnic History*, the *Journal of Military History*, and the *Radical History Review*. She is currently working on a book-length project on Vietnamese refugee camps in Southeast Asia between 1975 and 1997.

EDWIN A. MARTINI is professor of history at Western Michigan University, where he currently serves as associate dean of Extended University Programs. He is the author and editor of several books, including *Agent Orange: History, Science and the Politics of Uncertainty* and *Proving Grounds: Militarized Landscapes, Weapons Testing, and the Environmental Impact of U.S. Bases*.

BONNIE M. MILLER is associate professor of history at the University of Massachusetts-Boston. She is the author of *From Liberation to Conquest: The Visual and Popular Cultures of the Spanish American War*.

JENNIFER MITTELSTADT is professor of history at Rutgers University, New Brunswick, and author of *The Rise of the Military Welfare State*.

G. KURT PIEHLER is associate professor of history and director of the Institute on World War II at Florida State University. He is the author of multiple books and articles, including *Remembering War the American Way*, and serves as the consulting editor for the *Oxford Companion to American Military History*.

WILBUR J. SCOTT is professor of sociology in the Department of Behavioral Sciences and Leadership at the United States Air Force Academy. His areas of specialization include military sociology, the sociology of violence and war, and the sociology of veterans' issues.

RICHARD P. TUCKER is adjunct professor in the School of Natural Resources, University of Michigan. He is the author of numerous essays and coeditor of four multiauthor books on the environmental history of warfare, including *Natural Enemy, Natural Ally: Toward an Environmental History of War*.

KARA DIXON VUIC is Benjamin W. Schmidt Professor of War, Conflict, and Society at Texas Christian University. She is the author of *Officer, Nurse, Woman: The Army Nurse Corps in the Vietnam War*, the editor of *The Routledge Handbook on Gender, War, and the U.S. Military*, and coeditor of the University of Nebraska Press's series "Studies in War, Society, and the Military." Her book *The Girls Next Door: American Women and Military Entertainment* is forthcoming.

WILLIAM WATSON is adjunct professor of history at Kalamazoo Valley Community College (KVCC). He is also an active supporter of international education at KVCC, hosting numerous global awareness events on campus, as well as studying and teaching abroad.

MARK R. WILSON is professor of history at the University of North Carolina at Charlotte. He is the author of *The Business of Civil War: Military Mobilization and the State, 1861–1865* and *Destructive Creation: American Business and the Winning of World War II*.

NICK WITHAM is lecturer in U.S. political history at the Institute of the Americas, University College London, UK. He is the author of *The Cultural Left and the Reagan Era: US Protest and Central American Revolution* and coeditor (with Martin Halliwell) of *Reframing 1968: US Politics, Protest and Identity*.

Index